Social Inequality in Canada

Sixth Edition

Social Inequality in Canada

Dimensions of Disadvantage

Edited by

Edward Grabb | Jeffrey G. Reitz | Monica Hwang

OXFORD
UNIVERSITY PRESS

Oxford University Press is a department of the University of Oxford. It furthers the University's objective of excellence in research, scholarship, and education by publishing worldwide. Oxford is a registered trade mark of Oxford University Press in the UK and in certain other countries.

Published in Canada by
Oxford University Press
8 Sampson Mews, Suite 204,
Don Mills, Ontario M3C 0H5 Canada

www.oupcanada.com

Social Inequality in Canada: Patterns, Problems and Policies, Fifth edition was originally published in 2009 by Pearson Canada.

Library and Archives Canada Cataloguing in Publication
Social inequality in Canada : dimensions of disadvantage / edited by Edward Grabb, Jeffrey G. Reitz, and Monica Hwang. — Sixth edition.

Includes bibliographical references and index.
ISBN 978-0-19-902094-2 (paperback)

1. Equality—Canada—Textbooks. 2. Social classes—Canada—Textbooks. 3. Canada—Social conditions—1991- —Textbooks. I. Grabb, Edward G., editor II. Reitz, Jeffrey G., editor III. Hwang, Monica, editor

HN110.Z9S6 2016b 305.0971 C2016-902877-1

Cover image: Trina Dalziel/Getty Images; Chapter and Part opener image: © iStock/naqiewei

Oxford University Press is committed to our environment. This book is printed on Forest Stewardship Council® certified paper and comes from responsible sources.

Printed and bound in the United States of America
1 2 3 4 — 20 19 18 17

Contents

Contributors

Tracey L. Adams, Department of Sociology, Western University
Robert Andersen, Dean of Social Science, Western University
Rupa Banerjee, Ted Rogers School of Management, Ryerson University
Brenda Beagan, School of Occupational Therapy, Dalhousie University
Roderic Beaujot, Department of Sociology, Western University
Monica Boyd, Department of Sociology, University of Toronto
William Carroll, Department of Sociology, University of Victoria
Jim Conley, Department of Sociology, Trent University
Catherine Corrigall-Brown, Department of Sociology, University of British Columbia
Gillian Creese, Department of Sociology, University of British Columbia
Josh Curtis, Department of Sociology, Western University
Darren Cyr, Department of Sociology, McMaster University
James B. Davies, Department of Economics, Western University
Scott Davies, Department of Leadership, Higher and Adult Education, Ontario Institute for Studies in Education, University of Toronto
Pierre Fortin, Department of Economics, University of Québec at Montréal
Edward Grabb, Department of Sociology, Western University
Neil Guppy, Department of Sociology, University of British Columbia
Mabel Ho, Department of Sociology, University of British Columbia
Monica Hwang, Department of Sociology, St Thomas More College, University of Saskatchewan
Harvey Krahn, Department of Sociology, University of Alberta
Wolfgang Lehmann, Department of Sociology, Western University
Jianye Liu, Department of Sociology, Lakehead University
Nicole Malette, Department of Sociology, University of British Columbia
Vicky Maldonado, Department of Sociology, McMaster University
Charles R. Menzies, Department of Anthropology, University of British Columbia
Philip Oreopoulos, Department of Economics, University of Toronto
Tracy L. Peressini, Sociology and Social Development Studies Department, Renison University College, University of Waterloo
Zenaida Ravanera, Department of Sociology, Western University
Jeffrey G. Reitz, Department of Sociology and Munk School of Global Affairs, University of Toronto
Michael Rooyakkers, Department of Sociology, Western University
Lorne Tepperman, Department of Sociology, University of Toronto
Kim Shuey, Department of Sociology, Western University
Peter Urmetzer, History and Sociology Department, University of British Columbia (Okanagan)
Gerry Veenstra, Department of Sociology, University of British Columbia
Andrea Willson, Department of Sociology, Western University

Preface

This book brings together 25 substantial selections, written by leading experts studying the question of social inequality in Canada. The 25 chapters represent original research by prominent scholars in the field. Each paper, however, is written in a manner that makes it easily accessible to undergraduate and graduate students taking courses in a range of areas, including Social Inequality, Contemporary Class Structure, Social Stratification, Social Issues, Social Problems, and Canadian Society. The selections, which address virtually all of the major aspects of social inequality, are organized around a set of intersecting themes that explore the major dimensions of disadvantage and social injustice that currently exist in Canada and most other countries in the world.

In this new volume, we have sought to retain the core strengths of earlier editions, by including papers that reflect a broad range of theoretical perspectives and research approaches, with imaginative and clear expositions of both theoretical and empirical issues. The book is organized in major substantive sections, and we have endeavoured as well to ensure that interconnections among the four parts are identified and examined. Separate parts are organized around certain crucial concerns, including gender and the interrelated topics of race, ethnicity, language, and ancestry, for example. In addition, however, evidence and theories that pertain to these topics and others are provided across the other sections of the book, including those on the socio-economic bases and the consequences of social inequality, in particular. The section on social justice also includes, for the first time, studies that are specifically dedicated to inequalities related to sexual orientation and to disability. These new papers reflect the growing interest in, and importance of, these dimensions of disadvantage in contemporary Canadian society. We trust that the changes and additions make the book more comprehensive, more readable, and even more useful as a teaching tool.

While the book comprises works by many of the leading experts on social inequality in Canada, it was not possible, of course, to include many other outstanding studies dealing with the topic. Some of these additional sources are displayed in the lists of Recommended Readings that appear at the end of each chapter. We also have incorporated lists of Recommended Websites at the end of each selection, for students and colleagues who wish to pursue specific topics in greater depth. As well, the chapters conclude with Questions for Critical Thought, which we hope will be helpful to instructors.

The study of social inequality in Canada has moved forward in recent decades, towards a much better understanding of the phenomenon. Those of us who would like to see greater equality of opportunity and condition in Canada may be encouraged by this improved understanding. It is another matter, though, to turn understanding into action and positive social change. The research in this volume shows that, while some improvements have occurred in the recent past, many patterns of inequality are stubbornly resistant to change. Consequently, those readers who would prefer a more egalitarian Canada than currently exists will find reasons for both optimism and pessimism in the research presented here.

We would like to thank a number of people for their assistance with this project. First, of course, are the contributors to the volume. The strengths of the book are largely their doing. Second, we are indebted to numerous individuals for their helpful suggestions. These include the many students who have provided valuable feedback. Several colleagues have offered invaluable advice for this edition as well, including Rod Beaujot, Catherine Corrigall-Brown, Sylvia Fuller, Neil Guppy, Kim Luton, Jim Webb, and our anonymous reviewers. Finally, we appreciate the exceptional encouragement, support, and advice provided by the people at Oxford University Press, some of whom we do not even know by name! Those we do know include Suzanne Clark, Darcey Pepper, and Tanuja Weerasooriya. It has been a privilege to work with and learn from all of these talented and dedicated people.

Ed Grabb, Western University
Jeffrey G. Reitz, University of Toronto
Monica Hwang, St Thomas More College,
University of Saskatchewan

General Introduction

Social Inequality: Theoretical and Conceptual Issues

Edward Grabb

That human beings are often very different from each other is one of those basic truths about life that we can all recognize. We need only observe the various sizes, shapes, and colours of other people, the different group affiliations they adopt, and the distinct goals or interests they pursue, to be reminded of our numerous differences. Many of these differences have little or no lasting influence on our existence, but certain human differences have significant consequences for the lives we are able to lead in society.

The study of social inequality is really the study of these consequential human differences. In particular, inequality refers to differences that become *socially structured*, in the sense that they become a regular and recurring part of how people interact with one another on a daily basis. Structured inequality involves a process in which groups or individuals with particular attributes are more able than those who lack or are denied these attributes to control or shape rights and opportunities for their own ends. One major factor in this process is that advantaged groups or individuals tend to obtain greater access to the various rewards and privileges available in society. These benefits, in turn, serve to reinforce the control over rights and opportunities enjoyed by the advantaged factions, in a cyclical process that structures and *reproduces* the pattern of inequality across time and place.

In this book, we have brought together exemplary works by noted Canadian scholars who seek to understand consequential human differences and the inequalities they engender. The main goal of this Introduction is to provide an integrative background and context for the chapters that follow. This is not an entirely straightforward task, for there are clear divergences in theoretical orientations and research traditions in the study of inequality, just as in other vibrant and evolving areas of inquiry. Given these divergences, there is no single and universally accepted approach to analyzing the problem. We can, however, establish a general understanding of the major theoretical issues and empirical questions in the contemporary study of social inequality. This understanding will help us to appreciate important areas of agreement and dispute among leading scholars in the field.

The central questions addressed in this opening chapter are theoretical in nature. In particular, we assess the two most important ideas in most theories of social inequality: the concept of *class* and the concept of *power*, or *domination*. We will demonstrate that class and power are closely tied to questions of *economic control*, and also to questions of *ideological and political control*. The combined effects of these types of control give rise to the key bases for social inequality, or dimensions of disadvantage, that operate in Canada and other societies.

Social Inequality and the Concept of Class

If we asked what inequality is about, most people would put considerable stress on economic or material distinctions, on differences in economic rights, opportunities, rewards, and privileges between themselves and others. Although such differences might not be their sole focus, people show a notable interest, for example, in whether they earn as much money as others in different occupations; they might wonder if their own share of society's wealth is growing or shrinking over time; they might even raise questions about whether it is true that a small number of businesses increasingly controls more of their country's economic resources.

For many years, such questions about economic control and material privilege were the predominant concern among most social scientists interested in the topic of inequality. This focus is understandable, of course, since economic disparities involve the most immediate or fundamental inequality in social settings: people's differential access to the material necessities of life itself. Undoubtedly, this emphasis helps to explain the central role that the concept of economic class has always played in social analysis, particularly since the writings of Karl Marx and Max Weber (e.g., Marx 1867; Weber 1922).

The concept of class has provoked long-standing questions about its precise meaning and significance. Of these questions, five in particular will be raised in this opening section. First, scholars have questioned whether classes are just categories of individuals with similar economic circumstances, or whether the term "class" should refer only to an economic category that is also a real social group, a set of people with a sense of common membership or purpose. Second, analysts have debated whether classes are best thought of as the same as *social strata*—ranked layers of people separated according to income or occupation level, for instance—or whether the dividing lines between classes are less arbitrary, less variable, and more fundamental than such stratum distinctions suggest. Third, some writers question whether classes are best understood as sets of *people*, or whether they are really sets of *places* or *positions*, like boxes or containers in which the people are located. Fourth, theorists debate whether classes should be defined principally by differences in the amount of material rewards *distributed* to them for consumption purposes, or whether such differences are secondary to, and largely derivative from, structured economic *relationships*, especially relationships that give sustained control over material life to some and not others. For certain theorists, such control is the real means by which classes are defined and delineated. Finally, many writers disagree on how many classes there are in today's societies. Are there just two, a small dominant one and a large subordinate one? Are there instead some intermediate classes between top and bottom and, if so, how many? Or is it the case that there are no easily identifiable classes, but a continuous hierarchy without clear class distinctions?

The difficulties in answering these questions are obvious from the volume of work generated on the concept of class (for discussion, see Grabb 2007; McMullin 2010). The differing perspectives cannot be fully incorporated within a single conception or definition of class. Nevertheless, there is sufficient common ground for class to be viewed in a way that, at least in general terms, is consistent with most major works in the field, including those of the key classical writers, Marx and Weber, and of subsequent writers broadly sympathetic to either or both of these theorists (e.g., Poulantzas 1975; Carchedi 1977; Wright 1979, 1985, 1989, 1994, 1997, 2005; Wright and Rogers 2010; Parkin 1979; Giddens 1973, 1981, 1984, 1989, 1994, 2013: ch. 12).

Our approach to defining the concept of class involves the following answers to the five questions listed above:

1. Classes exist primarily as *categories* of people, and need not be defined as real *groups*. That is, classes typically will not be sets of people with a common sense of group membership and the capability to act together towards some collective goal. It is not that such united action is never possible; classes sometimes become groups, but only sometimes. As Giddens notes, class systems exist on a national or international scale, making such co-ordination and common purpose exceedingly difficult to generate, at least in the total population (Giddens 1973: 84). In those rare instances where simple economic classes acquire these group-like characteristics, some writers find it useful, following Weber, to refer to such groups as *social classes* (Weber 1922: 302–5; Giddens 1973: 78–9; Grabb 2007: 49).
2. While classes normally are not real groups, neither are they merely equivalent to strata, as certain writers suggest (Johnson 1960: 469; Barber 1957: 73; Parsons 1951: 172). Strata are usually ranked statistical aggregates, for which the ranking criteria are quite variable (e.g., income, education, occupation, or prestige level) and for which the choice of boundaries is an arbitrary decision of the researcher. In contrast, class divisions involve more fundamental, deep-seated, and uniform cleavages than those implied by these stratum distinctions.
3. Classes are most completely comprehended by recognizing that they are neither simple sets of people nor mere structural categories, the containers that separate or encapsulate sets of people; they really are both of these things in combination. This double meaning of class is one aspect of a more general process that Giddens has called the "duality" of social structures (Giddens 1981, 1984, 1989). Hence, classes exist as structural entities because certain enforceable rights or opportunities, e.g., the right to own and to exclude others from owning productive property, define them and distinguish them from each other. However, classes have almost no meaning if they are not also seen as real people, for people create the rights or opportunities that define classes in the first place, people enjoy or suffer the consequences of class inequalities, and people are capable of changing or consolidating class structures through social action.
4. Classes are most readily defined as *economically based* entities. However, as noted later, they also play an important part in the *political* and *ideological* spheres of society and can be said to exist, in a sense, within and across all social structures, not just the economic (see Wright 1978, 1989: 343–5; 1997: 303–4, 544–5). In delineating classes, we conform with Marx, Weber, and most leading contemporary theorists by treating

one distinction—between those who own or control society's productive property or resources and those who lack this attribute—as the initial and most fundamental division in class systems (Marx and Engels 1848a: 58, 92; Weber 1922: 927; Giddens 1973: 100; Poulantzas 1975: 14; Wright 1978: 73; Parkin 1979: 53).

While this basic division is the crux of class structures, other forms of economic inequality can occur. The relations of domination and exploitation established by this division are the primary factors in class formation, but the distribution of material benefits such as income can also serve to delineate classes. Such benefits can enhance or blur the division between the dominant and the subordinate classes, depending on whether or not these benefits are distributed so that the two classes have markedly distinct consumption habits and qualities of life.

Despite what some writers imply, the distribution of material benefits is a significant factor in the formation of classes. Some Marxist theorists tend to consider all wage and salary employees as simply members of the working class, or *proletariat*, because they depend for their livelihood on the sale of labour power to the propertied owning class, or *bourgeoisie*. However, some wage and salary employees earn sufficiently high incomes that they can accumulate surplus funds, over and above what they need for basic survival. This surplus can be, and often is, used to gain some control over productive resources, by acquiring such holdings as stocks, rental properties, interest-bearing bonds, annuities, and pension plans. These are relatively minor forms of economic control or ownership—compared to owning giant corporations, for example—and are somewhat like the economic control of the petty bourgeoisie, who own small-scale businesses or farms but employ few or no workers themselves. Nonetheless, having such resources means that distributive inequalities can give rise to economic categories that are distinct to some degree from both the large-scale bourgeoisie and the proletariat (Wright 1989: 325; 1994: 45–8).

A related point is that people with distributive surpluses can expend their funds in another manner: to help finance special educational qualifications or technical training for themselves or their children. Here again, distributive inequalities do not signify simple consumption differences. Some writers see educational credentials themselves as another form of productive "property." This may be true in the sense that educational certificates are tangible possessions that can generate material dividends all their own, providing a basis for economic control unattainable by those who lack such credentials (Giddens 1973; Collins 1979; Parkin 1979). Therefore, educational advantage or opportunity is yet another basis on which divisions can emerge in the class structure, and this advantage can be passed on or reproduced over generations. The important role of educational certification or "credential assets" in class formation has increasingly been acknowledged by some recent Marxist scholars (e.g., Wright 1985, 1989, 1994, 1997, 2005), in contrast to earlier Marxists who ignored or downplayed this factor.

5. Probably the most controversial question to address is: How many classes actually exist in current capitalist societies? While disagreement continues on this issue, most writers now concur that modern class systems are more complex and *pluralist*, with more elements than the single Marxist division between bourgeoisie and proletariat is able to represent. This may seem to contradict traditional Marxist treatments of class, especially those offered by Marx's early disciples. However, this more complex portrayal of class systems is really quite consistent with Marx's own analysis.

At several points in his writings, Marx clearly speaks of additional economic groupings that exist in real societies and that complicate the pure two-class model that he believes will ultimately emerge in advanced capitalism. Marx labels these complicating elements in various ways, calling them *Mittelstande* ("middle estates or strata"), *Mittelstufen* ("middle stages or ranks"), or *Mittelklassen* ("middle classes") (Marx and Engels 1848b: 472; Marx 1862: 368; 1867: 673, 688, 784, 791; 1894: 892). Most current Marxists note similar complications in contemporary class structures, although they often avoid referring to these additional elements as genuine classes (but see Carchedi 1977; Wright 1989, 1994, 1997, 2005). Complications include the traditional petty bourgeoisie of small-scale owners, but also a diverse range of salaried personnel who, because of their educational training, technical knowledge, administrative authority, and so on, persist as "fractions," "contradictory class locations," or similar elements within the basic two-class structure of capitalism (Poulantzas 1975: 196–9; Wright 1979: 46–7; 1985: 88–9; 1989: 301–48; 1994: 45–8).

Non-Marxist theorists readily acknowledge the existence of these intermediate class categories. Some recent theoretical work advocates a "neo-Durkheimian" approach to class analysis, which entails a greater appreciation of internal occupational complexities that exist apart from the "big" classes exemplified by the bourgeoisie and proletariat of Marxian theory (Grusky 2005). Other non-Marxists have argued that there are so many complexities and fine distinctions in today's economic or occupational structure that we really have a *continuous hierarchy* with no distinct classes at all (Nisbet 1959; Faris 1972). At times, non-Marxists have applied this notion of a continuum, while simultaneously retaining the concept of class in their analyses. In particular, the "structural functionalist school" argued that the continuum can be subdivided into classes that amount to clusters of occupations that share a similar level of *prestige*, because their jobs are supposedly of similar value to society (Parsons 1953; Barber 1957).

Most recent non-Marxist scholars, however, reject the latter conception, primarily because it confuses classes with statistical categories or strata. Instead, leading non-Marxists now generally conclude that key aspects of Marx's original conception of class should be retained, provided they are revamped and supplemented to account for newer developments in contemporary class systems.

The latter approach is reminiscent of that adopted by Max Weber, the best-known non-Marxist among major classical theorists of inequality, whose work represents a constructive critique of Marx's writings. Weber envisions a class structure broadly similar to Marx's, involving a dominant bourgeoisie or owning class at the top, a propertyless working class at the bottom, and a mix of "various middle classes" (*Mittelstandklassen*) in between (Weber 1922:303–5). There are, however, key differences between Marx and Weber. Perhaps the most crucial difference concerns their expectations for the eventual fate of some middle-class categories. Weber concurs with Marx's prediction that the petty bourgeoisie will disappear over time. Unlike Marx, though, Weber sees a growing need for intermediate bureaucratic and technical personnel in modern societies, which means that the educated middle class will not fall into the proletariat, but will endure as a significant force in the future. Ultimately, Weber is far less convinced than Marx that a growing split will emerge between the top and the bottom classes, or that an eventual revolution by the working class against capitalism is likely.

Weber's approach has influenced virtually all current non-Marxist theorists. Recent writers see classes arising because certain people can gain greater access to important "capacities" and "mobility chances" (Giddens 1973: 101–3) or to special "resources and opportunities" (Parkin 1979: 44–6) that exclude other people from advantaged positions, especially through their educational qualifications (also Scott 1996; Tilly 1998). Certainly, these more recent approaches are not identical, nor do they correspond precisely to the views of either Marx or Weber in their subtler details. Still, the class structures they portray are generally akin to one another and to the classical conceptions, for they all arrive at three key groupings: a *dominant class* composed mainly of those who own or control large-scale production; a *working class* of people who lack resources or capacities apart from their own labour power; and, in between, a *mixed intermediate range* that mainly includes professional, technical, or white-collar personnel with some degree of special training or education (Giddens 1973: 101–10; Parkin 1979: 47–58).

Even a brief review of classical and contemporary conceptions of class indicates that the main debate among most theorists is not whether complications exist in the class system, but whether these complexities, especially in the centre of the structure, constitute classes in their own right. Marxists usually say no, perhaps because they consider any middle segments as both transitional and heterogeneous, destined to fall eventually into the proletariat, and blurring only temporarily the real two-class system of capitalism. In contrast, non-Marxists routinely treat such central segments as a middle class, or set of middle classes, either because such writers use the term "class" differently, or because they genuinely believe that these intermediate categories are fundamental and persistent realities within modern class systems.

The view advocated here is that, for the current stage of capitalist development, the term "middle class" is a reasonable label for these central categories. There are at least three reasons for this position. First, there is nothing inherent in the word "class" to suggest that it must be reserved solely for permanent and lasting social categories. While Marxists treat the bourgeoisie as a real class within capitalism, Marxists also contend that this class is destined for eventual dissolution in future socialist societies. Similarly, then, whether or not the middle categories in the system are destined to be transitional entities should not be a crucial concern for deciding whether they form a class at present. Marx clearly saw this himself since, as noted above, he sometimes spoke of the existence of a middle class, but he had no doubt that its days were numbered.

Second, although the middle segments of the class structure are heterogeneous, this is insufficient grounds for denying that they form a distinct class. As leading Marxists and others acknowledge, the contemporary bourgeoisie and proletariat are also marked by considerable heterogeneity but are deemed to be classes all the same (Poulantzas 1975: 23, 139, 198).

Finally, between the proletarian or bourgeois classes, on the one hand, and the set of intermediate categories, on the other hand, there is some conceptual parity suggesting that the latter also can be seen as a class. The conceptual parity is that the middle class is definable using the very same criteria used to define the bourgeoisie and proletariat. These criteria concern people's relative control over society's material or productive resources, and the extent to which such control separates sets of individuals (and the positions they occupy) from one another. What is most distinctive about members of the middle class is their mixed or hybrid situation compared to people from other classes. As suggested in point 4 above, middle-class incumbents are unlike the proletariat, and similar to the bourgeoisie, because they retain some control over productive resources or assets, especially the acquisition of property and investments or educational credentials and skills. At the same time, however, middle-class members are unlike the bourgeoisie, and closer to the proletariat, because the resources they control are typically minor in scale and are often derived from a relatively small surplus fund accumulated from salaried or wage-based earnings. That these middle locations tend to commingle characteristics of the other two classes, and yet remain marginal to both of them, is what most clearly identifies the middle class as a separate entity (see Wright 1989: 333).

Therefore, we can address point 5 by suggesting that Canada, as well as most advanced capitalist countries, retains a class structure that, although highly complex and internally diverse, comprises at its core three basic elements. The first is a predominant class of large-scale owners of productive property, the so-called *capitalist class* or *bourgeoisie* in classical Marxian terminology. The second element is a subordinate class of workers, who live primarily through the sale of their labour power to the owning class, and who are usually termed the *working class* or *proletariat*. The third major element is a mixed and more heterogeneous middle category of small-scale business people, educated professional-technical or administrative personnel, and various salaried employees or wage earners possessing some certifiable credentials, training, or skills. The latter grouping, while for some writers just a set of complicating fractions or fragments within a basic two-class model, can be considered a third *middle class* for the reasons already outlined (Grabb 2007: 214–15). This characterization, while not providing a universally acceptable conception of modern class structures, offers a compromise view that establishes some level of agreement about how to think about the concept of class.

Notwithstanding the central focus that most analysts place on class, the majority of contemporary writers also recognize that any complete conceptualization of social inequality, one that addresses social inequality in all its forms, requires us to broaden our theoretical approach. This means moving beyond the concept of economic class alone and towards a wider range of concerns that build from the second key idea in most theories of social inequality—the concept of power or domination. To understand this concept, we must first discuss the ideas of political and ideological control.

Political and Ideological Control

We began with the suggestion that social inequality is primarily about consequential human differences, especially those that become structured and recurring features of our everyday lives. We then considered what may be the most familiar and fundamental illustrations of such differences: the inequalities deriving from differential *economic* control, or people's command over material and productive resources. In addition, however, many writers suggest at least two other major mechanisms that are crucial to the creation and continuation of social inequality. The first of these involves control over people and their conduct, or what some might call "human resources." Command over human resources is the essence of *political* control, as broadly defined by various analysts. The third major mechanism is *ideological* control, which entails command over ideas, knowledge, information, and beliefs, and which can also help to establish structured inequality between groups or individuals (Mann 1986, 1993; Runciman 1989; Grabb 2007).

A basic premise in the current discussion is that these two additional forms of control typically occur in conjunction with economic control, and with each other, but are not simply reducible to or a consequence of economic control. Both political control and ideological control have their own distinct origins. Consequently, individuals or groups can gain positions of dominance in society and establish inequalities between factions without relying purely on control over material resources.

For example, inequality can result from political control when enforceable policies, statutes, or laws are invoked to ensure that subordinates comply with the will of superiors. The government or *state* is most commonly identified with political control, because the state takes principal responsibility for creating the laws that govern the behaviour of people and can ensure compliance, if necessary, through the use of police or military force. However, political control in the broadest sense occurs whenever individuals' actions are constrained by rules of conduct established by others in authority over them in various organizations—when employees obey the work regulations imposed by employers, or when students follow the academic regulations of their university, for example. The most extreme or blatant form of political control is one that is typically exercised by the state: the use of physical force by one faction on another, what Poulantzas (1978: 28–9) literally calls the "coercion of bodies and the threat of violence or death."

In addition to economic and political control, inequalities also arise through, and are reinforced by, ideological forces. *Ideology* refers to the set of ideas, values, and beliefs that describe, explain, or justify various aspects of the social world, including social inequality (Porter 1965: chs 15, 16; Marchak 1988). Hence, a belief in racial superiority or inferiority is central to the ideological system that helped create and justify the unequal treatment of Blacks by Whites in the nineteenth-century institution of slavery in the United States and in the apartheid system in twentieth-century South Africa. Similarly, the belief in the divine right of kings was important in establishing and maintaining the rule of monarchs and nobles over commoners in much of medieval Europe. Of course, ideologies can also support *reductions* in inequalities among groups. The Canadian Charter of Rights and Freedoms is one relatively recent attempt in Canada to implement the belief in equal rights and opportunities for all people, regardless of "race, national or ethnic origin, colour, religion, sex, age or mental or physical disability" (Constitution Act, 1982, s. 15[1]). In these examples, ideas and beliefs about inequality were converted by governments into official policies and formal laws, illustrating the often close connection between politics and ideology in society.

We should also recognize, though, that ideology can be fundamental to the third major type of control, i.e., economic control. The belief that it is acceptable for people to own private property is clearly an essential ideological prerequisite for the existence of economic inequalities based on such ownership. Similarly, the belief that people with unequal talents or motivation should also be unequal in the material rewards they receive can be used as both an explanation and justification for the economic differences that arise among individuals. In both of these examples, whether people believe or reject ideas about themselves and their society has an important bearing on how much inequality exists, and how likely it is to change with time.

Political and Ideological Factors in Class Differences

The recognition of these multiple mechanisms of control and the distinct resources they entail suggests considerable pluralism in the processes that generate social inequality. This also implies that theories focusing solely on economic class are insufficient to capture this pluralism. Perhaps for this reason, some Marxists now include in their conceptions of class the sense that not only economic control but also political and ideological control are crucial to the formation of class structures (Poulantzas 1975; Wright 1979, 1985, 1989, 1994, 1997, 2005). The incorporation of these additional elements into their class conceptions is a significant innovation. Their inclusion permits us to recognize that classes, although they are primarily economic groupings, can also be important for other reasons and, in a way, are fundamentally embedded within and across all social structures, both economic and non-economic.

Here we should also note that, in addition to a revised notion of the class system, other complicating elements have come to be recognized in the multi-faceted structure of inequality that characterizes most societies. As both Marxists and non-Marxists now generally acknowledge, various patterns of inequality are at least partially independent of, and not reducible to, class inequality alone. The more prominent examples of these other bases or dimensions of inequality include gender, race, and ethnicity. Other important bases include age, region, language, religion, sexuality, and physical or mental ability/disability. Non-Marxists sometimes refer to such factors as different bases for "social closure" (Parkin 1979), while Marxists sometimes call them "multiple oppressions" (Wright 1985: 57). In either event, these forms of inequality represent important additional areas of inquiry, and require a broader conceptual approach than class theory alone can provide.

Social Inequality as Three Forms of Power

Many theorists recommend that the concept of power can be used in conjunction with class theory to develop a more general framework for comprehending social inequality in all its forms. Some Marxist scholars have been reluctant to take this approach, fearing that it might relegate class analysis to a secondary concern (Wright 1985: 57). Indeed, it is essential when analyzing other crucial problems in social inequality that we not ignore or downgrade the continuing importance of class in contemporary societies. Some have suggested that class is "dying" as a significant issue or concept in sociology (Clark and Lipset 1991; Clark et al. 1993), but existing research, including the studies presented in this book, make it clear that this suggestion is mistaken.

As noted already, however, class analyses are improved significantly by a fuller appreciation of the other forms of inequality and power relations in society. In other words, power can be a more generalizable, if not a more fundamental, concept than class, because it can be used to describe and analyze both class and non-class forms of inequality (Grabb 2007: 211–13). From this perspective, class is pivotal in any complete understanding of social inequality, but class differences represent just one manifestation of the more general structure of power that is responsible for generating the overall system of inequality in society. Other crucial manifestations of inequality, such as those based on gender and race, can therefore be understood as the results of differential access to the three different forms of power or domination—economic, political, and ideological (see Blalock 1989, 1991; Wilson 1973; Milkman 1987; Connell 1987; Collins 1988; Li 1988; Chafetz 1990, 1997; Walby 1990, 1997; Agger 1993; Andersen and Collins 1995).

Power serves this more general conceptual purpose, but what precisely is power? This is also not a simple question to answer, because power, like class, is an idea that has stimulated numerous debates over its definition and meaning (e.g., Weber 1922; Lukes 1974; Wrong 1979; Mann 1986, 1993; Runciman 1989; Scott 1996). For our purposes, *power* can be defined briefly as the differential capacity to command resources and thereby to control social situations. We have suggested there are three major types of resources operating in social settings (material, human, and ideological) and three mechanisms of control corresponding to them (economic, political, and ideological). These three mechanisms can be seen as the key forms of power in society.

Whenever differences in economic, political, or ideological power are sufficiently stable and enduring to promote regular, routinized relations of ascendance and subordination among people, the resulting pattern of interaction is a case of *structured power*, or what might be termed a *structure of domination* (Grabb 2007). Using abstract imagery, we can think of the overall system of inequality in society as a framework, involving all three forms of power and the three corresponding structures of domination—material, human, and ideological resources. In more concrete terms, the structures of domination exist mainly as bureaucratic or corporate organizations: business enterprises in the economic sphere; departments of government in the political sphere; church hierarchies, mass media, and institutions of higher learning in the ideological sphere. Within all these concrete settings, power differences among people, and the positions they occupy, are manifested, thereby producing organized patterns of inequality.

Another point about this abstract imagery is that there is no perfect one-to-one linkage between each of the three forms of power and each set of concrete structures. These are just the *primary* linkages, since each form of power can operate in at least a secondary fashion in any of the three structures. Thus, political power—control over people or human resources—is the principal jurisdiction of political or state organizations, but it also resides in the control that owners have over their workers in the workplace or economic structure. Similarly, the various political organizations composing the modern state do not derive all their power from the capacity to legislate or coerce human behaviour, because they also control material or economic resources through their command over tax revenues, government ownership of some business enterprises, and so on. Finally, ideological control—control over ideas, knowledge, and beliefs—is most obviously identified with such structures as the mass media, the education system, and religious organizations. However, as mentioned previously, ideological control is clearly a means for wielding power elsewhere, too, such as in the policy-making, information-gathering, and surveillance powers of the government, and in the control over technical ideas and knowledge that occurs in the economic sphere (Giddens 1981, 1985, 1989).

The combined operation of all three forms of power, through the concrete organizations to which they correspond, establishes the major contours of the overall structure of inequality. The organizations themselves are patterned according to formal rules, laws, and rights of office, with their personnel exercising power in accordance with these formal guidelines. In addition, however, inequalities can develop within organizations through informal practices or traditions, customs or habits, beliefs or prejudices. Not only formal rights or powers, but also informal privileges or advantages, tend to determine the nature and extent of inequality in society. The different forms of power, taken together, establish what the principal bases of social inequality will be and how much each of them will matter.

The Bases of Social Inequality: Dimensions of Disadvantage

This leads to the final conceptual issue, which is to identify the central bases of social inequality—and the major dimensions of disadvantage—that arise from the exercise of power in Canada. Researchers generally acknowledge a multiple set of human characteristics, or socially defined attributes, that have significant consequences for the quality of life experienced by most people. But what are these major bases for inequality?

Perhaps the more difficult question to ask, first, is: Why are some attributes of people more likely than others to lead to important inequalities? Why, for example, has colour of skin had such a sustained impact on people's rights, opportunities, and rewards historically, but not colour of eyes or hair? In general terms, we can address this question by looking once again at the idea of power, or domination, and by considering which factions within the population have historically been the most or the least successful in turning to their advantage the various economic, political, and ideological power mechanisms. If groups occupy positions of ascendancy on the basis of their class, gender, or race, for example, they will be able to use all three forms of power to establish and routinize structures of domination, and so will be relatively more successful in reproducing across time and place important advantages for themselves and others with similar background characteristics.

If we use class as our illustration, this means that, within capitalist societies, those individuals who retain private ownership or control over productive property will clearly enjoy special advantages and may well attempt to use their strategic position to encourage the further institutionalization of property rights in law, to foster belief systems favourable to such rights, and to employ whatever means they can to ensure that their privileges as property owners are maintained for themselves and succeeding generations of capitalists. Similarly, those who have recognized training and skills, notably those possessing formal credentials or degrees in such areas as medicine and law, will themselves benefit from the advantages such exclusive accreditation brings, and will favour continuing this system of special certification (and attendant privileges) for themselves and the cohorts who follow.

In both of these illustrations, we see how two important bases for inequality—property and educational credentials—also correspond to two important types of economic or productive resources in demand in most societies. In the present context, however, these are not just resources but socially defined human attributes, or capacities of real people. In this form, they become recognized by others as crucial characteristics for differentiating some individuals or factions from others and for determining the rights, opportunities, rewards, and privileges of those who do or do not have them. We should note that this distinction between resources, on the one hand, and human attributes, on the other, illustrates once again what has elsewhere been referred to as the duality of social structures.

And what are the other key dimensions of disadvantage in Canada? As mentioned previously, gender, race, and ethnicity may be the best contemporary examples. Inequalities based on these factors are neither identical to nor reducible to class inequality. Nevertheless, like class inequality, these dimensions can also be conceived of as the products of long-standing factional antagonisms, struggles, and contests, in which economic, political, and ideological power mechanisms have been significant for establishing and structuring advantages for one grouping of people relative to others.

The same can be said for the full range of human or socially defined attributes or capacities that are consequential for social inequality. In Canada, these include the set of class-related bases—property ownership, education, occupation, and possession of wealth or income—and numerous non-class bases—especially gender, race, ethnicity, language, region, age, sexual orientation, and physical or mental ability/disability (see Grabb 2007). As the chapters in this volume show, the evidence indicates that social groups can often gain advantages by distinguishing themselves from others along any or all of these dimensions.

In considering these dimensions, we should be aware that they will not be equally influential in shaping current patterns of inequality. It is also important to acknowledge that, in different historical periods or different places, there will be considerable variability in the influence or prevalence of some bases for inequality. One interesting example is religious affiliation. In centuries past, this social characteristic was a significant factor for generating inequality in Canada. Subsequently, many religious distinctions, such as that between Protestant and Catholic, became less consequential in influencing the power or rank of Canadians. In more recent times, however, it appears that some religious differences, such as that between Muslim Canadians and other Canadians, could be influential again in shaping Canada's system of social inequality, in part because such religious differences can overlap with and reinforce inequalities based on race or ethnicity (see Reitz et al. 2009; Breton 2012).

The recognition that different bases or dimensions of disadvantage can overlap with each other is another central aspect of leading theoretical approaches to social inequality in the present day. This is not an entirely new perspective, for it is evident in the work of certain classical writers, most notably Weber (1922). Nevertheless, prominent thinkers place much greater emphasis on this crucial insight than was true in the past. Sociologists today more fully appreciate the multi-dimensional nature of social inequality, and they also emphasize that these dimensions frequently "intersect" with each other (McMullin 2010; Zawilski 2010), producing what has been called a multi-faceted "matrix of domination and inequality" (Andersen and Collins 1995: 5; Grabb 2007: 200–1). Such a pattern would occur, for example, when a working-class, non-White woman experiences simultaneous economic and other disadvantages based on her subordinate locations within the class, race, and gender hierarchies. As the chapters in this book demonstrate, such complexities and interconnections are among the most important and intriguing aspects of recent research on social inequality in Canada.

Plan of the Book

The chapters presented here reflect the central role that the study of power and class has played in theory and research on inequality in Canada. The selections in Part I, entitled "Power and Class," emphasize how the power deriving from control over economic or productive property underlies the Canadian class structure and gives rise to a system that comprises our own large-scale capitalist class, working class, and middle class. Depicting these core features of Canada's system of inequality provides us with a context within which the other important bases of inequality can be located and analyzed.

We have discussed that significant inherited or attained socio-economic characteristics are also crucial for defining the main contours of inequality in Canada. This issue is the principal focus of Part II, which deals with the distribution of personal wealth or income, occupational status, and educational attainment. These three bases for inequality are distinct from each other and from economic ownership itself, but are also involved in shaping the system of economic classes. In particular, educational credentials and surplus wealth or income are, as we have noted, important for distinguishing the "middle class" from the two other major classes. The reason for including occupation in the same section may seem less obvious, but follows from two considerations. First, occupation has long been used in social research as an approximate indicator of class location, although methodological problems associated with this have been of concern to some writers, especially Marxists. Second, the analysis of occupational inequality is useful in a supplementary or residual sense, because occupation subsumes such phenomena as skill level, manual versus non-manual labour power, and so on, which are not fully captured in research restricted to the study of ownership, wealth or income, and education.

In Part III the central concern is with factors of social justice. The dimensions of inequality considered here are ethnicity, race, language, and ancestry; gender and sexual orientation; age; disability; and region of residence. These attributes are discussed separately from class and the socio-economic status characteristics for two reasons. First, these bases for inequality are conceptually independent of class distinctions, although, as we shall see, they are often correlated with class location and can give rise to important divisions *within* classes. Second, these attributes are what earlier theorists would call "ascribed" characteristics, involving statuses not typically achieved or attained by people. Instead they are largely "given," often at birth, and so are attributes over which people have little or no control. Such attributes are often central to questions of social justice or injustice, with people frequently enduring serious disadvantages and inequities simply because they happen to be born into subordinate groupings based on their race, gender, sexual orientation, and so on. Age is another social characteristic that, though constantly changing, is assigned or ascribed, being essentially beyond personal control. Language and region of residence also tend to be ascribed characteristics. Some might dispute this view because adults, at least, can choose to alter the language they speak or move to another place to live. However, even in adulthood, these attributes are more ascribed than they appear, because of the pressures upon many Canadians to retain the language and place of residence they are born into. Language barriers and regional divisions tend to reproduce themselves over time, much like other ascribed characteristics.

The first parts of the book concentrate on structural issues, on the nature of class divisions and the patterns of inequality developing from the other major dimensions of disadvantage. Part IV serves a different purpose, by providing a broad sampling of evidence to show how the various bases of inequality are consequential for the quality of life enjoyed or endured by Canadians. Of course, earlier parts of the book also deal with the consequences of inequality, including chapters examining the effects of class, gender, or ethnicity on education, occupation, or income inequality, for example. But the chapters in Part IV go beyond the earlier discussions to show the wide-ranging impact that social inequality can have on aspects of life as diverse as health and mortality, job discrimination, intolerance of sexual minorities, and people's beliefs about the causes of inequality. Taken together, the chapters in this volume provide a good sense of the array of critical issues that leading scholars have addressed in the study of social inequality in Canada.

References

Agger, Ben. 1993. *Gender, Culture, and Power.* Westport, Conn.: Praeger.

Andersen, Margaret, and Patricia Collins, eds. 1995. *Race, Class, and Gender.* Belmont, Calif.: Wadsworth.

Barber, Bernard. 1957. *Social Stratification.* New York: Harcourt Brace and World.

Blalock, H.M., Jr. 1989. *Power and Conflict: Toward a General Theory.* Newbury Park, Calif.: Sage.

———. 1991. *Understanding Social Inequality.* Newbury Park, Calif.: Sage.

Breton, Raymond. 2012. *Different Gods: Integrating Non-Christian Minorities into a Primarily Christian Society.* Montreal and Kingston: McGill-Queen's University Press.

Carchedi, Guglielmo. 1977. *On the Economic Identification of Social Classes.* London: Routledge.

Chafetz, Janet Saltzman. 1990. *Gender Equity: An Integrated Theory of Stability and Change.* Newbury Park, Calif.: Sage.

———. 1997. "Feminist theory and sociology: Underutilized contributions for mainstream theory." *Annual Review of Sociology* 23: 97–191.

Clark, Terry Nichols, and Seymour Martin Lipset. 1991. "Are social classes dying?"*International Sociology* 6: 397–410.

———, ———, and Michael Rempel. 1993. "The declining political significance of class." *International Sociology* 8: 293–316.

Collins, Randall. 1979. *The Credential Society.* New York: Academic Press.

———. 1988. *Theoretical Sociology.* San Diego: Harcourt Brace Jovanovich.

Connell, R.W. 1987. *Gender and Power: Society, the Person and Sexual Politics.* Cambridge: Polity Press.

Faris, Robert E.L. 1972. "The middle class from a sociological viewpoint." In G. Thielbar and S. Feldman, eds, *Issues in Social Inequality,* pp. 26–32. Boston: Little Brown and Company.

Giddens, Anthony. 1973. *The Class Structure of the Advanced Societies.* London: Hutchinson.

———. 1981. *A Contemporary Critique of Historical Materialism. Vol. 1, Power, Property, and the State.* London: Macmillan.

———. 1984. *The Constitution of Society.* Berkeley: University of California Press.

———. 1985. *A Contemporary Critique of Historical Materialism. Vol. 2, The Nation-State and Violence.* Berkeley: University of California Press.

———. 1989. "A reply to my critics." In D. Held and J. Thompson, eds, *Social Theory of Modern Societies,* pp. 249–301. Cambridge: Cambridge University Press.

———. 1994. *Beyond Left and Right: The Future of Radical Politics.* Stanford, Calif.: Stanford University Press.

———. 2013. *Sociology,* 7th edn. London: Polity Press.

Grabb, Edward G. 2007. *Theories of Social Inequality,* 5th edn. Toronto: Thomson Nelson.

Grusky, David. 2005. "Foundations of a neo-Durkheimian class analysis." In E.O. Wright, ed., *Approaches to Class Analysis,* pp. 51–81. Cambridge: Cambridge University Press.

Johnson, Harry M. 1960. *Sociology: A Systematic Introduction.* New York: Harcourt, Brace and World.

Li, Peter S. 1988. *Ethnic Inequality in a Class Society.* Toronto: Wall and Thompson.

Lukes, Steven. 1974. *Power: A Radical View.* London: Macmillan.

McMullin, Julie. 2010. *Understanding Social Inequality: Intersections of Class, Age, Gender, Ethnicity, and Race in Canada,* 2nd edn. Toronto: Oxford University Press.

Mann, Michael. 1986. *The Sources of Social Power, Vol.1.* Cambridge: Cambridge University Press.

———. 1993. *The Sources of Social Power, Vol.2.* Cambridge: Cambridge University Press.

Marchak, M. Patricia. 1988. *Ideological Perspectives on Canada.* Toronto: McGraw-Hill Ryerson.

Marx, Karl. 1862. *Theories of Surplus Value, Vol. 2.* Moscow: Progress Publishers.

———. 1867. *Capital, Vol. 1.* New York: International Publishers.

———. 1894. *Capital, Vol. 3.* New York: International Publishers.

——— and Friedrich Engels. 1848a. *The Communist Manifesto.* New York: Washington Square Press.

——. and ——. 1848b. *The Communist Manifesto* (German version). In *Marx Engels Werke, Vol.4.* Institut fur Marxismus-Leninismus Beim Zk Der Sed. Berlin: Dietz Verlag.

Milkman, Ruth. 1987. *Gender at Work.* Urbana: University of Illinois Press.

Nisbet, Robert A. 1959. "The decline and fall of social class." *Pacific Sociological Review* 2: 11–17.

Parkin, Frank. 1979. *Marxism and Class Theory: A Bourgeois Critique.* London: Tavistock.

Parsons, Talcott. 1951. *The Social System.* New York: Free Press.

——. 1953. "A revised analytical approach to the theory of social stratification." In T. Parsons, *Essays in Sociological Theory,* pp. 386–439. New York: Free Press.

Porter, John. 1965. *The Vertical Mosaic.* Toronto: University of Toronto Press.

Poulantzas, Nicos. 1975. *Classes in Contemporary Capitalism.* London: New Left Books.

——. 1978. *State, Power, Socialism.* London: New Left Books.

Reitz, Jeffrey, Rupa Banerjee, Mai Phan, and Jordan Thompson. 2009. "Race, religion, and the social integration of new immigrant minorities in Canada." *International Migration Review* 43: 695–726.

Runciman, W.G. 1989. *A Treatise on Social Theory. Vol. 2, Substantive Social Theory.* Cambridge: Cambridge University Press.

Scott, John. 1996. *Stratification and Power.* Cambridge: Polity Press.

Tilly, Charles. 1998. *Durable Inequality.* Berkeley: University of California Press.

Walby, Sylvia. 1990. *Theorizing Patriarchy.* Oxford: Basil Blackwell.

——. 1997. *Gender Transformations.* London: Routledge.

Weber, Max. 1922. *Economy and Society, Vols 1–3.* New York: Bedminster Press.

Wilson, William Julius. 1973. *Power, Racism, and Privilege.* New York: Macmillan.

Wright, Erik Olin. 1978. *Class, Crisis, and the State.* London: New Left Books.

——. 1979. *Class Structure and Income Determination.* New York: Academic Press.

——. 1985. *Classes.* London: Verso.

——. 1989. *The Debate on Classes.* London: Verso.

——. 1994. *Interrogating Inequality: Essays on Class Analysis, Socialism, and Marxism.* London: Verso.

——. 1997. *Class Counts: Comparative Studies in Class Analysis.* Cambridge: Cambridge University Press.

——, ed. 2005. *Approaches to Class Analysis.* Cambridge: Cambridge University Press.

—— and Joel Rogers. 2010. *American Society: How It Really Works.* New York: W.W Norton.

Wrong, Dennis. 1979. *Power: Its Forms, Bases and Uses.* New York: Harper and Row.

Zawilski, Valerie, ed. 2010. *Inequality in Canada. A Reader on the Intersections of Gender, Race, and* Class, 2nd edn. Toronto: Oxford University Press.

Part I

Power and Class

We begin the study of social inequality in Canada with three papers dealing with the interplay of power and class structure in our society. This is a logical starting point because, as was discussed in the general introduction, the concepts of class and power are pivotal to any general understanding of social inequality. In Part I, we are especially interested in the power that derives from ownership and control of productive property and resources, and in the nature of the class structure that is defined by such power. Some selections also explore the connections between economic classes and the state, most notably the role of government activities and policies in shaping the pattern of both ownership and class inequality in Canada.

In capitalist countries like Canada, and perhaps in all societies, ownership of property is arguably the key defining criterion for understanding the nature of material inequality and the emergence of economic classes. But what is really meant by the notion of property ownership? Most theorists agree that property does not refer to the possession of material resources used only for personal consumption, such as food, clothing, shelter, and the like. This is not to say that the distribution of these and other consumer items is unimportant to the study of inequality, nor is it to deny the tremendous significance of these items for those who experience a shortage or abundance of them in their daily lives. Rather, it is to recognize that the possession of material benefits or products is not only, or even primarily, what constitutes property ownership. Ownership of property, in its most crucial sense, entails the *right of disposition over the economic process in general.*

The essence of property ownership is having the capacity to command the various activities and organizational processes involved in producing, accumulating, investing, or expending society's material or economic resources. Ultimately, it is from this capacity that decisions are made about the distribution of economic benefits to people, and it is through this capacity that some groups and individuals can exclude others from economic control or influence. Perhaps the most important outcome of this process is that the class of people who own society's productive property is in a position to establish relations of domination and exploitation over the class of non-owners, who in turn must sell their labour to survive. The non-owners, or working class, may resist this pattern of relationships through political organization, unionization, and other forms of collective action.

However, as both classical and contemporary social theorists have often pointed out, the owning class is typically able to override or limit the success of such opposition, given the rights of this class to private productive property and the protection of these rights by the state or government.

The first chapter in this section, by Edward Grabb and Monica Hwang, assesses evidence on the concentration of economic power in Canada, in order to address three related questions: Has the share of Canada's economy controlled by private-sector corporations increased in recent decades? How significant for the ownership structure are the transnational connections that arise when foreign-controlled companies operate in Canada, and when Canadian companies operate in other countries? And how does the state's power and influence compare with that of private business interests when it comes to owning and directing the contemporary Canadian economy?

The second paper in this section, by William Carroll, offers an extensive assessment of several issues relating to the concentration of economic ownership in Canada and the nature of the Canadian capitalist class. He also links this discussion to the increasingly crucial problem of understanding the global capitalist economy and the role of Canada's corporate leaders and large-scale businesses within this broader international context. For many observers, the high concentration of economic control in relatively few hands is a potentially serious problem. The main concern is that far too much power has been wielded historically by the owners of productive property. Any further centralization of ownership, both within Canada and internationally, enhances the likelihood that such power could be abused, with the rest of the population facing increased exploitation and domination by the owning class.

In Chapter 3, Jim Conley considers the processes and forces that have been involved in the formation of the Canadian class structure. Beginning with Marx's and Weber's classical approaches to understanding capitalist class systems, and some discussion of Durkheim's perspective, the author then focuses on a review of Canadian evidence relating to a number of key topics. These include the alleged tendency for increased class polarization in modern capitalism, the changing organization of the workplace and its possible effects on working-class solidarity, the likelihood of increasing class awareness or class consciousness within the working class, and the prospects for mobilization, formal organization, and collective action among workers in Canada today.

The overall message conveyed in these chapters is that ownership of productive property or resources, especially through the mechanism of giant private-sector business enterprises, is perhaps the most fundamental force generating the overall pattern of social inequality, both in Canada and in the larger global arena. Moreover, the available evidence suggests that this will continue to be true in the foreseeable future.

1 Ownership Concentration, Transnational Connections, and State Involvement in the Canadian Economy

Edward Grabb and Monica Hwang

Introduction

A crucial feature of Canada's economic structure is the concentration of ownership among large-scale business enterprises. Researchers have studied this topic for many decades (Myers 1914; Creighton 1937), with John Porter's analyses in the 1950s and 1960s offering the first detailed evidence (Porter 1956, 1957, 1965). Porter found that fewer than 200 large corporations, controlled by boards of directors comprising roughly 1,000 individuals, dominated much of Canada's ownership structure. The next major body of research was Wallace Clement's studies of Canada's "corporate elite" (Clement 1975, 1977a, 1977b), which showed that, by the 1970s, economic control in Canada had probably become even more concentrated. Clement found that only 113 powerful companies, controlled by approximately 1,000 directors, accounted for the majority of business activity.

William Carroll has conducted more recent research suggesting that concentration of economic power has continued to increase. He found that, by the late 1990s, the dominant stratum of Canada's corporate elite included only 426 people, the directors of multiple interlocking enterprises at the top of the corporate structure (e.g., Carroll 2008, 2010; Carroll and Klassen 2011). Other academics, commentators, and journalists have also contributed to what has become a large literature on ownership of the Canadian economy (e.g., Newman 1979, 1981; Marchak 1979; Niosi 1981; Ornstein 1976; Brym 1985; Veltmeyer 1987; Laxer 1989; Fox and Ornstein 1986; O'Connor 1999; Brownlee 2005; Francis 1986, 2008). All of these studies suggest that the concentration of economic power continues to be very high.

Historically, many powerful companies were owned or controlled by a small number of people. A few prominent and long-established families formed a major component of Canada's economic elite (Newman 1979; Francis 1986, 2008). Over the years, they have included such well-known names as the Eatons, the Molsons, the Westons, the Thomsons, and the McCains. More recently, they have been joined or replaced by the Rogers family, the Saputos, and others. Another component of our economic elite involves individual entrepreneurs who, through what are commonly called "conglomerates" or "holding companies," control interrelated sets of large and often quite diverse businesses. An illustration is James Irving, who owns J.D. Irving, which is a conglomerate with interests in forestry, pulp and paper, newsprint, building supplies, frozen food, transportation, shipping lines, and shipbuilding. As the principal investors and shareholders in many of Canada's biggest businesses, these families and business leaders have had a sustained influence on the nature and overall direction of our economy.

Apart from private-sector companies, two other principal components of Canada's economic power structure can be identified. One involves transnational connections that link our economy to enterprises in other countries. The role of foreign owners in Canada's economy once captured the attention of leading researchers (e.g., Levitt 1970; Clement 1977a; Laxer 1989). More recently, another primary component has become the growth of reverse transnational links involving Canadian ownership of businesses outside Canada, as have the ways that transnational ownership connects the Canadian economy to the larger global capitalist system (Carroll 2010; see also Chapter 2 in this volume).

A third key component of economic ownership for some researchers involves the role of government. Especially since the 1970s, social scientists in various countries have been interested in government or state involvement in economic activity (Miliband 1973; Poulantzas 1978; Wright 1978; Offe 1984). In Canada, as well, observers have debated the extent of state intervention and its importance for shaping the system of economic power (Panitch 1977; Calvert 1984; Banting 1986; Fox and Ornstein 1986; Carroll 2010).

In this chapter, we review research on the pattern of ownership and economic control in Canada, focusing mainly on these three components: what is the evidence for ownership concentration in recent years, especially among Canada's large-scale private-sector corporations; what part do foreign or transnational connections play these days, and how have these connections changed over time; and how does the level of ownership by state-controlled agencies or enterprises compare with that of private-sector companies? Answering these questions will provide a much clearer picture of economic power and ownership concentration in Canada in the contemporary period.

Concentration of Ownership

Previous research on privately owned Canadian businesses has shown a high degree of ownership concentration. One study reported that, among the more than 400,000 companies operating in Canada in 1987, the largest 25 enterprises by themselves accounted for over 41 per cent of all corporate assets (O'Connor 1999: 36). This level of concentration was significantly greater than it had been just 10 years before (Francis 1986; Grabb 1990).

More recent evidence suggests some changes in the structure of corporate ownership. First, a number of the established family "dynasties," including the Eatons, the Reichmanns, and the Bronfmans, experienced a reduction in influence and the loss or sale of some corporate holdings. Consequently, whereas just 32 families, along with five conglomerates, controlled 40 per cent of Canada's top 500 companies in 1986, only 21 per cent of the top 500 were family controlled in 2007 (Francis 2008: 10–16). Nevertheless, some family-based enterprises continue to be very important. Examples include the Thomsons, who are a major force in publishing and media, the Irvings, with their powerful holdings in oil, pulp and paper, and transportation, and the Rogers family, who are key players in media and telecommunications. All of these families are central decision-makers on the Canadian economic scene, while also ranking among the wealthiest people in the country (Macdonald 2014; *Canada Business Review* 2011).

Government statistics and other evidence suggest a sustained pattern of high economic concentration. Between 1987 and 1998, the share of corporate assets controlled by the largest 25 enterprises continued to represent more than 40 per cent of the national total (Statistics Canada 1995: 50; 1998: 38–40). By 2000, large companies (those with assets above

$25 million) accounted for almost 80 per cent of all business assets (Statistics Canada 2001: 37, 44; also Carroll 2010; Brownlee 2005). Another study has looked at trends in the total value of all companies listed on the Toronto Stock Exchange (TSX), which includes the vast majority of all firms listed in Canada; this analysis revealed that the top 60 firms on the TSX accounted for 29 per cent of the total value in 1956, and that this proportion had doubled, to 57 per cent, as of 2010 (Brennan 2012: 28–9). Overall, these findings suggest an exceptionally high level of ownership concentration, which has almost certainly increased over recent decades.

Ownership concentration is apparent throughout most of the economy, but one area that has always stood out is the financial sector. Here only a handful of banks, trust companies, and insurance firms have predominated (Francis 1986, 2008). Mergers and acquisitions in the past two decades have added to this centralization. Prominent examples include the Bank of Nova Scotia's 1997 purchase of National Trust; Great West Life's 1997 takeover of London Life and 2003 purchase of Canada Life; Toronto-Dominion Bank's 2000 acquisition of Canada Trust; and Sun Life's 2002 acquisition of Clarica Life Insurance. The evidence of ownership concentration in the financial sector is truly striking. Data from Statistics Canada indicate that financial industries owned assets worth $2.214 trillion in 2005 (Statistics Canada 2007), and the *Financial Post* (2006: 64) reported that $1.727 trillion of these assets, or more than 78 per cent of the total for 2005, were held by the five largest Canadian banks: the Royal Bank, the Canadian Imperial Bank of Commerce, the Toronto-Dominion Bank, the Bank of Nova Scotia, and the Bank of Montreal. By 2012, the five largest banks accounted for about 90 per cent of all bank assets in Canada, a much higher level of concentration than in other developed nations, including the United States, the United Kingdom, Japan, and France (IMF 2014: 30).

The media are another prominent sector that has witnessed high and increasing ownership concentration. Findings for 2013 published by the Canadian Media Concentration Research Project (CMCRP) indicate that three companies—Rogers, Bell, and Telus—accounted for 92 per cent of the wireless media market; four companies—Shaw, Bell, Rogers, and Quebecor—controlled 79 per cent of cable and satellite business; and five companies—Bell, Rogers, Shaw, Videotron, and Telus—accounted for 75 per cent of Canada's Internet business (CMCRP 2014).

Transnational Connections and Foreign Influence

Transnational connections represent another significant feature of our ownership structure. These connections include those in which foreign enterprises own and control parts of Canada's economy, but also involve linkages in which Canadian corporations own and control businesses in other nations.

In Canada's early colonial development, our economy was marked by considerable outside control and influence, first from French, and later from British, commercial interests (Clement 1975). Subsequently, especially in the twentieth century, American-owned transnational companies were the most prominent foreign players. US involvement developed in a series of stages, becoming especially important during a period of about 25 years after World War II. By 1970, foreign ownership reached a peak, accounting for approximately 34 per cent of Canada's total economic assets and 38 per cent of total revenues (Statistics Canada 2005; Niosi 1981; Grabb 1990). During this era, our economy experienced higher levels of foreign control than most other developed nations, making Canada resemble less developed countries in this respect. Many researchers and observers at that time feared that Canada could lose control of its own economic destiny, becoming increasingly subject to decisions made by foreign corporations whose interests might not match the interests and needs of the Canadian people (Levitt 1970; Clement 1975, 1977a; Laxer 1989). More recently, however, foreign influence has decreased substantially. By 2012, the foreign share of total assets held in Canada had declined to just 18 per cent, while the foreign share of total revenues had also dropped, although it was still a sizable 29 per cent (Statistics Canada 2014b).

Another important change in recent years has been that our transnational connections mainly operate in the opposite direction, with Canadian businesses buying or investing in foreign countries more than the other way around. For each year between 1997 and 2013, the dollar value of Canadian direct investment abroad has exceeded foreign direct investment in Canada; the figures for 2013 show that Canadian businesses invested $779 billion in other countries, which is about 14 per cent higher than the $686 billion of foreign direct investment in Canada for that year (Statistics Canada 2014a). In fact, for some commentators, this reversal of the old pattern is a cause for concern. Some suggest that our higher investment abroad compared to foreign investment here is a sign that we may not be attracting sufficient outside interest in establishing businesses in Canada, which could negatively affect our employment opportunities, economic expansion, technological development, and general prosperity (e.g., Hejazi 2010; Bergevin and Schwanen 2011). In the current era, analysts increasingly see foreign investments, both in Canada and elsewhere, not as threats to the national economy but as a logical consequence of economic globalization and the worldwide expansion of capitalism (see Carroll 2010; Brownlee 2005; Francis 2008).

Over the years, the strongest evidence of foreign control in our economy could be found at the very top of the non-financial sector, where a few major non-Canadian corporations tended to predominate. In the mid-1980s, for example, six of the top 10 companies operating in Canada were foreign-owned. These included the Canadian subsidiaries of the three American automotive giants (General Motors of Canada, Ford of Canada, and Chrysler Canada), as well as two American-owned oil subsidiaries (Imperial Oil and Texaco Canada) and one Dutch-controlled oil company (Shell Canada) (*Financial Post* 1985). By 2013, however, there were only two foreign firms in the top 10 (Suncor Energy and Imperial Oil); among the top 100, foreign companies were still quite evident, especially in such areas as automobile manufacturing (e.g., Honda Canada, Ford of Canada, Chrysler Canada, General Motors of Canada) and retail (e.g., Walmart, Costco, Home Depot, Best Buy) (*Financial Post* 2014). These examples suggest that most of the foreign sector of our economy is still American.

Recent government statistics confirm this pattern. Companies based in the United States accounted for 49 per cent of the total foreign assets held in Canada in 2012 (Statistics Canada 2014b: Table 2). This proportion is down compared to previous years (e.g., it was 59 per cent in 2005) but still indicates a substantial American presence. Other countries with notable involvement in our economy include the United Kingdom, which accounted for 13 per cent of all foreign assets in Canada, the Netherlands (6 per cent), Germany (5 per cent), Japan (4 per cent), and France (3 per cent) (Statistics Canada 2014b: Table 2).

The State and Economic Power

The final topic to consider is the role of Canada's various levels of government in the contemporary Canadian economy. Historically, business activities have often been influenced by state involvement, although sometimes in contradictory ways. At certain times, for example, governments have promoted and protected Canadian companies, by lending money to Canadian capitalists and imposing tariffs and other trade restrictions on foreign competitors; at other times, however, governments have encouraged foreign business ventures, by offering tax reductions and other incentives to foreign companies in Canada, and also establishing state-run enterprises that compete directly with Canada's private-sector firms (Clement 1975, 1977b; Traves 1979; Marchak 1979; Laxer 1989).

Some discussions about the role of the Canadian state have centred on whether government intervention into the economy has become excessive in recent decades. Certain researchers question this claim, arguing that the state's role in the Canadian economy is actually rather small. These analysts usually acknowledge that the state spends a considerable portion of the national wealth, with governments covering the costs of providing and maintaining public education, health care, a wide range of social and protective services, transportation facilities, and the like. However, most of these writers also contend that, otherwise, the state has normally been a limited player in the Canadian economy, with private business interests still acting as the pre-eminent force (e.g., Calvert 1984; Fox and Ornstein 1986; O'Connor 1999). It is argued, as well, that a good deal of government activity has been directed towards assisting private-sector businesses, especially in their attempts to be more competitive in the global capitalist economy (Carroll 2010).

Other observers, however, have alleged that the various branches of the state have become too influential or intrusive within our economic system. These writers argue that governments at all levels too often use their considerable taxation and spending powers to fund poorly conceived endeavours, including expensive, loosely administered social programs and unprofitable, inefficient government enterprises (Palacios et al. 2008; Lammam 2013; Speer et al. 2014). Similar views have been voiced by many private-sector capitalists, who see the government as an unwelcome competitor in the business arena (Ornstein 1985; Ornstein and Stevenson 1999). Added to these perceptions is the belief that state-owned companies usually have an unfair advantage over private businesses, which need to turn a profit to survive and cannot rely on government financial assistance to bail them out of difficulty.

One direct means for measuring state economic power is to determine the proportion of government-controlled major enterprises within the national economy. Previous research found that, in both 1975 and 1985, only four of the top 25 non-financial corporations operating in Canada were state-owned, and fewer than 10 of the top 100 were state-owned (Grabb 1990: 79). More recent business rankings suggest an even smaller government presence at the highest level. For example, in 2013, no government-directed enterprises were among the leading 25 companies, although there were 11 in the top 100. These included four utilities—Hydro-Québec, Ontario's Hydro One, the British Columbia Hydro and Power Authority, and Ontario Power Generation; four financial services or compensation organizations—the Caisse de dépôt et placement du Québec, Canadian Mortgage and Housing Corporation, Ontario's Workplace Safety and Insurance Board, and Saskatchewan's Crown Investments Corporation; as well as Canada Post, the Ontario Lottery and Gaming Corporation, and the Liquor Control Board of Ontario (*Financial Post* 2014; see also Carroll 2010; Francis 2008). In general, then, it is difficult to argue that government enterprises dominate the Canadian economy.

A more comprehensive gauge of government economic influence is the share of the nation's total assets held by the various branches of the state. One early study, using government data on the "national balance sheet," estimated that the share of total assets in Canada owned by the government or public sector stood at 18.0 per cent in 1961, and declined to just 10.6 per cent by 2001 (Grabb 2004: 26). More recent data indicate that, by 2012, the asset value of government businesses and enterprises represented only 8.5 per cent of total corporate assets held within Canada (Statistics Canada 2014c: Table 24). Such findings reveal that government economic control in Canada is not nearly as great as some observers believe, is far lower than that enjoyed by the private business sector, and has been on the decline for several decades.

Although numerous factors probably account for decreasing state involvement, a major cause has been the changing policies of the federal government and many provincial administrations in recent years. In particular, state leaders encouraged private-sector economic expansion and have pursued the sale of various government-run enterprises to private interests. This pattern began in the mid-1980s, after the election of the federal Progressive Conservatives under Brian Mulroney. Despite suggestions to the contrary before their election in 1993, the federal Liberals, under Jean Chrétien, applied a similar set of policies into the early 2000s. From 2006 to 2015, Stephen Harper's Conservative government followed the same course (Sanger and Crawley 2008). Whether the recently elected federal Liberal government of Justin Trudeau will seek to expand or maintain direct state involvement in the economy remains to be seen, but any new government involvement is likely to remain limited, given the recent history of Liberal governments in Canada.

Conclusion

Our review of recent evidence on economic control and ownership in Canada has revealed many of the same patterns that existed in previous years. That is, there is still a high concentration of economic power in a small group of giant private-sector corporations operating at the top of the ownership structure. Trend data from different sources suggest, moreover, that that this high level of concentration has probably increased over the past several decades. It seems clear that large-scale financial and non-financial business enterprises, along with the principal shareholders and directors that control them, are as powerful as they have ever been in the Canadian economy.

We have also considered transnational connections and foreign involvement in Canada's ownership structure. We have found that non-Canadian businesses play a notable role in the economy, although substantially less than they did during the peak years of foreign influence around 1970. Another important change in recent decades has been that Canadian businesses now buy or invest in foreign countries more than the other way around. In contrast to researchers from years past, current analysts tend to see both types of transnational economic connections as logical developments in the continued growth and expansion of the globalizing capitalist system.

The final major issue we addressed was the level of state ownership and control in the Canadian economy. We have seen that the government role, though notable in some respects, is really quite minor in comparison with that played by private corporations. Moreover, the government's presence on the economic scene has declined in the past several decades, both in regard to its role as a director of large-scale business enterprises and in its share of national assets. Very few of Canada's largest enterprises are government-owned, and the proportion of Canadian assets owned by all branches of government is down to less than one-tenth of the total. In addition, for the past two decades or more, we have seen concerted drives by the federal and provincial governments to cut back on services in an effort to reduce government debts and deficits. These policies signal some curtailment of state economic activity in the spending area as well. The government strategy for the future appears to be one in which political leaders look primarily to the private sector, and not to state-sponsored programs, to promote economic activity. Overall, the current climate is one in which private-sector businesses continue to determine the major contours and direction of Canada's economic power structure.

Questions for Critical Thought

1. Some people think it is harmful for a few large companies to control a large proportion of Canada's economy. What are some of the arguments for and against this opinion?
2. Family businesses have been an important feature of Canada's corporate structure for many decades. What are your views on whether and why this is a positive or negative aspect of the economic and class systems?
3. Nowadays many analysts say that transnational interconnections between foreign involvement in the Canadian economy and Canadian involvement in the economies of other countries are both logical and potentially beneficial. What do you think about this claim?
4. Some business leaders contend that government involvement in Canada's economic activity is generally bad for business and for the general public. What are your thoughts concerning whether the government's role is useful or unnecessary, and whether it should be increased or decreased?

Recommended Readings

Brownlee, Jamie. 2005. *Ruling Canada: Corporate Cohesion and Democracy*. Halifax: Fernwood.

Carroll, William. 2010. *Corporate Power in a Globalizing World*, rev. edn. Toronto: Oxford University Press.

Francis, Diane. 2008. *Who Owns Canada Now?* Toronto: HarperCollins.

Healy, Teresa, ed. 2008. *The Harper Record*. Ottawa: Canadian Centre for Policy Alternatives.

Recommended Websites

Canadian Centre for Policy Alternatives:
https://www.policyalternatives.ca/

Corporations Returns Act:
http://www23.statcan.gc.ca/imdb/p2SV.pl?Function=getSurvey&SDDS=2503

The Daily, Statistics Canada's Official Release Bulletin:
http://www.statcan.gc.ca/dai-quo/

***The Financial Post*:**
http://www.financialpost.com/index.html

References

Banting, Keith. 1986. *The State and Economic Interests*. Toronto: University of Toronto Press.

Bergevin, Philippe, and Daniel Schwanen. 2011. "Reforming the Investment Canada Act." *C.D. Howe Institute Commentary* No. 337, Dec. http://www.cdhowe.org/pdf/commentary_337.pdf.

Brennan, Jordan. 2012. *A Shrinking Universe: How Concentrated Corporate Power Is Shaping Income Inequality in Canada*. Canadian Centre for Policy Alternatives research paper, Nov. http://www.policyalternatives.ca/sites/default/files/uploads/publications/National%20Office/2012/11/Shrinking_Universe_0.pdf.

Brownlee, Jamie. 2005. *Ruling Canada. Corporate Cohesion and Democracy.* Halifax: Fernwood.

Brym, Robert. 1985. *The Structure of the Canadian Capitalist Class.* Toronto: Garamond.

Calvert, John. 1984. *Government, Limited.* Ottawa: Canadian Centre for Policy Alternatives.

Canada Business Review. 2011. "Canadian billionaires and the conglomerates they lead." 11 Jan. http://www.businessreviewcanada.ca/leadership/8/Canadian-Billionaires-and-the-Conglomerates-They-Lead.

Canadian Media Concentration Research Project (CMCRP). 2014. "Media and internet concentration, 1984–2013." 26 Nov. http://www.cmcrp.org/2014/11/26/media-and-internet-concentration-1984-2013/.

Carroll, William. 2008. "The corporate elite and the transformation of finance capital: A view from Canada." *Sociological Review* 56 (S1): 44–63.

———. 2010. *Corporate Power in a Globalizing World,* rev. edn. Toronto: Oxford University Press.

——— and Jerome Klassen. 2011. "Transnational class formation? Globalization and the Canadian corporate network." *Journal of World-Systems Research* 17: 379–402.

Clement, Wallace. 1975. *The Canadian Corporate Elite.* Toronto: McClelland & Stewart.

———. 1977a. *Continental Corporate Power.* Toronto: McClelland & Stewart.

———. 1977b. "The corporate elite, the capitalist class, and the Canadian state." In L. Panitch, ed., *The Canadian State,* pp. 225–48. Toronto: University of Toronto Press.

Creighton, Donald. 1937. *The Commercial Empire of the St. Lawrence.* Toronto: Macmillan.

Financial Post. 1985. *The Financial Post 500,* Summer.

———. 2006. *The Financial Post Business FP500: Canada's Largest Corporations,* June.

———. 2014. *The FP500: 2014.* http://www.financialpost.com/news/fp500/2014/index.html?sort=rank&page=2.

Fox, John, and Michael Ornstein. 1986. "The Canadian state and corporate elites in the post-war period." *Canadian Review of Sociology and Anthropology* 23, 4 (Nov.): 481–506.

Francis, Diane. 1986. *Controlling Interest.* Toronto: Macmillan.

———. 2008. *Who Owns Canada Now?* Toronto: Harper Collins.

Grabb, Edward. 1990. "Who owns Canada? Concentration of ownership and the distribution of economic assets, 1975–1985." *Journal of Canadian Studies* 25: 72–93.

———. 2004. "Economic power in Canada." In J. Curtis, N. Guppy, and E. Grabb, eds, *Social Inequality in Canada: Patterns, Problems, Policies,* 4th edn, pp. 20–30. Toronto: Pearson Education Canada.

Hejazi, Walid. 2010. "Dispelling Canadian myths about foreign direct investment." Institute for Research on Public Policy, IRPP Study No. 1, 26 Jan. http://irpp.org/research-studies/study-no1/.

International Monetary Fund (IMF). 2014. *Canada—Financial Sector Stability Assessment.* IMF Country Report No. 14/29, Feb. https://www.imf.org/external/pubs/ft/scr/2014/cr1429.pdf.

Lammam, Charles. 2013. "Government waste cost Canadian taxpayers as much as $197 billion since 1988." *The Fraser Institute Research and News,* 31 Oct. http://www.fraserinstitute.org/research-news/overview.aspx.

Laxer, Gord. 1989. *Open for Business.* Toronto: Oxford University Press.

Levitt, Kari. 1970. *Silent Surrender.* Montreal and Kingston: McGill-Queen's University Press.

Macdonald, David. 2014. "Outrageous fortune: Documenting Canada's wealth gap." Canadian Centre for Policy Alternatives research paper, Apr. https://www.policyalternatives.ca/sites/default/files/uploads/publications/National%20Office/2014/04/Outrageous_Fortune.pdf.

Marchak, Patricia. 1979. *In Whose Interests?* Toronto: McClelland & Stewart.

Miliband, Ralph. 1973. *The State in Capitalist Society.* London: Quartet Books.

Myers, Gustavus. 1914. *A History of Canadian Wealth.* Toronto: James Lewis and Samuel.

Newman, Peter. 1979. *The Canadian Establishment.* Toronto: McClelland & Stewart-Bantam.

———. 1981. *The Acquisitors.* Toronto: McClelland & Stewart-Bantam.

Niosi, Jorge. 1981. *Canadian Capitalism: A Study of Power in the Canadian Business Establishment.* Toronto: Lorimer.

O'Connor, Julia. 1999. "Ownership, class, and public policy." In J. Curtis, N. Guppy, and E. Grabb, eds, *Social Inequality in Canada: Patterns, Problems, Policies*, 3rd edn, pp. 35–47. Scarborough, Ont.: Prentice-Hall Allyn Bacon Canada.

Offe, Claus. 1984. *Contradictions in the Welfare State.* Cambridge, Mass.: MIT Press.

Ornstein, Michael. 1976. "The boards and executives of the largest Canadian corporations: Size, composition, and interlocks." *Canadian Journal of Sociology* 1: 411–37.

———. 1985. "Canadian capital and the Canadian state: Ideology in an era of crisis." In R. Brym, ed., *The Structure of the Canadian Capitalist Class*, pp. 129–66. Toronto: Garamond.

——— and Michael Stevenson. 1999. *Politics and Ideology in Canada.* Montreal and Kingston: McGill-Queen's University Press.

Palacios, Milagros, Niels Veldhuis, and Michael Walker. 2008. *Tax Facts 15.* Vancouver: Fraser Institute.

Panitch, Leo, ed. 1977. *The Canadian State.* Toronto: University of Toronto Press.

Porter, John. 1956. "Concentration of economic power and the economic elite in Canada." *Canadian Journal of Economics and Political Science* 22: 199–220.

———. 1957. "The economic elite and the social structure of Canada." *Canadian Journal of Economics and Political Science* 23: 377–94.

———. 1965. *The Vertical Mosaic.* Toronto: University of Toronto Press.

Poulantzas, Nicos. 1978. *State, Power, Socialism.* London: New Left Books.

Sanger, Toby, and Corina Crawley. 2008. "Privatization under Harper." In Teresa Healy, ed., *The Harper Record*, pp. 389–401. Ottawa: Canadian Centre for Policy Alternatives. http://www.policyalternatives.ca/sites/default/files/uploads/publications/National_Office_Pubs/2008/HarperRecord/Privatization_Under_Harper.pdf.

Speer, Sean, Charles Lammam, Milagros Palacios, Hugh MacIntyre, and Feixue Ren. 2014. "The cost of government debt in Canada." *Fraser Research Bulletin*, Aug. http://www.fraserinstitute.org/uploadedFiles/fraser-ca/Content/research-news/research/publications/cost-of-government-debt-in-canada.pdf.

Statistics Canada. 1995. *Corporations and Labour Unions Returns Act. Preliminary 1993.* Catalogue no. 61-220.

———. 1998. *Corporations and Labour Unions Returns Act. Preliminary 1998.* Catalogue no. 61-220.

———. 2001. *Canada's International Investment Position, 2000.* Catalogue no. 67-202.

———. 2005. "Study: Trends in foreign investment and foreign control." *The Daily*, 18 Nov. http://www.statcan.gc.ca/daily-quotidien/051118/dq051118b-eng.htm.

———. 2007. "Foreign control in the Canadian economy." *The Daily*, 14 June.

———. 2014a. "Foreign direct investment, 2013." *The Daily*, 25 Apr. http://www.statcan.gc.ca/daily-quotidien/140425/dq140425a-eng.htm.

———. 2014b. "Foreign control in the Canadian economy, 2012." *The Daily*, 9 Dec. http://www.statcan.gc.ca/daily-quotidien/141209/dq141209a-eng.htm.

———. 2014c. *Corporations Returns Act 2012.* Catalogue no. 61-220-X. 9 Dec. http://www.statcan.gc.ca/pub/61-220-x/2012000/t075-eng.pdf.

Traves, Tom. 1979. *The State and Enterprise: Canadian Manufacturers and the Federal Government, 1917–1931.* Toronto: University of Toronto Press.

Veltmeyer, Henry. 1987. *Canadian Corporate Power.* Toronto: Garamond.

Wright, Erik Olin. 1978. *Class, Crisis, and the State.* London: New Left Books.

2 The Changing Face(s) of Corporate Power in Canada

William K. Carroll

In the contemporary world there is a close relationship between social power and social inequality: through the exercise of power, structures of inequality are reproduced, yet power itself is rooted in inequality. Underpinning the exercise of power are systemic inequities in the control of resources that enable dominant groups to frame agendas, make decisions, and secure compliance. These systemic inequities create a *unilateral dependence* that, for Peter Blau (1964: 117–18), is at the heart of power: the dependence of subordinates obliges them to comply with the requests of the powerful, lest the latter cease to provide for their needs.

Corporate power is the power that accrues to enormous concentrations of capital, or to large corporations in the late modern world. Workers, communities, and states depend on large corporations that may or may not choose to invest in a given place at a given time (Bowles and Gintis 1986); in this fundamental sense the concentration of corporate capital is a concentration of corporate power. Corporations had already emerged in Europe and North America by the middle decades of the nineteenth century, when Karl Marx (1967) drafted his prescient remarks on "the modern joint-stock company." But it was not until the twentieth century that corporate power was fully consolidated in advanced capitalist countries. Increasingly, corporate power has been projected beyond national states in the form of transnational corporations (TNCs), along with banks, a global capital market, and a complex of quasi-state institutions like the World Bank and the World Trade Organization (WTO) (Hart-Landsberg 2013; Hilary 2013).

Marx, of course, is the social theorist of capitalism *par excellence*. Marx gives us a starting point for the empirical analysis of corporate capitalism as a system of *class power*. Marx holds that control over the economic surplus is a decisive form of power. In any class society, the dominant class's control of economic resources—the means of production—enables it to appropriate the economic surplus produced by a subordinate class that depends on the dominant class for access to the means of production and subsistence (for jobs and wages, respectively).[1] Control of the surplus does more than fund an exorbitant standard of living for the dominant class. It also places the economic future largely at that class's disposal, and relegates others to positions of unilateral dependence.

As a form of class society, capitalism is distinctive in the market-mediated character of its social relations. Capital never exists as a unified entity but as many units, the most important of which are large corporations. Capitalists compete with each other for a sufficient share of the economic surplus to keep them "in the game": that is, maintaining an above-average profit. Moreover, in corporate capitalism the vast scale of production requires an elaborate apparatus for financing new production, getting commodities to final consumers, etc. Consequently, the economic surplus is competitively subdivided, not only among industrial corporations but also among all lines of investment, from finance and real estate to industry and retail commerce, with investors of whatever stripe striving for above-average rates of return. Workers within capitalism resist being exploited (e.g., through union activism), but also compete with each other for jobs and income. In the current era of globalizing capitalism, corporations have the structural power to play one national workforce off against another, so that union leaders and social activists worry about the prospect of a "race to the bottom," as workers in different countries undercut each other for the ultimate benefit of transnational capitalists and as TNCs troll the globe for countries offering tax breaks, low wages for workers, and lax environmental standards.

But how do we conceptualize corporate power in sociological terms? The most obvious place to begin is with the corporate directorate. Having final authority over the affairs of the corporation, the board of directors is at the apex of a hierarchy that reaches down to the shop floor. Directorates are *sites* of authority within corporate power structures, and directors are *agents* of corporate power. Also, through the cross-appointment of directors, the boards of major corporations overlap with each other. Such *interlocks* draw directorates into an inter-corporate network, while also drawing directors into a socially integrated corporate elite.

Corporate power is Janus-faced, with the two faces that include both *economic* and *cultural-political* facets. Corporate power is ultimately rooted in capitalist economic relations—the system of commodity production and exchange in which giant corporations and massive pools of money capital concentrate enormous social power in the capitalist class's top tier, so that workers, communities, and states must rely on the capitalist class for survival. This face of corporate power is inseparable from the accumulation of capital. Within corporate capitalism, it takes three forms:

- *Operational* power involves control of the labour processes within the firms that actually produce the economic surplus. It is the power of management, operating through a chain of command in which freedom to make decisions is increasingly circumscribed as we move from top management to the shop floor. Within large corporations, operational power displays a pyramidal shape: at the top is the chief executive officer, who reports directly to the board of directors; at the bottom are thousands of workers producing goods and services in workplaces that may be arrayed across dozens of countries.
- *Strategic* power involves control of the corporation itself, often through ownership of the largest bloc of shares. This is the power to set business strategies for the company or for a set of companies assembled under common control as an enterprise. This power is rooted in the non-democratic character of corporate capital. Directors are annually "elected" by the shareholders, but workers, communities, and consumers are entirely excluded from the election. Moreover, the election is not based on one vote per person, but on one vote per corporate share owned; in practice, then, corporations are controlled by the propertied few who own large concentrations of corporate shares. It has long been recognized that the dispersal of corporate shares across many small investors leads not to "people's capitalism" but to a stronger concentration of strategic power in the hands of major shareholders (Perlo

1958), whose ownership of a small proportion of voting shares can be sufficient to give them control of the board of directors (Scott 1997).
- Finally, *allocative* power stems from control of credit, or the money-capital on which large corporations depend; this power is particularly important when expanding or retooling operations, launching takeover bids, or coping with reduced revenue as a result of economic contraction. Allocative power entails various agents—non-financial capitalists but also governmental and non-governmental organizations—depending on the suppliers of financing, e.g., shareholders in a new public offering or lending institutions such as banks.

Each of these forms of economic power has its characteristic agents and sites in the accumulation process. As we have seen, operational power is wielded by managers within internal corporate management structures. Strategic power can involve complex alignments of major shareholders, whether individual or institutional: although it is centred in the board of directors, where major strategic decisions are made, it often cuts across individual companies through interlocking directorates and inter-corporate ownership (Berkowitz and Fitzgerald 1995; Carroll 2012). The situation is similar for allocative power, which accrues to agents and organizations controlling the financial assets that fund new investment. Allocative power may be centred in the institutions that control money-capital, but it entails complex relations between creditors and debtors, and these relations have often been visible in the structure of interlocking directorates between banks and other corporations.

The key point is that corporate boards of directors show traces of all three kinds of power. Much of the sociological research on corporate power has involved mapping the relations through which the largest corporations are linked together at the level of governance. Viewed from this angle, directorate interlocks, inter-corporate ownership, and the like are traces of allocative, strategic, and operational forms of economic power that, taken together, constitute a structure of *finance capital*: a coalescence of the forms of capital, particularly big industry and high finance, under conditions of monopolization and internationalization (Overbeek 1980; Carroll 2008). Thus defined, finance capital has been integral to advanced capitalism, pulling the largest corporations together into configurations of strategic control, capital allocation, and operational command.

But the exercise of corporate power is not simply a matter of commanding the heights of industry and finance. Its other face is cultural and political. In a way of life deeply marked by class inequality, by the juxtaposition of homeless people living on the street within blocks of the corporate offices at First Canadian Place in Toronto's financial district, the corporate elite strives to maintain hegemony or dominance. The consent of subordinates can never be assumed; although the work of organizing this consent might fall to various intellectuals—in the media, in policy planning think-tanks, in public relations, in academia, etc.—the corporate elite at the apex of the dominant class must exercise active leadership. This does not mean that the corporate elite, or the dominant class, "controls" the political process and its outcomes. Fred Block's (1977) famous claim that "the ruling class does not rule" is still appropriate, even after decades of globalization, during which neo-liberalism has diminished the relative autonomy of national states. Neo-liberalism refers to an economic approach in which national economies revert to old nineteenth-century ideas, including far less government regulation of capitalism, less direct government involvement in the economy through state enterprises, and freer markets.

Nevertheless, even if "the ruling class does not rule," business leadership *does reach* into civil society and into state institutions, recruiting support for a world view within which the interest of capital in profitable accumulation becomes universalized as the general interest of society, or even humanity. To be a leading, or hegemonic, cultural and political force, the corporate elite must achieve and maintain a certain *social cohesiveness* as a business community, with an internal basis of solidarity and a shared perspective on what is to be done.

Both faces of corporate power—the economic and the cultural-political—can be illuminated by studying the largest corporations and the corporate network (Carroll 2010). This chapter reviews findings from sociological research on the shape and form of Canadian corporate power in the era of neo-liberal globalization—from the late 1970s to the present. In the last quarter of the twentieth century, Canada's corporate elite underwent a number of significant transitions. Some of these transitions are closely associated with globalization and its political handmaiden, neo-liberalism, and all of them have been conditioned by these worldwide developments. In the early decades of the twenty-first century, the transitions have intensified. Yet, amid all the changes one constant has been a well-integrated corporate elite, which has continued to play directive roles within and beyond Canada's economy.

Concentration of Economic Power

Large and increasingly globalized corporations concentrate enormous economic power in the hands of those controlling the strategies of these dominant firms. Early in the twenty-first century, there were approximately 1 million incorporated businesses in Canada, yet the top 25 enterprises accounted for 41.2 per cent of all business assets. Across all economic sectors, large companies (firms generally with assets greater than $25 million or annual revenue greater than $100 million) claimed 79.4 per cent of all business assets (Statistics Canada 2001: 37, 44). The sheer concentration of corporate assets is not a new development, however. Ever since the era of the National Policy of protective tariffs established in 1879, capital has been highly concentrated, with a small elite of finance capitalists wielding extensive economic power. By the 1950s and the post–World War II era, the Canadian Pacific Railway—the largest corporate survivor of the old National Policy—still towered above all other corporations in the country, alone accounting for one-tenth of total national industrial assets (Carroll 1986: 65–6).

What is remarkable, however, is that the earlier pattern of extremely concentrated corporate capital was eroded in the post–World War II era with the rise of the welfare state, but was then re-established in the late twentieth century. A neo-liberal regime deregulated markets, reduced social provisioning, and thus redistributed wealth and income upward, based on a framework of continental accumulation that was consolidated in the North American Free Trade Agreement of 1994 (NAFTA). In 1961, the 60 largest corporations listed on the Toronto Stock Exchange (the TSX 60) received 35 per cent of aggregated net corporate profits of all firms in Canada, a figure that grew to an astonishing 60 per cent by 2010; this increase happened with the turn to neo-liberalism and the signing of continental "free trade" deals in 1989 and 1994, and occurred despite Canada being home to only 153,000 firms in 1965, compared to more than 1.3 million in 2009 (Brennan 2012: 19–20). *Most of the profits of 1.3 million companies were claimed by just 60 giant corporations.* Similarly, while in 1956 the top 60 corporations accounted for 29 per cent of the total market capitalization of the Toronto Stock Exchange,[2] by 2010 they claimed 60 per cent, indicating that those 60 firms now "dominate the Canadian political economy, driving the accumulation process" (Brennan 2012: 20)

The same pattern of concentrated ownership occurs for individuals and families. In 2012, the wealthiest 86 Canadian residents, representing just 0.0002 per cent of the population, owned wealth equivalent to the poorest 34 per cent of the population (11.4 million people) (Macdonald 2014). Much of the wealth of these 86 people consists in concentrated corporate shareholdings, placing many of them in a position of strategic control or influence over leading Canadian corporations.

Even more remarkable is the close relationship, over the past six decades, between the concentration of corporate capital and the extent of income inequality. Between 1950 and 2007, the average profit of the Toronto Stock Exchange's top 60 corporations grew from representing 234 times the average profit for all firms in Canada to 14,278 times the average profit, indicating ever-increasing capital concentration through high rates of accumulation by giant firms. Over the same period, the share of total income claimed by the top 0.1 per cent of income earners tripled, from 1.5 per cent to 4.5 per cent. The two time-series curves showed a correlation of 0.86, and the correlation between the concentration within the TSX 60 of corporate share value and the income share of the richest 0.1 per cent was 0.94 (Brennan 2012: 25–6). Particularly since the early 1990s, the *concentration of corporate capital* has closely tracked the *concentration of income* in the hands of an elite few, producing an "unprecedented concentration of both income and corporate power" (Brennan 2012: 40).

Across the same six decades, there was also a *geographical concentration* of corporate head offices in a few metropolitan command centres. In the early post–World War II period Montreal and Toronto were the cities that mattered for the corporate elite (and particularly for the financial sector), but many industrial corporations had head offices and physical plants outside the Toronto–Montreal axis. By the end of the twentieth century, however, the spatial organization of corporate power had been simplified into a bipolar configuration, with these two major urban centres and two lesser ones in the West—Calgary and Vancouver. Outlying areas were little involved, and Toronto decisively eclipsed Montreal as the country's corporate metropolis and terminus for continental and transnational interlocks. This shift meant the *further centralization of strategic control over capital* in the form of large, multi-divisional corporations, in which plant-specific operational aspects of management were subordinated to extra-local corporate strategies issuing from head offices located in these few "alpha" and "beta" world cities (Carroll 2010).[3]

Strategic Control, National Borders, and the Organization of the Corporate Elite

In a globalizing world, the concentration of corporate power cuts across national borders. Transnational investment is an important means through which capital becomes concentrated, and transnational corporations (TNCs) are the most powerful, with multifarious holdings enabling them to play one national or regional workforce (or state) off against another.

In studies of the social organization of Canadian corporate power, questions of corporate capital's *nationality* and the implications of the relatively high levels of foreign control of capital have loomed large (Naylor 1972; Clement 1975, 1977; Niosi 1981; Carroll 1986, 2010). In much of the global South, the process of colonization from the sixteenth century forward created a distinctive structure of class inequality and underdevelopment, as dominant classes in the colonizing states came to control much of the colonial economies, often in alliance with local elites. In the late 1960s and 1970s, a version of this narrative was applied to Canada, which Levitt (1970) famously described as "the world's richest underdeveloped country."

For Canada's corporate elite, the issue could be posed as two different scenarios. Has corporate power been organized around an alliance of Canadian banker/merchants and foreign-based industry, presiding over a cumulative process of silent surrender and underdevelopment, as argued by Levitt, Naylor, and Clement? Or has Canada's corporate elite been organized as in other advanced capitalist societies, with the dominant fraction controlling finance capital and showing the capacity to accumulate capital globally (Carroll 1986: xiv–xv)? Numerous empirical sociological investigations since the 1980s (see Carroll 2008) established the validity of the second scenario:

1. Leading industrial companies and financial institutions, heavily interlocked and controlled by Canadian capitalists, have comprised a dominant fraction of *indigenous finance capital*, i.e., Canadian-controlled capital centred in Toronto and Montreal but increasingly reaching westward.
2. Contrary to earlier notions of a "compradorization" process, in which Canada's capitalists act as agents allied with American TNCs (Clement 1975, 1977), foreign-controlled companies have not participated extensively in the corporate network.
3. Although American direct investment poured into Canada after World War II, it began to decline in the 1970s as American global hegemony weakened and as Canadian-based capitalists expanded their strategic control of domestic capital while investing massively abroad. "Silent surrender" turned out to be peculiar to an era, during which Canada's capitalists did not "surrender" but pursued opportunities within a US-centred regime that applied as much to Europe and Japan as to Canada (Carroll 2007: 5).

Broadly, then, corporate power in Canada has been organized in much the same way as in other developed capitalist societies: in a structure of finance capital that pulls the largest corporations together into configurations of strategic control, capital allocation, and operational command. Corporate capital's architecture has developed around extensive interlocks between the boards of big banks and non-financial corporations that are mainly controlled in Canada; this supports the inference that groups of interlocked capitalists who own or manage supra-corporate blocs of indigenous finance capital are at the centre of Canadian corporate power and at the apex of the Canadian bourgeoisie (Carroll 1984: 265; Carroll 1986, 2010).

By the close of the twentieth century, with American hegemony having partly yielded to a more multilateral pattern of "cross-penetration" among the advanced capitalist powers, the corporate network became recentred on a core of transnational banks and corporations controlled by capitalists based in Canada. Thus, "transnational financial capital" radiated from Canada in a way that did *not* disorganize the national network but *embedded* it more extensively in a circuitry of global accumulation (Carroll 2010: 85). Following the Swiss example (Rusterholz 1985), the Canadian network had become organized around an expanding sector of Canadian-based TNCs, both industrial and financial. In this transition, Canada's business community participated with other nationally based corporate elites in a global process of capital concentration and centralization.

However, in 2000 Arthurs revived the old *dependentist* interpretation, arguing that corporate Canada was becoming "hollowed out," as foreign parent corporations tightened control of their Canadian subsidiaries, closing down Canadian headquarters. Subsequent research has disputed this thesis. A comparison of the Canadian corporate network in early 1997 and 2007 (including the shifting composition of Canada's largest 250 corporations) showed that the many "rising stars" of corporate capital were overwhelmingly firms controlled in Canada, and that the elite network remained integrated primarily by interlocks among corporations controlled in Canada (Carroll and Klassen 2010). Across the same years, the national interlocking network became primarily a configuration of the boards of

Canadian-controlled TNCs, with elite connections that also extended transnationally. Noting that in the same period Canadian-based investment abroad continued its long-term expansion, we concluded that "Canadian TNCs have reinforced a national network of corporate power and simultaneously interlocked with foreign-based TNCs both inside and outside of Canada, in the grooves formed by transnational investment" (Klassen and Carroll 2011: 400). Rather than a hollowing out of corporate Canada, these trends suggest an increasing cross-penetration of capital across national borders. Through this process, which is integral to capitalist globalization, each local ruling class, including Canada's dominant class, cedes some control of its home market, but is also able to accumulate capital more effectively outside that market. The result in any one country might look like a hollowing out, as the national network becomes more transnationalized, but the larger pattern is an increasingly multilateral cross-penetration of capital and the formation of a transnational capitalist class, which includes Canada's leading capitalists (Carroll 2010).

Financialization, Corporate Governance Reform, and the Changing Shape of Finance Capital

The era of neo-liberal globalization has witnessed a dramatic deregulation of capital, which has unleashed vast amounts of "hot money"—mobile financial capital in search of short-term profit (Naylor 2004)—with intensifying competition for immediate returns. Such "financialization" has influenced the organization of corporate power. In a financialized economy, banks prefer liquidity over long-term loans: they shift from relationship-based finance—fostering durable ties with their corporate clients, including directorship interlocks, to transaction-based finance—as in marketing securitized debt as a tradable commodity. This shift weakens the basis for interlocks between banks and corporations. At the same time, financialization contributes to the increasing instability of capitalism, as larger volumes of footloose capital feed speculative bubbles.

In Canada, as in other advanced capitalist countries, the financial crises and scandals that accompanied financialization provoked corporate-governance reform initiatives. These reforms, first implemented by the Toronto Stock Exchange in 1995, sought to make corporate boards more active and effective as sites of strategic power and less subject to the cronyism of traditional elite practices or the whims of internal operational management. Among the reforms were calls for smaller corporate directorates and for directors to limit the number of directorships they hold (Carroll 2010: 33–5). Along with the weakening of relationship-based finance, the reforms had a dramatic impact on the structure of finance capital, as interlocks involving "insiders" (corporate officers, particularly lower-level executives) disappeared from the network. Most significantly, banks slimmed their elephantine directorates and bankers vacated the boards of industrial corporations. This left a looser elite structure in which the banks continued to participate alongside transnational corporations, in a network of information flows across outside directorships. Summarizing these developments, I noted that:

> finance capital becomes more loosely organized and more transnational in its circuitry. Yet national business communities such as Canada's persist, held together by a range of factors, including the need to exercise hegemony locally and to access the business scan that interlocking directorates enable. (Carroll 2008: 57)

This observation brings us back to the second face of corporate power distinguished at the outset: the *hegemonic*.

The Changing Face of Hegemony: From "Old Boys" to Meritocracy

Hegemony refers to cultural and political leadership that shapes the common-sense understandings of what is socially possible and what is deemed to be in the "common interest" (Gramsci 1971). For the corporate elite, the top tier of the capitalist class, such leadership requires: (1) a high level of internal *cohesion* as a solidaristic "business community" built through frequent interaction and sharing a common social vision; and (2) extensive *reach* into political and civil society, to recruit support for their hegemonic world view (Carroll 2010: 7). On both counts, recent decades have witnessed important transitions in the social organization of capitalist hegemony.

Classically, elite cohesion was maintained through forms of closure that created strong ties among the elect few and barriers to entry for the rest of society. Well into the late twentieth century, the corporate elite was organized this way—through private clubs, private schools, and other devices that supported a male-dominated and ethnically British "Canadian Establishment" (Newman 1975; Porter 1965; Clement 1975). However, with the advance of bourgeois society and its emphasis on individual achievement, aristocratic forms of closure have become culturally archaic. Recent decades witnessed an acceleration of this trend within the elite itself. Since the mid-1970s, the period of neo-liberal globalization has been one of *moral reform* within the corporate elite, with a transition to greater diversity and openness in the service of improved competitiveness. The governance reforms of the 1990s were part of this transition. As corporations empowered their boards to be independent and rational agencies, they mandated open recruitment of directors to mobilize talent from a wider pool. Smaller, leaner boards using "best practices" would further sharpen the competitive edge of companies.

One effect of these reforms was a shift in elite composition—an increase in the number of women and non-British (though almost exclusively European) ethnicities at the upper echelons of corporate power. For example, between 1976 and 1996, the proportion of women in the Canadian corporate elite grew from 0.6 per cent to 9.2 per cent,[4] while the proportion of non-British grew from 22.1 per cent to 36.2 per cent, including a rise from 12.7 per cent to 18.3 per cent among French members (Carroll 2010: 18). The corporate elite became less monocultural, less patriarchal, and less petrified, although its ethnic and gender composition still contrasted sharply with that of the general population. In its social profile, educational credentials became more important than exclusive club memberships, and advisers from academic and other fields of expert knowledge constituted a larger subgroup. These developments modernized the face of Canadian corporate capital and provided for a business leadership that was more in tune with contemporary society.

From Clubs to Business Activism

In the early 1970s, private clubs, mainly in Montreal and Toronto, were still the key sites for building elite cohesion. Such exclusive clubs existed to provide a space for comradely conversation among members. The leading directors of dominant corporations routinely belonged to several of these clubs, knitting the elite into a centralized "old boys' network." The culture of solidarity in the business community was primarily one of leisure, befitting a dominant, oligarchic elite. In the dense, centralized network of private clubs, and also on the capacious boards of the Big Five banks, the elite found its collective identity as an exclusive "confraternity of power" (Porter 1965).

In recent decades, however, as the corporate-interlock network has weakened, as elite participation in private clubs has declined, and as the culture of merit and diversity has increased, the elite's basis for solidarity shifted from the sphere of leisure to that of activism. Beginning in the 1970s, corporate elites in Canada, Britain, and the US created agencies of business activism—"councils," "round tables," "institutes"—that brought together for explicitly political purposes leading capitalists and so-called "organic" intellectuals who support capitalist interests; hence, the Anglo-Saxon world "led the way" in constructing and implementing the neo-liberal paradigm (Useem 1984). In Canada, business leaders recognized the need to legitimate a dramatic policy transition, from the Keynesian welfare state and associated state regulation of capital to the market-driven politics of neo-liberalism. With the founding in 1976 of the Business Council on National Issues, the corporate elite's basis for community began to shift, as noted above, from leisure pursuits to political activism. Elite policy-planning groups such as the Fraser Institute also sprang up, while older think-tanks such as the C.D. Howe Institute took a neo-liberal turn. An activist network emerged linking the directorates of Canada's largest corporations to a well-resourced complex of right-wing policy groups. This network extended into both the mainstream media and political circles, providing both internal cohesion and external reach (Carroll 2010). By the mid-1990s, the policy frameworks of both governments and political parties had been strongly conditioned by two decades of well-organized business activism. The CEO of the Business Council on National Issues, Thomas d'Aquino, summed up matters nicely:

> If you ask yourself, in which period since 1900 has Canada's business community had the most influence on public policy, I would say it was the last twenty years. Look at what we stand for and look at what all the governments, all the major parties . . . have done, and what they want to do. They have adopted the agendas we've been fighting for in the past two decades. (Quoted in Newman 1998: 151)

It is important to place the new business activism in a broader context. For the Canadian elite, that context is primarily North American. As a recent study of Canada, the US, and Mexico points out, beginning in the 1970s "the largest corporations in each of these countries organized new associations that developed understandings and policies that have become the new 'common sense' of the political elites, the media, and some sectors of the population" (Roman and Velasco Arregui 2015: 2–3). These elite groups were early advocates of neo-liberal "continentalism" under NAFTA; they formed the North American Forum in 2005 to encourage increased economic links between Canada and the US in particular, thereby taking the project of "deep integration" even further (Roman and Velasco Arregui 2015: 135).

More broadly still, we should keep in mind that regionalization is to globalization as a part is to the whole. NAFTA had important implications for the structure of corporate power in North America, because it secured the playing field for continentally integrated investment, production, and markets, while "locking in" the neo-liberal policies of the three regimes from future governmental changes (Roman and Velasco Arregui 2015: 58). But such agreements are not simply regional; they form an integral part of the globalization process (Schiller and Mosco 2001: 3). For instance, NAFTA's investor-rights provisions, which empower foreign investors to sue a government for compensation against measures that deprive them of future profits, were quickly picked up by the WTO as a new norm for international governance; these provisions now appear in other international agreements, including the Trans-Pacific Partnership and the Canada–EU Comprehensive Economic and Trade Agreement. Moreover, in integrating the North American market, NAFTA has stimulated an enormous inflow of foreign investment, further integrating the world economy. Driven by the complementary interests of American, Canadian, and Mexican corporate capital, "NAFTA is part of, facilitates, and advances globalization—the restructuring of economic and financial capital through international flows of production, trade, investment, and assets" (Du Boff 2001: 58).

Not surprisingly, elite business groups have strongly advocated these initiatives, further strengthening the power of corporate capital relative to workers, communities, and governments. In such transnational agreements, we find a convergence of the two faces of corporate power: the bid for hegemony, so as to present as the general interest what is actually the class interest of corporate capital; and the cementing of a system of rules enabling corporations and the capitalists who direct and control them to exercise strategic, operational, and allocative power within and across increasingly permeable national borders.

Questions for Critical Thought

1. Reflecting on your own day-to-day life, what are some of the key moments in which you come up against the economic and cultural-political faces of corporate power?
2. Read the business section of the *Globe and Mail* or *National Post*. How do the stories, and the way they are framed as news and analysis, exemplify the faces and forms of corporate power discussed in this chapter?
3. Neo-liberals view deregulated capitalism as a highly democratic form of society. Based on the analysis in this chapter, how might one respond to this claim?
4. Some people see localism—developing small-scale, locally controlled economic initiatives—as the alternative to the growing concentration of corporate power; others argue that continental and transnational corporate power must be countered with transnational movements for global justice. What, in your view, are the possibilities for resisting and perhaps transcending the rule of corporate capital?

Recommended Readings

Brownlee, Jamie. 2005. *Ruling Canada: Corporate Cohesion and Democracy.* Halifax: Fernwood.

Buxton, Nick, and Madeleine Bélanger Dumontier. 2015. *State of Power 2015: An Annual Anthology on Global Power and Resistance.* Amsterdam: Transnational Institute. http://www.tni.org/stateofpower2015.

Carroll, William K. 2010. *Corporate Power in a Globalizing World: A Study in Elite Social Organization,* 2nd edn. Toronto: Oxford University Press.

Hilary, John. 2013. *The Poverty of Capitalism.* London: Pluto Press.

Recommended Websites

Little Sis:
http://littlesis.org/

Canadian Centre for Policy Alternatives—Growing Gap:
https://www.policyalternatives.ca/projects/growing-gap

Corporate Power (part of the Economic Justice Program):
http://www.tni.org/work-area/corporate-power

Corporate Watch, Critical News and Research:
http://www.corporatewatch.org/

Notes

1. The complex circuitry through which the economic surplus is appropriated, circulated, and consumed as surplus value is examined closely in the three volumes of *Capital* (Marx 1967). For a more contemporary treatment, see Harvey (2007).
2. Total market capitalization is the value of all shares of all firms listed on the stock exchange.
3. As of 2012, Toronto ranked as an "alpha" world city (particularly central in the global economy) while Montreal, Vancouver, and Calgary ranked as "beta" world cities. See Globalization and World Cities Research Network, at: http://www.lboro.ac.uk/gawc/world2012t.html.
4. Moreover, by 2014, 21 per cent of the directors of TSX 60 corporations were women, placing Canada's corporate elite in the "middle of the pack" among advanced capitalist economies (Catalyst 2015).

References

Arthurs, Harry W. 2000. "The hollowing out of corporate Canada?" In J. Jenson and B. deSousa Santos, eds, *Globalizing Institutions*, pp. 29–51. Burlington, Vermont: Ashgate.

Berkowitz, S.D., and W. Fitzgerald. 1995. "Corporate control and enterprise structure in the Canadian economy: 1972–1987." *Social Networks* 17: 111–27.

Blau, Peter. 1964. *Exchange and Power in Social Life*. New York: John Wiley.

Block, Fred. 1977. "The ruling class does not rule: Notes on the Marxist theory of the state." *Socialist Revolution* 7, 3: 6–28.

Bowles, Samuel, and Herbert Gintis. 1986. *Democracy and Capitalism*. New York: Basic Books.

Brennan, Jordan. 2012. *A Shrinking Universe: How Concentrated Corporate Capital Is Shaping Income Inequality in Canada*. Ottawa: Canadian Centre for Policy Alternatives, Nov.

Carroll, William K. 1984. "The individual, class, and corporate power in Canada." *Canadian Journal of Sociology* 9: 245–68.

———. 1986. *Corporate Power and Canadian Capitalism*. Vancouver: University of British Columbia Press.

———. 2007. "From Canadian corporate elite to transnational capitalist class: Transitions in the organization of corporate power." *Canadian Review of Sociology* 44, 3: 265–88.

———. 2008. "The corporate elite and the transformation of finance capital: A view from Canada." *Sociological Review* 56 (S1): 44–63.

———. 2010. *Corporate Power in a Globalizing World: A Study in Elite Social Organization*, 2nd edn. Toronto: Oxford University Press.

———. 2012. "Capital relations and directorate interlocking: The global network in 2007." In Georgina Murray and John Scott, eds, *Financial Elites and Transnational Business: Who Rules the World?*, pp. 54–75. Northampton, Mass.: Edward Elgar.

——— and Jerome Klassen. 2010. "Hollowing out Corporate Canada? Changes in the corporate network since the 1990s." *Canadian Journal of Sociology* 35, 1: 1–30.

Catalyst. 2015. "2014 Catalyst Census of Women Board Directors," 13 Jan. http://www.catalyst.org/knowledge/2014-catalyst-census-women-board-directors.

Clement, Wallace. 1975. *The Canadian Corporate Elite*. Toronto: McClelland & Stewart.

———. 1977. *Continental Corporate Power*. Toronto: McClelland & Stewart.

Du Boff, Richard B. 2001. "NAFTA and economic integration in North America." In V. Mosco and D. Schiller, eds, *Continental Order? Integrating North America for Cybercapitalism*, pp. 35–63. New York: Rowman & Littlefield.

Gramsci, Antonio. 1971. *Selections from the Prison Notebooks of Antonio Gramsci*. New York: International Publishers.

Hart-Landsberg, Martin. 2013. *Capitalist Globalization*. New York: Monthly Review Press.

Harvey, David. 2007. *The Limits to Capital*, 2nd edn. London: Verso.

Hilary, John. 2013. *The Poverty of Capitalism*. London: Pluto Press.

Klassen, Jerome, and William K. Carroll. 2011. "Transnational class formation? Globalization and the Canadian corporate network." *Journal of World-Systems Research* 17: 379–402.

Levitt, Kari. 1970. *Silent Surrender*. Toronto: Macmillan of Canada.

Macdonald, David. 2014. *Outrageous Fortune: Documenting Canada's Wealth Gap*. Ottawa: Canadian Centre for Policy Alternatives.

Marx, Karl. 1967. *Capital*, 3 vols. New York: International Publishers.

Naylor, R.T. 1972. "The rise and fall of the third commercial empire of the St Lawrence." In G. Teeple, ed., *Capitalism and the National Question in Canada*, pp. 1–41. Toronto: University of Toronto Press.

———. 2004. *Hot Money and the Politics of Debt*, 3rd edn. Montreal and Kingston: McGill-Queen's University Press.

Newman, Peter C. 1975. *The Canadian Establishment, Volume 1*. Toronto: McClelland & Stewart.

———. 1998. *Titans: How the New Canadian Establishment Seized Power*. Toronto: Viking.

Niosi, Jorge. 1981. *Canadian Capitalism*. Toronto: Lorimer.

Overbeek, Henk. 1980. "Finance capital and the crisis in Britain." *Capital and Class* 2: 99–120.

Perlo, Victor. 1958. "'People's capitalism' and stock ownership." *American Economic Review* 48: 333–47.

Porter, John. 1965. *The Vertical Mosaic*. Toronto: University of Toronto Press.

Roman, Richard, and Edur Velasco Arregui. 2015. *Continental Crucible*, 2nd edn. Halifax: Fernwood.

Rusterholz, Peter. 1985. "The banks in the centre: Integration in decentralized Switzerland." In F.N. Stokman, R. Ziegler, and J. Scott, eds, *Networks of Corporate Power*, pp. 131–47. Cambridge: Polity Press.

Schiller, Dan, and Vincent Mosco. 2001. "Introduction: Integrating a continent for a transnational world." In V. Mosco and D. Schiller, *Continental Order: Interpreting North America for Cybercapitalism*, pp. 1–34. New York: Rowman & Littlefield.

Scott, John. 1997. *Corporate Business and Capitalist Classes*. New York: Oxford University Press.

Statistics Canada. 2001. *Canada's International Position, 2000*. Catalogue no. 67-202. Ottawa: Ministry of Industry.

Useem, Michael. 1984. *The Inner Circle*. New York: Oxford University Press.

3 Class Formation in Canada

Jim Conley

Two recent events have challenged traditional sociological understandings of the formation of social classes. First, after the 2008 financial crisis, the Occupy movement helped bring rising income inequality to public attention, with Canada, the US, and other wealthy countries appearing to be divided between a tiny elite (the 1 per cent) and everyone else (the 99 per cent). Second, the extensive historical and comparative analyses of income and wealth inequality portrayed in Thomas Piketty's bestselling book, *Capital in the Twenty-First Century* (2014), also suggested that societies are composed of income groupings and wealth strata that are massively unequal.

Movements like Occupy, which seek equality, and the existence of substantial income and wealth inequality, have long been central topics of sociological inquiry, where they have been linked to questions of power and social change. Among the many questions asked by sociologists, and also addressed in other chapters of this volume, are: Who has power? What are its institutional bases? How is it used? What conflicts does it create? Social classes have usually been understood as categories organized around social relations of economic domination, exploitation, and exclusion, which are bases for conflicts of interest, and also around processes of class formation and mobilization. While not denying this approach, Piketty's book redirects the attention of sociologists towards the long-term dynamics of wealth accumulation for understanding inequality and social change (Savage 2014).

These developments require a rethinking of class formation. In addition to shaping opportunities, resources, and power, does class inequality also lead to collective identity and collective action? To what extent are social conflicts organized around class differences? Are there symbolic and social boundaries separating classes, and are there solidarities within them? Do members of classes have a class identity? Are they disposed to act on that identity rather than on other social identities such as gender or ethnicity? Do organizations mobilize on the basis of class identities and undertake collective action in the name of a class?

Following a presentation of influential theories of class formation, this chapter examines the dynamics of class formation in Canada and concludes with an assessment of sociological theories of class formation.

Class Formation in Theory

The ideas of the three main "classical" sociological theorists, Karl Marx, Max Weber, and Émile Durkheim, continue to shape our understandings of class formation. This chapter begins by presenting their main ideas.

Marx

For Marx, class formation concerned the development of male industrial workers into a revolutionary force opposed to capitalist class power. Conflict between the working class and the capitalist class is an inherent feature of capitalism. The sources of conflict lie in workers' experiences of exploitative and alienating work, and in the consequences of capitalist profit-making strategies for working-class standards of life. The "general law of capitalist accumulation," Marx wrote, is "that in proportion as capital accumulates, the lot of the labourer, be his pay high or low, must grow worse . . . accumulation of wealth at one pole is, therefore, at the same time accumulation of misery, agony of toil, slavery, ignorance, brutality, mental degradation, at the opposite pole" (Marx 1867: 604). Either in absolute terms or compared to the capitalist class, the standard of living of workers falls as capitalism develops, and the conditions of work become more toilsome (Grabb 2007).

Marx believed that capitalism created the conditions of class formation and class power for workers to act to eliminate the sources of their distress. Specifically, he expected capitalism to create three conditions giving workers the organization and resources to resist capitalist power. First, changes in the production process would bring workers together in larger workplaces; a more co-operative production process would lead to solidarity between workers; and changes in production methods would obliterate skill differences. Together, these processes would make all workers into what are today called semi-skilled labourers. Mechanized production would also reduce the importance of physical strength, and gender differences between workers would lose significance. This process of homogenization would create "mechanical" solidarity for the working class, stemming from their similar jobs and conditions of employment (Sørensen 1994), making it possible and necessary for workers to organize on a broad, inclusive basis. The changing character of production also gave workers power: even as the demise of craft production and the introduction of machine-pacing deprived workers of control over the process of production as individuals, they gained power as a collectivity.

Second, Marx emphasized the power that derives from class size. The class structure in capitalism would polarize as the petty bourgeoisie of small proprietors disappeared, and the capitalist class would become smaller but more concentrated as large capitalists swallowed up smaller capitalists. As a consequence, the working class would become the largest class in capitalist societies, confronting a small capitalist class in a conflict without any intermediaries.

However, structural tendencies in capitalism towards homogenization of the working class and polarization of the class structure only furnish preconditions for working-class power. Solving the problem of collective action is the third condition: individual workers do not have the resources to counter the power of capitalists, and size is not enough for attaining power unless the workers are organized. Marx expected that, in the course of conflict with capitalists, workers would develop increasingly broad levels of organization: unions would form on local, then on industrial, and finally on national levels, at the same time as political parties representing workers and advancing their interests would grow (Marx and Engels 1848). In other words, out of the experience of conflict, increasingly inclusive and politicized forms of organization of workers would result, and increasingly broad struggles would follow between workers, on the one hand, and capitalists and the state, on the other.

Weber

Weber is often described as engaging in a debate with Marx's ghost. This certainly applies to Weber's approach to social inequality, which assumes much of what Marx had to say, but adds to and amends Marx's views (see Grabb 2007). Unlike Marx, who almost exclusively emphasized class, Weber considered classes, status groups, and parties as "phenomena of the distribution of power" within societies (Weber 1922: 927). Weber expected that, in addition to or instead of conflict occurring on class lines, there would be organized conflict based on status groups and factions competing for power in organizations, especially the state.

Like Marx, Weber thought that property was central to the concept of class. However, unlike Marx, Weber conceived of classes as based on opportunities in markets, not on exploitation in production. From this perspective, classes are distinguished by differences in the possession of marketable, income-producing goods and services. Thus, Weber's analysis points to possible lines of differentiation among workers based on possession of skills and other advantages in labour markets. Such differentiation in labour markets need not promote the general impoverishment of the working class that Marxian theory seems to suggest, because there would be distinct segments or strata within the working class, with different experiences, different interests, and different capacities for organization and collective action.

Even more importantly, Weber believed that the expansion of modern, bureaucratic forms of administration would lead to the development of a new middle class of "white-collar" employees, technical specialists, and professionals. This would provide an avenue for mobility out of the working class, and give people in these positions a distinct identity and interests (Weber 1922: 304). The formation of a middle class between the working class and the capitalist class contradicts the Marxian expectation that the class structure in capitalism would become polarized into just two classes over time.

Weber's concept of status identifies the second aspect of power that affects class formation. Rather than arising on the basis of class location, status groups form around processes such as shared consumption patterns and styles of life. The existence of status groups that cut across different classes complicates the increasing homogeneity of the working class that Marx envisioned. Thus, status groups based on gender, sexual orientation, ethnicity, region, religion, or education can divide members of one class and create solidarity between members of different classes. Because relations of domination between such status groups are typically more "transparent" than class relations, they are more readily available sources of group identity and collective action than class position.

Durkheim

Émile Durkheim is not usually considered a theorist of class, but his work has several elements that are relevant to understanding class formation. Unlike Marx, Durkheim (1893) expected the increasing division of labour in modern societies to lead, at least under certain circumstances (e.g., the absence of large inequalities in wealth and other obstacles to equality of opportunity), to organic solidarity between occupational groups. Closer in this respect to Weber than to Marx, Durkheim (1893, 1957) expected that even as mechanical solidarity, based on job sameness, disappeared at a societal level with the increasingly complex and differentiated division of labour, it would persist and be institutionalized at the level of occupations or professional groups. Developing Durkheim's ideas, Weeden and Grusky (2005) have proposed a "disaggregated" concept of classes. In this conception, occupational groups are the proper units of class analysis, fulfilling all the conditions usually attributed to "big" classes. These authors argue that relations of exclusion and exploitation, a common style of life, collective identity, and collective action are more likely to be found in occupational groups such as plumbers, teachers, transport truck drivers, and physicians than in aggregates like the "working class" or the "petty bourgeoisie."

Durkheim's analyses of collective representations and of rituals are also relevant to the question of class formation. To what extent do classes exist as shared mental constructs or "institutionalized social categories," for example, in government statistics, administrative classifications and policies, or in the mass media? Are these categories periodically renewed in collective, solidarity-generating rituals or in everyday interaction rituals (Goffman 1967), which create recognition and solidarity between members of the same class or institute boundaries between members of different classes?

Class Formation in Canada

What do we know about class formation in Canada in the second decade of the twenty-first century? Evidence on class formation and conflict will be presented with respect to the following issues: (1) the structural tendencies of class formation, with particular attention to the process of polarization expected by Marx; (2) changes in social organization in workplaces and labour markets that have affected class boundaries and solidarities; (3) the identities and dispositions of members of different classes; and (4) the mobilization and institutional representation of class interests (for example, in unions), along with conflict in social movements and strikes. Because the terms of debates about class formation have been set largely by Marx, the following discussion mainly considers societal trends that Marxists expected would create working-class solidarity and opposition to capitalism. In the conclusion, the results of this analysis will be used to raise questions about further theory and research.

Class Structure: Polarization?

Marxists have expected that the class structure in capitalism would polarize through the decline of the petty bourgeoisie; a growing income gap between the working class and the capitalist class; and a deskilling of work. While generally agreeing with Marxists on the declining petty bourgeoisie, Weber and others expected that polarization would be mitigated by the development of a new middle class of salaried technical, professional, and managerial employees possessing marketable educational credentials. In contrast to both, Durkheim expected a hierarchy of occupations within a complex division of labour, in which employment status would not matter. What does the Canadian evidence show?

Decline of the petty bourgeoisie?

Both Marx and Weber expected that the petty bourgeoisie, comprising self-employed artisans, farmers, shopkeepers, and the like, would disappear under the pressure of competition from larger, more efficient capitalist enterprises. For much of the twentieth century, that is what happened in Canada. Self-employment[1] fell from about 25 per cent of the total labour force in 1931 to about 12 per cent in the 1970s. Most of the historical decline of the petty bourgeoisie in Canada is due to falling employment in the agricultural sector, where levels of self-employment have always been very high and which now includes only 2 per cent of the labour force. Self-employment in the agricultural sector has also declined since the 1990s, to around 60 per cent. In the same period that self-employment in agriculture was falling, the overall share of the self-employed in Canada's workforce rose to about 15 per cent, as shown in Figure 3.1. Self-employment fluctuates according to the fortunes of the industries in which it is concentrated. Notable recent increases have occurred in financial services like real estate, in transportation, and in business support services. Along with farming, levels of self-employment have remained substantially higher than average in construction, professional services, scientific and technical services, business support services, personal services, and other services such as repair and maintenance. As both Marx and

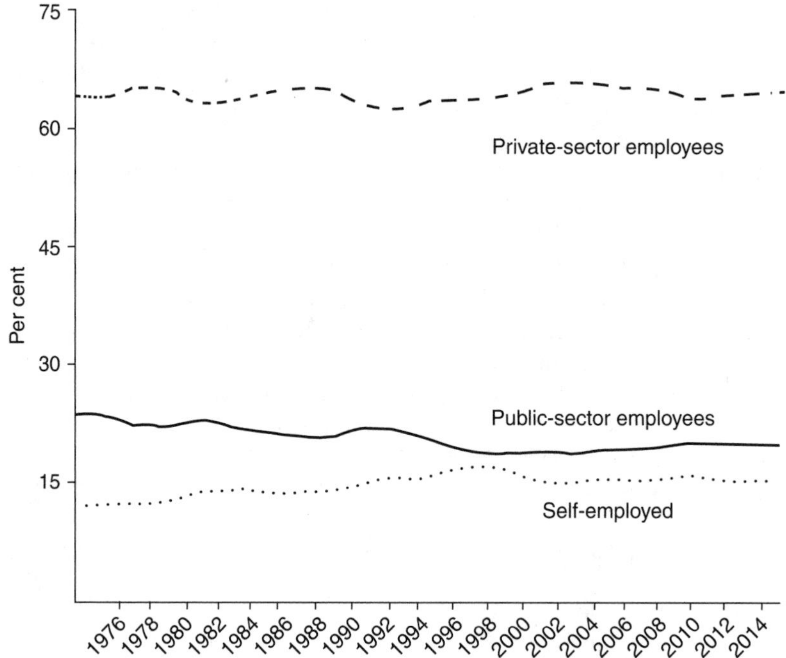

Figure 3.1 "Class" of Worker: Percentage of All Employed, 1976–2014

Source: Statistics Canada (2015c).

Weber would have expected, manufacturing has a very low level of self-employment (between 4 and 6 per cent since 1991), and self-employment is virtually non-existent in large bureaucratized fields like utilities, public administration, and education (Statistics Canada 2015c).

Approximately two-thirds of the self-employed have no employees. To the extent that they are actually dependent on a single buyer of their product or service, many of these people are employees in all but name. Because of its lack of benefits and legal protections to which employees are entitled, self-employment for many is a form of "precarious" employment, which is characterized by low earnings and insecurity. It is questionable, then, whether all the self-employed can be considered "middle class" in any meaningful way. The recent rise in the number of self-employed may represent an increase rather than a decrease in polarization.

A new middle class?

As noted earlier, Weberian understandings of class formation point to the growth of a new middle class that runs counter to Marxist predictions of polarization in the class structure. The new middle class is composed of employees who exercise authority within bureaucratic organizations, including the state, and who possess post-secondary educational credentials. Although the causes, characteristics, conceptualization, and future prospects of the new middle class have been much debated (see Grabb 2007), most researchers agree that the numbers of middle-level administrators, managers, professionals, and skilled technical employees constitute a significant and generally growing part of the post-industrial class structure, one that is relatively distinct from the bourgeoisie, the petty bourgeoisie, and the working class (e.g., Myles and Turegin 1994). In the only large-scale

Canadian study to use neo-Marxist class categories, the new middle class, defined as lower-level managers and supervisors with authority to impose sanctions on other employees, was found to represent about 25 per cent of the labour force in the early 1980s, compared to nearly 60 per cent for the working class, about 10 per cent for the petty bourgeoisie, and 6 per cent for employers (Clement and Myles 1994). Since then, however, some have suggested that the middle class has been declining. This position was given credibility by the wave of "downsizing" during the 1980s recession, involving well-publicized layoffs of middle managers in large corporations and reductions in the public sector. Figure 3.1 shows that public-sector employment declined somewhat from nearly one-quarter of the labour force in 1976 to a little over one-fifth in 2014. There has also been a recent decline in the share of managerial occupations (Statistics Canada 2015c).

Nevertheless, the occupations that most closely resemble what Marxists and Weberians consider the new middle class have grown steadily over the last several decades. For example, as Table 3.1 shows, the proportion of the labour force in "knowledge-based occupations"—professional, management, and technical occupations—grew from less than 14 per cent of the employed labour force in 1971 to more than 36 per cent in 2012, despite some recent declines in the management category.[2] Other research finds similarly that more than 40 per cent of employees in the non-market service sector (government, educational, and health and social services) are "knowledge workers" (Baldwin and Beckstead 2003).

Polarization between skilled and unskilled workers?

Despite the growth in the proportion of knowledge-based occupations, it is possible that long-term processes of routinization, deskilling, and loss of autonomy, which affected skilled manual and clerical work in previous stages of industrialization, now affect professional employees and middle-level administrators in the post-industrial period. In that case, polarization would mean a decrease in the share of high-skilled jobs (requiring complex decision-making skills and post-secondary degrees or diplomas), and an increase in both medium-skilled jobs (requiring at least high school diplomas and precise work routines), and low-skilled jobs (requiring only on-the-job training). Alternatively, as routine industrial and clerical jobs are taken over by computers and robots, there is the spectre of a post-industrial polarization between

Table 3.1 Knowledge Workers in Canada, 1971–2012

	Share of Employment* (%)						
	1971	**1981**	**1991**	**2001**	**1999**	**2007**	**2012**
All knowledge-based occupations	13.8	17.5	21.5	24.7	33.4	34.5	36.5
Management occupations	1.6	3.6	5.4	6.1	8.9	8.4	8.1
Professional occupations	8.7	9.9	11.3	14.3	16.2	17.6	19.3
Technical occupations	3.5	4.0	4.7	4.4	8.2	8.5	9.0
All other occupations	86.2	82.5	78.5	75.3	66.6	65.5	63.5
All occupations	100.0	100.0	100.0	100.0	100.0	100.0	100.0

* Defined as the employed labour force using the 1971 census labour force concept.

Note: Two different sources were used to construct Table 3.1. Burleton et al. (2013) used a more inclusive definition of knowledge-based workers than did Baldwin and Beckstead (2003), which partly accounts for the higher percentages in the Burleton et al. study. Nevertheless, the trend towards increasing proportions of knowledge-based workers over time is still evident.

Sources: 1971–2001: Baldwin and Beckstead (2003: 5, Table 1); 1999–2012: Burleton et al. (2013: 11, Table 3).

high-skilled jobs, on the one hand, and low-skilled, face-to-face, personal service jobs, on the other hand.

In Canada, evidence since the early 1980s has not supported the image of post-industrial polarization. Instead, the shift to a post-industrial service economy has created both skilled and unskilled jobs, but the share of the former (especially in technical and professional occupations) has grown more than that of both low- and medium-skilled jobs (Burleton 2013). The loss of medium-skilled jobs stemming from the decline of manufacturing occupations supports the polarization hypothesis, but this decline was partly counteracted by the boom in construction and resource jobs in mining and energy (Burleton 2013).

Polarization of incomes?

The growing inequality that has been observed in Canada and other advanced capitalist societies in the last 40 years has spawned a debate about whether the middle class has declined, not in numbers, but in income. In this case, the middle class is conceptualized in a gradational, distributive way, and is represented by individuals in the middle categories of the income structure, such as those between the fiftieth and ninetieth percentiles (Piketty 2014). Any shrinkage among middle-income earners could have important implications for class formation, because this group would include many members of both the new middle class and the more affluent part of the working class, as defined in Marxist or Weberian terms. In Canada, increases in average real incomes for men began after World War II, came to a stop in the early 1980s, and have been largely stagnant since (see also Chapter 4 in this volume). Among women, both labour force participation and earnings have risen, with the increasing prevalence of dual-income households helping to prevent declines in economic circumstances for many families. Income polarization based on age occurred in the last two decades of the twentieth century, with declines in the wages of younger workers relative to older workers; however, this trend has subsequently been partially reversed.

In addition, the resource extraction and construction boom in the 2000s drove increases in the wages of less-educated workers, narrowing the gap between them and university-educated workers (Morissette et al. 2013). Overall, there has been an across-the-board increase in earnings inequality, with workers at the bottom of the distribution losing ground compared to those in the middle, who themselves lost ground to those at the top (Green and Sand 2014). The increase in very high incomes corresponds to Marx's expectations. It has been caused in large part by extremely high levels of compensation for chief executives of large corporations and others in the top income percentile, especially in the top 1/10th and 1/100th of the top percentile (Veall 2012). Managerial occupations, in particular, experienced high rates of growth in wages in the first part of this century (Morissette et al. 2013).

The rise of precarious employment?

Another dimension of polarization that has received growing attention is an increase in "non-standard" or "precarious" work. Definitions of these terms vary (DePratto and Bartlett 2015; Vosko 2006; Lewchuk et al. 2013), but the core features of precarious employment include uncertainty about job tenure and unpredictable variations in income and work schedules. These features are most often found in self-employment and in casual, part-time, and temporary work. Workers in standard employment (full-time, full-year permanent jobs) may also experience uncertainty and insecurity, especially in vulnerable industries (Lewchuk et al. 2013), but the focus here is on the narrower conception of precarious or non-standard work.

In Canada, the share of temporary employment has increased in the last two decades, from about 11 per cent of all employment in 1997 to about 13 per cent in 2014; about half of these jobs are term or contract positions, and are mainly in health, education, and the high-skilled private sector (Statistics Canada 2015e). A growing proportion includes low-skilled casual positions, in which employees are called in to work only when the employer needs them. Most of the remainder are seasonal jobs. In general, temporary jobs provide lower wages, fewer benefits, less training, and less job security than permanent jobs (Burleton et al. 2013; Statistics Canada 2015f). Among young workers (aged 15–24), temporary employment has always been higher than it is among older workers, but the temporary proportion for young workers has continued to rise, from 25 per cent in 1997 to more than 30 per cent in 2014 (DePratto and Bartlett 2015).

As shown in Figure 3.2, part-time work has also increased substantially over time, from about 13 per cent in the 1970s to about 18 or 19 per cent for the period from 1992 to 2014. Figure 3.2 also reveals that part-time work has consistently been more frequent for women (fluctuating between 25 and 30 per cent) than for men, but the share for men has increased fairly steadily since the 1970s. Because there are many reasons why people work part-time, the best indicator of precarious work is probably involuntary part-time employment, situations in which a person working part-time would prefer to work full-time. Figure 3.3 shows that involuntary part-time work, which is consistently higher among men than among women, declined substantially from the 1970s to mid-2000s, but has trended upward somewhat for both sexes since then, and was in the 25–30 per cent range as of 2014.[3]

The future of precarious employment is uncertain. Optimistic accounts link it to the business cycle, increasing in downturns but decreasing in better times (DePratto and Bartlett 2015). Pessimists believe that it indicates the emergence of the "precariat," a new class of workers lacking the stable employment, rights, and benefits of the traditional working class. According to Standing (2014, 2015), members of the precariat include some disparate groups: less-educated workers who have fallen out of the old working class; immigrants and racialized minorities; and young, highly educated workers. Consequently, the implications of precarious employment for class formation are not entirely clear. In their map of the British class structure, Savage et al. (2013) considered such positions to be an emerging service class rather than a more deprived precariat. The variations in the situations of different people in precarious employment suggest that, while the existence of the precariat might mean polarization, it does not create a homogeneous group that is likely to develop solidarity and act collectively.

Conclusions on polarization

What can we conclude from the evidence on polarization in the class structure? First, Marx and Weber were broadly correct about the decline of the petty bourgeoisie, although its decline has not been uniform across all sectors of the economy, and the long-term trend has been reversed somewhat in the last 25 years. Second, there has been growth in new-middle-class positions within the class structure, as Weber expected. Moreover, although there has probably been a decline since the 1980s in job security of many middle-class workers in both the private and the public sectors—especially during the most recent recession—middle-class jobs have not decreased, either in absolute numbers or as a proportion of the labour force that they represent. Third, polarization of earned incomes has occurred, but this has happened along class lines mainly at the very top of the income distribution. For the majority of the labour force, polarization has involved falling incomes in the most vulnerable labour market positions, with those in more secure positions being somewhat better protected. The result has been, as Weber expected, a more complex class structure than classical Marxism tends to suggest.

Homogenization of the Working Class?

Marx expected capitalism to facilitate working-class solidarity through the concentration of

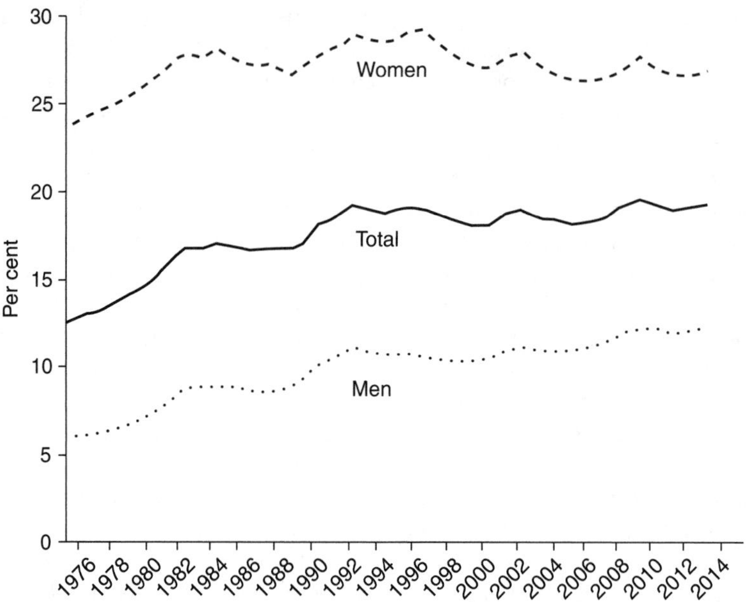

Figure 3.2 Part-Time Employees as Percentage of All Employees, by Gender, Canada, 1976–2014

Source: Statistics Canada (2015a).

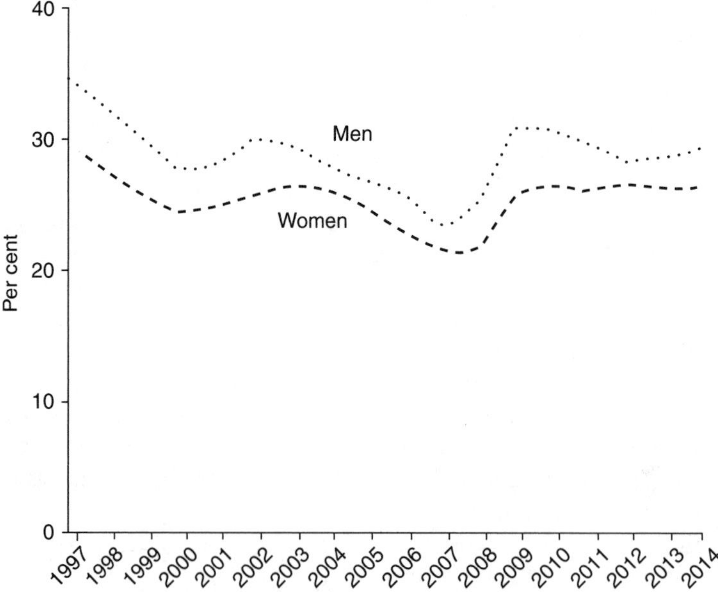

Figure 3.3 Percentage of All Part-Time Workers Who Involuntarily Work Part-Time, by Gender, 1997–2014

Source: Statistics Canada (2015d).

workers in larger workplaces. Weber expected that different labour market situations would persist within both the new middle class and the working class. We have seen that growth of the new middle class has meant that the class structure has not polarized into the two major classes that Marx anticipated. Moreover, evidence suggests that the recent increase in precarious work does not necessarily lead to working-class solidarity.

Regarding Marx's expectation that industrial workers would increasingly be concentrated in large factories, research indicates that, on average, workplaces did grow for much of the twentieth century, especially in manufacturing. Table 3.2 shows that, between 1925 and 1970, the proportion of manufacturing employees in large establishments (500 employees and over) rose, from less than 24 per cent to more than 31 per cent, while the proportion working in establishments with fewer than 100 workers declined. From 1975 to 2014, however, the pattern reversed, with the share of employment in large plants falling by half, to less than 15 per cent of manufacturing employment, and during the same period the share of employment in small plants increased. It is important to note, as well, that employment in manufacturing has also fallen sharply as a proportion of the total labour force, from 18.5 per cent in 1987 to less than 11 per cent in 2014 (Statistics Canada 2015g).

Not all of this shifting has involved blue-collar production workers. Consistent with Weber's expectations, the proportion of professional and managerial employees has generally risen with increases in workplace size (Morissette 1991: 37). Outside of manufacturing and utilities, workplaces tend to be smaller, especially in the private sector of the economy. About one-third of employees in the service sector work in the primarily public-sector services of education, health care and social assistance, and public administration. Between 1997 and 2014, more than one-fifth of the employees in these public-sector services worked in establishments with over 500 employees. These included jobs in government departments, hospitals, schools, and universities. In contrast, private-sector services, which employed 7.8 million women and men in 2014, are characterized by small workplaces: about four in 10 employees in the private-sector services worked in establishments with fewer than 20 employees, and three-quarters worked in establishments with fewer than 100 employees. Less than one in 12 were in establishments with more than 500 employees (Statistics Canada 2015g).

Thus, we find that the social organizational conditions for class formation envisaged by Marx have been only partly met in the sector where he expected them to develop, i.e., in manufacturing, where the share of total employment has declined. These conditions have also been partly met in the public sector, but not in the expanding private-sector service industries.

The increased share of private-sector employment accounted for by small establishments has significant implications for working-class formation. Workers in small workplaces receive less pay and fewer benefits than workers in larger firms, are less likely to receive on-the-job training, and are more likely to be laid off (Clement and Myles 1994: 57–9; Baldwin, Jarmin, and Tang 2002; Statistics Canada 2004). Nevertheless, the social relations and employment relationships in small firms tend to reduce class solidarities (Stinchcombe 1990). The social distance between employer and employee is likely to be smaller than in larger firms, because the employer is more likely to work alongside the employee, and employees can perceive opportunities for themselves to move up to the role of small employer. In smaller firms, there are also likely to be more individualized labour contracts and less routinized production. In contrast, larger companies tend to have more bureaucratized labour relations, with internal labour markets, standardized employment conditions, and extensive quasi-judicial procedures for grievances.

Class Consciousness

Both class polarization and the changing social organization of workplaces and labour markets are structural conditions affecting broad patterns

Table 3.2 Employees by Size of Establishment (Manufacturing), 1925–2014

A.	Year	Employees (%)		
		<100	100–499	500+
	1925	40.8	35.4	23.8
	1930	39.3	35.0	25.7
	1940	35.3	34.5	30.2
	1950	34.5	31.8	33.7
	1960	35.7	32.4	31.9
	1970	30.5	37.1	32.5
B.	**Year**	**Employees (%)**		
		<100	101–500	>500
	1975	30.7	38.6	30.7
	1980	32.0	37.8	30.2
	1985	34.9	37.9	27.2
	1990	39.4	36.2	24.4
	1995	36.8	39.5	23.7
C.	**Year**	**Employees (%)**		
		<100	100–500	>500
	1997	47.2	33.8	19.0
	2000	44.7	35.4	20.0
	2005	46.5	36.2	17.4
	2010	51.2	33.4	15.4
	2014	51.2	33.9	14.9

Sources:
A. *Historical Statistics of Canada*, rev. edn, Series R795–811, 812–25.
B. Baldwin, Jarmin, and Tang (2002: "Table 1. Distribution of Manufacturing Employment and Shipments by Plant Size Class: Canada").
C. Statistics Canada, CANSIM Table 282-0076, Labour force survey estimates (LFS), employees by establishment size, North American Industry Classification System (NAICS), sex and age group.

of social cleavage and solidarity in capitalist societies. The third feature of class formation to consider is how these structural conditions are interpreted by those who experience them, and the extent to which class-based outlooks follow from them. Despite some acknowledged methodological limitations, sample surveys of attitudes have provided much of the evidence for assessing and measuring class consciousness. These survey measures include people's estimates of their own class locations, their attitudes towards the role of corporations in the economy, their feelings about unions and strikes, and so on. Conceptually, researchers influenced by Marx have generally used a typology involving three types or degrees of class consciousness: class awareness or identity, oppositional class consciousness, and revolutionary or counter-hegemonic class consciousness (Giddens 1973; Livingstone and Mangan 1996). Class identity has been defined as awareness of membership in a distinct class, while class opposition entails the belief that the interests of workers and capitalists are opposed, and counter-hegemonic consciousness involves a belief in the possibility and desirability of a society organized along non-capitalist lines.

Assessing the results of attitude surveys is complicated by the variety of measures that have been used for both class position and class consciousness. When Canadians are asked to identify their own class position, they most often choose "middle class," less often "working class" (when it is one of the options), and rarely "poor," "lower class," or "upper class." Studies from the 1990s showed that members of the working class and petty bourgeoisie were more likely than members of other classes to choose a working-class identity, but the class identity adopted by the majority of respondents in all classes was still "middle class" (Livingstone and Mangan 1996, Johnston and Baer 1993). Recent evidence does suggest that the proportion of people self-identifying as middle class has declined, however, from about 67 per cent in 2002 to about 47 per cent in 2014 (Graves 2014).

As for oppositional class consciousness, surveys have found that, on such issues as the rights of labour unions and the redistribution of income from rich to poor, there are only small differences in the attitudes of members of different classes towards business and labour (Clement and Myles 1994; Livingstone and Mangan 1996; Langford 2002; see also Chapter 23 in this volume).

Finally, while little research has been conducted on hegemonic class consciousness, it generally shows that most people in all class positions rarely see an alternative to a capitalist economy. Members of the working class are somewhat more likely to do so, but even in this class the proportion represents a tiny minority (Livingstone and Mangan 1996; Johnston and Baer 1993).[4]

In Durkheimian terms, it appears that, despite a half-century of efforts by sociologists to underscore the inequalities in Canada's class structure (Porter 1965), the collective representation of Canadian society continues to be largely middle class.

Mobilization and Collective Action

For Marx and subsequent Marxists, increasing class polarization, growing working-class solidarity within changing workplaces, and rising class consciousness should all go hand-in-hand with higher levels of working-class organization. The primary role of labour unions is to defend the economic interests of their members. These interests include wages and benefits, working conditions, fair treatment by employers, and job security. Unions have largely succeeded in protecting these interests, because union jobs typically have higher wages and better benefits than do non-union jobs. This is not all that unions do, however. Many unions are also involved in movements and campaigns for broader objectives affecting working people more generally.

As Marx expected, unions have grown from small local organizations, based mainly on skilled craft workers, to large national and international bodies, often encompassing workers from a wide variety of different occupations. These comprise many members of the new middle class, including some of the more than one-in-three union members who have university degrees (Uppal 2011). The growth of unions in Canada occurred in three major waves: the organization of craft unions in the late nineteenth and early twentieth centuries, the spread of industrial unions in manufacturing in the 1940s, and the rapid growth of public-sector unionism in the 1960s. Union membership has expanded from 133,000 in 1911 to nearly 4.3 million in 2014.[5] In Canada, union density, or the percentage of paid workers who belong to unions, was nearly 38 per cent in 1981, but fell in the 1990s and was about 30 per cent at the turn of the century, where it still remains (Galarneau and Sohn 2013; Statistics Canada 2015f; Uppal 2011). In the majority of other advanced capitalist societies, union density has also fallen, sometimes to very low levels.

Canadian unionization rates have not declined as much as in other countries, including the US. As shown in Figure 3.4, this is largely because of the strength of public-sector unionism (e.g., civil servants, hospital workers, teachers). Public-sector workers make up more than half of all union members in Canada, and union density has held steady at more than 70 per cent; in contrast, it has fallen to just 15 per cent in the private sector (Statistics Canada 2015f). There are several reasons for this. First, private-sector employment has shifted towards service industries, where union density is lower, and away from goods-producing industries, such as manufacturing, forestry and mining, and construction, where union density is higher (but declining). Unions have had little success in organizing new growth industries, including those connected with information technology, or among "knowledge workers" in management and professional occupations. Second, as we have seen, establishment size in goods-producing industries has been declining, and unionization rates are generally lower in small firms; for example, unionization rates are four times higher in workplaces with over 500 employees than in workplaces with fewer than 20 employees. At the same time, union density has been declining even in larger enterprises, especially those with more than 100 employees. Third, precarious employment such as part-time and temporary jobs has grown, and these jobs are less likely to be unionized.

Partly as a consequence of declining unionization levels in goods-producing industries, union density has fallen among men, and women's unionization rate now exceeds men's (Figure 3.5) In 2014, over 52 per cent of union members were women, up from approximately 33 per cent in 1982 and only 16 per cent in 1962 (White 1993; Statistics Canada 2015f). It is also notable that unionization rates are also related to age, especially among women. The gains in unionization for women largely stem from increased employment of women over 45 in the highly unionized public sector, while unionization rates for younger women have declined (Galarneau and Sohn 2013); for men, unionization has fallen across

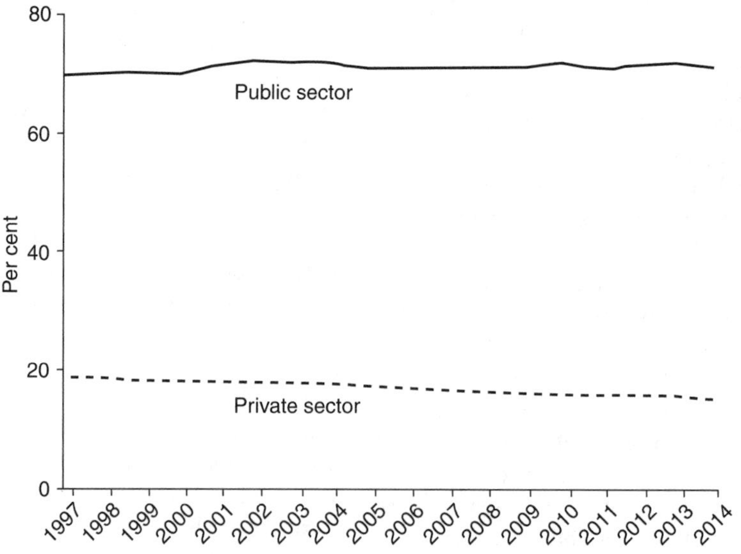

Figure 3.4 Public- and Private-Sector Unionization Rates, Canada, 1997–2014

Source: Statistics Canada (2015f).

all age groups. There are also large regional differences in unionization rates, which are highest in both Newfoundland and Labrador and Quebec, and lowest in Alberta (Galarneau and Sohn 2013).

Although unions in Canada have often supported left-leaning political parties, in particular the New Democratic Party, most of the opposition of workers to the power of capitalism or big business has been manifested in strike activity and political protest campaigns. Surges of union organization have corresponded historically with periods of heightened industrial conflict, with the two feeding off each other. The expansion of industrial unions in the 1940s and the rise of public-sector unionism in the 1960s both occurred amid waves of strikes that, at times, gave Canada among the highest rates of industrial conflict in the world (Cruikshank and Kealey 1987). As Figure 3.6 shows, since the 1980s the number of strikes and strikers, as well as the amount of time lost to strikes, has fallen to historically low levels (Uppal 2011).

Not surprisingly, given the high rate of public-sector unionization, public-sector unions have played prominent roles in protest campaigns against government cutbacks and attempts to restrict union power. Examples include the opposition to the federal government's imposition of wage controls in the 1970s, the Solidarity movement in British Columbia in the 1980s, opposition to the Harris government's "Common Sense Revolution" in Ontario in the 1990s, and conflict with the Campbell government in British Columbia in the early years of this century. At present, an important concern for unions, and for working-class organizations more generally, is the threat of increasing capital mobility in today's global economy, with companies moving their enterprises to other countries. Such possibilities have meant that unions, often in alliance with other groups, have fought free trade agreements and international institutions promoting corporate globalization. The combination of neo-liberal governments, globalization, and shifts in employment has weakened unions in all countries, although less so in Canada than elsewhere. Regional differences complicate the picture in Canada. For example, the loss of manufacturing jobs primarily affects Ontario and Quebec, and has little impact on the natural

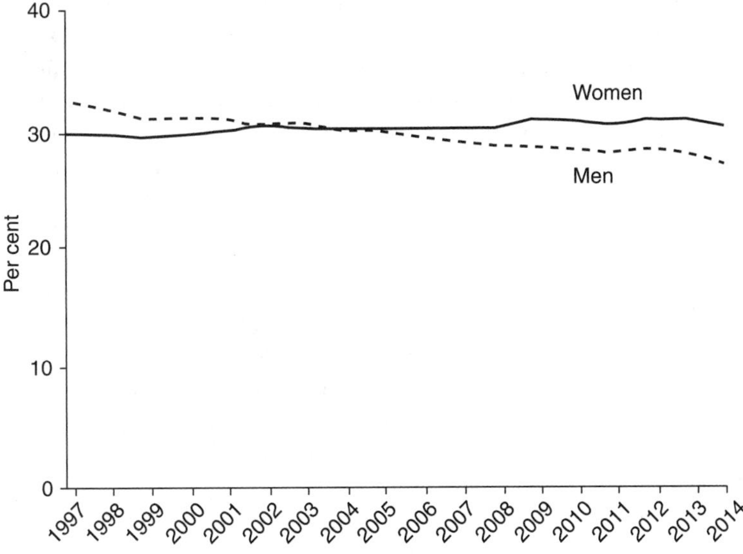

Figure 3.5 Unionization Rates by Gender, Canada, 1997–2014

Source: Statistics Canada (2015f).

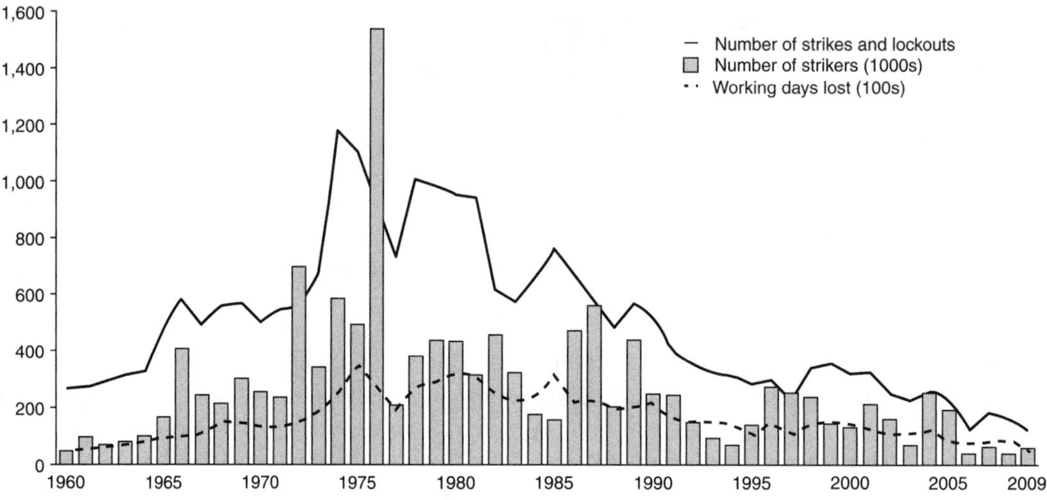

Figure 3.6 Strikes and Lockouts in Canada, 1960–2009

Source: "Work Stoppages" Administrative Data, Workplace Information Directorate, Human Resources and Social Development Canada. Data tabulated by Linda Briskin with contributions from Kristine Klement. http://libgwd.cns.yorku.ca/gwd/wp-content/uploads/hrsdc_table-11.pdf.

resources and construction industries that until recently were expanding in other provinces.

Despite union involvement in various protest campaigns and their support for other movements (Carroll and Ratner 1995), social movements in twenty-first-century Canada, including the environmental movement, Indigenous peoples' movements, the women's movement, and the LGBT movement, have generally not been organized along class lines (Staggenborg 2012; Ramos and Rogers 2015).

Conclusion

In this chapter, we have found that, although Marxist theory furnishes key ideas for an understanding of class formation and class conflict, the history of these two processes in Canada is more variable, contingent, and dependent on other conditions than Marx anticipated. Weber's ideas about the development of a new middle class, as well as Durkheim's conception of collective representations, are also needed to understand contemporary Canada. While the statistical overview presented here shows that Canada's class formation is very complex, it tells us nothing about how class is lived in workplaces or in leisure, community, and neighbourhood settings (Dunk 2003). In the absence of ethnographic and interview studies, we cannot examine issues such as the symbolic and social boundaries studied elsewhere by researchers like Lamont (1992, 2001) and Denis (2015). As the world currently struggles to emerge from the worst recession since the 1930s, and as income and wealth inequality show no sign of easing, there is plenty of work for students of class and social inequality to do.

Questions for Critical Thought

1. Outside of sociology classes, do you think of yourself and your family in terms of class? If so, what class? If not, what identity or identities are important to you?
2. What are the advantages and disadvantages of a Marxist conception of classes as positions in relations of production, a Weberian conception of classes as positions in markets, and a Durkheimian conception of classes as ranked occupational groups?
3. What makes an individual or family "middle class"? What distinguishes those in the middle class from others?
4. Can the "precariat" be considered a class with the potential for solidarity, consciousness, and collective action?

Recommended Readings

Dunk, Thomas. 2003 [1991]. *"It's a Working Man's Town": Male Working-Class Culture in Northwestern Ontario*, 2nd edn. Montreal and Kingston: McGill-Queen's University Press.

Grabb, Edward G. 2007. *Theories of Social Inequality*, 5th edn. Toronto: Nelson.

Lamont, Michèle, and Virág Molnár. 2002. "The study of boundaries in the social sciences." *Annual Review of Sociology* 28: 167–95.

Wright, Erik Olin, ed. 2005. *Approaches to Class Analysis*. Cambridge: Cambridge University Press.

Recommended Websites

Canadian Centre for Policy Alternatives:
https://www.policyalternatives.ca/

Gender and Work database:
http://www.genderwork.ca/gwd/

Marxists.org Internet Archive:
https://www.marxists.org/

Max Weber Studies:
http://www.maxweberstudies.org/

Notes

1. The concept of self-employment does not correspond strictly to Marx's concept of the petty bourgeoisie, as it includes both self-employed people who do not employ paid help, and those who do, i.e., employers or capitalists. There is debate about how many employees a self-employed person must have in order to be considered a capitalist.
2. Recent data sources using measures consistent with those used for 1971 to 2001 were unavailable. The conclusions presented here are drawn from Burleton et al. (2013) and the author's own analysis of data from Statistics Canada (2015b).
3. The most frequent reasons for women's part-time employment involve child care, personal responsibilities, and family responsibilities, which, given the gendered division of unpaid labour, can also be considered involuntary.
4. This pattern might be expected to vary according to the level of class conflict, but even in an

industrial city such as Hamilton, in a period of high strike activity, Livingstone and Mangan (1996) found that there was not much spontaneous recognition of class conflict. In his study of a postal workers' strike in the same city in the same time period, Langford (1994) found little enduring change in class consciousness as a result of participation in the strike.

5. Lack of consistent data series makes it difficult to construct exact measures over time. See Akyeampong (2004) and Morissette et al. (2005).

References

Akyeampong, Ernest. 2004. "The union movement in transition." *Perspectives on Labour and Income* 5, 8: 5–13.

Baldwin, John R., and Desmond Beckstead. 2003. "Knowledge workers in Canada's economy, 1971–2001." Statistics Canada Micro-economic Analysis Division. Insights on the Canadian Economy Analytical Paper No. 4.

———, Ron S. Jarmin, and Jianmin Tang. 2002. "The trend to smaller producers in manufacturing: A Canada/U.S. comparison." Statistics Canada Economic Analysis Research Paper Series No. 003.

Burleton, Derek. 2013. "Are medium-skilled jobs in Canada experiencing a hollowing out, U.S.-style?" *TD Economics Special Report*, 23 Feb. http://www.td.com/document/PDF/economics/special/AreMediumSkilledJobsInCanadaExperiencingAHollowingOut.pdf. Accessed 17 June 2015.

———, Sonya Gulati, Connor McDonald, and Sonny Scarfone. 2013. "Jobs in Canada: Where, what and for whom?" TD Economics. www.td.com/document/PDF/economics/special/JobsInCanada.pdf. Accessed 17 June 2015.

Carroll, William K., and R.S. Ratner. 1995. "Old unions and new social movements." *Labour/Le Travail* 35: 195–221.

Clement, Wallace, and John Myles. 1994. *Relations of Ruling: Class and Gender in Postindustrial Societies*. Montreal and Kingston: McGill-Queen's University Press.

Cruikshank, Douglas, and Gregory S. Kealey. 1987. "Canadian strike statistics, 1891-1950." *Labour/Le Travail* 20: 85–145.

Denis, Jeffrey S. 2015. "Contact theory in a small-town settler-colonial context: The reproduction of laissez-faire racism in Indigenous–White Canadian relations." *American Sociological Review* 80, 1: 218–42.

DePratto, Brian, and Randall Bartlett. 2015. "Precarious employment in Canada: Does the evidence square with the anecdotes?" *TD Economics Special Report*, 26 Mar. http://www.td.com/document/PDF/economics/special/PrecariousEmployment.pdf. Accessed 17 June 2015.

Dunk, Thomas. 2003. *"It's a Working Man's Town": Male Working-Class Culture in Northwestern Ontario*, 2nd edn. Montreal and Kingston: McGill-Queen's University Press.

Durkheim, Émile. 1893 [1933]. *The Division of Labor in Society*. Translated by George Simpson. New York: Free Press.

———. 1957. *Professional Ethics and Civic Morals*. Translated by Cornelia Brookfield. London: Routledge & Kegan Paul.

Galarneau, Diane, and Thao Sohn. 2013. *Long-Term Trends in Unionization*. Ottawa: Statistics Canada.

Giddens, Anthony. 1973. *The Class Structure of the Advanced Societies*. London: Hutchinson.

Goffman, Erving. 1967. *Interaction Ritual: Essays on Face-to-Face Behavior*. Garden City, NY: Anchor Books.

Grabb, Edward G. 2007. *Theories of Social Inequality*, 5th edn. Toronto: Nelson.

Graves, Frank. 2014. "From the end of history to the end of progress: The shifting meaning of middle class." Presentation to the Queen's University 2014 International Institute on Social Policy, Kingston, Ont., 19 Aug. http://www.ekospolitics.com/index

.php/2014/08/from-the-end-of-history-to-the-end-of-progress. Accessed 20 May 2015.

Green, David A., and Benjamin Sand. 2014. "Has the Canadian labour market polarized?" Canadian Labour Market and Skills Researcher Network Working Paper No. 133. http://www.clsrn.econ.ubc.ca/workingpapers/CLSRN%20Working%20Paper%20no.%20133%20-%20Green%20and%20Sand.pdf.

Johnston, William, and Douglas Baer. 1993. "Class consciousness and national contexts: Canada, Sweden and the United States in historical perspective." *Canadian Review of Sociology and Anthropology* 30, 2: 271–95.

Lamont, Michèle. 1992. *Money, Morals, and Manners: The Culture of the French and the American Upper-Middle Class.* Chicago: University of Chicago Press.

———. 2001. *The Dignity of Working Men: Morality and the Boundaries of Race, Class and Immigration.* Cambridge, Mass.: Russell Sage/Harvard University Press.

Langford, Tom. 1994. "Strikes and class consciousness." *Labour/Le Travail* 34: 107–37.

———. 2002. "Does class matter? Beliefs about the economy and politics in postindustrial Canada." In Douglas Baer, ed., *Political Sociology: Canadian Perspectives*, pp. 307–24. Toronto: Oxford University Press.

Lewchuk, Wayne, Michelynn Laflèche, Diane Dyson, Luin Goldring, Alan Meisner, Stephanie Procyk, Dan Rosen, John Shields, Peter Viducis, and Sam Vrankulj. 2013. *It's More Than Poverty: Employment Precarity and Household Well-being.* Toronto: United Way Toronto.

Livingstone, David, and J. Marshall Mangan, eds. 1996. *Recast Dreams: Class and Gender Consciousness in Steeltown.* Toronto: Garamond.

Marx, Karl. 1867 [1953]. *Capital: A Critical Analysis of Capitalist Production*, vol. 1. Moscow: Progress Publishers.

——— and Friedrich Engels. 1848 [1969]. "Manifesto of the Communist Party." In Marx and Engels, *Selected Works in Three Volumes*, vol. 1. Moscow: Progress Publishers.

Morissette, René. 1991. *Canadian Jobs and Firm Size: Do Smaller Firms Pay Less?* Research Paper No. 35. Ottawa: Analytical Studies Branch, Statistics Canada.

———, Grant Schellenberg, and Anick Johnson. 2005. "Diverging trends in unionization." *Perspectives on Labour and Income* 6, 4 (Apr.): 5–12.

———, Garnett Picot, and Yuqian Lu. 2013. *The Evolution of Canadian Wages over the Last Three Decades.* Ottawa: Statistics Canada Analytical Studies Branch Research Paper Series. www.statcan.gc.ca/pub/11f0019m/11f0019m2013347-eng.pdf.

Myles, John, and Adnan Turegin. 1994. "Comparative studies in class structure." *Annual Review of Sociology* 20: 103–24.

Piketty, Thomas. 2014. *Capital in the Twenty-First Century.* Translated by Arthur Goldhammer. Cambridge, Mass.: Harvard University Press.

Porter, John. 1965. *The Vertical Mosaic: An Analysis of Social Class and Power in Canada.* Toronto: University of Toronto Press.

Ramos, Howard, and Kathleen Rogers, eds. 2015. *Protest and Politics: The Promise of Social Movement Societies.* Vancouver: University of British Columbia Press.

Savage, Mike. 2014. "Piketty's challenge for sociology." *British Journal of Sociology* 65, 4: 591–606.

———, Fiona Devine, Niall Cunningham, Mark Taylor, Yaojun Li, Johs Hjellbrekke, Brigitte Le Roux, Sam Friedman, and Andrew Miles. 2013. "A new model of social class: Findings from the BBC's Great British Class Survey experiment." *Sociology* 47, 2: 219–50.

Sørensen, Aage B. 1994. "The basic concepts of stratification research: Class, status, and power." In David B. Grusky, ed., *Social Stratification in Sociological Perspective: Class, Race and Gender.* Boulder, Colo.: Westview.

Staggenborg, Suzanne. 2012. *Social Movements*, 2nd edn. Toronto: Oxford University Press.

Standing, Guy. 2014. "The Precariat." *Contexts* 13, 4: 10–12.

———. 2015. "A new class: Canada neglects the precariat at its peril." *Globe and Mail*, 13 June. http://www.theglobeandmail.com/report-on-business/rob-commentary/a-new-class-canada-neglects-the-precariat-at-its-peril/article24944758/. Accessed 17 June 2015.

Statistics Canada. 2004. *Workplace and Employee Survey Compendium*. Ottawa: Minister of Industry, Labour Statistics Division.

———. 2015a. CANSIM Table 282-0002, Labour force survey estimates (LFS), by sex and detailed age group, annual (persons x 1,000).

———. 2015b. CANSIM Table 282-0010, Labour force survey estimates (LFS), by National Occupational Classification for Statistics (NOC-S) and sex, annual (persons x 1,000).

———. 2015c. CANSIM Table 282-0012, Labour force survey estimates (LFS), employment by class of worker, North American Industry Classification System (NAICS) and sex, annually (persons).

———. 2015d. CANSIM Table 282-0014, Labour force survey estimates (LFS), part-time employment by reason for part-time work, sex and age group, annual (persons x 1,000).

———. 2015e. CANSIM Table 282-0080 5, Labour force survey estimates (LFS), employees by job permanency, North American Industry Classification System (NAICS), sex and age group, annual (persons x 1,000).

———. 2015f. CANSIM Table 282-0223, Labour Force Survey estimates (LFS), employees by union status, North American Industry Classification System (NAICS) and sex, Canada, annual (persons unless otherwise noted).

———. 2015g. CANSIM Table 282-0076, Labour force survey estimates (LFS), employees by establishment size, North American Industry Classification System (NAICS), sex and age group.

Stinchcombe, Arthur L. 1990. *Information and Organizations*. Berkeley: University of California Press.

Uppal, Sharanjit. 2011. "Unionization 2011." *Perspectives on Labour and Income* 23, 4 (Winter): 3–12, Data Table 4, Major wage settlements, inflation and labour disputes. http://www.statcan.gc.ca/pub/75-001-x/2011004/tables-tableaux/11579/tbl04-eng.htm. Accessed 16 June 2015.

Veall, Michael R. 2012. "Top income shares in Canada: Recent trends and policy implications." *Canadian Journal of Economics* 45, 4: 1247–72.

Vosko, Leah F. 2006. *Precarious Employment: Understanding Labour Market Insecurity in Canada*. Montreal and Kingston: McGill-Queen's University Press.

Weber, Max. 1922 [1968]. *Economy and Society: An Outline of Interpretive Sociology*. Edited by Guenther Roth and Claus Wittich. Berkeley: University of California Press.

Weeden, Kim A., and David B. Grusky. 2005. "The case for a new class map." *American Journal of Sociology* 111: 141–212.

White, Julie. 1993. *Sisters and Solidarity: Women and Unions in Canada*. Toronto: Thompson Educational Publishing.

PART II

Socio-economic Bases of Social Inequality

A. Income, Wealth, and Poverty
B. Occupation
C. Education

In Part I, we saw that the private ownership of large-scale businesses contributes to a fundamental division in Canadian society, between the small corporate elite—or capitalist class—and the rest of the population. Beyond ownership, however, three important socio-economic factors generate patterns of class difference and social inequality. The three factors are *income, wealth, and poverty*; *occupation*; and *education*.

These three bases of inequality are closely interrelated. A causal connection runs from education through occupation to income, because schooling typically affects job prospects, and people's jobs largely determine their income. Furthermore, income has consequences beyond people's own lifetimes, influencing the educational opportunities of their children, which in turn affect their jobs and incomes.

Several aspects of this interrelationship should be emphasized. First, when studying these forms of inequality, we need to clarify whether the focus is on individuals or on families. In seeking to explain the occupations or incomes of people, sociologists normally study individuals. However, when looking at intergenerational job mobility or the inheritance of wealth, the focus is mainly on families.

Second, discussions about inequality often involve transmission across generations. To what degree is social inequality *reproduced* over time? Research of this type investigates how people's family background can influence their own eventual educational, occupational, and income attainments. The openness or rigidity of opportunities in Canada is central here, as is the awareness that inequalities endure across generations.

Third, the relations among income or wealth, occupation, and education are not fixed, and the associations among them, while substantial, are not perfect. In other words, people with little education can sometimes earn large incomes, and people who are poor or unemployed will sometimes be highly educated. In other words, the connections linking these three types of inequality are not deterministic, but *probabilistic*.

Fourth, while social inequality is a feature of all societies, the *degree of inequality* will be higher or lower in different societies, and also at different times in the same society. Sociologists in Canada, therefore, are concerned with how inequality here compares with inequality elsewhere, and with how inequality in Canada changes over time.

As discussed in the General Introduction, explanations for social inequality vary. While the chapters in Part II of the book stress facts about inequality, issues of interpretation are equally important. For the analysis of socio-economic factors affecting social inequality, two competing perspectives are especially prominent.

First, some theorists explain inequality as an *individual achievement* issue and also point to inequality's positive consequences. This perspective holds that individuals will be motivated to acquire useful skills and to work at the most important jobs if they receive high rewards for doing so. Hence, people with drive, talent, and ability will use these attributes to benefit both themselves and society in general, but in return they must receive such tangible incentives as high incomes, prestige, and influence. Consequently, according to this perspective, there must and should be inequality in society, provided everyone has the same opportunity to achieve success.

A very different argument is offered by those who assert that *group conflict* is primarily responsible for social inequality. These theorists believe that equal opportunity generally does not exist, and so cannot explain patterns of inequality. Instead, inequality arises because tensions and disputes exist between opposing interest groups, who strive to control profit and privilege at the expense of others. For Marxist scholars, these interest groups are class-based; for some other writers, the opposing groups are defined mainly by non-class factors like gender or ethnicity. In all cases, however, the interpretation is that group conflict or struggle is crucial for understanding social inequality and is also the motor of social change.

The differences between these two perspectives underlie much of the writing on inequality, although there are several variants of each approach. In general, though, scholars who stress individual achievement focus on equality of opportunity, and also emphasize the freedom of individuals to pursue their own goals and interests. In contrast, theorists who stress group conflict typically favour equality of condition or outcome for all people, and the elimination of unfair advantages for some groups compared to others.

A. Income, Wealth, and Poverty

We begin this part of the book by exploring the distributions of income and wealth, including the extreme differences between Canada's rich and poor. The two chapters dealing with this topic also consider how these distributions have changed over time, as well as the role of Canada's governments in affecting income and wealth inequality.

Chapter 4, by Peter Urmetzer, explains that while the economic pie has generally grown for many decades, the sizes of the pie slices going to various income strata are quite different. He also shows that this pattern has been rather stable over time, although recent evidence suggests that the slices are becoming even more unequal than in the past. This has occurred despite government initiatives to redistribute incomes from the affluent to the poor, through taxation and various social welfare programs. Generally, Urmetzer shows that government programs have had only a minor impact in reducing income inequality and poverty in Canada. This is a particular concern, because the economic pie has not become substantially larger in recent years, with wages and salaries remaining stable or stagnant for many Canadians. Consequently, less affluent people, in particular, often must work harder and longer just to keep pace with inflation.

Income differences, of course, provide only a partial picture of economic inequality in Canada. For the very rich, accumulated assets or wealth is far more important than income alone. Wealth can be amassed and retained in the form of land, buildings, stocks, savings, pension plans, and so on. As James Davies reveals in Chapter 5, the distribution of wealth, in Canada and other countries, is far more unequal than the distribution of income, and wealth inequality has significantly increased in recent decades.

B. Occupation

It is clear that people's occupations are fundamentally important, because working is what most Canadians do with much of their waking lives. Job and career are often central to people's personal identities, frequently defining who they are to themselves and to others. Occupations also generate the incomes with which most Canadians provide for themselves and their families. In addition, occupation provides an approximate indication of where individuals stand on many other inequality dimensions, including income; education; skill level; degree of responsibility in the workplace; amount of authority over other workers; and overall prestige ranking.

Probably for these reasons, occupation is viewed by many researchers as the best single measure of a person's socio-economic ranking or class location. The relevance of occupation for understanding social inequality is evident from the numerous problems involving work or occupation that inequality researchers have addressed. These include, for example, the changing composition of the labour force, the extent to which occupational status depends on the attainment of educational credentials, the degree to which the occupational backgrounds of parents influence the occupational attainments of their children, and the problems posed by the changing nature of work in technologically advanced societies.

In the first chapter on occupation, Wolfgang Lehmann and Tracey Adams in Chapter 6 provide a detailed analysis of Canada's occupational structure, the nature of present-day labour markets, and the future of work. Among the major issues considered are the movement to a service-based economy in recent decades, the trend towards more "non-standard" work, including temporary and part-time employment, the prospects for a growing gap between "good" and "bad" jobs, and the question of gender segregation and gender inequality in the Canadian labour force. The authors also consider the implications of such issues for policy-makers in business and government.

Chapter 7 by Harvey Krahn, which also examines occupation, shows that family socio-economic status and parents' educational attainments have substantial predictive effects on the educational and occupational goals of children and on their ultimate occupational attainments. Using a research design that follows people from school into the workforce over a 25-year period, this study demonstrates the considerable importance of family background for the occupational outcomes and mobility of Canadians.

C. Education

Education is arguably the most important of the three socio-economic factors under discussion in Part II. Consider, for example, that education is among the best predictors of both occupational and income attainment. Especially for Canadians who are not born into wealth or affluence, higher education is typically the only avenue to the best jobs and the highest salaries.

Given the importance of education, researchers and policy-makers have looked for ways to achieve equality of educational opportunity. The first selection, Chapter 8 by Nicole Malette and Neil Guppy, addresses the issue of opportunity, by assessing whether family class background, gender, ethnicity, race, and ancestry affect educational attainment. If there is equal opportunity in Canada, these factors should have minimal effects, with each individual's education dependent mainly on personal effort and ability. Malette and Guppy's analysis shows mixed results on this question. Having a more advantaged class background is related to higher educational attainment, but gender and ethnicity or race have little impact; in fact, some disadvantaged groups, including women, visible minorities, and immigrants, tend to attain higher education than men, non-minorities, and the Canadian-born. A key finding, however, is that one disadvantaged ethno-racial group—Canada's Indigenous peoples—still faces considerable educational disadvantage in Canada.

Chapter 9, by Scott Davies, Vicky Maldonado, and Darren Cyr, examines the reasons why family class background has such an important impact on educational attainment. The authors make a significant contribution to the discussion by exploring an array of explanations, including economic resources, parental expectations, and differences in both cultural context and social capital.

A. Income, Wealth, and Poverty

4 Poverty and Income Inequality in Canada

Peter Urmetzer

Introduction

Misconceptions about income inequality are widespread. Frequently, information is tainted by personal impressions and media accounts. Thus, while the homeless are a common and all too visible feature of the urban landscape, they comprise only a small segment of Canada's population. The same is true of sport stars and executives earning the seven-figure salaries reported in the media: only a few Canadians fall into this multi-million-dollar club. These impressions, although powerful in influencing our perceptions about inequality, are unrepresentative. Most Canadians fall outside the extremes of excessive poverty and wealth and are not seen by the media's sensationalist eye.

Nevertheless, substantial inequality exists. Canada's economy has historically followed boom-and-bust cycles, which do not affect all Canadians equally. For example, economic downturns can create slowdowns in new housing construction, causing layoffs in the building industry, but universities and colleges may benefit from downturns, as more people upgrade their skills, creating more jobs for professors and teachers. These illustrations indicate that we need a more comprehensive approach to looking at inequality, one that does not focus narrowly on the rich and poor. We also need to move beyond personal and journalistic accounts that focus on unusual cases.

Inequality

Some people may question the relevance of studying income inequality, especially in a wealthy country like Canada. However, patterns of economic inequality are important, because they reveal the consequences of demographic changes, various social processes, and political decisions. Although seldom acknowledged, political debates often centre on issues of economic distribution, since social policies have consequences benefiting some while disadvantaging others. What is required is some way of assessing these outcomes. Social scientists and policy-makers need ways of evaluating claims about the superiority of market forces over government intervention, or vice versa. Evidence of how these policies affect income distribution is an indispensable tool. Invariably, social program cuts and changes in tax structure or monetary policy make some people richer and some people poorer.

A lowering or abolition of minimum wage legislation, resulting in higher profits for employers and lower pay for workers, does not affect everyone equally. Increases in the cost of borrowing and policies supporting high interest rates also have diverse consequences, because the borrower's larger interest payments end up as increased profits for investors. One person's loss is another person's gain. This holds true for the majority of economic policy decisions that Canadians have experienced over the past few decades: the struggle over the welfare state, free trade, the deficit, and globalization.

Statistics on poverty and income distribution demonstrate, at least indirectly, the outcomes of these policies. Careful examination of income distribution trends reveals important features of the organization of Canadian society. The key question that provides the primary focus of this chapter is: How has inequality changed in Canada in recent decades?

Poverty and Inequality

One challenge when measuring poverty and income inequality concerns the many ways of analyzing, presenting, and interpreting data. Some data can make the problem of poverty look worse, while other data can seem to downplay the issue. For example, should we examine household or individual income? In recent debates about the top 1 per cent of income earners, this distinction has not always been clear. We also need to know whether the income considered is before or after taxes, includes government transfers, and takes into account that the cost of living differs by place of residence. Twenty thousand dollars goes much further in most rural areas than in urban centres like Toronto or Vancouver. Furthermore, some poverty lines focus exclusively on the poor, while income distribution figures include all groups. Finally, in comparisons of the rich and poor, it is crucial to differentiate between income and wealth (see Chapter 5 in this volume).

Those who consider poverty, including academics, policy-makers, poverty advocates, and the general public, sometimes focus on various and often conflicting issues: child poverty, single mothers, homelessness, and so on. Moreover, not everyone recognizes poverty as a genuine problem, with some people more concerned that the taxation required to fund social programs is unjustified and that such programs act as labour market disincentives.

Absolute Poverty Line

A crucial distinction to recognize is the differences between the absolute and relative poverty lines. The relative line directly depends on the larger economic context; it is relative to what other people earn. The absolute poverty line ignores this context and introduces a metric that focuses on the minimum amount of resources required to survive (food, shelter). An absolute poverty line does not change as national income grows. This indicator is commonly used to measure Third World poverty, but it does have at least a few proponents in Canada. Christopher Sarlo, an economist with the conservative Fraser Institute think-tank, has long argued that relative poverty measures are arbitrary and overly generous, and overestimate the amount of poverty that occurs in Canada (Sarlo 2013). Sarlo's view is that a poverty line should show what is required to keep Canadians out of deprivation, not establish a standard for what is "expected" or considered "normal" in society. Proponents of an absolute poverty line might concede, for example, that having an Internet connection at home or having funds for children's sports activities is normal in Canada today, but would argue that these resources are not necessities.

In some ways, Sarlo is correct to suggest that relative indicators are arbitrary and subjective. However, it is debatable that an absolute poverty line is preferable to a relative measure. This seems especially true in affluent societies like Canada, where an acceptable standard of living presumably means more than surviving in squalor. There is a vast difference between mere survival and a healthy existence. Interpretations present a challenge in any ethical debate, and so it is with poverty policy. Differing preconceptions about what is "fair" are unavoidable, and sentiments often rely more on beliefs than science. Hence, choosing any poverty indicator tends to involve a value judgment, making debates about poverty continuous, highly political, and perhaps unresolvable.

In policy debates, the poverty line often serves as the opening salvo that defines the terms of subsequent debates. The choice of threshold determines how serious or unimportant the poverty problem appears to be: people are less likely to be concerned when 3 per cent of Canadians are deemed to be in poverty, compared to an instance where the poverty measure indicates a figure of 20 per cent. Clearly, the more people are categorized as poor, the greater the pressure for governments to act. In any event, absolute poverty lines have failed to gather much credence in Canada, with most discussions focusing on the relative well-being of low-income Canadians.

Relative Poverty Lines

Several measures of relative poverty are used in Canada. Most provinces have their own measures, as do larger cities like Toronto. In addition, some organizations, including the Canadian Centre for Social Development (CCSD) and Human Resources and Skills Development Canada (HRSDC), promulgate their own measurements. All relative poverty lines, as the name suggests, are comparative and calculated using a larger indicator, either median income or percentage of income spent on necessities. Therefore, the relative poverty line moves up or down as the economy grows or contracts.

Statistics Canada, which collects most of our economic and social data, has existed for nearly a century (1918), and has tracked low-income data since 1961. The advantage of having one institution collect this information is that the data are consistent and reliable from year to year. This enables accurate assessments of changes over time, that is, whether poverty in Canada has worsened, improved, or remained unchanged.

Statistics Canada collects income data using the low-income cut-off (LICO). The LICO is a relative figure that is "set to the income level where families spent 63 per cent of their after-tax income on necessities," according to Statistics Canada. It differs from other poverty measures in that it focuses on consumption rather than income. Canada does not have an official poverty line, and Statistics Canada is careful to insist that the LICO does *not* constitute a poverty line. Whether it is a poverty line is partly a matter of semantics, and hints at the political sensitivity of this topic. In fact, most researchers and commentators use "poverty" and "low income" interchangeably, and that is the convention followed here. LICO figures are the most widely used when it comes to issues of poverty in Canada, largely because they are consistent and freely available, and allow for extensive comparisons, especially over time. LICO data also provide flexibility, since they can be easily be broken down by family size (including unattached individuals), province, major metropolitan area, age group, and gender.

Table 4.1 provides just one snapshot of the data available, showing the dollar amounts required to avoid being categorized as low-income, according to city size and family size. Not shown in the table is the important finding that single adults under age 65 comprise the largest proportion of low-income Canadians. In 2011, this amounted to 30 per cent for males and 36 per cent for females. Hence, families are better able to avoid poverty than are individuals. Poverty is actually lowest for people over age 65, which arguably constitutes the biggest accomplishment of the welfare state since its inception following World War II (see also Chapter 18 in this volume). For children in two-parent families, the proportion living in poverty is a relatively low 5.9 per cent, but the figure quadruples to 23 per cent for children living in single, female-headed households; these findings also underscore the economic advantages of pooling incomes in households.

Another relative poverty indicator is the low-income measure (LIM), which is used by

Table 4.1 Low-Income Cut-Offs (LICOs) before Tax, by Community Size, 2013

Family Size	Rural Areas	Fewer than 30,000	30,000–99,999	100,000–499,999	500,000+
1	16,426	18,688	20,423	20,550	23,861
2	20,449	23,263	25,424	25,582	29,706
3	25,139	28,599	31,256	31,450	36,520
4	30,523	34,725	37,950	38,185	44,340
5	34,618	39,384	43,041	43,307	50,290
6	39,045	44,419	48,544	48,845	56,718
7+	43,470	49,453	54,047	54,381	63,147

Source: Statistics Canada (2014b).

international organizations such the Organisation for Economic Co-operation and Development (OECD) and the Luxembourg Income Study. The LIM is also collected and published by Statistics Canada, precisely for making international comparisons. The LIM is more intuitive and simpler to calculate than the LICO. It takes the median point of the national income and then divides that figure in half; hence, if the median family income is $60,000, then $30,000 is the threshold at which poverty is defined. The LIM is sometimes also pegged at 60 per cent of the median, and can be moved higher or lower depending on different rationales. As shown in Figure 4.1, the LICO and LIM followed a similar course between 1976 and 1990, but then began to diverge. According to the LICO, the percentage of Canadians considered low-income increased during the 1990s and improved considerably throughout the 2000s, falling to a low of 8.8 per cent in 2011. This may be unexpected, given the sometimes heated debates about poverty across Canada. The LIM exhibits significantly less variation than the LICO, displaying a smoother line and more consistent rate of poverty since the turn of the millennium. The LIM average is 12.5 per cent for the period 1976–2011, and was 12.6 per cent in the last year for which figures

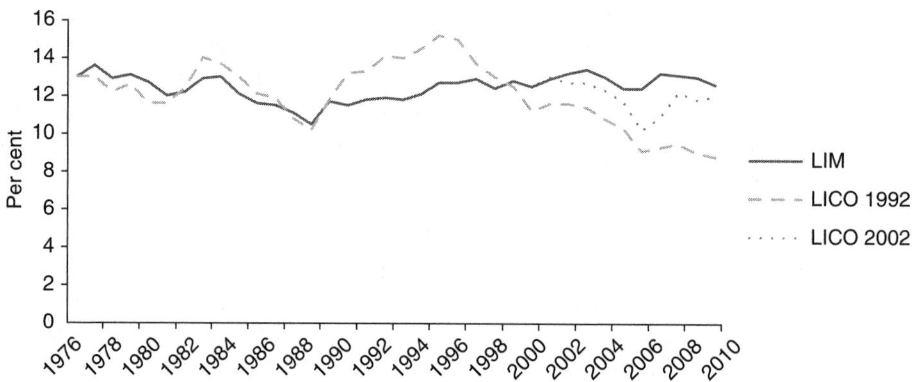

Figure 4.1 Percentage of People below LIM and LICO (after tax), Canada, 1976–2011

Source: Adapted from various Statistics Canada documents.

are available. It should be noted that, in 2002, Statistics Canada revised how it calculated the LICO and the figures since then are more in line with the LIM pattern. Overall, the indicators show no wild swings or significant trends in poverty, with the only discernible fluctuations involving dips triggered by the recessions of 1981, 1990, and 2008. This suggests there is no sustained trend showing that Canada's poor have become relatively worse off or better off over time.

While the absolute measure places poverty in Canada at around 5 per cent, Statistics Canada's LICO sets it at approximately 9 or 12 per cent depending on the measure, and the international LIM places it at 13 per cent (as shown in Figure 4.1). It is easy to see, then, that the perceived urgency of the poverty problem varies substantially, depending on the measure that is employed.

A major shortcoming of focusing only on the poverty line is that we can overlook how the large majority of Canada's national income is distributed. What about patterns and trends for the other nine-tenths of the population? To provide a more complete picture of economic inequality, we will next examine the distribution of income for all Canadians and how this distribution has changed over recent decades.

Income and Inequality

Since the poverty and hardship during the Great Depression of the 1930s, Canadians have experienced relative affluence. From the 1950s through the late 1970s, Canadians, as both individuals and families, enjoyed rising incomes and general economic prosperity. This is true even once inflation is taken into consideration.[1] Figure 4.2 charts the average real income of Canadian families from 1951 through to 2011, showing three distinct periods: (1) rising real incomes from 1951 to 1979; (2) income stagnation from 1980 to 1996; (3) a modest rise in the late 1990s until the recession of 2008. Although average earnings fluctuated somewhat, family purchasing power remained essentially flat from 1980 to 1996. In the late 1990s and throughout the following

Figure 4.2 Average Canadian Family Income, 1951–2011 (in 2011 dollars)

Source: Adapted from various Statistics Canada documents.

decade, family incomes rose more quickly, but not nearly as rapidly as in the decades immediately following World War II.

Real income growth for families from the 1950s through the 1970s reflects a period of sustained and unprecedented expansion in Canada's economy. Throughout this period, productivity levels rose, largely based on technological advances and an increasingly skilled labour force. Organized labour succeeded in tying wages to productivity and, consequently, earnings grew. However, in the early 1980s, earnings across the board began to stagnate. This occurred despite increasing numbers of women in the workforce (rising from 42 per cent in 1976 to 58 per cent in 2012). Note that these data reflect average income for families, not individuals, and the earnings of married women have been crucial for keeping family poverty rates down.

However, because averages only measure what statisticians call "central tendency," and are silent about dispersion or variation around that central point, we need another method of examining the *distribution* of earned income.[2]

Distribution of Income: Quintiles

The most common way to measure income distribution is to divide the population into equal-sized groups, usually fifths, and then examine each group's relative share of the total income. One way of perceiving this is to imagine a queue that contains all the families in Canada. At the head of the line is the family earning the highest income; at the tail is the family earning the lowest income. The line is then divided into five equal-sized groups called fifths or quintiles (each comprising 20 per cent of the population). Next, the sum of the combined incomes of each of the five groups is calculated. The resulting sum for each group is the portion of total income of all five quintiles (the total income of all families and unattached individuals in Canada).

If income were distributed perfectly equitably in Canada, every quintile would be allotted an identical share of income (i.e., 20 per cent). As Table 4.2 shows, the highest quintile acquires more than twice its 20 per cent share, while the lowest quintile receives less than a quarter of its theoretically allotted fifth. More precisely, the top quintile accounted for 47 per cent of all income in 2011. Of all the money earned among all Canadian families in 2011, nearly half accrued to the wealthiest 20 per cent of families. In contrast, the lowest income earners, the 20 per cent of families at the tail of the line, shared only 4.2 per cent of the national income.

Table 4.2 also tracks how income shares have changed over the six decades that span 1951 and 2011. At first glance, little change appears to have occurred in the income proportion that each quintile receives. Closer examination, however, reveals a gradual income shift from the three middle quintiles to the highest. In fact,

Table 4.2 Percentage of Total Before-Tax Income Going to Families and Unattached Individuals, by Quintile, 1951–2011

Income Quintile	1951	1961	1971	1981	1991	2001	2011
Lowest quintile	4.4	4.2	3.6	4.6	4.5	4.1	4.2
Second quintile	11.2	11.9	10.6	10.9	10.1	9.7	9.6
Middle quintile	18.3	18.3	17.6	17.6	16.5	15.6	15.4
Fourth quintile	23.3	24.3	24.9	25.1	24.7	23.8	23.8
Highest quintile	42.8	41.4	43.3	41.7	44.2	46.8	47.0

Source: Adapted from Statistics Canada (2014a).

between 1951 and 2011, the top quintile was the only grouping that saw a substantial increase in its share of the national income, with all other quintiles losing ground. This confirms what many middle-income Canadians are feeling: it is increasingly difficult to maintain their standard of living. It may be surprising, however, that the lowest quintile—the focus of most poverty studies—has been little affected. The majority of relative income decline has occurred in the middle, with all three of the middle quintiles experiencing losses. Between 1961 and 2011, these three quintiles saw a combined loss amounting to 5.7 per cent of the national income, a share that has gone entirely to the top quintile. The top quintile, which arguably needs it the least, has experienced the biggest increase in income, rising by 4.2 per cent since 1951 and 5.6 per cent since 1961. Given that the total annual income generated in Canada surpasses $1.5 trillion in 2011, the 5.6 per cent figure amounts to about $84 billion. If this money were to flow to the lowest quintile, its share would increase to 9.2 per cent of the national income, effectively eliminating poverty in Canada.

Compared to other industrialized countries, particularly the US, Canada has fared relatively well with respect to income inequality. However, the data in this chapter show that things have changed recently, with the gains of the economic expansion during the 1990s and 2000s going mainly to higher-income families (Picot and Myles 2005). The reasons for this upward redistribution are not entirely clear. Yalnizyan (2007) documents that it is not due to longer working hours among high-income earners; on the contrary, high-income earners work fewer hours now than in the 1980s, whereas all other income groups work more. Investment income is also unlikely to explain the upward redistribution, because incomes for top earners kept growing even after the major stock market corrections in 2001 and 2008. One answer is the less generous wage increases for middle-class workers in Canada, which explains much of the divergence even over a short time period. Another factor concerns changes in the labour market. With the baby boomers retiring, there are fewer people to fill many highly skilled occupations, resulting in even higher wages for people qualified to do these jobs. Because high-income earners are also more likely to retire early, employee shortages will be felt in this sector. One final explanation is that high-income professionals increasingly are marrying other high-income earners, and this pooling of high incomes has contributed significantly to an increasing income share for the top 1 per cent of households (Myles 2010).

Transfers and Taxes

The figures in Table 4.2 include all types of income. Especially for those families in the top quintile, earnings from stock market dividends, real estate holdings, pension plans, and professional salaries would be included. In contrast, considerable earnings in the bottom quintile come from employment insurance, pension plans, wages, and social assistance (or what is commonly referred to as "welfare"). The crucial difference here is between market income and government transfers. Income is either market-based (from wages, return on investments, etc.) or collected in the form of transfers (payments designed to assist people who are out of work or retired, including social assistance, employment insurance payments, and government pensions). Factoring in this important distinction changes the distribution of income dramatically.

As shown in Table 4.3, when only market income is considered, the lowest quintile received only 2.1 per cent of all income in 2011, compared to more than half (51.8 per cent) for the highest quintile. The second column in Table 4.3 shows that, once transfer payments were included, the lowest quintile's share doubled, from 2.1 per cent of market income to 4.2 per cent of total income.[3] The highest quintile, by contrast, experienced a loss, from 51.8 to 47 per cent.

Beyond the transfer system, the tax system can also be used for redistribution. Income tax,

Table 4.3 Percentage of Different Income Concepts Going to Families and Unattached Individuals, by Quintile, 2011

Income Quintile	Income before Transfers	Total Money Income	Income after Taxes
Lowest quintile	2.1	4.2	4.8
Second quintile	7.4	9.6	10.6
Middle quintile	14.4	15.4	16.3
Fourth quintile	24.4	23.8	24.1
Highest quintile	51.8	47.0	44.3

Source: Adapted from Statistics Canada (2014a).

at least in theory, is a progressive tax, because high-income earners are taxed at a higher rate than low-income earners.[4] The resulting revenues are then redistributed by the government to lower-income families. In this way, what high-income earners pay in the form of proportionally higher taxes goes to poorer families in the form of proportionally higher transfers. The outcome is a more equitable distribution of income.

The most recent data available, for 2011, reveal a redistribution effect of income taxation, although it is minor (see the far-right column in Table 4.3). Only the highest quintile experienced a decrease in its share (from 47 to 44.3 per cent), with all other quintiles gaining. Comparing the columns "Income before Transfers" and "Income after Taxes" shows the effect income tax has on the national income. This looks like good evidence that the state acts as the legendary Robin Hood, taking from the rich and giving to the poor.

However, this is not the full picture. As yet, we have only examined income taxes, but a significant share of government revenues comes from consumption taxes (e.g., sales taxes, excise taxes), property taxes, and, in some jurisdictions, garbage removal (bag tags). Consumption taxes are flat, not progressive, since everyone pays exactly the same rate regardless of their incomes (e.g., the 5 per cent Goods and Services Tax). Many economists and sociologists argue that, in practice, consumption taxes are actually *regressive*, with low-income earners paying an even higher proportion of their income in consumption taxes than do high-income earners. This conclusion is based on two related arguments.

One argument points out that sales taxes constitute a higher proportion of the income for a poor family than a well-off one. Consider, for example, two families, the Browns and the Greens, who are similar in many respects, but not in income. After income tax, the Greens earn half ($30,000) while the Browns earn ($60,000). Both families purchase a used car costing $10,000. The sales tax on this purchase, including GST and provincial sales tax (PST), would range between $500 and $1,500, depending on the province. At $1,200, for instance, the Greens would pay one-twenty-fifth of their income in sales tax ($1,200 from a total income of $30,000), while the Browns would pay only one-fiftieth ($1,200 from a total of $60,000). Whatever the numbers, the share for the lower-income family would be higher than for the higher-income one.

An obvious counter-argument here is that the wealthier family is likely to spend correspondingly more on a car, say $20,000, and thus end up paying the equivalent proportion of sales tax. The argument that consumption taxes are regressive gains credence, however, once spending patterns are taken into consideration. This brings us to the second argument. Families in lower-income brackets are forced, often out of necessity, to spend most (if not all) of their incomes and, consequently, contribute a higher proportion of their income to consumption taxes than do higher-income families. A family earning $30,000 a year is likely to spend all of its income on food, shelter, clothing, and other basics. By contrast, a family earning $300,000 a year can afford to save or invest a considerable proportion of its income in the stock market or real estate holdings. Money saved and invested is not subject to consumption taxes.

Moreover, not all products and services are taxed equally; for example, the purchase of a used home is not subject to consumption taxes (GST and PST, or the harmonized sales tax [HST] that the Atlantic provinces and Ontario participate in), and post-secondary tuition fees are not taxed by the provincial or federal government. We know that high-income earners are more likely to own homes and send their children to university, thus benefiting from these exemptions. Low-income earners, on the other hand, have less opportunity to take advantage of these tax breaks and therefore end up paying proportionally more of their income in taxes. Therefore, with consumption taxes the proportion of tax paid increases as earnings decrease, the direct opposite of what happens with the progressive income tax. Applying similar reasoning reveals that consumption taxes are regressive.

Once both income and consumption taxes are taken into consideration, the overall redistribution effect of the Canadian taxation system becomes less apparent. As Hunter (1993: 104) explains, "what taxes on income give, . . . taxes on spending take away." In other words, income taxes help redistribute money, but consumption taxes erode much of this redistributive effect. The final outcome is that after different taxes (and tax breaks) are considered, very little Robin Hood remains in the welfare state.

Income Distribution around the Globe

How fair is income distribution in Canada? In the abstract, the answer to this question is difficult, for it depends on all kinds of philosophical assumptions about merit, human rights, and property relations. In relative terms, though, we can address this question by comparing Canada's income distribution to those of other countries. Table 4.4 shows that Canada distributes its income more equally than the United States and the United Kingdom; these countries share cultural ties and economic philosophies with Canada, dating back to the days of the British Empire (with the exception of Quebec, of course). Canada has the same distribution as Australia, another former British colony. Focusing on the bottom quintile reveals that Canada has greater inequality than many nations, including Western European countries in general and Scandinavian countries in particular. Not surprisingly, Sweden, often heralded as the exemplar of the welfare state, has the most equitable distribution of income among Western nations. Japan, Germany, the Czech Republic, and India all have a more generous distribution towards the lowest quintile than Canada.

Table 4.4 also demonstrates that income can be distributed in a myriad of ways and follows no predetermined or consistent pattern. Income has long been most polarized in Latin America, which includes countries like Mexico and Brazil. However, this pattern is slowly changing, with incomes in Brazil and Mexico becoming more equal in recent years. Meanwhile, African countries have become less equal, exhibiting an even more lopsided distribution; South Africa is the only country reported in Table 4.4, but this pattern holds true for other countries in Africa as well. In most African and Latin American countries, a very wealthy top quintile occurs at the expense of relative impoverishment elsewhere, especially in the bottom quintile. It is worth mentioning how inequality has been affected in countries experiencing transformational changes over the past few decades. The Czech Republic and Russia, both members of the former Soviet Union, have charted diametrically opposing paths. Following the collapse of communism, Russia became one of the most unequal societies

Table 4.4 Income Distribution by Quintile, Selected Countries (various years)

	Lowest Quintile	Second Quintile	Middle Quintile	Fourth Quintile	Highest Quintile
Sweden	10	14	18	23	36
Japan	7	13	17	23	40
Germany	8	13	17	22	39
Canada	7	12	17	23	41
Australia	7	12	17	23	41
UK	6	11	16	23	44
US	5	10	16	23	46
Russia	6	11	15	21	47
Czech Rep.	9	15	18	22	36
Malaysia	5	9	14	22	51
Mexico	5	9	13	19	54
Brazil	3	8	12	19	57
South Africa	2	4	8	16	70
India	9	12	16	21	43
Iran	6	11	16	22	45

Note: Percentages are for after-tax income and adjusted for family size.
Source: World Bank (2014).

in the world, whereas the Czech Republic succeeded in becoming one of the most egalitarian. The collapse of the apartheid regime in South Africa in the early 1990s is another example of profound political and social change. Twenty years later, South Africa still exhibits some of the worst inequality in the world, with the lowest quintile having access to a mere 2 per cent of the country's income.

Compared to countries in Latin America, Africa, and to some extent Asia, Canada's distribution is appreciably more equitable. Nevertheless, this could change in the future if recent cuts to some government social programs continue. Many commentators fear that the elimination or reduction of social programs could dramatically alter the distribution of income in this country, and would most directly affect people in the lower quintiles. Some worry about the possible "Brazilianization" of our economy, a term that is meant to reflect the stark inequalities that plague Brazil, which essentially lacks a welfare state (Therborn 1986). The overarching concern is that by having too much faith in markets, some governments, including Canada's at times, have turned their backs on the poor. There is some reassurance, however, in the evidence reviewed here, which shows the relative stability of income shares in Canada over recent decades.

It is remarkable, in fact, just how stable the distribution of income has remained, given the numerous changes that Canadian society has undergone since World War II. These changes include increasing participation of women in the labour force, declines in industrial employment, and overall increases in government expenditures on social programs. The fact that income distribution has remained more or less constant for a half-century, despite greater government involvement, has led some commentators to question the efficacy of the welfare state as a mechanism for redistributing income. An often-quoted study by Hewitt (1977) argues that the redistributive effect of the welfare state is minimal at best. Hewitt's study also confirms that Canada's welfare state lags behind in its redistributive effectiveness, at least when compared with Western European countries.

On the face of it, it may seem inconceivable that Canadian society would be identical without the welfare state. However, the quintile evidence tends to confirm this conclusion: between the early 1950s and 2011, a period that saw an explosion of welfare state services, relative income shares changed little. Does this mean that the seemingly interminable political wrangling over social programs in Canada is essentially about nothing? The answer to this must be a resounding no. Those who claim that the welfare state is ineffective must consider that the quintile approach alone does not reveal important changes in Canada's income composition. As we have seen, the most common way to present quintiles is by total income—that is, market and transfer income combined. This approach ignores how the composition of income has changed over the years, specifically the ratio of market income to government transfers. Were it not for these transfers, the poorest quintile would receive very little income (see Table 4.3, column 1).

Another factor that quintiles ignore is Canada's most costly social programs, especially health and education, which are not included in income statistics because they are received in-kind (i.e., as a service rather than as monies). Nonetheless, these programs affect income distribution, because not having to pay for health care or education means a decrease in household expenditures. The resulting savings rise proportionally as income declines, which can be considered as contributing to greater equality. Consider, for example, that a $1,000 medical procedure represents a much bigger proportion of savings for someone in the bottom quintile than for someone in the top quintile.

These observations are not consistent with views that perceive little utility in the welfare state. The reason income shares have stayed so consistent over the years is precisely because the income transfers made through different social programs have steadily kept pace with declines in market income. In short, income distribution has remained relatively uniform because of the welfare state, not in spite of it.

Conclusion

This chapter is a short introduction to just some of the ways to study income inequality in Canada. We have examined how income varies among different quintile groups, but not the effects on income attainment of important sociological variables such as gender, ethnicity, and region (which are considered in other chapters in this volume). Another intriguing question is: Who occupies the different quintiles and at what moment in his or her life course? Individuals may occupy the lowest quintile, but only on a temporary basis. Many Canadians wander in and out of the lowest quintile at some points in their lives—as students, when first entering the labour force, or when temporarily unemployed—without suffering the long-term consequences normally associated with poverty. This dynamism is not reflected in the figures shown here. Conversely, some individuals are permanent occupants of the lower quintiles. This includes the homeless, who have increased their presence in most Canadian cities and yet are not included in this kind of study, primarily because they are notoriously difficult to track in income surveys and are unlikely to file income tax returns (see Chapter 22).

This chapter is also more descriptive than theoretical, and does not delve into detailed explanations for what lies at the root of income inequality (see, e.g., Grabb 2007). Even a cursory inventory shows that many theories abound: the advent of neo-liberalism, changes in the labour market, modifications to tax structures, deindustrialization, globalization, and so on. Whatever the issue, it is important to adopt a critical stance and ask who is likely to benefit or lose from these processes and policies.

Who benefits is not beyond empirical verification, of course. In this chapter, we have learned that although absolute incomes have risen substantially since the early 1950s, income distribution has stayed relatively stable. Closer inspection revealed, however, what many Canadians have experienced personally, which is that middle-income earners have been the least successful in holding on to their share. Much of this income has escaped upward to the highest quintile, giving credence to the claim that the rich are getting richer, although the poor seem not to be getting poorer, at least not in Canada these days. Other studies have shown that the top 1 per cent have made particularly large gains, and not always for reasons that some might expect, e.g., our finding that there is an exceptionally large proportion of high-income households that include high-earning couples.

We also saw that the primary statistic used to compare incomes, income quintiles, is not without problems. Its main shortcoming is that it obscures how the composition of income, in regard to market income versus government transfers, has changed over time. Still, despite the limitations associated with measuring inequality, it apparently does not matter much which metric is used. International comparisons show that, whether we employ quintiles, quartiles, deciles, or the Gini coefficient, similar patterns of inequality are revealed (Wilkinson and Pickett 2009).

Canada has a distribution of income that is fairly typical for an industrial economy. As studies consistently show, Canada is a wealthy country, but how this wealth should be divided remains a topic of considerable debate. In the end, definitive answers about what is fair continue to elude us; we are no closer today than when Karl Marx and Adam Smith debated this issue in centuries past. The lack of a conclusive answer, however, should not deter us from continuing to ask the question. Once we fail to do so, someone else's version of "what is fair" is sure to win out.

Questions for Critical Thought

1. Should the responsibility of avoiding privation fall solely on the shoulders of individual families? Or do governments have some responsibility when it comes to alleviating poverty?

2. While adults have some control over their economic circumstances, children do not. Should children in poor families have similar opportunities as children in middle- and upper-class families? How could we achieve some semblance of equality of opportunity for children from poor backgrounds?

3. In your opinion, what is a more appropriate indicator of deprivation: an absolute or relative poverty line? What are your reasons for your answer?

4. Take a close look at Table 4.1 and compare the different earning thresholds recommended for individuals and families. Do you think it would be manageable or nearly impossible to survive on the prescribed amounts? To make an informed decision, list some of the expenses required to survive: food, shelter, utilities, transportation, clothing, and entertainment. What about technology (cell phones, computers) or emergencies?

Recommended Readings

Grabb, Edward. 2007. *Theories of Social Inequality*. Toronto: Thomson Nelson.

Green, David A., W. Craig Riddell, and France St-Hilaire, eds. 2015. *Income Inequality: The Canadian Story*. Montreal: Institute for Research on Public Policy.

Milanovic, Branko. 2005. *Worlds Apart: Measuring International and Global Inequality*. Princeton, NJ: Princeton University Press.

Raphael, Dennis. 2011. *Poverty in Canada: Implications for Health and Quality of Life*. Toronto: Canadian Scholar's Press.

Stiglitz, Joseph. 2012. *The Price of Inequality*. New York: W.W. Norton.

Wilkinson, Richard, and Kate Pickett. 2009. *The Spirit Level: Why More Equal Societies Almost Always Do Better*. London: Allen Lane.

Recommended Websites

Canadian Centre for Policy Alternatives (CCPA):
https://www.policyalternatives.ca/

Canadian Council on Social Development (CCSD):
http://www.ccsd.ca/

Branko Milanovic Blog:
http://glineq.blogspot.co.uk/

Statistics Canada:
http://www.statcan.gc.ca

Notes

1. Inflation refers to rising prices. To remove the effect of inflation we use "real" or "constant" dollars, a common procedure in historical income comparisons. This method better reflects the purchasing power of money, i.e., what a dollar can buy. A bottle of soda pop costing 10 cents in the 1950s costs a dollar or more now. The purchasing power of each dollar has decreased. But then our incomes have also increased, so the question becomes, "Is a bottle of pop more affordable now than in the 1950s?" In Canada, we use the consumer price index (CPI) to evaluate price changes (and inflation). Purchasing a similar basket of goods and services (e.g., milk, haircuts) every month allows us to calculate price increases due to inflation. Incomes can then be adjusted to eliminate the effect of inflation, resulting in a measure of real purchasing power (as shown in Figure 4.2).
2. When Statistics Canada presents income findings, it provides both average (total earnings divided by the number of cases) and median incomes (the amount earned by the family located midway between the highest and lowest). Statistics Canada tracks both income types because averages can be inflated by even a few very high incomes. For example, a bank president earning $10 million a year (a realistic figure) and 100 bank clerks earning $25,000 a year would earn on average close to $125,000, vastly overstating the salary of the bank employees. Consequently, some believe median income is a better indicator of "typical" family income (which would be $25,000 for the bank employees in our example).
3. Between 2007 and 2011 (in constant 2011 dollars), market incomes for low-income (lowest quintile) families dropped by 12 per cent, from

$7,700 to $6,800. However, with government transfers included in the calculation, the drop was only 2 per cent, from $15,900 to $15,600 (Statistics Canada 2014a). This is solid evidence that the welfare state performed as intended, saving at least some Canadians from destitution.

4. The precise amount of income tax that individual filers pay depends on a complex array of factors, including the amount of money earned and the method by which the money was earned (e.g., wages, dividends, capital gains). The information below includes federal tax only. Each province also collects income tax. For 2015, Canadians pay no federal income tax on the first $11,327 they received. Beyond that threshold, any additional earnings up to $44,701 are taxed at a 15 per cent rate. The rate is 22 per cent for earnings between $44,702 and $89,401; 26 per cent for earnings between $89,402 and $138,586; and 29 per cent for earnings above $138,586. In this progressive fashion, as income rises, so does the rate of taxation.

References

Grabb, Edward. 2007. *Theories of Social Inequality*, 5th edn. Toronto: Thomson Nelson.

Hewitt, Christopher. 1977. "The effect of political democracy and social democracy on equality in industrial societies: A cross-national comparison." *American Sociological Review* 42: 450–64.

Hunter, Alfred. 1993. "The changing distribution of income." In James Curtis, Edward Grabb, and Neil Guppy, eds, *Social Inequality in Canada*, 3rd edn. Scarborough, Ont.: Prentice-Hall.

Myles, John. 2010. "The inequality surge." *Inroads* 26 (Winter): 66–73.

Picot, Garnett, and John Myles. 2005. *Income Inequality and Low Income in Canada: An International Perspective*. Ottawa: Statistics Canada.

Sarlo, Christopher. 2013. *Poverty: Where Do We Draw the Line?* Vancouver: Fraser Institute, Nov. http://ssrn.com/abstract=2354442 or http://dx.doi.org/10.2139/ssrn.2354442.

Statistics Canada. 2014a. "Income in Canada." CANSIM Table 202-0703.

———. 2014b. "Income Distribution by Size in Canada." CANSIM Table 202-080.

Therborn, Göran. 1986. *Why Some People Are More Unemployed Than Others*. London: Verso Books.

Wilkinson, Richard, and Kate Pickett. 2009. *The Spirit Level: Why More Equal Societies Almost Always Do Better*. London: Allen Lane.

World Bank. 2014. *2014 World Development Indicators*. Washington: World Bank..

Yalnizyan, Armine. 2007. *The Rich and the Rest of Us: The Changing Face of Canada's Growing Gap*. Ottawa: Canadian Centre for Policy Alternatives.

5 The Distribution of Wealth and Economic Inequality

James B. Davies

Introduction

This chapter addresses a series of questions about the distribution of wealth and economic inequality in Canada and also around the world. First, what is wealth and how is it distributed among Canadians? How does this compare with the picture elsewhere in the world? What determines how wealth is distributed—nationally and globally? Why should we care? And finally, how does wealth mobility affect our views about wealth inequality?

What Is Wealth?

The wealth of an individual or family equals the value of all their assets minus their debts at a moment in time. This concept is also referred to as "net worth." The assets that should be included cover a wide range. They include, for example, cash, bank deposits, owner-occupied housing, guaranteed investment certificates (GICs), registered savings plans (RSPs), private pension plans, stocks and shares, bonds, mutual funds, consumer durables, real estate, and machines and equipment used in unincorporated businesses. There is also a wide variety of debts—mortgages, credit card balances, personal loans, small business loans, and so forth.

Table 5.1 indicates the relative importance of the different forms of wealth at the end of 2006. Note, first, that 39.0 per cent of the total value of assets is made up of real estate, which is about evenly divided between buildings and land. Financial assets, at 55.2 per cent of the total, are more important than non-financial assets. Among financial assets, shares and bonds, whose ownership is relatively concentrated, make up 21.6 per cent of total assets. More widely distributed assets like cash, bank accounts, life insurance, and pensions make up the bulk of the total.

Some urge the use of a broader wealth definition—one that includes, for example, the value of public pension rights like Old Age Security (OAS), the Guaranteed Income Supplement (GIS), and the Canada Pension Plan/ Quebec Pension Plan (CPP/QPP). Estimates of such "social security wealth" in the US vary from about 40 per cent to 200 per cent of conventional net worth.[1]

Finally, it is often argued that the present value of future labour earnings—that is, "human wealth"—should be included. As for social security wealth, data availability is a barrier.

Table 5.1 Year-End National Balance Sheets at Market Value: Households and Non-profit Institutions Serving Households, Canada, 2014

	Assets (in millions $)	% of Assets
I. Non-financial Assets		
Residential structures	1,959,508	18.9
Non-residential structures	46,665	0.5
Land	2,024,702	19.6
Consumer durables	570,894	5.5
Machinery, equipment, & inventories	34,336	0.3
Total	4,638,377	44.8
II. Financial Assets		
Currency and deposits	1,329,437	12.8
Bonds	101,705	1.0
Life insurance and pensions	1,986,133	19.2
Shares	2,128,379	20.6
Other financial assets	164,442	1.6
Total	5,710,096	55.2
Total assets	10,348,473	100.0
III. Debt		
Mortgages	1,192,457	11.5
Other debt	708,325	6.8
Total	1,900,782	18.4
Net worth	8,447,691	81.6

Source: These data originate from the CANSIM Database, Table 378-0121. CANSIM is an official Mark of Statistics Canada.

Estimating human wealth requires projecting future earnings. Various estimates of aggregate human wealth are available. (See the appendix to Davies and Whalley 1991.) A best-guess estimate is that the total value of human wealth equals about three times that of non-human, or "physical" wealth.

How Is Wealth Distributed in Canada?

In Canada the major sources of information on the distributions of income and wealth among families are from Statistics Canada's household surveys. The most recent wealth survey, the Survey of Financial Security (SFS), was conducted in the early summer of 2012. There were earlier SFS surveys, in 1999 and 2005.[2] All surveys are subject to sampling and non-sampling error. These sources of error are especially important in wealth surveys.

Sampling error is the difference between the sample value of a statistic, e.g., average wealth, and its true *population* value. The larger the sample, the smaller this error is likely to be. For medians, it is generally small, since the sample sizes used by Statistics Canada are large. Without special sampling techniques, however, estimating the mean or the shape of the *distribution* of a highly skewed variable like wealth can involve significant sampling error.[3] Most samples will select too few rich households, although a few samples will have too many. This problem can be addressed by oversampling in the upper tail. This approach was not generally followed by the Survey of Consumer Finance (SCF), which is conducted every three years by the Federal Reserve Board in the US, but it is used in the SFS (Statistics Canada 2007; Morissette and Zhang 2007).

Non-sampling error is an especially serious problem in wealth surveys. It takes two forms. First, some people refuse to be interviewed. Studies indicate that the likelihood of non-response varies with age, region, and income. These problems can be corrected through weighting families according to their likelihood of being in the sample. Differential response across age groups, for example, can be almost entirely corrected. However, it is only when differential response according to wealth is highly correlated with differential responses according to observable characteristics (age, region, size of urban area, etc.) that this type of error can be adequately corrected by weighting. Since the correlation is far from perfect, differential response remains a problem.

Another form of non-sampling error—misreporting—occurs because people sometimes refuse to report certain items or make mistakes. In cases where people report that they own an asset but do not report its value, an imputed value can be assigned. However, no correction is possible if the interviewers do not know that the family owns an asset. American studies indicate that, on average, financial assets are often under-reported by up to 40–50 per cent. Other assets are more accurately reported. For example, the value of owner-occupied houses is, on average, reported with surprising accuracy (Davies 1979).

Keeping these reservations in mind, let us consider Table 5.2, which shows estimates of Canada's wealth distributions in 1999, 2005, and 2012. The table suggests that the real wealth of Canadian families has risen substantially in recent years. From 1999 to 2012, estimated mean wealth rose from $319,500 to $554,124 (in constant 2012 dollars), an increase of 73.4 per cent, or 4.3 per cent per year. This included an increase of 33.7 per cent from 2005 to 2012, despite the global financial crisis in 2008–9, which saw a major stock market crash and decreased house prices. After 2009, the stock market recovered, and has posted large gains, while Canadian house prices also resumed their upward trajectory.

The trends in wealth inequality from 1999 to 2012 in Table 5.2 are interesting, and in some ways troubling. From 1999 to 2005, the shares of the poor and middle groups declined. The share of the bottom four deciles fell from 2.5 to 2.0 per cent, and that of the next two deciles (percentiles 40–60) went down from 8.8 to 8.4 per cent. Meanwhile, the share of the top three deciles rose from 80.5 to 81.4 per cent. There was a slight improvement from 2005 to 2012 at the lower end, but the share of the bottom four deciles, at 2.2 per cent, remained below its 1999 level. Most interestingly, the middle and upper-middle groups each saw an increase in their share, while the top decile saw a fall from 50.9 to 47.9 per cent.

In view of the possible sources of error in survey results discussed above, it would be a mistake to make too much of the drop in the share of the top decile from 2005 to 2012.This drop may also reflect short-term trends that probably have reversed by now. In 2012, the stock market had recovered from its 2008–9 crash, but had not made large gains beyond that. On the other hand, house prices were rising steadily in Canada's largest cities. The share of the top decile is more sensitive to stock prices, and that of the middle and upper-middle deciles is more sensitive to house prices, which explains why the middle and upper-middle groups gained in their share while the top groups saw a decrease.

For the reasons discussed above, the figures shown in Table 5.2 are subject to significant sources of error. Although Statistics Canada tries hard to reduce these errors, and in particular now oversamples the upper tail in its SFS survey,

Table 5.2 Distribution of Wealth, Families and Unattached Individuals, Canada, 1999, 2005, and 2012

	Shares of Wealth		
Decile	1999 (%)	2005 (%)	2012 (%)
1	–0.3	–0.3	–0.2
2	0.2	0.1	0.1
3	0.7	0.6	0.6
4	1.9	1.6	1.7
5	3.3	3.2	3.4
6	5.5	5.2	5.7
7	8.1	8.1	8.7
8	12.0	12.2	12.8
9	18.9	18.3	19.5
10	49.6	50.9	47.9
Mean (2012 $)	319,500	414,332	554,124
Median (2012 $)	137,000	168,700	243,800

Source: Micro data from Statistics Canada's Survey of Financial Security.

the limitations of sample surveys mean that we should look at other information sources to get a complete picture. There are several alternative sources. Prominent examples include *Forbes* magazine's world list of billionaires, and *Canadian Business* magazine's list of the richest 100 Canadians, both of which are published annually.[4]

In February 2015, *Forbes* listed 1,826 billionaires around the world, of whom 39 were Canadian. Their average wealth was $3.5 billion and, in total, they had $134.8 billion, which is 1.6 per cent of Canada's total household wealth of $8,447.7 billion (Table 5.1). The wealthiest were David Thomson, at $25.5 billion, and Galen Weston, at $9.6 billion, ranking 25th and 131st in the world, respectively. By sector, the largest concentrations were in the retail sector (six billionaires) and media/communications/information technology (five).

Canada's relative showing on the *Forbes* list is evident in comparisons with the US, which has about 10 times Canada's population, and has 536 billionaires on the list, or about 14 times Canada's number. The American billionaires were also richer, averaging a net worth of $4.8 billion compared to the Canadians' $3.5 billion. These figures suggest that the upper tail of Canada's wealth distribution is a bit shorter and thinner than that in the US. Consequently, there may be less concentration of wealth in the upper tail in Canada than in the US, which is corroborated by other evidence discussed below. However, the apparent trend is that Canada's upper tail is becoming more similar to that of the US. As recently as 2007 (a good year for comparison, since it was the last year before the global financial crisis), there were 18 American billionaires for every Canadian on the *Forbes* list (405 Americans versus 23 Canadians). With the 2015 ratio of 14:1, we have gone halfway toward the 10:1 ratio that would indicate both countries had the same number of billionaires relative to their population sizes.

More information on the rich in Canada is provided by the annual list of the wealthiest 100 Canadians from *Canadian Business*. The 2015 list has 89 individuals or "families" with net worth of $1 billion or more.[5] This is more than double the 39 Canadian billionaires on the *Forbes* list. Part of the reason for the higher number is that *Canadian Business*'s wealth estimates tend to be higher than those of *Forbes*. For example, *Canadian Business* puts the David Thomson family at $30.8 billion versus $25.5 billion for David Thomson on the *Forbes* list. Galen Weston's fortune is estimated at $11.4 billion versus $9.6 billion in *Forbes*. In addition, the *Canadian Business* number is higher because it includes both families and individuals. Finally, *Canadian Business* also lists many more cases where wealth is just a little above $1 billion, which may mean that *Forbes* is less accurate in its lower ranges. In any case, there clearly is a significant group of very wealthy Canadians.

One of the most important reasons to look at "rich lists" is that the people on them are not captured in household surveys. The maximum wealth figures in such surveys are typically in the range of $10–$50 million. This affects the estimated shares of top groups. For example, the 2007 SFS indicated a share of the top decile equal to 47.9 per cent. Suppose the SFS captured the population with wealth up to $50 million accurately, but had no one above that level. Extrapolating the *Forbes* list down to $50 million would boost that share to 52 per cent, and doing the same with the *Canadian Business* list would raise it to 58 per cent.[6] More dramatically, the share of the top 1 per cent, which the SFS places at 16 per cent, would rise to 20 per cent based on *Forbes* and 26 per cent based on the *Canadian Business*.

International Comparisons and the World Distribution of Wealth

Recently there has been a great deal of interest in wealth inequality at a global level. It is interesting to try to put the Canadian wealth distribution in an international perspective. Over the last 10 years an international team of scholars has generated a series of estimates of the world distribution of household wealth, and also estimates for the world's major regions and individual countries (Davies et al. 2008, 2011; Shorrocks et al. 2010, 2011, 2012, 2013, 2014). Interest has also been piqued by Thomas Piketty's *Capital in the Twenty-First Century* (2014), which discusses the evolution of the distribution of wealth over time with a broad international and historical scope.

Table 5.3 shows estimated wealth distributions for the world as a whole, for its major regions, and for Canada and the US, taken from Shorrocks, Davies, and Lluberas (2014). One sees immediately that wealth inequality for the world as a whole is very high. The top 1 per cent has an estimated share of 48.2 per cent, while the bottom quintile (i.e., bottom 20 per cent) share is actually negative, at −0.2 per cent, indicating that on average their debts exceed their assets. Moreover, the Gini coefficient has the very high value of 0.911. The Gini is a popular measure of inequality, and ranges from zero, when there is perfect equality, to 1.0, when there is perfect inequality (one person owns everything). The value of 0.911 indicates that the world as a whole is uncomfortably close to the situation of maximum inequality.

Table 5.3 also shows that differences within countries and regions, and between them, are both important sources of inequality. Wealth per adult varies from $4,645 in India to $347,845 in the US.[7] Canada is in the upper-middle range, with mean wealth of $274,543. Some regions and countries have almost as much inequality within them as is evident for the world as a whole. This is reflected in Gini values of 0.846 for the US, 0.856 for Africa, and 0.895 for the Asia-Pacific region.[8] On the other hand, we see that Canada, which is roughly typical of OECD countries other than the US and UK in its level of wealth inequality, has a Gini of just 0.726. Interestingly, China's Gini of 0.719 is also relatively low in this context. This reflects that private wealth was of relatively little importance in China before its economic liberalization beginning in the late 1970s; it also reflects that formerly public housing generally, and land in rural areas, was distributed on an egalitarian basis, mainly in the 1980s and 1990s. Wealth inequality has recently increased in China, and the country has 213 billionaires on *Forbes*'s 2015 list. But the shares of lower groups are still higher than in most other regions and countries. India, which has always had large extremes of private wealth, shows a considerably higher level of wealth concentration.

Shorrocks, Davies, and Lluberas (2014) also found that the composition of wealth varies substantially from poor through middle- to high-income countries. The relative importance of non-financial assets—land, buildings, livestock, and equipment—is much greater in low-income countries. It is as high as 80 per cent of total wealth in the low-income countries of Asia and Africa. As development proceeds, the ratio of financial to non-financial assets increases, and is generally 1.0 or higher in OECD countries. Also, the relative importance of debt rises with country income and wealth. Among China, India, and Indonesia, for example, Shorrocks, Davies and Lluberas (2014) estimate that debt represents only about 5–7 per cent of total household assets. In contrast, a typical value in the OECD would be 15–17 per cent. This difference seems paradoxical, since we are all aware that indebtedness causes severe problems for some people in low-income countries. The resolution of the paradox is that it does not take very much debt in absolute terms to plunge poor people in low-income countries into misery. And, of course, in high-income countries there is a highly developed financial system that makes credit readily available, encouraging people to take on debt.

Finally, there is always much interest in trends in wealth inequality over time. As reported in Davies and Shorrocks (2000) and Roine and Waldenström (2014), several developed countries, not including Canada unfortunately, provide extensive time series evidence on wealth, starting in the early years of the twentieth century. Except for Switzerland, the countries all show a pattern of a long and very substantial decline in wealth inequality from the 1920s to the 1970s, with the share of the top 1 per cent declining from the 60–70 per cent range to the 20–30 per cent range. Since the 1970s, wealth inequality

Table 5.3 World Distribution of Wealth by Region and Selected Countries, 2014, per Adult

	Shares of Total Wealth							
Region/Country	**1st Quintile (%)**	**2nd Quintile (%)**	**3rd Quintile (%)**	**4th Quintile (%)**	**Top 10%**	**Top 1%**	**Gini**	**Mean (US dollars)**
Africa	0.1	0.9	2.9	7.9	78.3	46.1	.856	5,080
Asia-Pacific	0.1	0.5	1.3	4.0	85.3	70.9	.895	44,715
Canada	–0.1	1.9	7.5	17.6	57.0	24.4	.726	274,543
China	1.7	4.1	6.7	12.2	64.0	37.2	.719	21,330
Europe	–0.3	0.4	2.4	12.2	68.8	31.1	.827	145,977
India	0.6	2.1	4.4	9.5	74.0	49.0	.814	4,645
Latin America	0.1	1.4	4.5	11.4	70.8	40.5	.809	22,997
US	–0.5	0.7	3.2	9.8	74.6	38.4	.846	347,845
World	–0.2	0.4	1.3	4.0	87.4	48.2	.911	56,016

Source: Shorrocks, Davies, and Lluberas (2014: Tables 2-4, 6-5, 6-6).

has increased somewhat in Sweden, the UK, and the US, but the increase has not been extreme.[9] This contrasts with the strong increase in *income* inequality seen over the last three decades in the US, the UK, and many other countries. Suggested explanations are that changes in wealth naturally lag behind those in income, and that the increase in the number of very high incomes reflects, for example, increases in executive salaries rather than rising incomes due to wealth. Atkinson (2008) has also noted that the wealth of the rich has been rising quickly (and has become more concentrated), but this has not raised relative wealth inequality much, because ordinary people have also seen a rise in their wealth due to rising house prices and other factors.

What Determines How Wealth Is Distributed?

Wealth is the result of past accumulation, and comes from two main sources: labour income ("earnings"), and gifts and inheritances. Both provide resources that can be either saved or consumed. Resources that are saved can accumulate at different rates. Wise or lucky investors earn high rates of return; others, lower rates. Finally, given the lifetime path of earnings, savings, etc. up until retirement, the older the consumer, the greater tends to be his or her wealth. Thus, current wealth depends on past earnings, inheritances (including gifts), savings rates out of earnings and inheritances, rates of return, and age.

It is sometimes suggested that wealth differences might be largely explained by age. To illustrate this possibility, examples of egalitarian societies that also display considerable wealth concentration are sometimes devised. For instance, consider a society with zero population growth and a zero rate of interest, in which everyone works for 40 years and then retires for 10 years. Assume that, while earning a constant amount during their working years, people save at a constant rate, and then "*dissave*" at a constant rate during retirement, ending life with zero wealth. The wealthiest people would be those who were at stages just before and just after the retirement age. In this world, the share of the top 10 per cent of wealth-holders would be about 19 per cent.

At first glance, the fact that a 19 per cent share for the top 10 per cent could be generated from age differences alone might seem impressive. However, this does not mean that a large part of wealth concentration is explained by age in the real world, for at least two reasons. First, if we look at the top 1 per cent in the example, we find that their wealth share is just 2 per cent. By altering the details of the example, one could get this share to 3 or 4 per cent, but this would still be far short of the estimated real-world shares. Second, the assumed variation of wealth with age is not realistic. In the real world there is a less extreme pattern. On average, people save for the first few years after retirement and only dissave slowly beyond that point (Burbidge and Robb 1985).

A number of years ago I set out a microsimulation model that could be used to *decompose* wealth inequality (Davies 1982). That is, it is possible to see how wealth inequality would be reduced if we eliminated differences in earnings, inheritances, savings rates, rates of return, and age. The most important factor was inheritance, followed by differences in savings rates. Differences in earnings, rates of return, and age were of lesser importance and similar to each other in impact (Davies 1982: Table I).[10]

Recently, the aggregate importance and highly unequal distribution of inheritances have been emphasized by Piketty (2014). Piketty performed a careful analysis of the annual flow of inheritances between the generations in France over the last 100 years. He found that the flow fell from around 24 per cent of national income in the pre-World War II period to 4 per cent in 1950, due to the large-scale destruction of capital during the Depression of the 1930s and during World War II. Thereafter, private wealth was rebuilt and there is now an annual flow of inheritances equal to about 15 per cent of national income. On the basis of theoretical modelling combined with empirical work, Piketty (2014) predicts that the flow may rebound to the 24 per cent level over the course of this century, in the absence of war or great economic disturbances (see also Davies 2015).

There is other evidence on the importance of inheritance. Wedgwood (1929) investigated the wealth held by rich British descendants in 1924–5. Of 99 persons dying with wealth of at least £200,000, which was a fortune at the time, about 60 per cent had a predecessor, usually a parent, who had died leaving at least £50,000, and about 70 per cent had predecessors who left at least £10,000 (Wedgwood 1929: 138–9). This work was updated by Harbury and Hitchens (1979), who found similar results for the 1950s, 1960s, and 1970s. Studies by *Fortune* magazine in the US on top American wealth-holders concluded that about half were "self-made" (Brittain 1978). However, surveys indicate that a larger fraction—as many as 60 per cent—of those in top wealth groups had received some inheritance (Brittain 1978: 18). In both the UK and the US, at least half of the genuinely wealthy appear to have benefited to some extent from inheritance.

The American SCF asks respondents whether they have received gifts and inheritances and, if so, their value and when they were received.[11] Wolff and Gittleman (2014) used these data to chart trends in inheritance from 1989 to 2007. They found that the fraction of families receiving a transfer fell from 24 per cent in 1989 to 18 per cent in 2001 and then increased to 21 per cent in 2007. The SCF also shows that inheritances are quite large, and rise steeply in importance with income or wealth. From 1989 to 2007, transfers averaged $84,700, or 23 per cent of net worth, and $408,400 for those who had just received transfers. Of those with incomes over $250,000, 38 per cent had received a transfer, with an average amount of $3 million for recipients. For families in the top 1 per cent of the wealth distribution, the corresponding numbers were 44 per cent with a transfer and an average amount of $5 million. Transfers were more common, and larger, for Whites, the more educated, and older people.

What makes inherited wealth so concentrated? Ironically, the answer partly lies in the importance of human wealth. Most families tend to find that investing in their children's education is more effective than providing gifts and bequests. However, some families are in a position to provide more. First, some pass along family businesses. Second, some exhaust the opportunities for investing in their children's education before their benevolence has been used up. Third, the lure of bequests may elicit attention from children (Sussman et al. 1970; Cox 1987). The genuinely wealthy would almost all be in one of these three categories, and we therefore expect to see them making a considerable use of bequests.

The extent of concentration in inheritance depends on practices of estate division, fertility, and choice of marital partner (Atkinson 1983: 183–9). At one extreme, in some societies there is *primogeniture*. Under this arrangement, the entire estate passes to the eldest son (or daughter in the absence of a son). This keeps large estates intact and preserves wealth inequality over time. At the opposite extreme, many families practise equal division of estates. Especially where families are large, which was true in North America in the nineteenth and early twentieth centuries, this contributes to the rapid breakdown of wealth concentration. It appears that in Europe and North America today equal division of estates is the norm, although departures from this norm are observed.

Differences in fertility according to wealth can also have a sizable effect. If the wealthy had smaller families than others, their wealth would be broken up relatively slowly by division among heirs, and wealth concentration would tend to be preserved. While this factor may have been important in some societies at some times, in Canada today fertility differences across income and wealth groups are not large, so that it likely has a relatively small effect.

Finally, the extent of assortative mating is important. If wealthy sons marry wealthy daughters, inherited wealth can remain confined to a small minority of families. While there is positive sorting of mates according to wealth and income, the correlation in mates' backgrounds is far from perfect. Thus, there is a tendency for inequality to be broken down through wealthy children marrying non-wealthy spouses, and also through division of estates.

Why Should We Care How Wealth Is Distributed?

One reason some people are concerned about the distribution of wealth is that they believe it has much to do with the distribution of power in society. This concern has several facets, since power can take political, social, or economic forms. As an economist, I am not especially qualified to comment on the first two forms of power, but it is important not to exclude them entirely from the discussion.

Some believe that the wealthy exert vastly greater political influence than others. This could be achieved through funding political campaigns, by bribing politicians and civil servants, by control of media, and through funding researchers who obtain congenial findings. Similarly disproportionate *social* power may accrue to the wealthy, e.g., through the impact of advertising and media content on values and attitudes.

While not all would agree about the extent of political and social power conferred by wealth in Canada today, there is little doubt that the wealthy can exert considerable influence by the channels mentioned. But what of the economic power created by the concentration of wealth? At first blush it might appear that the concentration of corporate wealth observed in our society must imply great concentration of economic power. However, to the extent that we maintain internationally open and competitive markets, even the power of large corporations is limited by the rigours of the marketplace.

In competitive markets, business initiatives are governed by the logic of profit and loss. In order to survive, firms have to strive to make as much profit as possible. If they do not take advantage of opportunities, someone else will. Factors like technology, consumer preferences, supplies of productive inputs, the regulatory environment, and taxes and subsidies really determine what happens. The preferences of individuals who control even large corporations may ultimately be unimportant.

One should not be complacent about the limitations that competitive and open markets place on individuals' economic power. The wealthy do not like such limitations and, like trade unions, professional associations, and other groups, they may use their political power to try to achieve protection from competition. It is important for the electorate to be critical of weak competition policy, subsidies to private firms, special tax breaks, and other preferential treatment for private firms and wealthy individuals. Ultimately, such vigilance may be more effective in preventing unhealthy concentration of power in society, and indeed in preventing undue concentration of wealth itself, than a strategy that attacks wealth concentration directly.

I will now discuss the second reason why wealth inequality may matter, which concerns its implications for differences in economic well-being.

What determines the distribution of economic well-being at a moment in time? Often we attempt to summarize this distribution by looking at households' incomes over the calendar year. This is informative, but has limitations. If two families have equal incomes, but one has $1 million in non-human capital and the other just $100,000, their well-being is likely to be quite different. This realization has prompted many observers to argue that we should look at wealth as well as income.

Wealth differs from income in that it is a store of purchasing power for the future. While most income is consumed in the year it is received, consumption of wealth usually takes place gradually over the lifetime of consumers or, possibly, their heirs. Thus, when we turn to wealth, we must change our focus to the long run.

The long-run differences in well-being of a cohort of Canadians of similar age are determined largely by the sum of their human and non-human resources—that is, by "total wealth." We might try to estimate the distribution of this total wealth. Knowing net worth would be an important component of this exercise, but so also would be knowledge of the distribution of human wealth.

Since human wealth, on average, is considerably larger than non-human, is there any point in studying the distribution of non-human wealth by itself? The answer is that, while this is a limited exercise, it is important. Although there is not a perfect correlation, people with high labour income also tend to have high wealth, so that, overall, wealth differences tend to reinforce earnings inequality. Also, the extremes reached by wealth are not matched by the distribution of human wealth. Thus, at the highest reaches, one can almost say that the distribution of non-human wealth *is* the distribution of total wealth.

Finally, we may ask a deeper question about whether the observed differences in wealth are really important. To what extent are these differences inequitable? In other words, do they represent true *inequality*? There is a wide range of possible answers. Perspectives range from libertarian views on the right, to socialist views on the left.

Libertarians believe that, provided that wealth has been accumulated honestly, differences in wealth-holding are fair. Nobody has a right superior to that of the individual to enjoy the fruits of his or her past accumulation. Since there is no injustice, there is no "inequality."

Socialists have a very different viewpoint. The component of wealth that can be traced to inheritance, first of all, is considered undeserved. Second, some of the differences in past earnings and rates of return, which led to current differences in wealth, are regarded as unfair. In other words, aside from differences purely due to age, savings rates, or "reasonable" differences in rates of return and labour earnings, all wealth differences are regarded as unjustifiable by a true socialist.

Between the libertarian and socialist positions there is a large gap. What would a "typical" Canadian think about wealth differences? It would be interesting to answer this question using survey evidence. In the absence of such evidence, one can only conjecture. My guess is that most people believe that differences in inheritance are less justified than those in labour earnings. However, I would also guess that most people do not believe that differences in inheritance have *no* justification. Many feel that parents have the right to pass the fruits of their labour on to their children. Public concerns about tax loopholes are also widespread, so it is likely that the typical Canadian is also not entirely happy with differences in self-accumulated wealth. Thus, the average Canadian probably thinks that there is some true inequality involved in wealth differences.

How Does Wealth Mobility Affect Our Perceptions of Inequality?

Wealth mobility exists if people change their relative position in the wealth distribution over time. Mobility can take place both within a person's lifetime and from generation to generation. Within a lifetime, it is important to look at a person's wealth relative to others of about the same age. If this changes over time, and the change is not offset by changes in human wealth, then there is meaningful wealth mobility.

In fact, there is significant wealth mobility both within lifetimes and across generations. While most rich people have benefited from inheritance, there are numerous well-known, true-life "rags to riches" stories. Conversely, many wealthy heirs have squandered their fortunes. Moreover, over successive generations, there is even more mobility. Some claim that "shirtsleeves to shirtsleeves in three generations" is typical. This claim is exaggerated, as shown in recent work by Clark (2014) and others. However, research by Wedgwood (1929), Harbury and Hitchens (1979), Jianakoplos and Menchik (1997), Steckel and Krishnan (2006), and others does indicate significant intergenerational wealth mobility.

It is sometimes asserted that, given any level of wealth concentration, there will be less concern about inequality when there is substantial wealth mobility. This is not obvious, however, and may depend very much on what kind of mobility we are talking about. For example, although there is wide respect for those who build up their wealth by working hard, saving, and investing wisely, there can be great resentment of those who get rich through exploitative, questionable, or illegal activity. And, while the public probably has little sympathy for the downward mobility of spendthrift heirs, people may feel concern for those who are forced out of business by unexpected technological change, recession, or international trade shocks.

It seems likely that people regard wealth mobility as desirable only when it occurs for good reasons. This comes back to the earlier discussion. Upward mobility that occurs through moderate inheritance, working hard, saving carefully, and perhaps also bearing risk and having good luck in investments may be considered healthy and acceptable, just as the wealth differences created by these factors may not be resented. However, people may disapprove of mobility that stems from what are regarded as excessive inheritances or earnings differences, unequal tax treatment, and so on, just as they disapprove of wealth differences that are caused by these factors.

In summary, a reasonable degree of wealth mobility may be *necessary*, if the mechanisms that determine wealth differences in a society are to be regarded as fair. However, mobility by itself is not *sufficient*. The considerable wealth mobility in Canada and other Western countries shows that these societies are not caste-ridden, but it does not mean that the people of these nations should be unconcerned about wealth inequality.

Conclusion

In this chapter, I have tried to make clear the concept of wealth, have summarized the available evidence on how it is distributed in Canada and also globally, have discussed the determinants of wealth differences, and have asked whether these matter. The analysis has emphasized that, ideally, a comprehensive concept of wealth needs to be used—one that includes all financial and non-financial assets, ranging from consumer durables to pension wealth. We have seen that wealth differences are much greater than differences in income. Concentration in wealth-holding is the result of differences in inheritances, savings rates, labour earnings, rates of return, taxes, and age. Inheritance and the high rates of return earned by some entrepreneurs and investors together explain the extreme length of the upper tail of the wealth distribution. The great stock market booms of the 1990s and the early twenty-first century drew particular attention to the role of investment returns, which created a new crop of billionaires in Canada and lengthened the upper tail. Therefore, there may be a tendency at present to think of investment as the main source of riches in our society. However, stock market booms come and go. In 2002 there was a "meltdown" in high-tech and Internet share values, and the North American stock market overall lost all the gains it had created since 1997. Then, in 2008–9, a great crash was associated with the global financial crisis. Such downturns make it easier to appreciate the role of more stable factors, most notably inheritance, in creating the long upper tail of wealth-holding.

The chapter concluded by discussing why wealth differences matter. There are at least three key answers. The first is that great wealth may spell disproportionate power. Public vigilance and participation in politics can reduce this power difference, but public action is unlikely to eliminate it. A second reason is that differences in wealth have an important influence on the distribution of economic well-being. Finally, while some wealth differences reflect factors widely regarded as justifiable, including age, reasonable differences in labour income, and voluntary differences in savings rates, other wealth differences, such as those due to inheritance or extremes of executive compensation, do not win such wide approval.

Questions for Critical Thought

1. Should we be concerned about the distribution of wealth or is this a distraction from the main issue, which is income inequality?
2. If we think there is too much wealth inequality in Canada, what government policies might help to correct that?
3. Why is non-human capital different from human capital? In what ways is it more important? In what ways is it less important?
4. If there is more intergenerational wealth mobility, does that mean that high current wealth inequality is a less serious concern?

Recommended Readings

Davies, James B. 2015. "Book review of *Capital in the Twenty-First Century* by Thomas Piketty, Harvard University Press." *Journal of Economic Inequality* 13: 115–60.

——, Susanna Sandström, Anthony Shorrocks, and Edward N. Wolff. 2011. "The level and distribution of global household wealth." *Economic Journal* 121: 223–54.

Kopczuk, Wojciech. 2015. "What do we know about the evolution of top wealth shares in the United States?" *Journal of Economic Perspectives* 29: 47–66.

Roine, Jesper, and Daniel Waldenström. 2014. "Long-run trends in the distribution of income and wealth." In A.B. Atkinson and F. Bourguignon, *Handbook of Income Distribution*, vol. 2, pp. 469–592. Amsterdam: Elsevier.

Recommended Websites

International Association for Research in Income and Wealth:
http://www.iariw.org/

Thomas Piketty website for *Capital in the Twenty-First Century*:
piketty.pse.ens.fr/capital21C

United Nations University/World Institute for Development Economics Research:
http://www.wider.unu.edu/

The World Top Incomes Database:
http://topincomes.g-mond.parisschoolofeconomics.eu/

Notes

1. Feldstein (1976) estimated aggregate social security wealth in the US in 1962 at $382 billion. This was 54 per cent of conventional net worth ($711 billion) in his study. Wolff (1987) obtains a range of figures for 1969, when conventional net worth had risen to $2,904 billion. The estimates for social security wealth vary from $1,194 billion (41 per cent of net worth) to $5,649 billion (195 per cent of net worth), depending on assumptions about future growth in earnings and social security contributions and benefits (see Wolff 1987: 219, Table 9.1).
2. Prior to the SFS, wealth data were provided by Statistics Canada's Survey of Consumer Finance in 1970, 1977, and 1984.
3. A variable is skewed if its frequency histogram has one "tail" longer than the other. Distributions of income and wealth are positively skewed, meaning that they have long upper tails.

4. Earlier lists include Newman's (1975) 160 Canadian families with wealth over $20 million and Francis's (1986) 32 families with wealth over $100 million.
5. The concept of a "family" here is quite different from that in Statistics Canada's work. For Statistics Canada, a family is a group of two or more persons living in the same dwelling and related to each other by blood, formal or common-law marriage, or adoption. For *Canadian Business*, the "family" is the extended family, which is not limited by the requirement of a common dwelling unit.
6. These extrapolations were done using a Pareto distribution fitted to the data. It is widely found that this theoretical distribution fits the upper tail of reliable income and wealth data well. See, e.g., Davies and Shorrocks (2000).
7. Not shown in Table 5.3 are four smaller countries whose estimated wealth per adult exceeds that of the US. These are Switzerland ($580,686), Australia ($430,777), Iceland ($362,982), and Norway ($358,655).
8. Shorrocks, Davies, and Lluberas (2014) treat China and India as separate regions, and so Asia-Pacific excludes them.
9. There have been lively discussions in the US concerning the recent trend in wealth inequality. The main source of data is the Federal Reserve Board's Survey of Consumer Finance, most recently conducted in 2013. The data show a gradual increase in the share of the top 1 per cent, from 32.3 per cent in 2001 to 35.5 per cent in 2013. A faster increase has been estimated by Saez and Zucman (2014) using the investment income multiplier approach, but this methodology generally has not been considered very reliable in the past (Davies and Shorrocks 2000). For a good discussion of the evidence. see Kopczuk (2015).
10. Interestingly, the conclusions of Davies (1982) are consistent with the assessment of the famous University of Chicago economist Frank Knight. As Knight wrote in 1923, "the ownership of personal or material productive capacity is based upon a complex mixture of inheritance, luck, and effort, probably in that order of relative importance" (Brittain 1978: 1).
11. Other surveys ask similar questions in the US, and also in France, Sweden, and the UK (Klevmarken et al. 2003; Wolff and Gittleman 2014). However, the high frequency of the SCF and its long time span are unusual.

References

Atkinson, Anthony B. 1983. *The Economics of Inequality*, 2nd edn. Oxford: Clarendon Press.

———. 2008. "Concentration among the rich." In James B. Davies, ed., *Personal Wealth from a Global Perspective*, pp. 64–92. Oxford: Oxford University Press.

Brittain, John A. 1978. *Inheritance and the Inequality of Material Wealth*. Washington: Brookings Institution.

Burbidge, J.B., and A.L. Robb. 1985. "Evidence on wealth-age profiles in Canadian cross-section data." *Canadian Journal of Economics* 18 (Nov.): 854–75.

Clark, Gregory. 2014. *The Son Also Rises: Surnames and the History of Social Mobility*. Princeton, NJ: Princeton University Press.

Cox, Donald. 1987. "Motives for private income transfers." *Journal of Political Economy* 95: 508–46.

Davies, James B. 1979. "On the size distribution of wealth in Canada." *Review of Income and Wealth* 25 (Sept.): 237–59.

———. 1982. "The relative impact of inheritance and other factors on economic inequality." *Quarterly Journal of Economics* 47: 471–98.

———. 2015. "Book review of *Capital in the Twenty-First Century* by Thomas Piketty, Harvard

University Press." *Journal of Economic Inequality* 13: 155–60.

——, Susanna Sandström, Anthony Shorrocks, and Edward N. Wolff. 2008. "The world distribution of household wealth." In J.B. Davies, ed., *Personal Wealth from a Global Perspective*, pp. 395–418. Oxford: Oxford University Press.

——, ——, ——, and ——. 2011. "The level and distribution of global household wealth." *Economic Journal* 121: 223–54.

—— and A.F. Shorrocks. 2000. "The distribution of wealth." In A.B. Atkinson and F. Bourguignon, eds, *Handbook of Income Distribution*, pp. 605–75. Amsterdam: North-Holland/Elsevier.

—— and John Whalley. 1991. "Taxes and capital formation: How important is human capital?" In D. Bernheim and J. Shoven, eds, *National Saving and Economic Performance*, pp. 163–200. Chicago: University of Chicago Press.

Feldstein, M. 1976. "Social security and the distribution of wealth." *Journal of the American Statistical Association* 71: 800–7.

Francis, Diane. 1986. *Controlling Interest: Who Owns Canada?* Toronto: Macmillan.

Harbury, C.D., and D.M.W.N. Hitchens. 1979. *Inheritance and Wealth Inequality in Britain*. London: George Allen and Unwin.

Jianakoplos, N.A., and P. Menchik. 1997. "Wealth mobility." *Review of Economics and Statistics* 79, 1: 18–31.

Klevmarken, N.A., J.P. Lupton, and F. Stafford. 2003. "Wealth dynamics in the 1980s and 1990s: Sweden and the United States." *Journal of Human Resources* 38, 2: 322–53.

Kopczuk, Wojciech. 2015. "What do we know about the evolution of top wealth shares in the United States?" *Journal of Economic Perspectives* 29: 47–66.

Morissette, René, and Xuelin Zhang. 2007. "Revisiting wealth inequality." *Perspectives on Labour and Income* 19, 1: 5–16. http://www.statcan.ca/english/freepub/75-001-XIE/11206/art-1.pdf.

Newman, Peter C. 1975. *The Canadian Establishment*, vol. 1. Toronto: McClelland & Stewart.

Piketty, Thomas. 2014. *Capital in the Twenty-First Century*. Cambridge, Mass.: Harvard University Press.

Roine, Jesper, and Daniel Waldenström. 2014. "Long-run trends in the distribution of income and wealth." In A.B. Atkinson and F. Bourguignon, eds, *Handbook of Income Distribution*, vol. 2, pp. 469–592. Amsterdam: Elsevier.

Saez, Emmanuel, and Gabriel Zucman. 2014. "Wealth inequality in the United States since 1913: Evidence from capitalized income tax data." NBER Working Paper 20625, Oct.

Shorrocks, Anthony, James B. Davies, and Rodrigo Lluberas. 2010, 2011, 2012, 2013, 2014. *Global Wealth Databook*. Zurich: Credit Suisse Research Institute.

Statistics Canada. 2007. "The wealth of Canadians: An overview of the results of the Survey of Financial Security 2005." Pension and Wealth Research Paper Series. Statistics Canada Catalogue no. 13F0026MIE.

Steckel, R.H., and J. Krishnan. 2006. "The wealth and mobility of men and women during the 1960s and 1970s." *Review of Income and Wealth* 52, 2: 189–212.

Sussman, Marvin B., Judith N. Cates, and David T. Smith. 1970. *The Family and Inheritance*. New York: Russell Sage Foundation.

Wedgwood, Josiah. 1929. *The Economics of Inheritance*. London: George Routledge & Sons.

Wolff, Edward N. 1987. "The effect of pensions and social security on the distribution of wealth in the U.S." In Edward N. Wolff, ed., *International Comparisons of the Distribution of Household Wealth*. Oxford: Clarendon Press.

—— and Maury Gittleman. 2014. "Inheritances and the distribution of wealth, or whatever happened to the great inheritance boom?" *Journal of Economic Inequality* 12, 4: 439–68.

6 Labour Markets, Inequality, and the Future of Work

Wolfgang Lehmann and Tracey L. Adams

According to many commentators, the world of work is changing rapidly. Technological developments and globalization appear to be altering the nature and availability of work. Some argue that these changes create global winners and losers. The losers see their jobs eliminated by new technologies and/or by employees in the developing world who will work for less money (Rifkin 1995; Castells 2000). The winners, who can create and work with technology and innovate in flexible global markets, find employment, but they also face considerable uncertainty and must adapt continuously or risk losing their jobs (Castells 2000; Sennett 1998). For these commentators and others, the labour market has been polarizing over the last several decades into "good jobs" and "bad jobs." Even the good jobs are not as good as they once were, with skilled workers facing greater uncertainty and risk than in the past (Castells 2000; Sennett 1998).

As we show in this chapter, the Canadian labour market is more complex than this picture suggests, but the above arguments raise many real concerns about the future of work and the impact of social change on workers. Post-secondary education no longer guarantees access to a good job; youth unemployment is usually twice the national average; and, for at least part of this century, temporary jobs have grown at a faster rate than permanent jobs. Nevertheless, Canadian workers are more educated than ever before, and there is evidence that skilled, professional occupations "constitute a growing proportion of the employed labour force" (Livingstone 2014: 14). Moreover, some regions, like Alberta, have experienced labour shortages. What are we to make of these contradictory trends? Is there an expansion or a decline of good, stable jobs? Are jobs available or in short supply? Who gets the "good jobs" and what must Canadians do to obtain them?

In this chapter, we answer these questions by exploring Canadian labour market trends and considering their implications for social inequality.

Explaining Labour Markets

A labour market can be defined as the processes and institutions through which workers are allocated to paid jobs. Jobs provide income and other rewards, including pensions, paid vacations, opportunities for career advancement, and personal development and fulfillment. Consequently, jobs have a direct bearing on our standard of living and quality of life. People's jobs determine their "life chances." Sociologists often use occupation to gauge a person's location in the class structure. Labour market outcomes also reflect and reproduce gender and racial inequalities. Thus, labour markets are central to understanding broader issues of how inequality is structured in society.

To understand labour markets, it is helpful to review theoretical work on the subject. Below we consider some of the most influential perspectives: human capital theory; Bourdieu's work on social and cultural capital; and a set of related perspectives that include labour market segmentation theory, split labour market theory, dual systems theory, and queuing theory.

Human Capital Theory

Human capital theory draws on neo-classical economics (Becker 1975). This perspective assumes that the labour market is one large, open arena in which everyone with similar qualifications competes on the same basis for available jobs. The market rewards those individuals who have the greatest human capital, as measured by education, training, experience, and ability. A job's rewards are based on its economic contribution to society. By focusing on the supply of labour, in terms of workers' characteristics, this theory does not address the influence of employers' hiring practices or the organization of work on inequality. The theory simply assumes that employers make rational hiring and promotion decisions based on ability.

Human capital theory presents a consensus view of society; issues of class and power are ignored. The theory does accurately predict that those with higher levels of education typically have higher incomes, a lower risk of unemployment, and a generally higher probability of being in a good job, in comparison with individuals who have lower levels of education. Nevertheless, human capital theory cannot explain why men with university education typically make more money than women with the same level of education (Williams 2010), or why the returns to education are lower for the foreign-born than the Canadian-born (Statistics Canada 2015c). Moreover, the theory cannot explain why it is easier for some groups to attain high levels of education (Lehmann 2007). For example, young people from poor families often don't even get the opportunity to apply to a university and are at greater risk of dropping out of high school.

Social and Cultural Capital

Rather than an open arena in which individuals "exchange" their human capital (e.g., university credentials) for employment, some sociologists see the labour market as an area of social life infused with power and inequality. Pierre Bourdieu's (1977, 1990) theories about the value of social and cultural capital are especially useful in understanding the labour market as a field of unequal power relations.

Cultural capital describes individuals' access to cultural resources (e.g., books) but also the ease with which they understand and use forms of dominant culture (e.g., being articulate, doing well at school, and being at ease in social situations). Power and inequality come into focus here. For instance, children born into middle- and upper-class families have ready access to cultural resources (books, international travel), tend to do better at school (because schools value the knowledge gained from these cultural resources), and therefore often attend more prestigious educational institutions. Through these privileges, they also learn how to present themselves successfully to employers.

Social capital is the sum of individuals' social networks and connections, and the value these networks have in given social fields, such as the labour market. Once again, we can see how those from privileged backgrounds can more easily connect with people occupying influential positions in society. These individuals can help connect them with other influential people, who can provide information about good jobs and about individuals who can open up career opportunities for them. The wealthy and well-connected can trade on this social and cultural capital to find labour market success, whereas those who were raised without such capital, or who did not obtain it through their schooling, have fewer opportunities to attain good jobs.

While cultural capital explains educational success and social capital seems more important for access to good jobs, both types of capital intersect in the labour market. Consider the issue of credential inflation, which we will also discuss later in this chapter. The number of young people entering the labour market with university credentials has grown substantially in past decades, so that the value of the degree (i.e., the human capital it represents) has declined. Instead, existing contacts (social capital) are becoming increasingly important for securing good jobs. People from privileged families and those who attended prestigious high schools and universities are more likely to have contacts that lead to better employment. Furthermore, employers increasingly look at non-credential experiences in their applicants, such as studying abroad or doing career-related volunteer work. Again, people from more privileged backgrounds are more likely to have these items on their resumés (Brown, Lauder, and Ashton 2011; Lehmann 2011).

Labour Market Segmentation, Race, and Gender

A number of other theoretical approaches also view the labour market as an uneven playing field. Here we review four of them: labour market segmentation theory, split labour market theory, dual systems theory, and queuing theory.

Labour market segmentation theory depicts the labour market as comprising unequal segments, such that movement to a better or "primary" segment from a worse or "secondary" segment is often difficult. Jobs in the primary labour market offer security, good wages, and opportunities for promotion. In contrast, jobs in the secondary labour market offer little job security, low wages, and few opportunities for upward mobility (Adams and Welsh 2007: 170). Although these markets often characterize different types of work and industries, some firms may have both in their workforce at the same time, e.g., employees with good, permanent, and full-time jobs working alongside others on part-time or limited-term contracts. While sometimes individuals start as part-time employees and eventually attain full-time employment, workers often remain locked into a cycle of low-paying and temporary contracts (Fuller and Stecy-Hildebrandt 2014).

Segmentation theory suggests not simply one labour market but at least two; however, this perspective says little about how individuals are sorted into the different markets. Split labour market theory argues that employers play a significant role in these labour market divisions and sort people on the basis of race and ethnicity. Bonacich (1972) notes that people from different ethnic backgrounds are often paid differently for doing similar work. People from ethnic majorities have more favourable economic and political resources and access to information that enables them to obtain high-paying work. Once they obtain these jobs, they encourage employers to exclude or marginalize minority workers. For Bonacich, ethnic inequality is maintained and reproduced through this split labour market. Feminist scholars have argued that similar processes occur to reproduce gender inequality in labour markets. For example, Heidi Hartmann (1976) and other writers associated with dual systems theory contend that women are disproportionately locked into poorer jobs by the decisions of employers and the efforts of male workers to exclude or marginalize them.

Reskin and Roos's (1990) use of queuing theory lays out these same processes more clearly, and also accounts for social change in a more effective manner. Reskin and Roos claim that understanding the labour market and the distribution of people into jobs requires that we consider employers' decisions, i.e., their labour queues, and also workers' choices, i.e., their job queues. Employers are said to have opinions about which workers have the required attributes and skills, and about who will be more productive. Employers create mental lists of the "best" workers for their jobs, and the lists are ordered not only by education and training, but also by gender and race, as well as other criteria (age, disability, and so on). Historically, White men tended to be preferred employees at the top of the queue, especially for skilled and high-paying jobs. Whenever employers cannot hire White males, they move down the queue, choosing from other groups. For many white-collar and service occupations, the next group in the queue has been middle-class White women. For physical and manual labour, the next group in the queue typically has been minority men.

Reskin and Roos maintain that workers also have mental lists, or job queues. They rank the attractiveness of occupations, with the best-paying and most secure jobs typically at the top. Therefore, their conclusion is that labour market segmentation and occupational segregation are the combined result of employer and worker job queues. Traditionally, White men predominated in the best jobs, because they were employers' top choice and because these jobs were the workers' preference. However, by the late twentieth century, employers' labour queues had changed. With an increasingly diverse and educated labour force and the rise of anti-discriminatory legislation and societal values, employers established queues that were less affected by gender and race. The result has been less occupational segregation. However, studies suggest that factors like disability status and citizenship status are still important. Moreover, some race and gender segmentation persists, as we discuss later in this chapter.

Unions in Segmented Labour Markets

A consideration of social inequality in the labour market is incomplete without some discussion of unions. The existence of unions is characteristic of employment in the primary labour market. Unions promote the interests of their members through collective bargaining. Unionized workers typically earn higher wages and have better workplace benefits than their non-unionized counterparts. Unions protect their members from arbitrary and unfair workplace practices, and also provide workers with more job security (Adams and Welsh 2007: 76–7). Although unions were traditionally common in manufacturing jobs, today most unionized workers are in the public sector and some service sectors. Union membership has recently decreased, with only about 30 per cent of Canadians now unionized; the reduction has been especially steep for men in the declining manufacturing sector (Statistics Canada 2013a).

Labour Market Trends

At the beginning of this chapter, we noted that Canada's labour market has changed significantly over the last several decades. These changes have substantial implications for social inequality. In this section, we review several key topics: industrial shifts; occupational changes; job security and the expansion of non-standard work; working hours; and trends in employment, unemployment, and underemployment. We also explore the implications of these changes for social inequality, especially with respect to race, gender, and immigration status.

Industrial Shifts: Working in a Service Economy

Industry classifications focus on the types of economic activity within the workplace. Statistics Canada distinguishes between "goods-producing industries," which include natural resources, manufacturing, construction, and agriculture, and "service industries," which include retail and wholesale trade, health care, public administration, education, business services, information, and recreation (Statistics Canada 2015a). Over the last century or more, the percentage of Canadians working in the goods-producing sector has decreased, while the services sector has expanded significantly. Service industries account for much of the job growth in the labour market (Statistics Canada 2015a). Only one goods-producing industry—construction—has experienced significant job growth over the last decade (Statistics Canada 2015a). Currently 78 per cent of all Canadian workers are employed in service industries (Statistics Canada 2015a). The service sector includes a wide range of industries, and so it is useful to distinguish between upper-tier service occupations with the highest pay and educational qualifications, and lower-tier service jobs that generally involve lower incomes and educational requirements (Krahn, Lowe, and Hughes 2011). Looking at the sectors with the largest net job growth, we realize that they reflect both ends of the job spectrum: (1) high-skill jobs in education and in health care; and (2) less-skilled jobs in accommodation and food services (Statistics Canada 2015a). The latter jobs are often temporary, part-time, low-paid jobs, which are often referred to as "McJobs." These patterns support the notion of an increasingly polarized Canadian labour market.

Occupational Changes

We can also examine employment by looking at occupations, or the kind of work that individuals perform in their jobs. Most workers in goods-producing industries are classified as blue-collar (or manual) workers, while the growth of service industries is typically related to the expansion of white-collar occupations. Historically, white-collar occupations were usually viewed as having higher status. However, as service industries have grown and diversified, a majority of Canada's workers now hold white-collar occupations, and some of these jobs are not especially desirable. This is especially true of many clerical, sales, and personal service jobs, which are often called "pink-collar" occupations because they are mainly filled by women.

Some scholars see the growth of the services sector as a potential contributor to social inequality, because this sector comprises both "good" and "bad" jobs. Many jobs in upper-tier service industries require post-secondary education and are stable and well-paying. Jobs in the lower tier, however, often do not require education and are disproportionately low-paid, part-time, short-term, and dead-end. Scholars also argue that front-line service workers in the lower tier—those who work closely with customers—face additional layers of control, as employers direct not only their conduct on the job, but their appearance and demeanour as well (Macdonald and Sirianni 1996; Williams and Connell 2010). In addition, these workers are subject to control and discipline by customers, which often makes such jobs both challenging and unappealing (Macdonald and Sirianni 1996).

Job Security and Non-Standard Work

Despite public concerns about declining job security, most working Canadians still have full-time, year-round, permanent employment. Public worry about this issue has been fuelled by job losses and downsizing in certain industries, and by the significant expansion of temporary and contract jobs between 1997 and 2005. Non-standard work takes four main forms: part-time employment, multiple job-holding, own-account self-employment, and temporary work. In "standard" jobs individuals are assumed to work full-time, year-round, and for one employer (Adams and Welsh 2007; Kalleberg et al. 2000). At least one of these assumptions does not hold for each type of non-standard work, in which individuals may work fewer or more hours (part-time employment, multiple job-holding), on shorter-term contracts (temporary, self-employment), or for more than one employer (work through a temp agency, multiple job-holding). These four types of non-standard work account for roughly one-third of all employed Canadians (Krahn, Lowe, and Hughes 2011: 94–7); temporary, contract, and seasonal work alone accounted for 23 per cent of the employed in 2009. In recent years, contract positions have grown faster than temporary positions (Galarneau 2010).

Non-standard work varies. For some, it is low-paid and inherently precarious; for others, such as highly skilled IT workers and engineers, it means moving from contract to contract, which can yield valuable experience and a good income. Generally, though, contract workers make 14 per cent less than permanent workers, while temporary and seasonal workers make about 33 to 36 per cent less (Galarneau 2010). Non-standard work is appealing to employers, because they typically can offer lower income and benefits for non-standard work, and because they have the flexibility to increase or decrease quickly the size and skills of their workforce, depending on their needs (Kalleberg 2003; Shalla 2003). It is perhaps not surprising that women, people of colour, immigrants, and younger and older workers are over-represented in non-standard jobs (Fuller and Vosko 2008). Self-employment is the only form of non-standard work where men predominate. Nonetheless, it is worth noting that some workers embrace the flexibility and variety of non-standard jobs. Working part-time or on contract can free up time for other pursuits, including family responsibilities, education, or other meaningful activities (Adams and Welsh 2007). Others, however, do non-standard jobs involuntarily, because they cannot obtain standard occupations.

Non-standard work has obvious implications for social inequality, because the earnings of non-standard workers are usually substantially lower than those of individuals in standard jobs (Galarneau 2010; Fuller and Stecy-Heldebrandt 2014). In addition, finding oneself in non-standard work may also affect one's ability to move into standard employment. Of all non-standard workers in 1999, more than half (54 per cent) were still employed in non-standard work two years later, and an additional 10 per cent had returned to non-standard work, from either standard work or not working in the two intervening years (Kapsalis and Tourigny 2004: 8).

The low wages and precarious nature of non-standard work can mean that jobs, especially in sectors like agriculture, are difficult to fill. Generally, workers with few other options, such as recent immigrants or those without valued job skills, predominate in such jobs. When labour shortages persist, employers have joined forces with the Canadian government to bring in temporary foreign workers, who are imported to Canada on short-term contracts to work specifically in these positions. The Seasonal Agricultural Workers Program (SAWP) enables the importation of approximately 25,000 workers annually from Mexico and the Caribbean to work in Canadian agriculture (Preibisch and Grez 2010). Lacking good employment opportunities in their countries of origin, these workers, most of them men, come to Canada to earn money for their families (Basok 2002; Preibisch and Grez 2010). They work extremely long hours for low wages, under poor working and living conditions. Health problems are common (Basok 2002). When language barriers exist, workers are often more vulnerable and subject to abuses. If a position does not work out, workers lack the ability to leave one employer for another; instead, they must endure the situation or risk being sent home and not brought back in another year (Basok 2002). Workers in the SAWP are also unable to migrate permanently to Canada. Other temporary foreign workers are employed in a variety of other industries, e.g., women working as nannies, housekeepers, and home health-care aides. These workers share low wages and vulnerability with agricultural workers, but they do have the opportunity to settle in Canada eventually.

Although the sociological literature has focused on temporary foreign workers in extremely vulnerable jobs, there are temporary foreign workers in almost every sector of the economy. Some of these workers (unpaid interns) are also in vulnerable positions, but others have access to good jobs.

Hours of Work

Canada established a standard 40-hour work week in the late 1950s. Despite expectations of more leisure time due to the productivity gains from computers and other new technologies, the average length of the work week has continued to hover around 40 hours up to the present day (Usalcas 2008). In the late 1990s and early 2000s there was evidence of a growing polarization of working hours, as part-time jobs increased at the same time as did jobs with long hours. More recently, however, this trend has reversed. Average hours worked in part-time jobs has continued to increase, but fewer full-time workers are working 50 or more hours a week. The end result is a slight decline in weekly hours worked, from 38.6 in 1972 to 36.5 in 2006, including both full-time and part-time workers (Usalcas 2008: 5).

Changes in both women's and men's working hours are driving the trends. The number of women (including mothers) working full-time has increased over time, but women are less likely than men to work more than 40 hours weekly. Women have long spent fewer hours than men in paid work, because women spend more time doing unpaid domestic labour. However, more women than ever now work full-time. While women's working hours have increased over time, men's have decreased slightly; in particular, fewer men are working over 40 hours per week (Usalcas 2008; see also Chapters 15 and 16 in this volume). These trends might reflect the growing commitment of men and women to achieve work–family balance. One study of dual-earner families found that women and men worked a combined average of 77 hours per week, a number that had not changed substantially since the 1970s; this report identified a convergence, whereby married women were working more hours, while married men were working fewer (Marshall 2009). Most Canadian workers (72 per cent) work 30 to 48 hours per week on average (Usalcas 2008).

Unemployment and Underemployment

To assess labour market trends, experts rely on several different but related measures. The employment rate is simply a ratio of people 15 years of age and older who are working, to the overall population in this age group. Over time, the employment rate has increased slightly, from 57 per cent in 1976 to 61.8 per cent in 2012 (Statistics Canada 2015d). As Figure 6.1 shows, there is a gender difference in employment rate trends. Although men have always had a higher employment rate than women, the men's rate has

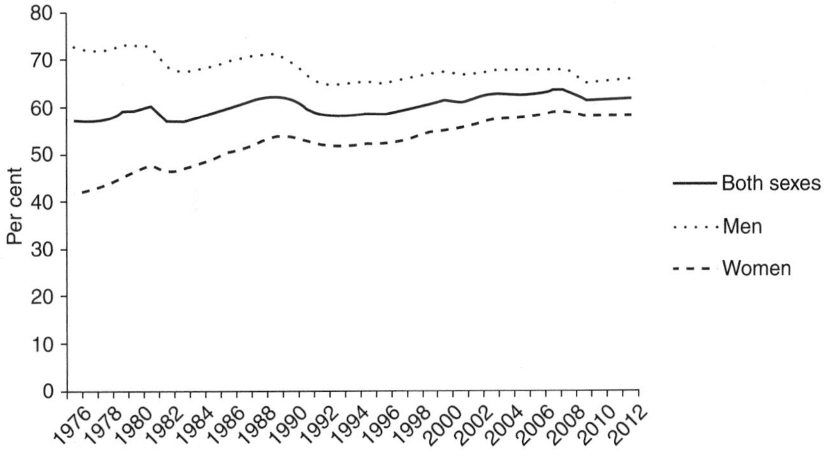

Figure 6.1 Employment Rate by Gender, 1976–2012

Source: Statistics Canada (2015d).

declined slightly in the past three decades while women's has increased substantially. The overall increase in employment rate mentioned above can therefore be attributed to the growth in women's employment. This change is due to several factors, including the shift in employment from the industrial to the service sector, and the increase in women's educational attainment.

The unemployment rate is a calculation of the number of people not working who are looking for work as a percentage of the total labour force. In contrast to the employment rate, the unemployment rate fluctuates with the economic cycle and other broader economic trends (Figure 6.2).

In 2014–15, the Canadian unemployment rate hovered around 6.8 per cent (Statistics Canada 2015a). The unemployment rate is lowest for men and women aged 25 to 54 (5.6 per cent for men, 5.3 per cent for women). The unemployment rate is significantly higher for youth aged 15–24, at 13.5 per cent. Unemployment remains fairly low at 5.1 per cent for those older than 55, reflecting a significant drop in labour force participation (Statistics Canada 2015a). Furthermore, unemployment rates are strongly related to educational attainment. As shown in Figure 6.3, young Canadians' chances of being unemployed decline as their educational attainment increases. For those Canadians aged 25–29 who have not completed high school, the unemployment rate in 2012 was 16.4 per cent, compared to only 5.8 per cent for those in this age group with a university degree.

Unemployment and employment rates vary across region: in 2014, unemployment rates were highest (11.8 per cent) in Newfoundland and Labrador, and lowest in Saskatchewan (3.7 per cent) and Alberta (4.7 per cent) (Statistics Canada 2015a). Rates also vary by industrial sector. Goods-producing industries have a higher unemployment rate (8.6 per cent) than services (4.0 per cent); some sectors like fishing and forestry have high unemployment, while fields like finance, education, and health care have quite low unemployment rates (Statistics Canada 2015b).

Employment and unemployment rates also vary by ethnicity and country of origin. Aboriginal workers, visible minority workers, and immigrants have lower employment rates and higher unemployment rates than others. Aboriginal workers' employment rate was only 53.7 per cent in 2010 (Usalcas 2010). Aboriginal workers living off-reserve had an unemployment rate of almost 15 per cent in 2010 (Usalcas 2010); Aboriginal workers living on-reserve have even

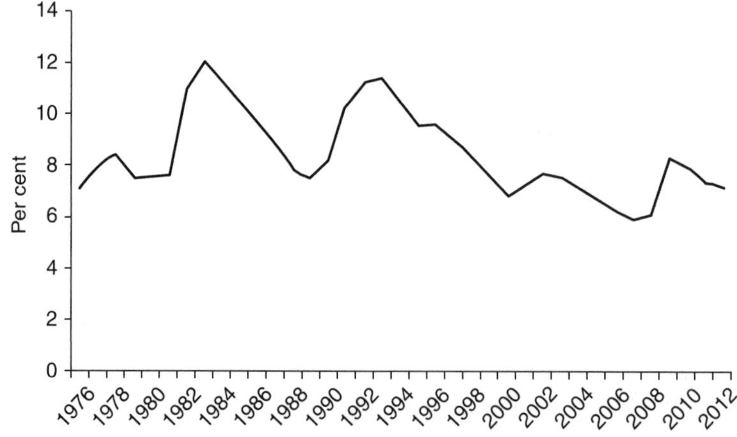

Figure 6.2 Unemployment Rate, Canada, 1976–2012

Source: Statistics Canada (2015e).

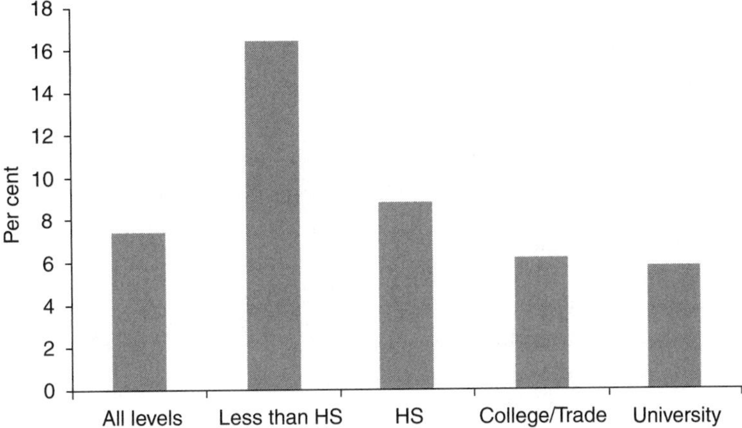

Figure 6.3 Unemployment Rates of 25- to 29-year-olds, by Educational Attainment, Canada, 2012

Source: Statistics Canada (2013b).

lower employment rates and higher unemployment rates than those living in cities (White et al. 2003). These poorer labour market outcomes partly reflect Aboriginals' lower average levels of education and limited regional labour market opportunities. Immigrants also have lower employment rates and higher unemployment rates, especially within their first five years in Canada (Statistics Canada 2015c). Visible minority immigrants are particularly disadvantaged, and their employment rates have declined significantly over time (Tran 2004). Canadian-born visible minorities face similarly poor outcomes, with lower employment rates and higher unemployment rates. Systemic barriers and discrimination play a significant role in the labour market outcomes of all these groups.

In addition to unemployment and employment, sociologists also consider underemployment, which occurs when workers have obtained more education than their jobs require (Livingstone 1999). Underemployment has increased over time for all types of employees, as workers pursue more education and try to keep up with credential inflation. The proportion of the workforce with a university degree increased from 7 per cent to about 28 per cent between 1975 and 2014, and over half of all workers have now completed some form of post-secondary education (Conference Board of Canada 2014). For younger workers and women, these percentages are even higher. In 2011, nearly 40 per cent of employed women aged 25–34 had a university degree, compared with 27 per cent of employed men (Uppal and LaRochelle-Côté 2014).

At the same time, there is little evidence of jobs becoming significantly more complex. Thus, it is not surprising that a significant number of university-educated workers are underemployed. In 2011, approximately 18 per cent of university-educated men and women aged 25–34 were employed in occupations requiring a high school education or less. This reflects a relatively large gap between educational and occupational achievement. In the same year, approximately 40 per cent of university-educated men and women aged 25–34 were in occupations for which a college degree would have been sufficient. Underemployment is higher for service workers and visible minority immigrants than others (Uppal and LaRochelle-Côté 2014).

Income and Benefits

As discussed in the previous sections, the labour market is a competitive arena in which some people fare better than others. This is especially evident if we look at income. The Occupy movement sought to draw public attention to the substantial income inequality in societies like Canada and the US. The incomes of the richest 1 per cent have increased, and they now hold more than one-third of the country's wealth. In 2014, the average annual income for Canadian company directors was $1.6 million (Lamontagne 2014), while the average Canadian, according to the most recent census figures, earned just $38,700 (CBC 2013). Newer workers have particular difficulty, especially young men without a university education. This is probably due to the disappearance of traditional, unionized, blue-collar jobs in manufacturing. Many jobs in the services sector, especially for people with little education, pay 20 per cent less than jobs in the goods-producing industries.

Employment income varies by gender. The gender gap in wages has decreased over time, partly because of increases in women's wages, but also because men's real earnings have declined slightly (Krahn, Lowe, and Hughes 2011). Nevertheless, among full-time workers, women still earned only about 71 per cent of men's earnings (Williams 2010; see also Chapter 15 in this volume). Research reveals a wage gap based on race as well, with visible minority Canadians, especially Blacks, earning significantly less than other Canadians (Gosine 2000; see also Chapter 13 in this volume). Immigrants who hold foreign degrees also tend to earn less than similarly educated Canadians. Clearly, then, employment earnings are a significant factor shaping social inequality.

Occupational Segregation

We have highlighted how labour market outcomes have led to disadvantages based on race, gender, and immigration status in Canada. Studies have also identified labour market disadvantages for people with disabilities (Shier et al. 2009). Research shows that some of these inequalities result from occupational segregation—the fact that people with different social characteristics work in different jobs—and also from systemic discrimination. In this section, we examine both of these factors and consider how they contribute to labour market and social inequality.

Occupational segregation is an enduring characteristic of Canada's workforce. The place where people work and the work they perform tend to vary by gender, race, and ethnicity. Occupational segregation by gender has decreased over time. Fifty years ago, men and women rarely did the same jobs, in the same industries and firms. In the 1960s, creating a non-segregated labour force would have required 70 per cent of women to change their jobs (Fox and Fox 1987). By the turn of the twenty-first century, this percentage had dropped to about 50 per cent, and more recently has dropped closer to 35 per cent (Brooks et al. 2003; Tomaskovic-Devey et al. 2006). Researchers often distinguish between vertical segregation and horizontal segregation (Charles and Grusky 2004). Vertical segregation exists within industries. For example, when women work mainly as support staff, while men work mainly as managers in the same industry, we have a situation of vertical segregation. Horizontal segregation exists across industries. Thus, when women predominate in nursing and daycare jobs, while men predominate in truck driving and construction work, we have horizontal segregation. Over time, vertical segregation has decreased. For example, women's movement into high-status occupations in medicine and management has resulted in declining occupational segregation (Jarman et al. 2012). Nonetheless, women still have difficulty reaching the truly upper echelons: for example, only 13 per cent of company directors are women (Lamontagne 2014). Horizontal segregation across industries, however, has proven more resilient. For instance, there has been little parallel movement of women into truck driving and construction, or of men into nursing or early childhood education. Although it is helpful to distinguish between the different types of segregation, to understand these contradictory trends we need to recognize that horizontal segregation, defined in this manner, still has implications for social inequality. As Jarman et al. (2012) have shown, these implications are often complex, in that men's jobs tend to pay more than women's, but women's jobs are often safer, because men predominate in jobs that are among some of the lowest-status and the highest-risk occupations.

As for the most common jobs for men and women, women are most likely to work in clerical occupations, child care and support, nursing and teaching, while men are most likely to work in transportation, computer and information systems, engineering, manufacturing, and trades (Adams and Welsh 2007). Although it is helpful to look at segregation using these broad occupational categories, research suggests that if we look at the level of more specific jobs, segregation rates are actually higher. For instance, women have moved into management occupations in higher numbers, but they still tend to be segregated in certain sub-areas, such as hospital management and human resources.

Occupations are also still segregated by race and ethnicity. Different estimates suggest that between 35 and 45 per cent of people would have to change jobs to have a racially desegregated labour force (Tomaskovic-Devey et al. 2006). Studies show that members of visible minorities are over-represented in service and semi-skilled manual jobs, and under-represented in management, especially in the upper echelons. While racial segregation has decreased over time, most of the main gains were made decades ago (Tomaskovic-Devey et al. 2006). Only 3.4 per cent of top executives in Canada were members of visible minorities in 2014, and this percentage actually decreased between 2010 and 2014 (Lamontagne 2014).

Occupational segregation is significant because it contributes to inequalities in income and employment opportunity. The gender gap in wages is partly accounted for by occupational segregation, as are inequalities by race and ethnicity. The jobs in which women and minorities are concentrated typically pay less, are less likely to lead to promotions, and are less likely to include employment benefits.

How can we account for occupational segregation? Studies point to a complex intersection of factors (Adams and Welsh 2007). Gender socialization and personal choices play a role, as do differences in education, especially area of study. Women's responsibilities for family and child care affect their employment patterns. Research has also identified the presence of discrimination in the labour market. Significantly, women receive lower returns from their post-secondary education than do men (Ferguson and Wang 2014), and the same is true for members of visible minorities. Ideologies of gender difference, including the belief that men and women are inherently different and have different skills and abilities, also play a part in influencing employers' hiring decisions, as well as workers' job choices. Research has shown that employers' beliefs and prejudices about productivity and skill differences by gender and race affect their hiring practices (Reskin and Roos 1990). Studies have found that when presented with identical resumés, employers are more likely to hire applicants who appear to be White and Canadian-born (Henry and Ginzberg 1985; see also Chapter 25 in this volume). Labour market biases still persist, leading to different outcomes on the basis of race, gender, and ethnicity.

To counteract these persistent biases, the Canadian government implemented employment equity policies, beginning in the mid-1980s. The goal of employment equity policies is to eliminate barriers to the recruitment or advancement of four social groups that historically have been disadvantaged in the labour market: women, visible minorities, Aboriginal peoples, and persons with disabilities. Pay equity promotes the principle of equal pay for work of equal value. This policy uses job evaluation systems to compare predominantly female jobs with predominantly male jobs within the same organization, in an attempt to redress any undervaluing of women's work. These policies have had some effect in promoting equity in the labour market, but inequalities by gender, race, citizenship status, and other characteristics have been stubbornly persistent (see also Chapter 15 in this volume).

Conclusion

Considerable debate continues about whether the rise of a service economy and other labour market changes have created more good jobs than bad jobs, and whether such changes influence social inequality. We have seen that good jobs have expanded over time, and gender inequality has declined. Nevertheless, rising executive salaries still exacerbate income inequalities, and labour market inequalities by age, race, gender, and immigration status persist. Non-standard jobs foster feelings of risk and uncertainty; the labour market appears to be polarizing, creating winners and losers. Even in prosperous economic times, inequality continues. These developments have a direct impact on society, as more of the risks associated with economic change are transferred to individuals, families, and communities, and as the divide widens between Canada's "haves" and "have-nots."

This chapter has focused on paid work and social inequality in Canada. Still, it is important to recognize that a fully comprehensive discussion of work should include unpaid work performed in households and in volunteer-based community organizations, and also paid work in the informal or underground economy that operates outside government regulation. In addition, a thorough discussion of work and social inequality requires a global lens. Work and rewards are unevenly distributed around the world. Industrial labour has long been outsourced to developing nations that offer manufacturers extremely low labour costs and few labour market or environmental regulations, which are seen as costly restrictions in industrial nations. This development has led to what many consider a vicious cycle of worker exploitation in sweatshops in developing nations. Recent events have brought these global labour inequalities to public attention. These include the worker suicides at Foxconn—the Chinese company assembling iPhones and iPads—and the deaths in 2013 of more than 1,000 workers after the collapse of a Bangladesh factory that produced clothes for the Canadian label Joe Fresh. Sadly, though, these tragedies have done little to change the conditions of workers in these nations. In recent years, jobs outside of manufacturing have also moved to developing countries. With advanced communication technology, professional employment such as book production, engineering, and software design can be outsourced even more easily to an increasingly qualified but lower-paid workforce in nations such as India and China (Brown, Lauder, and Ashton 2011). These trends exacerbate the exploitation of workers in developing countries, but they also create employment losses and downward pressure on salaries in industrialized societies like Canada, with jobs leaving the country or workers having to accept lower salaries to remain competitive.

As we have shown in this chapter, access to and experiences with employment remain stratified in Canada. Rather than being the outcomes of a meritocratic process, people's jobs, income, and quality of employment are significantly affected by their gender, ethnicity, race, and class background. Although the focus of the chapter has been on Canada, we can see that labour market inequalities are truly a global phenomenon. Workers around the globe are exploited, while top executives in developed nations earn unprecedented high incomes. The challenges and trends facing Canadian workers must be understood in the context of these increasingly global labour market trends.

Acknowledgement

The authors would like to thank Graham S. Lowe for his significant contributions to previous versions of this chapter, upon which some of our work is based.

Questions for Critical Thought

1. Based on the available labour market data, do you think labour market trends will lead to greater or lesser social inequality?
2. How do you think labour market trends contribute to the changing nature of social inequality in Canadian society and around the world?
3. To what extent are labour market inequalities the result of the capitalist system, and to what extent are they the result of other social forces?
4. Can labour market inequalities be resolved by giving more Canadians the opportunity to go to university?

Recommended Readings

Adams, Tracey, and Sandy Welsh. 2007. *The Organization and Experience of Work*. Scarborough, Ont.: Nelson Canada.

Brown, P., H. Lauder, and D. Ashton. 2011. *The Global Auction: The Broken Promises of Education, Jobs and Incomes*. Oxford and New York: Oxford University Press.

Williams, Christine L., and Catherine Connell. 2010. "'Looking good and sounding right': Aesthetic labor and social inequality in the retail industry." *Work & Occupations* 37: 349–77

Recommended Websites

Centre for Policy Alternatives:
https://www.policyalternatives.ca/

Conference Board of Canada:
www.conferenceboard.ca

Employment and Social Development Canada:
http://www.esdc.gc.ca/eng/home.shtml

Statistics Canada:
www.statscan.ca

References

Adams, Tracey, and Sandy Welsh. 2007. *The Organization and Experience of Work*. Scarborough, Ont.: Nelson Canada.

Basok, Tanya. 2002. *Tortillas and Tomatoes: Transmigrant Mexican Harvesters in Canada*. Montreal and Kingston: McGill-Queen's University Press.

Becker, Gary S. 1975. *Human Capital: A Theoretical and Empirical Analysis with Special Reference to Education*. 2nd edn. Chicago: University of Chicago Press.

Bonacich, Edna. 1972. "A theory of ethnic antagonism: The split labor market." *American Sociological Review* 37, 5: 547–59.

Bourdieu, Pierre. 1977. *Outline of a Theory of Practice*. New York: Cambridge University Press.

———. 1990. *The Logic of Practice*. Cambridge: Polity.

Brooks, Bradley, Jennifer Jarman, and Robert M. Blackburn. 2003. "Occupational gender segregation in Canada, 1981–1996: Overall vertical and horizontal segregation." *Canadian Review of Sociology and Anthropology* 40, 2: 197–213.

Brown, P., H. Lauder, and D. Ashton. 2011. *The Global Auction: The Broken Promises of Education, Jobs and Incomes*. Oxford and New York: Oxford University Press.

Canadian Broadcasting Corporation (CBC). 2013. "Wealthiest 1% earn 10 times more than average Canadian." http://www.cbc.ca/news/business/wealthiest-1-earn-10-times-more-than-average-canadian-1.1703017. Accessed 14 Apr. 2015.

Castells, Manuel. 2000. "Materials for an exploratory theory of the network society." *British Journal of Sociology* 51, 1: 5–24.

Charles, Maria, and David B. Grusky. 2004. *Occupational Ghettos: The Worldwide Segregation of Women and Men*. Stanford, Calif.: Stanford University Press.

Conference Board of Canada. 2014. "How Canada performs: University completion." http://www.conferenceboard.ca/hcp/details/education/university-completion.aspx.

Ferguson, Sarah Jane, and Shunji Wang. 2014. *Graduating in Canada: Profile, Labour Market Outcomes and Student Debt of the Class of 2009–2010*. Ottawa: Statistics Canada, Catalogue no. 81-595-M No. 2014101.

Fox, Bonnie J., and John Fox. 1987. "Occupational gender segregation of the Canadian labour force, 1931–1981." *Canadian Review of Sociology and Anthropology* 24, 3: 374–97.

Fuller, Sylvia, and Leah Vosko. 2008. "Temporary employment and social inequality in Canada: Exploring intersections of gender, race, and immigration status." *Social Indicators Research* 88: 31–50.

——— and Natasha Stecy-Hildebrandt. 2014. "Lasting disadvantage? Comparing career trajectories of matched temporary and permanent workers in Canada." *Canadian Review of Sociology* 51, 4: 293–323.

Galarneau, Diane. 2010. *Temporary Employment in the Downturn*. Ottawa: Statistics Canada.

Gosine, Kevin. 2000. "Revising the notion of a 'recast' vertical mosaic in Canada: Does a post-secondary education make a difference?" *Canadian Ethnic Studies* 32, 3: 89–104.

Hartmann, Heidi. 1976. "Patriarchy, capitalism and job segregation by sex." *Signs* 1: 137–68.

Henry, Frances, and Effie Ginzberg. 1985. *Who Gets Work? A Test of Racial Discrimination in Employment*. Toronto: Urban Alliance on Race Relations and the Social Planning Council of Metropolitan Toronto.

Jarman, Jennifer, Robert M. Blackburn, and Girts Racko. 2012. "The dimensions of occupational gender segregation in industrial countries." *Sociology* 46, 6: 1003–19.

Kalleberg, Arne. 2003. "Flexible firms and labor market segmentation: Effects of workplace restructuring on jobs and workers." *Work & Occupations* 30, 2: 154–75.

———, Barbara Reskin, and Ken Hudson. 2000. "Bad jobs in America: Standard and non-standard employment relations and job quality in the United States." *American Sociological Review* 65, 2: 256–78.

Kapsalis, C., and P. Tourigny. 2004. "Duration of non-standard employment." *Perspectives on Labour and Income* 5, 12: 5–13.

Krahn, Harvey, Graham S. Lowe, and Karen D. Hughes. 2011. *Work, Industry & Canadian Society*, 6th edn. Toronto: Thomson Nelson.

Lamontagne, Elyse. 2014. *Canadian Directors' Compensation Practices*, 20th edn. Ottawa: Conference Board of Canada.

Lehmann, Wolfgang. 2007. *Choosing to Labour? School–Work Transitions and Social Class*. Montreal and Kingston: McGill-Queen's University Press.

———. 2011. "Extra-credential experiences and social closure: Working-class students at university." *British Educational Research Journal* 38, 2: 203–18.

Livingstone, D.W. 1999. *The Education–Jobs Gap: Underemployment or Economic Democracy*. Toronto: Garamond Press.

———. 2014. "Interrogating professional power and recognition of specialized knowledge: A class analysis." *European Journal for Research on the Education and Learning of Adults* 5, 1: 13–29.

Macdonald, Cameron Lynne, and Carmen Sirianni. 1996. "The service society and the changing experience of work." In C.L. Macdonald and C. Sirianni, eds, *Working in the Service Society*, pp. 1–26. Philadelphia: Temple University Press.

Marshall, Katherine 2009. "The family work week." *Perspectives on Labour and Income* 10, 4: 5–13.

Preibisch, Kerry L., and Evelyn Encalada Grez. 2010. "The other side of *el Otro Lado*: Mexican migrant women and labor flexibility in Canadian agriculture." *Signs* 35, 2: 289–316.

Reskin, Barbara, and Patricia Roos. 1990. *Job Queues, Gender Queues: Explaining Women's Inroads into Male Occupations*. Philadelphia: Temple University Press.

Rifkin, Jeremy. 1995. *The End of Work: The Decline of the Global Labor Force and the Dawn of the Post-Market Era*. New York: Putnam.

Sennett, Richard. 1998. *The Corrosion of Character: The Personal Consequences of Work in the New Capitalism*. New York: W.W. Norton.

Shalla, Vivian. 2003. "Part-time shift: The struggle over the casualization of airline customer sales and service agent work." *Canadian Review of Sociology and Anthropology* 40, 1: 93–109.

Shier, M., J. Graham, and M. Jones. 2009. "Barriers to employment as experienced by disabled people: A qualitative analysis in Calgary and Regina, Canada." *Disability & Society* 24, 1: 63–75.

Statistics Canada. 2013a. "Study: Long-term trends in unionization, 1981 to 2012." *The Daily*, 26 Nov.

———. 2013b. *Education Indicators in Canada: Report of the Pan-Canadian Education Indicators Program*. Ottawa: Statistics Canada, Catalogue no. 81-582-X.

———. 2015a. *Labour Force Survey: 2014 Year-End Review*. Ottawa: Statistics Canada.

———. 2015b. CANSIM, Table 282-0007, "Unemployment by industry, sex and age group."

———. 2015c. CANSIM, Table 282-0106, "Labour force characteristics by immigrant status of population aged 25 to 54, and by educational attainment."

———. 2015d. CANSIM, Table 282-0002, "Labour force survey estimates (LFS), by sex and detailed age group, annual (persons unless otherwise noted)." Database, accessed 14 Apr. 2015.

———. 2015e. CANSIM, Table 282-0086, "Labour force survey estimates (LFS), supplementary unemployment rates by sex and age group, annual (rate)." Database accessed 14 Apr. 2015.

Tomaskovic-Devey, D., K. Stainback, T. Taylor, C. Zimmer, C. Robinson, and T. McTague. 2006. "Documenting desegregation: Segregation in American workplaces by race, ethnicity, and sex, 1966–2003." *American Sociological Review* 71, 4: 565–88.

Tran, Kelly. 2004. "Visible minorities in the labour force: 20 years of change." *Canadian Social Trends* (Summer): 7–11.

Uppal, Sharanjit, and Sébastien LaRochelle-Côté. 2014. *Overqualification among Recent University Graduates in Canada*. Ottawa: Statistics Canada.

Usalcas, Jeanine. 2008. "Hours polarization revisited." *Perspectives on Labour and Income* 9, 3: 5–15.

———. 2010. *Aboriginal People and the Labour Market: Estimates from the Labour Force Survey 2008–10*. Ottawa: Statistics Canada Catalogue no. 71-588-X No. 3.

White, J., P. Maxim, and S.O. Gyimah. 2003. "Labour force activity of women in Canada: A comparative analysis of Aboriginal and non-Aboriginal women." *Canadian Review of Sociology and Anthropology* 40, 4: 391–415.

Williams, Cara. 2010. *Women in Canada: Economic Well-being*. Ottawa: Statistics Canada, Catalogue no. 89-503-X.

Williams, Christine L., and Catherine Connell. 2010. "'Looking good and sounding right': Aesthetic labor and social inequality in the retail industry." *Work & Occupations* 37: 349–77.

7 Choose Your Parents Carefully: Social Class, Post-secondary Education, and Occupational Outcomes

Harvey Krahn

Introduction

Advances in the science of genetics have made it possible for parents to pre-select the sex of their children (Wertz and Fletcher 1998). With cloning specialists shifting their attention from the animal world to the human species, it may be only a matter of time before someone chooses to bring a copy of her- or himself into existence. While the ethical implications of such actions need to be seriously debated (Harris 1997), science has brought us to the point where parents literally can choose their children. What if the laws of time and physics could be reversed and we could choose our parents? Given the opportunity, whom would you choose? Famous parents? Gorgeously beautiful parents? A loving, caring mother and father? Someone who would get off your back? This chapter concludes that, if you are concerned about your own educational and career future, and if you really could select your parents, you would clearly benefit from making them better educated and more affluent.

Social Class and Life Chances

Over the past century, sociologists from different theoretical camps have debated the extent to which *social class*—one's position in an economic hierarchy defined by occupation, education, or income—affects people's life chances (Grabb 2007). There has generally been agreement that, compared with their working-class counterparts, middle-class North Americans and Europeans enjoy a more comfortable and worry-free existence, tend to live longer and healthier lives (Wilkinson and Pickett 2010; Raphael 2011), fare better in the criminal justice system (King and Winterdyk 2010), and are more likely to pass such advantages on to their children (Turcotte 2011).

Even so, some have argued that the importance of social class in Western industrial societies has declined. The rapid expansion of colleges and universities during the 1960s and 1970s allowed many talented young people, including some born into poor families, to acquire post-secondary credentials and, thus, move into better-paying professional careers. On the basis of this and related trends, Daniel Bell (1973) argued that, in post-industrial society, rigid social inequalities based on accidents of birth (e.g., were you born into a wealthy or a poor family?) were replaced by more fluid and less severe income differences based on educational attainment. More recently, social theorists such as Anthony Giddens (1991) and Ulrich Beck (1992) have suggested that the rapid social and economic change characteristic of globalized, postmodern society have provided young people with more opportunities to shape their own destinies, even though postmodern society has also generated more risks. In short, the argument goes, social class is no longer as relevant an explanation of social inequality as it once was; rather, it has become "an increasingly outmoded concept" (Clark and Lipset 1991: 397).

However, the labour market in Western industrial societies has been changing in recent decades, and many full-time, well-paying, and secure jobs have been replaced by much more precarious (e.g., part-time, temporary, lower-paying) forms of employment (Vosko 2005; Kalleberg 2011; Krahn et al. 2015). Researchers examining the connections between individuals' educational accomplishments and their family of origin have continued to report persistent patterns of intergenerational reproduction of social inequality. Specifically, young people from more advantaged backgrounds are more likely to finish high school (Tanner et al. 1995) and succeed in the post-secondary education system (Davies and Guppy 1997; Knighton and Mirza 2002; Lehmann 2007; Turcotte 2011; Bukodi and Goldthorpe 2013; Frenette and Chan 2015). The most obvious explanation is that wealthier parents can pay for better and more post-secondary education.

In addition, children from more advantaged backgrounds are less likely to participate in non-academic (vocational) secondary school programs that typically leave graduates without the high school credits required for university entrance (Taylor and Krahn 2009). This "streaming" may be a function of teachers and advisers providing more encouragement and advice to middle-class youth compared with their less advantaged peers. It may also reflect the educational choices of working-class youth, who typically report lower educational and occupational aspirations (Andres et al. 1999) than do their middle-class peers. The latter are more likely challenged by parents and teachers to "aim higher."

Related to these patterns is the differential distribution of *cultural capital* (Bourdieu 1986). Children from more affluent backgrounds are more likely to have been exposed to the experiences (e.g., preschool education, a "book" culture in the home, exposure to the fine arts) and beliefs (e.g., "You have to get a university degree to be successful in life") that are valued in the formal education system (Sullivan 2001) and, so, are more likely to enjoy and do well in high school and university (Lehmann 2007, 2014). In contrast, working-class youth without such advantages are more likely to do poorly.

Thus, despite the observations of those who forecasted the declining relevance of social class, research clearly shows that social class continues to matter. The most convincing evidence comes from longitudinal studies that track individuals as they move into, through, and out of the formal educational system into their adult occupational careers. The rest of this chapter discusses research findings from a unique longitudinal study that tracked the educational and occupational ambitions and experiences of a large sample of Canadians over a 25-year period, from when they were completing high school in 1985 until they were 43 years old in 2010.

Research Design

The Edmonton Transitions Study (ETS) began in 1985 with a survey of 983 high school seniors from six different Edmonton high schools located in both middle- and working-class sections of the city.[1] Since most of these young people were born in 1967, they would be considered part of "Generation X," while their parents would have been early "baby boomers" (Krahn and Galambos 2014). Survey participants (17 or 18 years old) completed questionnaires in class in May and early June, before they wrote their final examinations. Follow-up surveys were conducted by mail in 1986, 1987, 1989, and 1992 (by now, study participants were 25 years old, on average). In each follow-up survey, only those individuals who had participated in the previous wave of data collection were contacted.

In 1999 (ETS sample members were now 32 years old), yet another follow-up survey was conducted, this time by telephone, since many of the postal addresses recorded in 1992 were out of date. This survey attempted to interview as many of the baseline (1985) respondents as possible, whether or not they had participated in all four intervening waves of data collection. In 2010, when ETS sample members were in early mid-life (43 years old, on average), a seventh survey involving both telephone and web survey technologies, was completed, again targeting all of the 1985 original study participants. In total, 405 ETS respondents were interviewed in 2010 (41 per cent of the complete 1985 sample).[2] Almost all of the non-participants in the 2010 study could not be located or, if located, could not be reached by telephone, e-mail, or Facebook, despite repeated attempts. Very few (only 6 per cent of the potential respondents) refused to participate in the 2010 survey after being contacted.[3]

2010 Sample Characteristics

Fifty-three per cent (n = 213) of the 405 ETS respondents (in 2010) were female, and 47 per cent (n = 192) were male. Eighty-six per cent had been born in Canada, while 14 per cent were immigrants, much like the proportion of immigrants in the city of Edmonton in the mid-1980s. Ten per cent of those who answered the survey question about race indicated that their mother was either Aboriginal or a member of another visible minority group, and a similar proportion said the same about their father's racial origin.[4]

Thirty-seven per cent of the 2010 ETS sample members (who had answered this question in 1985) indicated that their mother had acquired at least some post-secondary education; 16 per cent said their mother had a university degree. Half of the 2010 respondents reported that their father had participated in the post-secondary system following high school, with 28 per cent indicating that their father had completed university.[5] In total, 29 per cent of the 2010 ETS sample members reported that at least one of their parents had completed a university degree. In the following analyses (all of them based on the 405 ETS sample members who responded in 2010), this simple binary variable—whether or not at least one parent had completed a university degree—is used to measure family socio-economic status (SES), a proxy for the concept of social class.

Socio-economic Status (SES) and Education Values

When first surveyed in 1985, the 18-year-old study participants were asked to indicate how much they agreed or disagreed (on a 1–5 scale where 1 meant "strongly disagree" and 5 meant "strongly agree") with a range of statements about different aspects of education and work. In total, almost three out of four (73 per cent) of the 2010 sample members agreed (scores of 4 or 5) that "overall, I have enjoyed my time in high school." While ETS participants from higher SES families were somewhat more likely to agree (79 per cent) than were those whose parent(s) had not completed university (70 per cent), the difference between the two groups was not statistically significant.[6]

While this first statement focused on individuals' personal reaction to school, a second changed the topic to whether or not they felt it would be useful for future employment. More than three-quarters (78 per cent) of the 2010 ETS sample agreed that "continuing my education will help me get a good job." There was virtually no difference between sample members from higher SES (79 per cent agreed) and lower SES families (77 per cent agreed), although those with university-educated parents were a little more likely to "strongly agree" with this statement (57 per cent versus 49 per cent). This difference, however, was not statistically significant.

These findings reinforce those reported by other researchers (e.g., Tanner et al. 1995) who have concluded that there is very little evidence of outright rejection of, or "resistance" to, formal education among high school students in Canada, or of greater rejection among young people from less advantaged backgrounds. Thus, if we find that lower SES study participants eventually acquire less post-secondary education, it is likely not because they failed to recognize the value of higher education.

Socio-economic Status (SES) and High School Education

In 1985, two-thirds (68 per cent) of the ETS sample members were enrolled in academic high school programs that should, if successfully completed, provide graduates with the course credits needed for university entrance. The rest were enrolled in a range of non-academic programs. Table 7.1 shows a strong relationship between family social status (SES) and the type of high school program in which youth participated. Almost nine out of 10 (87 per cent) students from higher SES families were enrolled in academic high school programs, compared with only 60 per cent from families in which neither parent had completed university. While this study cannot explain the process whereby "streaming" into different high school programs occurs, it can tell us, as we will see below, whether the type of high school program a young person completes makes a difference for subsequent educational and occupational attainment.

Table 7.1 also demonstrates a strong relationship between family SES and students' performance in high school. One-half (51 per cent) of the survey respondents from families where at least one parent had acquired a university degree reported average grades of 70 per cent or higher in their senior year in high school, compared with only 35 per cent of the young people from less advantaged family backgrounds.

As noted above, young people from lower SES families, like their more advantaged peers,

Table 7.1 High School Program and Grades by Parent(s)' University Education, Edmonton High School Seniors, 1985

Parent(s)' Education	No Degree (%)	Degree (%)	Total (%)
*High School Program**			
Academic	60	87	68
Non-academic	40	13	32
*Grades in Past Year**			
< 60%	17	9	14
60–9%	48	40	46
70–9%	27	34	29
80%+	8	17	11
Total %	100	100	100
(N)	(289)	(116)	(405)

*Differences in percentages are statistically significant ($p < 0.05$; chi-square test).

generally recognize the value of higher education. Even so, other research (e.g., Sullivan 2001) has suggested that the greater "cultural capital" available to middle-class youth is part of the explanation for differences in school performance. University-educated parents may provide more encouragement to their children to do well in high school, and can likely provide more advice and, also, additional resources (e.g., paying for tutoring) that would lead to higher grades. In turn, teachers may expect more from young people from more affluent families and, as a result, pay more attention to them. Better grades in high school improve one's chances of being accepted into university and, furthermore, into "better" (higher-status) universities and into programs that lead to higher-paying careers.

Socio-economic Status (SES) and Young People's Aspirations

While young people whose parents did not attend university recognize the value of higher education, we now know that, on average, they are less likely to be enrolled in academic high school programs that "stream" students into university. Compared to their peers with parents who did attend university, they are also less likely to have high grades in high school. Do these differences perhaps translate into lower post-secondary educational and future occupational aspirations?

When asked in 1985, virtually all of the ETS sample members indicated that they intended to acquire some post-secondary education—only 7 per cent of the total sample said they intended to finish high school and nothing more (Table 7.2). One-half (49 per cent) planned a college (or technical school) education,[7] while almost as many (44 per cent) expected to acquire a university degree, including 16 per cent who intended to complete a second degree.

The 1985 survey participants were also asked, "What kind of job or career do you want eventually?" and answered with responses like "teacher," "mechanic," "rock star," "engineer," "hairdresser," and "lawyer." Recognizing that many high school seniors may not have firm career plans, their answers to a question like this still signal general preferences for employment in the future. To simplify the analysis, the many different specific occupational aspirations recorded by sample members in 1985 have been collapsed into

Table 7.2 Post-secondary Education Plans and Occupational Aspirations by Parent(s)' University Education, Edmonton High School Seniors, 1985

Parent(s)' Education	No Degree (%)	Degree (%)	Total (%)
*Post-secondary Educational Plans**			
Finish high school	9	–	7
1–2 years college/university	57	31	49
3–4 years university	24	39	28
5+ years university	10	30	16
*Occupational Aspirations**			
Managerial/professional	60	77	64
Other occupations	40	23	36
Total %	100	100	100
(N)	(289)	(116)	(405)

*Differences in percentages are statistically significant ($p < 0.05$; chi-square test).

two basic categories, "managers/professionals" (managers of all kinds and professionals such as nurses, lawyers, teachers, engineers, and artists) and "other occupational aspirations" (included here are all other lower-status occupations as well as the "don't know" responses provided by a small minority of respondents).

Table 7.2 demonstrates that, when finishing high school, almost two-thirds (64 per cent) of the total sample hoped to someday be in a managerial or professional occupation, the type of job that typically pays better, provides more fringe benefits, and is generally more rewarding (Krahn et al. 2015). Since, by 2012, only about 40 per cent of all employed Canadians were in managerial or professional occupations (Krahn et al. 2015: 67), it is again apparent that not all of these high career aspirations would have been attained. Along with the high educational and occupational aspirations of the total sample, what also stands out in Table 7.2 are the statistically significant SES differences. Specifically, over two-thirds (69 per cent) of the survey respondents from university-educated families expected to acquire one or more university degrees, compared with only one-third (34 per cent) from families where neither parent had completed a university degree. The SES differences in occupational aspirations are not quite as large, but are still pronounced: More than three-quarters (77 per cent) of the Grade 12 students from more advantaged backgrounds hoped to become a manager or professional someday, compared with 60 per cent of the high school seniors from lower SES backgrounds. Thus, family socio-economic status (or social class, using another related term) does matter for education and career aspirations. Does it also matter for post-secondary education and subsequent career outcomes?

Socio-economic Status (SES) and Educational Attainment

By 2010, when ETS study participants were in early midlife (43 years old, on average), a large majority (76 per cent) were married or in a long-term relationship, and over three-quarters (78 per cent) were parents (of children living with them or someone else). Sixty per cent were still living in the Edmonton region, 23 per cent were living elsewhere in Alberta, and 17 per cent had moved out of the province (including 6 per cent who were living outside Canada).

Over the previous 25 years, sample members had been extensively involved in the post-secondary education system. Only one in six (16 per cent) had not gone beyond high school, and another 13 per cent had completed some college, technical school, or university training. One-third (34 per cent) had acquired a college or technical school diploma, one-quarter (25 per cent) had received a university undergraduate degree, and 12 per cent had received an advanced or graduate degree. In total, 71 per cent reported a diploma or a degree as their highest level of education. A majority of those with post-secondary credentials (a diploma or a degree) had received them by age 25 (in 1992), and most of the others had done so by age 32 (in 1999). Only a small minority had returned to school or completed a degree or diploma later.

Male ETS participants were somewhat more likely to have completed a degree or diploma (74 per cent, compared to 68 per cent of women), but this gender difference was not statistically significant. A more detailed analysis of earlier data from this study (results not shown), however, demonstrated that women were somewhat more likely to receive community college diplomas and university undergraduate degrees, while men were more likely to receive technical school diplomas (including completed apprenticeships).

It is interesting to note that, 25 years earlier when they were completing high school, 93 per cent of these ETS participants had planned to obtain post-secondary credentials (Table 7.2). The central question addressed in the following analyses is whether family SES or, in other words, class background had an impact on post-secondary educational attainment. As Figure 7.1 demonstrates, the answer very clearly is "yes."

By 2010, only 18 per cent of ETS participants from higher SES families (one or both parents with a university degree) had not acquired some kind of post-secondary educational credential, compared to 34 per cent of those from less advantaged family backgrounds. Six out of 10 (59 per cent) of those with university-educated parents had completed a degree themselves (including 23 per cent who had completed graduate or advanced degrees), compared to less than half as many (only 28 per cent) of those without a university-educated parent. ETS sample members from such lower SES families were somewhat more likely to have acquired a technical school or college diploma (38 per cent compared to 23 per cent).

These longitudinal survey findings highlight the remarkably strong impact of family

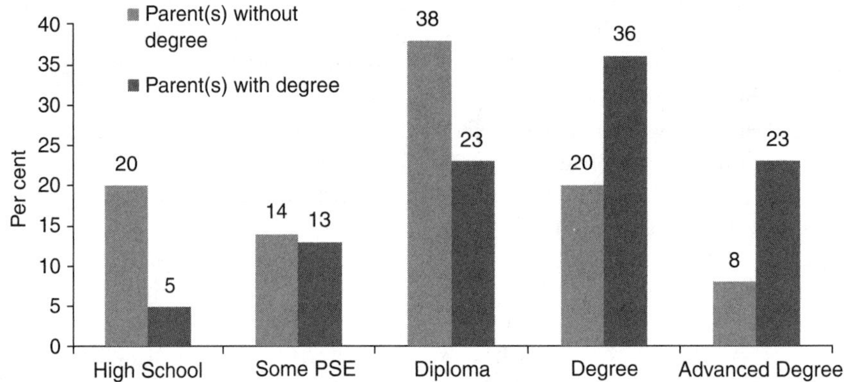

Figure 7.1 Post-secondary Educational Attainment by 2010, by Parent(s)' University Education*

*N = 405; differences by parent(s)' education are statistically significant ($p < 0.05$).

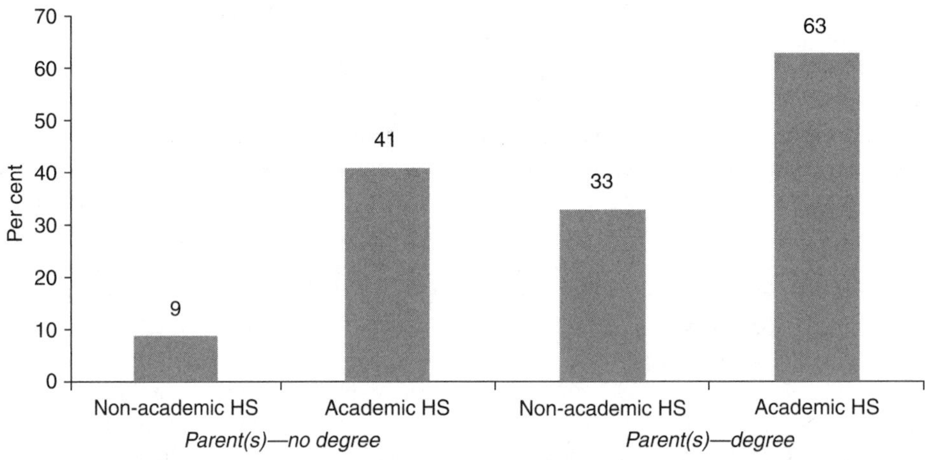

Figure 7.2 University Degree by 2010, by High School Program* by Parent(s)' University Education

*N = 405; differences by parent(s)' education are statistically significant ($p < 0.05$).

socio-economic status (SES), but they cannot directly explain the differences. However, we know that educational ambitions differed significantly between young people in lower- and higher-SES families (Table 7.2), and it is likely that familiarity with academic systems and institutions did as well, along with access to a range of educational resources. Furthermore, as we have already noted (Table 7.1), children from more advantaged backgrounds were much more likely to complete an academic high school program that provided all of the necessary prerequisites for university education.

Thus, Figure 7.2 reveals that only 9 per cent of the 1985 sample members whose parents had not completed university and who had been enrolled in non-academic high school programs had completed a university degree by 2010. In sharp contrast, 63 per cent of the higher SES graduates of academic high school programs had a degree by 2010. The additional cultural capital that would result from completion of an academic high school program was, no doubt, augmented by additional financial resources that more affluent parents could provide, with the result being that middle-class youth were much more likely to have obtained university credentials by 2010.

Socio-economic Status (SES) and Occupational Outcomes

How well had the "class of 1985" turned its post-secondary credentials into satisfactory and rewarding employment? By 2010, at age 43, 92 per cent of the ETS participants were employed (including 13 per cent who were holding at least two jobs). Only 2 per cent were unemployed (out of work and actively seeking work), while the remaining 6 per cent were out of the labour force (likely for family-raising reasons). Almost half (48 per cent) of the employed study participants were in managerial or professional jobs, including 20 per cent in managerial positions, 6 per cent in science or engineering professional positions, 6 per cent in professional positions in the health-care sector, and 9 per cent in education and social science professions. Just over one-quarter (27 per cent) of the 2010 ETS sample members held jobs usually requiring at least a technical school or college diploma or a completed apprenticeship, while almost as many (25 per cent) were working in lower-status, lower-skill clerical, sales, service, or manual labour jobs.

In 2010, male ETS respondents were over-represented in management positions (24 per cent of employed men, compared to 15 per cent of employed women), while women were somewhat more likely than men (31 per cent versus 27 per cent) to be holding a professional job. Men were also over-represented in jobs requiring a diploma or apprenticeship (32 per cent compared to 21 per cent of women), while women were more likely than men to be in lower-skill jobs (33 per cent compared to 17 per cent of men). In short, the occupational distribution of these ETS study participants at age 43 had a distinct gendered pattern, as does the occupational distribution of Canada's total labour force (Krahn et al. 2015: 82). Figure 7.3 documents the extent to which family background (SES) and respondents' own educational attainment had influenced their career outcomes. While 48 per cent of all employed sample members were in managerial/professional occupations, the odds of having acquired a higher-status occupation were considerably higher (67 per cent) for young people from families where at least one parent had completed university. Within this subgroup, over three-quarters (77 per cent) of those who had acquired a university degree were in a managerial or professional position when surveyed in 2010, compared to about half (52 per cent) of sample members without a degree.

Among ETS sample members from non-university families, those who had acquired a university degree had much the same chances (73 per cent) of working in a managerial or professional occupation by early mid-life (age 43) as did degree-holders from higher SES families (77 per cent). In contrast, only 28 per cent of ETS participants without a degree and from lower SES families were in managerial or professional

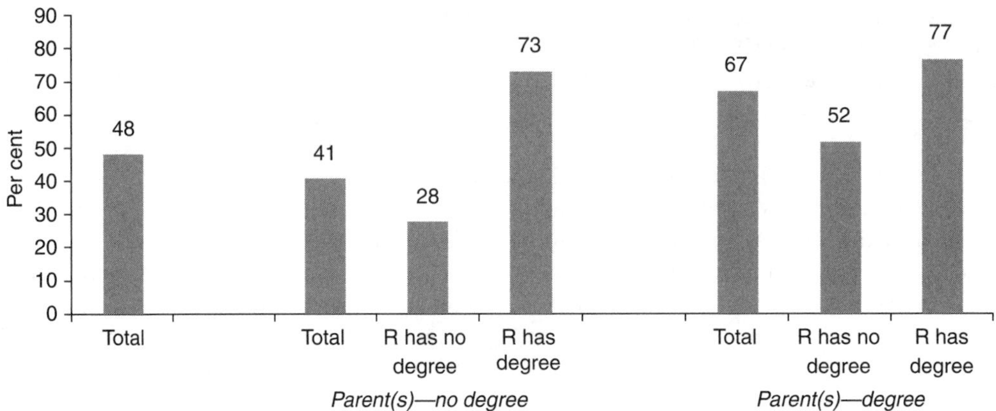

Figure 7.3 Managerial/Professional Occupation in 2010, by Respondents' University Education* by Parent(s)' University Education

*N = 372; differences between respondents with and without degrees are statistically significant ($p < 0.05$).

occupations by age 43, compared to 52 per cent of their equivalently educated peers with higher SES backgrounds.

In short, a university degree can help less advantaged youth get ahead in the labour market but, as we saw in Figure 7.1, less than half as many lower SES youth compared to young people from university-educated families (28 per cent compared to 59 per cent) manage to obtain university degrees. In contrast, focusing only on ETS sample members who did not complete a university degree, those from more advantaged backgrounds were almost twice as likely (52 per cent compared to 28 per cent of those whose parents had not completed university) to move into a managerial or professional occupation by midlife.

Socio-economic Status (SES) and the Match between Aspirations and Outcomes

In Table 7.2 we observed that 64 per cent of ETS participants had aspired to managerial or professional occupations when completing high school in 1985. Our 2010 follow-up study revealed that only 34 per cent had *both* aspired to a managerial/professional occupation and then, eventually, moved into such a career. Having now shown how SES strongly influences both educational attainment and occupational outcomes, we turn to a final research question: Does SES also influence one's chances of finding the type of employment one had hoped to obtain? Figure 7.4 provides a clear answer. As already noted, 64 per cent of the total 2010 sample (259 individuals) had aspired to managerial or professional occupations when they were completing high school at age 18. Fifty-seven per cent of these "high-goal" individuals had attained their goal by 2010 (Figure 7.4). However, by age 43, only half (51 per cent) of "high-goal" sample members from less advantaged families were employed in a managerial or professional occupation, compared to 7 out of 10 (69 per cent) of "high-goal" study participants from higher SES families.

This big difference is largely explained by the previous findings that the children of university-educated parents were more than twice as likely as their less advantaged peers to obtain a university degree (Figure 7.1), and that a university degree significantly enhances one's chances of employment in a professional or managerial occupation (Figure 7.3). In fact, with a university degree,

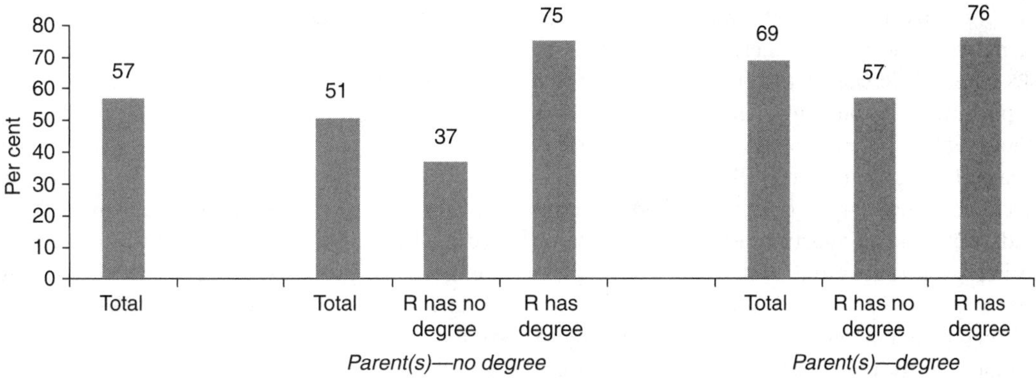

Figure 7.4 Managerial/Professional Occupation in 2010, by Respondents' University Education* by Parent(s)' University Education: "High Goals" in 1985 Subgroup

*N = 241 respondents who aspired to a managerial or professional occupation in 1985; differences between respondents with and without degrees are statistically significant ($p < 0.05$).

young people from both lower and higher SES backgrounds had similar chances (75 per cent and 76 per cent, respectively) of reaching their occupational goal (Figure 7.4). Without a degree, however, young people from non-university educated families were much less likely (37 per cent) than their more advantaged peers (57 per cent) to find themselves in the managerial or professional type of career to which they had aspired 25 years earlier.

Summary and Policy Implications

Summarizing the findings from this longitudinal study of school–work transitions, we have seen that middle-class youth typically do better in high school and are more likely to complete academic high school programs that will improve their chances of gaining entry to university. Even though young people from both lower and higher SES families recognize the value of higher education, the latter tend to have higher educational and occupational aspirations. In the 25 years following high school completion, members of this ETS sample acquired an impressive array of post-secondary credentials; 71 per cent reported holding either a college/technical school diploma or a university degree. These longitudinal survey data show that children of university-educated parents were much more likely to obtain a university degree themselves and, as a result, were much more likely to move into managerial or professional employment and to find the type of higher-status employment to which they had originally aspired when leaving high school. In short, this study clearly demonstrates that social class, as measured by SES (parents' university education in this study), continues to matter. In fact, it matters a great deal. So choose your parents carefully!

Class matters as a result of "streaming" into academic and non-academic programs in high school. It matters because of the different educational and occupational aspirations of teenagers from lower and higher SES families. It matters because more educated and affluent parents can provide more cultural capital, including knowledge of the post-secondary system and more financial support for their children. Ultimately, class matters the most because of the different post-secondary educational "choices" made by young people from more and less advantaged backgrounds since, in our credential-focused society, a university degree continues to be the prerequisite required to compete for most of the better-paying, higher-status, and often more satisfying types of employment.

If social class matters this much, should we, as members of society, do something to reduce these SES-based differences in education and career opportunity? If you begin with the premise that public policy interventions are always inappropriate, then your answer would be "no." Alternatively, you might argue that unequal educational and employment opportunities as a result of family background are unfair. You might also propose that an economy in which some potentially very talented people do not have equal opportunity to compete for the best jobs is an economy that is less productive than it could be. Both the fairness and the economic productivity arguments invite suggestions for public policy responses.

Having observed the impact of "streaming" in the high school system—and specifically the much higher probability of obtaining a university degree if one completes an academic high school program—we should look carefully at how high school programs are organized and how young students are channelled into them. On one hand, it is difficult to reject the argument that some young people may not have the ability or aptitude to complete highly challenging high school courses that lead to university entrance. High school programs that lead into non-university careers are a useful and important alternative. On the other hand, it is possible that some young people who could complete academic high school programs are not encouraged to try, or are even actively discouraged, perhaps because of cultural capital deficits.

High school counsellors and others involved in advising young people about educational and career choices need to be acutely conscious of the significant impacts they can have on students' futures. In addition, high school programs, both academic and non-academic, need to be designed in such a way that young people in them can continue to make choices. For example, several Canadian provinces have designed youth apprenticeship programs that allow high school students to apprentice for trades while still obtaining the high school credits needed for university entrance, should they decide to go that way in the future (Lehmann 2005).

The longitudinal survey data examined in this paper highlight a substantial class effect on occupational outcomes via post-secondary educational attainment. In other words, children of university-educated parents are much more likely to complete university themselves and, as a result, are more likely to obtain higher-status and more rewarding occupations. Greater access to cultural capital among middle-class youth is part of the explanation, but material capital—money—also plays an important role. Most of the Edmonton youth in this study had completed university by the late 1980s or early 1990s. As we might expect, many had taken out student loans, and many took years to pay back these loans. And, no doubt, many had relied heavily on parents to help finance their post-secondary education.

However, the cost to students of a university education in the late 1980s was relatively low compared with the situation today. In 1980, Canadian universities received only 13 per cent of their total revenue from students' tuition fees. By 1995, this had risen to 24 per cent (Little 1997: 2), and tuition fees have continued to rise steadily in almost all provinces since then. For example, by 2010–11, in Ontario, student tuition made up 44 per cent of universities' total operating costs (Macdonald and Shaker 2012). As tuition costs continue to increase across the country, universities and provincial governments are promising to put in place funding programs to assist the less advantaged to attend university and other post-secondary institutions. It remains to be seen whether these new sources of financial assistance will be sufficient and, furthermore, whether they will really be directed towards those who are most needy. If not, we can expect to see an even more pronounced impact of social class on educational and occupational attainment in the future. As we have observed, class already matters a great deal with respect to post-secondary education. Without appropriate policy interventions of the type discussed above, it may matter even more in the future.

Questions for Critical Thought

1. What are some of the key social and cultural factors that led to you attending college or university? Was your family's socio-economic status (SES) one of them?
2. Many post-secondary institutions across Canada are raising tuition rates, arguing that this is necessary to maintain high-quality education as provincial governments cut back on funding. What effect might this have on patterns of educational inequality in Canada? What other policy alternatives might be used to reduce the likelihood of growing educational inequality?
3. Aboriginal youth in Canada are among the least likely to complete college or university. What might explain this fact, and what might be done about this problem?
4. Larger proportions of Canadian youth are attending and completing university, but the numbers of jobs requiring university education are increasing less quickly. What are the implications of this trend for patterns of social inequality in Canada, and what, if anything, might be done about it?

Recommended Readings

Davies, Scott, and Neil Guppy. 2014. *The Schooled Society: An Introduction to the Sociology of Education*, 3rd edn. Toronto: Oxford University Press.

Lehmann, Wolfgang. 2007. *Choosing to Labour: School–Work Transitions and Social Class.* Montreal and Kingston: McGill-Queen's University Press.

Macdonald, David, and Erika Shaker. 2012. *Eduflation and the High Cost of Learning.* Ottawa: Canadian Centre for Policy Alternatives.

Wotherspoon, Terry, and Bernard Schissel. 2003. *The Legacy of School for Aboriginal People: Education, Oppression and Emancipation.* Toronto: Oxford University Press.

Recommended Websites

BC Teachers' Federation:
http://www.bctf.ca/PovertyResearch.aspx

Canadian Federation of Students:
http://cfs-fcee.ca/

People for Education:
http://www.peopleforeducation.ca/pfe-news/is-inequality-growing-in-canadas-public-schools/

The Wealth Paradox:
http://www.theglobeandmail.com/news/national/time-to-lead/our-time-to-lead-income-inequality/article15316231/

Notes

1. The author of this chapter has directed this study since 1985. Dr Graham S. Lowe (Professor Emeritus, Department of Sociology, University of Alberta) was co-principal investigator from

1985 until 2002. Dr Nancy Galambos (Professor of Psychology, University of Alberta) became co-principal investigator several years later. The initial study involved surveys of both high school and university graduates in three cities (Edmonton, Toronto, Sudbury). The Edmonton high school sample is the only component of the original study that has been tracked for 25 years (http://www.artsrn.ualberta.ca/transition). The Population Research Laboratory, Department of Sociology, University of Alberta, has been responsible for data collection and processing. The primary funding source has been the Social Sciences and Humanities Research Council of Canada (SSHRC), followed by the government of Alberta.

2. Since only 894 of the original 983 respondents provided their name and address for follow-up purposes back in 1985, the 2010 sample (N = 405) represented 45 per cent of the original respondents who could have participated.
3. Additional analysis of attrition bias in this longitudinal study indicates that female respondents were somewhat more likely to remain in the study from start to finish, as were 1985 respondents with higher educational aspirations.
4. Thirteen per cent of the sample members did not answer these questions (or respond to the 1986 follow-up survey when the question was first included).
5. Ten per cent of the 405 sample members (in 2010) did not answer these questions, presumably because they were unsure about how much education their parent(s) had acquired.
6. When we say that a difference between two groups is statistically significant, we mean that, with a sample of this size, the probability of differences this large occurring by chance alone is less than 5 per cent ($p < 0.05$).
7. Included in this category are about 5 per cent of the total sample who stated that they expected to complete one or two years of university.

References

Andres, Lesley, Paul Anisef, Harvey Krahn, Dianne Looker, and Victor Thiessen. 1999. "The persistence of social structure: Cohort, class, and gender effects on the occupational aspirations and expectations of Canadian youth." *Journal of Youth Studies* 2, 3: 261–82.

Beck, Ulrich. 1992. *Risk Society: Towards a New Modernity.* London: Sage.

Bell, Daniel. 1973. *The Coming of Post-Industrial Society.* New York: Basic Books.

Bourdieu, Pierre (R. Nice, trans.). 1986. "The forms of capital." In J.C. Richardson, ed., *Handbook of Theory and Research for the Sociology of Education*, pp. 241–58. New York: Greenwood Press.

Bukodi, Erzebet, and John Goldthorpe. 2013. "Decomposing 'social origins': The effects of parents' class, status, and education on the educational attainment of their children." *European Sociological Review* 29, 5: 1024–39.

Clark, Terry Nichols, and Seymour Martin Lipset. 1991. "Are social classes dying?" *International Sociology* 6: 397–410.

Davies, Scott, and Neil Guppy. 1997. "Fields of study, college selectivity, and student inequalities in higher education." *Social Forces* 75, 4: 1417–38.

Frenette, Marc, and Ping Ching Winnie Chan. 2015. "Academic outcomes of public and private high school students: What lies behind the differences?" Ottawa: Statistics Canada, Analytic Studies Branch, Catalogue no. 11F0019M-no. 367.

Giddens, Anthony. 1991. *Modernity and Self-Identity: Self and Society in the Late Modern Age.* Oxford: Polity Press.

Grabb, Edward G. 2007. *Theories of Social Inequality*, 5th edn. Toronto: Thomson Nelson.

Harris, J. 1997. "'Goodbye Dolly?' The ethics of human cloning." *Journal of Medical Ethics* 23, 6: 353–60.

Kalleberg, Arne. 2011. *Good Jobs, Bad Jobs: The Rise of Polarized and Precarious Employment Systems in the United States, 1970s to 2000s.* New York: Russell Sage Foundation.

King, Douglas E., and John A. Winterdyk. 2010. *Diversity, Inequality, and Canadian Justice.* Whitby, Ont.: de Sitter Publications.

Knighton, Tamara, and Sheba Mirza. 2002. "Post-secondary participation: The effect of parents' education and household income." *Educational Quarterly Review* 8, 3: 25–32.

Krahn, Harvey, and Nancy Galambos. 2014. "Work values and beliefs of 'Generation X' and 'Generation Y'." *Journal of Youth Studies* 17, 1: 92–112.

———, Karen D. Hughes, and Graham S. Lowe. 2015. *Work, Industry and Canadian Society*, 7th edn. Toronto: Nelson Education.

Lehmann, Wolfgang. 2005. "Choosing to labour: Structure and agency in school–work transitions." *Canadian Journal of Sociology* 30, 3: 325–50.

———. 2007. "'I just don't feel like I fit in': The role of habitus in university drop-out decisions." *Canadian Journal of Higher Education* 37, 2: 89–110.

———. 2014. "Habitus transformation and hidden injuries: Successful working-class university students." *Sociology of Education* 87, 1: 1–15.

Little, Don. 1997. "Financing universities: Why are students paying more?" *Education Quarterly Review* 4, 2: 10–26.

Macdonald, David, and Erika Shaker. 2012. *Eduflation and the High Cost of Learning*. Ottawa: Canadian Centre for Policy Alternatives.

Raphael, Dennis. 2011. *Poverty and Policy in Canada: Implications for Health and Quality of Life*, 2nd edn. Toronto: Canadian Scholars' Press.

Sullivan, Alice. 2001. "Cultural capital and educational attainment." *Sociology* 35: 893–912.

Tanner, Julian, Harvey Krahn, and Timothy F. Hartnagel. 1995. *Fractured Transitions from School to Work: Revisiting the Dropout Problem*. Toronto: Oxford University Press.

Taylor, Alison, and Harvey Krahn. 2009."Streaming in/for the new economy." In Cynthia Levine-Rasky, ed., *Canadian Perspectives on the Sociology of Education*. Toronto: Oxford University Press.

Turcotte, Martin. 2011. "Intergenerational education mobility: University completion in relation to parents' education level." *Canadian Social Trends* (Winter): 38–44.

Vosko, Leah, ed. 2005. *Precarious Employment: Understanding Labour Market Insecurity in Canada*. Montreal and Kingston: McGill-Queen's University Press.

Wertz, Dorothy C., and John C. Fletcher. 1998. "Ethical and social issues in prenatal sex selection: A survey of geneticists in 37 nations." *Social Science & Medicine* 46, 2: 255–73.

Wilkinson, Richard, and Kate Pickett. 2010. *The Spirit Level: Why Equality Is Better for Everyone*. London: Penguin Books.

C. Education

8 Educational Attainment among Canadians: Open and Competitive or Closed and Sponsored?

Nicole Malette and Neil Guppy

Introduction

Experience in the education system shapes your future. Education is important for honing skills and abilities. These influence your occupational attainment—whether you achieve good or bad jobs—and your mobility either up or down the distribution of inequality. In contrast to societies with little mobility, where people's fates are determined at birth (e.g., an inflexible caste system), more open societies like Canada allow people the chance to alter their position in the hierarchy of inequality, based on success or failure in schooling.

However, for education to influence upward and downward mobility, it is also important that schooling is fair and neutral, i.e., that it promotes equality of educational opportunity. Children from all backgrounds should have about the same likelihood of moving up or down the inequality hierarchy, independent of their family origins. Put simply, people's adult destinations (e.g., job, income, residence) should be at most only modestly related to their origins. If adult destinations are determined primarily by childhood background, then success is closed to most, and the children of well-placed elites have sponsored access to a prosperous future. In that case, the education system merely acts to reproduce and legitimate existing inequalities.

Considerable research suggests that, on some dimensions, personal background matters less today in shaping educational destinations than it did previously, but, on other dimensions, background is still quite important. In this chapter we provide supporting evidence that, for women and many ethnic groups, educational attainment is much more equally distributed than it once was. However, regarding social class or socio-economic background (terms that we use interchangeably), there has been virtually no change over time. This is also true for Indigenous Peoples, with Aboriginal educational success remaining low. Therefore, education still serves to reproduce class and ancestral inequality, even though it now contributes to a fairer distribution of outcomes for women and some ethnic and racial minorities.

Educational Attainment by Socio-economic Background

Young people spend more time in school now than in the past. Average years of schooling have increased and high school dropout rates have diminished. But averages can deceive. For example, averages conceal differences in years of schooling or dropout rates for people with different class backgrounds. Parental education, income, and occupation are good indicators of class background, and they all strongly influence children's school success. Furthermore, the educational inequality resulting from this relationship has persisted in Canada and most other Western nations (Blossfeld and Shavit 1993; Wanner 1999). Rather than more openness and equality of opportunity, the evidence suggests the social reproduction of inequality. Thus, over generations, education does little to alter the position of family members along the hierarchy of inequality.

Figure 8.1 provides recent Canadian evidence demonstrating this pattern. For individuals whose parents did not hold a university degree, the likelihood of attending university is less than one in four (17.2 per cent in 2000, and 23.0 per cent in 2009). However, among those that had even one parent who attended university, the likelihood of attending university is about one in two (51.1 per cent in 2000, and 55.8 per cent in 2009). The probability of pursuing a university degree is more than twice as high for people with one parent who attended university, compared to those whose parents did not study beyond high school.

The patterns in Figure 8.1 undermine any strong sense that education is a great equalizer for Canadians from disadvantaged class backgrounds. In addition, differences in the success rates of students from private versus public schools are almost entirely due to the advantaged class backgrounds of private-school students, and not something special about the networks or education that private schools provide (Frenette and Chan 2015). Some evidence does suggest, however, that in Canada post-secondary access is more equitably distributed across classes than in the US (Frenette 2005).

Many possible explanations could underlie the strong link between the education levels of parents and children, including differences in family structure, ethnic composition, work ethic, or academic achievement. However, even when these other factors are taken into account, the strong class-based parent–child link persists.

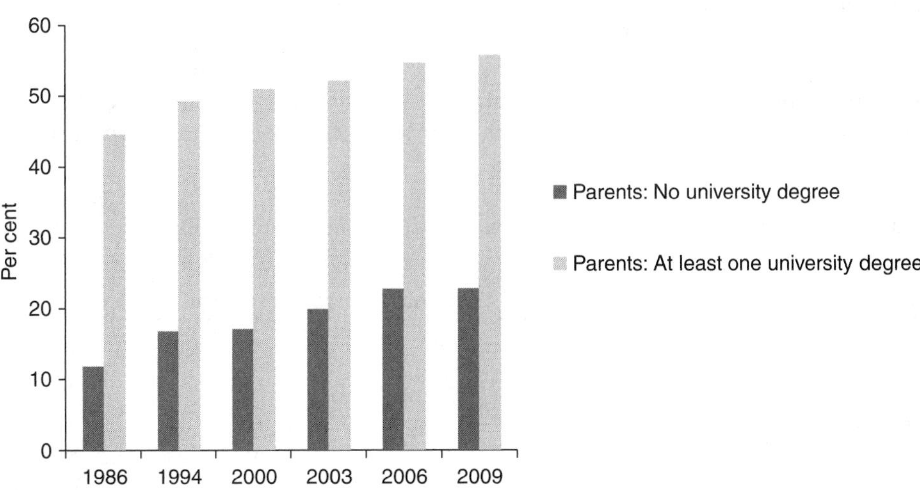

Figure 8.1 Percentage of People Aged 25–39 Who Hold a University Degree, by Parental Education, 1986–2009

Source: Adapted from Turcotte (2011).

Using definitions slightly different from those in Figure 8.1, Finnie et al. (2005: 22) state that "the relative university attendance rates for those whose parents have a high school diploma and those with at least some university education are 29 versus 53 percent in the case of men, and 37 versus 65 percent for women," controlling for other factors.

Hertzman (2000: 14) has argued persuasively that the higher educational attainment among children of more educated parents represents a "socio-economic gradient." As people move up the gradient—along dimensions of education, income, or wealth, for example—the children of families of higher socio-economic status generally attain higher education.

Four important factors underlie this gradient. First, it represents a causal linkage between family background and educational attainment. No matter how many other factors are taken into account (e.g., ethnicity, region, family structure), the effect of socio-economic level on educational attainment persists. Second, the gradient is robust across different measures of education; for example, if instead of university attendance we look at high school dropouts, we find that parents' education has a causal influence on high school completion rates. Third, the linkage between family origin and school attainment is robust across different measures of socio-economic status or social class (e.g., comparing working, middle, and upper classes, or comparing people by family income level). Finally, the gradient persists across time and place: it has endured for generations and in all industrial countries, although its steepness varies both cross-nationally and historically.

Another way to understand this gradient is to consider the skills and abilities children bring with them to their first days of schooling. Children's readiness to learn is influenced by their home and neighbourhood environments, which are in turn linked to family socio-economic status. Verdon (2007) has shown that, among five-year-old children, family income was positively related to differences in readiness to learn, as measured by vocabulary, communication skills, knowledge of numbers, copying and using symbols, attention, and co-operative play.

Table 8.1 shows a final way to understand the gradient. Using data from Statistics Canada's Youth in Transition Survey, Krahn and Taylor (2007) examined the options open to Grade 10 students for post-secondary study. Taking the right English, mathematics, and science courses was critical for college and university admission. These researchers found that family income influences the likelihood that students choose such courses in their early high school years. In Ontario, for example, only 49 per cent of Grade 10 students from families with annual incomes below $30,000 were enrolled in high school courses that permitted enrolment

Table 8.1 Percentage of Grade 10 Students with Post-secondary Access Options Open, by Family Income and Province, 2000

Family Income	British Columbia	Alberta	Saskatchewan	Ontario
Less than $30,000	59	50	83	49
$30,000 to $44,999	60	52	83	52
$45,000 to $59,999	60	53	88	59
$60,000 to $74,999	70	56	93	65
$75,000 to $89,999	69	62	89	70
$90,000 or more	73	68	89	73
Total	66	59	87	64

Source: Krahn and Taylor (2007).

in post-secondary programs. Among students in families with incomes of $90,000 or more, the corresponding figure was 73 per cent (see also Chapter 7 in this volume).

In summary, evidence consistently shows that educational attainment in Canada differs systematically by social class or socio-economic status. Moreover, this distribution of educational inequality shows no sign of significant change in recent decades.

Educational Attainment by Gender

Reporting in 1970, Canada's Royal Commission on the Status of Women argued that "education opens the door to almost every life goal. Wherever women are denied equal access to education, they cannot be said to have equality" (1970: 161). At that time, far fewer women than men were advancing to higher education, but this pattern has changed. By 1982 more women than men were earning undergraduate degrees. The women's movement and greater female labour force participation were critical factors explaining these changes. Now, as Figure 8.2 shows, more women than men are earning both undergraduate and master's degrees, with the gender gap at the Ph.D. level also narrowing substantially.

What explains this change in university attendance rates by women over the last half-century? The key answers lie in women's higher scholastic achievements relative to men (both in school grades and on standardized tests), women's study habits and school engagement, and parental expectations (Frenette and Zeman 2007). Another factor is that high-paying jobs are more plentiful for men who lack university credentials than for women with the same education, especially in resource-rich provinces (Guppy and Luongo 2015).

However, while more women than men attain undergraduate degrees today, women are still under-represented in science, technology, engineering, mathematics, and computer sciences (STEM) (Hango 2013). Previous studies sought to understand why women are less likely

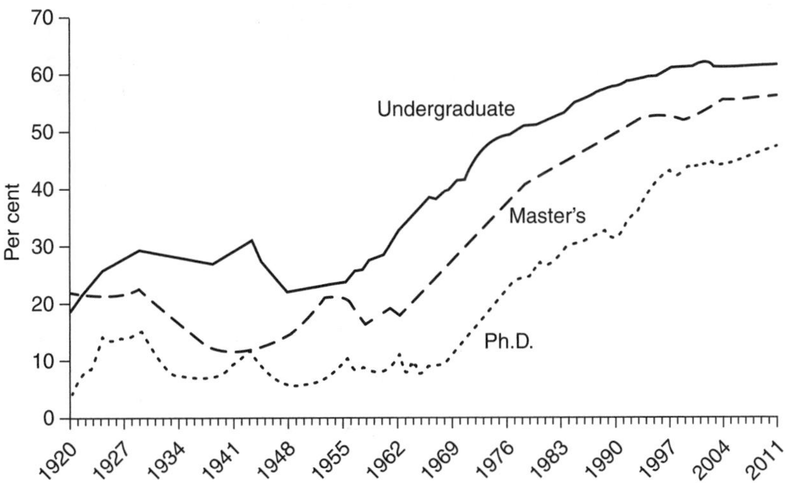

Figure 8.2 Percentage of Women Receiving Undergraduate, Master's, and Ph.D. Degrees, 1920–2011

Sources: Statistics Canada, CANSIM Table 477-0020 for 1992 to 2011; *Education in Canada*, selected years for 1975 to 1991; *Historical Statistics* for 1920–74.

than their male counterparts to enter and complete STEM university programs. Some studies suggest that the gender gap is a by-product of different social values (OECD 2012; Kane and Mertz 2012), while others argue for differences in mathematical ability (Summers 2005). Recent work by Darcy Hango (2013) has demonstrated that young women with high mathematic abilities are significantly less likely to enter STEM fields than young men, even for men with lower levels of mathematic ability. These outcomes suggest that the gender gap in STEM fields is not due to differential ability, but perhaps reflects various social influences (Villar and Guppy 2015).

Overall, schools are now places where traditional gender roles have been challenged and changed. Indeed, Arnot, David, and Weiner (1999: 150) call these changes "one of the most extensive inversions of social inequality in contemporary times." The labour market and associated workplaces are far more segregated and gendered than are schools. Certainly, some gender segregation and stereotyping still occur in schooling, but the massive changes within the education system should not be ignored. When the report of the Royal Commission on the Status of Women was published in 1970, women were a minority in both medical schools and law schools, but now they comprise the majority in both medicine and law programs. The greater representation of women in these professional schools is symptomatic of the massive changes in educational attainment by gender.

Educational Attainment by Ancestry, Ethnicity, and Race

One approach to examining educational attainment by ethnicity is to contrast educational outcomes for young people from visible minority and non-visible minority backgrounds. Table 8.2 summarizes evidence on this question from Shaienks and Gluszynski (2007). Their findings show that, among those aged 24–26, the likelihood of having attended any post-secondary institution was higher for people with visible minority backgrounds (87 per cent) than for those with non-visible minority backgrounds (78 per cent). University attendance was also higher for visible minority Canadians (62 per cent) than for non-visible minority Canadians (49 per cent).

Another approach to the question of whether educational attainment is unevenly distributed by ethnicity or race is to examine the educational experiences of children born in families who immigrated to Canada, as opposed to children born into families of Canadian residents (i.e., non-immigrants). Both McMullen (2004) and Worswick (2004) have shown that while children from immigrant families are more likely to start school with less developed educational abilities, especially in reading and writing, rapid gains by immigrant children in the early years mean that the performances of immigrant and Canadian-born students converge fairly quickly. Although the educational

Table 8.2 Post-secondary Participation Rates of Canadians Aged 24 to 26, by Visible Minority Status, December 2005

	Participation Rate	Type of Post-secondary Institution Attended		
	Attended Post-secondary	University	College/CEGEP	Other Type of Post-secondary
Visible minority	87	62	27	11
Not visible minority	78	49	34	17

Source: Shaienks and Gluszynski (2007).

system cannot take all the credit for this pattern, the convergence is good evidence that the experiences in school of immigrant children are positive for developing key scholastic abilities (see also Guppy and Lyon 2012).

The comparisons so far are imprecise in one way. By creating two broad dichotomies—visible minority and others—the comparisons lump together many different groups, implying that the experiences of all people identified as visible minorities are similar. For example, the visible minority category includes people from China and the West Indies, yet the experiences of young people from these two groups are very different (Abada and Tenkorang 2009; Lyon et al. 2014). However, the finding that visible minority status is not an impediment to schooling in Canada is not eclipsed, despite these variations in the experiences of different minority groups.

First Nations Peoples, who are not considered as part of the "visible minority" category by the Canadian government, continue to be haunted by the legacy of residential schooling, which led to generations of children being wrenched from their families and communities and shipped to boarding schools. While many individuals from First Nations backgrounds have been very successful, as judges (Alfred Scow), physicians (Nadine Caron), musicians and educators (Buffy Sainte-Marie), or playwrights (Tomson Highway), people from Aboriginal backgrounds have generally experienced much lower levels of schooling than have other Canadians.

Figure 8.3 shows high school completion rates for young people aged 20–24 in 2006. Among the non-Aboriginal population, 88 per cent of young people completed high school, compared to 60 per cent for Aboriginal people. Figure 8.3 also demonstrates that completion rates vary systematically among Aboriginal Peoples, with Métis more likely to graduate (75 per cent), than either First Nations (52 per cent) or Inuit youth (40 per cent). Region of residence is one factor explaining this variation: Inuit live in the more remote Arctic and Métis tend to live in urban centres. However, the colonial legacy remains a crucial factor for First Nations Peoples, who were subjected to residential schooling. By 2011, the National Household Survey, which for this year replaced the long-form census, showed that 38 per cent of Aboriginal people had some post-secondary experience, compared to 55 per cent of non-Aboriginal people (Fong and Gulati 2013).

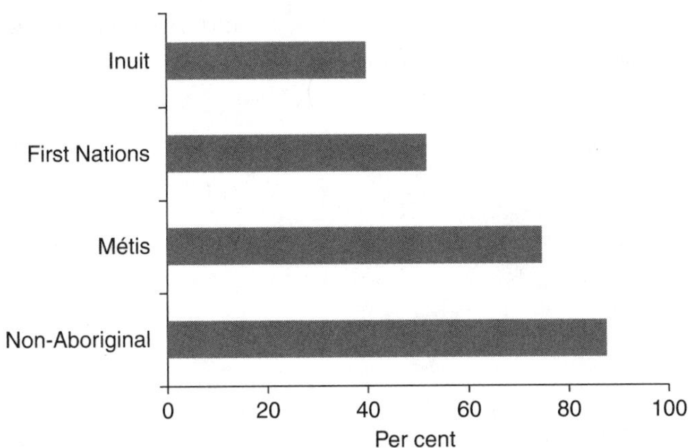

Figure 8.3 Percentage of People Aged 20–24 Graduating from High School, by Aboriginal/Non-Aboriginal Status

Source: Authors' calculation from 2006 Canadian census data.

Conclusion

Post-secondary schooling has increased in Canada, and a proliferation of credentials are now offered, including certificates, diplomas, and degrees granted by colleges, institutes, and universities. The value of these credentials for labour market outcomes, including employment security and income level, varies enormously, e.g., between a medical degree from an elite university and a child-care diploma from a small community college. Thus, we now see far more diversity in post-secondary credentials, with the value differing both by field of study and by type of institution (Davies and Guppy 2014). Individuals who are privileged enough to earn credentials from higher-ranked post-secondary institutions and degrees in the "right" field of study are likely to enjoy a leg up for economic success, while less advantaged people are more likely to struggle.

Clearly, education has important consequences for the lives of Canadians (see Davies and Guppy 2014 for a fuller discussion). Among students who drop out of high school, finding sustainable, good-paying work is apt to be very difficult over the life course. Among students who graduate from law or medical school, on the other hand, secure and well-paid employment is much easier to attain. In Canada today, children from different social classes still have quite different likelihoods of dropping out of school or attaining professional educational credentials. For women, school attainment is now much more equitably distributed than in previous generations. School success is also a reality for members of many immigrant and visible minority groups. Unfortunately, this pattern is far less evident among Aboriginal Peoples and those from disadvantaged class backgrounds. For these two groups, in particular, schooling remains comparatively more closed and less accessible than for other Canadians.

Questions for Critical Thought

1. Are too many young people going to university? Could it be argued, persuasively, that we should restrict access to university more, and encourage more young people to pursue training in colleges and institutes where more practical skills development is stressed?
2. If public policy were to be introduced to reduce the social reproduction of inequality that arises via education, what would be the two or three most effective policy interventions?
3. How might education change in future decades to either reinforce or erode the inequality of education that currently exists in Canada and other industrialized countries?
4. The authors show that educational attainment among most visible minorities is as high as, or even higher than, attainment among non-visible minority backgrounds. However, Aboriginal and Black students struggle to attain post-secondary degrees. Is it possible to reconcile these findings?

Recommended Readings

Davies, Scott, and Neil Guppy 2014. *The Schooled Society: An Introduction to the Sociology of Education*, 3rd edn. Toronto: Oxford University Press.

Lehmann, Wolfgang. 2015. "Habitus transformation and hidden injuries: Successful working-class university students." *Sociology of Education* 87, 1: 1–15.

Sadovnik, Alan, Peter Cookson, and Susan Semel. 2013. *Exploring Education: An Introduction to the Foundations of Education*. New York: Routledge.

Wotherspoon, Terry. 2015. *The Sociology of Education in Canada: Critical Perspectives*, 4th edn. Toronto: Oxford University Press.

Recommended Websites

Canadian Education Association:
http://www.cea-ace.ca/

Canadian Teachers' Federation:
http://www.ctf-fce.ca/en/

Council of Ministers of Education:
http://www.cmec.ca/en/

Statistics Canada:
http://www.statcan.gc.ca/

References

Abada, Teresa, and Eric Y. Tenkorang. 2009. "Pursuit of university education among the children of immigrants in Canada: The roles of parental human capital and social capital." *Journal of Youth Studies* 12, 2: 185–207.

Arnot, Madeleine, Miriam David, and Gaby Weiner. 1999. *Closing the Gender Gap: Postwar Education and Social Change*. Cambridge: Polity Press.

Blossfeld, H.P., and Y. Shavit. 1993. *Persistent Inequality: Changing Educational Attainment in Thirteen Countries*. Boulder, Colo.: Westview Press.

Davies, Scott, and Neil Guppy. 2014. *The Schooled Society: An Introduction to the Sociology of Education*, 3rd edn. Toronto: Oxford University Press.

Finnie, Ross, Eric Lascelles, and Arthur Sweetman. 2005. "Who goes? The direct and indirect effects of family background on access to post-secondary education." Statistics Canada, Analytical Studies Branch Research Paper Series, Catalogue no. 11F0019MIE No. 237.

Fong, Frances, and Sonya Gulati. 2013. *Employment and Education among Aboriginal Peoples*. Toronto: TD Economics, Special Report.

Frenette, Marc. 2005. "Is post-secondary access more equitable in Canada or the United States?" Statistics Canada, Analytical Studies Branch Research Paper Series, Catalogue no. 11F0019MIE No. 244.

——— and Ping Ching Winnie Chan. 2015. *Academic Outcomes of Public and Private High School Students: What Lies Behind the Difference*. Ottawa: Statistics Canada, Catalogue no. 11F0019M No. 367.

——— and Klarka Zeman. 2007. "Why are most university students women? Evidence based on academic performance, study habits and parental influences." Statistics Canada, Analytical Studies Branch Research Paper Series, Catalogue no. 11F0019MIE No. 303.

Guppy, Neil, and Katherine Lyon. 2012. "Multiculturalism, education practices, and colonial legacies: The Canadian case." In Christos Kassimeris and Marios Vryonides, eds, *The Politics of Education: Challenging Multiculturalism*, pp. 114–35. London: Routledge.

——— and Nicole Luongo. 2015. "The rise and stall of Canada's gender-equity revolution." *Canadian Review of Sociology* 52, 3: 241–65.

Hango, Darcy. 2013. "Gender differences in science, technology, engineering, mathematics and computer science (STEM) programs at university." *Insights on Canadian Society*. Ottawa: Statistics Canada, Catalogue no. 75-006-X.

Hertzman, Clyde. 2000. "The case for an early childhood development strategy" ISUMA (Autumn): 11–18.

Kane, Jonathan, and Janet Mertz. 2011. "Debunking myths about gender and mathematics performance." *Notices of the AMS* 59, 1: 10–21.

Krahn, Harvey, and Alison Taylor. 2007. "'Streaming' in the 10th grade in four Canadian provinces in 2000." *Education Matters: Insights on Education, Learning and Training in Canada* 4, 2. Statistics Canada, Catalogue no. 81-004-XIE.

Lyon, Katherine, Helene Frohard-Dourlent, Paul Fripp, and Neil Guppy. 2014. "Canada." In Peter Stevens and Gary Dworkin, eds, *The Palgrave Handbook of Race and Ethnic Inequalities in Education*, 170–204. Basingstoke: Palgrave Macmillan.

McMullen, Kathryn. 2004. "Children of immigrants: How well do they do in school?" *Education Matters: Insights on Education, Learning and Training in Canada* 1, 2. Statistics Canada, Catalogue no. 81-004-XIE.

Organisation for Economic Co-operation and Development. 2012. *Closing the Gender Gap: Act Now.* Paris. OECD, p. 352.

Royal Commission on the Status of Women. 1970. *Report of the Royal Commission on the Status of Women in Canada* Ottawa: Information Canada.

Shaienks, Danielle, and Tomasz Gluszynski. 2007. "Participation in postsecondary education: Graduates, continuers and drop outs—results from YITS Cycle 4." Statistics Canada Research Paper, Catalogue no. 81-595-MIE No. 059.

Summers, Lawrence. 2005. "Remarks at NBER Conference on Diversifying the Science and Engineering Workforce, 14 Jan. Cambridge, Mass., Harvard University.

Turcotte, Martin. 2011. "Intergenerational education mobility: University completion in relation to parents' education level." *Canadian Social Trends* (24 Aug.): 37–43. Statistics Canada Catalogue no. 11-008-X.

Verdon, Lisa. 2007. "Are 5-year-old children ready to learn at school? Family income and home environment contexts." *Education Matters: Insights on Education, Learning and Training in Canada* 4, 1. Statistics Canada, Catalogue no. 81-004-XIE.

Villar, Paz, and Neil Guppy. 2015. "Gendered science: Representational dynamics in science textbooks over the last half century." *Canadian Journal of Education* 38, 3.

Wanner, Richard. 1999. "Expansion and ascription: Trends in educational opportunity in Canada, 1920–1994." *Canadian Review of Sociology and Anthropology* 36: 409–42.

Worswick, Christopher. 2004. "Adaptation and inequality: Children of immigrants in Canadian schools." *Canadian Journal of Economics* 37, 1: 53–77.

9 Changing Times, Stubborn Inequalities: Explaining Socio-economic Stratification in Canadian Schooling

Scott Davies, Vicky Maldonado, and Darren Cyr

Introduction

Schools are a central arena for social inequality, where children compete from early ages and eventually are sifted and sorted into stratified career paths. Social scientists have long demonstrated that socio-economic background strongly shapes students' educational success, from early primary school to post-graduate studies. Generally, poor or working-class youth fare less well than their more affluent peers, whether measured by standardized test scores, high school completion rates, or university attendance. Within any socio-economic category, there has always been a range of outcomes, so that thousands of underprivileged youths have enjoyed success in Canadian schools. On average, however, aggregate disparities across socio-economic strata have been remarkably durable over the past half-century. Indeed, this repeated pattern across time and space may be as close as sociologists have come to discovering a scientific law.

This chapter seeks to explain these durable patterns. We review trends in Canadian educational attainment, and provide an explanatory framework based on both classic and recent theories. Sociologists have proposed various cultural and structural forces that, in their view, hinder the educational expectations and academic success of working-class youth (Duncan and Murnane 2011; Karabel and Halsey 1977; Reardon 2014; in Canada, see Anisef 1974; Davies and Guppy 2013; Murphy 1979; Porter, Porter, and Blishen 1979). We prioritize Canadian research, but also draw on influential international studies from Britain and the US, where the patterns are fairly similar.

Recent Trends in Educational Attainment

A striking trend over the past five decades has been higher school attainment for Canadians from all walks of life. A century ago, higher education was mainly the preserve of the elite, with only 5 to 10 per cent of people attending universities or colleges. By 2008, 64 per cent of young Canadians had completed some form of post-secondary education (Shaienks and Glusynski 2009; Statistics Canada 2011). Consequently, most young adults, regardless of social origin, now possess more school credentials than their parents or grandparents (Corak et al. 2003). This Canadian trend parallels a broader pattern throughout much of the globe (Baker 2013; Schofer and Meyer 2005). About one-quarter of the population aged 25 to 64 has a university degree, making Canada one of the world's most highly educated societies (OECD 2013).

Canadians from all socio-economic backgrounds now attend some form of post-secondary schooling (Finnie, Lascelles, and Sweetman 2005). College or university education is increasingly the norm, even among the disadvantaged, and more than 80 per cent of Canadian parents, even from the lowest income and educational categories, expect their children to go to college or university (Davies 2005).

Equally striking, however, is the durability of educational inequality. While all strata now achieve more years of schooling, the gap between the more and less affluent persists because increases in attainment among advantaged youth have kept pace with increases among the less advantaged. The gap is apparent using various indicators at the primary, secondary, and post-secondary levels. For preschool children, socio-economic gaps appear on several cognitive measures. Those from low-income households are four times more likely to experience delays in vocabulary development than are more affluent children (Farkas and Hibel 2008). Elementary schools with larger proportions of students living in affluent and stable neighbourhoods fare much better on standardized tests (Johnson 2007). Teenagers with university-educated parents score considerably higher on reading, mathematics, and science tests (Willms 2002; Statistics Canada 2005). About 50 per cent of youth from the top income quartile of families attended university, but only 31 per cent from the bottom quartile did so (Dooley, Payne, and Robb 2009). Moreover, university attendance among students from the highest income quartile has steadily risen since 2002, while attendance among the three lowest income quartiles has stagnated (Deller and Oldford 2011). Even for students with comparable skill levels and grades, youth from higher socio-economic origins are more likely to finish high school, enter higher education, and attend higher-ranked universities (Radford 2013; Davies, Maldonado, and Zarifa 2014).

These trends have continued despite decades of educational expansion and reform, and are found in many nations beyond Canada (Shavit et al. 2007). How can we explain this persistent inequality in an era of rising attainment?

A Framework for Explaining Disparities

We organize the literature into three parts, highlighting the roles of resources, contexts, and expectations. "Resources" are tangible possessions (i.e., finances) or personal attributes (i.e., skills) that offer advantages in school competitions. "Contexts" are characteristics of schools and neighbourhoods that can influence attainment over and above resources. Finally, "expectations" are the processes by which people make educational decisions. The latter concept aligns with a lengthy theoretical tradition that seeks to understand how individuals convert social structure into social action, and by which social action aggregates into concrete social structures (see van den Berg 1998).

Resources

The most elemental explanation for socio-economic disparities in school concerns economic resources. Years ago, Porter et al. (1979) concluded that "money matters" in education, even though K–12 public schools charge no tuition. Finding clear differences in school attainment for children from different income categories, Porter et al. reasoned that effective school performance often requires additional costs, whether for books and other learning materials, trips to museums and galleries, or perhaps private tutors. More importantly, post-secondary institutions charge tuition. Porter et al. found that, even controlling for their academic ability, students' socio-economic background affected their decisions to attend university (Porter et al. 1979). Further, most private schools, which are unaffordable for lower-income families, outperform public schools in sending most of their graduates to universities, but these advantages apparently arise mainly because of the higher socio-economic origins of students attending private schools (Frenette and Chan 2015).

Another factor is variation in the quality of public schooling across neighbourhoods. While Canadian data are not conclusive, American students from more affluent neighbourhoods experience higher achievement, net of their family resources, probably because their schools enjoy superior resources and attract better teachers (Duncan and Murnane 2011). While it has been difficult for researchers to demonstrate that superior school resources directly raise learning outcomes, better-funded schools may nurture an environment that enhances the academic climate and students' expectations.

Nevertheless, for several reasons, the role of money did not figure strongly in classic explanations of education disparities. Socio-economic gaps in student performance appear from the earliest primary grades, before most families are required to pay tuition fees or bear additional school expenses. Most Canadian high school students who take part-time jobs have done so not out of dire necessity, but for extra disposable income. For much of the post–World War II era, Canada's post-secondary tuition fees were relatively affordable, while nations like Great Britain, France, and Australia, which had abolished these fees, still had comparable (or worse) socio-economic inequalities in university participation. Furthermore, researchers have long found that parental education is a better predictor of various student outcomes than is parental income. While financial resources—whether used for tuition, transportation, or private tutors, or to avoid part-time work—affect school outcomes, they do not fully determine student success. Therefore, classic studies usually sought non-material explanations of educational disparities.

Many sociologists have considered cultural forces and the structure of schooling. One focus is children's informal learning within their families. Researchers have discussed how more educated parents provide their children with "human capital"—basic reading, writing, and vocabulary skills, along with disciplined work habits—that bring distinct advantages in school. Several classic studies showed that exposure to reading material in households, for instance, improved the chances of a student completing high school and attending university (reviewed in Sewell and Hauser 1980). More recent research has confirmed that socio-economic disparities in cognitive skills can be detected among students from the earliest school years (Farkas and Hibel 2008; Janus and Duku 2007). Among older age categories, socio-economic gaps in literacy appear to *widen* during the summer months, when children are not in school (Davies and Aurini 2013; Downey et al. 2004), and these gaps have been shown to predict eventual socio-economic disparities in high school completion and university attendance (Alexander, Entwisle, and Olson 2007). A key conclusion from such research is that children's experiences during school time are actually more equal than their experiences during non-school time in their homes and neighbourhoods. This equalizing effect of school influences not only learning opportunities, but also extracurricular activities and exposure to disorder, crime, and violence (e.g., Bennett et al. 2012; Cyr 2014; Paulle 2013). These studies suggest that schools in dangerous neighbourhoods can be "oases" that temporarily shield youth from the harsher conditions outside school.

Do youth from higher socio-economic origins enjoy other cultural advantages? Some sociologists have focused on cultural aesthetics as another type of family resource. "Cultural capital," the signature concept of the French sociologist, Pierre Bourdieu (Bourdieu and Passeron 1990), refers to the possession of sophisticated (as opposed to merely competent) conversational abilities and tastes for literature and the arts. Writing from Paris between the 1970s and 1990s,

Bourdieu contended that schools reward children who possess a certain type of cultural sophistication that is less often found in the working class. Schools, he reasoned, borrow their styles of speech, dress, and cultural references from the professional middle class. Teachers were seen to value the aesthetic sensibilities and vocabularies possessed by middle-class children, yet "misrecognized" those cultural styles as badges of intelligence and natural ability. Essentially, Bourdieu argued that socio-economic disparities in education stemmed from the tendency of schools to reward middle-class culture.

To test this theory, sociologists have attempted to correlate school outcomes with various indicators of cultural capital, such as whether students have attended art galleries or museums, are familiar with the works of famous authors and artists, or have engaged in various extracurricular lessons. On the whole, however, these studies suggest that the link between cultural capital and class background is not exactly as Bourdieu imagines. Some find that possessing cultural capital per se does not boost school performance or teacher evaluations; instead, teachers simply reward literacy skills and good work habits (see Goldthorpe 2007; Kingston 2001). Moreover, not all middle-class youth participate in high-status culture—far from it—and not all working-class children are excluded from this culture (Kingston 2001). Finally, it is difficult to argue that North American school curricula simply mirror upper middle-class culture, as Bourdieu contended in the French context.

Partly responding to this research, Lareau (2011) suggests that middle-class cultural advantages lie not in their aesthetic dimensions, but instead in their superior knowledge of school requirements and their ability to develop competitive strategies that facilitate academic success. She suggests that successful middle-class parents "activate" their resources through their knowledge of school processes and how to intervene effectively on behalf of their children. Several studies inspired by Lareau's work suggest that, in recent decades, highly educated parents, despite being employed for longer hours, are spending more time on educational activities with their children, producing a growing socio-economic gap in home learning resources (Aurini et al. 2016; Duncan and Murnane 2011; Schaub 2015).

Another line of research on cultural capital highlights the importance of actually "activating" these resources (Looker 1994). Exposing children to music, art galleries, and world travel may offer potential advantages, but that potential must be actualized through strategic action (Aurini et al. 2016). For instance, many Asian-American immigrant parents possess little cultural capital in Bourdieu's sense (e.g., English-language skills, dominant aesthetics, or directly intervening at schools), but strongly push their children towards academics while continually monitoring their children's homework and school performance (Jimenez and Horowitz 2013). Furthermore, children themselves need to activate their capital. McCrory-Calarco (2014) found in elementary schools that middle-class children, who themselves were products of intensive parenting, activated their capital by making far more requests for teachers' help than did working-class children, and so were more successful at eliciting assistance.

Contexts

Notwithstanding these family resources, how do surrounding contexts affect school attainment? While at one level, motivation is an individual, idiosyncratic matter, individual effort does not occur in a social vacuum but in broader social contexts. The formal structure of schools, along with informal relationships among students, teachers, parents, and neighbours, can channel an individual's actions.

One key aspect of school structure is the practice of streaming. In Canada, as in many countries, working-class youth are more likely than their middle-class counterparts to be streamed into less challenging, terminal high school programs (Krahn and Taylor 2007). The very existence of streaming systems, critics contend, disadvantages working-class students (Clanfield et al. 2014). These youth arguably would fare better in a non-streamed high school environment offering the same curricula and expectations; instead, enrolment in lower tracks steers students to less challenging work, lowering their expectations and aspirations. Fatalistic frames of reference are reinforced, as opportunities to rise in school and learn are limited. The incentives of available jobs and/or impending domestic roles, when combined with streaming, lead these youth to perceive school as irrelevant to their future roles in life.

"De-streaming" movements have emerged that seek to abolish differential groups, mixing students of all abilities. In the early 1990s, Ontario removed streams in Grade 9 and planned eventually to phase out all streaming. However, the government ended the experiment for several reasons, especially teacher complaints about the practical difficulties of teaching students with heterogeneous abilities. Nevertheless, de-streaming could ease class disparities in schooling, if practical problems associated with student heterogeneity can be overcome.

Streaming highlights a larger question: how does the complexity of school systems shape attainment? Even when students from humble origins have high aspirations and are academically gifted, the complex and numerous post-secondary options they have can sometimes impede their success. Choosing among the many community colleges and universities, the various types of degrees, and the wide variety of programs available within any institution can be a daunting task.

Making wise choices and maximizing their benefits requires individuals to understand how the system operates, as they navigate through a maze of programs and institutions. Decades ago, Boudon (1974) reasoned that such navigational savvy is held disproportionately by students from middle-class origins, so that more complex educational systems tend to generate more socio-economic disparities in schooling outcomes. In keeping with Boudon's argument, research suggests that, in nations with more differentiated and complex secondary structures, schools have a significant influence on student aspirations, whereas, in nations with less complex systems, families and peers are more influential (Buchmann and Dalton 2002). By international standards, Canadian K–12 schooling is not particularly hierarchical (Kerckhoff 2001). The large majority of Canadians attend comprehensive secondary schools, rather than purely academic institutions (e.g., British grammar schools) or purely vocational schools (e.g., Germany's *Hauptschulen*). Streaming in Canadian schools starts relatively late, and our provincial systems offer many opportunities for high school dropouts to re-enter schooling. Access to post-secondary education is more equitable in Canada than in the US, for example (Frenette 2005), perhaps because the US has a larger private system and an astonishing variety of institutions. Nevertheless, while the Canadian system offers broader opportunities for working-class youth, informal processes can create advantages for middle-class youth, who may have superior information or knowledge about the academic marketplace, which fields offer lucrative rewards, and how to find competitive advantages.

Research on streaming and school structures has been complemented by a broader strand of theorizing about "neighbourhood effects." This literature emphasizes that children's school attainment is influenced by surrounding circumstances that are independent of personal and family characteristics. Communities can generate social capital (Coleman 1988) by forging norms of reciprocity and mutual obligation among parents, youth, and schools; such norms breed strong bonds of trust, co-operation, and mutual respect, and channel students' motivation and effort. In contrast, disadvantaged communities can foster less commitment to educational goals. Research shows that advantaged neighbourhoods produce superior educational outcomes, net of other family resources (Boyle et al. 2007; Cyr 2014); this effect can even aid working-class students who attend schools in such neighbourhoods, presumably because these students are exposed to an enriched academic environment, to high-status role models, and to aspiring peers. Conversely, children in crime-stricken neighbourhoods can be diverted from school-sponsored activities because of worries about daily survival and safety (Paulle 2013). Schools with unhealthy social climates tend to lower student motivation, heighten disengagement and frustration, and ultimately lessen achievement (Cyr 2014).

Expectations

Because our consumer-driven, success-striving society encourages people to pursue the "North American dream" of a prestigious, well-paying job, almost everyone "values" education in an abstract sense. Through surveys, interviews, or policy statements, virtually all Canadians place great importance on education. However, expressing an appreciation for education is one thing; converting desires into reality is another.

The process by which educational desires become firm and motivating expectations is the bridge between their resources and their surrounding social contexts. We develop expectations by comparing ourselves to similar people, aligning our aspirations and efforts accordingly. Significant others shape our frames of reference for the jobs and lifestyle we want and the role school plays in our desires. For instance, when asked what they want to be when they grow up, very young children often reply "police officer," "nanny," or "teacher." But as they grow older and learn about other jobs, their choices change.

Sociologists apply ideas about expectations in two broad ways. One tradition, known as a "rational-choice perspective," assumes that people make educational decisions by calculating the costs, anticipated benefits, probability of success, and attractiveness of alternatives (Goldthorpe 1996; Morgan 2005). Students' socio-economic origins shape how much they value schooling, because different social locations mean unequal costs, benefits, and chances of success. While average attainments have risen for all groups, socio-economic disparities persist, partly because the cost–benefit balances have remained stable for different strata. For working-class youth, the prospect of paying high university tuition fees, only to suffer a bout of unemployment later, may simply be too costly, because their families are less able to subsidize them and they have fewer social connections to help them land a white-collar job.

A second tradition, associated with Pierre Bourdieu, emphasizes that people's perceptions are rooted in their pre-existing dispositions and surrounding influences. This tradition de-emphasizes the strategic and calculating aspect of social action, instead focusing on its more habitual and instinctive qualities. For Bourdieu, people are oriented by cultural repertoires and social scripts, which are historical products of groups internalizing their objective conditions. Thus, young people with lower socio-economic origins may decide not to attend university, not because of any rigorous cost–benefit calculation but because they see university as alien territory, particularly if no one from their family had ever attended such an institution. This perspective emphasizes how youths' job aspirations tend to mirror the kinds of jobs held by their parents or other people like themselves (see Lehmann 2007). Hence, younger people from lower socio-economic backgrounds may tend to view relatively secure blue-collar jobs, requiring lower educational credentials, as viable options; in contrast, more affluent students would tend to reject such choices, instead seeking entrée into elite universities, largely because they feel that only such locations are worthy (Mullen 2010). In general, this perspective emphasizes that social upbringing shapes our preferences and whether we see various life options as enticing, impossible, or unacceptable. In Bourdieu's terms, people's past experience and current social position (or "habitus") encourage them to "come to terms" with their circumstances and adjust their expectations to what is "realistic." We learn to largely desire only what we can expect, Bourdieu emphasizes.

While these two traditions are not entirely incompatible, they place differing emphases on whether actors' schooling decisions are based on a knowing assessment of probable costs and benefits, or on prevailing group norms, scripts, and cultural values. Both traditions acknowledge that our sense of desirable, yet possible and realistic, life options shapes our educational expectations, and that immediate family and friends greatly influence our mental horizons.

Research on educational expectations suggests a nuanced reality. Studies have long found that student aspirations are influenced by family and friends, net of their own economic and academic resources (Morgan 2005). Nevertheless, socio-economic background only partly determines people's educational expectations. Some poor and working-class students do develop high expectations. Evidence suggests that middle-class and working-class families have only incrementally different outlooks, not profoundly dissimilar values and norms. Today, rational-choice theorists would comprehend the rising post-secondary expectations of Canadians from all walks of life as reflective of how the changing economy has shifted the relative costs and benefits of schooling, replacing solid blue-collar opportunities with jobs requiring higher school credentials. Rational-choice perspectives are useful for understanding rising absolute levels of school attainment.

But what about persisting disparities? In previous eras, many sociologists pointed to a fundamental mismatch between the cultural orientations that schools required and the culture of lower socio-economic groups. In the 1950s and 1960s, some sociologists held that families from lower socio-economic strata failed to embrace "middle-class" orientations, like valuing school competition and aspiring to upward social mobility. They saw working-class families as behind the times, mired in pre-modern values (Hyman 1953).

Between the 1970s and 1990s, some sociologists redefined working-class orientations as instances of cultural "resistance." In the most popular version of this idea, the British ethnographer Paul Willis (1977), drawing on fieldwork among young people in the West Midlands, argued that class disparities in school stem from working-class youth rejecting the ethic of status, striving instead towards working-class mores of solidarity, which had been historically forged through struggles with capitalist employers. A working-class upbringing was said to instill pride in heavy, manual labour (at least among boys), preference for solidarity over competitiveness, disparagement of the "pencil-pushing" that pervades school work, and general antagonism towards institutional authority. For Willis, these habits encourage working-class youth to reject school and eagerly anticipate the "real world" of factory employment. However, today's economy forces us to confront a key question: if fewer youth today can look forward to traditional blue-collar jobs, are such stances still prevalent among working-class youth? If not, is there still a working-class "habitus" that can help us to understand persisting disparities in educational expectations? We return to this issue in the conclusion.

A flip side to research on student expectations is the classic notion, as articulated by Bourdieu, that teachers, who are themselves middle class, hold higher expectations for middle-class students than for working-class students. According to this argument, teachers generalize, perhaps unconsciously, from students' physical and social attributes (e.g., dress, demeanour, and speech style) to their abilities, subtly assuming that well-dressed, presentable, and articulate children are good students, and those with the opposite traits are poor students. This typecasting is said to create a self-fulfilling prophecy. Through their subtle body language and attention, teachers' differential treatment is said to be internalized by students. Students for whom teachers have low expectations are said to develop poor self-images, leading eventually to poor academic performance. Proof of this thesis was originally thought to be provided by the famous "Pygmalion in the classroom" experiment (Rosenthal and Jacobson 1968) with a group of California elementary students and teachers, in which teachers were told that certain (named) students were expected to be intellectual "bloomers" in that school year, and these children did especially well. Subsequent analyses, however, suggest that the study's conclusions went far beyond the evidence, with later attempts to replicate the study producing mixed results at best (Farkas et al. 1990; Kingston 2001).

Conclusion: Theorizing Persisting Inequality in a Changing System

Socio-economic gaps persist, albeit at higher average rates of attainment. Documenting these trends is relatively easy, but devising convincing and well-grounded explanations is harder. Sociologists have explained these disparities by pointing to unequal resources, contexts that advantage some groups over others, and how both of these factors shape student expectations. However, the relative weight of these factors is changing, as rising levels of attainment stimulate new government policies and new family strategies. We end this chapter by discussing how prevailing explanations may need to be revised.

Are some resources becoming more important with time? We have found that research confirms the importance of middle-class parents' ability to pass on skills and to intervene strategically for their children, but studies are less supportive of the more aesthetic explanations focusing on class culture. Furthermore, while some earlier research downplayed the role of finances, the past decade has seen a steep rise in university tuition fees and a deregulation of tuition for professional programs in some provinces. Evidence suggests that deregulation may discourage lower socio-economic groups from entering professional programs (Frenette 2005). Hence, family finances may re-emerge as a prime factor shaping educational outcomes, at least in terms of accessing some university fields. Policy-makers are attempting to counteract this situation by making loans and bursaries more readily available, but it is too early to judge their impact.

Understanding inequality requires that we recognize not only the barriers faced by working-class youth, but also the evolving advantages and strategies of middle-class families. Even if working-class frames of reference change and school biases are removed—which would render working-class students more competitive—middle-class families appear to be developing new strategies to keep ahead. Research shows marked rises in the use of private tutors, private schools, educational consultants, and educational toys, all of which seem likely to give middle-class families continued educational advantages (Aurini 2006; Davies and Quirke 2007), and may also reflect increasingly intensive and competitive parenting (Lareau 2011; Quirke 2006).

In what ways are contexts changing? Policy-makers want colleges and universities to expand and differentiate. To encourage more post-secondary attendance, Canadian policy-makers are reducing non-academic streaming in high schools and devising policies to allow more flexibility for dropouts to re-enter school systems at various levels. To encourage post-secondary expansion, governments are extending new funds to colleges and universities, while also allowing tuition to rise. This strategy has expanded the number of available slots in universities, particularly in graduate-level programs, but has also placed a greater financial burden on families. To encourage differentiation, governments and market forces appear to be increasing the structural hierarchy within post-secondary programs. Politicians are encouraging programs and institutions to raise more of their own funds, with governments creating pools of research monies that are distributed quite unequally across educational institutions. These changes could be triggering a steeper prestige pecking order among universities (Davies and Zarifa 2012), and could shift the "streaming" process from secondary to post-secondary levels (see Davies, Maldonado, and Zarifa 2014).

If middle-class families are responding to these trends with new competitive strategies, how will lower socio-economic groups respond? Some sociologists have seen "working-class culture" as an enduring and coherent entity that discouraged post-secondary aspirations. However, partly because of deindustrialization, that cultural form is probably fading. Until the mid-1980s, blue-collar jobs in resources and manufacturing, which required few educational credentials, attracted many working-class Canadians, particularly males, to leave school. But now the stock of such jobs is smaller. Instead, more school leavers are entering service-sector jobs, which often require educational credentials but may not involve high levels of skill or pay. Moreover, women, who are generally marrying and bearing children at later ages today, are achieving substantially higher levels of educational attainments among all classes. Thus, two viable alternatives that previously attracted many working-class students out of school have been undercut. In response, working-class families have boosted their attainments, even though the gap between them and the middle class persists. In the contemporary period, we can no longer presume that working-class families do not value higher education, or that their children will follow the habits of their parents and opt for factory work.

The theoretical challenge, therefore, is to combine rational-choice and habitual understandings of educational decision-making in this era of change. As our society embraces the "knowledge-based economy," lifetime learning is being hailed as the next source of educational expansion. People of all descriptions, so the argument goes, will return to school numerous times over their employment lifetimes to upgrade their skills. Middle-class families, it appears, are largely discounting any options they deem to be inferior (a reflection of their "habitus"), yet they are also consciously devising new competitive strategies to pass on educational advantages. Fewer working-class children will be employed in settings that are similar to those of their parents, since many industrial and agricultural forms of employment are declining. Even if these youth are not very upwardly mobile, they will work in non-farm and non-factory settings.

To understand persisting inequalities in education, we need to acknowledge important social changes. Parental resources like cognitive skills and competitive strategies are increasingly vital, and family finances may re-emerge as an important determinant of post-secondary participation. Contexts will evolve, as the "streaming" of students migrates upward from high schools to the expanded and increasingly differentiated post-secondary sector. This context will elicit high educational expectations among most families, further weakening traditional blue-collar ambivalence towards school. Still, disparities among families according to their possession of key resources will make unequal educational outcomes persist.

Questions for Critical Thought

1. When you decided to apply to university, was your decision based on a "rational choice," that is, an explicit cost–benefit calculation? Or was it something "habitual," that is, something you always "knew" you would do? Did money ever factor into your decision to attend university? Explain.
2. Recall your elementary and secondary school experience: do you think children's "cultural capital" affected their school success? Which kind of cultural capital—Bourdieu's version or Lareau's version—seems to matter more?
3. In your childhood, did your parents ever do any home activities, formal or informal, that

aimed to sharpen your literacy and/or numeracy skills? Did these activities affect your school performance?

4. This chapter argues that relative disparities in educational attainment have been maintained despite rising attainments among all groups. Will school attainments continue to increase in the next decade? Are there limits to growth? If so, what causes those limits?

Recommended Readings

Duncan, Greg J., and Richard J. Murnane, eds. 2011. *Whither Opportunity? Rising Inequality, Schools, and Children's Life Chances*. New York: Russell Sage.

Davies, Scott, and Neil Guppy. 2013. *The Schooled Society: An Introduction to the Sociology of Education*, 3rd edn. Toronto: Oxford University Press.

Lareau, Annette. 2011. *Unequal Childhoods: Class, Race, and Family Life, Second Edition with an Update a Decade Later*. Berkeley: University of California Press.

Paulle, Bowen. 2013. *Toxic Schools*. Chicago: University of Chicago Press.

Recommended Websites

Council of Ministers of Education Canada:
http://www.cmec.ca/en/

Programme for International Student Assessment (PISA):
http://www.oecd.org/pisa/

Sociology of Education Section of the American Sociological Association:
http://www.asanet.org/sectioneducation/education.cfm

Statistics Canada: Educational Statistics:
http://www5.statcan.gc.ca/subject-sujet/theme-theme.action?pid=1821&lang=eng&more=0

References

Alexander, Karl L., Doris R. Entwisle, and Linda Steffel Olson. 2007. "Lasting consequences of the summer learning gap." *American Sociological Review* 72, 2: 167–80.

Anisef, Paul. 1974. *The Critical Juncture*. Toronto: Ministry of Colleges and Universities.

Aurini, Janice. 2006. "Crafting legitimation projects: An institutional analysis of private education businesses." *Sociological Forum* 21, 1: 83–112.

——, Emily Milne, and Cathelene Hillier. 2016. "The two sides of vigilance: Parent engagement and its relationship to school connections, responsibility and agency." In W. Lehmann, ed. *Education and Society: Canadian Perspectives*. Toronto: Oxford University Press.

Baker, David. 2013. *The Schooled Society*. Stanford, Calif.: Stanford University Press.

Bennett, Pamela R., Amy C. Lutz, and Lakshmi Jayaram. 2012. "Beyond the schoolyard: The role of parenting logics, financial resources, and social institutions in the social class gap in structured activity participation." *Sociology of Education* 85, 2: 131–57.

Boudon, Raymond. 1974. *Education, Opportunity, and Social Inequality: Changing Prospects in Western Society*. Toronto: John Wiley and Sons.

Bourdieu, Pierre, and Jean-Claude Passeron. 1990. *Reproduction in Education, Society and Culture*, 2nd edn. London: Sage.

Boyle, Michael H., Kathy Georgiades, Yvonne Racine, and C. Mustard. 2007. "Neighbourhood and family influences on educational attainment: Results from the Ontario Child Health Study follow-up 2001." *Child Development* 78, 1: 168–89.

Buchmann, Claudia, and Ben Dalton. 2002. "Interpersonal influences and educational aspirations in twelve countries: The importance of institutional context." *Sociology of Education* 75: 99–122.

Clanfield, David, Bruce Curtis, Grace-Edward Galabuzi, Alison Gaymes San Vicente, David W. Livingstone, and Harry Smaller. 2014. *Stacking the Deck: The Streaming of Working Class Kids in Ontario Schools*. Toronto: Our Schools/Our Selves.

Coleman, James S. 1988. "Social capital in the creation of human capital." *American Journal of Sociology* 94: s95–s120.

Corak, Miles, Garth Lipps, and John Zhao. 2003. "Family income and participation in post-secondary education." Analytical Studies Branch Research Paper Series, no. 210. http://www.statcan.ca/english/research/11F0019MIE/11F0019MIE2003210.pdf. Accessed 26 Oct. 2007.

Cyr, Darren. 2014. "Physical graffiti and school ecologies: A new look at disorder, neighbourhood effects and school outcomes." Ph.D. dissertation, McMaster University.

Davies, Scott. 2005. "A revolution of expectations? Three key trends in the SAEP data." In Robert Sweet and Paul Anisef, eds, *Preparing for Post-secondary Education: New Roles for Governments and Families*, pp. 149–65. Montreal and Kingston: McGill-Queen's University Press.

——— and Janice Aurini. 2013. "Summer learning inequality in Ontario." *Canadian Public Policy* 39, 2: 287–307.

——— and Neil Guppy. 2013. *The Schooled Society: An Introduction to the Sociology of Education*, 3rd edn. Toronto: Oxford University Press.

———, Vicky Maldonado, and David Zarifa. 2014. "Effectively maintaining inequality in Toronto: Predicting university destinations of Toronto District School Board graduates." *Canadian Review of Sociology* 51, 1: 22–53.

——— and Linda Quirke. 2007. "The impact of sector on school organizations: The logics of markets and institutions." *Sociology of Education* 80, 1: 66–89.

——— and David Zarifa. 2012. "The stratification of universities: Structural inequality in Canadian and American higher education." *Research in Social Stratification and Mobility* 30, 2: 143–58.

Deller, Fiona, and Stephanie Oldford. 2011. "Participation of low-income students in Ontario." Issue Paper No. 11, Higher Education Quality Council of Ontario. Toronto.

Dooley, Martin D., A. Abigail Payne, and A. Leslie Robb. 2009. "University participation and income differences: An analysis of applications by Ontario secondary school students." Toronto: Higher Education Quality Council of Ontario.

Downey, Douglas B., Paul T. von Hippel, and Beckett Broh. 2004. "Are schools the great equalizer? Cognitive inequality during the summer months and the school year." *American Sociological Review* 69: 613–35.

Duncan, G.J., and R.J. Murnane, eds. 2011. *Whither Opportunity? Rising Inequality, Schools and Children's Life Chances*. New York: Russell Sage Foundation.

Farkas, George, Robert P. Grobe, Daniel Sheehan, and Yuan Shuan. 1990. "Cultural resources and school success: Gender, ethnicity, and poverty groups within an urban school district." *American Sociological Review* 55, 1: 127–42.

——— and J. Hibel. 2008. "Being unready for school: Factors affecting risk and resilience." In A. Booth and A.C. Crouter, eds, *Disparities in School Readiness: How Families Contribute to Transitions into School*, pp. 3–30. New York: Lawrence Erlbaum Associates.

Finnie, Ross, Eric Lascelles, and Arthur Sweetman. 2005. "Who goes? The direct and indirect effects of family background on access to post-secondary education." Analytical Studies Branch Research Paper Series, no. 237. http://www.statcan.ca/english/research/11F0019MIE/11F0019MIE2005237.pdf. Accessed 25 Oct. 2007.

Frenette, Marc. 2005. "The impact of tuition fees on university access: Evidence from a large-scale price de-regulation in professional programs." Analytical Studies Branch Research Paper Series, no. 263. http://www.statcan.ca/english/research/11F0019MIE/11F0019MIE2005264.pdf.

——— and Ping Ching Winnie Chan. 2015. "Academic outcomes of public and private high schools: What lies behind the difference?" Analytic Studies Branch Research Paper Series, no. 367. Ottawa: Statistics Canada.

Goldthorpe, John H. 1996. "Class analysis and the re-orientation of class theory: The case of persisting differentials in educational attainment." *British Journal of Sociology* 47, 3: 481–505.

———. 2007. "Cultural capital: Some critical observations." *Sociologica* 2.

Hyman, Herbert H. 1953. "The value systems of different classes: A social psychological contribution to the analysis of stratification." In Reinhard Bendix and Seymour Martin Lipset, eds, *Class, Status and Power: A Reader in Social Stratification*, pp. 426–42. Glencoe, Ill.: Free Press.

Janus, Magdalena, and Eric Duku. 2007. "The school entry gap: Socioeconomic, family, and health factors associated with children's school readiness to learn." *Early Education and Development* 18, 3: 375–403.

Jimenez, Tomas R., and Adam L. Horowitz. 2013. "When white is just alright: How immigrants redefine achievement and reconfigure the ethnoracial hierarchy." *American Sociological Review* 78, 5: 849–71.

Johnson, David. 2007. *Signposts of Success: Interpreting Ontario's Elementary School Test Scores (updated version)*. Toronto: C.D. Howe Institute.

Karabel, Jerome, and A.H. Halsey. 1977. "Introduction." In Jerome Karabel and A.H. Halsey, eds, *Power and Ideology in Education*. New York: Oxford University Press.

Kerckhoff, Alan C. 2001 "Education and social stratification processes in comparative perspective." *Sociology of Education* (extra issue): 3–18.

Kingston, Paul. 2001. "The unfulfilled promise of cultural capital theory." *Sociology of Education* (extra issue): 88–99.

Krahn, Harvey, and Alison Taylor. 2007. "'Streaming' in the 10th grade in four Canadian provinces in 2000." *Education Matters: Insights on Education, Learning and Training in Canada* 4, 2. http://www.statcan.ca/english/freepub/81-004-XIE/2007002/stream.htm. Accessed 30 Oct. 2007.

Lareau, Annette. 2011. *Unequal Childhoods*. Berkeley: University of California Press.

Lehmann, Wolfgang. 2007. *Choosing to Labour: School–Work Transitions and Social Class*. Montreal and Kingston: McGill-Queen's University Press.

Looker, E. Dianne. 1994. "Active capital: The impact of parents on youths' educational performance and plans." *Sociology of Education in Canada: Critical Perspectives on Theory, Research and Practice*. Toronto: Copp Clark Longman.

McCrory-Calarco, Jessica. 2014. "Coached for the classroom: Parents' cultural transmission and children's reproduction of educational inequalities." *American Sociological Review* 79: 1015–37.

Morgan, Stephen. 2005. *On the Edge of Commitment*. Stanford, Calif.: Stanford University Press.

Mullen, Ann. 2010. *Degrees of Inequality*. Baltimore: Johns Hopkins University Press.

Murphy, Raymond. 1979. *Sociological Theories of Education*. Toronto: McGraw-Hill Ryerson.

Organisation for Economic Co-operation and Development. 2013. "OECD education rankings—2013 update." https://ourtimes.wordpress.com/2008/04/10/oecd-education-rankings/. Accessed 21 May 2015.

Paulle, Bowen. 2013. *Toxic Schools*. Chicago: University of Chicago Press.

Porter, Marion, John Porter, and Bernard Blishen. 1979. *Does Money Matter?* Downsview, Ont.: Institute for Behavioural Research.

Quirke, Linda. 2006. "'Keeping young minds sharp': Children's cognitive stimulation and the rise of parenting magazines, 1959–2003." *Canadian Review of Sociology* 43, 4: 387–406.

Radford, Alexandria Walton. 2013. *Top Student, Top School? How Social Class Shapes Where Valedictorians Go to College*. Chicago: University of Chicago Press.

Reardon, Sean F. 2014. "Education." In *The Poverty and Inequality Report 2014*, pp. 53–9. Stanford, Calif.: Stanford Center on Poverty and Inequality.

Rosenthal, R., and L. Jacobson. 1968. *Pygmalion in the Classroom*. New York: Rinehart and Winston.

Schaub, Maryellen. 2015. "Is there a home advantage in school readiness for young children? Trends in parent engagement in cognitive activities with young children, 1991–2001." *Journal of Early Childhood Research* 13, 1: 47–63.

Schofer, Evan, and John W. Meyer. 2005. "The world-wide expansion of higher education in the twentieth century." *American Sociological Review* 70: 898–920.

Sewell, William, and Robert Hauser. 1980. "The Wisconsin longitudinal study of social and psychological factors in aspirations and achievements." *Research in Sociology of Education and Socialization* 1: 59–99.

Shaienks, Danielle, and Tomasz Gluszynski. 2009. "Education and labour market transitions in young adulthood." Statistics Canada Catalogue no. 81-595-M—No. 075, July.

Shavit, Yossi, Richard Arum, and Adam Gamoran. 2007. *Stratification in Higher Education: A Comparative Study*. Stanford, Calif.: Stanford University Press.

Statistics Canada. 2005. "Student achievement in mathematics—the roles of attitudes, perceptions and family background." *Education Matters* 2, 1. http://www.statcan.ca/english/freepub/81-004-XIE/2005001/math.htm.

———. 2011. *Education in Canada: Attainment, Field of Study and Location of Study*. Catalogue no. 99-012-XIE2011001.

van den Berg, Axel. 1998. "Is sociological theory too grand for social mechanisms?" In Peter Hedstrom and Richard Swedberg, eds, *Social Mechanisms*, ch. 9. Cambridge: Cambridge University Press.

Willis, Paul. 1977. *Learning to Labour*. Farnborough, UK: Saxon House, Teakfield.

Willms, J. Douglas. 2002. *Vulnerable Children*. Edmonton: University of Alberta Press.

PART III

Social Justice and Inequality

A. Ethnicity, Race, Language, and Ancestry
B. Gender and Sexual Orientation
C. Age
D. Disability
E. Region

In Parts I and II we concentrated on class and socio-economic inequality, focusing especially on corporate ownership, income, wealth, occupation, and education. In this third section, our attention shifts to a range of other crucial bases of inequality: ethnicity, race, language, and ancestry; gender and sexual orientation; age; disability; and region.

These topics fall under the general heading of "social justice," a term that has become popular in recent sociological analysis as a rubric for these other kinds of inequality. Of course, problems of class and socio-economic inequality are also matters of social justice, especially the inequities experienced by the poor and destitute. Nevertheless, the term "social justice" is closely linked with these other forms of inequality. Certain categories of people within these dimensions experience substantial and enduring *in*justice. Sadly, this happens even in societies like Canada, where all citizens are theoretically equal under the law, and where all are supposed to enjoy equal treatment, or at least equal opportunity, as they pursue their life's dreams.

Virtually every dimension of inequality assessed in Part III involves what social scientists refer to as *ascribed* social statuses. This term captures the idea that these statuses are not generally attributes of our own making. Unlike educational attainment or occupational status—which can be seen as at least partly the result of our personal choices, efforts, or *achievements*—ascribed statuses are not typically under our personal control. For example, our gender, ethnic heritage, racial background, first language, and age cohort are given to us at birth. Moreover, with few exceptions, these are not attributes we can change through our own actions.

Ascribed statuses become issues of social justice when attributes beyond people's control are used as pretexts for legally granting or denying fundamental human rights. The enslavement of racial minorities, which long ago was legal in Canada and unofficially still exists in some parts of the world, is a prime example of the denial of social justice to certain individuals purely on the basis of an ascribed status or attribute. Other examples include denying women the right to vote, own property, or work in certain occupations; these injustices once existed in Canada and still exist in some countries today. The banning of gay marriage, which no longer occurs in Canada but continues to happen in many other countries, is another illustration. So too is the simple right to have equal access to buildings or public transit, which is an everyday injustice for many disabled people even today. These instances provide some idea of the number, the variety, and the depth of challenges that Canadians have faced, and continue to face, when it comes to achieving social justice and equality in our society.

A. Ethnicity, Race, Language, and Ancestry

Part III begins with four chapters that demonstrate the multi-faceted nature of ethnic and racial inequality in our society: the so-called "vertical mosaic." More than 50 years ago, John Porter coined this now famous metaphor to symbolize the rich diversity of Canada's cultural groups, but also the significant inequalities that exist among these groups. The four selections presented here examine the related issues of ethnicity, race, language, and ancestry.

The first analysis, by Charles Menzies and Monica Hwang in Chapter 10, considers Aboriginal ancestry, showing the many inequalities and injustices faced by Canada's Aboriginal peoples. The chapter discusses the historical dislocation of the First Nations by the encroachment of European settlers. For centuries, Aboriginal peoples were trapped in a position of dependency, their land claims often unheeded and their calls for self-determination largely ignored. The authors describe some improvements and progress in recent years, but caution that much remains to be done.

In Chapter 11, Pierre Fortin assesses how Canada's French-language minority, especially French Quebecers, have seen dramatic changes in their circumstances over the past half-century. His analysis reveals that French Canadians have come a long way towards catching up, both socio-economically and otherwise, with the English-speaking majority that traditionally dominated Canadian society. Since the 1960s, the French have solidified their language rights and political pre-eminence in Quebec, and have also moved much closer to economic parity with the English population.

As much as any country in the world, Canada is a nation of immigrants. In Chapter 12, Monica Boyd and Michael Vickers present detailed evidence on the changing nature of immigration. Among the important patterns discussed is the movement away from European immigration and towards mainly non-European visible minority immigration since the 1960s. The authors also consider the ebb and flow in the number of immigrants across different time periods, and discuss the main explanations for these patterns.

In Chapter 13, the final chapter in this subsection, Jeffrey Reitz and Rupa Banerjee address crucial problems of racial inequality and discrimination in Canada, presenting extensive evidence derived from the Ethnic Diversity Survey. They consider the effects of racial and ethnic inequality on social cohesion, and discuss social policies to improve the sense of inclusion and shared citizenship of Canada's minority citizens.

B. Gender and Sexual Orientation

Social scientists typically distinguish between sex—a biological concept referring to physiological differences between females and males—and gender—a social concept referring to *socially constructed* differences between women and men. This distinction underscores that differences between women and men are not about biological "destiny" as much as they are about how the social world is organized along gender lines. Hence, women still experience serious disadvantages on some inequality dimensions, e.g., income level and occupational status, but these disadvantages have nothing to do with biology, or "natural" ability, and everything to do with social structures that make it difficult, and sometimes impossible, for women to compete on an equal basis with men. As noted in the introduction to this volume, economic, political, and ideological control by privileged groups—in this case, males—underlies the structural inequalities that many women still experience in Canada.

In Chapter 14, Tracey Adams and Michael Rooyakkers offer a detailed review of important theoretical and conceptual developments in the study of gender, gender inequality, and sexual identity. The chapter provides a concise history of feminism and of the theories that have driven the development of gender studies more broadly, including the recent study of "masculinities."

In Chapter 15, Gillian Creese and Brenda Beagan present extensive evidence on the employment opportunities of Canadian women, and discuss specific policy changes to assist women's job prospects. They examine employment rates, female–male earnings ratios, occupational segregation, and policies to encourage pay equity and employment equity.

Roderic Beaujot, Zenaida Ravanera, and Jianye Liu, in Chapter 16, consider gender inequality in the family setting. The analysis addresses several questions, including who does the domestic labour in Canadian households. Findings show that couples have a more equal partnership in the sharing of household responsibilities than in the past, but women continue to do more than men.

In the final chapter in this subsection, Lorne Tepperman and Josh Curtis in Chapter 17 explore the issue of sexual orientation, which has become pivotal in discussions of the social construction of gender and gender identities. Sexual orientation is clearly a significant social justice concern, and an understanding of its various manifestations is essential in any comprehensive assessment of social inequality. Among other concerns, the authors look at legal issues confronting the gay community, homophobia, hate crimes, and the problems faced by same-sex families.

C. Age

Age is another ascribed attribute that has important implications for social inequality. Chapter 18, by Neil Guppy, discusses how age is not simply a biological concept, but a social construction as well. He considers such questions as whether society should construct legal age limits on fundamental rights like the right to work. He also provides evidence on how age is related to economic inequality over the life course, and explores the prospect of age-based conflict between different generations of Canadians.

D. Disability

Kim Shuey, Andrea Willson, and Katherine Bouchard, in Chapter 19, consider how different forms of disability affect the life chances of many Canadians and their opportunities to achieve a full and rewarding life. The obstacles placed in the path of those with physical and mental disabilities, or differences, range from physical barriers to accessibility to the stigmatization and discrimination they often experience in such areas as education, the workforce, and housing.

E. Region

In the last chapter of Part III, Mabel Ho and Catherine Corrigall-Brown in Chapter 20 offer extensive information on regional inequality in Canada, based on such indicators as income, unemployment level, health, life expectancy, and educational attainment. The authors also review key explanations for regional inequalities and discuss government policies that have been implemented to alleviate problems of regional disparity.

Region is included in the social justice section because the place where we live, to some degree, is another ascribed status that affects our life chances and opportunities to succeed. It might seem dubious to contend that region is an ascribed attribute: after all, people can choose to move throughout Canada, and are not legally bound to stay in one place. Consider, however, that region of birth is not our personal choice, and it is also a strong predictor of our ultimate place of residence; people born in one region tend to settle there as adults because of the community allegiances, regional identities, and social or family ties that usually develop early in life. Region is also included in this part because it correlates closely with other important ascribed statuses, most notably ethnicity and language. This is especially evident for French Canadians living in Quebec and for Indigenous peoples living in the northern territories and the northern regions of most provinces. But the power of regional ties is apparent throughout the country, as illustrated by the residents of the Atlantic provinces, for example, who retain an enduring identity with, and affection for, their home region.

A. Ethnicity, Race, Language, and Ancestry

10 First Nations, Inequality, and the Legacy of Colonialism

Charles R. Menzies and Monica Hwang

. . . it would not be accurate to assume that even pre-contact existence in the territory was in the least bit idyllic. The plaintiffs' ancestors had no written language, no horses or wheeled vehicles, slavery and starvation was not uncommon, wars with neighbouring peoples were common, and there is no doubt, to quote Hobbes, that Aboriginal life in the territory was, at best, "nasty, brutish and short." —BC Appeal Court Chief Justice Allan McEachern, *Delgamuukw: Reasons for Judgment*, 1991

Racism is racism, and racism stings. All the good intentions in the world do not take away the sting and do not take away the pain. —Patricia Monture-Angus, *Thunder in My Soul* (1995)

Introduction

The First Nations' response to Justice Allan McEachern's decision in *Delgamuukw* was angry and tearful. For the First Nations people living in the Gitksan and Wet'suwet'en territories, the four-year-long court case was about the right to live as they and their ancestors had for millennia. From the point of view of the governments of British Columbia and Canada, a large tract of land full of crucial economic resources was at stake and had to be defended. By opening their box of stories and experience to a court, the Gitksan and Wet'suwet'en people, elders, and chiefs had placed their trust in an institution they saw as foreign. In return, they felt they had been repaid with insult and disdain. While McEachern's decision stands out from recent court rulings and to a certain extent was overturned on appeal,[1] his basic interpretations of First Nations people as having existed without "real" social organization or culture until the arrival of Europeans in the Americas is itself a product of the colonial encounter.

Canada is built upon a colonial system in which Aboriginal lands have been expropriated, Aboriginal institutions banned, and Aboriginal Peoples relegated to marginal sectors of the mainstream economy. Put simply: Colonialism involves a relationship which leaves one side dependent on the other to define the world. At the individual level, colonialism involves a situation in which one individual is forced to relate to another on terms unilaterally defined by the other (McCaskill 1983: 289). Five hundred years of European settlement in the Americas is painfully and tragically represented in standard indices of social pathologies such as high rates of suicide, unemployment and underemployment, and substance abuse. This is not to deny impressive and significant examples of successful First Nations people. Rather, it is important to underline the fact that the structure of social inequality experienced by First Nations people is directly linked to the processes of colonialism and government policies directed at undermining Aboriginal institutions and social organization. In this chapter we describe the contemporary structure of inequality, outline the general process of colonialization and expropriation of First Peoples in Canada, and suggest strategies for improving the current situation.

Stories to Cry Over

Social inequality cannot simply be captured in a set of cold, apparently objective numbers (although you will see some numbers below). Think of the everyday stories we tell among friends, in school, or at work. These stories form the basis of our regular communication. They are important sources of knowledge and cultural codes. For the social scientist, these stories are also important places to search out experiences and expressions of inequality. Who is telling the story? Where is it being told? Who is excluded from the audience? We recognize that some stories are not public, that they are in some sense restricted to special places or social settings.

In his writing on the subject of First Nations inequality, an important part of Charles Menzies's work has involved detailing the semi-private stories of Euro-Canadian men and the role their storytelling plays in the maintenance of colonial structures (see, e.g., Menzies, 1994, 1997). These are emotionally wrenching stories. While one may wish to deny or ignore them, it is more important to listen to these stories. How does it feel to be the target, the butt of the joke, the object of ridicule? A cousin of Charles told him, some years after he had given her a copy of *Stories from Home* (Menzies 1994), that the stories of hate recounted in this work had made her cry. She said: "I know these men, or men just like them. My husband has worked alongside of them. We raised our children in the same community as them. To hear how they talk about us [First Nations people] in your paper still makes me cry." The telling of these stories is important to this woman, even though they are painful to hear. They reveal, more than any graph, the everyday experience of racism and inequality. Here is a version of a story Menzies first heard while sitting on the deck of a fishing boat one summer afternoon in a northern British Columbia port.

A small gathering of men were relaxing in the quiet time between the end of work and heading up town or home for the night. Ed, a crew member from an adjacent boat, joined the circle and began to talk about his exploits of the previous evening. He had spent most of his time at a 20-year high school reunion—by all accounts it had been a smashing success. Ed is a respected member of the local fishing community,[2] an accomplished storyteller, and an effective public speaker (the public here being a group of predominantly Euro-Canadian fishermen). As the author began to tune out—he had heard this story before, at least versions of it—drink, party, and drink . . . he had almost decided to leave when Ed's story took an unexpected turn.

"Jim had all this paint up at his place, so we loaded it into my car and drove back downtown. Parked off Third, took a look for the cops and then went to it."

"Doing what?" the author asked.

"Hey? What do you think we were doing?"

"Painting the town red," somebody said to a chorus of laughs.

"No," said Ed, "we were painting the town white. Yeah, we painted a bloody white crosswalk from the Belmont [Hotel] right into the Empress. Help all those drunken Indians make it across the street."

"I wondered who did that when I came down to the boat this morning," Menzies said. "But why is it so jagged? It's crooked."

"That's the beauty of it," said Ed. "It's designed just right. Your Indian stumbles out of the bar, into the street. 'Hey, look, he says, 'a crosswalk.' And he's right over into the other bar. First class."

The irony of Ed's own drunkenness seemed to have escaped him. He plays up a popular explanation of the so-called "Indian problem": the drunken Indian. Yet his story is only one example in a multitude of narratives of colonialism in which the disparate threads of racial superiority and intolerance are wound. Ed's story is part of the day-to-day experience of social inequality felt by people of Aboriginal descent.

The Contemporary Structure of Inequality

Social scientists typically measure inequality using social indicators such as income level, rate of participation in employment and education, and quality-of-life measures such as health and housing. To demonstrate inequality objectively, it is necessary to show that significant differences between groups of people do in fact exist. In this section, statistics concerning income, education and employment, health, and justice are presented. You will notice that, despite some very successful First Nations individuals (in business, entertainment, politics), many First Nations people are relatively impoverished when compared with mainstream Canadian society. Social statistics can be produced in an ad hoc manner, and co-ordination among producers of social statistics can be insufficient, resulting in inconsistent statistics. For example, some statistics are available for all First Nations people, but some only for on-reserve or urban populations. Further distinctions may be made among Inuit, Métis, and registered or non-registered First Nations or Indian populations. As the evidence below will show, regardless of which group or indicator of inequality is considered, and despite a few signs of improvement in certain areas, the inequities and disadvantages remain substantial, and actually have increased, not decreased, on some dimensions.

Income

One indicator that has always revealed significant inequality is income. First Nations and other Aboriginal Peoples have consistently earned lower incomes than non-Aboriginal Canadians. This has been shown to be true for as long as representative evidence has been collected. Notable income inequalities exist, moreover, whether we consider individual income, household income, average income, median income, or other measures. The one finding that provides some modest reason for optimism is that, in recent decades, the income gaps between Aboriginal Peoples and other Canadians have declined somewhat. For example, in a study of Canadian census data sponsored by the Canadian Centre for Policy Alternatives, which used median employment income as the indicator, Wilson and Macdonald (2010: 8) found that Aboriginal people's incomes were only 56 per cent of those earned by other Canadians in 1995, but that this percentage had increased to 63 per cent by 2000 and 70 per cent by 2005. While this pattern suggests some improvement, the researchers still concluded that "disturbing levels of income inequality persist" (Wilson and Macdonald 2010: 3). Another study, by the Canadian Council of Aboriginal Businesses (2010), found that the income gap was smaller when only full-time, and not part-time, workers were considered, but that the evidence of a decreasing gap over time was very slight, moving up only marginally from 77 per cent in 2000 to 78 per cent in 2005.

A more technical and detailed analysis by Pendakur and Pendakur (2011) reported similar slight declines in the income gap for the period 1995–2005, and concluded that Aboriginal Peoples "face disparity on par with the most disadvantaged non-Aboriginal ethnic minorities in Canada" (Pendakur and Pendakur 2011: 80). In a similar vein, Scott Gilmore, writing in *Maclean's* magazine, compared Canada's Aboriginal people with the most disadvantaged minority in the US—African Americans—on income, and also on a range of other economic and social indicators; he showed that, in almost every case, Canada's Aboriginal people were more unequal, leading him to conclude that Canada's race problem "is even worse than America's" (Gilmore 2015).

The most recent income data available come from the 2011 National Household Survey (NHS), which replaced Canada's long-form census. Based on measures that consider both households and individuals, the survey revealed that the median income of Aboriginal households was 86 per cent of the Canadian household median in 2010, but that the median income of individual Aboriginal people was still only 69 per cent of Canadian individual income (Statistics Canada 2011a, 2011b). Therefore, despite some indication that income inequalities are slowly declining, significant income disparities still remain, especially for individuals as opposed to households. For this reason some researchers have concluded that, at the current rate of change in the pattern of income inequality, "it would take 63 years for the gap to be erased" (Wilson and Macdonald 2010: 3). While a number of factors influence this income disparity, it clearly reflects structural aspects of the national economy, which continues to be predicated on the colonial expropriation of Indigenous lands and on legal frameworks that have historically restricted and constrained Indigenous economic activities.

There are also some notable internal income variations within the broad Aboriginal Peoples category. Research generally shows that First Nations people who are registered under the Indian Act face larger income inequalities than do those who are not registered (Maxim et al. 2001; Pendakur and Pendakur 2011), and that Inuit and Métis usually fare better than First Nations people as a whole (Canadian Council of Aboriginal Businesses 2010; Wilson and Macdonald 2010).

Another way to look at income is to examine evidence based on the low-income cut-offs (LICOs). The overall prevalence of low income is significantly higher among Aboriginal people than among the non-Aboriginal population. One study conducted by the Canadian Parliament found that, as of 2005, about 19 per cent of Aboriginal families experienced low income, as did 43 per cent who were unattached individuals; the comparable figures for non-Aboriginal Canadians were much lower, at just 8 per cent for families and 28 per cent for individuals (Collin and Jensen 2009; also Murphy et al. 2012). More recent data from the 2011 NHS, which used a different indicator, called the after-tax low-income measure (LIM-AT), showed that, by 2010, 25 per cent of Aboriginal households were surviving on low incomes, compared to just 15 per cent of Canadian households as a whole (Statistics Canada 2011a, 2011b).

The sources of people's incomes also provide important information about the structure of inequality. Data for 2010 show that, for the population aged 15 or older, government transfer payments accounted for about 19 per cent of income in private households for Aboriginal people, compared to just 12 per cent for other Canadians; among these government transfers, Aboriginal people's households were more likely than other households to derive income from child benefits and employment insurance (Statistics Canada 2011a, 2011b). The on-reserve population is especially likely to receive its funding revenues from government sources; however, one change in recent years is that First Nations have increasingly generated "own-source revenues," with additional funds coming from land claims settlements and a range of business ventures that have included wineries, shopping centres, casinos, hotels, conventions centres, and so on (Schwartz 2013).

Education and Employment

Two other indicators of inequality linked closely with income are education and employment. For most Canadians, educational attainment is an important factor influencing both the type of employment they pursue and, in turn, the amount of income they earn. As discussed later in this chapter, historically the educational experiences of Canada's Aboriginal Peoples were deeply scarred by the infamous system of residential schools, which were funded by the federal government and administered by Christian churches, especially the Roman Catholic Church, as well as the Anglican and United churches. Under this system, which existed for almost a century beginning in the 1870s, children were forced to attend, and often to live and work in, institutions marked by punitive and brutal environments, where they endured the systematic undermining of their own culture and identity, and where they also could be subjected to the worst forms of both physical and sexual abuse (e.g., Haig-Brown 1988; White et al. 2009; Frideres and Gadacz 2011; Gordon and White 2014).

In spite of the terrible injuries and injustices inflicted by the residential schools, Aboriginal people have increasingly shown in recent times that they retain the same motivations and aspirations to succeed in the larger education system as do other Canadians; hence, there have been notable increments in educational participation and achievement for Aboriginal people over time. For example, among adults aged 25–64, the proportion of Aboriginal people with some post-secondary education rose from 28 per cent in 1996 to 42 per cent in 2011 (Gordon and White 2014). At the same time, however, the comparable proportions for the non-Aboriginal population were even higher, and also increased at a more rapid rate: for adults aged 25–64, the proportion of non-Aboriginal people with some post-secondary education rose from an already high 43 per cent in 1996 to 62 per cent in 2011 (Gordon and White 2014). This means that, although Aboriginal educational attainments have increased in *absolute* terms, unfortunately, *relative* to other Canadians, they have actually fallen a bit further behind (see also Fong and Gulati 2013, and Chapter 8 in this volume).

Research does show that the income gap separating highly educated Aboriginal people and highly educated non-Aboriginal people is smaller than the gap separating less educated members of these two populations; even so, the evidence is worrisome because some inequalities in both income and employment continue to exist, even among the Aboriginal people who have attained the same high education levels as other Canadians (Wilson and Macdonald 2010; Pendakur and Pendakur 2011). Evidence from the 2011 NHS also shows that the unemployment rate for working-age Aboriginal people was more than twice the rate for other Canadians of the same age (13 per cent versus 6 per cent); in this case, however, the gap between the two populations narrowed, albeit slightly, going from a difference of 8 per cent in 2006 to 7 per cent in 2011 (Statistics Canada 2011c; see also Gilmore 2015). Overall, though, any optimism about the education, employment, and income levels of Aboriginal people must be tempered by the realization that the gaps separating them from other Canadians have either reduced very slowly or, in some cases, increased a bit in recent years.

Health

Although the basic health of First Nations people has improved over the last several decades, the available evidence indicates that significant differences remain between the health of Aboriginal people and members of mainstream Canadian society. In regard to life expectancy, for example, a Health Canada profile showed that, between 1980 and 2001, average life expectancy at birth among registered Indians rose from 60.9 to 70.4 years for males, and from 68.0 to 75.5 years for females; even so, life expectancies were much higher for other Canadians throughout this period, rising from 71.7 to 77.0 years for males, and from 78.9 to 82.0 years for females (Health Canada 2003: Figure 8). Calculations using population projections from Statistics Canada (for both males and females combined) suggest that the average life expectancy of Aboriginal people will be about 74 years by 2017, compared to about 81 years for the non-Aboriginal population (Statistics Canada 2010: Chart 13). Overall, these figures suggest that the gap in life expectancy between Aboriginal people and other Canadians has been declining somewhat over time, but continues to be substantial.

Apart from lower life expectancy, illnesses resulting from poverty, overcrowding, poor housing, and other social determinants of health have long led to serious health problems for Aboriginal people. Recent reports by the National Collaborating Centre for Aboriginal Health (2012, 2013) confirm these patterns for chronic and acute respiratory diseases, infectious diseases, cardiovascular diseases, hypertension, and so on (see also Chapter 21 in this volume). Another concern is infant mortality, which is more than twice as high for Aboriginal people compared to the rate for other Canadians, and four times as high for some First Nations groups (Gilmore 2015; CBC News 2013).

Deaths related to violence are another area of stark differences between Aboriginal people and other Canadians, as recent investigations into murdered and missing Aboriginal women and girls have underscored (Innes 2015). The RCMP has reported that, between 1980 and 2012, Aboriginal females accounted for 16 per cent of all female homicides in that period, even though they represented only about 4 per cent of Canada's female population as of 2011 (RCMP 2014). During the same period, Aboriginal males account for 17 per cent of all male homicides, even though they represented only about 4 per cent of Canada's male population (Andrew-Gee 2014; see also Innes 2015). Deaths by suicide are also much higher for Aboriginal people. The Centre for Suicide Prevention (2013) reports that suicides among Aboriginal youth are about six times the national average, and that suicide and self-inflicted injuries continue to be the leading causes of death, both for First Nations youth and for adults under age 45. Such statistics highlight the significant discrepancies between Aboriginal and non-Aboriginal people in Canada.

The Law

The interaction between First Nations people and Canadian law occurs at a collective and individual level. Collectively, particular social institutions in the past have been banned or restricted (such as the feast or potlatch system among Northwest Coast groups). The right to vote in federal elections was denied to all status Indians until 1960. Between 1927 and 1951 activity related to land claims (e.g., protesting) was illegal (Tennant 1990; Cole and Chaikin 1990). As mentioned previously, many Aboriginal children were forcibly removed from their home communities and placed in residential schools. Industrial residential schools, run primarily by Christian church organizations, were used through much of the twentieth century as part of a government assimilationist policy. The evidence is now clear that an inordinate number of children died while incarcerated in these schools, under what the Truth and Reconciliation Commission has called a cultural genocide (2015: 1). The impact of these assimilationist policies on First Nations individuals is clearly seen in the over-representation of First Nations people incarcerated in the criminal justice system.

In 2001, Aboriginal people accounted for about 3 per cent of the total Canadian population, but represented 18 per cent of federal and 14 per cent of provincial admissions to prison (Correctional Services Canada 2001). This over-representation has existed for many decades and continues to increase. By 2011, the Office of the Correctional Investigator (2013) found that Aboriginal people, who now account for about 4 per cent of Canada's population, currently represent more than 23 per cent of the federal prison population, and are incarcerated at a rate 10 times that for non-Aboriginal Canadians (see also Gilmore 2015). This pattern has been especially pronounced in western Canada. For example, evidence from the Prairies Region of the Correctional Service of Canada shows that Aboriginal people now represent more than 46 per cent of the inmate population in Manitoba, Saskatchewan, and Alberta (Office of the Correctional Investigator 2013).

Patricia Monture-Angus (1996: 335) has highlighted an important difficulty with this statistical picture: "The overrepresentation of Aboriginal people in the system of Canadian criminal justice is all too often seen as an Aboriginal problem (that is, a problem with Aboriginal people)." In a careful examination of all aspects of the Canadian criminal justice system, Ponting and Kiely (1997: 155) concluded that "each stage of the judicial process is punctuated with a disproportionate number of Aboriginal people. [Their data] suggest that Aboriginal people are victims of a discriminatory criminal justice system."

Given these experiences, recent research understandably reveals a relatively low level of trust in judicial agencies and government institutions among Aboriginal people. Using sample data from the 2008 General Social Survey, Hwang (2015) found that only a minority of Aboriginal people expressed "a great deal" or "quite a lot" of trust in the justice system and the courts, or in government leaders in the federal Parliament. In contrast, other traditionally disadvantaged groups, including visible minorities and the French, were the most trusting of government institutions among all the ethnic and racial groups that were compared, including more privileged groups like the British. These findings suggest that government agencies and the justice system may be doing a comparatively good job of protecting the rights and aspirations of other cultural minorities, but are doing a far worse job in the case of Aboriginal people. One possibly surprising finding is that a clear majority (75 per cent) of Aboriginal people expressed a high level of trust in the police, although this was still below the average in the sample as a whole (Hwang 2015; see also Perreault 2011). The relatively high trust in the police could also relate to the fact that First Nations people now increasingly deal with officers who themselves have Indigenous backgrounds. In particular, on-reserve policing is performed primarily by Indigenous officers under First Nations policing policy agreements (Clairmont 2006; Lithopoulos 2007).

The federal government has recently promoted alternative justice strategies to address the special issues that confront Aboriginal people in their experiences with the justice system; a central concern has been to increase community involvement in the local administration of justice, in order to reduce rates of crime, incarceration, and victimization among Aboriginal people (Department of Justice 2011). "Restorative justice" is one community-based strategy that has been employed, in which victims, offenders, and community members come together to discuss a particular crime's impact and to decide collectively on how the offender can make amends (Public Safety Canada 2015). While some evidence suggests that these strategies have merit, the key solution is to remove the underlying causes of over-representation of Aboriginal people in prisons and involvement in the criminal justice system in general. If we are to see substantial improvements in this situation, Canadian government officials must take greater responsibility for addressing these causes, including poverty, family disruption and disorganization, and the sad legacy of the residential school system (Innes 2015; Office of the Correctional Investigator 2013).

Explaining Inequalities: Colonialism's Legacy

The socio-economic context of First Nations people is clearly disadvantaged in comparison with mainstream society. Popular explanations of this imbalance of power and resources typically blame the victim. Such explanations fail to take into account the rich, vibrant way of life that pre-existed European arrival in the Americas, or the many examples of individual and community success (more on this below). By focusing on individuals, popular explanations deny the overpowering dominance of European traditions and economic processes that were forced upon Aboriginal Peoples. An important and powerful set of explanations roots social inequality in the historical and cultural phenomena of colonialism, the expropriation of First Nations land and resources, and government policies designed to undermine Aboriginal social institutions. This is clearly illustrated by the historical experience of Northwest Coast groups in British Columbia.

Colonial History: A Northwest Coast Illustration

On the northwest coast of British Columbia, people of European and First Nations descent have come together and separated over the years as the result of the historical movement of capital. Initial contact revolved around the exchange of commodities such as fur, iron, beads, or other trade goods.

In British Columbia, a maritime-based fur trade structured the early contacts between Europeans and First Nations (1774–1858). In this period a European-based mercantile capitalism interacted with an Indigenous kin-ordered mode of production,[3] in which the control over labour power and the production of trade goods remained under the control of the Native traders who were for the most part "chiefs." They "mobilized their followers and personal contacts to deliver . . . otter skins, and [their] power grew concomitantly with the development of the trade" (Wolf 1997 [1982]: 185). The merging of these two modes of production—one based on the family and one based on European capitalism—produced new wealth and intense inflation for both First Nations and Europeans (Fisher 1977: 8–20, Codere 1961: 443–67, Wolf 1997 [1982]:184–92). However, as Europeans prospered from this fur trade and developed industrial enterprises, First Nations people lost control over trade and were displaced by a settler-based industrial capitalism.

This was also a period of massive demographic transition, with non-Indigenous diseases such as smallpox, measles, and flu leading to what can only be described as waves of death washing along the coast and interior of the province (Campbell, Menzies, and Peacock 2003). To understand the social changes that followed, we must take into account, in a serious manner, the devastation to communities caused by this microbial form of colonialism. In many cases, European settlers to British Columbia took land that had been "cleared" of people by disease. In other cases, diseases erupted from what at best was callousness, or at worst was an intentional spread of disease. The survival and active participation in the developing industrial economy of the colony of British Columbia are testaments to the power and reliance of First Nations society and culture.

As European settlement extended into First Nations territories, marriages between Euro-Canadian businessmen and First Nations women became increasingly common. According to several commentators, these early marriages followed customary First Nations practices and were ostensibly designed to facilitate trade and co-operation between groups (Fisher 1977).

Vancouver Island, and British Columbia more generally, began to change from a locale in which Europeans exploited Indigenous labour power to become colonies of settlement in the 1850s, following the discovery of gold in the interior of the province. With the exception of the fishing industry, First Nations' labour power "was only of marginal significance in the economic concerns of the Europeans" (Fisher 1977: 96, 109). Mining, forestry, and fishing supplanted the fur trade and became the backbone of British Columbia's economy.

The extension of industrial capitalism into this region fundamentally altered the basis for alliance. No longer valued as trading partners, First Nations were slotted into the developing resource economy as a subordinate part of the growing industrial labour force, in which workers were segregated by race and gender. Union organizers and social activists have attempted, with little success, to overcome these structural divisions.

By the mid-1880s, Indigenous control of commercially valuable land and resources was almost completely destroyed through a variety of legal (and extra-legal) measures introduced by Canada and the provinces (McDonald 1994). One of the most insidious changes was the creation of the legal category of "food fishing" in the 1880s, which prohibited Aboriginal fishers from catching fish without a permit from the federal government (Newell 1993). At the same time, First Nations people were integrated "into virtually every major resource industry in [British Columbia] as workers and owner-operators" (Knight 1996: 10).

Alliances between First Nations and non-Aboriginal resource workers have played a major role in shaping British Columbia's union movement, especially in the fishing industry. Although union organizers have attempted to include them in pan-racial organizations, First Nations workers ultimately found themselves in conflict with many of their Euro-Canadian co-workers. The major point of contention between non-Aboriginal and First Nations resource workers has been the issue of land claims. Despite their common confrontation with capital as workers, non-Aboriginal workers' associations have not been able to develop a united policy for redressing the expropriation of First Nations territories and Eurocentric attacks against First Nations social institutions. While unions have been successful in addressing some aspects of First Nations experiences as workers, they seemed incapable of effectively confronting and overcoming the racism and segregation of twenty-first century industrial society.

Assimilation and Government Policies

Colonialism is not simply an economic process. It also involves social policy and regulation. In Canada, the underlying premise of most twentieth-century social policies directed at Aboriginal people has been assimilation, and the central instrument of assimilationist policy was the residential school. "By taking children away from the old ways and 'civilizing' them into European ways, so the argument ran, 'the Indian problem' would be solved" (Barman 1996: 273). However, residential schools did not fulfill their stated goals. Instead, they "served as vehicles for marginalizing generations of young men and women from the Canadian mainstream and from home environments" (Barman 1996: 273).

In the early 1900s, attempts were also made to assimilate mobile Aboriginal people by settling them into agricultural communities. From the government point of view, forcing nomadic First Nations people into settlements would allow other instruments of assimilation, such as local government, church, and school, to be more easily brought into effect. Settlement also freed up large tracts of land that could then be developed by non-Aboriginal people.

Success Stories

The story of First Nations is not all social pathology and economic disadvantage. First Nations people have maintained a strong sense of their social identity and their place within their traditional territories. On the northwest coast of Canada, for example, First Nations cultural institutions have been maintained despite concerted attempts by missionaries, government offices, and economic interests to dislodge them. The Nisga'a, Tsimshian, Gitksan, and Haida in north-coastal British Columbia have persisted in asserting their Aboriginal rights and title from the moment Europeans first arrived to occupy their land.

Examples of political organization are not restricted to British Columbia. The James Bay Cree, for example, won an important battle in the 1970s against the government of Quebec so that it could not proceed unilaterally with its massive James Bay hydroelectric project without Aboriginal approval. The subsequent 1975 James Bay and Northern Quebec Agreement guaranteed the Cree and Inuit their respective homelands. The Native Women's Association of Canada fought for a redress of sexual discrimination under the Indian Act and played an important role in the passage of Bill C-31, which in 1985 reinstated status to First Nations women (and their children) who had married non-Aboriginals (see Frideres and Gadacz 2011).

The 1973 Supreme Court *Calder* case, named after Frank Calder (an important Nisga'a leader and former member of the BC legislature for the New Democratic Party), began the legal process in British Columbia that led the way to the 2000 Nisga'a Final Agreement between the Nisga'a and Canada and British Columbia. Throughout the 1980s, the Gitksan and Wet'suwet'en people waged a strategic struggle for the recognition of their Aboriginal rights, a struggle that included tactical blockades, legal actions, and economic restraints. BC Appeal Court Chief Justice

Allan McEachern's harshly worded 1991 decision against these Indigenous groups' claim to Aboriginal title to their traditional lands was overturned by the Supreme Court of Canada in its 1997 *Delgamuukw* decision. Taken together, the concerted political actions of First Nations people have forced Canada and non-Aboriginal Canadians to take notice (as witnessed, for example, by the apology to First Peoples in January 1998 by the federal government of Canada, an apology that was enlarged and formalized in the June 2008 apologies in Parliament by the Prime Minister and the leaders of the other federal parties). The policy initiatives presented in the report of the Truth and Reconciliation Commission of Canada (2015) will hopefully lead to further successes in redressing injustice and protecting the rights and interests of First Nations people.

Strategies for the Future

In *What Is the Indian Problem?*, Noel Dyck (1991: 162) cogently argues that "the only way to rectify the ravages that Indian bands have suffered is to stop looking for 'experts' and 'masterplans' and to refuse to accept the presumption that Indians do not know what is in their best interests." Mainstream Canadian society has to accept its collective responsibility for the legacy of colonialism. An important first step is to accelerate the process of treaty negotiations and, finally, to dismantle the colonial apparatus of the Canadian state. The Truth and Reconciliation Commission and the 2008 federal apology to Aboriginal Peoples for Canada's role in residential schools go partway towards resolution. However, without a strong affirmation of Aboriginal rights and title, such actions will remain largely symbolic.

Self-determination is not a panacea for all the past wrongs. It is, however, an important place to start. Nevertheless, for self-determination to have any meaningful remedial effect on the experience of social inequality among First Nations, it must be built upon a solid economic and resource base. The 1997 Supreme Court ruling in *Delgamuukw* established the basis for a fundamental change in Canadian law that could vastly improve the economic situation of First Nations. These rights were reaffirmed and strengthened by the 2014 Supreme Court *Tsilhqot'in Nation* decision, which found that the Tsilhqot'in people of central BC held Aboriginal title to a large portion of their claimed traditional territory, and also stated that their jurisdiction and authority had to be respected. In these decisions, the Court found that Aboriginal people have a right to fair compensation for lands expropriated by the Canadian state, that they have a right to use their traditional lands as they see fit, and that their oral traditions should be accorded the same evidentiary weight as written sources. These decisions, it is hoped, will usher in a new era of economic and political co-operation between First Nations and the non-Aboriginal people of Canada. At the very least, they can be part of the beginning of a process of national reconciliation, in which mainstream Canada finally accepts its complicity in the process of colonialism.

Questions for Critical Thought

1. What are the points of difference and similarity between social inequality as experienced by Aboriginal people in Canada, and inequality as experienced by new immigrants? Do social class and economic status play a role in how inequality is experienced?
2. How would the affirmation of Aboriginal title and rights contribute to the economic well-being of Aboriginal communities?
3. The Truth and Reconciliation Commission calls the residential school system and its associated government policies "cultural genocide."

Examine the ways in which this issue has been treated in the mainstream press versus the alternative Aboriginal press. Is there a difference? If so, what does that difference of representation suggest in terms of ongoing issues of colonialist ideology in Canada?

4. How likely is it that the inequalities and injustices faced by Aboriginal Peoples will be reduced or eliminated in the future? What do you believe are the best strategies for achieving this goal?

Recommended Readings

Bunten, Alexis C. 2015. *So, How Long Have You Been Native? Life as an Alaska Native Tour Guide*. Lincoln: University of Nebraska Press.

Coultard, Glen. 2014. *Red Skin, White Masks: Rejecting the Colonial Politics of Recognition*. Minneapolis: University of Minnesota Press.

King, Tomas. 2012. *The Inconvenient Indian: A Curious Account of Native People in North America*. Toronto: Doubleday Canada.

Lawrence, Bonita. 2004. *Real Indians and Others: Mixed-Blood Urban Native Peoples and Indigenous Nationhood*. Vancouver: University of British Columbia Press.

Niezen, Ronald. 2013. *Truth and Indignation: Canada's Truth and Reconciliation Commission on Indian Residential Schools*. Toronto: University of Toronto Press.

Recommended Websites

Assembly of First Nations, Canada:
http://www.afn.ca/index.php/en

Indigenous Foundations, UBC:
http://indigenousfoundations.arts.ubc.ca/

Native Women's Association of Canada:
http://www.nwac.ca/

Truth and Reconciliation Commission of Canada:
http://www.trc.ca/

Notes

1. In 1997, the Supreme Court of Canada decided that Aboriginal rights had not been extinguished and that Justice McEachern's decision was flawed because he did not accept the Gitksan and Wet'suwet'en *adaawk* (oral history).
2. The physical location of this fishing community is not specifically relevant to the main issue of this chapter. Nor does this one man's storytelling necessarily reflect widespread opinion within the larger community.
3. The kin-ordered mode of production is one in which access to and control of labour power is mediated by kinship. For an elaboration of this concept, see Wolf (1997 [1982]: 88–96).

References

Andrew-Gee, Eric. 2014. "Aboriginal men murdered at higher rate than aboriginal women." *Toronto Star*, 22 Aug. http://www.thestar.com/news/gta/2014/08/22/aboriginal_men_murdered_at_higher_rate_than_aboriginal_women.html.

Barman, Jean. 1996. "Aboriginal education at the crossroads: The legacy of residential schools and the way ahead." In David Alan Long and Olive Patricia Dickason, eds, *Visions of the Heart: Canadian Aboriginal Issues,* pp. 271–303. Toronto: Harcourt Brace and Company.

Campbell, Kenneth, Charles R. Menzies, and Brent Peacock. 2003. *BC First Nations Studies*. Victoria: BC Ministry of Education.

CBCNews.2013."EarlyinfantmortalityinCanadacalled 2nd worst in developed world." 8 May. http://www.cbc.ca/news/health/early-infant-mortality-in-canada-called-2nd-worst-in-developed-world-1.1314423.

Canadian Council of Aboriginal Businesses. 2010. "Aboriginal income gap." https://www.ccab.com/uploads/File/One%20Pagers/Aboriginal-Income-Gap.pdf.

Centre for Suicide Prevention. 2013. *Suicide Prevention Resource Toolkit*. https://suicideinfo.ca/LinkClick.aspx?fileticket=MVIyGo2V4YY%3D&tabid=563.

Clairmont, Don. 2006. *Aboriginal Policing in Canada: An Overview of Developments in First Nations.* Report for the Attorney General of Ontario and the Canadian Department of Justice, Sept. https://www.attorneygeneral.jus.gov.on.ca/inquiries/ipperwash/policy_part/research/pdf/Clairmont_Aboriginal_Policing.pdf.

Codere, Helen. 1961. *Fighting with Property: A Study of Kwakiutl Potlatching and Warfare 1729–1930.* American Ethnological Society Monograph No. 18. New York: J.J. Augustin.

Cole, Douglas, and Ira Chaikin. 1990. *An Iron Hand upon the People.* Vancouver: Douglas & McIntyre.

Collin, Chantal, and Hilary Jensen. 2009. *A Statistical Profile of Poverty in Canada*. Ottawa: Parliament of Canada, Social Affairs Division, 28 Sept. http://www.parl.gc.ca/content/lop/researchpublications/prb0917-e.htm#a9.

Correctional Services Canada. 2001. "Aboriginal offender statistics." http://www.csc-scc.gc.ca/text/prgrm/correctional/abissues/know/4_e.shtml. Accessed 3 Sept. 2002.

Department of Justice. 2011. *Aboriginal Justice Strategy Evaluation, Final Report*. http://justice.gc.ca/eng/rp-pr/cp-pm/eval/rep-rap/11/ajs-sja/p2.html#sec2.

Dyck, Noel. 1991. *What Is the Indian Problem? Tutelage and Resistance in Canadian Indian Administration*. St. John's: ISER Books.

Fisher, Robin. 1977. *Contact and Conflict: Indian–European Relations in British Columbia, 1774–1890.* Vancouver: University of British Columbia Press.

Fong, Frances, and Sonya Gulati. 2013. "Employment and education among Aboriginal Peoples." Toronto: TD Economics, Special Report.

Frideres, James, and Rene Gadacz. 2011. *Aboriginal Peoples in Canada: Contemporary Conflicts*, 9th edn. Toronto: Pearson Canada.

Gilmore,Scott.2015."Canada'sraceproblem?It'sworsethan America's." *Maclean's*, 22 Jan. http://www.macleans.ca/news/canada/out-of-sight-out-of-mind-2/.

Gordon, Catherine, and Jerry White. 2014. "Indigenous educational attainment in Canada." *International Indigenous Policy Journal* 5, 3: Article 6.

Haig-Brown, Celia. 1988. *Resistance and Renewal: First Nations People's Experiences of the Residential School.* Vancouver: University of British Columbia Press.

Health Canada. 2003. *A Statistical Profile on the Health of First Nations in Canada: Vital Statistics for Atlantic and Western Canada, 2001/2002.* First Nations and Inuit Health Branch in-house statistics. http://www.hc-sc.gc.ca/fniah-spnia/pubs/aborig-autoch/stats-profil-atlant/index-eng.php#fig9.

Hwang, Monica. 2015. "Understanding differences in political trust among Canada's major ethno-racial groups." Paper presented at the Canadian Sociology Association annual meetings, Ottawa, 3 June.

Innes, Robert A. 2015. "Moose on the loose: Indigenous men, violence, and the colonial excuse (with errata)." *Aboriginal Policy Studies* 4, 1: 46–56.

Knight, Rolf. 1996. *Indians at Work*, 2nd edn. Vancouver: New Star Books.

Lithopoulos, Savvas. 2007. *International Comparison of Indigenous Policing Models.* Ottawa: Public Safety Canada. http://www.publicsafety.gc.ca/cnt/rsrcs/pblctns/cmprsn-ndgns-plcng/index-eng.aspx.

McCaskill, D. 1983. "The urbanization of Indians in Winnipeg, Toronto, Edmonton, and Vancouver: A comparative analysis." *Culture* 1: 82–9.

McDonald, James A. 1994. "Social change and the creation of underdevelopment: A northwest coast case." *American Ethnologist* 21, 1: 152–75.

McEachern, Justice Allan. 1991. *Delgamuukw: Reasons for Judgment.* BC Supreme Court.

Maxim, Paul S., Jerry P. White, Dan Beavon, and Paul C. Whitehead. 2001. "Dispersion and polarization of income among Aboriginal and non-Aboriginal Canadians." *Canadian Review of Sociology and Anthropology* 38, 4: 465–76.

Menzies, Charles R. 1994. "Stories from home: First Nations, land claims, and Euro-Canadians." *American Ethnologist* 21, 4: 776–91.

———. 1997. "Indian or white? Racial identities in the British Columbian fishing industry." In Anthony Marcus, ed., *Anthropology for a Small Planet: Culture and Community in a Global Environment*, pp. 110–23. St James, NY: Brandywine Press.

Monture-Angus, Patricia. 1995. *Thunder in My Soul: A Mohawk Woman Speaks.* Halifax: Fernwood.

———. 1996. "Lessons in decolonization: Aboriginal overrepresentation in Canadian criminal justice." In David Alan Long and Olive Patricia Dickason, eds, *Visions of the Heart: Canadian Aboriginal Issues*, pp. 335–54. Toronto: Harcourt Brace and Company.

Murphy, Brian, Xuelin Zhang, and Claude Dionne. 2012. *Low Income in Canada: A Multi-line and Multi-index Perspective.* Income Research Paper Series, Mar. Catalogue no. 75F0002M—No. 001. Ottawa: Minister of Industry.

National Collaborating Centre for Aboriginal Health. 2012. *The State of Knowledge of Aboriginal Health: A Review of Aboriginal Public Health in Canada.* http://www.nccah-ccnsa.ca/Publications/Lists/Publications/Attachments/52/The%20State%20of%20Knowledge%20of%20Aboringal%20Health%20(EN).pdf.

———. 2013. "An overview of Aboriginal health in Canada." http://www.nccah-ccnsa.ca/Publications/Lists/Publications/Attachments/101/abororiginal_health_web.pdf.

Newell, Diane. 1993. *Tangled Webs of History: Indians and the Law in Canada's Pacific Coast Fisheries.* Toronto: University of Toronto Press.

Office of the Correctional Investigator. 2013. "Backgrounder: Aboriginal offenders—A critical situation." http://www.oci-bec.gc.ca/cnt/rpt/oth-aut/oth-aut20121022info-eng.aspx.

Pendakur, Krishna, and Ravi Pendakur. 2011. "Aboriginal income disparity in Canada." *Canadian Public Policy* 37, 1: 61–83.

Perreault, Samuel. 2011. "Violent victimization of Aboriginal people in the Canadian provinces, 2009." *Juristat*, 11 Mar. Catalogue no. 85-002. Ottawa: Statistics Canada. http://www.statcan.gc.ca/pub/85-002-x/2011001/article/11415-eng.htm.

Ponting, J. Rick, and Jerilynn Kiely. 1997. "Disempowerment: 'Justice,' racism, and public opinion." In J. Rick Ponting, ed., *First Nations in Canada: Perspectives on Opportunity, Empowerment, and Self-Determination*, pp. 152–92. Toronto: McGraw-Hill Ryerson.

Public Safety Canada. 2015. "Restorative justice." http://www.publicsafety.gc.ca/cnt/cntrng-crm/crrctns/rstrtv-jstc-eng.aspx.

RCMP. 2014. *Missing and Murdered Aboriginal Women: A National Operational Overview.* In collaboration with Statistics Canada. Catalogue no. PS64-115/2014E-PDF. http://www.rcmp-grc.gc.ca/pubs/mmaw-faapd-eng.pdf.

Schwartz, Daniel. 2013. "How does native funding work? It's a combination of federal contributions and 'own-source revenue'." CBC News, 6 Feb. http://www.cbc.ca/news/canada/how-does-native-funding-work-1.1301120.

Statistics Canada. 2010. "Life expectancy." Catalogue no. 89-645-X. http://www.statcan.gc.ca/pub/89-645-x/2010001/life-expectancy-esperance-vie-eng.htm.

———. 2011a. "National Household Survey Aboriginal population profile, Canada, 2011." https://www12.statcan.gc.ca/nhs-enm/2011/dp-pd/aprof/details/page.cfm?Lang=E&Geo1=PR&Code1=01&Data=Count&SearchText=Canada&SearchType=Begins&SearchPR=01&A1=Income%20of%20households&Custom=&TABID=1.

———. 2011b. National Household Survey profile, Canada 2011. http://www12.statcan.gc.ca/nhs-enm/2011/dp-pd/prof/details/page.cfm?Lang=E&Geo1=PR&Code1=01&Data=Count&SearchType=Begins&SearchPR=01&A1=All&B1=All.

———. 2011c. “Fact sheet—2011 National Household Survey—Aboriginal demographics, educational attainment, and labour market outcomes.” https://www.aadnc-aandc.gc.ca/eng/1376329205785/1376329233875.

Tennant, Paul. 1990. *Aboriginal Peoples and Politics: The Indian Land Question in British Columbia, 1849–1989.* Vancouver: University of British Columbia Press.

Truth and Reconciliation Commission of Canada. 2015. *Honouring the Truth, Reconciling for the Future: Summary of the Final Report of the Truth and Reconciliation Commission of Canada.* Winnipeg: Truth and Reconciliation Commission of Canada.

White, Jerry, Julie Peters, Dan Beavon, and Nicholas Spence, eds. 2009. *Aboriginal Education: Current Crisis and Future Alternatives.* Toronto: Thompson Educational Publishing.

Wilson, Daniel, and David Macdonald. 2010. *The Income Gap between Aboriginal Peoples and the Rest of Canada.* Ottawa: Canadian Centre for Policy Alternatives, Dec. http://www.policyalternatives.ca/sites/default/files/uploads/publications/reports/docs/Aboriginal%20Income%20Gap.pdf.

Wolf, Eric R. 1997 [1982]. *Europe and the People without History*, 2nd edn. Berkeley: University of California Press.

11 French Canada and Inequality: Quebec's Quiet Revolution, Fifty Years Later*

Pierre Fortin

When Jean Lesage and his *équipe du tonnerre* ("tiger team") came to power in 1960, two-thirds of young adults in Quebec didn't have high school diplomas.[1] Throughout the 1950s the Quebec economy had surfed on the global post-war expansion, but Quebec had not been able to narrow the 20 per cent gap between its standard of living and that of neighbouring Ontario.[2] Although Francophones made up 80 per cent of Quebec's population, only 47 per cent of Quebecers were employed in Francophone-owned businesses.[3] When writer Pierre Vallières called French Canadians the "white niggers of America" in 1968, he was widely dismissed for making a ridiculous overstatement. In fact, he was telling the truth. In 1960, French-origin men earned less relative to British-origin men in Quebec (52 per cent) than Black men did relative to White men in the United States (54 per cent).[4]

To his credit, Lesage insisted that improving the relative economic position of Francophone Quebecers was urgent. Here is an excerpt from his April 1962 budget speech:

> We constitute an ethnic minority that has been able to survive till now, but whose material power is far from corresponding to that of our English compatriots. In certain fields, we have accumulated the delays of at least one generation. It is for this reason that we have so much to accomplish today and that we have to realize it so quickly. We possess a common lever, the state of Quebec. We would be guilty if we did not use it. . . . The needs of our people can be grouped in three categories: those that arise from the effort that we should make in matters of education and culture, those that arise from the necessity of increasing the welfare and health of our population, and those that are connected with the development of our economy.[5]

The Lesage Liberals used the provincial government to achieve four goals:

- raise the general level of schooling,
- accelerate economic development,
- share the increased income widely, and
- improve the relative economic position of Francophones.

* Abridged from Pierre Fortin, "Quebec's Quiet Revolution, 50 Years Later," *Inroads* 291 (Summer-Fall 2011), pp. 90–99. Reprinted with permission.

With the passage of a half-century, it is a good time to ask whether these goals have been broadly achieved. In sum, the answer is "yes." In what follows, I lay out evidence that the goals have been realized, largely as a result of the active role played by the Quebec provincial government during and after Lesage's terms in office. At the end, I mention a few areas where more progress has to be made and a number of new problems that remain to be addressed.

Quebec Government Activity Has Expanded Greatly

Lesage's deeds matched his words. A long-delayed set of accelerated changes took place during his two terms in office from 1960 to 1966. Political scientist Dale Thompson was the first to describe this as the "Quiet Revolution."[6] This period has left a lasting imprint on Quebec's institutions and shaped the culture of the entire generation of baby boomers who were entering adult life in the 1960s.

Beginning in 1960, government activity increased rapidly. The provincial public service was modernized and allowed to unionize and expand. Education and health were secularized, professionalized, and centralized. New programs were launched, such as hospital insurance (a federal–provincial shared-cost program), school allowances, and the Quebec Pension Plan. Regional high schools were launched throughout the province. A host of state enterprises were created, such as the Société Générale de Financement (SGF), the steel company Sidbec, the Société Québécoise d'Exploration Minière (SOQUEM), and the Caisse de Dépôt et Placement du Québec (CDPQ). In 1963, all large private power companies were nationalized, enabling the old Hydroelectric Commission to be transformed into modern-day Hydro-Québec.

From 1960 to 1966 provincial government expenditures and tax revenues tripled, while gross domestic income increased by 65 per cent. The rapid change in institutions coupled with the sharp increase in the tax burden generated a voter backlash that led Lesage to electoral defeat in 1966. Out went "*Ti-Jean la taxe*" (little Jean, the taxman), as he was called during the campaign.

Nevertheless, after 1966 the new Union Nationale Premier, Daniel Johnson, Sr, and his successors decided to carry on with the Quiet Revolution. From 1966 until today, Quebecers' lives have been changed by family allowances, health insurance, and social assistance (two additional federal–provincial shared-cost programs), the development of CEGEPs, many more new state enterprises (SOQUIP, SOQUIA, REXFOR, Loto Quebec, National Asbestos Corporation, Madelipêche, Nouveler, Quebecair, among others), the James Bay hydroelectric project, language legislation to protect French within the province, no-fault automobile insurance, provincial economic summits, many forms of financial assistance to business, a few privatizations, support for the free trade agreement with the United States, a large number of tax credits, and a new wave of social programs in the 1990s.

Figure 11.1 summarizes the impact all these measures have had on total provincial and local government (P&L) expenditure from 1961 to 2007.[7] From 13 per cent in 1961, Quebec's P&L spending increased to 34 per cent of GDP in the mid-1980s, and it has hovered around this level ever since. From the same starting point in 1961, Ontario's P&L spending has stabilized around 24 per cent of provincial GDP, 10 points below the Quebec level. Put another way, Quebec's P&L expenditure in 2007 was $30 billion more than if the province had spent at the same rate as Ontario.[8] Consistent with its high ratio of P&L spending to GDP, total taxes paid by Quebecers to all levels of government amounted to 38 per cent of GDP in 2008, compared to 30 per cent in provinces other than Quebec.

An interesting question is how much of the excess of Quebec's P&L spending over the national average has been financed from own-source revenues and how much has come from above-average federal transfers. The answer for 2007 is that 84 per cent came from own-source revenues and 16 per cent from above-average federal transfers.[9] In contrast, for the three Maritime provinces, 5 per cent of above-average P&L spending came from own-source revenue and 95 per cent from above-average federal transfers.

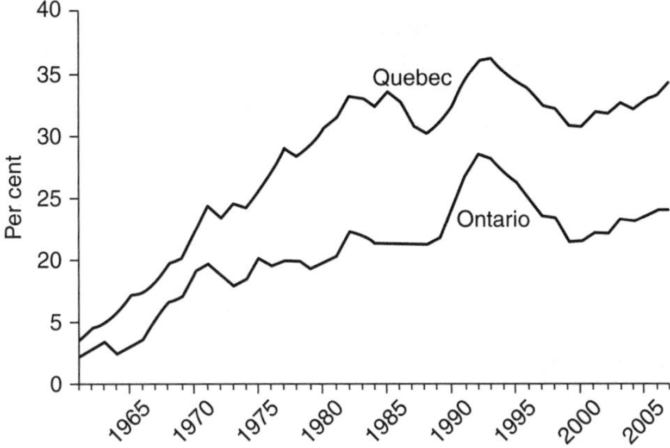

Figure 11.1 Total Provincial and Local Government Expenditure in Quebec and Ontario, 1961–2007 (% of GDP)

Source: Statistics Canada, CANSIM Table 384-0004.

Quebec's Educational Attainment Now Matches the National Average

How effective has expanded government activity been in helping Quebec achieve the goals set by Lesage? Table 11.1 shows that Quebec's average level of schooling was more than a year under the national average 50 years ago; by 2001 it had closed the gap.

Table 11.2 compares educational attainment of the 25–44 population in Quebec and Ontario, the best-performing province. Basically, Quebec is weaker in the tails but stronger in the middle. First, Quebecers are more likely to lack a high school certificate than Ontarians (11 versus 7 per cent). This is particularly significant since it takes 11 years to complete high school in Quebec and 12 in Ontario. Second, a smaller percentage of Quebecers than Ontarians hold university degrees (30 versus 34 per cent). However, Quebecers lead at the trades and college level (43 versus 35 per cent), which includes vocational, college, and technical studies. As a result, the probability of having some form of post-secondary training beyond high school is higher in Quebec than in Ontario (73 versus 69 per cent).

What about the quality of education? Table 11.3 summarizes the evidence from the 2009 study of student skills at age 15 conducted by the OECD Programme for International Student Assessment (PISA). It turns out that youth from the four largest Canadian provinces

Table 11.1 Average Years of Completed Schooling for Population Aged 25–34, Quebec, Ontario, and All Other Provinces, 1961 and 2001

Region	1961	2001	Change
Quebec	9.5	14.4	+4.9
Ontario	11.0	14.7	+3.7
All other provinces	10.7	14.3	+3.6

Note: 2001 is the last census year for which data on years of schooling were collected. The 1961 data for the 25–34 age group are assumed to be the same as the 1991 census data for the 55–64 age group.

Source: Statistics Canada, *Census of Canada* (1991, 2001).

Table 11.2 Distribution of Population Aged 25–44 by Highest Educational Attainment, Quebec and Ontario, 2010 (% of Total Population)

	Quebec	Ontario
Incomplete high school	11	7
High school certificate	16	24
Trades certificate and college diploma	43	35
University degree	30	34
Total	100	100

Source: Statistics Canada, CANSIM Table 282-0004.

Table 11.3 Average PISA Scores of 15-Year-Olds in Reading, Mathematics, and Science, Selected Provinces and the United States, 2009

Region	Reading		Mathematics		Science	
	Score	Rank	Score	Rank	Score	Rank
Quebec	522	9	543	5	524	13
Ontario	531	6	526	12	531	10
Alberta	533	4	529	10	545	4
British Columbia	525	8	523	15	535	8
United States	500	21	487	41	502	30
Study Median	486	37	488	37	495	37

Note: Results are available for 65 countries (including the 30 members of the OECD) and the 10 Canadian provinces. Rank is based on the scores of 74 units, which include the 10 provinces and all countries except Canada.
Source: Tamara Knighton, Pierre Brochu, and Tomasz Gluszynski, Measuring Up: Canadian Results of the OECD PISA Study, The Performance of Canada's Youth in Reading, Mathematics and Science, 2009 First Results for Canadians Aged 15. Catalogue no. 81-590-XPE-no. 4 (Ottawa: Statistics Canada, with HRSDC and CME, 2010).

(including Quebec) are doing well in reading, mathematics, and science relative to those from the United States and other countries. Among provinces, Alberta is first in reading and science, and Quebec is the best in mathematics.

To sum up, while the quantity and quality of education in Quebec can still be improved, among Canadian regions the province is no longer the laggard it was 50 years ago when Lesage and his "tiger team" launched the Quiet Revolution. Moreover, since education is a provincial responsibility under the Canadian Constitution, credit for closing the educational gap lies essentially with the policies and institutions Quebec itself has put in place over the last 50 years. Major challenges remain: reducing the high school dropout rate (among Francophone boys in particular) and increasing the university graduation rate further.

Quebec's Standard of Living Has Caught Up with Ontario's

A key concern of Premier Lesage was economic development. His objective was to develop the economy so that Quebec's standard of living could one day catch up with that of its "English compatriots." Has this challenge been met in the last 50 years?

Figure 11.2 answers this question affirmatively, taking Ontario as the economic reference as most public documents did in the 1960s. It shows that Quebec's standard of living increased from 81 per cent of Ontario's in 1961 to 96 per cent in 2009.[10] During the first 30 years, progress was slow and rocky. In particular, the temporary "bubble" in 1976–84 was a consequence of the James Bay megaproject. In 1989, the Quebec/Ontario ratio was 85 per cent, still only 4 points above the 1961 level. But over the next 20-year period, Quebec gained 11 points, reaching 96 per cent in 2009. The remaining 4-point gap can be explained by the fact that Quebecers choose to work fewer hours per capita than Ontarians. They have shorter work weeks, more holidays, more leaves and longer vacations, and they retire earlier. *La joie de vivre* is a choice that has a cost. But in a basic sense, the two provinces are on a par in standard of living.

The surge in Quebec's relative standard of living after 1989 is not the result of fast-growing output per worker (productivity), but of rapid increase in the employment rate (proportion of people aged 15 and over with jobs). Quebec's employment rate increased from 86 per cent of Ontario's in 1989 to exact parity with Ontario's in 2010.[11] Given the close connection between rising educational attainment and employment, and given that it requires decades to raise the education level of an entire population, much of this development can be seen as a delayed consequence of the Quiet Revolution. The "culture" of the Quiet Revolution has also produced progressive legislation such as low-fee child care and the Parental Insurance Plan. Both programs are popular and have pushed Quebec women's labour force participation in the 25–54 age group above the national average.[12] Another "cultural" factor to appreciate is that, after a string of major labour conflicts between 1972 and 1983, Quebecers have now learned to manage peacefully the system of industrial relations put in place by the Quiet Revolution.

Given that from now on aging will reduce the employed fraction of Quebec's population, future advances in standard of living will crucially depend on what happens on the productivity front. So far, Quebec's performance on this score is not impressive. Although currently 5 per cent higher than that of Ontario,[13] its productivity level is 16 per cent lower than that of the United States. It is also far behind productivity levels of countries such as France, Germany, Norway, the Netherlands, and Belgium.

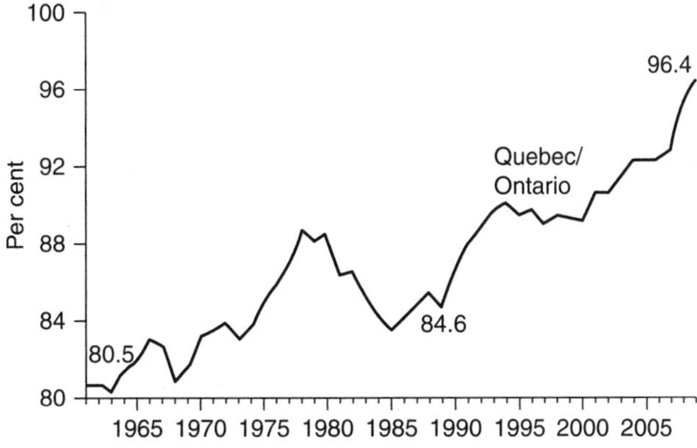

Figure 11.2 Fifty-Year Trend in Relative Standard of Living: Quebec as a Percentage of Ontario, 1961–2009

Source: Calculations based on Statistics Canada data.

There Is Less Poverty and Income Inequality in Quebec Than Elsewhere

"Increasing the welfare and health of our population" was another stated objective of the Lesage government. How successful has Quebec been in building its welfare state since then?

According to data shown in Table 11.4, by the late 2000s Quebec had arguably become the most egalitarian society in North America. Whether in absolute or relative terms, there is generally less poverty in Quebec than elsewhere in Canada and the United States. By the late 2000s, among Canadian provinces, only Alberta had an absolute poverty rate (7.4 per cent) lower than Quebec's (8.5 per cent). This difference is small in view of the fact that, in recent years, real income per capita in the oil-rich province has been 60 per cent higher. Broad measures of income inequality reported in Table 11.4, such as the Gini coefficient and the top 1 per cent income share, give the same message: there is less inequality in Quebec.

The fact that Quebec has less poverty and income inequality—even as the province is far from being one of the richest jurisdictions in North America—suggests that its tax/transfer system must, by design, be more redistributive than that of other jurisdictions. Table 11.5 shows that this is indeed the case. The two left-hand columns report that market income for the lowest quintile is lower in Quebec than in other provinces. However, once government transfers are added and income taxes subtracted, the poorest 20 per cent wind up with greater purchasing power in Quebec than in other parts of the country.[14] The implication of this redistributive effort is that Quebec's income tax system must be more progressive. This is illustrated by the two right-hand columns of Table 11.5: among the highest-earning fifth of Quebecers and Canadians overall, both groups pay the same tax rate (21 per cent), despite Quebecers' market incomes in this group being 15 per cent lower.

Quebec's tax, transfer, and social policies have their roots in the Quiet Revolution of the 1960s. They reflect Lesage's vision as well as the shared social democratic bent of his Liberal and Parti Québécois successors. Even as the welfare state was pronounced dead in conservative circles around the world in the 1990s, Quebec's *État providence* was beginning a second life with a new wave of social programs such as universal

Table 11.4 Poverty and Income Inequality, Quebec, Canada, and the United States, Various Years

Measure	Quebec	Canada	United States
Absolute poverty rate			
(market basket measure 2007)	8.5%	10.1%	n.a.
Relative poverty rate			
(low-income measure 2006)	9.0%	11.4%	17.3%
Gini coefficient (2008)	0.30	0.32	0.37
Top 1% income share (2007)	11%	14%	24%

Note: The absolute poverty rate is the percentage of population that cannot buy a fixed subsistence-level basket of goods and services. The relative poverty rate is the percentage living in households with less than 50 per cent of the median disposable income of the region. The Gini coefficient is a number between 0 and 1 that is a broad measure of the degree of income inequality. The income referred to in "Top 1% income share" is total income less government transfers (in other words, market income) as reported in income tax statistics.

Sources: Human Resources and Skills Development Canada, *Low Income in Canada: 2000–2007 Using the Market Basket Measure, Final Report* (Ottawa, 2009); Statistics Canada, CANSIM Table 202-0709; Stéphane Crespo, Annuaire de statistiques sur l'inégalité de revenu et le faible revenu (Quebec City: Institut de la Statistique du Québec, 2008); Luxembourg Income Study, "Key figures," at www.lisproject.org; Canada Revenue Agency, Final Statistics, 2009 edition (for 2007 tax year), www.cra-arc.gc.ca; United States Internal Revenue Service, "Tax statistics," www.irs.gov.

Table 11.5 Redistributive Effect of Tax/Transfer System, Quebec and Canada, 2008

	Lowest Fifth		Highest Fifth	
Element	**Quebec**	**Canada**	**Quebec**	**Canada**
Average annual market income ($)	8,200	9,800	88,700	104,700
Plus: Transfers less taxes ($)	8,000	6,600	−18,900	–22,300
Equals: Disposable income ($)	16,200	16,400	69,800	82,400
PPP-based disposable income ($)	17,100	16,400	73,500	82,400
Net-of-transfer tax rate	−98%	−67%	21%	21%

Note: Data are for individuals in lowest and highest quintiles of economic families with two persons or more, where each individual is represented by adjusted family income. Disposable income based on purchasing power parity (PPP) is disposable income adjusted for differences in the cost of living between Quebec and the national average. Statistics Canada's October 2008 survey of city retail prices estimates that consumer prices in Quebec were 95 per cent of the national average. Transfers and taxes are total federal and provincial transfers and personal income taxes.

Source: Statistics Canada, CANSIM Tables 202-0706 and 326-0015.

drug insurance, low-fee child care, extended parental leaves, new family allowances, and pay equity. Given population aging and the current state of public finances, the challenge from now on will probably be to pay for and maintain these programs rather than to adopt new ones.

The Relative Economic Position of Francophones Has Been Normalized

Lesage was concerned not only with economic development of Quebec overall, but with the relative position of Francophones within the province. Has their position improved in the last 50 years?

Unambiguously yes. There are two dimensions to consider: relative earnings and business ownership. On the first, Table 11.6 reports 2000 earnings, using an index in which the earnings of unilingual Anglophones are set to 100 and the earnings of other groups compared to this value. The findings show that the earnings of Quebec Francophones were equal to or greater than earnings of Anglophones of the same gender, language skills, level of education, number of years of experience, and number of weeks worked. This is a far cry from the 52 per cent ratio of wages of French-origin to British-origin men in Quebec in 1960. Faster economic integration of allophones, particularly those who are unilingual, remains a major challenge.

On the second dimension, François and Luc Vaillancourt have estimated that Francophone-owned businesses in Quebec increased their share of provincial employment from 47 per cent in 1961 to 67 per cent in 2003.[15] They found that foreign control over provincial employment was 10 per cent. This implies that, foreign-owned firms aside, 75 per cent of domestic Canadian control over Quebec employment derives from Francophone-owned firms—not far from the Francophone percentage in Quebec's population (80 per cent). Taking foreign ownership as a given, Quebec Francophones have become *maîtres chez nous* (masters in their own house).

Challenges Remain, and New Ones Have Arisen

Over fifty years ago, Jean Lesage and his Liberal government launched the Quiet Revolution. The basic goal was the modernization—the *mise à jour*—of Quebec society. The Liberals wanted to use the provincial government to raise the level of schooling, accelerate economic development,

Table 11.6 Index of Earnings, by Gender, Mother Tongue, and Language Skills, Quebec, 2000 (unilingual Anglophones = 100)

Language Skills	Men	Women
Unilingual Anglophones	100	100
Bilingual Anglophones	122	107
Unilingual Francophones	122	100
Bilingual Francophones	137	117
Unilingual-English Allophones	85	100
Unilingual-French Allophones	81	81
Bilingual Allophones	108	105

Note: Data are controlled for level of education, years of experience, and number of weeks worked.
Source: François Vaillancourt, Dominique Lemay, and Luc Vaillancourt, *Laggards No More: The Changed Socioeconomic Status of Francophones in Quebec*, Backgrounder No. 103 (Toronto: C.D. Howe Institute, 2007), Tables 3 and 4. Results are from Lemay's M.Sc. thesis (Université de Montréal, 2005), based on 2001 census microdata.

share the increased income widely, and improve the relative economic position of Francophones.

The goals Lesage set out have been met to a large extent. Government activity has expanded greatly; educational attainment is up to the national average; the standard of living has caught up with Ontario's; there is less poverty and income inequality than elsewhere in North America; and the relative economic position of Francophones has been normalized. In each case, the origin of progress can be found in the Quiet Revolution—in the culture and institutions it put in place in the first half of the 1960s, and in the inspiration it gave Lesage's successors. There is no question that national and international factors have simultaneously influenced Quebec's evolution during the last half-century, but the conclusion that the Quiet Revolution has played a fundamental role is inescapable.

Naturally, there is more to accomplish. In education, there remain the important tasks of reducing the high school dropout rate (particularly for Francophone boys) and increasing the university graduation rate. In the economy, the main challenges are to increase productivity (while showing respect for the environment), remain a sharing society, pay the bills of existing programs before adding new ones, and facilitate the economic integration of immigrants and Aboriginals.

There are also new problems to address. Lesage had high hopes for what the "state of Quebec" could accomplish. Indeed, the provincial "state" has helped Quebec reach the goals Lesage set out. But 50 years later, the reach of the provincial government into every corner of Quebec life has become a cause for concern. Although more peaceful than in the 1970s and 1980s, labour relations in the public sector are still very adversarial. Administrative, professional, and union bureaucracies block the slightest proposed change in the health and education sectors. Bridges and overpasses threaten to collapse, and human lives have been lost in a few incidents. Too many teenagers drop out of high school. Timely access to health care seems out of reach despite billions of additional dollars being poured into the sector each year. Public construction projects are rarely completed on schedule or within budget. Rumours of corruption in politics and construction are widespread. Interest group lobbyists are everywhere, extracting maximum benefits for their clients at the expense of taxpayers. The government is the wet nurse of businesses and the Santa Claus of regions. Large protected sectors such as electricity, agriculture, health, and construction post disturbingly high production costs.

Welcome to the twenty-first century.

Questions for Critical Thought

1. What aspects of French–English relations have changed over the 50 years since the Quiet Revolution?
2. What forces have produced change in French–English inequality in Quebec since the Quiet Revolution? What was the role of the Quiet Revolution in those changes?
3. How have the relations between Quebec and Canada changed over the same 50-year period? What is the relationship between changes within Quebec and changes in the relations between Quebec and the rest of Canada?
4. What have been the results of the changes in French–English relations as described by Fortin?

Recommended Readings

Behiels, Michael. 1985. *Prelude to Quebec's Quiet Revolution: Liberalism and Neo-Nationalism*. Montreal and Kingston: McGill-Queen's University Press.

Fortin, Pierre. 2010. "Quebec is fairer: There is less poverty and inequality in Quebec." *Inroads* 26: 58–65.

Haddow, Rodney. 2015. *Comparing Quebec and Ontario: Political Economy and Public Policy at the Turn of the Millennium*. Toronto: University of Toronto Press.

McRoberts, Kenneth. 1993. *Quebec: Social Change and Political Crisis*. Toronto: McClelland & Stewart, 3rd edn, with a postscript.

Noël, Alain. 2013. "Quebec's new politics of redistribution." In Keith Banting and John Myles, eds, *Inequality and the Fading of Redistributive Politics*, pp. 234–55. Vancouver: University of British Columbia Press.

Porter, John. 2015. *The Vertical Mosaic: An Analysis of Social Class and Power in Canada, 50th Anniversary Edition*. Toronto: University of Toronto Press.

Vaillancourt, François, Dominique Lemay, and Luc Vaillancourt. 2007. *Laggards No More: The Changed Socioeconomic Status of Francophones in Quebec*. Backgrounder No. 103. Toronto: C.D. Howe Institute.

Recommended Websites

Association for Canadian Studies:
http://www.acs-aec.ca/en/; http://www.acs-aec.ca/fr/

Centre d'étude sur la pauvreté et l'exclusion:
http://www.cepe.gouv.qc.ca/

English-language introduction to Centre d'études ur la pauvreté et l'exclusion:
http://www.cepe.gouv.qc.ca/Index_en.asp

Government of Canada, Office of the Commissioner of Official Languages:
http://www.ocol-clo.gc.ca/en; http://www.ocol-clo.gc.ca/fr

Notes

1. Data are for population aged 25–34. In Ontario and other provinces, the percentage without a high school degree was 49 per cent. Statistics Canada's CANSIM Table 282-0004 gives the educational attainment of the 55–64 age group in 1990, which should be the same as that of the 25–34 age group in 1960.
2. From 1947 to 1960, the average growth rate of net-of-transfer personal income per capita was 5 per cent in both Quebec and Ontario. As a result, the Quebec level adjusted for purchasing power parity remained unchanged at around 80 per cent of the Ontario level. The data are from CANSIM Tables 380-0043, 380-0047, and 380-0050.
3. From François Vaillancourt, Dominique Lemay, and Luc Vaillancourt, *Laggards No More: The Changed Socioeconomic Status of Francophones in Quebec*, Backgrounder No. 103 (Toronto: C.D. Howe Institute, 2007), Table 5.
4. The Quebec figure is from Vaillancourt, Lemay, and Vaillancourt, *Laggards No More*, note 2. The US figure is from David Card and Alan Krueger, "Trends in relative Black–White earnings revisited," *American Economic Review* 83, 2 (1993): 85–91.
5. Quebec, *Budget Speech* (Quebec City, 12 Apr. 1962), 37, 39.
6. Dale C. Thomson, *Jean Lesage and the Quiet Revolution* (Toronto: Macmillan, 1984).
7. Total P&L expenditure is defined here as non-federal current and capital expenditure. It includes Canada and Quebec Pension Plan benefits and capital spending by government. Given that the responsibilities of local governments differ across provinces, meaningful interprovincial comparisons have to be based on the aggregate P&L sector.
8. The 2007 P&L expenditure/GDP ratio was 29 per cent in Atlantic Canada, 23 per cent in British Columbia, and 18 per cent in the Prairie provinces.
9. In this calculation, federal transfers to Quebec include the value of the tax abatement granted by the federal government to Quebec taxpayers in lieu of an equal amount of transfers to the government of Quebec. The data are from Statistics Canada's CANSIM Tables 384-0002 and 384-0004 and Canada Revenue Agency, *Final Statistics*, 2009 edition (for 2007 tax year).
10. The standard of living in Figure 11.2 is defined as real domestic income per capita. Real domestic income is equal to gross domestic product (GDP) divided by the average price of what people buy, which includes private and public consumption and investment goods and services. This average price is allowed to differ between the two provinces. "Per capita" means that the result is divided by total population.
11. To avoid any purely demographic distortion caused by the population 65 and over, the employment rate is defined here as total employment of the population 15 and over as a percentage of the 15–64 population.
12. In 2010, the labour force participation rate of women aged 25–54 was 83.6 per cent in Quebec, 82.3 per cent in Ontario, and 81.5 per cent in all other provinces.
13. In purchasing-power-adjusted US dollars, productivity levels (GDP per work hour) in 2009 were $53.10 in the United States, $44.80 in Quebec, and $42.60 in Ontario. This implies that Quebec leads Ontario by 5 per cent, but lags behind the United States by 16 per cent.
14. Low-income Quebecers also have access to greater amounts and variety of public goods and services than other low-income Canadians.
15. François Vaillancourt and Luc Vaillancourt, *La propriété des employeurs au Québec en 2003 selon le groupe d'appartenance linguistique* (Quebec City: Conseil Supérieur de la Langue Française, 2005), Table 3.1.

12 Immigration Trends and Integration Issues: More Than a Century of Change*

Monica Boyd and Michael Vickers

Introduction

Record numbers of immigrants came to Canada in the early 1900s. During World War I and the Depression years, numbers declined, but at the beginning of the new millennium they again approached those recorded 100 years earlier (Figure 12.1). Despite the superficial similarities at the beginning and the end of a century of immigration, the characteristics of immigrants are quite different. This change reflects many factors: developments and modifications in Canada's immigration policies; the displacement of peoples by wars and political upheaval; the cycle of economic "booms and busts" in Canada and other countries; Canada's membership in the Commonwealth; and the growth of communication, transportation, and economic networks linking people around the world.

These forces have operated throughout the twentieth century to alter the basic characteristics of Canada's immigrant population in five fundamental ways. First, the numbers of immigrants arriving each year have waxed and waned, meaning that the importance of immigration for Canada's population growth has fluctuated. Second, immigrants increasingly chose to live in Canada's largest cities. Third, the predominance of men among adult immigrants declined as family migration grew and women came to represent slightly over half of immigrants. Fourth, the marked transformation in the countries in which immigrants had been born enhanced the ethnic diversity of Canadian society. Fifth, alongside Canada's transition from an agricultural to a knowledge-based economy, immigrants were increasingly employed in the manufacturing and service sectors of the economy. In addition, immigrants also had children; how they are integrating is another measure of the legacy of immigration. This chapter provides an overview of these important changes over the last 110 years.

The Early Years: 1900–1915

The twentieth century opened with the arrival of nearly 42,000 immigrants in 1900. Numbers quickly escalated to a record high of over 400,000 in 1913. Canada's economy was growing rapidly during these years, and immigrants were drawn by the promise of good job prospects. The

* Adapted and updated from "100 Years of Immigration in Canada." *Canadian Social Trends*. Statistics Canada. Catalogue 11-008, Autumn 2000, pp. 2–11. Reprinted with permission.

building of the transcontinental railway, the settlement of the prairies, and expanding industrial production intensified demand for labour. Aggressive recruitment campaigns by the Canadian government to boost immigration and attract workers also increased arrivals: between 1900 and 1914, more than 2.9 million people entered Canada, nearly four times as many as had arrived in the previous 14-year period.

Such volumes of immigrants quickly enlarged Canada's population. Between 1901 and 1911, net migration (the excess of those arriving over those leaving) accounted for 38 per cent of population growth, a level not reached again for another 75 years (Figure 12.2). The share of the overall population born outside Canada also increased, so that while immigrants accounted for 13 per cent of the population in 1901, by 1911 they made up 22 per cent.

Most of the foreign-born population lived in Ontario at the start of the century, but many later immigrants headed west. By 1911, 41 per cent of Canada's immigrant population lived in the Prairie provinces, up from 20 per cent recorded in the 1901 census. This influx had a profound effect on the populations of the western provinces. By 1911, immigrants represented 41 per cent of people living in Manitoba, 50 per cent in Saskatchewan, and 57 per cent of those in Alberta and British Columbia. In contrast, they made up less than 10 per cent of the population in the Atlantic provinces and Quebec, and only 20 per cent in Ontario.

Men greatly outnumbered women among people settling in Canada in the first two decades of the twentieth century (Urquhart and Buckley 1965). The 1911 census recorded 158 immigrant males for every 100 females, compared with a 103:100 ratio for Canadian-born males and

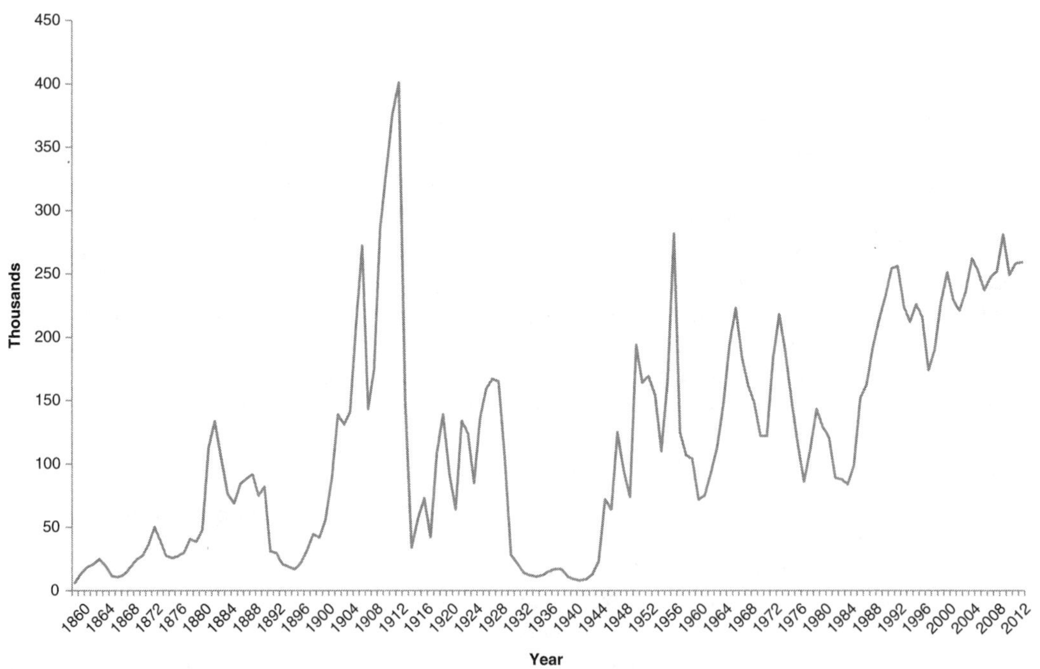

Figure 12.1 Total Number of Immigrants to Canada, 1860–2013

Sources: Canada, Citizenship and Immigration, *Facts and Figures 2002*, http://publications.gc.ca/collections/collection_2010/cic/MP43-333-2003-eng.pdf; Canada, Citizenship and Immigration, Facts and Figures 2013, http://www.cic.gc.ca/english/resources/statistics/facts2013/permanent/01.asp.

females. These unbalanced gender ratios are not uncommon in the history of settlement countries such as Canada, Australia, and the United States. They often reflect labour recruitment efforts targeted at men rather than women, as well as the behaviour of immigrants themselves. In migration flows, particularly those motivated by economic reasons, men frequently precede women, either because the move is viewed as temporary and there is no need to uproot family members, or because the man intends to become economically established before being joined by his family. By the time of the 1921 census, the gender ratio for immigrants had become less skewed, standing at 125 immigrant males for every 100 immigrant females. It continued to decline throughout the twentieth century, reaching 91 per 100 in 2011.[1]

Of course, women also immigrated for economic reasons in the early decades of the twentieth century. There was strong demand for female domestic workers, with women in England, Scotland, and Wales being most often targeted for recruitment. Between 1904 and 1914, "domestic" was by far the most common occupation reported by adult women immigrants (almost 30 per cent) arriving from overseas. Men immigrating from overseas during that period were more likely to be unskilled and semi-skilled labourers (36 per cent) or to have a farming occupation (32 per cent) (Urquhart and Buckley 1965). Historians observe that, contrary to the image of immigrants being farmers and homesteaders, immigrants at the turn of the century were also factory and construction workers. And although many did settle in the western provinces, many

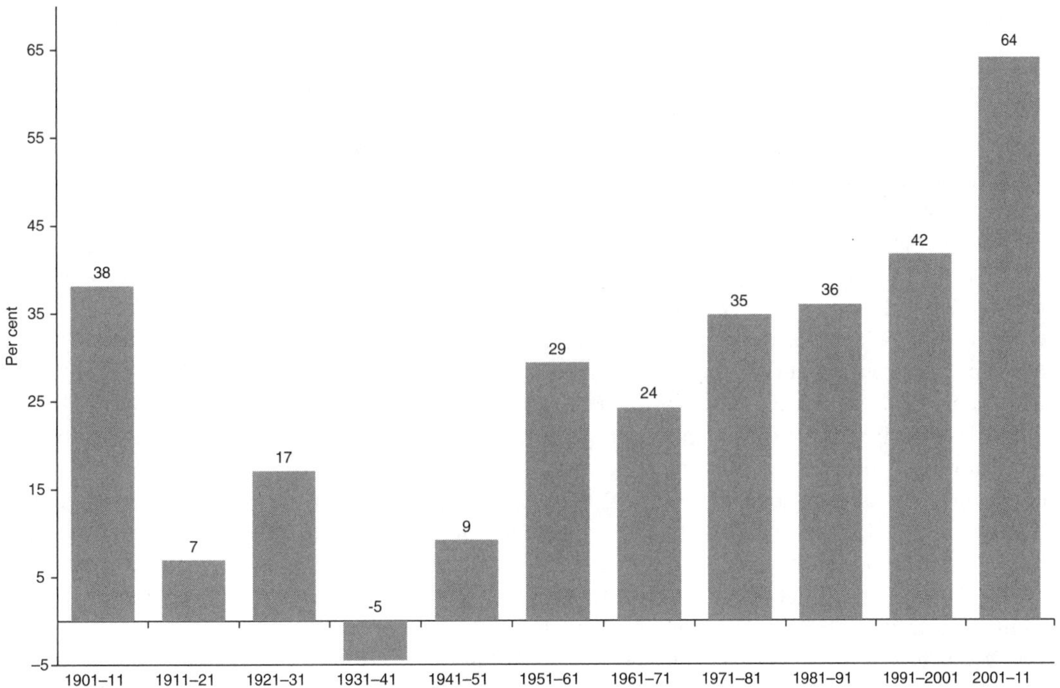

Figure 12.2 Immigration as a Percentage of Total Population Growth, 1901–11 to 2001–11

Source: Personal communication, Statistics Canada, Apr. 2015; based on Figure 1 in Statistics Canada, "Canadian Demographics at a Glance," 2014, Catalogue no. 91-003-x, http://www.statcan.gc.ca/pub/91-003-x/2014001/c-g/desc/desc03-eng.htm.

also worked building railroads or moved into the large cities, fuelling the growth of industrial centres.

Immigration from outside Britain and the US Begins to Grow in the 1910s

At the start of the century, the majority of immigrants to Canada had originated in the United States or the United Kingdom. However, during the 1910s and 1920s, the number born in other European countries began to grow, slowly at first, then rising to its highest levels in 1961 and 1971.

This change in countries of origin had begun in the closing decades of the nineteenth century, when many new groups began to arrive in Canada—Doukhobors and Jewish refugees from Russia; Hungarians; Mormons from the US; Italians; and Ukrainians. This flow continued until World War I. It generated public debate about who should be admitted to Canada: for some writers and politicians, recruiting labour was the key issue, not the changing origins of immigrants; for others, British and American immigrants were to be preferred to those from Southern or Eastern European countries.

By comparison, immigration from Asia was very low at this time, in dramatic contrast to the situation at the end of the twentieth century. Government policies regulating immigration had been rudimentary during the late 1800s, but when legislation was enacted in the early 1900s, it focused primarily on preventing immigration on the grounds of poverty or mental incompetence, or on the basis of non-European origins. Even though Chinese immigrant workers had helped to build the transcontinental railroad, in 1885 the first piece of legislation regulating future Chinese immigration required every person of Chinese origin to pay a tax of $50 upon entering Canada. At the time, this was a very large sum. The "head tax" was increased to $100 in 1900 and to $500 in 1903. This fee meant that many Chinese men could not afford to bring brides or wives to Canada. As evidence of this fact, the 1911 census recorded 2,790 Chinese males for every 100 Chinese females, a figure far in excess of the overall ratio of 158 immigrant males for every 100 immigrant females.

The Act of 1906 prohibited the landing of persons defined as "feebleminded," having "loathsome or contagious diseases," "paupers," persons "likely to become public charges," criminals, and "those of undesirable morality." In 1908, the Act was amended to prohibit the landing of those persons who did not come to Canada directly from their country of origin. This provision effectively excluded the immigration of people from India, who had to book passage on ships sailing from countries outside India because there were no direct sailings between Calcutta and Vancouver. Also in the early 1900s, the Canadian government entered into a series of agreements with Japan that restricted Japanese migration (Calliste 1993; Kelley and Trebilcock 2010; Troper 1972). It should be noted that although Asians were the most severely targeted by efforts to reduce immigration by non-Europeans, other ethnic groups such as Blacks from the United States and the Caribbean also were singled out.

The Wars and the Great Depression: 1915–1946

With the outbreak of World War I, immigration quickly came to a near standstill. From a record high of over 400,000 in 1913, arrivals dropped sharply to less than 34,000 by 1915. Although numbers rebounded after the war, they never again reached the levels attained before 1914. As a result, net immigration accounted for about 7 per cent of Canada's population growth between 1911 and 1921, considerably less than the contribution made in the previous decade. However, the influence of earlier foreign-born arrivals continued, reinforced by the more modest levels of wartime and post-war immigration. At the time of the 1921 census, immigrants still comprised 22 per cent of the population (Figure 12.3).

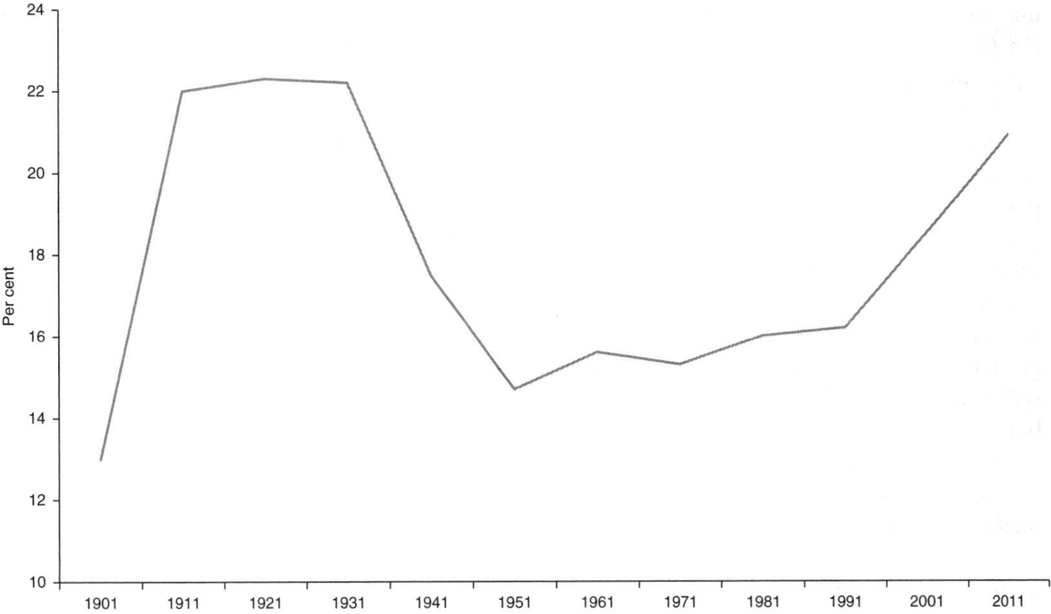

Figure 12.3 Immigrants as a Percentage of Total Canadian Population, 1901–2011

Sources: Statistics Canada, Catalogue nos 99-936, 97-557-XCB2006006, and 99-010-X2011026.

The number of immigrants coming to Canada rose during the 1920s, with well above 150,000 per year entering in the last three years of the decade. But the Great Depression and World War II severely curtailed arrivals during the 1930s and early 1940s—numbers fluctuated between 7,600 and 27,500. Furthermore, there was actually a net migration loss as more people left Canada than entered between 1931 and 1941. The 1930s is the only decade in the twentieth century in which this occurred. By the time of the 1941 census, the percentage of the total population that was foreign-born had fallen to just under 18 per cent.

While more men than women had immigrated to Canada in the first three decades of the century, the situation was reversed when immigration declined in the 1930s and 1940s. During this period, women outnumbered men, accounting for 60 per cent of all adult arrivals between 1931 and 1940, and for 66 per cent between 1941 and 1945 (Urquhart and Buckley 1965). As a result of these changes, the overall gender ratio of the immigrant population declined slightly.

While lower numbers and the predominance of women among adult immigrants represented shifts in previous immigration patterns, other trends were more stable. The majority of immigrants continued to settle in Ontario, Manitoba, Saskatchewan, Alberta, and British Columbia. Increasingly, though, they gravitated to urban areas, foreshadowing the pattern of recent immigration concentration in large cities that became so evident in the last years of the twentieth century.

Britain was still the leading source of immigrants, but the arrival of people from other parts of the globe also continued. During the 1920s, the aftershocks of World War I and the Russian Revolution stimulated migration from Germany, Russia, Ukraine, and Eastern European countries including Poland and Hungary (Kelley and Trebilcock 2010). During the Depression, the majority of immigrants came from Great Britain, Germany, Austria, and Ukraine. Fewer than 6 per cent were of non-European origin.

Public debate over whom to admit and the development of immigration policy to regulate admissions was far from over. Regulations passed in 1919 provided new grounds for deportation and denied entry to enemy aliens, to those who were enemy aliens during the war, and to Doukhobors, Mennonites, and Hutterites (Kalbach 1970). The 1923 Chinese Immigration Act restricted Chinese immigration still further (Avery 2000). Responding to labour market pressures following the stock market crash of 1929 and the collapse of the prairie economy in the drought-stricken 1930s, farm workers, domestics, and several other occupational groups, as well as relatives of landed immigrants, were struck from the list of admissible classes. Asian immigration was also cut back again (Kalbach 1970).

Then, with the declaration of war on Germany on 10 September 1939, new regulations were passed to prohibit the entry or landing of nationals of countries with which Canada was at war. In the absence of a refugee policy that distinguished between immigrants and refugees, the restrictions imposed in the inter-war years raised barriers to those fleeing the chaos and devastation of World War II. Many of those turned away at this time were Jewish refugees attempting to leave Europe (Abella and Troper 1982). War-related measures also included the forced relocation—often to detention camps—of Japanese Canadians living within a 100-mile area along the British Columbia coastline. It was argued that they might assist a Japanese invasion.

The Boom Years: 1946–1970

The war in Europe ended with Germany's surrender on 6 May 1945; in the Pacific, Japan surrendered on 14 August. With the return of peace, both Canada's economy and immigration boomed. Between 1946 and 1950, over 430,000 immigrants arrived, exceeding the total number admitted in the previous 15 years.

The immediate post-war immigration boom included the dependants of Canadian servicemen who had married abroad, refugees, and people seeking economic opportunities in Canada. Beginning in July 1946 and continuing throughout the late 1940s, Orders-in-Council paved the way for the admission of people who had been displaced from their homelands by the war and for whom return was not possible (Kalbach 1970; Knowles 2007). The ruination of the European economy and the unprecedented boom in Canada also favoured high immigration levels.

Numbers continued to grow throughout most of the 1950s, peaking at over 282,000 admissions in 1957. By 1958, immigration levels were beginning to fall, partly because economic conditions were improving in Europe, and partly because, with the Canadian economy slowing, the government introduced administrative policies designed to reduce the rate of immigration. By 1962, however, the economy had recovered and arrivals increased for six successive years. Although admissions never reached the record highs observed in the early part of the century, the total number of immigrants entering Canada in the 1950s and 1960s far exceeded the levels observed in the preceding three decades.

During this time, net migration was higher than it had been in almost 50 years, but it accounted for no more than 30 per cent of total population growth between 1951 and 1971. The population effect of the large number of foreign-born arrivals was muted by the magnitude of natural growth caused by the unprecedented birth rates recorded during the baby boom from 1946 to 1965.

Many of the new immigrants settled in cities, so that by 1961, 81 per cent of foreign-born Canadians lived in urban areas, compared with 68 per cent of the Canadian-born. The proportion of the immigrant population living in Ontario continued to grow, accelerating a trend that had begun earlier in the century; in contrast, the proportion living in the Prairie provinces declined (Figure 12.4).

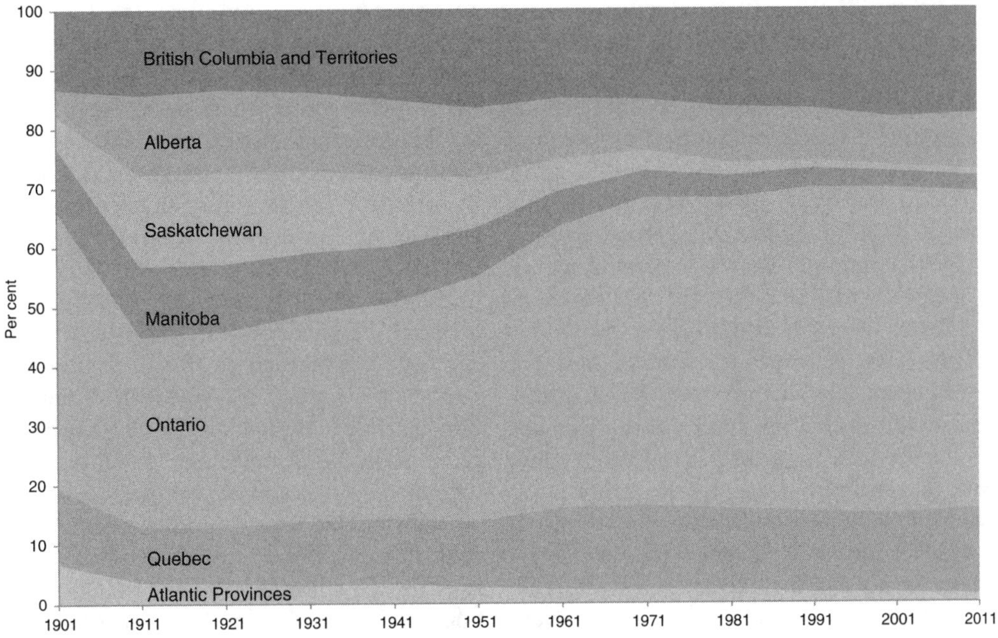

Figure 12.4 Provincial Distribution of Immigrants, 1901–2011

Source: Statistics Canada, *1901 Census of Population* (Bulletin VIII), and Product nos 93F0020XCB, 97F0009X2001040, and 99-010-X2011033.

Such shifts in residential location went hand in hand with Canada's transformation from a rural agricultural and resource-based economy in the early years of the century to an urban manufacturing and service-based economy in the later years. Post-war immigrants were important sources of labour for this emerging economy, especially in the early 1950s. Compared with those arriving at the turn of the century, the post-war immigrants were more likely to be professional or skilled workers, and they accounted for over half of the growth in these occupations between 1951 and 1961.

Although the largest numbers of immigrants arriving after World War II were from the United Kingdom, people from other European countries were an increasingly predominant part of the mix. During the late 1940s and 1950s, substantial numbers also arrived from Germany, the Netherlands, Italy, Poland, and the USSR. Following the 1956 Soviet invasion of Hungary, Canada also admitted over 37,000 Hungarians, while the Suez Crisis of the same year saw the arrival of almost 109,000 British immigrants (Kalbach 1970; Kelley and Trebilcock 2010; Avery 2000). During the 1960s, the trend increased. By the time of the 1971 census, less than one-third of the foreign-born population had been born in the United Kingdom; half came from other European countries, many from Italy.

New Policies Help Direct Post-War Immigration Trends

Much of the post-war immigration to Canada was stimulated by people displaced by war or political upheaval, as well as by the weakness of the European economies. However, Canada's post-war immigration policies also were an important factor. Because they were statements of who would be admitted and under what conditions, these policies influenced the numbers of arrivals, the types of immigrants, and the country of origin of new arrivals.

Within two years of the war ending, on 1 May 1947, Prime Minister Mackenzie King reaffirmed that immigration was vital for Canada's growth, but he also indicated that the numbers and country of origin of immigrants would be regulated. Five years later, the Immigration Act of 1952 consolidated many post-war changes to immigration regulations that had been enacted since the previous Act of 1927. Subsequent regulations that spelled out the possible grounds for limiting admissions included national origin; on this basis, admissible persons were defined to be those with birth or citizenship in the United States, the United Kingdom, Australia, New Zealand, the Union of South Africa, and selected European countries.

In 1962, however, new regulations effectively removed national origin as a criterion of admission. Further regulations enacted in 1967 confirmed this principle and instead introduced a system that assigned points based on the age, education, language skills, and economic characteristics of applicants. These policy changes made it much easier for persons born outside Europe and the United States to immigrate to Canada.

The 1967 regulations also reaffirmed the right, first extended in the 1950s, of immigrants to sponsor relatives to enter Canada. Family-based immigration had always coexisted alongside economically motivated immigration, but now it was clearly defined. As wives, mothers, grandmothers, aunts, and sisters, women participated in these family reunification endeavours: women accounted for almost half of all adult immigrants entering Canada during the 1950s and 1960s. As a result of this gender parity in immigration flows, sex ratios declined over time for the foreign-born population.

Growth and Diversity: 1970–2011

In the 1960s, changes in immigration policy were made by altering the regulations that governed implementation of the Immigration Act of 1952. But in 1978, a new Immigration Act came into effect. This Act upheld the principles of admissions laid out in the regulations of the 1960s: family reunification and economic contributions. For the first time in Canada's history, the new Act also incorporated the principle of admissions based on humanitarian grounds. Previously, refugee admissions had been handled through special procedures and regulations. The Act also required the minister responsible for the immigration portfolio to set annual immigration targets in consultation with the provinces. The most recent legislation, the Immigration and Refugee Protection Act, effective in June 2002, keeps these three criteria of admission. However, refugee and humanitarian admissions are only a small share of yearly immigration, representing between 9 and 14 per cent during the 2000–14 period. That share is likely to increase in 2015–16, as it has before when global crises have displaced people, with the admission of 25,000 Syrian refugees. Since the mid-1990s economic migrants have outnumbered those entering on the basis of family reunification or humanitarian concerns (Boyd and Alboim 2012; Kelley and Trebilcock 2010). Since 2008 the policy emphasis on recruiting migrants to meet labour needs and to stimulate the economy has increased with the enactment of additional regulations, including new guidelines for the admission of economic migrants (Boyd and Alboim 2012; Picot and Sweetman 2012).

From the 1970s through the 1990s, immigration numbers fluctuated. The overall impact, however, continued to be a significant contribution to Canada's total population growth that increased as the century drew to a close. With consistently high levels of arrivals after the mid-1980s, immigration accounted for over 40 per cent of the population growth between 1991 and

2001 and nearly two-thirds between 2001 and 2011. These percentages exceeded those recorded in the 1910s and the 1920s. The cumulative effect of net migration from the 1970s onward was a gradual increase in the percentage of foreign-born Canadians. By the time of the 2011 National Household Survey,[2] immigrants comprised just under 21 per cent of the population, the largest proportion in more than 60 years. The number of temporary migrants living in Canada also grew; by 2011, they represented 1 per cent of Canada's population. When combined, immigrants and non-permanent residents made up almost 22 per cent of the 2011 population, approximately the percentages of foreign born found in 1911 and 1921.

Having an immigration policy based on principles of family reunification and labour market contribution also recast the composition of the immigrant population. It meant that people from all nations could be admitted if they met the criteria as described in the immigration regulations. The inclusion of humanitarian-based admissions also permitted the entry of refugees from countries outside Europe. As a result, the immigrants who entered Canada from 1966 onward came from many different countries and possessed more diverse cultural backgrounds than earlier immigrants. Each successive census recorded declining percentages of the immigrant population that had been born in European countries, the United Kingdom, and the United States.

Meanwhile, the proportion of immigrants born in Asian countries and other regions of the world began to rise, slowly at first and then more quickly from the 1980s on (Figure 12.5). By 2001, 36.5 per cent of the immigrant population in Canada had been born in Asia and another 17 per cent came from places other than the United States, the United Kingdom, or Europe. Ten years later, just under half of the immigrant population

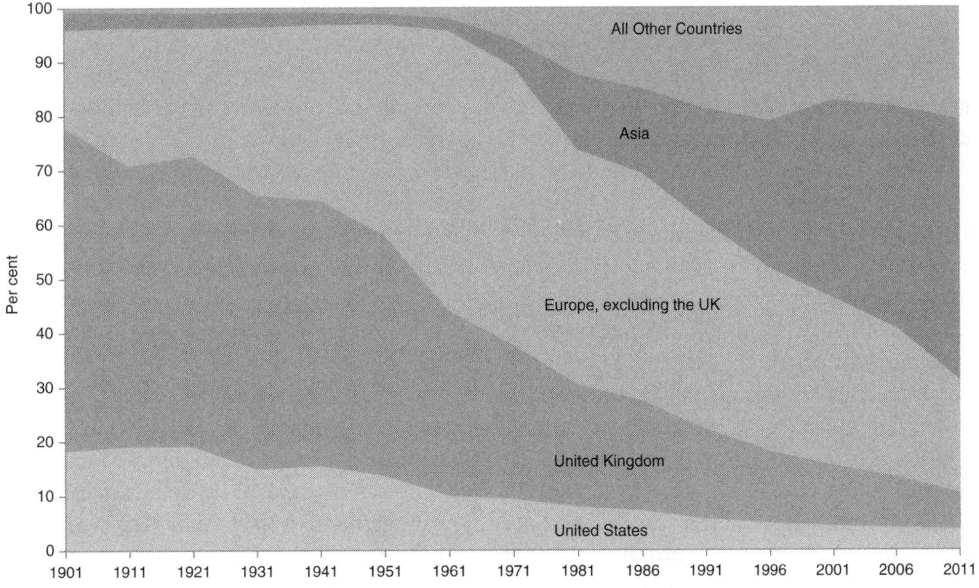

Figure 12.5 Birthplaces of Immigrants to Canada, 1901–2011

Source: Statistics Canada, Catalogue nos 99-517 (Vol. VII, Part 1), 92-727 (Vol. I, Part 3), 92-913, Catalogue no. 97F0009XCB2001002 97-557-XCB2006007, and Product nos 93F0020XCB and 99-010-X-2011026.

had been born in Asia. According to the 2011 National Household Survey, the top three places of birth for immigrants arriving between 2001 and 2011 were the People's Republic of China, India, and the Philippines. Together, these three countries accounted for almost one-quarter of all immigrants who arrived in that decade.

Immigration and Canada's Growing Visible Minority Population

The visible minority population[3] has grown dramatically in the last two decades. In 2011, just over 19 per cent of Canada's population—nearly 6.3 million people—identified themselves as members of a visible minority group, up from under 5 per cent in 1981. Immigration has been a big contributor to this growth: nearly two-thirds of visible minorities are immigrants, with four out of 10 arriving between 2001 and 2011.

Most immigrants live in Canada's big cities, with the largest numbers concentrated in the census metropolitan areas (CMAs) of Toronto, Montreal, and Vancouver. This continues the trend established earlier in the century. Proportionally more immigrants than Canadian-born have preferred to settle in urban areas, attracted by economic opportunities and by the presence of other immigrants from the same countries or regions of the world. In 2011, 91 per cent of all immigrants lived in one of Canada's 33 CMAs, compared with 63 per cent of the Canadian-born population. As a result, the largest CMAs have a higher percentage of immigrants than the country as a whole. In 2011, 46 per cent of Toronto's population, 40 per cent of the Vancouver population, and 23 per cent of Montreal's population were immigrants. Newcomers are even more likely to live in Canada's large urban areas (Statistics Canada 2013). The attraction to urban centres helps to explain the provincial distribution of immigrants. Since the 1940s, a disproportionate share has lived in Ontario and the percentage has continued to rise over time. By 2011, 53 per cent of all immigrants lived in Ontario, compared with nearly 18 per cent in British Columbia and 14 per cent in Quebec.

Recent Immigrants' Adjustment to the Labour Force

Just as immigrants have contributed to the growth in Canada's population, to its diversity, and to its cities, so too have they contributed to its economy (Figure 12.6). During the last few decades, most employment opportunities have shifted from manufacturing to service industries, and immigrants are an important source of labour for some of these industries. However, compared with non-immigrants, they are more likely to be employed in the personal services industries, manufacturing, and construction. Moreover, the likelihood of being employed in one industry rather than another often differs depending on the immigrant's sex, age at arrival, education, knowledge of English and/or French, and length of time in Canada.

Living in a new society generally entails a period of adjustment, particularly when a person must look for work, learn a new language, or deal with an educational system, medical services, government agencies, and laws that may differ significantly from those in his or her country of origin. The difficulty of transition may be seen in the labour market profile of recent immigrants: Compared with longer-established immigrants and with those born in Canada, many may experience higher unemployment rates, hold jobs that do not reflect their level of training and education, and earn lower incomes. Further, studies of immigrant earnings indicate that recent arrivals are not doing as well as newly arrived groups that entered Canada in previous decades. Comparisons of the earnings of new arrivals to those of the Canadian-born indicate lower earnings for immigrants, especially for those arriving in the 1990s. The earnings gap between

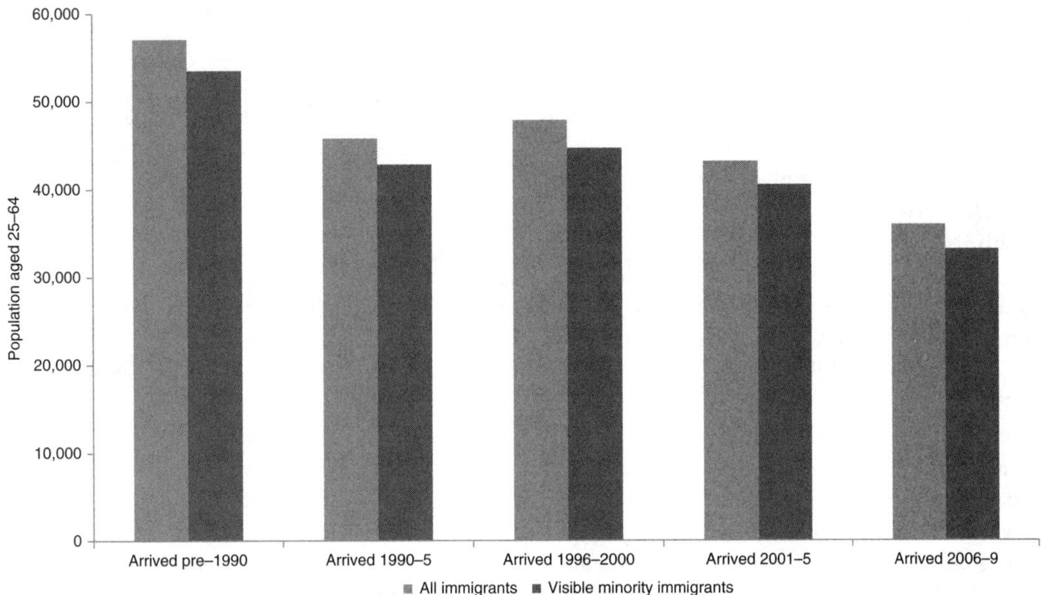

Figure 12.6 Average Annual Wages and Salaries of All Immigrants and Visible Minority Immigrants, pre–1990 to 2006–9

Source: Statistics Canada, 2011 National Household Survey Public Use Microdata File for Individuals; special tabulations by Monica Boyd.

immigrant and Canadian-born men widened from 11 per cent in 1980 to 33 per cent in 1995, before declining to 22 per cent in 2000. Similar trends exist for the earnings gap between Canadian-born and immigrant women. The time necessary for the wages of new cohorts to catch up to those of the Canadian-born also is getting longer (Aydemir and Skuterud 2005; Frenette and Morissette 2005). During the recessionary period of 2008–9, the economic outcomes for immigrants arriving within the previous five years deteriorated (Picot and Sweetman 2012).

In the past, the disparities between recent immigrants and the Canadian-born have often disappeared over time, indicating that initial labour market difficulties reflect the adjustment process. The differences in the 1990s and in the early 2000s may also result from the diminished employment opportunities available during recessions, which also affect the Canadian-born who were new entrants to the job market. Nevertheless, other possible explanations include changing countries of origin, which in recent years are associated with non-English/non-French language skills, non-recognition of professional and trades credentials by employers and professional associations, and employer discounting of foreign experience. In other words, immigrants often are treated as if they are new entrants to the labour force instead of being simply new arrivals in Canada (Picot and Sweetman 2005, 2012).

The Immigrant Legacy: Children of Immigrants

Immigrants either bring children with them or build their families in Canada. As a result, a growing population either immigrated as children (the 1.5 generation) or are Canadian-born and had at least one foreign born parent. On the whole, the 1.5 and second generations are younger than the third-plus generation and this is especially true for visible minorities. Reflecting the settlement patterns of their parents, the 1.5 and second generations are more likely to live in Canada's largest provinces and cities (Dobson et al. 2013).

One of the main reasons why people choose to uproot themselves and immigrate to another country is their desire to provide greater opportunities for their children. Thus, one measure of the success of an immigrant's adaptation to Canadian society is the degree of success their children achieve. This focus is consistent with the "straight-line" theory of the process of immigrant integration, which asserts that integration is cumulative: with each passing generation since immigration, the measurable differences between the descendants of immigrants and the Canadian-born are reduced until they are virtually indistinguishable. However, this theory's dominance has been challenged in recent years by analysts who argue that it is based primarily on the experiences of immigrants who were largely White and European, and whose children grew up during a period of unprecedented economic growth. They argue that this theory applies less well to more recent immigrants because it ignores changes in the social and economic structure of Canada in the latter half of the twentieth century. Also, it discounts the impact of barriers facing young immigrants, who are predominantly visible minorities.

Evidence of barriers to the socio-economic integration of the children of immigrants is not uniform, varying by the indicator (i.e., education, occupation, or earnings), age, sex, residential location, and visible minority membership or parental country of origin. However, if the

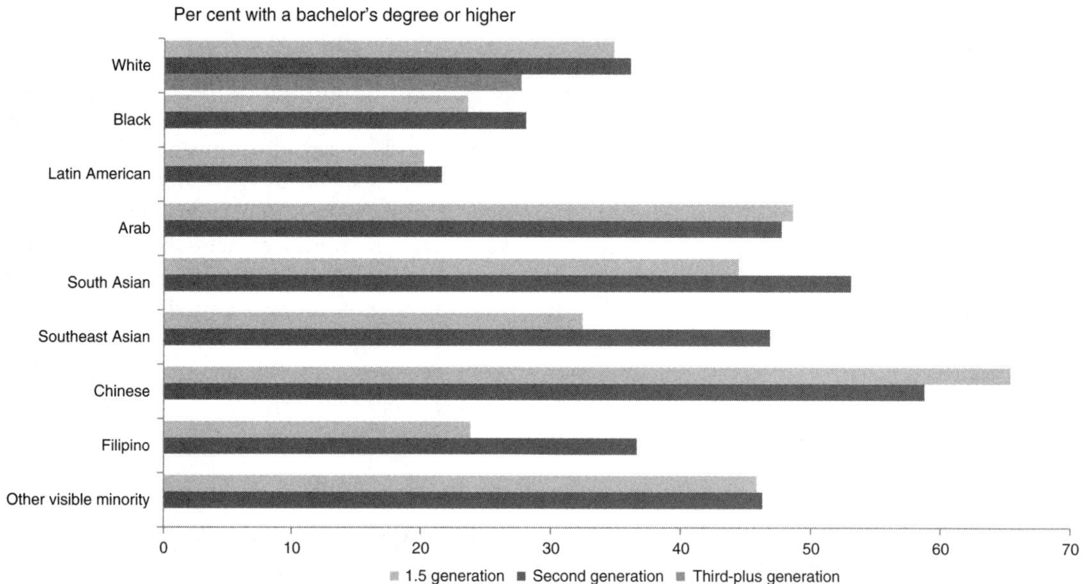

Figure 12.7 University Education of 1.5 and Second-Generation Whites and Visible Minorities Compared to the Third-plus Generation White Population, Ages 25–39

Source: Statistics Canada,. 2011 National Household Survey Public Use Microdata File for Individuals; special tabulations by Monica Boyd.

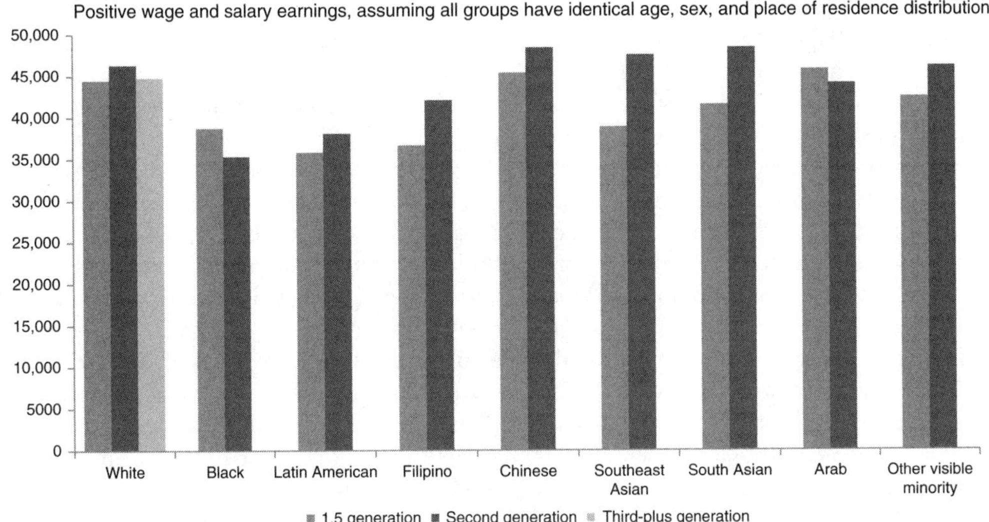

Figure 12.8 Average Earnings of 1.5 and Second-Generation Whites and Visible Minorities Compared to the Third-plus Generation White Population, Ages 25–39

Source: Statistics Canada, 2011 National Household Survey Public Use Microdata File for Individuals; customized multivariate MCA analysis by Monica Boyd.

third-plus generation whites, which consists of the Canadian-born with Canadian-born parents, is taken as the standard, the 1.5 generation (those immigrants who arrived as children) and the second generation have higher educational attainments, and this is particularly true for some—but not all—visible minority groups, as shown in Figure 12.7 (Boyd 2002; Picot and Sweetman 2012). One reason for the variation is that educational attainments of children are influenced by the education of parents. In recent years, highly educated immigrants are coming to Canada and they may pass on high educational expectations and aspirations to their children.

The least consensus exists on the similarity of wages between generation groups (Figure 12.8). Some studies find lower wages for the children of immigrants than for the third-plus generation. However, others do not. Such differences between studies depend on the age, gender, country of origin or visible minority status, place of residence in Canada, and educational attainments of the immigrant offspring (Picot and Sweetman 2012).

New Trends and Issues on the Horizon

Most arrivals to Canada are admitted as legally entitled to reside permanently in Canada. However, people also enter on a temporary basis. The architecture of the current temporary admissions program began in 1973 with the introduction of the Employment Visa Regulations; but in addition to persons destined to the labour force, students and those seeking admission on humanitarian grounds are allowed to reside in Canada temporarily. In addition, some people may be in Canada without legal authorization; the size of the undocumented migrant population (sometimes called illegal migrants) is not known with any certainty, but is popularly thought to be between 200,000 to 500,000 persons.

The number of temporary residents is increasing over time (Figure 12.9). A sharp increase in the number of humanitarian admissions occurred in the early 1990s as a result of the dissolution of the former USSR and the 1989 Tiananmen Square massacre in China. Thereafter, growing numbers of international students and workers also increased the size of the temporary resident migrant population. The temporary worker program is highly diverse, consisting of two small groups entering as live-in caregivers and as agricultural workers, a larger group admitted under bilateral or trade agreements such as NAFTA, and a group recruited by employers for jobs where local labour is scarce and where the government authorizes such employment. Some of the more highly skilled international students and workers are permitted to transition and become permanent residents in Canada. Others are expected to return to their countries when their visas expire.

Temporary workers do not necessarily receive the same employment rights, such as employment insurance, as others in Canada, and they may not access other benefits, such as health care, because they fear employment-related consequences (Nakache 2012). In addition, low-skilled temporary migrant workers may be in jobs that are poorly paid and have bad working conditions, and these workers have precarious employment where they lack guarantees about the permanency of the work and are subject to changing hours of work. Undocumented workers are thought to be at risk for such employment conditions as well. These precarious work conditions appear to persist even if permanent residency is granted (Goldring and Landolt 2012).

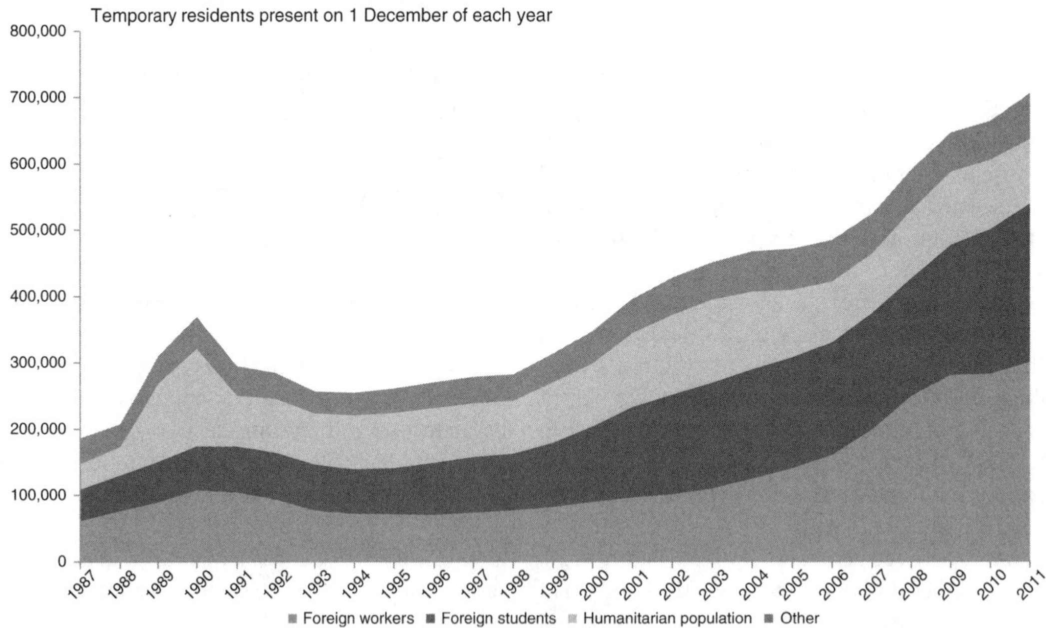

Figure 12.9 Temporary Migrant Population, 1987–2011

Source: Canada Citizenship and Immigration, *Facts and Figures 2011—Immigration Overview: Permanent and Temporary Residents,* "Temporary residents present on December 1st by gender and yearly status, 1988–2011," http://www.cic.gc.ca/English/resources/statistics/facts2011/index.asp.v

Summary

Few would quarrel with the statement that the twentieth century in Canada was an era of enormous change. Every area of life, ranging from the economy to family to law, was altered over the course of 100 years. Immigration was not immune to these transformative forces. The size and character of immigration flows were influenced by economic booms and busts, by world wars and national immigration policies, and indirectly by expanding communication, transportation, and economic links around the world.

The ebb and flow of immigration has presented volatile changes over the last 115 years. The twentieth century began with the greatest number of immigrant arrivals ever recorded. Thereafter, levels fluctuated, often with dramatic swings from one decade to the next. The lowest levels were recorded in the 1930s during the Depression. By 2011, though, the number of immigrants arriving annually was again sufficiently large that net migration accounted for nearly two-thirds of Canada's population growth.

Other changes in immigration are better described as trends, for they followed a course that was cumulative rather than reversible. The high ratio of men to women immigrants dropped steadily throughout the century. There were two main reasons for this decline. First, the number of men immigrating fell during the two wars and the Depression; and second, the number of women immigrants increased in the last half of the century as a result of family reunification after World War II and of family migration, in which women, men, and their children immigrated together.

Even in the 1900s and 1910s, the foreign-born were more likely to live in urban areas. After the initial settlement of the prairies in the early 1900s, the trend towards urban settlement accelerated. By 2011, the vast majority of recent immigrants were residing in census metropolitan areas, mainly those of Toronto, Vancouver, and Montreal, although immigrants also were settling in smaller cities such as Edmonton, Calgary, and Hamilton.

Government policies regulating who would be admitted and under what conditions also evolved. Much of the effort during the first 50 years of the century focused on restricting immigration from regions of the world other than the US, Britain, and Europe. This position changed in the 1960s, when national origin was removed as a criterion for entry. The policies enacted thereafter entrenched the basic principles guiding admissions, such as family reunification, economic contributions, and humanitarian concerns. With these changes, the source countries of immigrants to Canada substantially altered. By 2011, 69 per cent of the foreign-born in Canada were from places other than the UK, the US, and Europe.

As a result of these changes, Canada at the close of the twentieth century contrasted sharply with Canada 100 years before. Immigrants had increased the population; they had diversified the ethnic and linguistic composition of the country; and they had laboured both in the agrarian economy of old and in the new industrial and service-based economy of the future. Their children, the 1.5 and second generations, are also part of the Canadian fabric and their experiences illustrate the multi-generational process of integration. Those admitted on humanitarian grounds, as well as students and temporary workers, further add to the complexity of Canada as the twenty-first century unfolds.

Questions for Critical Thought

1. The countries of origin of Canada's immigrants have changed greatly over time. Indicate why it changed. What do these changes imply for Canada as a nation and for the immigrants themselves?

2. Immigration regulations and laws always have the potential for creating inequalities. Looking at the history of Canada, can you identify inequalities in the treatment of people that made it easier or harder for some to be admitted to Canada?
3. Discuss the inequalities between immigrants and the Canadian-born in the labour force—what are they and what are the explanations for these inequalities?
4. Who are the children of immigrants? How are they doing in terms of educational attainments and what are the possible reasons?
5. What types of temporary residents exist? Why does a concern exist about the low-skilled temporary workers?

Recommended Readings

Abada, Teresa, Feng Hou, and Bali Ram. 2009. "Ethnic differences in educational attainment among the children of Canadian immigrants." *Canadian Journal of Sociology* 34, 1: 1–28.

Boyd, Monica. 2009. "Social origins and the educational and occupational achievements of the 1.5 and second generation." *Canadian Sociological Review* 46, 4: 339–69.

——— and Naomi Alboim. 2012. "Managing international migration: The Canadian case." In Dan Rodríguez-García, ed., *Managing Immigration and Diversity in Canada: A Transatlantic Dialogue in the New Age of Migration*, pp. 123–50. Montreal and Kingston: McGill-Queen's University Press.

Ferrer, Ana M., Garnett Picot, and William Craig Riddell. 2014. "New directions in immigration policy: Canada's evolving approach to the selection of economic immigrants." *International Migration Review* 48, 2:846–67.

Goldring, Luin, and Patricia Landolt. 2012. "The impact of precarious legal status on immigrants' economic outcomes." Institute for Research on Public Policy (IRPP) Study No. 35, Oct. http://irpp.org/research-studies/study-no35/.

Marsden, Sarah. 2012. "The new precariousness: Temporary migrants and the law in Canada." *Canadian Journal of Law and Society* 27, 2: 209–29.

Recommended Websites

Citizenship and Immigration Canada:
http://www.cic.gc.ca/

Institute for Research on Public Policy:
http://irpp.org

Maytree Foundation:
http://maytree.com/

Statistics Canada:
http://www.statcan.gc.ca/

Notes

1. Prior to the 1991 census, data combined people who were immigrants with those who were non-permanent residents. Immigrants are people who are granted the right to live in Canada permanently by the immigration authorities. Some are recent arrivals; others have resided in Canada for many years. Non-permanent residents are people from another country who live

in Canada and have permission from the immigration authorities to work or study or to claim refugee status. They are not included in the immigrant population after 1986 except in growth projections.

2. The 2011 National Household Survey was a voluntary survey of one in three Canadian private households; it replaced the previous long form of Canada's quiennial censuses where respondents were required by law to answer the census questionnaire. The new Trudeau Liberal government has promised to return to the mandatory long-form census for the collection of more reliable and complete demographic data.
3. The Employment Equity Act defines visible minorities as "persons, other than Aboriginal peoples, who are non-Caucasian in race or non-white in colour." The visible minority population includes the following groups: Blacks, South Asians, Chinese, Koreans, Japanese, Southeast Asians, Filipinos, Arabs and West Asians, Latin Americans, and Pacific Islanders.

References

Abella, Irving, and Harold Troper. 1982. *None Is Too Many: Canada and the Jews in Europe, 1933–1948*. Toronto: Lester & Orpen Dennys.

Avery, Donald. 2000. "Peopling Canada." *The Beaver* 80, 1: 28–38.

Aydemir, Abdurrahman, and Mikal Skuterud. 2005. "Explaining the deteriorating entry earnings of Canada's immigrant cohorts, 1966–2000." *Canadian Journal of Economics* 38, 2: 641–72.

Boyd, Monica. 2002. "Educational attainments of immigrant offspring: Success or segmented assimilation?" *International Migration Review* 36 (Winter): 1037–60.

——— and Naomi Alboim. 2012. "Managing international migration: The Canadian case." In Dan Rodríguez-García, ed., *Managing Immigration and Diversity in Canada: A Transatlantic Dialogue in the New Age of Migration*, pp. 123–50. Montreal and Kingston: McGill-Queen's University Press.

Calliste, Agnes. 1993 "Race, gender and Canadian immigration policy: Blacks from the Caribbean, 1900–1932." *Journal of Canadian Studies* 28, 4: 131–48.

Dobson, Jarod, Helene Maheux, and Tina Chui. 2013. "National Household Survey, 2011. Generation status: Canadian-born children of immigrants." Catalogue no. 99-010-X2011003. Ottawa: Statistics Canada.

Frenette, Marc, and Rene Morissette. 2005. "Will they ever converge: Earnings of immigrant and Canadian-born workers for the last two decades." *International Migration Review* 39, 1: 229–58.

Goldring, Luin, and Patricia Landolt. 2012. "The impact of precarious legal status on immigrants' economic outcomes." Institute for Research on Public Policy (IRPP) Study No. 35, Oct. http://irpp.org/research-studies/study-no35/.

Kalbach, Warren. 1970. *The Impact of Immigration on Canada's Population*. Ottawa: Dominion Bureau of Statistics.

Kelley, Ninette, and M.J. Trebilcock. 2010. *The Making of the Mosaic: A History of Canadian Immigration Policy*, 2nd edn. Toronto: University of Toronto Press.

Knowles, Valerie. 2007. *Strangers at Our Gates: Canadian Immigration and Immigration Policy, 1540–2006*, rev. edn. Toronto: Dundurn Press.

Nakache, Delphine. 2012. "The Canadian Temporary Foreign Worker Program: Regulations, practices and protection gaps." In Luin Goldring and Patricia Landolt, eds, *Producing and Negotiating Non-Citizenship: Precarious Legal Status in Canada*, pp. 71–95. Toronto: University of Toronto Press.

Picot, Garnett, and Arthur Sweetman. 2005. "The deteriorating economic welfare of immigrants and possible causes: Update 2005." Statistics Canada: Analytical Studies Branch. Research Paper Series No. 262. http://www.publications

.gc.ca/Collection/Statcan/11F0019MIE/11F0019 MIE2005262.pdf.

——— and ——— 2012. "Making it in Canada: Immigration outcomes and policies." Institute for Research on Public Policy (IRPP) Study No. 29, Apr. http://irpp.org/research-studies/study-no29/.

Statistics Canada. 2013. "Immigration and ethnocultural diversity in Canada." Catalogue no. 99-010-X2011001.

Troper, Harold. 1972. *Only Farmers Need Apply: Official Canadian Government Encouragement of Immigration from the United States, 1896–1911.* Toronto: Griffin House.

Urquhart, Malcolm, and Kenneth Buckley. 1965. *Historical Statistics of Canada.* Toronto: Macmillan.

13 Racial Inequality, Social Cohesion, and Policy Issues in Canada*

Jeffrey G. Reitz and Rupa Banerjee

Immigration has substantially increased the racial diversity of the Canadian population. Since the 1960s, when discriminatory selection policies were eliminated, questions about immigration's impact on the cohesiveness of Canadian society have become more prominent. Although few predict a breakdown in social cohesion as a result of racial diversity, concerns about racial tensions have been expressed from a variety of political standpoints by a number of commentators, including advocates for minority rights (Lewis 1992; Omidvar and Richmond 2003) and advocates of reduction in immigration (Economic Council of Canada 1991; Stoffman 2002; Collacott 2002; Francis 2002). In this chapter, we review some research findings specifically related to racial inequality and discrimination in Canada as well as to the social integration of racial minorities in Canadian society; we then examine the relation between the two. Our review suggests that racial inequality is a significant issue in Canada, and that the extent of discrimination is a point of dispute between racial groups. This creates a potentially significant racial divide and prompts us to ask whether existing policy responses are adequate to bridge the gap.

The shift towards non-European sources of immigration to Canada after the late 1960s was marked. Immigrants arriving before 1970 were overwhelmingly from Europe and the United States, and in the 1950s and 1960s many came from Southern and Eastern Europe, as well as from Northern Europe, the United Kingdom, and the United States. Of those arriving in the 1960s or before, only 10.2 per cent were racial or visible minorities (based on 2001 census data). However, this figure rises dramatically to 51 per cent for 1970s arrivals, 65.4 per cent for 1980s arrivals, and nearly 75 per cent for 1990s arrivals. In the new millennium, the trend towards racial minority immigrants continued. According to the 2011 National Household Survey (NHS), 82 per cent of new immigrants arriving between 2006 and 2011 were racial minorities. The Philippines was the leading source country for immigrants arriving between 2006 and 2011. As a result, racial or visible minorities have grown

* Abridged from Jeffrey G. Reitz and Rupa Banerjee, "Racial Inequality, Social Cohesion, and Policy Issues in Canada." In Keith Banting, Thomas J. Courchene, and F. Leslie Seidle (eds.), *Belonging? Diversity, Recognition and Shared Citizenship in Canada*. Montreal: Institute for Research on Public Policy, 2007, pp.489–545. Updated, 2015. Reprinted with permission.

from constituting less than 1 per cent of the population in 1971 to 13.4 per cent in 2001 to 19.1 per cent in 2011. The largest groups according to the 2011 NHS are South Asians (4.8 per cent), Chinese (4.0 per cent), and Blacks (2.9 per cent). They were followed by Filipinos, Latin Americans, Arabs, Southeast Asians, West Asians, Koreans, and Japanese.

The increasing impact of racial diversity in Canada is magnified because of the concentration of minorities in certain immigrant-intensive cities, especially Toronto and Vancouver. In the Toronto Metropolitan Area, racial minorities constituted only about 3 per cent of the total population of 2.6 million in 1971, but by 2011 the figure had grown to 47 per cent of 5.5 million. In both Toronto and Vancouver, racial minorities comprised nearly half of the population by 2011, well on the way to becoming "majority-minority" cities.

Ethnic and racial diversity may adversely affect a society's cohesiveness in two ways. When diversity results in inequality, it may undermine the sense of fairness and inclusion among individuals and groups. Racial diversity may also weaken the commonality of values, commitments, and social relations among individuals and groups, thereby affecting their capacity to co-operate in the pursuit of common objectives. Each dimension is important in its own right, and they may have a combined effect on social cohesion.

Given the long history of ethnic and linguistic diversity in the Canadian population, both issues—fairness and shared values—have always been of great significance. However, in many countries breakdowns in interracial relations have most often been seen as linked to the issue of fairness, racial inequality, and discrimination. Witness the United States in the 1960s (Kerner Commission 1968) or Britain in the 1980s (Scarman 1986). And in Canada in recent years, responses to increasing racial diversity have gradually shifted; more attention is being paid to equality. For example, although equality has always been an objective of Canada's multiculturalism initiative, it was sought initially through an emphasis on culture—specifically, recognition of the cultural contribution of various ethnic groups and the promise of government support for culture. This was intended to help break down barriers to equal participation in society (as Prime Minister Pierre Trudeau suggested in his speech announcing the policy [Canada, House of Commons 1971: 8545–6]). But since the 1980s, multiculturalism has included an explicit anti-racism component. Racial equality is now a focus of other policies, as well, such as the federal employment equity policy adopted in 1986.

In this chapter, we examine evidence of racial inequality and discrimination and consider their relation to the social integration of racial minorities in Canada. In doing so, we have used very helpful data from Statistics Canada's landmark Ethnic Diversity Survey (EDS), conducted in 2002.[1] This survey provides economic data and is an invaluable source of indicators of social integration such as intercultural friendships, participation in voluntary activities in the community, social trust, sense of belonging, and feeling Canadian.

The analyses we present distinguish recent immigrants, immigrants with longer experience in Canada, and the children of immigrants—the so-called second generation. Most racial minorities in Canada are immigrants, but a born-in-Canada generation is emerging: by 2011, it constituted 30.9 per cent of the racial minority population. As the children of relatively recent immigrants, most of these Canadian-born members of racial minorities are young: the median ages of the second generation for Canada's three largest visible minorities were 12.2 years for South Asians, 16.8 for Chinese, and 14.5 for Blacks. Still, because they constitute an emerging young adult population with a perspective that differs from that of immigrants, this second generation is critical to an assessment of the long-term impact of immigration (Boyd 2000). On the one hand, as Canadian-born, they will not confront many of the obstacles their parents faced as arriving immigrants. On the other hand, their expectation of social acceptance, economic opportunity, and equal participation may be greater than that of their parents.

An analysis of the existing literature and EDS findings indicates that racial minority immigrants integrate into Canadian society relatively slowly, and that discriminatory inequalities are at least part of the reason. This prompts a consideration of existing Canadian policies on racial inequality and their adequacy to address this challenge to the cohesiveness of Canadian society.

Racial Inequalities and Discrimination

Overall Economic Situation and Employment of Racial Minorities

Generally speaking, visible minorities have much lower relative household incomes and higher poverty rates than do ethnic groups of European origin (Kazemipur and Halli 2001, 2000: 107–9; Ornstein 2000). Data from the EDS (Table 13.1, column 1) show mean individual-equivalent household incomes for ethnic groups,[2] relative to the mean for the census metropolitan area of residence. For visible minorities, incomes are $7,686 less than the local average, while for Whites incomes are $1,895 above the local average; thus, the gap is $9,581. In relation to the national mean individual-equivalent household income of $41,330, this gap is 23.2 per cent. Relative household incomes of virtually all racial minority groups—including Chinese, South Asians, and Blacks, as the largest groups—are substantially lower than those of almost all White groups (for further details, see Reitz and Banerjee 2007).[3] In 2001, the poverty rate for racial minorities was nearly double that for the rest of the population (Table 13.1, column 2, from census data): 26.6 per cent compared with 14.2 per cent; some racial minorities had higher rates than others.[4] White immigrant groups experience inequality as well, but not nearly to the same extent.

The main economic problem for new racial minority immigrants is, of course, finding adequate employment (Li 2000). There are a number of reasons they experience difficulties in doing so. Some of these difficulties—but by no means all—are associated with the period of adjustment or "entry effect" that all immigrants must confront. Entry problems may be particularly severe for immigrants arriving during a recession, as was the case for many in the early 1900s. All immigrants do better as they settle in and become more accustomed to their new environment. Furthermore, adverse experiences linked to economic recession may be offset by a later rebound in the economy, as the immigrants who arrived in the early 1980s discovered (Bloom et al. 1995; Grant 1999). In short, economic disadvantage and high rates of poverty may attenuate over time, and the entry effect will disappear.

There are a number of other reasons for immigrants' employment difficulties. Perhaps the most important are urban settlement, the discounting of qualifications, and race. With respect to the first reason, in seeking employment, immigrants find that any educational advantage they might have due to Canada's skill-selective immigration policy is offset by the fact that most settle in major urban areas where jobs are plentiful but competition is intense from new native-born labour market entrants, who tend to be young and also highly educated. In terms of the second reason, immigrants' skills tend to be discounted in the labour market, while those of the native-born are not (Li 2001; Reitz et al. 2014); as for the third reason, racial minority immigrants face more obstacles than immigrants of European origin or native-born workers (Pendakur and Pendakur 1998, 2002). Other possible reasons for employment difficulties include isolation in minority occupational enclaves and the fact that minority group social networks lack the linkages necessary to find good jobs.

The obstacles to immigrant success appear to have increased, and the greatest impact has been felt by those arriving most recently, even though the late 1990s and early 2000s were a period of strong labour demand. In fact, underlying the ups and downs of several business cycles, there has been a downward trend in the employment rates and earnings of successive cohorts of newly arrived immigrants, both male and female (Frenette and Morissette 2003; see Reitz 2007). Whereas immigrant men arriving in the

Table 13.1 Objective and Perceived Ethnoracial Inequality in Canada by Ancestry

	IE Income (mean $1)[1]	Poverty Rate (%)[2]	Perceived Discrimination (%)	Perceived Vulnerability (%)	N
Non-Visible Minorities (by Ancestry)[3]					
Canadian	1,258.7	16.4	10.7	14.3	10,293
French	750.5	16.6	9.1	19.2	592
British	3,386.1	11.8	10.7	15.0	1,744
Northern and Western European	2,238.2	12.5	10.0	11.2	4,356
Russian and Eastern European	405.7	16.2	12.5	16.5	299
Other Southern European	−2,778.6	14.3†	14.7	16.8	2,098
Jewish	11,637.7	13.3†	20.0	38.7	276
Arab and West Asian	−6,058.4	29.2	18.9	21.2	125
Latin American	−7,416.6	25.1	24.2	23.8	5,893
Greek	−617.4	16.3†	13.6	15.6	291
Italian	1,278.0	12.2†	11.5	19.2	207
Portuguese	−5,832.7	12.8†	8.9	15.9	568
Other European	9,453.1	12.5	16.2	16.0	4,109
Total non-visible minorities	1,895.3	14.2	10.6	16.0	30,851
Visible Minorities (All Ancestries)					
Chinese	−6,730.2	26.9	33.2	33.6	513
South Asian	−5,815.8	21.7	33.1	38.7	1,424
Black	−10,607.2	31.1	49.6	43.0	2,421
Filipino	−5,063.5	16.4†	35.8	48.8	653
Latin American	−10,270.3	29.3	28.6	30.0	362
Southeast Asian	-6,829.3	25.6	34.5	37.7	148
Arab and West Asian	−13,359.4	40.8	29.8	27.0	386
Korean	−17,145.0	40.8†	40.5	49.0	209
Japanese	4,079.5	n/a	42.8	34.2	1,892
Other visible minorities	−7,115.5	23.7	33.3	36.8	331
Multiple visible minorities	−4,304.2	n/a	41.5	28.7	283
Total visible minorities	−7,686.4	26.6	35.9	37.3	8,622
Total					**39,473**

1 Individual-equivalent household income, relative to the census metropolitan area (CMA) mean. The individual-equivalent income adjusts household incomes for household size, and is calculated by dividing household income by the square root of household size.

2 Data on poverty rates are from the 2001 Census Public Use Microdata File, 2.7 per cent sample, for people aged 15 and over, and are based on Statistics Canada's low-income cut-offs. In those data, visible minorities are identified only as Black, South Asian, Chinese, and other visible minorities. In this table "other visible minorities" are further identified as Filipino, Latin American, Southeast Asian, Arab and West Asian, and Korean, based on ancestry.

3 The origins of this group in the "non-visible minorities" category include Arab, West Asian, and Latin American, and these also appear in the "visible minority" group. Those who are considered in the "non-visible minority" category described themselves as White in the visible minority question. Those who did not identify any ancestry or visible minority group or did not report household income or perceived inequality were excluded.

† Data exclude Maritime provinces.

Source: *Ethnic Diversity Survey 2002* (Ottawa: Statistics Canada, 2003).

five-year period before the 1981 census earned 79.6 per cent of the earnings of native-born men, by 1996 this figure had dropped to 60 per cent. For women, it dropped from 73.1 per cent to 62.4 per cent. By 2001, as a result of the improved labour demand of the late 1990s, relative earnings for the most recently arrived immigrants were higher than they had been in the mid-1990s, but they remained about 15 percentage points below 1970 levels (Frenette and Morissette 2003: 7). Notably, despite earnings mobility experienced by immigrants as their time in Canada increases, the general trend towards declining earnings also affects immigrants who have been in Canada longer.

New immigrants have seen reduced employment success even though immigrant education levels are at an all-time high (Frenette and Morissette 2003; see also Statistics Canada 2003; Citizenship and Immigration Canada 1998). Marc Frenette and René Morissette (2003: 4) show that the proportion of immigrant men arriving in the late 1990s who possessed at least the equivalent of a bachelor's degree was over 40 per cent, more than twice the figure of 18.6 for native-born Canadian men; the corresponding figures for women were 37.5 per cent and 21.7 per cent. Yet, as we have mentioned, this has not translated into employment success. Only some of the reasons for these trends are well understood. The shift towards immigrants originating from outside Europe, with the resulting change in the racial composition of immigration, explains some of the reduced employment success, particularly during the 1970s and 1980s. Abdurrahman Aydemir and Mikal Skuterud (2005: 648–9) show that when we consider immigrant trends throughout the period following the policy changes of the 1960s and focus on earnings in relation to levels of education, we see that the decline in earnings to 2000 is as much as 50 per cent for both men and women. As much as one-third of this decline stems from origin shifts and the disadvantages associated with racial minority status.

Broader labour market changes affect immigrants as well—particularly racial minorities. David Green and Christopher Worswick (2004) have shown that, to some extent, the downward trend in immigrant employment parallels the trend among the native-born entering the workforce for the first time, in the sense that both groups fared worse in the 1990s than in earlier decades. While the causes of the trend may or may not be the same for immigrants and native-born, the consequences are greater for immigrants, since a larger proportion are pushed into poverty, and racial minorities are disproportionately affected.

Increased difficulties for immigrants may also be related to the move towards a knowledge economy, the transformation of the occupational structure, and an overall increase in earnings inequality. One aspect of this is the rise in native-born education levels, which, since the 1970s, has been generally faster than the rise in immigrant education levels. Reitz (2001) shows that the discounting of the foreign-acquired education of immigrants in the labour market compounds their difficulties in keeping pace. Furthermore, the increased earnings disadvantages of immigrants are related to their reduced access to professional-level employment (Reitz 2003) and to their growing difficulty in obtaining well-paying jobs outside professional fields, where educational qualifications are becoming more important. Finally, there is a noticeable decline in the value of foreign experience in the labour market, though the origins of this decline are not yet known (Green and Worswick 2004; Aydemir and Skuterud 2005; Reitz 2007).

In addition, the economic situation of immigrants may be affected by broader institutional changes in Canadian society (Reitz 1998). Specifically, social services have been reduced, affecting immigrants who are in the early stages of settlement, and costs for public services are rising, including costs for retraining and educational upgrading.

Clearly, the racial dimension of economic inequality in Canada today is significant, and its social implications require scrutiny. In any society, a noticeable association of racial status and economic success over extended periods raises questions about social and political integration. A critical aspect of this, which we will now consider, is the significance of discriminatory treatment.

Perceptions of Racial Prejudice and Discrimination: A Racial Divide?

The fact that immigrants experience inequality and disadvantage may not in itself be divisive if it is regarded as the result of understandable circumstances—such as newcomer status, lack of sufficient language skills, or training that does not match Canadian job requirements. Simply stated, inequality may not become a social problem if it is perceived as legitimate. However, racism, prejudice, and discrimination are another matter. Not surprisingly, discriminatory treatment is more likely to be perceived as unjust and to lead to serious intergroup antagonism, as Gunner Myrdal has noted. In his classic—and prescient—examination of racial inequality in the United States, Myrdal (1944) points out the significance of the contradiction between the ideal of equal opportunity and the reality of inequality reinforced by discrimination.

But how significant is racial discrimination in Canada? Let us begin by considering the way this problem is perceived in Canadian society. Within certain minority groups, perceptions of racial discrimination are fairly widespread. In the 2002 Ethnic Diversity Study, which includes reports of personal experiences of racial and ethnic discrimination, respondents were asked, "In the past 5 years [or, for more recent immigrants, since arriving in Canada], do you feel that you have experienced discrimination or been treated unfairly by others in Canada because of your ethnicity, race, skin colour, language, accent, or religion?" To capture perceptions of vulnerability to discrimination, two other questions were asked. The first concerned the respondent feeling "uncomfortable or out of place in Canada" because of race or cultural background; the second concerned the respondent worrying about becoming a victim of a hate crime.[5]

As Table 13.1 shows, of the members of visible minorities who responded to this survey, 35.9 per cent reported experiences of discrimination, compared with 10.6 per cent of Whites. The highest rate is for Blacks, at 49.6 per cent, but there are substantial rates also for the other visible minority groups, including Chinese at 33.2 per cent and South Asians at 33.1 per cent. Among most White groups, experiences of discrimination are reported by fewer than 15 per cent.[6] Experiences of perceived vulnerability are reported by 37.3 per cent of visible minority groups and 16 per cent of White groups. These are personal experiences and the EDS does not report perceptions of discrimination against the group as a whole. However, earlier surveys indicate that individuals are even more likely to perceive discrimination against their group as a whole than against themselves personally: over one-third of Chinese respondents felt that way, as did a clear majority of Blacks.

Despite improvement in the economic circumstances of immigrants as they adjust to Canadian society and labour markets and the generally more positive employment experiences of the second generation, a racial gap in perception of discrimination is notable among immigrants with longer experience in Canada. This gap is even greater among the children of immigrants. Data from the EDS, reported in Table 13.2, show that among recent immigrants (those arriving during the previous 10 years), 33.6 per cent of racial minorities report having experienced discrimination, compared with 19.2 per cent of those of European origin. Among immigrants arriving earlier, perceptions of discrimination are less common for those of European origin; at a rate of 10.2 per cent, it is about the same as it is for the children of European immigrants and for the broader Canadian population of third generation and greater. But among racial minority immigrants who arrived earlier, perceptions of discrimination are, if anything, more common, at 35.5 per cent; and among the children of racial minority immigrants, the percentage experiencing discrimination is still greater, at 42.2 per cent.

Table 13.2 Objective and Perceived Inequality by Origin, Immigration Cohort, and Generation, 2002

	Immigrants			
	Recent[1]	**Earlier**[2]	**Second Generation**[3]	**Third Generation and Higher**[4]
IE *Income (Mean)*[5]				
White	−8,467.5	2,190.6	3,497.2	3,656.7
All visible minorities	−14,630.7	1,535.2	−1.6	
Chinese	−16,500.8	1,523.3	4,670.0	
South Asian	−13,103.3	1,938.1	417.9	
Black	−15,872.1	−6,840.0	-3,782.8	
Other visible minorities	−13,726.9	−3,779.5	-1,680.3	
Perceived Discrimination (%)				
White	19.2	10.2	10.9	9.9
Visible minorities	33.6	35.5	42.2	
Chinese	35.4	30.9	34.5	
South Asian	28.2	34.1	43.4	
Black	44.8	47.7	60.9	
Other visible minorities	32.5	34.8	36.2	
Perceived Vulnerability (%)				
White	26.2	17.0	14.8	16.1
Visible minorities	41.8	37.8	27.0	
Chinese	40.8	32.3	20.2	
South Asian	40.7	39.9	28.4	
Black	49.8	44.5	37.2	
Other visible minorities	41.0	37.6	25.2	

1 Immigration between 1992 and 2002. *N*'s (depending on the outcome measure): Whites 740–70; Chinese 603–22; South Asians 455–79; Blacks 174–81; other visible minorities 563–85; all visible minorities 1,795–1,867.
2 Immigrated in 1991 and before. *N*'s (depending on the outcome measure): Whites 4,992–5,186; Chinese 758–69; South Asians 643–75; Blacks 401–25; other visible minorities 999–1,032; all visible minorities 2,801–928.
3 *N*'s (depending on the outcome measure): Whites 11,949–12,069; Chinese 889–97; South Asian 713–23; Blacks 677–91; other visible minorities 1,062–73; all visible minorities 3,341–84.
4 *N*'s for Whites of third generation and higher (depending on the outcome measure): 14,247–875. Third-generation visible minorities are excluded.
5 Mean individual-equivalent household income, relative to the census metropolitan area (CMA) mean. The individual-equivalent income adjusts household incomes for household size, and is calculated by dividing household income by the square root of household size.
Source: *Ethnic Diversity Survey 2002* (Ottawa: Statistics Canada, 2003).

The racial gap in perceptions of discrimination, which is 14.4 per cent for recent immigrants, is 25.3 per cent for earlier immigrants, and 31.3 per cent for the children of immigrants. In other words, greater experience in Canada seems to lead to a larger racial gap in the perception of discrimination. This widening racial gap is observed among Chinese, South Asians, Blacks, and other visible minority groups. In these groups, the percentage of those born in Canada who report experiences of discrimination varies between 34.5 per cent for Chinese, 43.4 per cent for South Asians, and 60.9 per cent for Blacks, compared with 10.9 per cent for the children of immigrants of European origin.

Members of minority groups also express serious concerns about the non-recognition of immigrant qualifications. In some cases, the educational qualifications may be equivalent to those of native-born Canadians yet not recognized by employers. Complaints about barriers to licensed trades and professions have been voiced for many years, and the first wave of the Longitudinal Survey of Immigrants to Canada, based on interviews with approximately 12,000 immigrants arriving between October 2000 and September 2001 and released in 2003 (Statistics Canada 2005), shows that the lack of recognition of foreign credentials or experience is one of the most commonly reported employment problems—along with lack of Canadian job experience and official language knowledge. The earnings lost due to this long-standing problem are potentially quite large, amounting to about $2 billion annually (Reitz 2001; Watt and Bloom 2001).

The broader Canadian population remains skeptical of the significance of racial discrimination affecting minorities, and there is a prevailing view that racism is marginal in Canada (Reitz and Breton 1994). Even so, many members of the majority population recognize that discrimination exists. A CRIC–*Globe and Mail* survey entitled *The New Canada* shows that about three in four Canadians—both White and visible minority—agree that "there is a lot of racism in Canada" (Centre for Research and Information on Canada [CRIC]–*Globe and Mail* 2003; see also Breton 1990: 210–21). However, there are differences with respect to how significantly prejudice affects opportunities in key arenas such as employment. The survey shows that 42 per cent of visible minorities think that prejudice affects opportunities, compared with 30 per cent of Whites. Moreover, the actual racial divergence in perceptions of the significance of discrimination is greater than is reflected in this difference in percentages, because some Whites say it is Whites who lose opportunities because of discrimination (17 per cent)—sometimes called "reverse discrimination"—whereas this perception is less common among visible minorities (7 per cent).

The view that racial discrimination is not a significant problem in Canada undoubtedly contributes to a belief that existing government policies on the subject are adequate, so that further action is not needed. Official policies on multiculturalism and human rights are seen as sufficient to maintain what most Canadians would describe as a favourable environment for immigrants and minority groups, particularly by international standards. Only a minority of the White population think that prejudice is something that the Canadian government should address with more determination.

Evidence of Discrimination against Racial Minority Immigrants

These are the perceptions, but what are the facts? In some ways, the research community is as divided as the general population. While the available research confirms that racial discrimination does exist, it allows for divergent interpretations of its significance.

Four types of evidence are cited in discussions of the extent of discrimination: prejudiced attitudes; evidence of discrimination in human rights cases; field tests of discrimination; and discrimination as revealed by statistical analysis of earnings gaps in labour market surveys. While each is useful, each is also problematic. Prejudiced attitudes could lead to discrimination, but not necessarily. Human rights case evidence may be persuasive, and the circumstances of a particular case may be suggestive of broader patterns, but it remains case-specific. Field trials show patterns of discrimination but not its consequences in the aggregate for minority inequality. Finally, statistical analyses of labour force data are open to diverse interpretations. However, when considered together, the four types of evidence suggest that the possibility of significant discrimination should be taken seriously. We deal with each in turn.

Attitudinal research

Research on attitudes reveals prejudice in Canada and a corresponding potential for discrimination. Not all attitudes towards minorities are negative, of course. Attitudes towards immigration in general tend to be more favourable in Canada than in societies receiving fewer immigrants (Simon and Lynch 1999). Gallup polls conducted almost every year between 1975 and 2001 have shown majority support for either maintaining or increasing Canada's emphasis on immigration (the exception being 1982, a recession year); other polls show continuing support to 2010 (see Reitz 2014a: 101). Yet research also makes it clear that racial boundaries are a reality of Canadian social life. For example, while most Canadians deny harbouring racial views, they maintain a "social distance" from minorities—that is, they say they prefer not to interact with members of other racial groups in certain social situations (Reitz and Breton 1994). Although an Environics Focus Canada poll showed that a large majority (93 per cent in 2000) reject the proposal that "non-whites should not be allowed to immigrate to Canada" (Esses et al. 2002: 72), there is much evidence that Canadians are more comfortable with groups of European origin than with non-European groups, and these preferences carry implications for group status (Angus Reid Group 1991; Berry and Kalin 1995; Esses and Gardner 1996).

Racism and racial bias help determine attitudes towards immigration (Henry et al. 1998; Satzewich 1998), and concerns about the threat to jobs are related to racial attitudes (Palmer 1991, 1996; Esses et al. 2001; Kalin and Berry 1994; Berry and Kalin 1995). Some research suggests that Canadians see immigrants as posing an economic threat, and this view fuels a prejudicial backlash (Esses et al. 2001). If the political acceptability of immigration derives from the economic success of immigrants, then a dip in that success rate could politically undermine the program of immigration. There is little evidence as yet that this is occurring in Canada, demonstrating that the economic problems of the newly arrived do not quickly affect the overall tone of intergroup relations.

The potential impact of racial attitudes on discrimination is complex, however. Although prejudicial attitudes do not necessarily lead to discriminatory behaviour, they may be associated with such behaviour. For example, psychological research by Victoria Esses, Joerg Dietz, and Arjun Bhardwaj (2006) shows that assessments of foreign qualifications tend to be lower among persons who show other evidence of racial bias or prejudice. Discrimination may be displayed by persons who are not overtly prejudiced because of social pressure. For example, systemic discrimination arises when established practices in an organization exclude minorities. A complex phenomenon, systemic discrimination is only beginning to be understood, and its significance is being debated. A 1997 Canadian Human Rights Tribunal decision that found systemic racial discrimination in the federal public service illustrates the complex nature of evidence required for legal proof (Beck et al. 2002).

Human rights cases

The Human Rights Tribunal decision just cited serves as an example of the kind of evidence we can draw from human rights complaints, but, while compelling, it is only one case. It involved allegations that there was a glass ceiling for minorities in a particular federal department—that is, that systemic discrimination was practised by those responsible for promoting staff to senior managerial positions. There was evidence of statistical under-representation of minorities at the senior management level; evidence derived from a survey on human resource practices of discrimination in the promotion process; and testimony about the attitudes of officials responsible for promotion decisions. The case is remarkable, partly because the respondent was a mainstream employer—the government of Canada—generally considered an opponent of racial bias and discrimination.

Field tests of discrimination

Experimental field studies (or "audit" studies) have been conducted to find out if there is a variance in employer responses to people from different racial groups applying for the same jobs and presenting the same qualifications, and the results have offered persuasive evidence of discrimination. In Canada, the study by Oreopoulos (2011; also in this volume, Chapter 25) involved sending nearly 13,000 resumés to employers in response to advertised jobs. Resumés containing English or British names prompted employer calls for an interview 39 per cent more often than resumés with Chinese, Indian, Pakistani, and Greek names, even when the latter indicated Canadian education and Canadian experience. (Callback rates were far lower for those with minority names whose education and experience came from outside Canada.) Although this evidence refers to only the very first phase of the employment process, it is significant because it is based on direct observation of the behaviour of employers (see an earlier study by Henry and Ginsberg, 1985, which included job offers). Such studies should be repeated regularly, in the manner of the program organized by the International Labour Office in Geneva (Zegers de Beijl 2000). Yet even audit studies do not address the question of the extent to which discrimination accounts for the overall economic inequalities experienced by racial minorities.

Statistical studies

A large number of statistical studies show that within the labour force as a whole—relative to measured job qualifications, such as education or work experience, and with differences in knowledge of official languages taken into account—visible minority immigrants have lower earnings than their European counterparts or native-born Canadian workers of European origin. Some studies are Canada-wide (Li 2001; Pendakur and Pendakur 2002, 2011; Skuterud 2010); others are specific to immigrant-intensive settings, such as Toronto (Reitz and Sklar 1997; Ornstein 2000). In either case, the amount of earnings disadvantage varies among minority groups and between genders. For immigrant men, it varies between 10 per cent and 25 per cent. Inequalities are greater for Blacks than for some Asian groups. Earnings disadvantages exist for immigrant women, although the amounts are less, as the comparison group is native-born Canadian women, themselves a disadvantaged group compared with men.

Such analyses are useful in identifying potential discriminatory earning gaps, but the earnings disadvantages of minorities are open to interpretation not just in terms of discrimination but also in terms of deficiencies in qualifications that cannot be measured in the survey data. Foreign-acquired educational qualifications might be lower in quality, foreign experience might not be relevant in Canada, or language skills might be deficient in subtle but significant ways.

Education and Employment for the Children of Immigrants

The education and employment experiences of Canadian-born children of immigrants (or of immigrants who arrive so young that their formative experiences occur in Canada) are regarded as critical to the long-term integration of racial minorities. In fact, their experiences may be a better test of the prevalence of racial discrimination. Earnings disadvantages for immigrants, even when controls for years of formal education or experience are applied, may be attributed to differences in the quality of Canadian relevance of foreign-acquired education or experience, or to language difficulties that are difficult to measure. Hence, several studies of discrimination have focused on experiences of racial minorities born in Canada, as their labour market experiences would not be affected by such characteristics.

Overall, the education levels of the racial minority second generation in Canada are fairly high—even relative to parental education levels—despite complaints of cultural and racial bias in Canadian schools, including universities. Since the federal government introduced multiculturalism as a policy framework, provincial authorities responsible for education have addressed this issue with multicultural, and then anti-racist, policies (Davies and Guppy 1998; Dei 2000). While education researchers still point to racial biases among teachers and in the curriculum (Henry et al. 1998; James 1998), Scott Davies and Neil Guppy (1998: 136) show, using the 1991 census, that among persons 20 years of age and older, both immigrant and native-born visible minorities have significantly higher rates of high school graduation than the majority population. Analyses of more recent data show that rates of university degree attainment are also fairly high (Boyd and Grieco 1998, Boyd 2002; see Reitz, Zhang, and Hawkins 2011 for a comparison of Canada with the United States and Australia in this regard).

It is important, however, to distinguish descriptive findings on educational attainment from findings that bear on equality of opportunity in the school system. The emerging second generation are children of relatively well-educated immigrants, many of whom arrived with the earlier minority immigrant cohorts of the 1970s and, despite difficulties, earned relatively high incomes. The education levels attained by their children do not necessarily reflect equality of opportunity, and barriers hidden in the analyses may subsequently come to light.

Regarding the critical question of employment discrimination, analysis of the employment experiences of the children of immigrants suggests that racial disadvantage for native-born racial minorities is significant, albeit less so than for the immigrant generation. Derek Hum and Wayne Simpson (1999) suggest that among native-born racial minorities, only Black men suffer employment discrimination. While most studies agree that Blacks experience significant disadvantage in the second generation, they also find that other visible minorities are also affected (see Li 2000; Reitz 2001; Pendakur and Pendakur 1998, 2002, 2011; Skuterud 2010).

Summary

Among the various ethnic groups in Canada, racial minorities have the lowest incomes and highest rates of poverty, and many members of these groups believe they have experienced discrimination based on their minority racial origins. Although the economic situation is somewhat better for those who have been in Canada longer and for the Canadian-born generation, the perception that they have been affected by discrimination is more widespread among the latter two groups. In fact, a racial divide exists regarding perceptions of discrimination. In this context, the research on the extent of discrimination—although it does not conclusively point to discrimination as a significant cause of racial inequality—does not conclusively resolve the questions.

Social Cohesion and the Social Integration of Racial Minorities

Analysis of the social consequences of racial inequality and perceptions of discrimination may have many different aspects. Ultimately, our concern in this chapter is with the cohesion of society and the impact of minorities on that cohesion. Here, "cohesion" refers to the capacity of society to set and implement collective goals. Lack of cohesion may be reflected in conflict, sometimes violent conflict. Instances of civil disorder involving immigrants or minorities in other countries—most recently, France and the United Kingdom—have reinforced these concerns. We should remember, however, that conflict does not necessarily detract from cohesion: it may actually help resolve problems of intergroup relations and, hence, be an essential part of social life in a cohesive society. Finally, lack of social cohesion is manifested in other less dramatic but equally important ways, including lack of participation in decision-making, withdrawal of support for decisions, and lack of organizational capacity to participate in constructive social activities.

The following discussion focuses on the integration of racial minorities as an important aspect of the Canadian social fabric. It also considers the impact of inequality and discrimination on minority social integration. Here, "social integration" refers to the extent to which individual members of a group form relationships with people outside the group—relationships that help them to achieve individual economic, social, or cultural goals. Social integration, in this sense, is relevant to the broader question of social cohesion: groups whose members look to the broader society as a means to private ends are more likely to become engaged in common objectives; similarly, groups that are well integrated into society become resources for the constructive resolution of conflicts.

In the Ethnic Diversity Survey, which provides data on individuals, the analysis focuses on those attitudes and behaviours that are expected to reflect integration into society. Three of these seem especially relevant here: strength of individual ties to the group, overall satisfaction with life (presumably a reflection of a sense of having achieved personal goals), and extent of civic participation.

Several EDS survey questions tap into these aspects. Regarding individual ties to Canadian society, there are measures of sense of belonging to Canada, trust in others, self-identification as Canadian, and acquisition of Canadian citizenship. Regarding the second aspect—overall life satisfaction—there is a single question. The third aspect—civic participation—is reflected in the following two items: participation in voluntary organizations and voting in federal elections. The survey question on participation in voluntary organizations probes deeper than simple membership, asking whether the respondent contributes on a voluntary basis to the activities of the organization. The question on voting asks about federal elections. Voting is a meaningful indicator of participation in the Canadian community, but as citizenship is a prerequisite to voting and acquisition of citizenship reflects various circumstances, it is important to restrict analyses of voting to an examination of those who are Canadian citizens and were eligible to vote in the last federal election prior to the survey date.

Table 13.3 compares the results for all seven indicators for Whites and visible minorities. On six of the seven indicators, visible minorities appear less integrated. The greatest gap between visible minorities and Whites is in self-identification as Canadian (30.7 percentage points). There are also significant gaps in citizenship (18.3 percentage points) and in voting (11.1 percentage points). The gap in citizenship undoubtedly reflects, at least in part, the significantly higher proportion of immigrants among visible minorities. There are smaller racial gaps in life satisfaction (5.5 percentage points) and volunteering (7.2 percentage points). On two indicators—sense of belonging and trust in others—there does not appear to be a significant overall racial difference. Visible minorities, in fact, express a somewhat stronger sense of belonging than Whites.

Some of these generalizations apply to most visible minorities; others do not. The most pervasive pattern affecting all visible minorities is the substantially lower level of Canadian identity and voting. All also have lower rates of citizenship. Regarding life satisfaction and trust, there are clear variations among groups. Lower life satisfaction affects Chinese in particular, while the other groups are closer to the White average. Less trust in others affects Blacks, while South Asians and other visible minorities are near the White average; Chinese are more than 10 percentage points above the White average. Some groups have lower levels of integration in most aspects, particularly Blacks and Chinese. Blacks have the highest rate of volunteer work, followed by South Asians and other visible minorities; Chinese are lower than Whites.

Recency of Immigration and the Second Generation

Findings from the Ethnic Diversity Survey also permit us to make a systematic assessment of the effects of immigration and generational status

Table 13.3 Integration of Visible Minorities into Canadian Society, 2002 (%)

	Belonging[1]	Trust[1]	Canadian Identity[1]	Citizenship[1]	Life Satisfaction[1]	Volunteering[1]	Voted in Federal Election[2]
Whites	54.8	49.9	64.3	97.3	47.2	33.8	81.9
All visible minorities	58.6	47.9	33.6	79.0	41.7	26.6	70.8
Specific Minority Origins							
Chinese	52.7	60.1	40.5	83.9	30.8	20.7	68.1
South Asian	64.9	49.0	30.5	73.3	48.4	29.1	76.1
Blacks	60.6	30.6	29.0	80.8	43.5	34.6	71.8
Other visible minorities	58.3	45.5	32.0	78.0	45.2	26.1	69.5

1 *N*'s (depending on the outcome measure): Whites: 31,341–32,660; all visible minorities: 8,149–8,622; Chinese: 2,267–2,421; South Asians: 1,755–1,892; Blacks: 1,347–1,424; other visible minorities: 2,757–2,885.

2 The analysis of voting is restricted to eligible voters, namely, citizens and those at least 20 years old. N's: Whites: 28,250; all visible minorities: 5,581; Chinese: 1,646; South Asians: 1,159; Blacks: 888; other visible minorities: 1,888.

Source: *Ethnic Diversity Survey 2002* (Ottawa: Statistics Canada, 2003).

on the integration of visible minorities. We can summarize our finding under three points. (For complete details and statistics, see Reitz and Banerjee 2007.) First, Whites who have greater experience in Canada are better integrated into society than their visible minority counterparts. The negative effects on visible minorities of greater experience living in Canada are most pronounced with regard to their self-identification as Canadian and their voting, but are also found in their sense of belonging, trust in others, and life satisfaction. Still, visible minorities are more likely than Whites to become citizens, and there are no major differences in volunteering.

Second, although visible minority immigrants have lower earnings than Whites at an individual level, low earnings alone contribute little or nothing to these trends in social integration. Rather, negative trends in integration reflect more pronounced experiences of discrimination and vulnerability, which become, or remain, pronounced for the second generation.

Third, many of the most important trends affect all visible minorities. Perhaps most significantly, in the second generation, all visible minority groups are more negative on all indicators. Nevertheless, some groups consistently show more negative patterns than others. In the second generation, Blacks and South Asians are least likely to self-identify as Canadian; Blacks and other visible minorities are least likely to vote; Blacks, Chinese, and other visible minorities are least likely to have a sense of belonging in Canada.

In sum, improvement in immigrants' earnings may contribute to successful integration, but higher earnings alone do not smooth the path to integration. The analysis here suggests that experiences of discrimination and vulnerability remain, slowing the social integration of minorities. Furthermore, these effects may be intensified for the children of immigrants, whose expectation of equality may be greater than was the case for their parents.

Among visible minorities, Blacks consistently experience the greatest inequality, and their integration into Canadian society is slower. However, the fact that none of the indicators of inequality fully explains the slower integration of visible minorities suggests that the awareness of one's group standing as problematic may affect how individuals feel about society, even those not focusing on specific disadvantages.

Policy Issues: Managing Diversity under Conditions of Inequality

Our findings on racial inequality and the social integration of minorities carry implications for broader issues of multiculturalism and pluralism in Canada. We may well ask whether existing policies are adequate to address potential threats to social cohesion. The following discussion points to one feature of existing policy that may affect potential threats—namely, policy goals and the processes of setting them.

Goals of Canadian Multiculturalism and Anti-racism

Multiculturalism is the centrepiece of Canada's policy on inter-ethnic relations, and its focus is on broad ideals rather than specific goals and objectives. Canada has been an innovator in multiculturalism policies, which have been embraced at all levels of government since their initial proclamation in 1971 (Quebec does not embrace the label "multiculturalism," even though its policies have similar goals). The initial formulation articulated very broad equity objectives (Canada, House of Commons 1971: 8545–6), but there were few specifics. Reactions to the policy of multiculturalism have been varied: some have supported it as the essence of modern conceptions of equality (Kymlicka 1995); others have criticized it as divisive (Bissoondath 1994; Schlesinger 1992). Despite the lack of consensus, since the Canadian policy has developed with the passage of explicit legislation and the multicultural character of the country is protected in the Constitution, the emphasis on broad ideals has held firm.

Racial barriers have been identified across a range of institutions in Canada, and many policy arenas touch on this issue of race relations. These include immigration and settlement policy; human rights policy; employment policy, including that which addresses discrimination and recognition of immigrant qualifications; policies for minority equality in public services; and policies for policing and the administration of justice in minority communities. But policies designed to address the special needs of visible minorities and to promote racial equality have been developed without an emphasis on specifics and with perhaps an even smaller consensus on objectives. When race relations was introduced under the rubric of multiculturalism in the 1980s, it was not recognized in principle as a separate concern.

Governments have responded to race issues as they have arisen, but with little co-ordination or continuity. For example, in 2005 the federal government announced *A Canada for All: Canada's Action Plan against Racism*, which attempted to co-ordinate existing policies, and involved a number of initiatives (Department of Canadian Heritage 2005). However, although a subsequent evaluation (Citizenship and Immigration Canada 2010) suggested that little had been accomplished, only minor adjustments followed.

Policy related to racial minorities is spread throughout agencies and levels of government. One example of lack of co-ordination is the policies that address the deteriorating employment situation of newly arrived immigrants (Reitz 2005; Reitz et al. 2014). A number of relevant policies are in place, but they have not been developed in a co-ordinated way. At the federal level, Citizenship and Immigration Canada is responsible for immigrant selection and settlement; Canadian Heritage, Employment and Social Development Canada, and various other departments are responsible for related policies. Most policies involve activities for which responsibility is divided among various levels of government, and the responsible parties have taken approaches that in some respects are complementary and in others are divergent—even contradictory. A recent example is the federal government's Foreign Credential Recognition Program, which funds projects aimed at innovation, while making no provision for co-ordination with existing provincial agencies. What is needed is a comprehensive approach that addresses the range of issues such as immigrant employment, settlement programs, recognition of immigrant qualifications, bridge training, and employment discrimination. All of this should be considered in relation to maintaining the overall success of the immigration program. Co-ordination might be enhanced by the creation of a unit within the federal government (perhaps directed by a cabinet minister) responsible for all immigration-related policies and with the authority to initiate discussions with provincial and municipal governments to promote greater consistency and effective policy-making.

Provincial and municipal governments do not consider race relations in a consistent manner. In fact, the general direction of policy has been away from issues of race. In the mid-1990s, the Ontario government under Mike Harris abolished the provincial Employment Equity Act on the grounds that it gave undue preference to racial minorities. Its Job Quotas Repeal Act, 1995 was described as "an Act to repeal job quotas and to restore merit-based employment practices in Ontario," implying that discrimination such as has been described in this paper does not exist. The Harris government also abolished an Anti-racism Secretariat advisory group within the Minister of Citizenship. Similarly, a network of Toronto municipal committees on community and race relations functioned for many years but disappeared in the wake of municipal amalgamation and budget reductions mandated by the province in the late 1990s. In more recent years, policy has addressed race only occasionally, and only rarely has it confronted the issue of discrimination explicitly.

Illustrative of the lack of policy specificity regarding goals is the absence of provision for their formal evaluation. Evaluation requires explicit goals, and these are not in place. Multiculturalism policy itself has never been evaluated in the specific social sciences sense of the word, which implies direct observation of program impact. Jeffrey Reitz and Raymond Breton (1994) have shown that intergroup relations involving immigrants (including racial minority ones) in Canada are not markedly different from those in the US, a finding that casts doubt on the notion that Canada's multiculturalism has a dramatic impact. In fact, a perception of multiculturalism as largely symbolic and incapable of creating a major social impact has been reinforced by the fact that program expenditures are very small (see also Reitz 2014b).

Public Information and Setting Goals

Canadians agree on the primacy of equal opportunity in principle but differ on the question of putting it into practice. The gap between the widespread perception among racial minorities of problems with equal opportunity and skepticism among political leaders about the need to address such problems is, to some extent, a gap in perception of fact; hence, consensus might be assisted by clarification of relevant facts. In this context, the lack of credible research information on which to base political decision-making poses difficulties.

Universities, research centres, public foundations, and interest groups could provide an adequate research base from which to address these needs, but university-based research on immigration and race relations is a low-priority activity, often conducted with few resources. The "Metropolis" international immigration research network was launched in 1996 and remains active, though direct government funding for Canadian participation ended in 2012. In the past, royal commissions have focused attention on topics of national priority, and the Commission on Systemic Racism in the Ontario Criminal Justice System (which published its report in 1995) made significant contributions to knowledge. In 2015, Ryerson University launched a "Global Diversity Exchange" to promote the transfer of research on diversity and immigration into policy.

Political Participation

Immigrants have high rates of citizenship acquisition, but minority access to electoral office has been limited (Black 2001; Pal and Choudhry 2007). Their small size in any political constituency and low voting rates contribute to this. Avenues of access to political decision-making for minority groups include the ethnic community itself—through its leaders' connections to individual politicians—or advisory groups established to provide minority input into decision-making (Breton 1990). The effectiveness of such means of representation is debated.

These problems of access may be related to the low rates of voting among racial minorities, as shown by the EDS data cited earlier. If racial minorities experience distinctive problems but have difficulty gaining a voice within Canada's political institutions, then proactive measures are needed to ensure that their viewpoints are reflected in decision-making. Here, a national advisory council would be useful. Such a council could address concerns about the impact of immigration on race relations and social cohesion. An effective council would have the means for independent fact-finding, which would allow it to explore the most divisive issues in an authoritative manner. One such issue is racial discrimination.

Conclusions

This discussion has combined existing research on racial inequality in Canada with an analysis of the social integration of racial minorities based on the 2002 EDS, raising questions about Canadian policies directed at racial minorities and arriving at three basic conclusions. First, the rapidly growing racial minority populations in Canada experience much greater inequality than do traditional European-origin immigrant groups, and discrimination is a widespread concern for racial minorities. The debate among researchers over the significance of racial discrimination, so far inconclusive, is paralleled by a broader debate across society, and this debate seems to divide racial groups.

Second, social integration into Canadian society for racial minorities is slower than it is for immigrants of European origin, partly as a result of their sense of exclusion, represented by perceived discrimination. It is striking that indications of lack of integration into Canadian society are so significant for second-generation minorities, since they are regarded as the harbinger of the future. Educational and employment success for many within these racial minority groups may not be the only matter of social and political relevance. The evidence suggests that economic integration does not guarantee social integration, although it may contribute to such integration.

Third, based on a brief overview, we conclude that it is far from clear that existing policies are adequate to address the evident racial divide in Canadian society. Policies have emphasized the laudable ideals of equal opportunity and opposition to racism, but they lack the features that would enable them to effectively bridge that racial divide. More specifically, existing policies are weakened by their failure to present clear objectives, reflecting a lack of interracial consensus on the significance of the problem of discrimination and a lack of will to create such a consensus. These policies also lack the means to ensure effective implementation, intergovernmental co-ordination, or evaluation.

Underlying these circumstances is a lack of effective participation by racial minorities themselves in the political decision-making process. Given the salience of equality issues for these groups, such issues may require more attention in the future. Without a new recognition of the significance of racial equality issues within the majority population, the most important precondition for improved policy may be the creation of more effective means for minority group participation.

Questions for Critical Thought

1. What is the significance of racial discrimination in accounting for racial inequality in Canada?
2. Under what circumstances does racial discrimination or inequality pose a threat to social cohesion in Canada?
3. What are some aspects of racial inequality in Canada that most need further research?
4. What policies are needed to address racial inequality in Canada? How close do existing policies come to meeting those needs?

Recommended Readings

James, Carl. 2010. *Seeing Ourselves: Exploring Race, Ethnicity, and Culture*, 4th edn. Toronto: Thompson Educational Publishing.

Pendakur, Krishna, and Ravi Pendakur. 2011. "Colour by numbers: Minority earnings." *Journal of International Migration and Integration* 12, 3: 305–29.

Reitz, Jeffrey G., Raymond Breton, Karen Kisiel Dion, and Kenneth L. Dion. 2009. *Multiculturalism and Social Cohesion: Potentials and Challenges of Diversity*. Amsterdam: Springer.

Statistics Canada. 2003. *Ethnic Diversity Survey: Portrait of a Multicultural Society*. Catalogue no. 89-593-XIE. Ottawa: Minister of Industry.

Recommended Websites

Canadian Race Relations Foundation:
http://www.crr.ca/en/; http://www.crr.ca/fr/

Centre d'études ethniques des universités montréalaises:
http://www.ceetum.umontreal.ca/

Global Migration Research Institute:
http://munkschool.utoronto.ca/ethnicstudies/gmri/

United Nations Office of the High Commissioner for Human Rights:
http://www.ohchr.org/EN/

Urban Alliance on Race Relations (Toronto):
http://urbanalliance.ca/

Notes

1. The Ethnic Diversity Survey was a post-census telephone survey conducted between April and August of 2002 using a sample of 41,695 persons aged 15 and over, excluding Aboriginal persons.
2. Individual-equivalent household incomes adjust household incomes for household size and are calculated by dividing household incomes by the square root of household size.
3. Among racial minorities, Japanese are the sole exception in having relatively high incomes. Of those identifying as White, the ones belonging to either a Latin American group or an Arab/West Asian group have relatively low incomes. In these two categories, the majority actually do not identify as White. In the census data, these two groups appear both as White and as visible minorities.

4. Rates of poverty are relatively high for the largest visible minorities—Blacks (44.6 per cent), Chinese (29.4 per cent), and South Asians (34.6 per cent)—but they are highest for Ethiopians, Ghanaians, Afghans, and Somalis, among whom poverty rates reach 50 to 80 per cent and higher (Ornstein 2000).
5. The respondent was read the following: "Using a scale from 1 to 5, where 1 is not worried at all and 5 is very worried, how worried are you about becoming the victim of a crime in Canada because of someone's hatred of your ethnicity, culture, race, skin colour, language, accent, or religion?"
6. One exception is the Jewish group: 20 per cent reported experiences of discrimination. The other exceptions are Latin Americans and Arab/West Asians.

References

Angus Reid Group. 1991. *Multiculturalism and Canadians: Attitude Study 1991*. Ottawa: Multicultural and Citizenship Canada.

Aydemir, Abdurrahman, and Mikal Skuterud. 2005. "Explaining the deteriorating entry earnings of Canada's immigrant cohorts, 1966–2000." *Canadian Journal of Economics* 38, 2: 641–72.

Beck, J. Helen, Jeffrey G. Reitz, and Nan Weiner. 2002. "Addressing systemic racial discrimination in employment: The Health Canada case and implications of legislative change." *Canadian Public Policy* 28, 3: 373–94.

Berry, John W., and Rudolf Kalin. 1995. "Multicultural and ethnic attitudes in Canada: An overview of the 1991 survey." *Canadian Journal of Behavioural Science* 27, 4: 17–49.

Bissoondath, Neil. 1994. *Selling Illusions: The Cult of Multiculturalism in Canada*. Toronto: Penguin Books.

Black, Jerome. 2001. "Immigrants and ethnoracial minorities in Canada: A review of their participation in federal electoral politics." *Electoral Insight* 3, 1: 8–13.

Bloom, David E., Gilles Grenier, and Morley Gunderson. 1995. "The changing labour market position of Canadian immigrants." *Canadian Journal of Economics* 28, 4b: 987–1005.

Boyd, Monica. 2000. "Ethnicity and immigrant offspring." In Madeline A. Kalbach and Warren E. Kalbach, eds, *Perspectives on Ethnicity in Canada*, pp. 137–54. Toronto: Harcourt Canada.

———. 2002. "Educational attainments of immigrant offspring: Success or segmented assimilation?" *International Migration Review* 36, 4: 1037–60.

——— and Elizabeth M. Grieco. 1998. "Triumphant transitions: Socioeconomic achievements of the second generation in Canada." *International Migration Review* 32, 4: 521–51.

Breton, Raymond. 1990. "The ethnic group as a political resource in relation to problems of incorporation: Perceptions and attitudes." In Raymond Breton, Wsevolod W. Isajiw, Warren E. Kalbach, and Jeffrey G. Reitz, eds, *Ethnic Identity and Equality: Varieties of Experience in a Canadian City*, pp. 196–255. Toronto: University of Toronto Press.

Canada, House of Commons. 1971. *House of Commons Debates*, 3rd sess., 28th Parliament, 8 Oct., vol. 8. Ottawa: Queen's Printer.

Centre for Research and Information of Canada (CRIC)–*Globe and Mail*. 2003. *The New Canada*. Montreal and Toronto: CRIC, Globe and Mail, Canadian Opinion Research Archive.

Citizenship and Immigration Canada. 1998. *The Economic Performance of Immigrants: Immigration Category Perspective*. IMDB Profile Series. Ottawa: Citizenship and Immigration Canada, Dec.

———, Evaluation Division. 2010. *Evaluation of Canada's Action Plan against Racism*. Ottawa: Citizenship and Immigration Canada, Dec.

Collacott, Martin. 2002. *Canada's Immigration Policy: The Need for Major Reform*. Vancouver: Fraser Institute.

Davies, Scott, and Neil Guppy. 1998. "Race and Canadian education." In Vic Satzewich, ed., *Racism and Social Inequality in Canada: Concepts, Controversies and Strategies of Resistance*, pp. 131–56. Toronto: Thompson Educational Publishing.

Dei, George J.S. 2000. *Removing the Margins: The Challenges and Possibilities of Inclusive Schooling.* Toronto: Canadian Scholars' Press.

Department of Canadian Heritage. 2005. *A Canada for All: Canada's Action Plan against Racism: An Overview.* Ottawa: Minister of Public Works and Government Services Canada.

Economic Council of Canada. 1991. *Economic and Social Impacts of Immigration.* Ottawa: Supply and Services Canada.

Esses, Victoria M., Joerg Dietz, and Arjun Bhardwaj. 2006. "The role of prejudice in the discounting of immigrant skills." In Ramiswami Mahalingam, ed., *Cultural Psychology of Immigrants*, pp. 113–30. Mahwah, NJ: Lawrence Erlbaum.

——, John F. Dovidio, and Gordon Hodson. 2002. "Public attitudes toward immigration in the United States and Canadian response to the September 11, 2001, 'Attack on America.'" *Analysis of Social Issues and Public Policy* 2: 69–85.

——, John F. Dovidio, Lynn M. Jackson, and Tamara L. Armstrong. 2001. "The immigration dilemma: The role of perceived group competition, ethnic prejudice, and national identity." *Journal of Social Issues* 57, 3: 389–412.

——and Robert C. Gardner. 1996. "Multiculturalism in Canada: Context and current status." *Canadian Journal of Behavioural Science* 28, 3: 145–52.

Francis, Diane. 2002. *Immigration: The Economic Case.* Toronto: Key Porter Books.

Frenette, Marc, and René Morissette. 2003. *Will They Ever Converge? Earnings of Immigrant and Canadian-Born Workers over the Last Two Decades.* Analytical Studies Branch Research Paper Series. Catalogue no. 11F0019MIE B no. 215. Ottawa: Statistics Canada.

Grant, Mary L. 1999. "Evidence of new immigrant assimilation in Canada." *Canadian Journal of Economics* 32, 4: 930–55.

Green, David, and Christopher Worswick. 2004. "Earnings of immigrant men in Canada: The roles of labour market entry effects and returns to foreign experience." http://www.econ.ubc.ca/green/chrfexp4.pdf). Accessed 7 Nov. 2006.

Henry, Frances, and Erne Ginsberg. 1985. *Who Gets the Work? A Test of Racial Discrimination in Employment.* Toronto: Urban Alliance on Race Relations, Social Planning Council of Metropolitan Toronto.

——, Carol Tator, Winston Mattis, and Tim Rees. 1998. *The Colour of Democracy: Racism in Canadian Society*, 2nd edn. Toronto: Harcourt Brace.

Hum, Derek, and Wayne Simpson. 1999. "Wage opportunities for visible minorities in Canada." *Canadian Public Policy* 25, 3: 379–94.

James, Carl. 1998. "'Up to no good': Black on the streets and encountering police." In Vic Satzewich, ed., *Racism and Social Inequality in Canada*, pp. 157–76. Toronto: Thompson Educational Publishing.

Kalin, Rudolf, and John W. Berry. 1994. "Ethnic and multicultural attitudes." In John W. Berry and Jean A. Laponce, eds, *Ethnicity and Culture in Canada: The Research Landscape*, pp. 293–321. Toronto: University of Toronto Press.

Kazemipur, Abdolmohammad, and Shiva S. Halli. 2000. *The New Poverty in Canada: Ethnic Groups and Ghetto Neighbourhoods.* Toronto: Thomson Educational Publishing.

—— and ——. 2001. "Immigrants and new poverty: The case of Canada." *International Migration Review* 35, 4: 1129–56.

Kerner Commission. 1968. *Report of the National Advisory Commission on Civil Disorders.* Toronto: Bantam.

Kymlicka, Will. 1995. *Multicultural Citizenship: A Liberal Theory of Minority Rights.* Toronto: Oxford University Press.

Lewis, Stephen. 1992. *Report to the Office of the Premier.* Toronto: Government of Ontario.

Li, Peter S. 2000. "Earnings, disparities between immigrants and native-born Canadians." *Canadian Review of Sociology and Anthropology* 37, 3: 289–311.

——. 2001. "The market worth of immigrants' educational credentials." *Canadian Public Policy* 27, 1: 23–38.

Myrdal, Gunner. 1944. *An American Dilemma: The Negro Problem and Modem Democracy.* New York: Harper and Row.

Omidvar, Ratna, and Ted Richmond. 2003. *Immigrant Settlement and Social Inclusion in Canada.* Laidlaw Foundation Working Papers Series, Perspectives on Social Inclusion. Toronto: Laidlaw Foundation.

Oreopoulos, Philip. 2011. "Why do skilled immigrants struggle in the labor market? A field experiment with thirteen thousand résumés." *American Economic Journal: Economic Policy* 3, 4: 148–71.

Ornstein, Michael. 2000. *Ethnoracial Inequality in Metropolitan Toronto: Analysis of the 1996 Census.* Toronto: Institute for Social Research, York University.

Pal, Michael, and Sujit Choudhry. 2007. "Is every ballot equal? Visible-minority vote dilution in Canada." *IRPP Choices* 13, 1: 1–30.

Palmer, Douglas. 1991. "Prejudice and tolerance in Canada. In *Social and Economic Impacts of Immigration*, pp. 103–19. Ottawa: Economic Council of Canada.

———. 1996. "Determinants of Canadian attitudes towards immigration: More than just racism?" *Canadian Journal of Behavioural Science* 28, 3: 180–92.

Pendakur, Krishna, and Ravi Pendakur. 1998. "The colour of money: Earnings differentials among ethnic groups in Canada." *Canadian Journal of Economics* 31, 3: 518–48.

——— and ———. 2002. "Colour my world: Have earnings gaps for Canadian-born ethnic minorities changed over time?" *Canadian Public Policy* 28, 4: 489–512.

——— and ———. 2011. "Colour by numbers: Minority earnings." *Journal of International Migration and Integration* 12, 3: 305–29.

Reitz, Jeffrey G. 1998. *Warmth of the Welcome: The Social Causes of Economic Success for Immigrants in Different Nations and Cities.* Boulder, Colo.: Westview Press.

———. 2001. "Immigrant skill utilization in the Canadian labour market: Implications of human capital research." *Journal of International Migration and Integration* 2, 3: 347–78.

———. 2003. "Occupational dimensions of immigrant credential assessment: Trends in professional, managerial, and other occupations, 1970–1996." In Charles Beach, Alan Green, and Jeffrey G. Reitz, eds., *Canadian Immigration Policy for the 21st Century*, pp. 469–506. Kingston, Ont.: John Deutsch Institute for the Study of Economic Policy, Queen's University.

———. 2005. "Tapping immigrants' skills: new directions for Canadian immigration policy in the knowledge economy." *IRPP Choices* 11, 1: 1–18.

———. 2007. "Immigrant employment success in Canada, part II: Understanding the decline." *Journal of International Migration and Integration* 8, 1: 37–62.

———. 2014a. "Canada: New initiatives and approaches to immigration and nation building." In J.F. Hollifield, P.L. Martin, and P.M. Orrenius, eds, *Controlling Immigration: A Global Perspective*, 3rd edn, pp. 88–116. Stanford, Calif.: Stanford University Press.

———. 2014b. "Multiculturalism policies and popular multiculturalism in the development of Canadian immigration." In Jack Jedwab, ed., *The Multiculturalism Question: Debating Identity in 21st Century Canada*, pp. 107–26. Montreal and Kingston: McGill-Queen's University Press.

——— and Rupa Banerjee. 2007. "Racial inequality, social cohesion, and policy issues in Canada." In Keith Banting, Thomas Courchene, and F. Leslie Seidle, eds, *Belonging? Diversity, Recognition and Shared Citizenship in Canada*, pp. 489–545. Montreal: Institute for Research on Public Policy.

——— and Raymond Breton. 1994. *The Illusion of Difference: Realities of Ethnicity in Canada and the United States.* Toronto: C.D. Howe Institute.

———, Josh Curtis, and Jennifer Elrick. 2014. "Immigrant skill utilization: Trends and policy issues." *Journal of International Migration and Integration* 15, 1: 1–26.

——— and Sherilyn M. Sklar. 1997. "Culture, race, and the economic assimilation of immigrants." *Sociological Forum* 12, 2: 233–77.

———, Heather Zhang, and Naoko Hawkins. 2011. "Comparisons of the success of racial minority immigrant offspring in the United States, Canada and Australia." *Social Science Research* 40, 4: 1051–66.

Satzewich, Vic, ed. 1998. *Racism and Social Inequality in Canada: Concepts, Controversies and Strategies of Resistance.* Toronto: Thompson Educational Publishing.

Scarman, Leslie George. 1986. *The Brixton Disorders: 10–12 April 1981. The Scarman Report: Report of an Inquiry by the Right Honourable the Lord Scarman.* Harmondsworth, UK: Penguin Books.

Schlesinger, Arthur M., Jr. 1992. *The Disuniting of America: Reflections on a Multicultural Society.* New York: W.W. Norton.

Simon, R.J., and J.P. Lynch. 1999. "A comparative assessment of public opinion toward immigrants and immigration policy." *International Migration Review* 33, 2: 445–67.

Skuterud, Mikal. 2010. "The visible minority wage gap across generations of Canadians." *Canadian Journal of Economics* 43, 3: 860–81.

Statistics Canada. 2003. *Earnings of Canadians: Making a Living in the New Economy.* 2001 Census Analysis Series, Catalogue no. 96F00-30XIE2001013. Ottawa: Statistics Canada.

———. 2005. "Longitudinal survey of immigrants to Canada: A portrait of early-settlement experiences." Catalogue no. 89-614-XIE. Ottawa: Statistics Canada.

Stoffman, Daniel. 2002. *Who Gets In: What's Wrong with Canada's Immigration Program—and How to Fix It.* Toronto: Macfarlane Walter and Ross.

Watt, Douglas, and Michael Bloom. 2001. *Exploring the Learning Recognition Gap in Canada: Phase 1 Report. Recognizing Learning: The Economic Cost of Not Recognizing Learning and Learning Credentials in Canada.* Ottawa: Conference Board of Canada.

Zegers de Beijl, Roger. 2000. *Documenting Discrimination against Migrant Workers in the Labour Market: A Comparative Study of Four European Countries.* Geneva: International Labour Office.

B. Gender and Sexual Orientation

14 Theorizing Gender Inequality

Tracey L. Adams and Michael Rooyakkers

> The people who oppose democratic principles tell us that there is no such thing as equality—that, if you made every person exactly equal today, there would be inequality tomorrow. . . . but what we plead for is equality of chance, equality of opportunity. —Nellie McClung (1915: 100)

In Canada, theories of gender inequality have long been wrapped up with the women's movement. First-wave feminists such as Nellie McClung fought for women's right to vote, for access to higher education, for fair treatment in the labour market and access to good jobs, and for the right to have a voice in social debates, in governance, and in the home. They fought for equal pay for work of equal value, and they fought to increase the social value attached to women's work. They developed and advanced explanations for gender inequality in order to reverse it.

These middle-class women's movements of the late nineteenth and early twentieth centuries shared many of the same goals as the feminist movements of the 1960s and 1970s and the more recent activities of feminists and gender scholars in the twenty-first century. The equality of opportunity advocated by McClung remains an important goal. Nevertheless, the explanations provided for gender inequality, and ideas about gender difference, have changed substantially over time. Strategies proposed for bringing about positive change have altered accordingly.

In this chapter we review trends and developments in theories of gender inequality, focusing on those that were particularly influential among sociologists, especially those based in Canada. We begin by noting the key principles and tensions underlying nineteenth- and twentieth-century women's movements and the explanations and assumptions implicit within them. Then we consider theories of gender inequality that became popular in sociology in the 1970s and 1980s, emphasizing those theories that adapted Marx and Weber to shed light on women's and men's experiences. Subsequently, we identify the limitations associated with these theories and review the various ways that scholars have sought to overcome these limitations by broadening and developing gender theory in multiple directions. Among these developments, we pay particular attention to those theories that see social institutions and interactions as gendered, approaches that look at the reproduction of gender and inequality at the level of interaction, theories of intersectionality, and theories of masculinity. We also highlight the contributions of prominent theorists such as Dorothy Smith and Judith Butler.

Maternal/Cultural Feminism and Liberal/Equity Feminism

For the feminist movement in Canada, as elsewhere, there have long been two linked, but nonetheless distinguishable, perspectives. In Canada, historically, "maternal" or cultural feminism was slightly more predominant (Prentice et al. 1996: 189). According to this view, women's experiences, and their family roles as wives and mothers, give them a perspective distinct from men's. Women have skills, abilities, and concerns that men typically do not possess. Gender inequality, at least in part, results when women's perspectives, skills, and work are undervalued. When nineteenth-century women fought for the vote, they argued that women knew better than men what would be best for other women, children, and families. With a political voice they could enact change that would improve lives and better society. When women in the late twentieth century fought for better wages for women, it was often with the argument that women's jobs were paid less than men's jobs because women's skills were undervalued. Maternal and cultural feminism tends to see men and women as inherently different, but argues that those differences should not be a source of gender inequality.

In contrast, liberal or equity feminism holds that men and women are more similar than different. Men and women are equally smart and capable, and hence should have equal access to opportunities. While this approach acknowledges a history of difference, it argues that men are just as capable as women of raising children, while women are equally skilled at carpentry, rocket science, and brain surgery. Or they would be, if given the opportunity. Women's disadvantages in the labour market and other social institutions stem primarily from discrimination; women have been denied the opportunities that men have had. Removing barriers to women in politics, the workplace, and other social institutions is required if equality is to be achieved.

These different views historically coexisted in tension. Although they are somewhat contradictory, they are not always perceived as such. As Prentice et al. (1996: 190) argue of first-wave feminists, "most accepted both types of arguments, emphasizing one or the other as seemed most useful or appropriate, apparently without feeling any contradiction." The same appears true for generations of feminists and gender scholars; these different viewpoints continue to shape both scholarly and everyday perceptions of gender and inequality.

Twentieth-Century Developments

First-wave feminists in Canada fought for the vote for Canadian women and for the ability to hold political office. They sought access to post-secondary education and to male-dominated professions like medicine and law. They fought for family reform, and endeavoured to improve the well-being of women and children in part through temperance; that is, they saw men's use of alcohol as a contributing factor to poverty and domestic abuse (Prentice et al. 1996). Feminists' activities were fundamentally shaped by their race, class, and religion. Their writings, arguments, and organizations were shaped by Protestantism in particular, and had a decidedly evangelical tone.

Second-wave feminism was more secular, but still predominantly a middle-class movement. In the 1960s and 1970s, women were especially concerned with equality of opportunity in the labour market and other arenas of social life. Many first-wave feminists believed that they could create real change for women by asking men for "fair play" and to do their "Christian duty" (McClung 1915). For some second-wave feminists, significant change required more substantial action, akin to social revolution. In this era, radical and especially Marxist feminism became more influential.

Radical Feminism

In the 1970s and early 1980s, radical feminists tended to see gender inequality as being tied to reproduction. For instance, for Shulamith Firestone (1970: 9), it was "the natural reproductive difference between the sexes [that] led directly to the first division of labor." These reproductive differences relegated women to the private sphere of home and family, while allowing men to engage in a variety of productive activities outside the home. For Firestone and some others, gender equality could not be achieved while these reproductive differences remained. Mary O'Brien (1981: 8) also linked gender inequality to reproduction, but with a Marxian twist. For O'Brien, women experience reproduction as an embodied experience, while men—physically separated from their sperm, the fetus, and the child—see reproduction as an alienating experience. To overcome this alienation, men seek to "appropriate" their children and control women, in part to limit women's sexual activity and ensure that the children are theirs. O'Brien was not alone in linking women's oppression to men's control of women's bodies and reproduction. Other writers located women's oppression in sexuality, sexual violence, and men's efforts to control and regulate human sexuality.

These ideas did not resonate widely with sociologists, many of whom argued that they had limited explanatory power (Armstrong and Armstrong 1990; Fox 1988). Further, these theories typically cannot account for social change in gender relations or illuminate how women can bring about a more equal society. More influential for gender scholars in Canada was Marxist feminism, which focused on family relations and the labour market (Armstrong and Armstrong 1990; Luxton 1980).

Marxist Feminism

Marx's critique of the social order, and his conviction that social inequality could be eradicated with social action, resonated with many feminists in the 1970s and 1980s. So did his location of social inequality in the organization of labour and the family. Marxist feminists took Marx's analysis in two related directions. First, they drew upon Marx's analysis of productive labour under capitalism as a source of class inequality to explore women's (reproductive) labour in the home and its relationship to gender inequality. Second, they developed aspects of Marx's (1987 [1867]) work that were only alluded to in passing in *Capital*, so as to examine how class and gender inequalities are intertwined through women's role in social reproduction.

Canadian researchers were very active in what became known as "the domestic labour debate" (Armstrong and Armstrong 1990; Fox 1988). This debate cast women's work in the home in Marxian terms, seeing women's domestic labour and child-rearing activities as work that benefited both men within families and the capitalist system more broadly. For some, men were like capitalists, exploiting women by reaping the rewards of women's domestic labour; women were exploited within both the home and the labour market (Guettel 1974, in Armstrong and Armstrong 1990: 69). In this sense, women could be seen as members of a class, who could band together to achieve equality by fighting the capitalist and patriarchal systems that oppressed them.

Domestic labour was viewed slightly differently by scholars like Meg Luxton (1980, 2006). For Luxton, women's work in the home was productive labour, in which their product was not a good for sale in the labour market (Marx's focus), but workers or labour power for the capitalist system. In his discussion on "the buying and selling of labour power" in *Capital*, Marx (1987 [1867]) emphasizes that labour power must be reproduced on both a daily and generational basis.[1] After a long day at work, workers must rest and eat to regain their strength, in order to work again another day. Women's domestic labour, then, ensures that their family members are rested, fed, and ready to labour. Furthermore, women raise children who will eventually take their place in the labour market, thereby reproducing labour power on a generational basis. For these researchers, the family unit was both a locus of production for women and a locus of consumption where goods were purchased and used (in part to produce workers). This is described most clearly in Luxton's *More Than a Labour of Love* (1980). Luxton (1980: 18) identifies four components of domestic labour: (1) reproduction of labour power on a daily basis; (2) child-bearing and child-rearing (producing future labour power); (3) housework to maintain the household; (4) and the transformation of wages into goods and services for the household (money management, shopping, and so on). Luxton (2006) problematizes the production/reproduction dichotomy, arguing that "reproduction" should not be seen as separated from the economic workings of society. The family (i.e., the social reproductive work that occurs within the family) is understood as central to the capitalist mode of production. For Marxist feminists, then, women's experiences are intimately bound up with the capitalist system, even when they are not employed outside the home.

For many Marxist feminists, gender and class are intertwined to such an extent that we cannot really speak of class without attention to gender, and vice versa. Moreover, gender equality is unlikely to be achieved without greater class equality.

Dual-Systems Theory

Dual-systems theorists had much in common with Marxist feminists, in that they typically located gender inequality in the hierarchical division of labour in both the home and the capitalist economy (Hartmann 1976). In addition, dual-systems theorists were influenced by the work of classical social theorists, especially Marx and Weber. However, while many Marxist feminists came to view class and gender as intertwined, dual-systems theorists saw them—and the systems of capitalism and patriarchy that shaped them—as separate, though interacting (Baron 1991; Hartmann 1976). One of the most influential dual-systems theorists was Heidi Hartmann (1976). Hartmann argued that gender inequality was the result of the intersection of historical trends in patriarchy and capitalism. She defined patriarchy as "a set of social relations which has a material base and in which there are hierarchical relations between men, and solidarity among them, which enable them to control women" (1976: 138). Patriarchy predated capitalism and, under this system, men learned to control the labour of women and children in the family. When capitalism developed as a system sometime later, "men's domination was already established" (152), and "capitalism proceeded in a way that built on [this existing] authority structure" (150). The actions of male workers, used to having authority in the home, reinforced this process. Men "viewed the employment of women as a threat to their jobs," so they organized against them and sought their exclusion (Hartmann 1976: 155). This process benefits capitalists because it divides the working class and prevents class unity, by creating a subordinate group of workers who will work for less money.

Thus, for Hartmann (1976: 168), "capitalism grew on top of patriarchy." Women's subordinate position in society is the result of both patriarchy and capitalism, or the combined activity of working men and their employers. Like Marxist feminists, then, dual-systems theorists like Hartmann emphasize women's family and labour roles as being central to gender inequality. Furthermore, they believe that for equality to be achieved, we must challenge both patriarchy and capitalism. Hartmann's analysis was influential, but not without its detractors. For instance, critics argued that Hartmann overstated the ability of men to organize and exclude women, and overstated the harmony between men's goals and those of capitalists (Witz 1992).

Two British scholars, Sylvia Walby (1990) and Anne Witz (1992), sought to extend Hartmann's analysis, in part by emphasizing and elaborating on processes of social closure. Social closure is a neo-Weberian concept, which describes efforts by members of some groups to cut off others' opportunities and access to rewards in order to maximize their own status and rewards. Walby (1990) extended Hartmann's analysis by showing how patriarchy operates not only in the home and labour market, but in politics, and through violence and sexuality as well. Processes of exclusion and segregation—processes of social closure—are central to the reproduction of inequality in society. The application of Weber to dual-systems theory was elaborated further by Anne Witz (1992) in her analysis of gender and participation in professions. Witz showed that social closure processes contributed to gender inequality and limited labour market opportunities in several different ways. Not only were women "excluded" from some positions, but "demarcationary" processes also segregated women's labour in a narrow range of occupations. As well, Witz demonstrated how marginalized individuals could use processes of social closure themselves to improve their own position and potentially wrest power back from those in dominant positions. Overall, the addition of Weberian theory improved the ability of dual-systems scholars to understand the processes through which gender inequality was enacted and perpetuated, as well as the strategies through which subordinate women could fight back.

Critiques of Dual-Systems and Marxist-Feminist Accounts

Many scholars worked within a dual-systems framework in the 1980s and 1990s, and each elaborated a different variation of the approach. In the previous section, we presented a fairly simplified summary, but one that captures the main tenets. Both dual-systems and Marxist-feminist approaches illuminated processes of gender inequality by showing how gender and class were interrelated and how central gender was to capitalist societies. These approaches also demonstrated the challenge of eradicating gender inequality in societies rife with inequality generally, and suggested tactics that feminists could employ in the battle against discrimination and oppression. Nevertheless, by the 1990s, dual-systems theory was under attack, with gender scholars identifying many limitations associated with it (Baron 1991). In this section, we outline those limitations, since each has spurred further theorizing that has enhanced our understanding of the changing nature of gender inequality in society.

First, both dual-systems and Marxist-feminist theories tended to emphasize broad social forces and structured social relations. Their concern was with systems of patriarchy and capitalism. While both theories sought to document how inequality was reproduced at a more local level (the workplace and the family), they tended not to consider how gender is reproduced through micro-processes and social interaction. Scholars influenced by symbolic interactionism and related perspectives sought to document how gender is reproduced (and challenged) at the level of everyday interaction.

Second, dual-systems theories akin to that proposed by Hartmann locate gender inequality in the family, and depict it as a set of social relations imported by men into other forms of social organization. Thus, this approach assumes that capitalism and organizations are, at least theoretically, gender-neutral (Baron 1991). Since the 1990s, scholars have explored more concretely how social institutions are themselves gendered (Acker 1990, 1992), arguing that gender infuses social practices and organizations; hence, gender is not simply a characteristic of individuals that they carry around with them.

Third, the theories tend to depict men's lives simplistically. Men are a focus when they are acting to restrict women's opportunities, or when they are being exploited by their capitalist employers. Differences among men (other than the acknowledgement of class differences) are not elaborated (Fox 1988). In dual-systems theory, men are often portrayed as a unified group that acts in concert to restrict women (O'Brien 1981; Hartmann 1976). The complexity of men's lives and the importance of inequalities among men have been revealed through subsequent theory and research on men and masculinities.

Fourth, Marxist-feminist and dual-systems theories highlight the intersection of gender and class, but ignore other social relations and characteristics. In response, intersectional approaches (as discussed below) have emerged, and they show the value of looking beyond class to consider the intersection of gender with race, ethnicity, age, citizenship, sexual orientation, and other statuses and social factors (McMullin 2010; Glenn 2002).

Last, scholars began to argue that the basic terms used by feminist theorists needed to be questioned and challenged. What exactly was "gender" and should it be viewed as synonymous with biological sex? By the late 1980s, scholars argued that gender was best viewed as a social construction in which social meanings were attached to biological sex differences (Scott 1988; Armstrong and Armstrong 1990). While this view is still predominant, research has shown that sex itself is also socially constructed (Laqueur 1990). In a similar vein, scholars challenged the use of the term "patriarchy," finding it imprecise, ill-specified, and at times ahistorical (Fox 1988). Several scholars advocated alternative concepts like "sex-gender system" (Fox 1988), but this term, too, has fallen by the wayside with the rise of theories of intersectionality and gendered organizations.

In the rest of this chapter we review many of these theoretical developments. First, though, it is helpful to examine the ideas of Dorothy Smith, whose theorizing addresses several of these concerns.

Dorothy Smith and Standpoint Theory

Dorothy Smith (1987, 1990) challenged feminist sociologists and gender scholars to move beyond their concern with gender roles, and the adaptation of traditional sociological knowledge, to examine social experience through an alternative lens. It was not enough simply to investigate women's experiences and add these to research done previously on men—what Baron (1991: 8) labelled the "add women and stir" approach. Rather, Smith proposed that sociologists begin from women's standpoint, thereby making "our direct embodied experience of the everyday world the primary ground of our knowledge" (Smith 1990: 22). She argues that traditional approaches, from men's perspectives, have been abstract, bound up with the relations of ruling (power), and too divorced from the everyday embodied experiences of living. Traditional approaches provide a distorted view: dominant men's experiences appear to be the *only* experiences when the marginalized are hidden from view (Smith 1987, Acker 1990). For Smith (1990: 22), "the only way of knowing a socially constructed world is knowing it from within." Moreover, when we begin with our experiences, we become more aware of our social location and how that location shapes our reality and our own understanding of it. For Smith (1990: 27), a sociology from women's standpoint "makes the everyday world its problematic."

Through her work, Dorothy Smith is not simply seeking to identify the forces that establish and reproduce social inequality, but also to show how power distorts the ability of sociologists and others to see the social world clearly. When we start with everyday experiences, and especially the experiences of those traditionally marginalized in academic discourse, we improve our understanding of social life and are in a better position to fight the "relations of ruling" that shape our social practices and institutions. Smith's work has informed a generation of academic researchers who seek to understand gender and inequality, and her research has informed many of the theoretical approaches and views reviewed in the following sections.

"Doing Gender"

In accord with Smith's (1990) push to begin sociological analysis with attention to everyday experience, some researchers have adopted a social constructionist perspective to understand how gender identity is created through action and interaction (Connell 2005; Kimmel 2004). For scholars like West and Zimmerman (1987), gender is something we "do," not something we have or something we are. Gender is an activity situated in social interaction. We routinely accomplish gender "recurrently" and "in interaction with others" (140). We "do" gender because we are always subject to assessment. "Doing gender" is unavoidable: whether one conforms to or rejects normative understandings of gender, one is "doing" gender.

For West and Zimmerman (1987), doing gender is about "doing difference." Doing gender means "creating differences between girls and boys and women and men, differences that are not natural, essential, or biological"—differences that, once constructed, "are used to reinforce the 'essentialness' of gender" (137). The resources for doing gender and expressing our "essential" differences can include physical features in our social settings, such as sex-segregated public washrooms. "Standardized social occasions," such as organized sports, are also arenas where we highlight gender difference through action and social interaction. Ultimately, we *all* do gender in everyday interactions.

While the way we do gender reproduces gender difference, it also reproduces gender inequality. For West and Zimmerman (1987: 145–7), when we "do gender appropriately, we simultaneously sustain, reproduce, and render legitimate" the prevailing gender order, so that the subordination of women to men is upheld. Nevertheless, we can do gender in a way that disrupts conventional norms and potentially challenges gender inequality.

There are several reasons why the "doing gender" approach has been influential. It recognizes that gender is not a "natural" force, or something simply imposed on us, but that we actively construct gender through our actions and interactions. Similarly, this perspective moves away from the heavily deterministic structural approaches of the past. Finally, an important implication of the "doing gender" approach is that gender can be undone and, consequently, there is the possibility for change (Deutsch 2007). When we emphasize both the "doing" and "undoing" of gender, we draw attention to human agency, and illustrate how social inequality can be reduced through our actions and interactions (Deutsch 2007; Risman 2009).

West and Zimmerman's (1987) "doing gender" approach has been very influential in North America; however, it has been criticized for potentially neglecting power and inequality by focusing attention on the meanings attached to gender and social interaction. As we discuss in the next section, gender also operates at, and is embedded within, the institutional and organizational level (Smith 2009; Acker 1990).

Gendered Organizations and Institutions

As far back as 1915, feminists argued that social institutions had been "made by men, and for men's advantage" (McClung 1915: 84). However, traditionally, sociological theory has depicted social institutions as gender neutral—a perspective that some gender scholars adopted as their own, as we have seen with dual-systems theory. A growing literature identifying barriers to women's advancement in the workplace and politics, when combined with theoretical innovations from scholars like Dorothy Smith, has spurred changes in thinking.

Joan Acker's (1990, 1992) concepts of gendered organizations and gendered institutions have been particularly influential. Acker argues that gender relations and ideologies have been embedded in organizations and social practices. She identifies at least five interacting processes through which gendering occurs: (1) the construction of divisions by gender (for example, at work, in physical space, behaviourally); (2) symbols and images surrounding these divisions (ideology, language, culture, dress); (3) interactions between men and women (in which male dominance is often reinforced); (4) the identity and presentation of self; (5) organizational logics and practices within organizations. Acker's (1990) work concentrates on the latter processes, and she documents these processes through an analysis of job evaluations.

Acker (1990) explains that job evaluations describe jobs, not the workers who fill them. These jobs are assessed in terms of the tasks associated with them; the workers who fill the jobs are merely "hypothetical" at this point. Workers' personal characteristics are deemed irrelevant. For the purpose of the job evaluation and description, the abstract workers who fill the abstract jobs have no gender, no families, no sexuality, no responsibilities outside of work, because none of these are deemed relevant. The abstract worker exists only for the work. Acker (1990: 149) argues that the very "concept of 'a job' assumes a particular gendered organization of domestic labour and social production." Historically, most men could fit the mould of the abstract worker and devote themselves to work, because they had women in their lives who could handle the family and other responsibilities outside of work. Women have been less able to meet this abstract worker ideal, and so appear to be less than ideal workers. The end result is fewer rewards and promotions for women. The literature on gendered organizations has concentrated on work and employment, but it can also be applied to other areas of social life.

This theory has been very influential in understanding gender inequality, especially in the workplace, but it has been criticized for its implicit assumption that all men are equally capable of meeting the "abstract worker" ideal and for its limited ability to account for variations in experience across other dimensions of social inequality.

Masculinities

While many theorists and researchers have considered the ways that women are structurally and systematically disadvantaged and subordinated to men, other scholars have focused on men and masculinities. These scholars emphasize that men and masculinities are diverse; that there are hierarchies of masculinities that reflect relations of dominance and subordination; and that masculinities are not fixed, but actively constructed, and so are fluid and changing.

R.W. Connell, a leading gender theorist, explains that a variety of masculinities exist, as boys and men occupy different social locations (Connell 1987, 2005). Connell (1996: 208) states that, "within any workplace, neighbourhood, or peer group, there are likely to be different understandings of masculinity and different ways of 'doing' masculinity." For example, there are masculinities associated with different minority ethnic groups as well as homosexual masculinities. These competing forms of masculinity are not all on an equal footing; rather, a hierarchy of masculinities exists, with some being more valued than others. Homosexual masculinities, for instance, are less valued in contemporary Western culture, where more valued forms of masculinity are typically connected to heterosexuality (Connell 1987).

Another common theme in masculinity theory entails the concept of hegemony (Connell 2001). *Hegemonic* masculinity is the "idealized form of masculinity in a given historical setting" (Messerschmidt 1993). It is "culturally dominant" and it takes on "a position of cultural authority and leadership" (Connell 1996: 209). The hegemonic form is not necessarily the "normal" or "most common" form of masculinity, because only a small number of men may ultimately perform or achieve it; however, it is a very visible form and the most respected form of masculinity around which men position themselves (Connell 2005; Connell and Messerschmidt 2005). Also, "the majority of men gain from its hegemony, since they benefit from the patriarchal dividend, the advantage men in general gain from the overall subordination of women" (Connell 2005: 79). Relations of (what Connell terms) *complicity* characterize the groups of men that benefit from hegemony.

Thus, hegemonic masculinity involves "the maintenance of practices that institutionalize men's dominance over women" and is "constructed in relation to women and to subordinate masculinities" (Connell 1987: 185–6). Hegemonic masculinity is defined as superior to other masculinities, and also to femininity, reflecting the "privilege men *collectively* have over women" (Connell 1996: 209).

In this view, then, masculinity is about rejecting the "feminine"—one of the key rules of manhood, accordingly, is that men must completely reject the feminine and not be like women. The failure to embody any of the rules of manhood and "to affirm the power of the rules and one's achievement of them is a source of men's confusion and pain" (Kimmel 1994: 126). Such a model is unrealizable for almost any man. Gay men, for example, don't measure up to this definition of manhood, as they are stereotypically understood as being "feminine" and are attracted to the "wrong" sex. Gay masculinity is an example, then, of a subordinated masculinity. As Connell explains, this entails not just a "cultural stigmatization of homosexuality or gay identity [but also] an array of quite material practices," including violence and discrimination at both the individual and institutional level (Connell 2005: 78).

Therefore, masculinity is a "configuration of practice *within* a system of gender relations"—masculinity is not a system itself, but rather is part of the larger system (Connell 2005: 84). Understanding this larger structure is key to understanding hegemonic masculinity, and more broadly, recognizing that masculinities are plural and hierarchical. Hegemonic masculinity is simultaneously powerful and *vulnerable*, insofar as hegemonic masculinity must be continually constructed and reconstructed (Connell 2005). The continual production of masculinities results in many forms of inequality, including violence against women and against other men. Violence is a tool to maintain men's dominance over women and a way to assert or reaffirm men's masculinity while simultaneously subordinating other men, as occurs with violence against gay men, for example.

Moreover, masculinities and gender more broadly can only be understood relationally, because masculinities are not just a series of "alternative lifestyles" (Connell 2001: 141), but instead exist in relation to each other. By examining the relations between multiple masculinities (and between masculinities and femininities), we can recognize and better understand the relations of dominance and subordination that create and sustain inequalities, not only between men and women, but among men and among women (Connell 2005).

This leads us to a final theme, which is that masculinities are actively constructed and contested, and so are not fixed categories. Connell (2005: 35) explains that "gender is not fixed in advance of social interaction, but is constructed in interaction," and "rather than treat [the way masculinity is done] as pre-existing [gender] norms which are passively internalized and enacted, the new research [on masculinity] explores the making and remaking of conventions in social practice itself."

This approach to recognizing gender as a social practice is in keeping with the social construction of gender approach found in gender theory; it also suggests that masculinities are actively done rather than a set of character traits, as is commonly understood. Therefore, masculinities are fluid rather than fixed. How masculinities are produced and reproduced varies according to race and class, and according to the different institutional settings in which they are enacted, including schools, sports, and the military. Masculinities are constructed collectively within these institutions, and culturally produced images of masculinity exist (Connell 2001, 2005).

Up to this point, we have mainly discussed gender itself: the production of gender at the level of the individual and institution, and how this produces inequality. In the following section, we address theories of intersectionality and the ways feminist theorists have been challenged to recognize gender as only one set of social relations that include many other dimensions of inequality.

Intersectionality

The term "intersectionality" is used to capture the idea that multiple axes of inequality exist, including gender, race, class, and others, and that these amount to interlocking oppressions which cannot be analytically separated from each other. That is, gender cannot be understood in isolation, because it intersects with race, class, sexual orientation, age, and so on (Smith 2009; Andersen and Collins 1995). When we study gender separately from other dimensions, we tend to ignore the experiences of other marginalized groups. Only by considering the intersection of these multiple dimensions can we truly and fully comprehend social inequality.

Choo and Ferree (2010) identify three ways in which intersectionality has been theorized. The first is concerned with "giving voice to the oppressed" (131). This stance tries to counteract traditional approaches to gender and inequality that have privileged middle-class white women's experiences while marginalizing others. The goal here is to "give voice to the particularity of the perspectives and needs of women of colour" by highlighting their standpoint. Patricia Hill Collins (1990) is the most influential of the theorists behind this position. Her work highlights the specific challenges faced by women of colour, and shows how adopting their standpoint sheds light on inequality more broadly. While "giving voice" in this manner is valuable, it can downplay the importance of gender and race for members of dominant groups, and may reinforce the prevailing tendency to see white men as possessing neither gender nor race.

The second approach to intersectionality centres on interaction effects and select cases. That is, gender, race, and class are seen to be important dimensions of inequality that interact in concrete settings and specific circumstances, thereby shaping social experience (Choo and Ferree 2010). In these models, gender, class, and race may interact selectively at certain points in time. Some proponents of this approach see gender, class, and race as being socially constructed, but they would see this social construction as occurring differently in different social contexts (Choo and Ferree 2010). This approach can be useful in highlighting how gender, class, and race interact in concrete circumstances, but it tends to assign primacy to some dimensions over others. For example, some researchers identify class as a primary dimension of inequality that is occasionally cross-cut by other "secondary" dimensions, such as race, gender, or sexual orientation, depending on the context. In addition, some critics question whether it is truly possible to identify situations where gender does not interact with other dimensions of social inequality.

A third approach to intersectionality sees gender, class, and race as co-constructed systemic inequalities (Glenn 2002; Choo and Ferree 2010). In these accounts, gender and race (and other dimensions of inequality) are seen as "fundamentally embedded in, working through, and determining the organization" of capitalism and social life (Choo and Ferree 2010: 135). Gender and race are not secondary effects added on to class to shape experience under capitalism, but their combination influences the establishment and functioning of the capitalist system. Such approaches assess specific socio-historical locations and events to determine how gender, class, and race are co-created and intersect (Glenn 2002; Choo and Ferree 2010). For Choo and Ferree (2010: 136), this approach is the most fruitful because it treats "intersectionality as a complex system," and it examines how gender, class, and race combine in everyday life, in multiple if differing ways, to produce social inequality and shape social experience.

Gender, class, and race tend to receive the most attention as structured social relations or axes of inequality. Age relations are often ignored completely, which is problematic because power relations are embedded in age relations just as they are in gender relations (McMullin 2010). Consequently, feminists have been criticized for ignoring age relations and for failing to examine the intersection of age and gender.

Sexual orientation is also often overlooked, or else is inaccurately assumed to be subsumable under gender relations (Risman 2004). Thus, feminist sociology has also been criticized for assumptions of heterosexuality, for failing to look at gender and sexuality together, failing to see their connections, and unwittingly presenting heterosexuality as the normal way of being (Ingraham 1996).

Postmodern Feminism: Judith Butler

Theories of intersectionality have helped to usher in the idea that there is no single common female experience. Female identity varies by race, class, and other axes of inequality. By the early 1990s, postmodern feminists rejected the idea of a singular category of woman and challenged the dichotomies of "male" and "female," "men" and "women." Judith Butler is probably the most influential scholar within this school of thought.

Butler (1990) contends that gender is a performance, and therefore that the categories of men and women are constructed. This notion of "performativity" implies that we are not naturally male or female, but that, through the repetition of performance, we learn how to act as if we are men or women. We learn how to talk, walk, and dress as men and women, and the repetitive act of doing so creates the illusion of "natural"-born men and women.

By emphasizing the artificial and performative quality of gender identity, Butler aims to "trouble" the way gender is defined. For Butler, gender identity is regulatory, a way to control people. The act of performing gender, of engaging in masculine or feminine behaviours, makes it appear that we are enacting a true gendered self—that we have core gender identities. Even when feminists recognize gender as being socially constructed, many still see a core gender identity. For Butler, this notion of real "men" and "women" is a fiction, and the dichotomous categories of sex, gender, and sexuality are categories of knowledge that limit ways of being. This can produce inequality, because such categories marginalize other identities, behaviours, and desires (Butler 1990).

Alternatively, by thinking differently about gender and sexuality, by being open and "troubling" the system, we can give a voice to those whose ways of being are marginalized (Butler 2004). This encourages us to think more critically and ethically about the categories of sex, gender, and sexuality that are presented to us as natural and normal.

Butler's view that gender is a performance, and that gender identity is an illusion, has significant implications for both feminist theory and politics. Many feminists find this postmodern perspective problematic, because it implicitly challenges more traditional women's movements. How do women fight for equality if there is no coherent category of "women" to begin with? Feminists and sociologists continue to grapple with such fundamental questions.

Conclusion

This chapter has provided an overview of how sociologists have developed gender theory in order to understand, and potentially undermine, gender inequality. Gender scholars agree that, if we are to combat gender inequality, we need to question long-standing assumptions and conceptualizations regarding gender roles and gender differences. In addition, many scholars concur that gender inequality cannot be overcome unless we simultaneously challenge other forms of inequality involving class, race, sexual orientation, age, and so on. Moreover, we must recognize that gender operates on multiple levels, including the individual, interactional, institutional, and systemic levels. And we also need to understand that gender inequality in any one sphere of social life—in the family or the workplace, for example—typically affects inequality in the other spheres as well. Only by comprehending gender in all its complexity can we effectively challenge gender inequality and bring about a more just and egalitarian society.

Questions for Critical Thought

1. Does gender difference always translate into gender inequality?
2. Are femininities structured in a hierarchical way, and related to power, in the same way that masculinities are?
3. Which of the theories discussed in this chapter do you believe captures gender inequality best?
4. What are some ways, derived from theories discussed in this chapter, that we might help to reduce gender inequality?

Recommended Readings

Frye, Marilyn. 2000. "Oppression." In A. Minas, ed., *Gender Basics: Feminist Perspectives on Women and Men*, pp. 10–16. Belmont, Calif.: Wadsworth/Thomson Learning.

Glenn, Evelyn Nakano. 2002. *Unequal Freedom: How Race and Gender Shaped American Citizenship and Labor*. Cambridge, Mass.: Harvard University Press.

Kimmel, Michael. 2004. *The Gendered Society*. New York: Oxford University Press.

Walby, Sylvia. 1990. *Theorizing Patriarchy*. Oxford: Basil Blackwell.

Recommended Websites

Canadian Women's Foundation:
http://canadianwomen.org/improve-equality

Center for the Study of Men and Masculinities:
http://www.stonybrook.edu/commcms/csmm/

Men Against Violence Against Women:
http://mavaw.org/

National Council of Women of Canada:
http://www.ncwcanada.com/

Note

1. "If the owner of labour-power works to-day, to-morrow he must again be able to repeat the same process in the same condition as regards health and strength. . . . The owner of labour-power is mortal. If then his appearance in the market is to be continuous . . . the seller of labour-power must perpetuate himself . . . by procreation. The labour-power withdrawn from the market by wear and tear and death, must be continually replaced by, at the very least, an equal amount of fresh labour-power" (Marx 1987 [1867]: 168).

References

Acker, Joan. 1990. "Hierarchies, jobs, bodies: A theory of gendered organizations." *Gender & Society* 4, 2: 139–58.

———. 1992. "Gendered institutions: From sex roles to gendered institutions." *Contemporary Sociology* 21: 565–9.

Andersen, Margaret, and Patricia Hill Collins, eds. 1995. *Race, Class, and Gender*. Belmont, Calif.: Wadsworth.

Armstrong, Pat, and Hugh Armstrong. 1990. *Theorizing Women's Work*. Toronto: Garamond Press.

Baron, Ava. 1991. "Gender and labor history: Learning from the past, looking to the future." In A. Baron, ed., *Work Engendered: Toward a New History of American Labor*, 1–46. Ithaca, NY: Cornell University Press.

Butler, Judith. 1990. *Gender Trouble: Feminism and the Subversion of Identity*. New York: Routledge.

———. 2004. *Undoing Gender*. New York: Routledge.

Choo, Hae Yeon, and Myra Marx Ferree. 2010. "Practising intersectionality in sociological research: A critical analysis of inclusions, interactions, and institutions in the study of inequalities." *Sociology Theory* 28, 2: 129–49.

Collins, Patricia Hill. 1990. *Black Feminist Thought*. New York: HarperCollins.

Connell, R.W. 1987. *Gender and Power*. Stanford, Calif.: Stanford University Press.

———. 1996. "Teaching the boys: New research on masculinity, and gender strategies for schools." *Teachers College Record* 98, 2: 206–35.

———. 2001. "Masculinities and men's health." In B. Baron and H. Kotthoff, eds, *Gender in Interaction*, pp. 139–52. Amsterdam/Philadelphia: John Benjamin Publishing.

———. 2005 [1995]. *Masculinities*. Berkeley: University of California Press.

——— and James Messerschmidt. 2005. "Hegemonic masculinity: Rethinking the concept." *Gender & Society* 19, 6: 829–59.

Deutsch, Francine. 2007. "Undoing gender." *Gender & Society* 21, 1: 106–27.

Firestone, Shulamith. 1970. *The Dialectic of Sex*. New York: Bantam.

Fox, Bonnie J. 1988. "Conceptualizing 'patriarchy'." *Canadian Review of Sociology and Anthropology* 25, 2: 163–82.

Glenn, Evelyn Nakano. 2002. *Unequal Freedom: How Race and Gender Shaped American Citizenship and Labor*. Cambridge, Mass.: Harvard University Press.

Hartmann, Heidi. 1976. "Capitalism, patriarchy, and job segregation by sex." *Signs* 1, 3: 137–67.

Ingraham, Chrys. 1996. "The heterosexual imaginary: Feminist sociology and theories of gender." In S. Seidman, ed., *Queer Theory/Sociology*, pp. 168–93. Malden, Mass.: Blackwell.

Kimmel, Michael. 1994. "Masculinity as homophobia: Fear, shame, and silence in the construction of gender identity." In H. Brod and M. Kaufman, eds, *Theorizing Masculinities*, pp. 119–41. Thousand Oaks, Calif.: Sage.

———. 2004. *The Gendered Society*, 2nd edn. New York: Oxford University Press.

Laqueur, Thomas. 1990. *Making Sex: Body and Gender from the Greeks to Freud*. Cambridge, Mass.: Harvard University Press.

Luxton, Meg. 1980. *More Than a Labour of Love: Three Generations of Women's Work in the Home*. Toronto: Women's Press.

———. 2006. "Feminist political economy in Canada and the politics of social reproduction." In K. Bezanson and M. Luxton, eds, *Social Reproduction: Feminist Political Economy Challenges Neo-Liberalism*, pp. 11–44. Montreal and Kingston: McGill-Queen's University Press.

McClung, Nellie L. 1915. *In Times Like These*. New York: D. Appleton and Company.

McMullin, Julie Ann. 2010. *Understanding Social Inequality: Intersections of Class, Age, Gender, Ethnicity, and Race in Canada*, 2nd edn. Toronto: Oxford University Press.

Marx, Karl. 1987 [1867]. "Chapter VI: The buying and selling of labour-power." In *Capital*, vol. 1, pp. 164–72. New York: Free Press.

Messerschmidt, James W. 1993. *Masculinities and Crime: Critique and Reconceptualization of Theory*. Lanham, Md: Rowman & Littlefield.

O'Brien, Mary. 1981. *The Politics of Reproduction*. Boston: Routledge & Kegan Paul.

Prentice, Alison, Paula Bourne, Gail Cuthbert Brandt, Beth Light, Wendy Mitchinson, and Naomi Black. 1996. *Canadian Women: A History*, 2nd edn. Toronto: Harcourt Brace Canada.

Risman, Barbara J. 2004. "Gender as a social structure: Theory wrestling with activism." *Gender & Society* 18, 4: 429–50.

———. 2009. "From doing to undoing: Gender as we know it." *Gender & Society* 23, 1: 81–4.

Scott, Joan Wallach. 1988. *Gender and the Politics of History*. New York: Columbia University Press.

Smith, Dorothy E. 1987. *The Everyday World as Problematic.* Milton Keynes, UK: Open University Press.

———. 1990. *The Conceptual Practices of Power: A Feminist Sociology of Knowledge.* Toronto: University of Toronto Press.

———. 2009. "Categories are not enough." *Gender & Society* 23, 1: 76–80.

Walby, Sylvia. 1990. *Theorizing Patriarchy.* Oxford: Basil Blackwell.

West, Candace, and Don Zimmerman. 1987. "Doing gender." *Gender & Society* 1, 2: 125–51.

Witz, Anne. 1992. *Professions and Patriarchy.* London: Routledge

15 Reproducing the Gender Gap: Work, Inequality, and Neo-liberalism

Brenda Beagan and Gillian Creese

Introduction: Gender, Paid Work, and Domestic Labour

Women's rates of paid employment are very similar to men's. Paid employment, however, is only part of the work most adults do. Domestic labour is unpaid work that must be done to sustain household members. In 2010, women with full-time jobs and an employed partner spent on average 13.9 hours per week on household domestic work, compared with 8.6 hours for men in the same circumstances (Statistics Canada 2011: 43). In dual-earner heterosexual couples with children, women, when employed full-time, also spent 49.8 hours per week on child care, compared with 27.2 hours for men (Statistics Canada 2011: 42). This means that women with children spend an extra 1,451 hours on domestic work annually, the equivalent of 181 extra eight-hour shifts (see also Chapter 16 in this volume).

Women have done the lion's share of unpaid household work for decades, although this pattern is slowly changing. A 2011 study shows that when hours spent on household work are examined for young adults across three generations, the differences between women and men have narrowed steadily since the 1980s. Men's contributions have increased slightly, and younger women are doing less housework compared to their mothers' and grandmothers' generations (Marshall 2011: 8).

The uneven division of unpaid domestic work significantly affects gender inequalities in the labour market. Moreover, unless Canadian governments alter neo-liberal reforms that downsize the public sector, cut social programs and services, and move "caring work" back into private households, gendered work disparities will likely grow. This chapter explores the major trends in women's paid work, considers the impact of neo-liberal reforms on gender equality, and identifies strategies to achieve greater gender equity in the workplace.

Trends in Women's Labour Force Participation

The proportion of women in the labour force has increased steadily since World War II, when only one in four women were employed (Calzavara 1993: 312). In 2014, population estimates showed that 57.6 per cent of women were employed, compared to 65.4 per cent of men (Statistics Canada 2015a). Women make up 47 per cent of the workforce (Statistics Canada 2015a). While women have increased their rates of labour force participation, men's participation has decreased, from 84 per cent in 1951 to 65 per cent in 2014 (Calzavara 1993: 312; Statistics Canada 2015a). These combined trends mean that the participation rates of women and men are now more similar than different.

One key difference that remains, however, concerns part-time versus full-time employment. In 2014 more than 2 million women—27 per cent of the female labour force—were employed part-time, compared to only 12 per cent of men (Statistics Canada 2015a). Women were more likely to report working part-time to care for their children (12 per cent of women part-time workers, 1.3 per cent of men), while men were more likely to work part-time to attend school (35.5 per cent of male part-time workers, 25.4 per cent of female) (Statistics Canada 2015b).

It is worth noting some significant employment variations among different groups of women (Tables 15.1 and 15.2). Immigrant women have lower levels of employment than Canadian-born women. Recent immigrants have the highest unemployment rates in the country, with women faring worse than men. In that group, women with less than high school education faced 24.4 per cent unemployment in 2014, compared with 14.5 per cent for Canadian-born women with the same education (Statistics Canada 2015c). Yet the earnings gap has narrowed over the past two decades, so that by 2010 immigrant women averaged 93 per cent of the annual earnings of Canadian-born women (Morissette and Sultan 2013).

Visible minority women also experience higher levels of unemployment than other women (10.6 per cent versus 6.7 per cent) (Table 15.2), earning on average about $4,000 less per year when working full-time, full-year (Block and Galabuzi 2011: 12). Similarly, unemployment rates for Aboriginal women are almost double those for all Canadian women (13.3 per cent compared with 7.4 per cent), with Aboriginal men's unemployment even higher. In 2011, Aboriginal women earned substantially less than the average for all Canadian women ($26,341 versus $33,000), while Aboriginal men averaged $15,000 per year less than the $48,594 average for Canadian men (Statistics Canada 2013).

Disability also disadvantages women in employment and earnings. In 2011, the employment rate for adults with disabilities was 49 per cent, compared with 79 per cent for those without

Table 15.1 Employment and Unemployment Rates, by Immigration Status, 2014

	Women		Men	
	% Employed	% Unemployed	% Employed	% Unemployed
Very recent immigrants, 5 years or less	47.8	15.4	68.0	11.0
Recent immigrants, 5–10 years	59.1	10.5	73.4	8.1
Established immigrants, 10-plus years	50.4	6.3	59.7	6.4
Canadian-born	59.8	5.8	66.2	7.4

Source: Statistics Canada, CANSIM Table 282-0104, "Labour force survey estimates (LFS), by immigrant status, sex and detailed age group, Canada, annual (persons unless otherwise noted)" (accessed 1 Apr. 2015).

Table 15.2 Employment and Unemployment Rates, Visible Minority and Aboriginal, by Gender, 2011

	Women		Men	
	% Employed	% Unemployed	% Employed	% Unemployed
Visible minority	55.2	10.6	64.8	9.3
Non-visible minority	57.4	6.7	65.0	7.8
Aboriginal	50.4	13.3	53.9	16.8
All Canadians	57.0	7.4	64.9	8.0

Sources: Statistics Canada, 2011 National Household Survey, Statistics Canada Catalogue no. 99-012-X2011038 (accessed 1 Apr. 2015); Statistics Canada, 2013 Canada (Code 01) (table), National Household Survey (NHS) Profile, 2011 National Household Survey, Statistics Canada Catalogue no. 99-004-XWE (accessed 1 Apr. 2015).

disability (breakdown by gender is not available). The same year, among full-time, full-year workers, women with disabilities earned 86–92 per cent of the average wages of women without disabilities, depending on severity of disability (Turcotte 2014: 6).

Occupational Segregation and the Income Gap

As we have seen, some women fare better than others in the labour market, with greater disadvantages connected to immigrant status, visible minorities, Aboriginal women, and those with disabilities. Differences among groups of women, however, are less marked than the gender differences between women and men, which remain a defining characteristic of the Canadian labour market.

Women are employed in a much broader range of occupations than at any previous time. In the last three decades, women have made major inroads into such prestigious and traditionally masculine professions as medicine, dentistry, law, and corporate management. Despite these successes, gendered occupational segregation persists in Canada. Compared with men, women remain concentrated in occupations with lower pay and less social prestige.

A majority of women (54.4 per cent) are employed in just three occupational sectors: sales and services, clerical, and health (see Table 15.3). Similarly, men are concentrated in specific occupations, with a majority (58.7 per cent) employed in trades and transport, sales and services, and natural and applied sciences. As Table 15.3 shows, most occupational sectors are dominated by either men or women, patterns that have remained remarkably stable over the past decade. Only three occupational fields were gender-balanced in 2014—professional occupations in business and finance; occupations in art, culture, recreation, and sport; and sales and service occupations. These three fields include one-third of employed women and a quarter of employed men; the remainder of Canadian workers are employed in gender-segregated fields. Furthermore, these three gender-balanced fields contain internal gender divisions. For example, while sales and services occupations are gender-balanced overall, within that category women comprise 21 per cent of workers in protective services, 27 per cent of those in wholesale and specialist sales, 67 per cent of those in retail sales, and 91 per cent of child-care and home support workers (Statistics Canada 2015d).

Gendered occupational segregation would not be so noteworthy if not for the marked economic consequences for many women. The jobs where women dominate typically earn lower pay, and, as Table 15.4 shows, women also earn less than men within each occupational sector. This pattern holds even in occupations where

Table 15.3 Distribution of Employment in Canada, by Occupation and Gender, 2014

Occupation	% of Women	% of Men	Women as Percentage of Workers
Financial, secretarial, and administrative	8.5	1.8	81.1
Health occupations	11.6	2.6	80.3
Social sciences, government service, and religion	8.3	2.6	74.3
Clerical, including supervisors	13.3	5.2	70.0
Teachers and professors	5.7	2.4	68.1
Art, culture, recreation, and sport	4.1	2.7	57.7
Sales and services	29.5	20.6	56.5
Professional business/finance	3.6	3.1	51.4
Other management	5.8	9.4	35.8
Senior management	0.2	0.4	32.1
Processing, manufacturing, and utilities	2.6	6.3	27.7
Natural and applied science and related	3.5	11.3	22.1
Primary industries	1.3	4.8	19.7
Trades, transport, equipment operators, related	2.0	26.8	6.3
Total of workforce	100%	100%	47.6%

Source: Statistics Canada, CANSIM Table 282-0010, "Labour force survey estimates (LFS), by National Occupational Classification for Statistics (NOC-S) and sex, annual (persons unless otherwise noted)" (accessed 1 Apr. 2015).

Table 15.4 Women's Earnings as a Ratio of Men's, by Occupation, 2011

Occupation	Women as Percentage of Workers	Women's Earnings as a Percentage of Men's
Natural and applied science and related	22.1	83.5
Art, culture, recreation, and sport	57.7	76.1
Management	35.7	72.0
Social science, education, government, religion	71.6	68.5
Business, finance, and administrative	69.7	67.2
Processing, manufacturing, and utilities	27.7	64.4
Trades, transport, equipment operators, related	6.3	55.3
Sales and services	56.5	54.7
Health occupations	80.3	47.0
Primary industries	19.7	42.3

Source: Statistics Canada, CANSIM Table 202-0106, "Earnings of individuals, by selected characteristics and National Occupational Classification (NOC-S), 2011 constant dollars, annual," (accessed 1 Apr. 2015).

women predominate, such as health care, partly because of internal gender divisions; thus, while health care is dominated by women (80 per cent), women comprise only 38 per cent of physicians but more than 90 per cent of nurses (National Physician Survey 2014; Canadian Institute for Health Information 2013).

Across occupational categories, women's wages steadily increased through the 1970s and 1980s, narrowing the wage gap with men. Since the 1990s, the gendered wage gap has narrowed more slowly. For full-time, full-year workers, women's earnings as a ratio of men's have remained fairly stable at 69–72 per cent since 1991 (see Table 15.5). In 2011, women employed full-time, full-year earned 72 cents for every dollar men earned. When part-time workers are included, women's average earnings drop to 66.7 cents for every dollar men earn.

The gender wage gap has narrowed, but this is significantly due to men's wages stagnating. From 2001 to 2011, men's wages fluctuated up and down, with a cumulative increase of only 3.1 per cent over 10 years, while women's wages saw a larger cumulative increase of 10.3 per cent (Statistics Canada 2015e). Neither men's nor women's earnings increased enough to keep up with inflation, but women's wages were less stagnant than men's, narrowing the gap slightly.

As Table 15.6 illustrates, the gendered wage gap appears across all educational levels, including the university-educated. For the past decade, women have made up over half (56 per cent) of enrolments in post-secondary education (Statistics Canada 2014a). In 2013, women outnumbered men in university programs in education (77 per cent), health professions (74 per cent), social sciences, and law (68 per cent), but remained a minority in science and mathematics; computer and information sciences (26 per cent); and architecture, engineering, and related fields (19 per cent) (Statistics Canada 2014b). Differences in educational fields result in different occupational opportunities.

Even within identical occupations requiring specialized educational qualifications, gendered wage gaps remain. In higher-paying professions (where women make up 32–40 per cent of the workforce), women's earnings are still lower than men's: general practice physicians, 88 per cent; university professors, 86 per cent; lawyers, 80 per cent; dentists, 74 per cent; and specialist physicians, 69 per cent (Krahn, Hughes, and Lowe 2015: 199). Some of these wage gaps stem from women in these fields generally being younger and having fewer years of experience. However, a recent analysis showed that less than one-third of the gap is explained by differences in educational

Table 15.5 Women's Earnings as a Ratio of Men's Earnings

	Women's Earnings as a Percentage of Men's	
Year	**All Earners**	**Full-Time, Full-Year Workers**
1976	46.8	59.4
1981	53.2	63.5
1986	57.2	65.6
1991	60.1	68.7
1996	63.6	72.8
2001	62.1	69.9
2006	64.7	71.9
2011	66.7	72.0

Source: Statistics Canada, CANSIM Table 202-0102, "Average female and male earnings, and female-to-male earnings ratio, by work activity, 2011 constant dollars" (accessed 1 Apr. 2015).

Table 15.6 Average Annual Earnings, by Education and Gender, Full-Time, Full-Year Workers, 2011

Educational Attainment	Women's Earnings as a Percentage of Men's
Less than Grade 9	56.9
Some secondary school	64.6
Graduated high school	72.1
Some post-secondary	77.1
Post-secondary certificate or diploma	67.9
University degree	68.8
All education levels	72.0

Source: Statistics Canada, CANSIM Table 202-0104, "Female-to-male earnings ratios, by selected characteristics, 2011 constant dollars, annual (per cent)" (accessed 1 Apr. 2015).

levels, occupation, years of experience, number of hours worked, or employment sector (Vincent 2013: 3).

Women's wages remain lower than men's partly because work traditionally seen as feminine is socially devalued, merely an extension of mothering and nurturing roles. But horizontal and vertical gender forms of segregation also affect women's wages. Horizontal segregation occurs when women and men are typically found in different occupations, such as clerical versus construction work. Vertical segregation exists within occupational categories (Krahn, Hughes, and Lowe 2015: 193–4). For example, women make up 84 per cent of elementary school and kindergarten teachers, but only 42 per cent of secondary school teachers, who have higher status and higher pay. In medicine, the three highest-paid specialties (urology, neurosurgery, and cardiovascular/thoracic surgery) remain 85–90 per cent male, while women predominate in lower-status, lower-income specialties such as family medicine and pediatrics (Canadian Medical Association 2015).

Overall, the most important factors explaining the continuing gender wage gap are educational and occupational choices (or streaming); women's greater family responsibilities, particularly for mothers, who earn less than women without children; and gender stereotypes (Vincent 2013: 3–4). The World Economic Forum's *Global Gender Gap Report 2014* ranked Canada twenty-seventh out of 142 countries for wage equality, a key factor in a disappointing overall equality ranking of 19. Canada sits well behind the Nordic countries—Iceland, Finland, Norway, Sweden, and Denmark—the top five countries for gender equality.

Seeking Solutions: Strategies for Achieving Gender Equality

We outline five strategies to achieve greater gender equality in the labour market: (1) policies to hire more women in higher-paying jobs traditionally held by men (employment equity); (2) programs to raise the monetary value of work traditionally performed by women (pay equity); (3) attempts to organize a larger segment of the low-wage workforce (unionization); and (4) strategies to accommodate and redistribute domestic responsibilities in the household (sharing domestic labour). These four strategies promise some improvement in the situation of women workers, but each one has limitations. The fifth strategy, (5) reversing the erosion of the public sector, is critical because the neo-liberal erosion of this sector, including the contracting out of work formerly done in the public sector, has undermined all other gender equity initiatives, threatening to increase rather than decrease gender inequality in the labour market.

Employment Equity

Given the degree of gendered occupational segregation, employment equity programs are crucial for eliminating barriers to hiring and promotion. In Canada the federal Employment Equity Act, passed in 1986 and revised in 1996, applies to women, Aboriginal peoples, people with disabilities, and visible minority groups. Employers with 100 or more employees in the federal public sector and the federally regulated private sector are required to develop plans to ensure their staff represents the qualified workforce available. For example, if women make up 40 per cent of trained biologists, eventually 40 per cent of biologists employed in a government department should be women. Under the Federal Contractors Program, companies with contracts to provide goods or services worth at least $1 million are also subject to the employment equity program. Altogether, however, the federal program applies to less than 1 per cent of employers, and only about 13 per cent of Canadian workers (Weiner 2014).

Seven provinces (British Columbia, Manitoba, Saskatchewan, Quebec, Nova Scotia, New Brunswick, and Prince Edward Island) developed employment equity *guidelines* for the provincial public service. Only Ontario introduced employment equity *legislation*, in 1994, which applied to most employers (public and private sector) in the province. However, in 1995 a newly elected Ontario Progressive Conservative government repealed the legislation, arguing that "special measures" are themselves discriminatory. Similarly, in 2001 a new Liberal government in British Columbia eliminated employment equity in its public service (Armstrong 2007; Bakan and Kobayashi 2004).

The success of employment equity in achieving its goals has been modest (Agocs 2014). Until the early 1990s, improvements were minimal; since 1996, stronger enforcement mechanisms have meant some improvements (Employment and Social Development Canada 2013). Nevertheless, women, visible minorities, and Aboriginal peoples remain under-represented in upper management, while women, people with disabilities, and Aboriginal people are under-represented in professional and middle management positions (Jain et al. 2012). Overall, "visible minorities and women still face glass ceilings in higher level occupations" (Jain et al. 2012: 15). Aboriginal women and women with disabilities have seen the least improvement in the workplace (England 2014).

Several limitations affect the impact of employment equity in equalizing job opportunities for women and other disadvantaged groups. First, employment equity covers only a fraction of the workforce, almost entirely in the public sector, whereas most Canadians work for private-sector employers; furthermore, recent neo-liberal moves in some provinces (e.g., Ontario and British Columbia) have eliminated employment equity policies. Second, at the federal level, employment equity is weakly enforced with very few firms subject to audits (Agocs 2014; Jain et al. 2012). Third, equality is defined as the proportion of women employed relative to the proportion of women available in the trained workforce. This fails to address systemic gender segregation that, as we have seen, results in very small proportions of women being qualified for some occupations.

Pay Equity

While employment equity policies aim to improve women's representation in male-dominated occupations, pay equity policies address the consistent underpaying of "women's jobs" relative to comparable "men's jobs." As early as the 1950s, legislation was passed in most provinces requiring equal pay for equal work, but occupational segregation meant that women and men seldom did the same work. Beginning in the late 1970s, the federal government and several provinces introduced legislation requiring "equal pay for work of equal value," meaning equal pay for jobs that are comparable in terms of skill, effort, working conditions, and responsibility. This allows very different job categories to be compared across segregated occupations in the same company (e.g., comparing male janitors and female clerical staff working at a university).

Federally, pay equity is addressed through the Canadian Human Rights Act, section 11, which prohibits wage discrimination between male and female employees performing work of equal value. It uses a complaints-based model, with pay practices scrutinized only if a complaint is made. Cases can take years, even decades, to process through the courts, at enormous cost (Côté and Lassonde 2007). The burden is on workers as complainants to bear the cost of the court process, so that, in practice, only workers represented by large unions have recourse to this measure (Armstrong 2007).

Some provinces (Manitoba, Ontario, Quebec, Nova Scotia, Prince Edward Island, and New Brunswick) developed more proactive pay equity legislation requiring employers to develop pay equity plans, which promoted fairer job classification systems in some workplaces (Armstrong 2007). Except in Ontario and Quebec, provincial pay equity legislation only applies to the public sector. These policies compare job classes, not male and female workers within job classes. Furthermore, there is little enforcement by government. Iyer (2002) notes that, among Ontario private-sector employers with 50 or fewer employees, non-compliance with the Pay Equity Act is as high as 90 per cent.

Pay equity has led to significant pay settlements for some groups of women, mostly in large public-sector unions, but it has not resulted in a significant reduction of the gendered wage gap (Armstrong 2007; Côté and Lassonde 2007). It is usually limited to comparisons within a site, so that, in predominantly female workplaces, there may be no appropriate male jobs for comparison. Moreover, most of the workforce is not covered by pay equity legislation. Some provinces have never passed such legislation, while others, such as British Columbia, repealed these initiatives (Iyer 2002). In addition, contracting out public-sector work to private companies has eliminated hard-won gains. For example, when the BC government contracted out housekeeping, laundry, security, and food services in provincial hospitals in 2002, wages dropped by 40 per cent and "more than 30 years of pay equity gains for women" disappeared (Cohen and Cohen 2004: 4).

Unionization

Another potential solution is to increase rates of unionization in low-wage sectors, where jobs disproportionately are occupied by women. On average, unionized workers enjoy better wages and benefits than non-union workers, and the gap is greatest for women workers. Among men, the average wage for unionized workers in 2014 was $28.94 an hour, compared with $25.29 for non-union workers; while women earned less than men overall, unionized women workers averaged $27.48 per hour, while non-union women earned $20.38 (Statistics Canada 2015f). Unionization, then, reduced the gendered wage gap from $4.91 per hour to $1.46.

Historically, unions were male-dominated and were most common in industries like manufacturing, construction, forestry, and mining. Beginning in the 1970s, large numbers of public-sector workers also formed unions, bringing civil servants, nurses, teachers, and postal workers into the labour movement. Today, the majority of union members are public-sector workers and more women than men are union members (32.8 per cent versus 30.3 per cent) (Employment and Social Development Canada 2015). While unionization decreases the gendered wage gap for the same job, unions have not decreased workplace gender segregation.

Still, most employees, nearly 70 per cent, are not unionized and so not covered by collective agreements. Also, during the last two decades, governments across the country—especially in Ontario, Saskatchewan, Alberta, and British Columbia—have adopted neo-liberal policies to reduce public-sector employment, contract out public services to private companies, and curtail the ability to organize unions and to strike. Such policies are intended to decrease rates of unionization and lower public-sector wages. As long as such policies continue to dominate the political agenda, the ability to raise women's wages through unionization will remain limited.

Sharing Domestic Labour

One of the most important dimensions of the gendered division of work is the uneven distribution of domestic labour in most households. Even when women work full-time in the labour force, most retain primary responsibility for child care, elder care, housework, shopping, and food preparation. As discussed earlier, women with children, on average, devote 1,451 hours more than men do to domestic work (Statistics Canada 2011: 42–3). This extra domestic burden limits women's ability to compete for jobs or promotions that require long hours, relocation for employment, or further education to upgrade skills. The uneven division of domestic labour disadvantages women in the workplace, making it difficult to compete with male colleagues who may have the advantage of a female partner performing most domestic responsibilities.

Meanwhile, neo-liberal policies have intensified domestic work by cutting back on services once provided in the public sector and downloading these responsibilities to individual households. Hospital patients are released earlier to be cared for at home (usually by wives, mothers, or daughters). Home-care services are cut for the elderly, who must turn to relatives for support (usually daughters or daughters-in-law). Public funding for daycare is cut and subsidies reduced, forcing some parents (usually mothers) out of the labour market or into lower-paying part-time jobs. Policy decisions that reduce public services mean that domestic work falls disproportionately on women's shoulders.

Levelling the playing field for women and men in the workplace requires public programs that meet the needs of employed women and their families, including government-supported low-cost daycare; better maternity and paternity leave provisions; adequate social services in areas such as health, education, and home care; "family-friendly" employee programs like on-site daycare, flex-time, and family leave; and a work culture that does not tie promotion to excessive overtime or frequent relocation. Such measures would improve the situation of all parents, especially single mothers, who are the heads of one in every five families with children (Statistics Canada 2011: 34). In the long run, however, men must also take on an equal share of domestic responsibilities. Redefining the domestic division of labour so that it is equally men's and women's work should help to break down the sharp gendered distinctions attached to most jobs in the labour market.

Conclusion: Reversing the Neo-liberal Erosion of the Public Sector

By the first decades of the twenty-first century, the labour force participation rates of women and men have become more similar than different, but major differences remain in the gender segregation of occupations, in the wages earned by women and men, and in the uneven distribution of unpaid work in the household. Gender segregation and a significant income gap are deeply entrenched in the labour market and are not easy to overcome, as suggested by the limited effect of decades of employment equity programs, pay equity policies, and unionization. Moreover, the legacy of the neo-liberal policies embraced by federal and provincial governments in Canada since the 1990s pose a significant barrier to achieving greater gender equality.

The philosophy of neo-liberalism prioritizes private-sector growth, limits government economic regulation, cuts taxes for corporations and high-income earners, diminishes public-sector employment, and reduces access to social programs. Consequently, Canada has witnessed the erosion of (mostly women's) public-sector employment and restricted access to social programs and benefits (McBride and McNutt 2007). Neo-liberal principles are used as a rationale for not developing national child care and other programs that are essential for gender equality. As Brodie and Bakker (2008) point out, neo-liberal policies have largely jettisoned the concept of "gender justice" from public policy decisions, so that the gendered impact of neo-liberalism is rarely acknowledged. The countries with the best performance in *The Global Gender Gap Report* (World Economic Forum 2014) all have strong social programs to support women's equality.

Reversing the neo-liberal erosion of the public sector and reinstituting gender-based assessments of public policies are critical strategies for attaining greater gender equality in the labour market and society at large. Measures proposed to provide women access to more and higher-paying jobs, including employment equity, pay equity, and others, must be supplemented with expanded publicly funded social programs to support employed women and their families. Although none of these proposals alone resolves existing forms of gender inequality, in combination these five strategies could substantially improve the situation of women in the workplace.

Postscript: A Note on the Complexity of Gender

Gender is distinct from sex, though the two terms are usually treated as indivisible. Everyone has a biological sex (female, male, or intersex), gender identity (an internal sense of self as woman, man, neither, or both), and gender expression (communication of gender to others through appearance and behaviour). These concepts are all generally understood as binary—someone is either male *or* female, masculine *or* feminine. In fact, though, they are all non-binary, because many people live outside these two categories. Gender identity is not always aligned with a person's biological sex, or the gender assigned at birth. For example, some are biologically female and raised as girls, but know themselves to be men. The umbrella term "transgender" captures the range of experiences arising from this lack of alignment. Some refuse binary gender notions altogether, experiencing their gender identity as non-binary, neither masculine *nor* feminine. They may self-identify in numerous ways, including "gender fluid" and "gender queer." The term "cis-gender" is used for those who experience their sex, gender at birth, and gender identity as fully aligned.

Statistics about employment and work apply almost exclusively to cis-gender people, using the binary male–female categories. Most Canadian labour statistics come from large-scale surveys offering only the two gender options. What research does exist suggests that transgender and gender non-conforming people face higher levels of employment discrimination and unemployment in Canada and the US, and are far more likely than the national average to live below the poverty line (Bauer et al. 2010, 2011; Grant et al. 2011).

We acknowledge the inadequacy of treating gender as binary, but do so here because of limitations in the available evidence.

Questions for Critical Thought

1. Why are labour markets largely segregated into "women's jobs" and "men's jobs"? What causes some jobs to be associated with men (such as engineers or construction workers) and others with women (like nurses or secretaries)? Should these patterns be changed? Why? How?

2. Over the past quarter-century, there has been little reduction in the gendered wage gap, despite pay equity and employment equity programs. At the current rate, it will take 200 years to attain gender equity. Why have these equity programs had such minor impacts?
3. Why do you think some groups of women (Aboriginal, visible minority, immigrant women, and women with disabilities) are particularly disadvantaged in employment rates and income levels? What ideas do you have about how this could change?
4. Explain how the division of domestic labour in households and the organization of paid labour in employment reinforce each other. What different consequences does the division of paid and unpaid labour have for men and women?

Recommended Readings

Agocs, Carol, ed. 2014. *Employment Equity in Canada: The Legacy of the Abella Report*. Toronto: University of Toronto Press.

Armstrong, Pat, and Hugh Armstrong. 2010. *The Double Ghetto: Canadian Women and Their Segregated Work*, 3rd edn. Toronto: Oxford University Press.

Statistics Canada. 2011. *Women in Canada: A Gender-based Statistical Report*, 6th edn. Ottawa: Minister of Industry, July. Catalogue no. 89-503- X. http://www.statcan.gc.ca/pub/89-503-x/89-503-x2010001-eng.pdf.

Vincent, Carole. 2013. "Why do women earn less than men? A synthesis of findings from Canadian microdata." *The Canadian Research Data Centre Network (CRDCN) Synthesis Series*, Sept.

Recommended Websites

National Association of Women and the Law:
http://nawl.ca/en/

Status of Women Canada:
http://www.swc-cfc.gc.ca/index-eng.html

Women Suffrage and Beyond: Confronting the Democratic Deficit:
http://womensuffrage.org

World Economic Forum, *The Global Gender Gap Report 2014*:
http://www.weforum.org/reports/global-gender-gap-report-2014

References

Agocs, Carol, ed. 2014. *Employment Equity in Canada: The Legacy of the Abella Report*. Toronto: University of Toronto Press.

Armstrong, Pat. 2007. "Back to basics: Seeking pay equity for women in Canada." *Labour & Industry* 18, 2: 11–32.

Bakan, Abigail, and Audrey Kobayashi. 2004. "Backlash against employment equity: The British Columbia Experience." *Atlantis* 29, 1: 61–70.

Bauer, Greta, Michelle Boyce, Todd Coleman, Matthias Kaay, Kyle Scanlon, and Robb Travers. 2010.

"Who Are Trans People in Ontario?" *Trans PULSE e-Bulletin* 1, 1.

——, Nicole Nussbaum, Robb Travers, Lauren Munro, Jake Pyne, and Nik Redman. 2011. "We've got work to do: Workplace discrimination and employment challenges for trans people in Ontario." *Trans PULSE e-Bulletin* 2, 1 (30 May).

Block, Sheila, and Grace-Edward Galabuzi. 2011. *Canada's Colour Coded Labour Market: The Gap for Racialized Workers.* Ottawa and Toronto: Canadian Centre for Policy Alternatives and The Wellesley Institute.

Brodie, Janine, and Isabella Bakker. 2008. *Where Are the Women? Gender Equity, Budgets, and Canadian Public Policy.* Ottawa: Canadian Centre for Policy Alternatives.

Calzavara, Liviana. 1993. "Trends and policy in employment opportunities for women." In James Curtis, Edward Grabb, and Neil Guppy, eds, *Social Inequality in Canada*, 2nd edn, pp. 311–26. Toronto: Prentice-Hall Canada.

Canadian Institute for Health Information. 2013. *Regulated Nurses 2012—Summary Report.* https://secure.cihi.ca/free_products/Nursing-Workforce-2013_EN.pdf. Accessed 1 Apr. 2015.

Canadian Medical Association. 2015. "Canadian specialty profiles." https://www.cma.ca/En/Pages/specialty-profiles.aspx. Accessed 1 Apr. 2015.

Cohen, Marjorie Griffin, and Marcy Cohen. 2004. *A Return to Wage Discrimination: Pay Equity Losses through the Privatization of Health Care.* Ottawa: Canadian Centre for Policy Alternatives.

Côté, Andrée, and Julie Lassonde. 2007. *Status Report on Pay Equity in Canada.* Ottawa: National Association of Women and the Law.

Employment and Social Development Canada. 2013. *Employment Equity Act: Annual Report 2013.* http://www.labour.gc.ca/eng/standards_equity/eq/pubs_eq/annual_reports/2013/index.shtml. Accessed 12 Apr. 2015.

——. 2015. "Work—Unionization rates." http://www4.hrsdc.gc.ca/.3ndic.1t.4r@-eng.jsp?iid=17. Accessed 12 Apr. 2015.

England, Kim. 2014. "Women, intersectionality, and employment equity." In Agocs (2014: 71–98).

Grant, Jaime M., Lisa A. Mottet, Justin Tanis, Jack Harrison, Jody L. Herman, and Mara Keisling. 2011. *Injustice at Every Turn: A Report of the Transgender Discrimination Survey.* Washington: National Center for Transgender Equality and National Gay and Lesbian Task Force.

Jain, Harish, Frank Horwitz, and Christa Wilkin. 2012. "Employment equity in Canada and South Africa: A comparative review." *International Journal of Human Resource Management* 23, 1: 1–17.

Iyer, Nitya. 2002. *"Working Through the Wage Gap": Report of the Task Force on Pay Equity.* Victoria, BC: Attorney General's Office.

Krahn, Harvey, Karen Hughes, and Graham Lowe. 2015. *Work, Industry and Canadian Society*, 7th edn. Toronto: Nelson.

McBride, Stephen, and Kathleen McNutt. 2007. "Devolution and neoliberalism in the Canadian welfare state: Ideology, national and international conditioning frameworks and policy change in British Columbia." *Global Social Policy* 7, 2: 177–201.

Marshall, Katherine. 2011. "Generational change in paid and unpaid work." *Canadian Social Trends* no. 92. Statistics Canada Catalogue no. 11-008-X. http://www.statcan.gc.ca/pub/11-008-x/2011002/article/11520-eng.htm. Accessed 27 July 2011.

Morissette, René, and Rizwan Sultan. 2013. *Twenty Years in the Careers of Immigrant and Native-born Workers.* Economic Insights No. 032. Ottawa: Statistics Canada Catalogue no. 11-626-X. http://www.statcan.gc.ca/pub/11-626-x/11-626-x2013032-eng.pdf. Accessed 1 Apr. 2014.

National Physician Survey. 2014. "National results." http://nationalphysiciansurvey.ca/result/2013-national-results. Accessed 1 Apr. 2015.

Statistics Canada. 2011. *Women in Canada Sixth Edition: A Gender-based Statistical Report.* Ottawa: Minister of Industry, July. Catalogue no. 89-503-X.

——. 2013. Canada (Code 01) (table). National Household Survey (NHS) Profile. 2011 National Household Survey. Catalogue no. 99-004-XWE. Ottawa. Accessed 18 Feb. 2015.

——. 2014a. "Canadian postsecondary enrolments and graduates, 2012/2013." *The Daily*, 25 Nov. 2014. Catalogue no. 11-001-X.

———. 2014b. Table 477-0019—Postsecondary enrolments, by registration status, Pan-Canadian Standard Classification of Education (PCSCE), Classification of Instructional Programs, Primary Grouping (CIP_PG), sex and immigration status, annual (number), CANSIM (database). Accessed 1 Apr. 2015.

———. 2015a. Table 282-0002—Labour force survey estimates (LFS), by sex and detailed age group, annual (persons unless otherwise noted), CANSIM (database). Accessed 1 Apr. 2015.

———. 2015b. Table 282-0014—Labour force survey estimates (LFS), part-time employment by reason for part-time work, sex and age group, annual (persons), CANSIM (database) Accessed 1 Apr. 2015.

———. 2015c. Table 282-0106—Labour force survey estimates (LFS), by immigrant status, educational attainment, sex and age group, Canada, annual (persons unless otherwise noted), CANSIM (database). Accessed 1 Apr. 2015.

———. 2015d. Table 282-0010—Labour force survey estimates (LFS), by National Occupational Classification for Statistics (NOC-S) and sex, annual (persons unless otherwise noted), CANSIM (database). Accessed 1 Apr. 2015.

———. 2015e. Table 202-0102—Average female and male earnings, and female-to-male earnings ratio, by work activity, 2011 constant dollars, CANSIM (database). Accessed 1 Apr. 2015.

———. 2015f. Table 282-0074—Labour force survey estimates (LFS), wages of employees by job permanence, union coverage, sex and age group, annual (current dollars unless otherwise noted), CANSIM (database). Accessed 1 Apr. 2015.

Turcotte, Martin. 2014. *Persons with Disabilities and Employment*. Ottawa: Minister of Industry, Catalogue no. 75-006-X

Vincent, Carole. 2013. "Why do women earn less than men? A synthesis of findings from Canadian microdata." *Canadian Research Data Centre Network (CRDCN) Synthesis Series*, Sept.

Weiner, Nan. 2014. "Employment equity in Canada: What do the data show about its effectiveness?" In Agocs (2014: 29–50).

World Economic Forum. 2014. *The Global Gender Gap Report 2014*. http://www.weforum.org/reports/global-gender-gap-report-2014. Accessed 13 Apr. 2015.

16 Gender Inequality in the Family Setting

Roderic Beaujot, Jianye Liu, and Zenaida Ravanera

Introduction

Families are arenas for sharing and caring, but they are also arenas of power relations. Both love and exploitation can occur in families. The balance of these dynamics depends considerably on socio-economic dimensions that give rise to differential access to resources on the basis of gender and age. It also depends on the extent to which people can enter and exit from relationships. The potential for exploitation is much higher if some members control decisions about the formation or dissolution of the family, and if there is limited alternative support for those who remove themselves from their family setting.

In this chapter, we first consider change and diversity across the various types of families. We then assess gender differences in the entry and exit from relationships and gender differences in living with children. Because gender issues in families are most apparent in the central activities of earning a living and caring for each other, we also look at gender inequalities in the division of paid and unpaid work. The concluding section addresses certain policy questions associated with gender inequality in family settings.

Family Diversity

Families have become increasingly diverse. In the "Leave it to Beaver" era of the 1950s there was one predominant family model: the heterosexual nuclear family with a traditional division of labour. Recent census reports reveal the diversity across family types today. In the 2011 census, families with two married parents and children at home represented only 31.9 per cent of families, while 7.3 per cent were cohabiting couples with children, and 16.3 per cent were lone-parent families (Statistics Canada 2012). Therefore, almost half (44.5 per cent) of families did not include children at home. Among couple families with children at home, 12.6 per cent were stepfamilies (Statistics Canada 2012: 11). Stepfamilies were also more likely to involve cohabitation rather than marriage: among families with children, common-law couples comprised 14.0 per cent of intact families but 50.1 per cent of stepfamilies. Same-sex couples comprised 0.8 per cent of all families.

These trends towards greater diversity across families have been linked to weakening norms against divorce, premarital sex, cohabitation, voluntary childlessness, and same-sex relationships. The trends are also linked to the gender revolution and the growing importance of individual autonomy for both women and men.

Value change has promoted individual rights, along with less regulation of the private lives of individuals by the larger community (Dagenais 2008). There is a heightened sense that both women and men should make their own choices about relationships and child-bearing. Diversity is valued in living arrangements and in family forms. While most people do not live in same-sex relationships themselves, the majority support the right to equal treatment for gay and lesbian relationships and marriages.

A key change has been greater flexibility in the entry and exit from relationships, as represented by cohabitation and divorce. Cohabitation first changed premarital relationships, but also changed post-marital relationships; cohabitation effectively changed marriage itself, by introducing less rigid understandings of unions. Common-law couples represented 6.3 per cent of all couples in 1981, but this number had risen to 19.9 per cent by 2011. In recent times, as well, evidence indicates that more than one-third of marriages end in divorce within the first 25 years (Milan 2013: 14).

Besides the greater flexibility in entry and exit from relationships, we have seen a delay in family formation. The mean age at first marriage was 23 for women and 25 for men in 1961–71, but by 2008 it had risen to age 29 for women and 31 for men (Kerr and Beaujot 2015). In 1965, 30.8 per cent of first-time brides were under 20 years of age, compared to 3.5 per cent in 2000. Of more significance, the age at women's first giving birth increased from a mean of 23.6 years in 1961 to 28.5 in 2011.

The family transitions associated with home leaving and union formation have involved not only a delay, but also more fluidity through less defined transitions and variability from case to case. The trajectories have diverged from the traditionally preferred pathway of finishing schooling, leaving the parental home, entering the labour force, and then getting married (Ravanera et al. 2006; Ravanera and Rajulton 2006).

Educational attainment has increased, leading to a later completion of education and later entry into full-time employment, which has also occurred because of insecurities in the labour market (Beaujot 2006). Since both men and women need to position themselves in relation to the labour market, Oppenheimer (1988) speaks of a "career entry theory" of marriage timing. To make the most profitable match, prospective partners need to know how each will be positioned for earning income. Two incomes have become important for maintaining stable middle-class standing (Coltrane 1998). Consequently, the completion of education and higher income prospects have come to be positively related to women's probability of getting married, a pattern that has always been the case for men (Sweeney 2002; Ravanera and Rajulton 2007).

Family diversity can be found in the variety of living arrangements evident today: alone or in a family; married or cohabiting; two parents or a lone parent; opposite-sex or same-sex; couples with children or without; and intact families or stepfamilies. Diversity is also evident in how earning and caring responsibilities are shared: single breadwinner versus dual earners, and a traditional gender division of work and care versus a more equal division by gender. Because of significant cultural and political changes, many Canadians now celebrate this diversity, because it means more family options beyond the once-predominant heterosexual couple with children and a traditional gender division of labour.

Another important indicator of change is that Statistics Canada decided not to publish the vital statistics of marriage after 2008. Of course, divorce statistics do not include separations of relationships that were not official marriages, or persons who are separated but not divorced. Consequently, Statistics Canada data on families generally do not differentiate married and cohabiting unions. In this chapter, we do the same: our tables combine married and cohabiting families.

Gender Differences in the Entry and Exit from Relationships

While sharing a common culture, ethnicity, or religion was once the dominant factor in union formation, education now plays a much more important role. Potential mates often socialize in similar educational settings, and persons with similar educational assets are more likely to enter into marital unions.

Since 1970, there has been an increase in educational homogamy, i.e., in people marrying others with a similar level of education. Hou and Myles (2008) found that this increase was more about changing patterns of mate selection than about the growing similarity in educational attainments of men and women. Among men with a university degree, 67 per cent were married to women with a university degree in 2006, compared to only 38 per cent in 1981 (Martin and Hou 2010: 71). These results reflect what can be called assortative mating, in which people form relationships with others having a similar level of education, leading to an accentuation of the differences across couples.

Selectivity in Union Formation

In their analysis of the propensity to marry in the United States, Goldscheider and Waite (1986) found that, before 1980, stable employment increased the likelihood of marriage for men but not for women. In that period, women apparently were more likely to use a higher personal income to "buy out of marriage," because higher income gave women greater options outside of marriage and so reduced their relative preference for marriage. These patterns would change in the 1980s, as economic prospects became positively related to marriage for both men and women (Sweeney 2002; Pew Research Center 2010). In a comparison of the propensity to marry by level of education in 25 European countries, Kalmijn (2013) found that more highly educated women were less likely to be married in countries with traditional gender roles, but more likely to be married in countries with relatively egalitarian gender roles.

Such findings suggest that socio-economic characteristics have long been important for men's marriageability, but that this pattern now applies to women as well. In Canada, as well, Ravanera and Rajulton (2007) analyzed data for 1993–8 to show that increased education is the main factor in the postponement of marriage, and that greater economic assets increase the propensity to marry for both men and women.

Selectivity into Union Dissolution

Using Swedish data for 1970–99, Kennedy and Thomson (2010) determined that educational differences in family instability were small in the 1970s, but then increased due to the rising union disruption among less-educated parents. Sweden now conforms to the patterns in other countries in showing socio-economic differences in family stability, with more separations for those with lower socio-economic status. Using longitudinal data from Canada over the period 2002–7, Bohnert (2011) also found evidence of these patterns: employment difficulties were associated with increases in the relative risks of union dissolution, while home ownership had the opposite effect.

In a study of multi-partner fertility among Norwegian men born between 1955 and 1984, Lappegard and her colleagues (2009) showed that men's education and income are positively related to the likelihood of having a first birth, and also to the probability of a second birth with the same partner, while men with lower education are more likely to have a subsequent birth with a new partner. That is, men with lower status are less likely to retain a stable partnership.

Proportions Living in Couples by Gender, Education, and Age

For people over age 30, the evidence on the proportion living as couples confirms that those with more education are more likely to be in union. For instance, at ages 40–4, 83.6 per cent of men with a university degree are part of a couple, compared to 71.4 per cent of men without a university degree (Table 16.1). For women of the same ages, the differences are smaller but in the same direction: 78.5 per cent of those with university degrees live in couples, compared to 71.1 per cent of those without a university degree. For people in their twenties, those with no university degree are more likely to be living in couples. That is, those who complete their education sooner are also more likely to cohabit or marry sooner. More generally, within given cohorts, later marriage is associated with higher socio-economic status (Ravanera et al. 1998; Ravanera et al. 2006; Ravanera and Rajulton 2006). The patterns at ages over 30 imply that higher human capital increases the propensity to union formation, and higher education also increases the likelihood to remain in union or to form a subsequent union.

Table 16.1 also confirms that union formation typically occurs earlier for women: for instance, at ages 25–9, 54.2 per cent of women are married or cohabitating, compared to 40.8 per cent of men. However, the opposite occurs at ages over 40, where a higher proportion of men than women are in union. While there are increased gender similarities in the formation and dissolution of unions, men are advantaged by later entry into relationships and by the higher propensity to be in union at ages 40 and above.

Table 16.1 Percentages Living in Couples, for Population Aged 15+, by Gender, Education, and Age, Canada, 2011

	Male			Female		
	Total	No University Degree	University or Higher	Total	No University Degree	University or Higher
15+	60.4	56.8	71.9	57.5	54.4	66.0
15–19	0.4	0.4	1.7	1.6	1.7	1.3
20–4	11.2	11.6	8.7	21.1	22.3	17.4
25–9	40.8	42.3	37.3	54.2	55.8	51.9
30–4	64.3	62.7	67.7	69.9	67.9	72.7
35–9	74.4	71.8	79.6	74.3	71.1	79.0
40–4	75.3	71.4	83.6	73.8	71.1	78.5
45–9	74.0	71.0	82.1	72.5	71.2	75.7
50–4	74.9	72.8	81.4	72.5	72.0	73.8
55–9	76.4	74.7	81.5	70.5	70.6	70.3
60–4	78.8	77.3	82.8	68.4	68.4	68.5
65–9	79.9	78.8	83.2	64.8	64.4	66.3
70–4	79.8	78.8	83.3	58.0	58.1	58.0
75–9	77.6	76.6	81.9	46.0	45.7	48.3
80–4	72.3	71.2	78.1	33.0	32.2	40.7
85+	60.2	58.8	66.8	16.1	15.7	21.2

Notes:
1 Persons living in couples are persons who are married or common-law, as defined by "marital status" and "common-law status."
2 Total number of cases aged 15+ is 762,879 and there are 34,807 (4.6 per cent) missing cases.
Source: 2011 NHS micro-file (data are weighted).

Parenting and Gender Inequalities

The median age at birth of the first child has increased for both women and men, but the median age remains four years older for men than women (Ravanera and Hoffman 2012: 29). There are also important gender differences in the proportions living with children. Table 16.2 shows that in 2011, at ages 20–64, 38.6 per cent of men compared to 43.7 per cent of women were living with children. For persons living in couples, at each age group from 20–4 to 40–4, women were more likely than men to be living with children, and the opposite occurred at ages 45–9 to 60–4, where the men were more likely to be living with children. The contrasts are greater for persons not living in couples, where, up to ages 55–9, women were considerably more likely to be living with children. At ages 30–54, over 30 per cent of women not in couples were living with children. For men not in couples, the highest proportions living with children were at ages 40–54, with about 13–15 per cent living with children.

These patterns of parenting by age indicate that women are more likely than men to be living with children. The gender differences are especially noteworthy at younger ages, and especially for people who are not in couples. While parenting brings various life satisfactions, parenting also competes with other activities. In particular, there are trade-offs between investing in reproduction and investing in one's own productive abilities. Later entry into relationships, and especially later child-bearing, makes young people more able to handle the trade-offs. In contrast, persons who make transitions early can be relatively disadvantaged. Based on census data from 2006, Ravanera and Hoffman (2012: 31) found that at ages 20–39, fathers had less education than non-fathers, but the opposite applied at ages 40–64 where fathers had more education than non-fathers.

In a study of men born between 1926 and 1975 and women born between 1922 and 1980,

Table 16.2 Percentages Living with Children, Persons in Couples and Not in Couples, Population Aged 20–64, by Gender and Age, Canada, 2011

	Male			Female		
Age	Total	Persons in Couples	Persons Not in Couples	Total	Persons in Couples	Persons Not in Couples
20–64	38.6	58.1	5.9	43.7	55.5	23.0
20–4	3.2	26.2	0.5	10.5	33.3	4.6
25–9	16.9	40.6	1.4	32.2	48.7	13.9
30–4	42.8	65.9	3.7	59.8	73.4	30.3
35–9	61.1	80.4	8.9	74.1	84.7	45.1
40–4	65.4	83.2	14.2	75.4	84.6	51.1
45–9	61.3	78.1	15.4	65.8	73.6	46.1
50–4	49.2	61.9	12.9	43.7	49.2	30.0
55–9	28.3	34.8	7.7	18.8	20.6	14.7
60–4	12.2	14.5	4.2	5.0	5.3	4.3

Notes:
1 Children are defined as persons under 25 who are living with at least one parent.
2 Persons in couples are married spouses or common-law partners. Persons not in couples are all other people aged 20–64.
3 Total number of cases aged between 20 and 64 is 552,577 and there are 3,526 (0.6 per cent) missing cases.
Source: 2011 NHS micro-file (data are weighted).

based on the 2001 Canadian General Social Survey, Ravanera and colleagues (Ravanera et al. 2006; Ravanera and Rajulton 2007) found that men and women with high social status were more likely to have delayed their entry into parenthood, having first completed post-secondary education. In contrast, men and women with low social status were more likely to become parents at a younger age, often without first completing post-secondary education or having a period of regular full-time work.

Since women typically carry more of the parenting burden, these socio-economic differences in the timing of parenthood affect women more than men. Only at older ages (45+ for men living in union, and 60+ for men not in union) are men more likely to be living with children. By these ages, there is less difficulty in handling the trade-offs between investing in production and investing in reproduction.

Earnings Inequality across Family Types

Diversity can mean differential risks and inequality across families and individuals. In 1980, the average employment earnings of married mothers were highest when husbands had intermediate earnings; however, by the 1990–2000 period, employment earnings of married mothers were higher when husbands were in the higher earnings categories (Myles 2010: 69). Similarly, Gaudet and her colleagues (2011) found that the proportion of women working within two years of a first birth was highest for women whose husbands earned the highest incomes.

Especially important is the contrast between two-earner couples, on the one hand, and breadwinner and lone-parent families, on the other hand. For instance, among couples without children, those with one full-time, full-year worker had only 55.5 per cent of the median earnings of those with two full-time, full-year workers in 2005 (Statistics Canada 2008). For couples with children, those with one earner had only 54.9 per cent of the income of those with two earners. As measured by Statistics Canada's low-income cut-off (LICO), after taxes and transfers, the 2011 poverty rate was 5.1 per cent for two-parent families with children, compared to 21.2 per cent for female lone-parent families and 12.4 per cent for male lone-parent families (Statistics Canada 2013). The low-income rates are also high for non-elderly persons who are "unattached," that is, living either alone or not in a family setting. The poverty rates for the non-elderly unattached are 29.9 per cent for men and 36.0 per cent for women. In contrast, the poverty rates are less than 3 per cent for couples with two earners and for elderly couples. Among one-earner couples, there are much higher rates of poverty when children are present (Beaujot et al. 2014).

It is important to observe the significant decline in the low-income proportion among people in lone-parent families over time, from 49.3 per cent in 1996 to 19.7 per cent in 2011 (Statistics Canada 2013). However, the disadvantages of lone-parent families remain significant, at almost four times the rate for two-parent families with children. Further analyses indicate that older female lone parents made significant income gains over the period 1980–2000. This may be partly because they have fewer and older children, they have increased their education, and they are working longer hours (Myles et al. 2007; see also Richards 2010). At the same time, the income gains for married female parents are even stronger, especially through increases in hours worked.

The income situation of younger lone parents did not improve over the period 1980–2000. Lone parenthood is a significant risk factor for women who marry early. For instance, among women under age 25, the proportion with children is highest for the formerly married, as opposed to women who are currently married, cohabiting, or single (Ravanera and Beaujot 2010).

Compared to intact families with children, stepfamilies are more likely to have both parents in paid employment and also working full-time (Vézina 2012). However, stepfamilies are more likely to be financially stressed, with 18 per cent being "unable to meet a financial obligation at least once in the previous year," compared to 11 per cent for intact families and 31 per cent for lone parents. The complex nature of financial obligations, within and beyond the immediate family, contributes to this greater financial stress in stepfamilies and lone-parent families.

Some of the gender inequality that we see in families derives from the relative disadvantage of women compared to men in a given family arrangement. The 2011 low-income rate is higher for female (21.2 per cent) than for male (12.4 per cent) lone parents; for female (36.0 per cent) than for male (29.9 per cent) unattached non-elderly; and for female (16.1 per cent) than for male (12.2 per cent) unattached elderly (Beaujot et al. 2014). Gender inequality also stems in part from the higher probability of women being lone parents, while men are more likely to be living as part of a couple.

Families, Earnings, and Gender Inequality

Although inequality persists, employment and earnings have been moving in a converging direction by gender. For instance, women's labour force participation rate increased from 22.9 per cent in 1951 to 62.3 per cent in 2011, while men's rate declined from 84.1 per cent to 71.5 per cent in the same period (Beaujot et al. 2014). Another example of this converging trend concerns income changes for men and women among couples with children; the median income for husbands declined by 5 per cent between 1980 and 2005 but increased for wives by more than 500 per cent (Statistics Canada 2008: 26). For all couples, wives earned more than husbands in only 10 per cent of couples in 1976, compared to 30 per cent in 2008 (Statistics Canada 2011).

While there has been movement in a converging direction, important differences remain. At ages 20–64, 78.8 per cent of men and 64.1 per cent of women were employed in 2011 (Table 16.3). For those working, the mean hours worked were 42.5 for men and 35.2 for women.

Table 16.3 further differentiates employment rates and mean work hours, by both marital status (married/cohabiting versus other) and parental status (not living with children versus living with children). There is less evidence of the traditional pattern, in which men's labour force involvement is higher and women's lower, when they are married with children. Nonetheless, men still have the highest employment rate when they are married or cohabiting with children at home. However, women's employment rate is no longer suppressed when they are living with children. For married or cohabiting women, employment rates are the same for those living with and without children at home (66.1 per cent versus 66.3 per cent). For women who are not in relationships, employment rates are higher if they are living with children, as is the case for men. In terms of average hours worked, men's hours are highest if there are children at home, especially if they are married or cohabiting. Married/cohabiting women have slightly higher average work hours if they have no children, while women who are not in relationships have the highest hours if they have children.

Thus, for both men and women, employment rates are higher for those in relationships. For men, and for women not in relationships, the employment rate and the hours worked are higher when they have children. For women in relationships, the employment rates are the same when comparing those with and without children.

Table 16.3 also shows economic differences, as measured by the proportions of men and women who are in poverty (below the LICO). For the 20–64 age group, the poverty rate is 11.5 per cent for men and 12.2 per cent for women. The poverty rates are lowest and the gender differences are small for persons who are married or cohabiting, with 7.0 per cent of men and 6.8 per cent of women below the LICO. For persons not in relationships, the rates are much higher: 19.3 per cent for men and 22.0 per cent for women. It can also be seen that the poverty rates are highest for those not in union and not living with

Table 16.3 Employment Rate, Hours Worked at All Jobs in a Week, and Percentage with Low-income Status, by Gender, Marital, and Parental Status, Ages 20–64, Canada, 2011

		Male			Female		
		Employment Rate	Mean Work Hours	% with Low Income*	Employment Rate	Mean Work Hours	% with Low Income*
Married/ cohabiting	Total	86.4	43.9	7.0	66.2	35.2	6.8
	No child	78.1	42.6	6.7	66.3	35.8	6.2
	Child(ren)	91.0	44.6	7.2	66.1	34.8	7.4
Other	Total	61.9	39.1	19.3	59.5	35.2	22.0
	No child	60.7	38.9	23.6	56.4	34.5	25.7
	Child(ren)	77.6	42.0	8.7	68.1	37.2	16.9
Total	Total	78.8	42.5	11.5	64.1	35.2	12.2
	No child	68.7	40.6	15.0	61.6	35.2	14.3
	Child(ren)	90.4	44.4	7.5	66.4	35.2	10.1

*For "% with Low Income," the number of missing cases is 2,283 or 0.3% of total sample size. The definition of low-income status is based on after-tax low-income cut-offs (LICO-AT).

Sources: "Employment Rate" and "Mean Work Hours" are based on 2011 General Social Survey (data are weighted); "% with Low Income" are based on 2011 National Household Survey micro-file (data are weighted).

children: 23.6 per cent for men and 25.7 per cent for women. Nonetheless, the rates are also high for women with children but not in union, at 16.9 per cent compared to 8.7 per cent for men.

Therefore, except for women who are living with children and not in union, the gender differences in poverty rates are not large across marital and parental statuses. On the whole, men are advantaged by being more likely to be in union, while women are disadvantaged by being more likely to be not in union but living with children.

Families, Caring, and Gender Inequality

It is especially in caring activities that family status differentiates men and women (Beaujot 2000). However, there has been some change, with men doing more housework and child care than in the past (Doucet 2006; Ranson 2010).

For this section, we rely on time-use surveys that measure each person's activities over a 24-hour day. Time use provides a means of gauging both earning and caring activities on the basis of the same metric (see Marshall 2006, 2011, 2012; Turcotte 2007; Milan et al. 2011). The activities that take place over a 24-hour day can be grouped into four categories: (1) paid work (including commuting to and from work, and education), (2) unpaid work (including housework, household maintenance, child care, elder care, and volunteer work), (3) personal care (including eating and sleeping), and (4) leisure or free time (including active and passive leisure).

The tables presented here use the categories of paid work and unpaid work, which together can be seen as productive activities, in contrast to the down time associated with personal care and leisure. In the period 1986–2010, women's paid work hours increased and men's unpaid hours increased (Beaujot et al. 2014). In 1986, women's paid work plus education represented 58.9 per cent of men's time in these activities, compared to 74.0 per cent in 2010. For unpaid work, men's time in 1986 represented 46.3 per cent of women's time, compared to 65.9 per cent in 2010. Therefore, for the whole population, men's unpaid work time represented less than half of women's unpaid work time in 1986, compared to two-thirds in 2010.

Based on time-use surveys in 1986, 1992, 1998, and 2005, Marshall (2006) used the title of "Converging gender roles" to describe the trends in paid and unpaid work. Marshall (2011) showed this convergence by comparing the division of work across three generations: late baby boomers (born 1957–66), Generation X (1969–78), and Generation Y (1981–90). She found increasing gender similarity in the involvement in paid work and housework from the earlier to the later generation. For young adults (ages 20–9) in dual-earner couples, she found increased sharing of economic and domestic responsibilities over generations, as women increased their hours of paid work and men increased their share of household work. However, even for the younger generations, the presence of dependent children reduced the woman's contribution to the couple's total paid work time, and increased her relative time in housework.

When paid work and unpaid work are added, the average total productive activity of men and women is found to be very similar in each of the survey years. For instance, in 2010, for ages 15–64, the average total productive hours per day (paid plus unpaid) were 8.4 hours for men and 8.8 hours for women (Table 16.4). For both men and women, and at each of the age groups shown, the total productive hours increase as we move from those not in relationships with no children, to those in relationships without children, to those in relationships with children.

The younger married or cohabiting parents have rather complementary patterns of time use: men did an average of 6.5 hours of paid work and 4.0 hours of unpaid work, while women did an average of 6.5 hours of unpaid work and 3.7 hours of paid work, with average total hours of 10.5 for men and 10.2 for women (Table 16.4). At ages 45–64, the average hours of unpaid work increased for the four marital and

Table 16.4 Average Daily Hours in Paid Work and Unpaid Work, Ages 15–64, by Gender, Age, Marital, and Parental Status, Canada, 2010

	Men				Women			
	Total	Paid	Unpaid	N	Total	Paid	Unpaid	N
15–44								
Unmarried no children	6.9	5.4	1.4	1,152	7.7	5.8	1.9	1,044
Married no children	9.2	6.8	2.4	377	9.0	5.6	3.4	449
Married parents	10.5	6.5	4.0	968	10.2	3.7	6.5	1,317
Lone parents	10.0	6.4	3.7	56	10.3	4.5	5.8	107
45–64								
Unmarried no children	7.1	4.3	2.8	755	8.0	4.1	3.9	1,105
Married no children	8.0	4.8	3.2	1,347	8.1	3.7	4.5	1,729
Married parents	9.7	6.5	3.2	478	9.5	4.3	5.1	390
Lone parents	8.7	4.6	4.1	51	9.5	3.9	5.6	125
Total	8.4	5.7	2.7	5,184	8.8	4.5	4.3	6,542

Married includes cohabiting.
Source: 2010 General Social Survey (data are weighted).

parental categories shown: unmarried with no children, married no children, married parents, and lone parents.[1] The lone parents, both women and men, have the longest hours of unpaid work. At ages 15–44, the increase occurs only over the first three marital/parental categories, with both male and female lone parents having less unpaid work than married parents of the same gender.

The converging trend in gender roles is also seen through the increased number of dual-earner couples between 1986 and 2005 (Marshall 2006). In 2005, among dual-earner couples, husbands put in 54 per cent of the total time that couples spent at jobs, and wives did 62 per cent of the time that couples spent on housework. Marshall (2006) observes that "children widen the gap" and "education narrows it." In dual-earner couples, the division of labour becomes more equal as wives have higher incomes. For couples with the wife's income at $100,000+, the division was equal, with each partner spending some 6.5 hours per day on paid work and 1.5 hours on housework.

Table 16.5 presents figures on time use in productive activities by employment status, for men and women. It is noteworthy that the average total productive hours are again very similar, at 9.3 hours for men and 9.4 hours for women, for the total age group 25–54. As average paid hours are reduced over the categories of full-time, part-time, and not employed, the average unpaid hours increase over these same categories, for both men and women. Nonetheless, for both men and women, the average total hours are lowest for those who are not employed and highest for those working full-time. For men, the average hours of child care are quite similar over these categories of employment; for women, however, the average hours of child care increase from those working full-time, to working part-time, to not employed. Thus, among persons working full-time the average hours of child care are lowest, and are most similar for men and women.

Another way of measuring the variability in earning and caring is at the couple level. By comparing spouses, we can determine whether a given person does more, the same amount, or less of both paid work and unpaid work (Table 16.6). For couples where neither is a full-time student and neither is retired, we have combined the patterns into five models for the division of paid and unpaid work.[2] The most predominant model is complementary traditional, where the man does more paid work and the woman does more unpaid work; however, this model's proportion has declined over time, from 43.5 per cent of persons in couples in 1992 to 33.4 per cent in 2010. The female double burden, in which women do more unpaid work and at least as much paid work compared to men, has remained rather constant over time, involving

Table 16.5 Average Daily Hours of Paid Work and Unpaid Work, Ages 25–54, by Gender and Labour Force Status, Canada, 2010

	Male					Female				
	Paid work	Child Care	Other Unpaid	All Unpaid	Total Paid and Unpaid	Paid Work	Child Care	Other Unpaid	All Unpaid	Total Paid and Unpaid
Total	6.2	0.6	2.4	3.0	9.3	4.5	1.2	3.7	4.9	9.4
Full-time	7.0	0.6	2.3	2.9	9.9	5.9	0.8	3.2	4.1	10.0
Part-time	4.2	0.6	2.7	3.3	7.5	3.5	1.6	4.0	5.6	9.1
Not employed	2.6	0.7	3.0	3.7	6.3	1.5	2.0	4.7	6.8	8.3

Source: 2010 General Social Survey (data are weighted).

Table 16.6 Distribution of Couples by Models of Division of Work, Canada, 1992–2010

	Persons in Couples			
Models of Division of Work (%)	**1992**	**1998**	**2005**	**2010**
Complementary traditional	43.5	39.1	32.9	33.4
Complementary gender-reversed	1.7	2.7	3.0	3.2
Women's double burden	26.5	26.8	26.8	25.9
Men's double burden	5.8	7.6	10.7	8.8
Shared roles	22.6	23.8	26.5	28.8

Sources: Beaujot et al. (2013: Table 6) and authors' calculation based on 2010 General Social Survey.

some 26 to 27 per cent of couples. The shared-role model, in which women and men do about the same amount of unpaid work, has increased, from 22.6 per cent of couples in 1992 to 28.8 per cent in 2010. The male double burden, in which men do more unpaid work and at least as much paid work compared to women, has increased over time, from 5.8 per cent to 8.8 per cent. The complementary gender-reversed model is the least common, but it has increased from 1.7 per cent to 3.2 per cent of couples during the period 1992–2010.

Other analyses indicate that the models in which women do more unpaid work (complementary traditional or women's double burden) are more common when there are young children present, while the models in which men do a more equal share of unpaid work are more likely when women have more education and other resources (Ravanera et al. 2009). Other analyses using these models of the division of work indicate that, in 2005 and 2010, average household incomes are highest in the shared-roles model, intermediate in the models involving the double burden, and lowest in the complementary-roles model (Beaujot et al. 2014). Thus, contrary to the theory that shared roles are an inefficient approach to the division of paid and unpaid work, couples in the shared-roles model have the highest average incomes.

Discussion

The greater variability and fluidity in family transitions and family patterns have brought considerable diversity in the families and family experiences of individual children, women, and men. This has been celebrated as evidence of less rigidity and more pluralism in family forms, but has also brought other forms of inequality in the earning and caring ability of families. It is noteworthy that, among families with children, 27.2 per cent are lone-parent and 12.6 per cent are step-parent families.

Some family trends have moved in the direction of reduced gender inequalities, especially a greater sharing of paid work, and towards men's greater participation in unpaid work. However, the differences remain large, and the inequalities are accentuated by the presence of young children.

Across family types, those with the highest poverty rates involve people who are unattached to families, and also lone-parent families. A significant portion of gender inequality in family settings derives from the higher likelihood of women being lone parents. Until age 50, women are more likely than men to be living with children, while men over age 40 are more likely to be living in a couple.

The patterns for entering marital or cohabiting unions have become more similar for women and men, with socio-economic status positively related to union formation for both men and women. There is also higher union dissolution among those with lower socio-economic status. The delays in union formation and parenthood have also benefited both men and women, who profit from a longer period of human capital accumulation. This also implies that those who form unions early, and especially those who have children early, are more likely to be disadvantaged. These patterns of early union and early parenthood affect women more than men.

In the context of diverse and less stable families, what directions should social policy take? In our view, equality across gender would especially benefit from the promotion of a model of gender equity in the division of both earning and caring. As a report for the United Nations Economic Commission for Europe proposes: "transforming gender norms is vital to the success of family policies" (United Nations 2013: 11). In particular, the two-income model should be promoted at the expense of the breadwinner model.

In the past, family policy followed the breadwinner model, with an emphasis on men's family wage and associated pension and health benefits, along with widowhood and orphanhood provisions in the case of the premature death of breadwinners. That is, the focus of family policy was on dealing with the loss of a breadwinner and supporting the elderly who were beyond working age. The challenge of current policy is to accommodate children who receive lower parental investments; young lone parents who have difficulty coping with both the earning and caring functions; the disadvantages faced by couples where neither has secure employment; and the difficulties of unattached persons at older labour force ages who have limited employment potential.

As we move towards a two-income model, we should discuss putting aside widowhood benefits, tax deductions for dependent spouses, and pension-splitting. Similarly, while income-splitting for taxation purposes promotes more equality across two-parent families with children, it provides no benefit to lone-parent families. These provisions, based on a breadwinner model, can promote dependency, especially for women. If the aim is to reduce inequality across all families and not just across two-parent families, then policies should take the form of the Child Tax Credit, the Working Income Tax Credit, and the Guaranteed Income Supplement, where the strongest transfers occur for those who have the lowest incomes.

Across family types, lone parents are especially disadvantaged. The widowhood and orphanhood provisions are clearly inadequate when the death of the breadwinner is infrequently the reason for lone parenthood. The policies promoting the employment of the lone parent are important, as are the child tax benefits and child-care subsidies tailored to families with lower income. There is also an "equivalent to spouse tax credit" that, for tax purposes, counts the first child of a lone-parent family as equivalent to a dependent spouse. We would propose that tax deductions for dependent spouses should be abolished and replaced, for all families, with a tax deduction for the first dependent child. That would leave room for an alternative like that used in Norway, such as doubling the child tax benefit for the first child of a lone-parent family.

We should promote a more egalitarian type of family that includes greater common ground between women and men in family activities. Just as policy has promoted the de-gendering of earning, we would argue for approaches that increase equal opportunity through the de-gendering of child care (Beaujot 2002). We should discuss the types of social policy that would further modernize the family in the direction of co-providing and co-parenting. Key questions here include parental leave and child care. Parental leave supports the continuing earning roles of parents, and public support for child care reduces the costs for working parents. The Quebec model for parental leave, including greater flexibility and a dedicated leave for fathers, has promoted the greater participation of men in parental leave (Beaujot et al. 2013). At the same time, the higher Quebec support for child care has promoted women's earning activities.

Questions for Critical Thought

1. How has the changing composition of family units brought more diversity among families? How has this diversity affected inequality by gender?
2. In what ways has gender inequality in the broader society affected gender inequality in family settings?
3. In what ways has gender inequality in family settings affected gender inequality in the broader society?
4. In terms of breadwinner and two-income models, which type of family should policy promote, and why?
5. Which family types are most disadvantaged? How does this relate to gender? Which social policies would be most helpful?

Notes

1. As elsewhere in the chapter, the married category includes cohabiting, while the unmarried category is neither married nor cohabiting.
2. These models are based on questions regarding time use in the previous week for the respondent and the respondent's spouse. Combining the paid and unpaid work hours for the couple, we first divided both the paid and unpaid work hours of respondent and spouse into three categories: respondent does more (over 60 per cent of the total), respondent does less (under 40 per cent of the total), and they do the same (40–60 per cent of the total). From the nine models in terms of a given partner doing more, the same, or less of both paid and unpaid work, we derived the five models as specified in Table 16.6. The 2010 questionnaire used categories rather than the exact number of hours for spouse's time use over the week. Using the respondents of given sexes and presence of children, we established point estimates from these categories.

Recommended Readings

Beaujot, Roderic. 2000. *Earning and Caring in Canadian Families*. Peterborough, Ont.: Broadview Press.

Doucet, Andrea. 2006. *Do Men Mother? Fathering, Care, and Domestic Responsibilities*. Toronto: University of Toronto Press.

Milan, Anne. 2013. "Marital status: Overview, 2011." Report on the Demographic Situation in Canada. Ottawa: Statistics Canada, Catalogue no. 91-209-X.

Statistics Canada. 2012. *Portrait of Families and Living Arrangements in Canada: Families, Households and Marital Status, 2011 Census of Population*. Ottawa: Statistics Canada, Catalogue no. 98-312-X2011001.

———. 2012. *Living Arrangements of Young Adults Aged 20 to 29*. Ottawa: Statistics Canada, Catalogue no. 98-312-X-2011003.

Vézina, Mireille. 2012. *General Social Survey: Overview of Families in Canada—Being a Parent in a Stepfamily: A Profile*. Ottawa: Statistics Canada, Catalogue no. 89-650-X—No. 002.

Recommended Websites

Canadian Policy Research Network, "Children, youth and families" tab:
http://www.cprn.org/

Families and Work Institute (FWI):
http://www.familiesandwork.org

Report on the Demographic Situation in Canada:
http://www.statcan.gc.ca/pub/91-209-x/91-209-x2014001-eng.htme

Vanier Institute of the Family:
http://www.vanierinstitute.ca/

References

Beaujot, Roderic. 2000. *Earning and Caring in Canadian Families*. Peterborough, Ont.: Broadview Press.

———. 2002. "Earning and caring: Demographic change and policy implications." *Canadian Studies in Population* 29: 195–225.

———. 2006. "Delayed life transitions: Trends and implications." In K. McQuillan and Z. Ravanera, eds, *Canada's Changing Families: Implications for Individuals and Society*, pp. 105–32. Toronto: University of Toronto Press.

———, Ching Du, and Zenaida Ravanera. 2013. "Family policies in Quebec and the rest of Canada: Implications for fertility, child care, women's paid work and child development indicators." *Canadian Public Policy* 39, 2: 221–39.

———, Jianye Liu, and Zenaida Ravanera. 2014. "Family diversity and inequality: The Canadian case." *Population Change and Life-course Cluster Discussion Paper* 1, 1. http://ir.lib.uwo.ca/pclc/vol1/iss1/7/.

Bohnert, Nora. 2011. "Examining the determinants of union dissolution among married and common-law unions in Canada." *Canadian Studies in Population* 38, 3–4: 93–104.

Coltrane, Scott. 1998. *Gender and Families*. Thousand Oaks, Calif.: Pine Forge Press.

Dagenais, Daniel. 2008. *The (Un)making of the Modern Family*. Vancouver: University of British Columbia Press.

Doucet, Andrea. 2006. Do Men Mother? *Fathering, Care, and Domestic Responsibilities*. Toronto: University of Toronto Press.

Gaudet, Stéphanie, Martin Cooke, and Joanna Jacob. 2011. "Working after childbirth: A life-course transition analysis of Canadian women from the 1970s to the 2000s." *Canadian Review of Sociology* 48, 2: 153–80.

Goldscheider, Frances, and Linda J. Waite. 1986. "Sex differences in the entry into marriage." *American Journal of Sociology* 92, 1: 91–109.

Hou, Feng, and John Myles. 2008. "The changing role of education in the marriage market: Assortative marriage in Canada and the United States since the 1970s." *Canadian Journal of Sociology* 33, 2: 337–66.

Kalmijn, Matthijs. 2013. "The educational gradient in marriage: A comparison of 25 European countries." *Demography* 50, 4: 1499–1520.

Kennedy, Sheela, and Elizabeth Thomson. 2010. "Children's experiences of family disruption in Sweden: Differentials by parent education over three decades." *Demographic Research* 23, 17: 479–508.

Kerr, Don, and Roderic Beaujot. 2015. *Population Change in Canada*, 3rd edn. Toronto: Oxford University Press.

Lappegard, Trude, Marit Ronsen, and Kari Skrede. 2009. "Socioeconomic differentials in multi-partner fertility among fathers." Paper presented at the International Population Conference of the International Union for the Scientific Study of Population, Marrakesh, 27 Sept.–2 Oct.

Marshall, Katherine. 2006. "Converging gender roles." *Perspectives on Labour and Income* 18, 3: 7–19.

———. 2011. "Generational change in paid and unpaid work." *Canadian Social Trends* 92: 13–24.

———. 2012. "Paid and unpaid work over three generations." *Perspectives on Labour and Income* 24, 1: 5–17.

Martin, Laetitia, and Feng Hou. 2010. "Sharing their lives: Women, marital trends, and education." *Canadian Social Trends* 90: 70–4.

Milan, Anne. 2013. "Marital status: Overview, 2011." *Report on the Demographic Situation in Canada.* Ottawa: Statistics Canada, Catalogue no. 91-209-X.

———, Leslie-Anne Keown, and Covadonga Robles Urquijo. 2011. *Families, Living Arrangements and Unpaid Work.* Ottawa: Statistics Canada, Catalogue no. 89-503-X.

Myles, John. 2010. "The inequality surge." *Inroads: The Canadian Journal of Opinion* 26: 66–73.

———, Feng Hou, Garnett Picot, and Karen Myers. 2007. "Employment and earnings among lone mothers during the 1980s and 1990s." *Canadian Public Policy* 33, 2: 147–72.

Oppenheimer, Valerie. 1988. "A theory of marriage timing." *American Journal of Sociology* 94, 3: 563–91.

Pew Research Center. 2010. *The Decline of Marriage and Rise of New Families.* A Social & Demographic Trends Report. Washington: Pew Research Center.

Ranson, Gillian. 2010. *Against the Grain: Couples, Gender, and the Reframing of Parenting.* Toronto: University of Toronto Press.

Ravanera, Zenaida R., and Roderic Beaujot. 2010. "Childlessness and socio-economic characteristics: What does the Canadian 2006 General Social Survey tell us?" Paper presented at the meetings of the Canadian Sociological Association, Montreal, June.

———, ———, and Jianye Liu. 2009. "Models of earning and caring: Determinants of the division of work." *Canadian Review of Sociology* 46, 4: 319–37.

———, Thomas K. Burch, and Fernando Rajulton. 2006. "Men's life course trajectories: Exploring the differences by cohort and social class." *Social Biology* 53, 3–4: 120–39.

——— and John Hoffman. 2012. "Canadian fathers: Demographic and socio-economic profiles from census and national surveys." In J. Ball and K. Daly, eds, *Father Involvement in Canada: Diversity, Renewal, and Transformation*, pp. 26–49. Vancouver: University of British Columbia Press.

——— and Fernando Rajulton. 2006. "Social status polarization in the timing and trajectories to motherhood." *Canadian Studies in Population* 33, 2: 179–207.

——— and ———. 2007. "Changes in economic status and timing of marriage of young Canadians." *Canadian Studies in Population* 34, 1: 49–67.

———, ———, and Thomas Burch. 1998. "Early life transitions of Canadian women: A cohort analysis of timing sequences, and variations." *European Journal of Population* 14: 179–204.

Richards, John. 2010. "Reducing lone parent poverty." C.D. Howe Institute Commentary No. 305. http://www.cdhowe.org.

Statistics Canada. 2008. *Earnings and Incomes of Canadians over the Past Quarter Century, 2006 Census.* Ottawa: Statistics Canada, Catalogue no. 97-563-X.

———. 2011. *Women in Canada.* Ottawa: Statistics Canada.

———. 2012. *Portrait of Families and Living Arrangements in Canada. Families, Households and Marital Status, 2011 Census of Population.* Ottawa: Statistics Canada, Catalogue no. 98-312-X2011001.

———. 2013. CANSIM Table 202-0804. Ottawa: Statistics Canada.

Sweeney, Megan. 2002. "Two decades of family change: The shifting economic foundations of marriage." *American Sociological Review* 67: 132–47.

Turcotte, Martin. 2007. "Time spent with family during a typical workday, 1986 to 2005." *Canadian Social Trends* 83: 2–11.

United Nations. 2013. *Report of the UNECE Regional Conference on ICPD beyond 2014: Enabling Choices: Population Priorities for the 21st Century.* United Nations, Economic and Social Council, Economic Commission for Europe ECE/AC.27/2013/2.

Vézina, Mireille. 2012. 2011 *General Social Survey: Overview of Families in Canada—Being a Parent in a Stepfamily: A Profile.* Ottawa: Statistics Canada, Catalogue no. 89-650-X—No. 002.

17 Sexual Orientation and Social Inequality*

Lorne Tepperman and Josh Curtis

Introduction

People with alternative sexual orientations have long faced discrimination, ridicule, exclusion, and even violence. In the past, many Canadians considered homosexual behaviour as problematic, but Canadian public opinion has since changed dramatically. Attitudes towards same-sex intimacy and marriage have become more liberal. Fewer Canadians now view homosexuality as immoral or criminal. In particular, people with homosexual relatives, friends, acquaintances, or workmates are more accepting of and knowledgeable about the homosexual community (Osterlund 2009). In Canada today, most people consider *anti*-homosexual behaviour a social problem, potentially violating hate laws and human rights codes. Understanding changes in Canadian attitudes to sexual orientation requires that we first consider some key terms.

Sexual Orientation

Sexual orientation is about sexual attraction, and homosexuality is a physical and emotional attraction to people of the same sex. Views vary about whether homosexuality is an act, a preference, or an identity, and whether it is occasional, regular, or permanent. The word "queer," though once thought offensive by gays, has been embraced by the gay community as an umbrella term for people who identify as anything other than hetero-normative (Hammers 2009; Walcott 2009). Because the term is still not comfortably accepted in the heterosexual community, here we refer to the non-heterosexual community by the acronym "LGBT," which stands for lesbian, gay, bisexual, transgender, or transsexual.

In early twentieth-century North America, most people saw sexuality as fixed, binary, and categorical. People were thought to be entirely heterosexual or entirely homosexual. However, by the 1940s and 1950s, the American sexologist Dr Alfred Kinsey showed that human sexual orientation lies on a continuum, between heterosexuality at one end and homosexuality at the other. Kinsey also noted that people often do not act on their sexual desires, for fear of censure or stigma (Gebhard and Reece 2008). Therefore, some people who think of themselves as heterosexual, but feel attracted to people of the same sex, may not act on this attraction. Similarly, people who

* Abridged from "Sexualities," Chapter 5 in *Social Problems: A Canadian Perspective,* 4th edition, by Lorne Tepperman and Josh Curtis. Toronto: Oxford University Press, 2016.

identify as homosexual, but feel attracted to people of the opposite sex, may not respond either, believing that they should be sexually consistent. Both behaviours reflect a misconception that people are *either* heterosexual *or* homosexual.

Numbering the Homosexual Population

Acceptance of homosexuality is widespread today, although the practice remains relatively rare. The gay community has long claimed to comprise 10 per cent of the population, but studies in the US, Great Britain, France, and elsewhere suggest lower levels. In the US, about 2–3 per cent of sexually active men and 1–2 per cent of sexually active women indicate that they are homosexual, but about 8 per cent report engaging in same-sex relations, and 11 per cent report some same-sex attraction at some time (Gates 2011). According to Statistics Canada (2004), 1.1 per cent of Canadians aged 18–59 report being homosexual and 0.9 per cent see themselves as bisexual. This research defined homosexuality in terms of identity rather than sexual behaviour. In Canada, as well, the proportion of people who report having a previous same-sex partner, or some same-sex attraction, is probably higher than the proportion who actually identify as homosexual. Researchers agree that homosexuals concentrate in larger numbers in some communities more than others, e.g., in cities rather than rural areas, and that they could represent as much as 10 per cent of the population in concentrated areas. Male homosexuals are more numerous than females, but the reasons for this are unknown.

One study (McCabe et al. 2009) shows the difficulties in enumerating the homosexual population. The researchers sought to assess rates of substance use and dependency among heterosexuals and homosexuals, using a US sample of 35,000 adults collected in the 2004–5 National Epidemiologic Survey on Alcohol and Related Conditions. The study showed that 2 per cent of the sample self-identified as lesbian, gay, or bisexual. However, 4 per cent reported at least one same-sex sexual partner, and 6 per cent reported same-sex attraction. Non-heterosexual orientation was associated with an above-average risk of substance use and dependence (Brubaker et al. 2009; Gillespie and Blackwell 2009), but the risks varied greatly, depending on how sexual orientation was defined. This underscores the problems in defining and measuring homosexuality (Uzzell and Horne 2006).

Coming Out

Sociologically, the most important step in the sexual "career" of an LGBT person is "coming out"—disclosing a previously secret sexual identity to family, friends, and others (Bogaert and Hafer 2009). Until people come out, they have difficulty fully entering the LGBT community. People's identities are linked to their social roles (Corrigan et al. 2009), and they cannot fully enter a new identity until they fully embrace the new role that it entails. Coming out is a statement people make as much to themselves as to others. Disclosure is important at the workplace, as well, but many worry it could harm their job security and relations with workers (DeJordy 2008; King et al. 2008).

LGBT people may delay coming out for years (Frost and Bastone 2008), and may even marry and raise children with someone of the opposite sex, as camouflage. They may come out in middle age after leading a secret life, which, needless to say, potentially disrupts relationships and the entire life they have constructed. Many grieve the loss of a "normal" life. Coming out requires courage, but courage is also needed to preserve secrecy (Wang et al. 2009). It also does not occur in a vacuum, affecting many others as well. For example, parents with a child who comes out may have to face a reality that may be incomprehensible and morally unacceptable to them (Potoczniak et al. 2009). Not all parents can immediately accept their children's sexual identities, and some never do (Potoczniak et al. 2009).

Attitudes and Laws

Most people conduct their sexual activities privately and, most of the time, people treat as private the sexual inclinations of others. Still, people generally are aware of homosexuality and prominent homosexuals. For example, a great many people knew and accepted Oscar Wilde (1854–1900), the celebrated Irish playwright, as being homosexual long before anyone charged and imprisoned him for this then-criminal offence. It was the disapproving father of Lord Alfred Douglas, Wilde's aristocratic lover, who discredited the playwright in court and made his homosexuality a public issue.

In contrast, the ancient Greeks considered sexual relations between two men as regular and "normal" (Harris 2009). Adult males, as citizens, were free to have sex with other males, including young boys. Moreover, behaviour that we would consider homosexual today was not assumed to indicate a person's sexual *identity* (Halperin 1990). The Greeks felt that sexual identity could not be inferred from sexual actions, making the line between homosexuality and heterosexuality even more blurred than it is today, and not an important social issue. In Christian Europe during the early Middle Ages, the Catholic Church largely ignored or tolerated homosexual behaviour, but hostility and resentment eventually surfaced. Thomas Aquinas (1225–74) saw homosexuality as unnatural and undesirable, and said Christians must condemn it (Richlin 2005; Findlay 2006).

Even today, homosexual behaviour is either illegal or highly regulated in many countries. Restrictive morality laws (e.g., in Singapore and Saudi Arabia) treat homosexual behaviour as morally wrong and threatening to society. Punishments can include imprisonment, whippings, even death. In some countries, laws only apply to homosexual relations between two men (Bahreini 2008; Whitehead 2010). Sri Lanka's law, for example, doesn't even mention lesbian relations (Ottosson 2009). Not all religions opposed homosexuality. It was not banned in Confucian philosophy, unless the family forbade it and unless it interfered with reproduction (Liu 2009; Rosker 2009). Still, there are restrictions on homosexual behaviour in Chinese communities like Singapore. Israel, by contrast, has shown support for homosexual citizens, despite opposition by Orthodox Jews.

Homosexual Culture

In recent decades, the perspectives on homosexuality among social scientists have also shifted. Sociologists changed from seeing homosexuality as learned social behaviour, instead suggesting biological causes and the influences of nature, not nurture (Engle et al. 2006). This promoted the belief that people should not criticize or try to change someone's sexual orientation, any more than they should someone's skin colour.

The dramatic changes in outlook owe a lot to gay rights activism. In the 1950s and 1960s, underground bars and clubs had begun to shape the experience of gays and lesbians, but mainstream culture viewed homosexuality as a deviant and dangerous lifestyle. Police regularly raided gay establishments and arrested patrons merely for being present. In June 1969, after yet another police raid in New York City, the homosexual community fought back, resisting as a group and thus starting the long battle for equal rights (Gillespie 2008). Toronto's gay and lesbian communities also had been routinely victimized by police harassment. In February 1981, during the "Toronto bathhouse riots," the city police raided four bathhouses and arrested 300 men. The community fought back, marking a turning point in Canada's LGBT movement. Eventually, the Ontario government recommended improvements in relations between police and the LGBT community. Everyone recognized the need to promote a peaceful and harmonious Toronto (Valverde and Cirak 2003).

These protests happened in the wake of previous movements promoting civil rights and women's rights, especially in the United States. Women and racial minorities taught gays and lesbians about social mobilization and the importance of *institutional completeness*—the creation of communities that are fully self-supporting and self-aware. In this way, minority *communities* survived and, in turn, minority *identities* survived.

LGBT and Native Communities

The Canadian Aboriginal approach offers a way to think about homosexuality that solves or avoids many problems. Researchers use the term "two-spirit" or "two-spirited" to refer to North American Aboriginal thinking about sexuality and gender (Stimson 2006). This term was devised by Native activists in 1990 to reconnect Aboriginal people with their cultural traditions. It signals a fluid sexual identity, moving beyond conventional binary distinctions between gay and straight, or male and female (Walters et al. 2006).

Unfortunately, Aboriginal people who identify as two-spirited not only encounter heterosexism and sexism but also often can experience racial discrimination from both society at large and queer identity movements (Walters et al. 2006). Nevertheless, the two-spirit concept is useful because it involves both sexual and gender identities, helps to unify the Aboriginal queer movement, and removes the need for separate gay, lesbian, bisexual, and transsexual organizations, thereby lending empowerment and support to many sexual causes (Meyer-Cook and Labelle 2004). People identifying as both Aboriginal and LGBT can face particular problems due to the intersection of these two minority statuses. This could explain why one study in Manitoba found that two-spirited Aboriginals were especially likely to experience serious illnesses, poverty, emotional distress, hostility, and violence.

Homophobia and Heterosexism

Homophobia—fear or hatred of homosexuals—takes various forms, including social distance (e.g., unwillingness to form a close friendship), stereotyping (e.g., the view that all gays are the same), bullying and harassment, and hate crimes (Balkin et al. 2009; Harris 2009; O'Higgins-Norman 2009). One feature of homophobia is essentialism: the belief that all homosexuals have fundamentally the same characteristics (Haslam and Levy 2006; Tomsen 2006). Psychologist Gordon Allport (1979 [1954]) concluded that this belief in group "essences" points to a prejudiced personality and a rigid cognitive style that rejects ambiguity or changeability.

Essentialist ideas about sexuality vary along two dimensions: "immutability" and "fundamentality." Immutability is the belief that one cannot change a personal feature. Fundamentality is the belief that a certain feature is central to personal character. Research finds that hostile attitudes towards lesbians and gay men are correlated positively with fundamentality but negatively with immutability. That is, people are more likely to hold anti-gay attitudes if they believe homosexuals have a choice in their sexual orientation, and if they believe homosexuality is an essential feature of a person, overshadowing all other qualities (Waldner et al. 2006).

Today's gay rights activists and gays themselves generally agree that being gay is inborn, that homosexuality is immutable (VanderLaan and Vasey 2008). This idea is also gaining acceptance from the heterosexual public. In addition, people are coming to realize that homosexuals vary as widely, socially and psychologically, as heterosexuals do. What, then, is the source of prejudice and discrimination?

Attribution-value theory maintains that people develop prejudices against groups seen as morally responsible for their stigmatized behaviour (Haider-Markel and Joslyn 2008). This theory suggests two causes of the behaviour: biological causes that people cannot control, and behavioural causes that they can control (Boysen and Vogel 2007). When a stigma is thought to be due to voluntary action, like AIDS or drug abuse, people are more likely to react with hostility than for a stigma seen as biological, like Alzheimer's disease. Therefore, homophobia develops when people believe that homosexuality is both socially harmful and a choice.

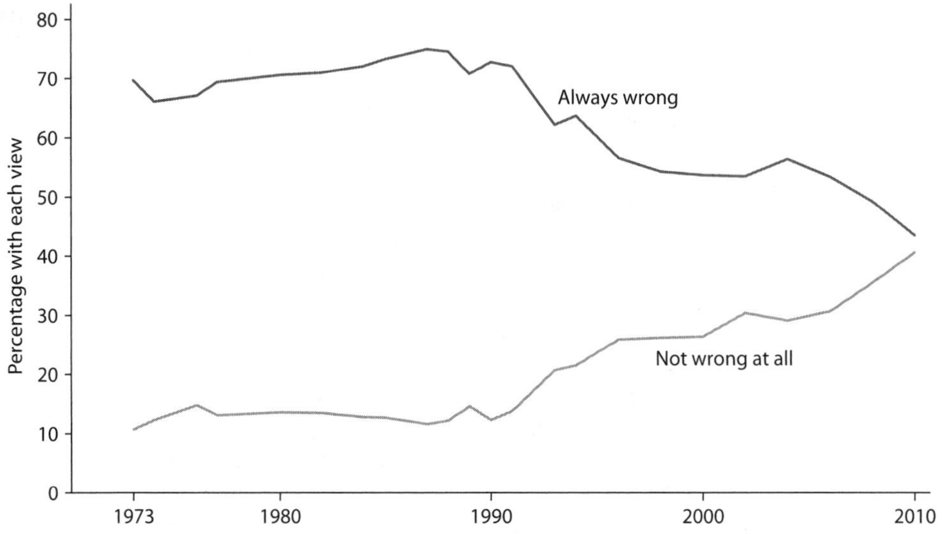

Figure 17.1 Stated Attitude to Sexual Relations between Two Adults of Same Sex

Source: Based on data from Tom W. Smith, "Public attitudes toward homosexuality." www.norc.org/PDFs/2011%20GSS%20Reports/GSS_Public%20Attitudes%20Toward%20Homosexuality_Sept2011.pdf, pp. 2, 3.

George Weinberg (1983 [1972]) introduced the term "homophobia" to denote the problem of anti-gay prejudice and stigma. Weinberg stressed the irrationality and harmfulness of this prejudice, which is no more acceptable than racism or sexism. However, the term has limitations, including the implication that, as a "phobia," anti-gay prejudice is based mainly on fear and is thus an irrational defence mechanism (Dermer et al. 2010: 327). This psychoanalytic approach does not account for social and historical changes in how homosexuality and heterosexuality are viewed. Gregory Herek (2004) uses three concepts to capture the most important sociological aspects of homophobia: (1) *sexual stigma*—the shared knowledge of society's negative regard for any non-heterosexual behaviour, identity, or community; (2) *heterosexism*—the cultural ideology that perpetuates sexual stigma; and (3) *sexual prejudice*—people's negative attitudes about sexual orientation. It is unclear whether recent declines in anti-homosexual attitudes resulted from changes in these ideas (see Figure 17.1).

Social Consequences of Homophobia

Same-Sex Families

Parents of homosexual or bisexual children can have difficulty accepting this reality, which can lead to harsh words, broken relationships, and depression. Parents often believe they know what is best for their children and fear that their children will miss valuable opportunities or suffer discrimination. Parents may even ask "Why did you do this to me?" even though the situation has little to do with them (Seidman 2002).

Fortunately, such attitudes have been changing, in part because same-sex families have altered the dominant view of what "normal" families are and do. The theoretical tradition, Queer Theory, seeks to deconstruct some of the false dichotomies shaping our lived experiences, which "give the impression of fixity and permanence where none 'naturally' exists" (Crawley and Broad 2008: 551). As shown in Figure 17.2,

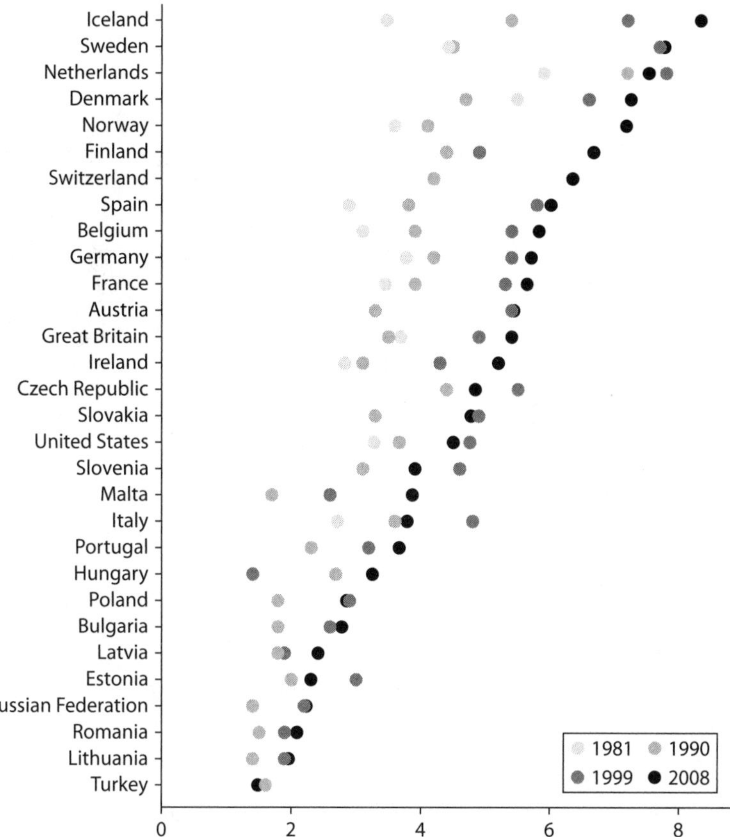

Figure 17.2 Change in Attitudes towards Homosexuality, European Values Survey

Note: Respondents were asked to rate on a scale from 1 to 10 whether homosexuality is "justifiable," where 1 means "never" and 10 means "always."
Source: www.washingtonmonthly.com/ten-miles-square/2012/05/changes_in_public_attitudes_to037429.php.

attitudes towards homosexuality have liberalized all over the Western world, as have attitudes towards same-sex families. A Canadian study used World Values Survey data to show that, for the period 1991 to 2006, acceptance of having gay neighbours rose from 70 per cent to 86 per cent, and that favourable views increased about homosexuals generally (Grabb 2010).

The existence of same-sex couples, especially those with children, forces us to re-examine preconceived ideas about the family. Same-sex parents, especially lesbian parents, behave much like heterosexual families, in that both practise child-centred parenting and both try to parent children using socially produced scripts. Lesbian families also have special strengths, e.g., being more likely than straight families to engage in egalitarian decision-making (Savin-Williams and Esterberg 2000; Moore 2009; Röndahl et al. 2009).

As more countries legalize gay and lesbian unions and as homosexuality becomes more broadly acceptable (Figure 17.3), the number of same-sex couples wishing to adopt and raise children should increase. Some have feared that children in homosexual households will also be homosexual, but there is no evidence to support this concern. Among LGBT families, parents'

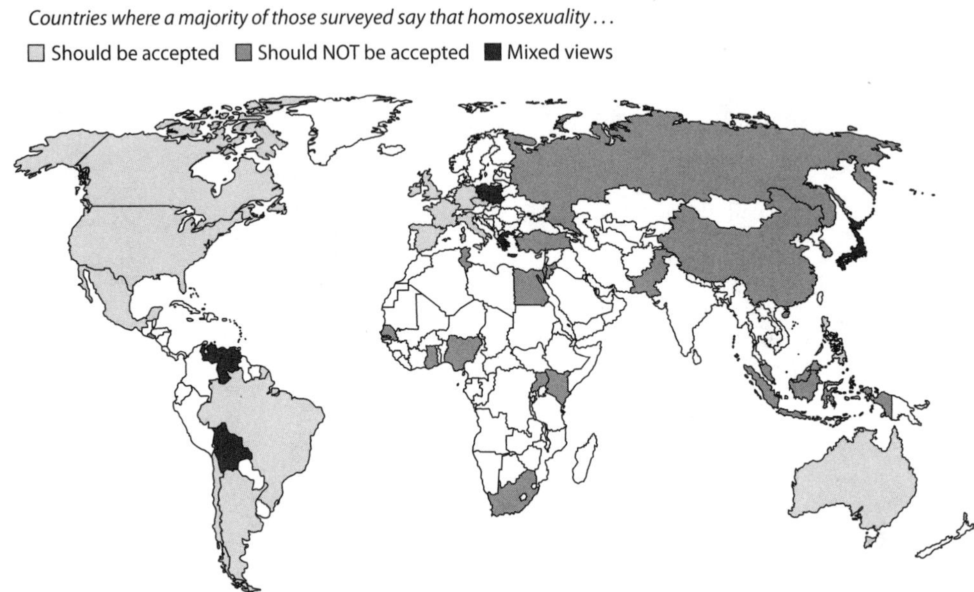

Figure 17.3 Societal Acceptance of Homosexuality

Note: The Pew Research Center surveyed 39 countries for its study of global attitudes towards homosexuality; countries shown in white on the map were not included in the survey.
Source: Accessed at: www.pewresearch.org/fact-tank/2013/06/04/global-snapshot-sex-marriage/.

sexual orientation does not determine children's gender development or increase the likelihood of psychological problems (Bos and Sandfort 2010; Volpp and Drescher 2011; Tasker 2005). Instead, the quality of family relationships is what influences the child's well-being (Patterson 2006). Many studies also indicate that gay and lesbian parents are as capable at child-rearing as heterosexual parents. Children of homosexual parents do not differ in behavioural and educational outcomes from children of heterosexual parents, and do not feel less loved or accepted (Mattingly and Bozick 2001).

Some critics claim that lesbian unions lack a father figure, which could affect the children's growth. Biblarz and Stacey (2010) argue that such criticisms conflate gender with other variables. For example, critics often cite data comparing heterosexual two-parent families to single-mother families, whereas there is no real difference between homosexual and heterosexual two-parent families. Many children with same-sex parents said they gained important insights about gender relations and more inclusive definitions of family as a result (Crowl et al. 2008; Biblarz and Stacey 2010).

More people now accept homosexuals, but attitudes about gay parents remain conservative, especially among older and rural people. Only about 20 per cent of Canadians surveyed in Miall and March's (2005) study, for example, supported homosexuals adopting children, compared with 92 per cent supporting adoption by traditional married couples.

Harassment and Hate Crimes

Schools are crucial for passing on attitudes about homosexuality. The classroom and the schoolyard are where most children experience their peers' attitudes about sexuality. Boys often learn homophobic terms at school, and often learn to use these homophobic terms against others. This commonly occurs before puberty, before boys gain an adult sexual identity and before they know much, if anything, about homosexuality. The early school experience is where powerful homophobic codes are first learned (Plummer 2001).

Not surprisingly, then, hate and fear persist about homosexuality. To combat this, Bill C-250 was passed in 2004, making it a crime to spread hate concerning sexual orientation. Homosexuals are now among the groups protected under the Criminal Code, a list that includes racial, religious, and ethnic minorities. Unfortunately, hate crimes continue. A study of gay and lesbian victims found that strangers in public places were the most likely to commit hate crimes. Victimization also occurs in other locales, perpetrated by neighbours, schoolmates, co-workers, and even relatives. Unfortunately, because people fear police bias or public disclosure of their sexual orientation, many are reluctant to report anti-gay crimes. They also worry that perpetrators will go unpunished anyway or take revenge.

Workplace Discrimination

Today companies often claim to support workplace diversity and equal opportunity for all minority employees, including gays and lesbians. However, not all companies keep their promises. Consequently, many gays and lesbians hide their sexual identity at work to avoid discrimination (O'Ryan and McFarland 2010). Most people want to keep their personal lives private, but reporting discrimination can lead to unwanted attention. Nevertheless, queer rights groups warn that if harassment goes unreported, nothing will change. Homosexuals subjected to discrimination have a difficult decision, but the law is on their side. Provincial human rights codes and the Canadian Charter of Rights and Freedoms make it illegal to discriminate based on sexual orientation.

Employers can improve the environment for homosexual workers through policies to prevent discrimination, the presence of LGBT employee networks, and a non-heterosexist organizational climate (Ragins et al. 2003). Conditions that can keep a person "in the closet" at work include a lack of racial and gender balance in work teams. Having a male supervisor also increases the likelihood that homosexual employees will stay in the closet, as people report more discrimination and homophobia under male supervisors. The military has been a particularly problematic workplace for LGBT minorities. Only recently have Canadian and US military services knowingly permitted enlistment by homosexual people and protected them against discrimination.

Solutions to the Homophobia Problem

One of the greatest social changes in recent years has been the establishment of sexual orientation as a personal domain legally protected from discrimination. In *Vriend v. Alberta*, a 1997 Supreme Court of Canada case, Delwin Vriend claimed that he was unjustly fired from his job because of his sexual orientation. This challenge was necessary because sexual orientation was not included under the Canadian Charter of Rights and Freedoms. Gay and lesbian activists in the early 1980s had sought specific inclusion in the Charter of Rights and Freedoms and in the Alberta Individual Rights Protection Act as a basis for legal protection against discrimination, but they had not succeeded.

Vriend successfully argued that sexual orientation is similar to the other grounds stated in section 15 of the Charter, including race, religion, sex, and ability/disability. Consequently, no one today can legally discriminate against homosexuals because of sexual orientation, just as they cannot discriminate against Blacks because of skin colour, or Jews or Muslims because of religion. Nonetheless, this important legal precedent is not as powerful as the explicit constitutional protection afforded other groups. More remains to be done to achieve true equality based on sexual orientation.

Increases in the direct personal experiences between LGBT people and other Canadians should improve relations. Some acts once considered sexually deviant, including homosexual acts, are now increasingly accepted in the general population. Today, homosexuals also have more recognition and inclusion, as governments show greater concern about fair and equal treatment for the LGBT minority. In 1997, the Quebec government sought to erase heterosexist attitudes prevalent in the provision of health and social services, highlighting problems for which LGBT people are vulnerable, including psychological distress, substance abuse, suicide, and HIV/AIDS. Officials focused especially on access to public services and organizations for the LGBT community, and established new policies and interventions. In 1999, the British Columbia government published a similar document, which focused on lesbian and gay experiences in the health-care system and included tips for health planners, policy-makers, and practitioners.

In 2001, the federal government, for the first time, included a question about same-sex relationships in the census. This census found 34,000 same-sex couples, a number that has probably increased with Canada's subsequent legalization of same-sex marriage. The 2001 census also revealed that 15 per cent of lesbian couples and 3 per cent of gay couples are raising children. These data are important for a number of reasons, including their potential influence on the extent of government funding that the LGBT community may receive in future. Equally important, however, is that they represent a significant element in the formal recognition and normalizing of homosexual people in Canada.

Questions for Critical Thought

1. In this chapter, we see how homosexuality has become normalized in Canadian society. What other types of sexual activity have also been normalized recently, and what were the processes behind this normalization?
2. Think about the double standard concerning the expected sexual behaviours of males and females. Has this double standard affected research on homosexuality?
3. Why is homosexual activity often limited to distinct parts of cities? What purpose might this geographic segregation serve?
4. How is the LGBT community similar to other stigmatized communities, e.g., Aboriginals, visible minorities, homeless people, or the unemployed? How is it different?
5. What are the possible problems and benefits of including transgender and transsexual people with the LGBT community?
6. Does sexuality get more attention than many other inequality issues? If so, why is this true? If not, why might some people think this is so?

Recommended Readings

Butler, Judith. 1990. *Gender Trouble: Feminism and the Subversion of Identity*. New York: Routledge.

Laqueur, Thomas W. 2003. *Solitary Sex: A Cultural History of Masturbation*. New York: Zone Books.

Laumann, Edward O., Stephen Ellingson, Jenna Mahay, Anthony Palk, and Yoosik Youm, eds. 2004. *The Sexual Organization of the City*. Chicago: University of Chicago Press.

Nelson, Claudia, and Michelle H. Martin, eds. 2004. *Sexual Pedagogies: Sex Education in Britain, Australia, and America, 1879–2000*. New York and Basingstoke: Palgrave Macmillan.

Recommended Websites

Egale Canada:
http://www.prevnet.ca/partners/organizations/egale-canada

Human Rights Watch:
https://www.hrw.org/topic/lgbt-rights

Parliament of Canada, Sexuality and Legal Rights:
http://www.parl.gc.ca/content/lop/researchpublications/prb0413-e.htm

Stanford Center on Poverty and Inequality, Sexual Orientation:
http://web.stanford.edu/group/scspi/issue_sexual_orientation.html

References

Allport, Gordon. 1979 [1954]. *The Nature of Prejudice*. Reading, Mass.: Addison-Wesley.

Bahreini, Raha. 2008. "From perversion to pathology: Discourses and practices of gender policing in the Islamic Republic of Iran." *Muslim World Journal of Human Rights* 5, 1 (article 2, electronic publication).

Balkin, Richard S., Lewis Z. Schlosser, and Dana H. Levitt. 2009. "Religious identity and cultural diversity: Exploring the relationships between religious identity, sexism, homophobia, and multicultural competence." *Journal of Counseling & Development* 87, 4: 420–7.

Biblarz, Timothy J., and Judith Stacey. 2010. "How does the gender of parents matter?" *Journal of Marriage and the Family* 72, 1: 3–22.

Bogaert, Anthony F., and Carolyn L. Hafer. 2009. "Predicting the timing of coming out in gay and bisexual men from world beliefs, physical attractiveness, and childhood gender identity/role." *Journal of Applied Social Psychology* 39, 8: 1991–2019.

Bos, Henry, and Theo Sandfort. 2010. "Children's gender identity in lesbian and heterosexual two-parent families." *Sex Roles* 62, 1–2: 114–26.

Boysen, Guy A., and David L. Vogel. 2007. "Biased assimilation and attitude polarization in response to learning about biological explanations of homosexuality." *Sex Roles* 57, 9–10: 755–62.

Brubaker, Michael D., Michael T. Garrett, and Brian J. Dew. 2009. "Examining the relationship between internalized heterosexism and substance abuse among lesbian, gay, and bisexual individuals: A critical review." *Journal of LGBT Issues in Counseling* 3, 1: 62–89.

Corrigan, Patrick W., Jonathon E. Larson, Julie Hautamaki, Alicia Mathews, Sachi Kuwabara, Jennifer Rafacz, Jessica Walton, Abigail Wassel, and John O'Shaughnessy. 2009. "What lessons do coming out as gay men or lesbians have for people stigmatized by mental illness?" *Community Mental Health Journal* 45, 5: 366–74.

Crawley, S., and K.L. Broad. 2008. "The construction of sex and sexualities." In J. Holstein and J. Gubrium, eds, *Handbook of Constructionist Research*, pp. 545–66. New York: Guilford Press.

Crowl, Alicia, Soyeon Ahn, and Jean Baker. 2008. "A meta-analysis of developmental outcomes for children of same-sex and heterosexual parents." *Journal of GLBT Family Studies* 4, 3: 385–407.

DeJordy, R. 2008. "Just passing through—Stigma, passing, and identity decoupling in the work place." *Group & Organization Management* 33, 5: 504–31.

Dermer, Shannon B., Shannon D. Smith, Korenna K. Barto. 2010. "Identifying and correctly labeling sexual prejudice, discrimination, and oppression." *Journal of Counseling and Development* 88, 3: 325–31.

Engle, M.J., J.A. McFalls Jr, B.J. Gallagher III, and K. Curtis. 2006. "The attitudes of American sociologists toward causal theories of male homosexuality." *American Sociologist* 37, 1: 68–76.

Findlay, James F., Jr. 2006. "Glimpses of recent history: The National Council of Churches, 1974–2004." *Journal of Presbyterian History* 84, 2: 152–69.

Frost, David M., and Linda M. Bastone. 2008. "The role of stigma concealment in the retrospective high school experiences of gay, lesbian, and bisexual individuals." *Journal of LGBT Youth* 5, 1: 27–36.

Gates, G.J. 2011. "How many people are lesbian, gay, bisexual and transgender?" The Williams Institute. http://williamsinstitute.law.ucla.edu/wp-content/uploads/Gates-How-Many-People-LGBT-Apr-2011.pdf (accessed 6 Jan. 2013).

Gebhard, Paul H., and Michael Reece. 2008. "Kinsey and beyond: Past, present, and future considerations for research on male bisexuality." *Journal of Bisexuality* 8, 3–4: 175–89.

Gillespie, Wayne. 2008. "Thirty-five years after Stonewall: An exploratory study of satisfaction with police among gay, lesbian, and bisexual persons at the 34th Annual Atlanta Pride Festival." *Journal of Homosexuality* 55, 4: 619–47.

——— and Roger L. Blackwell. 2009. "Substance use patterns and consequences among lesbians, gays, and bisexuals." *Journal of Gay & Lesbian Social Services: Issues in Practice, Policy & Research* 21, 1: 90–108.

Grabb, Edward. 2010. "Cultural convergence or divergence? Reassessing the debate over Canadian and American values." The 2010 James E. Curtis Memorial Lecture, 21 Oct.

Haider-Markel, Donald P., and Mark R. Joslyn. 2008. "Beliefs about the origins of homosexuality and support for gay rights: An empirical test of attribution theory." *Public Opinion Quarterly* 72, 2: 291–310.

Halperin, David M. 1990. *One Hundred Years of Homosexuality and Other Essays on Greek Love*. London and New York: Routledge.

Hammers, Corie. 2009. "Space, agency, and the transfiguring of lesbian/queer desire." *Journal of Homosexuality* 56, 6: 757–85.

Harris, Angelique C. 2009. "Marginalization by the marginalized: Race, homophobia, heterosexism, and 'the problem of the 21st century'." *Journal of Gay & Lesbian Social Services* 21, 4: 430–48.

Haslam, Nick, and Sheri R. Levy. 2006. "Essentialist beliefs about homosexuality: Structure and implications for prejudice." *Personality and Social Psychology Bulletin* 32, 4: 471–85.

Herek, Gregory M. 2004. "Beyond 'homophobia': Thinking about sexual prejudice and stigma in the twenty-first century." *Sexuality Research and Social Policy* 1, 2: 6–24.

King, E.B., C. Reilly, and M. Hebl. 2008. "The best of times, the worst of times—Exploring dual perspectives of 'coming out' in the workplace." *Group & Organization Management* 33, 5: 566–601.

Liu, Ting. 2009. "Conflicting discourses on boys' love and subcultural tactics in Mainland China and Hong Kong." *Intersections: Gender and Sexuality in Asia and the Pacific* no. 20. intersections.anu.edu.au/issue20/liu.htm.

McCabe, Sean Esteban, Tonda L. Hughes, Wendy B. Bostwick, Brady T. West, and Carol J. Boyd. 2009. "Sexual orientation, substance use behaviors and substance dependence in the United States." *Addiction* 104, 8: 1333–45.

Mattingly, Marybeth J., and Robert N. Bozick. 2001. "Children raised by same-sex couples: Much ado about nothing." Paper presented to Southern Sociological Society conference.

Meyer-Cook, Fiona, and Diane Labelle. 2004. "Namaji: Two-spirit organizing in Montreal, Canada." *Journal of Gay & Lesbian Social Services* 16, 1: 29–51.

Miall, C., and K. March. 2005. "Open adoption as a family form: Community assessments and social support." *Journal of Family Issues* 26, 3: 380–410.

Moore, M.R. 2009. "New choices, new families: How lesbians decide about motherhood." *Journal of Marriage and the Family* 71, 5: 1350–2.

O'Higgins-Norman, James. 2009. "Straight talking: Explorations on homosexuality and homophobia in secondary schools in Ireland." *Sex Education: Sexuality, Society and Learning* 9, 4: 381–93.

O'Ryan, Leslie W., and William P. McFarland. 2010. "A phenomenological exploration of the experiences of dual-career lesbian and gay couples." *Journal of Counseling & Development* 88, 1: 71–9.

Osterlund, Katherine. 2009. "Love, freedom and governance: Same-sex marriage in Canada." *Social & Legal Studies* 18, 1: 93–109.

Ottosson, Daniel. 2009. *State-sponsored Homophobia: A World Survey of Laws Prohibiting Same Sex Activity between Consenting Adults*. International Lesbian and Gay Association (ILGA): 14.

Patterson, Charlotte J. 2006. "Children of lesbian and gay parents." *Current Directions in Psychological Science* 15, 5: 241–4.

Plummer, David C. 2001. "The quest for modern manhood: Masculine stereotypes, peer culture, and the social significance of homophobia." *Journal of Adolescence* 24, 1: 15–23.

Potoczniak, Daniel, Margaret Crosbie-Burnett, and Nikki Saltzburg. 2009. "Experiences regarding coming out to parents among African American, Hispanic, and white gay, lesbian, bisexual, transgender, and questioning adolescents." *Journal of Gay & Lesbian Social Services: Issues in Practice, Policy & Research* 21, 2–3: 189–205.

Ragins, Belle Rose, John M. Cornwell, and Janice S. Miller. 2003. "Heterosexism in the workplace: Do race and gender matter?" *Group and Organization Management* 28, 1: 45–74.

Richlin, Amy. 2005. "Eros underground: Greece and Rome in gay print culture, 1953–65." *Journal of Homosexuality* 49, 3–4: 421–61.

Röndahl, Gerd, Elisabeth Bruhner, and Jenny Lindhe. 2009. "Heteronormative communication with lesbian families in antenatal care, childbirth and postnatal care." *Journal of Advanced Nursing* 65, 11: 2337–44.

Rosker, Jana S. 2009. "The golden orchid relationships: Female marriages and same-sex families in the Chinese province of Guangdong during the 19th century." *Socialno Delo* 48, 1–3: 99–110.

Savin-Williams, R.C., and K.G. Esterberg. 2000. "Lesbian, gay, and bisexual families." In D.H. Demo, K.R. Allen, and M.A. Fine, eds, *Handbook of Family Diversity*. New York: Oxford University Press.

Seidman, Steven. 2002. *Beyond the Closet: The Transformation of Gay and Lesbian Life*. New York: Routledge.

Statistics Canada. 2004. *The Daily*, 15 June.

Stimson, Adam. 2006. "Two spirited for you: The absence of 'two spirit' people in western culture and media." *West Coast Line* 40, 1: 69-81.

Tasker, Fiona. 2005. "Lesbian mothers, gay fathers, and their children: A review." *Journal of Developmental Behavioral Pediatrics* 26, 3: 224–40.

Tomsen, Stephen. 2006. "Homophobic violence, cultural essentialism and shifting sexual attitudes." *Social & Legal Studies* 15, 3: 389–407.

Uzzell, David, and Nathalie Horne. 2006. "The influence of biological sex, sexuality and gender role on interpersonal distance." *British Journal of Social Psychology* 45, 3: 579–97.

Valverde, Mariana, and Miomir Cirak. 2003. "Governing bodies, creating gay spaces: Policing and security issues in 'gay' downtown Toronto." *British Journal of Criminology* 43, 1: 102–21.

VanderLaan, D.P., and P.L. Vasey. 2008. "Born gay: The psychobiology of sex orientation." *Archives of Sexual Behavior* 37, 4: 673–4.

Volpp, Serenayuan, and Jack Drescher. 2011. "What has the lesbian family structure taught us about child rearing by gay adults?" *Clinical Psychiatry News* 39, 3: 7.

Walcott, Rinaldo. 2009. "David Rayside, queer inclusions, continental divisions: Public recognition of sexual diversity in Canada and the United States." *Labour/Le Travail* 64: 227–30.

Waldner, L.K., H. Martin, and L. Capeder. 2006. "Ideology of gay racialist skinheads and stigma management techniques." *Journal of Political & Military Sociology* 34, 1: 165–84.

Walters, K.L., T. Evans-Campbell, J. Simoni, T. Ronquillo, and R. Bhuyan. 2006. "'My spirit in my heart': Identity experiences and challenges among American Indian two-spirit women." *Journal of Lesbian Studies* 10, 1–2: 125–49.

Wang, Frank, Herng-Dar Bih, and David Brennan. 2009. "'Have they really come out?' Gay men and their parents in Taiwan." *Culture, Health and Sexuality* 11, 3: 285–96.

Weinberg, George. 1983 [1972]. *Society and the Healthy Homosexual*. New York: St Martin's Press.

Whitehead, A.L. 2010. "Sacred rites and civil rights: Religion's effect on attitudes toward same-sex unions and the perceived cause of homosexuality." *Social Science Quarterly* 91, 1: 63–79.

Young, Lisa, and Keith Archer, eds. 2002. *Regionalism and Party Politics in Canada*. Toronto: Oxford University Press.

C. Age

18 Age and Social Inequality

Neil Guppy

Over the course of our lives we all share the same chronology of aging—age one, age two, . . . age 20, . . . age 42, and so on. Therefore, as an inequality dimension, age is different from our biological sex or our ethnic roots, because the latter are inequality dimensions that we generally share with only a limited number of others: for age, we all move through the same sequence of years, but for sex and ethnicity we do not all experience what life is like in each category. Age is also unlike inequality dimensions such as income or education, because we have no control over the chronological aging process, whereas we have at least limited control over how much schooling or income we accrue.

So, if we all share the experience of moving through age categories, how is age connected to inequality? First, social expectations shape the rights and opportunities we have at different ages. Clear age-related normative or cultural schemas enable or constrain our behaviour—from voting, to renting a car, to obtaining seniors' discounts on movie tickets. Second, age cohorts, or generations, also find their opportunities or privileges shaped by the relative size of their own and other generations, as well as by the period of history in which they were born. For example, health care is a demand of the elderly and schooling a need of the young. In societies with a disproportionate number of elderly people consuming public health dollars, there can be a strain on the funding available to support the young via public education. This is the current situation in Canada, where a large baby-boom generation, born principally in the 1950s, is now reaching senior age. As another example, think about how different your life might have been if you had been born in the 1920s and subsequently found yourself in your twenties involved with the horrors of World War II.

Notice in the above statements that one focus is on what individuals can or cannot do, as in renting a car or getting cheaper movie admission. In contrast, the second focus highlights cohorts or age groups. The latter concept centres on the collective distribution of individuals, as opposed to the rights or opportunities of any one individual. In effect, aging happens to individuals as they grow older, but aging also happens among individuals as age cohorts receive disproportionate advantages or disadvantages (Dannefer 2003). For individuals in some cohorts, it is easier to establish entry-level careers, and the advantages of that initial job security accumulate over the lifetime of those cohort members. Such a generation can then find itself far better off, as a group, than members of other age cohorts who, in a bad economy, struggle even to find a job, let alone a promising career in their early labour market experiences (Gill, Knowles, and Stewart-Patterson 2014). For some cohorts, "advantages accumulate"; for other generations, "disadvantages persist."

Inequality, Individual Age, and Age-Grading

In more traditional societies, prior to the rise of industrialization, the elderly were more powerful. Older people not only controlled property, but also had the experience and knowledge necessary to ensure group prosperity, as exemplified in decisions about the timing of nomadic movements, the planting of crops, or the seasonality of hunting and trapping. Industrial societies differ; the power and subsequent social standing of the elderly are lower in these societies. This is a function of two primary factors. Rapid social change has diluted the value of traditional wisdom: think smartphones and most elderly people. Older people also now typically do not live with their children, so their control of family resources is diminished. Certainly, respect for the elderly varies cross-culturally, but, overall, the social standing of the elderly is lower in modern industrial societies, where retirement can marginalize older people from key institutions, especially economic production, and where geographic mobility often fractures close family ties.

Age-Grading

Beyond respect for the elderly, an individual's age defines many rights and privileges. For instance, obtaining a driver's licence before the age of 16 is impossible, and many large car rental firms will not lease vehicles to anyone under 25. Age also shapes our working lives. Provincial wage laws often contain clauses allowing employers to pay lower minimum wages to workers under 18 than to adults. Both a Canadian Human Rights Tribunal and the Federal Court of Appeal recently upheld the right of Air Canada to require two of their pilots, George Vilven and Neil Kelly, to retire at age 60 even though both wanted to continue working. Minimum wage laws and mandatory retirement provisions may seem unfair, because one or two years of age make little difference in how individuals can function. However, just as with the right to drive or to vote, age may be used as an automatic trigger affecting both wages and democratic input.

In these examples, age is an inflexible decision-making criterion limiting what we can or cannot do. This process, often called "age-grading," can seem unfair. Determining access to rights and privileges based solely on age, regardless of individual merit or ability, runs against the premise of equal opportunity and merit-based decision-making. Using chronological age to fix a date in our lives at which point we can, or cannot, be counted on to act reliably or responsibly makes a huge assumption. However, as we have just seen, this applies to a host of formal rights, ranging from voting or running for public office, to serving in the armed forces or drinking alcohol.

On the face of it, these examples highlight age discrimination. Someone is being denied something solely on the basis of age. The Canadian Charter of Rights and Freedoms (s. 15[1]) explicitly legislates against discrimination based on age:

> Every individual is equal before and under the law and has the right to the equal protection and equal benefit of the law without discrimination and, in particular, without discrimination based on race, national or ethnic origin, colour, religion, sex, age or mental or physical disability.

Section 15(1) states that using age to decide the rights and privileges of individual Canadians is discriminatory. How, then, can age be used as an automatic trigger effectively barring someone from obtaining a driver's licence at the age of 14 or voting in provincial elections at 15? Similarly, if someone is not hired for a job simply because she/he is too young or too old, this would clearly seem to contravene the Charter, as would forcing an airline pilot to retire at age 60.

Typically, when age-grading determines rights and privileges, the argument is that these practices place reasonable limits on people's activity. In obtaining a driver's licence or renting a car, for example, age-grading is justified as a reasonable criterion to invoke by citing the higher accident rates of younger drivers. Age restrictions on buying alcohol are similarly justified. Alcohol consumption impairs judgment, so that restricting access to alcohol for young people is viewed as reasonable.

Unequal access is thought to be justified in these circumstances, because the infringement of individual rights and privileges is beneficial for the whole of society. In special circumstances, the rights of the individual are given lower priority than the rights of the community, and this too is reflected in the Canadian Charter, which guarantees "the rights and freedoms set out [herein] subject only to such *reasonable limits* prescribed by law as can be *demonstrably justified* in a free and democratic society" (section 1, emphasis added).

Sometimes age can be a barrier to rights and privileges, not because of laws but through social convention. In the workplace, for example, mere seniority often takes precedence over performance or merit in determining pay (e.g., in teaching), layoffs (e.g., last hired, first fired), or promotions (e.g., where loyalty is often rewarded). Less formally, such activities as leaving home, having children, or investing in retirement savings plans may be constrained by age. This constraint occurs because people come to believe that these and other behaviours typically should take place at certain stages in the life course, but not at others.

Whether resulting from legal regulations or social norms, such age-based delineations of human behaviour are primarily social creations. In other words, while aging can be partly understood as a physiological process, it is also a social process. Age, in this latter sense, is used as a socially constructed criterion for classifying and ranking people (age-grading), a process with significant implications for generating and sustaining patterns of inequality.

Dependency and Aging

Age-grading is also related to dependency (Turner 1988). The judgments others hold of us, or the entitlements others grant us, depend on whether we are believed to be responsible citizens, capable of making rational decisions about the welfare of ourselves and others. Ariès (1962 [1960]) has argued that childhood, as a recognizable feature of the life course, only began to emerge in European societies through the late 1600s. Children came to be seen as a group with special needs who were especially susceptible to poverty, vagrancy, and social and moral corruption. Various child protection laws were thus enacted at this time to safeguard children. Debate continues over children's rights. In the Canadian justice system, for example, policy-makers have attempted to grant special rights to young offenders (aged 12 to 17), while also requiring young persons to be accountable for their actions.

The elderly, as a group, are also frequently defined as dependent. Partially, this is a consequence of degenerative diseases, such as Alzheimer's, that erode an individual's ability to function independently (see Gilmour and Park 2006). However, the social arrangements of work and family are also consequential for relations of dependency or independence. As discussed below, retirement and pension arrangements may make it difficult for many Canadians, especially women, to support themselves economically in their later years. Many elderly people also find that their traditional support systems—their children and other relatives—no longer live in close enough proximity to provide substantial care.

Aging and dependency are also related to other inequality dimensions. Figure 18.1 shows this by displaying the average total income that

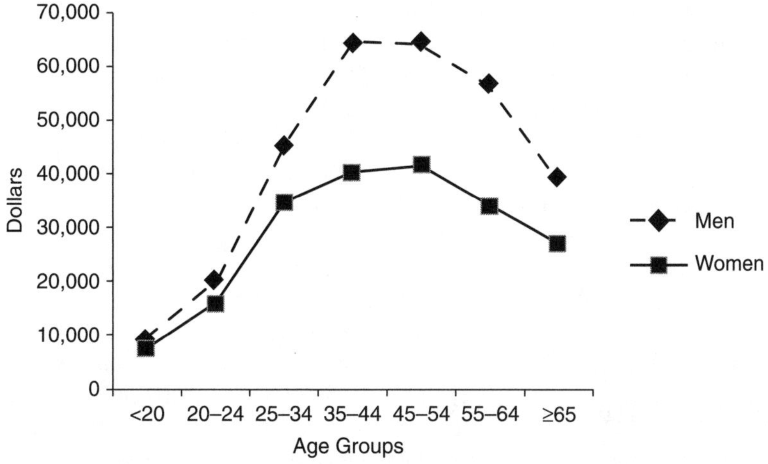

Figure 18.1 Average Total Individual Income by Age Group and Sex, 2011

Source: Author calculations from Statistics Canada, CANSIM Table 202-0407.

Canadians receive over the life course. The graph shows that in our years of dependency, i.e., in our early years and our later years, incomes are significantly lower than during the middle years of our lives. This is true for both men and women, although the figure also emphasizes the familiar inequality pattern of lower incomes for women compared to men.

Dependency, and the intersection of age and gender, can be seen in other ways. One manifestation of this is portrayed in Figure 18.2, which graphs the likelihood of women and men, 65 and over, living with a partner or living alone (excluded here are people living in seniors homes, with relatives, etc.). In their senior years, men are much more likely than women to live with

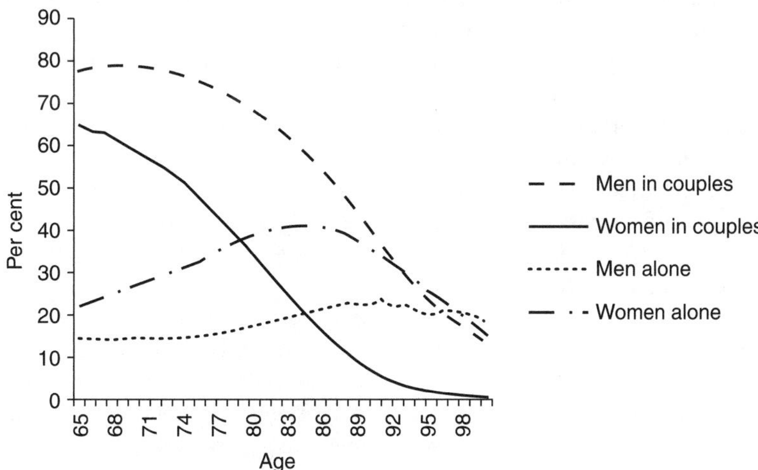

Figure 18.2 Living Arrangements of Canadian Seniors by Family Type and Age

Source: Statistics Canada, Census of Population, 2011.

a partner, married or common-law. Women are almost twice as likely as men to experience living alone as a senior. Both of these outcomes are largely a function of women living longer than men and women being younger than men when they marry. Consequently, as men become older and more dependent, they typically have partners who can care for them, whereas most women are not so fortunate.

Inequality and the Collective Distribution of Individuals

Inequality also occurs between generations. The reason that rights and opportunities differ across generations typically has to do with two interrelated issues: differential cohort power and historical period. The baby-boom generation of the 1950s is one example of a cohort with differential power. People born between 1948 and 1962 represent the largest collective group in Canadian history. During no other equivalent time span were as many Canadians born. The sheer number of people makes this group a powerful cohort, as I will show below. Historical period also factors into the power of this generation, coming as they did just after World War II. The subsequent period of history saw, at least in North America, a long economic boom. Broadly, it has been sweet times for the baby-boom generation. In contrast, as noted above, being born in the 1910s and 1920s placed that generation of people in a historical period where many families struggled to survive through the Great Depression of the 1930s and then many individuals suffered death, severe injury, or loss of loved ones during World War II. The importance of historical period is easy to comprehend from this example.

The concept of cohort power also can be illustrated using the spring 2015 federal budget, which again highlights intergenerational justice. In 2015, young people born in the 1990s were completing school but experiencing some of the toughest economic times in recent decades. They also often were carrying large student debts and facing steep housing costs as they contemplated starting families. For example, in 2014 the unemployment rate for those aged 20 to 24 was among the highest in Canadian history, running at double that of workers 25 and older (author's calculations, CANSIM Table 282-0002). Therefore, we might have expected a federal budget that offered younger Canadians some government support. The 2015 budget, however, was labelled as a senior-friendly financial plan by most media outlets, including the Canadian Broadcasting Corporation and the *Globe and Mail*. The budget targeted tax adjustments, tax savings, and tax credits for the elderly, with next to nothing provided directly for the young.

The reasons for this generational imbalance are easy to understand, especially once we recall that this was a pre-election budget. First, seniors make up a sizable and growing proportion of the voting age population. For example, in 1971, there were over 2 million more people of ages 15–24 than those aged 55–64; by 2015, however, there were about 150,000 more people aged 55–64 than those of ages 15–24. Second, seniors are also much more likely than the young to vote. Consider that, in the federal election of 2011, 38.8 per cent of 18–24-year-olds voted, compared to 71.5 per cent of 55–64-year-olds (Elections Canada 2012). Consequently, any federal political party is likely to propose legislation that favours the elderly over the young, simply because older people are more numerous than the young, and also more likely to vote.

If this generational imbalance was restricted solely to the 2015 federal budget, the issue would be fairly minor. However, the 2015 budget is illustrative of a larger pattern of intergenerational imbalance that has occurred because of the differential cohort power of generations. The distribution of individuals is such that, overall, there are far more seniors these days. Even though these seniors are relatively well-off compared to previous generations of seniors and to the current younger generations, the seniors are nevertheless receiving much more than their share of rewards and privileges. The Conference Board of Canada recently demonstrated this imbalance in noting that the share of total income, both before and after taxes, going to younger Canadians versus older Canadians has been deteriorating for every year from 1984 to the present (Gill, Knowles, and Stewart-Patterson 2014; for a more nuanced view for the young, see Galarneau, Morissette, and Usalcas 2013). The old are getting richer and the young poorer. Put another way, the income gap between the young and the old is now greater than the income gap between women and men.

Table 18.1 provides a second illustration of generational inequity. It shows how government spending has shifted over the last three decades or more. The top panel of the table focuses on government spending that goes strictly to the elderly, while the bottom panel highlights spending that largely benefits younger generations. Between 1976 and 2011, the amount of inflation-adjusted money going to programs supporting the elderly increased by $58 billion, while government spending for the young declined by $15 billion. To be fair, as noted above, the proportionate size of the elderly population has increased, and so some spending rise for the elderly is logical because of this demographic shift in aging. Kershaw (2015) argues, however, that this spending allocation is disproportionate, effectively squeezing younger generations unfairly. Not only has this spending gap widened, but consider also that the federal debt has been expanding over this period, and it is the younger generations who will have to pay the debt, not the baby boomers. Couple this with the environmental debt that continues to grow, both through climate change and through human-created toxicity and pollution, and the challenges to generational justice are even higher.

Government spending allocations that support the elderly also occur at the municipal level. Most transit systems, for example, provide discounts for seniors, as do most community and recreational centres. Furthermore, and at even greater cost, most municipalities discount property taxes for the elderly. In effect, these subsidies for seniors are picked up by younger generations—someone has to pay taxes. A good question is: Why were senior subsidies ever introduced in the first place? The answer is that

Table 18.1 Change in Government Spending by Age Group, 1976 and 2011

Government Spending Programs	$ Change 1976 to 2011 (2011 dollars)
Elderly	
Medical care for 65+	32,476,000
Old Age Security	343,000
Canada/Quebec Pension Plan	25,254,000
Total for older generation	58,073,000
Younger Generations	
Child-care services	2,982,000
Parental leave	1,872,000
Family income support	–4,472,000
K–12 education	–18,985,000
Post-secondary education	2,449,000
Medical care for <45	680,000
Total for younger generations	–15,475,000

Source: Author's calculations from Kershaw (2015); constant 2011 dollars to account for inflation.

they came about as urban planners and politicians tried to address poverty among older citizens, a problem that was quite widespread in the 1960s and 1970s. However, as shown below, seniors' poverty has abated significantly in recent decades. Generally, the across-the-board, flat senior benefits from property tax discounts or subsidized rates are no longer needed; even so, because of the sizable elderly voting constituency, only a brave municipal politician would change this pattern, although it is a change that is drastically needed (Kitchen 2015). Moving from universal property tax discounts to income or wealth-based subsidies seems prudent, given that some seniors still live in poverty but that an expanding population of seniors do not. There is a danger here, though, in that targeted benefits may be economically wise but politically vulnerable, open to being scaled back in periods of austerity (Myles 2013).

Pensions and Income Security among the Elderly

One of the sharpest and most progressive changes in inequality in Canada has been the rapid decline over the last few decades in the poverty rates for elderly people, whether living alone or living as couples. In important ways, this is a good news story that has not been matched by subsequent policy changes.

Poverty among the elderly, as noted previously, was an issue of national concern in the 1970s and 1980s. It was an especially acute problem for women, who on average live significantly longer than men. Table 18.2 shows, however, a significant drop in poverty rates for seniors over time. In 1976, the rate of poverty for seniors was double that of children under age 18, but by 1994 and even more so by 2011, the seniors' rate had dropped below the poverty rate for children. In 2011, about 5.2 per cent of seniors lived in poverty, compared to 8.5 per cent of children. Of course, you can read the table as though the poverty rates are too high for both children and the elderly, and advocates for each will do that, but it is important to recognize the positive change that has occurred among elderly Canadians. Life for seniors has dramatically improved between 1976 and 2011, although room for improvement remains.

Inside this good news lurks some bad news. The poverty rate for elderly Canadians has fallen in large measure because of the government spending changes noted in Table 18.1 and especially the changes related to pensions. While all Canadians who have been in the labour force receive some Canada/Quebec Pension Plan (C/QPP) coverage, this funding is especially important for the many Canadians who work in jobs without employer-provided pension plans. What is perhaps most important, however, is how the C/QPP is funded.

Like other income security programs for the elderly, including health care and Old Age Security (OAS), C/QPP is funded on a pay-as-you-go basis. For health care and OAS the funds come from tax revenues; for C/QPP the funds come from payroll contributions, which is a form of tax paid by employers and employees. The important point is that today's workforce is paying the taxes that support the income payments going to today's seniors. I exaggerate here slightly because, for pensions, there has been a surplus saved from payroll contributions, but this surplus will run out very soon unless some drastic changes are made (Wolfson 2013).

The C/QPP was introduced in 1966. Fifty years later it needs fixing. The fixes are necessary for four basic reasons. First, Canadians are living longer, and so the Plan not only has to cover more people, but also has to cover those people for more years. Second, the surplus currently in the Plan is woefully inadequate to cover the expectations of this growing population of eligible recipients. Third, the Plan is supported by the payroll contributions of current members of the labour force, and this group is shrinking in size. Fourth, the maximum benefit payable to recipients is currently $12,000 per year, which is totally inadequate as a low-income threshold to support a person in the present day.

Table 18.2 Canadians with Low Income, by Age, Family Type, and Year

	1976	1994	2011	
	%	%	%	Number
Seniors (over age 65)	29.0	8.6	5.2	249,000
Senior couples	15.0	2.3	1.5	50,000
Senior unattached females	68.1	25.6	16.1	149,000
Senior unattached males	55.9	13.3	12.2	50,000
Children (under 18)	13.4	16.3	8.5	571,000

Source: Author calculations from CANSIM Table 202-0802. Low income based on standardized 1992 basket of goods: Statistics Canada definition.

The C/QPP was introduced to help ensure Canadians had adequate incomes in old age. It was part of a package of welfare reforms introduced by government to support Canadian citizens. However, since its inception in 1966, the role of governments in supplying income support has been questioned. One alternative is that individuals ought to plan for their own future and not rely on government. In an ideal world, where everyone received a good employment income, this might work. In Canada, however, many people have low family incomes even though one or more family members work full-time, full-year. Furthermore, millions of Canadians don't have jobs where employers provide pensions (Drolet and Morissette 2014). And where, one might ask, are those without pensions located? Again, the intersectionality of inequality shows itself—employees in the bottom 10 per cent of wage earners are significantly less likely than those in the top 10 per cent of wage earners to have a work-based pension plan (Drolet and Morissette 2014; Messacar and Morissette 2015).

Conclusions

Canada's seniors now compose 15 per cent of the population, but this cohort will grow to around 25 per cent of the population by 2030. One in four Canadians will be 65 or over in the near future. The median age of Canadians was 25 in 1965 but will be 42 by 2042. The aging of Canada will present two fundamental problems. First, the responsibility for economic growth will fall to a proportionately smaller and smaller contingent of Canadians. Second, the economic and health-related security needs of the elderly cohort will rise. One solution to both issues is delayed retirement, so that older workers remain in the labour force longer and thus contribute to economic growth, tax revenue, and stronger pensions. A possible corollary of this is that higher-paid, more highly educated workers may opt more frequently to work past age 65; such a development would increase inequality in Canada, as people in lower-paying manual jobs choose to retire or are unable to continue working past age 65. This could also exacerbate the growing inequality between age cohorts, since older workers earn more in wages and salaries than their young counterparts.

Older people will not only be more numerous in Canada than they have been in the past, but because they vote more frequently they will have increasing political clout. This may mean, as the 2015 federal budget illustrated, even more political priority given to the aged and the affluent.

These possibilities suggest that more thoughtful and prudent long-term policy planning is required. The social practices we use in regard to age-grading and dependency will have to change. As well, the democratic forces at play between age cohorts must be dealt with in ways that provide for the well-being of both younger and older Canadians.

Questions for Critical Thought

1. Disentangle the influences of age, period, and cohort in explaining to someone how the social processes of aging relate to income inequality.
2. What would be the key planks in a political platform that focused on public policies you could support to deal with issues of aging and inequality?
3. What are the pros and cons of an argument that said the welfare of the aged ought to be left to individuals and their families?
4. What does it mean to say that, for cohorts, advantages accumulate or disadvantages persist?

Recommended Readings

Ferraro, Kenneth, and Tetyana Pylypiv Shippee. 2009. "Aging and cumulative inequality: How does inequality get under the skin?" *Gerontologist* 49, 3: 333–43.

Myles, John. 2013. "Income security for seniors: System maintenance and policy drift." In K. Banting and J. Myles, eds, *Inequality and the Fading of Redistributive Politics*. Vancouver: University of British Columbia Press.

Novak, Mark, and Lori Campbell. 2010. *Aging and Society: A Canadian Perspective*, 6th edn. Toronto: Nelson

United Nations, Department of Economic and Social Affairs, Population Division. 2013. *World Population Ageing 2013*. ST/ESA/SER.A/348.

Vincent, John, Chris Phillipson, and Murna Downs. 2006. *The Futures of Old Age*. London: Sage.

Recommended Websites

CARP (formerly Canadian Association of Retired Persons):
http://www.carp.ca/

Generation Squeeze:
http://www.gensqueeze.ca/

National Seniors Council:
http://www.seniorscouncil.gc.ca

World Health Organization, Population Aging:
http://www.who.int/ageing/en/

References

Ariès, P. 1962 [1960]. *Centuries of Childhood: A Social History of Family Life*. R. Baldick, trans. New York: Alfred A. Knopf.

Dannefer, Dale. 2003. "Cumulative advantage/disadvantage and the life course: Cross-fertilizing age and social science theory." *Journal of Gerontology* 58B, 6: S327–S337.

Drolet, Marie, and René Morissette. 2014. *New Facts on Pension Coverage in Canada*. Ottawa: Statistics Canada, Catalogue no. 75-006-X.

Elections Canada. 2012. *Estimation of Voter Turnout by Age Group and Gender at the 2011 Federal General Election*. Ottawa: Elections Canada.

Galarneau, Diane, René Morissette, and Jeannine Usalcas. 2013. "What has changed for young people in Canada?" *Insights on Canadian Society*. Ottawa: Statistics Canada, Catalogue no. 75-006-X.

Gill, Vijay, James Knowles, and David Stewart-Patterson. 2014. *The Bucks Stop Here: Trends in Income Inequality between Generations*. Ottawa: Conference Board of Canada.

Gilmour, Heather, and Jungwee Park. 2006. *Dependency, Chronic Conditions and Pain in Seniors*. Ottawa: Statistics Canada, Health Statistics Division.

Kershaw, Paul. 2015. "Population aging, generational equity, and the middle class." Vancouver: Generation Squeeze. http://www.gensqueeze.ca/evidence_base.

Kitchen, Harry. 2015. "No seniors' specials: Financing municipal services in aging communities." *Institute for Research on Public Policy* 51 (Feb.).

Messacar, Derek, and René Morissette. 2015. *Employer Pensions and the Wealth of Canadian Families*. Ottawa: Statistics Canada, Catalogue no. 75-006-X.

Myles, John. 2013. "Income security for seniors: System maintenance and policy drift." In K. Banting and J. Myles, eds, *Inequality and the Fading of Redistributive Politics*. Vancouver: University of British Columbia Press.

Statistics Canada. 2011. *Living Arrangements of Seniors*. Ottawa: Statistics Canada, Catalogue no. 98-312-X.

Turner, Bryan. 1988. "Ageing, status politics and sociological theory." *British Journal of Sociology* 40, 4:588–606.

Wolfson, Michael. 2013. *Not-So-Modest Options for Expanding the CPP/QPP*. IRPP Study 41. Montreal: Institute for Research on Public Policy.

19 Disability and Social Inequality in Canada

Kim Shuey, Andrea Willson, and Katherine Bouchard

Introduction

The inequalities experienced by persons with disabilities have become major issues for policy-makers, scholars, and social activists. Historically, individuals with disabilities have struggled to live full, dynamic, and autonomous lives because of stigma, discrimination, and numerous social, environmental, and institutional barriers. Social institutions, cultural beliefs, and everyday practices shape the lives of people with disabilities across the life course, affecting their personal relationships, educational attainment, employment opportunities, and economic security. Academic research, work by grassroots organizations, and personal accounts all demonstrate the serious need for people with disabilities to be granted greater inclusion and participation in society.

There are many identifiable challenges to achieving this goal. The first is the long-standing labelling of people with disabilities—through legislation, policies, and practices—as either sick, resource-consuming, or functionally limited (Quinn 1995). Within sociology, Erving Goffman (1963) wrote in the 1960s about the physical stigma and stigma of character experienced by persons with physical or mental disabilities, and how possessing "non-normal" traits can result in disqualification from full social acceptance. Negative attitudes and behaviours spread fear, perpetuating oppressive stereotypes that become embedded in social institutions and raise barriers to employment, educational attainment, housing, and social relationships for persons with disabilities. Anti-stigma programs in the media, schools, and the workplace, and a greater awareness among health-care professionals, are necessary to counteract these problems.

Unfortunately, as we discuss below, Canadians living with a disability or multiple disabilities are more likely to face unemployment, involuntarily work part-time, earn lower wages, and have lower educational attainment than their counterparts without disabilities. Additional factors, including disability severity, age of onset and duration (and the associated experience of aging *with* versus aging *into* disability), and the intersection of disability with other sources of disadvantage such as social class and race/ethnicity, can exacerbate the degree of inequality associated with disability.

In this chapter, we review issues related to disability and inequality in Canada. First, we consider the changing perceptions of disability and the importance of the social model of disability as articulated by disability theorists. Then we provide a detailed depiction of the prevalence of disability in Canada. We also discuss how the social model of disability has shaped disability policy, and address the fact that social oppression is embedded in social institutions, leading to important social inequalities for persons with disabilities.

Our approach is informed by a life course perspective, which encourages a holistic view of social phenomena. This perspective considers the macro level of the state and historical forces of social change, the meso level of organizations such as workplaces and the family, and the micro level of individual experience and perception. This allows us to highlight how individual outcomes are shaped by accumulated experiences across the entire life course and by the ever-changing social context within which people live and age (Elder et al. 2003). Inequality is generated within the context of social forces such as history, state policy, culture and norms, and social institutions, which in turn differentially shape the risks and opportunities available to individuals across their life course according to their social location. Therefore, the experiences of people with disabilities change over time as they age, varying from one birth cohort to the next and within birth cohorts.

The discussion to follow incorporates demographic evidence describing trends in levels of inequality in education and employment, as well as results from qualitative studies that provide rich detail on the experiences of living with a disability. As with other social phenomena, both quantitative and qualitative approaches to understanding disability and inequality in Canada are necessary to help us to address new questions and design better policies.

Defining and Theorizing Disability

Here we provide a brief introduction to the theoretical developments that have led to the emergence of disability studies as an academic discipline (see Oliver and Barnes 2012; Thomas 2007). Most important is the distinction between approaches focusing primarily on the individual (the "individual" or "medical model" of disability) and those focusing on society and the social environment ("social" models of disability). Individual and medical approaches have historically dominated academic understandings of disability; however, beginning with the important work of Oliver (1983) that emerged from the disabled people's movement of the 1970s, a social interpretation of disability arose, reinforced by the radical policy agenda of equality and full participation formulated by disability activists (Priestley 2005). Oliver (1983, 1996) emphasized that an individual or medical model sees the "problem" of disability as an issue of individual functional limitations and psychological consequences. Responsibility and accountability lie with the individual, in what is often referred to as "personal tragedy theory" (Oliver 1983). This approach cultivates an image of suffering, passivity, and dependence, in which people with disabilities must rely on personal social networks and state assistance through welfare benefits and services. As a sub-approach within this model, psychological perspectives emphasize individual adaptation and coping strategies; they consider the influence of impairment and societal stigma on personal identity, and often stress the need for assistance from health and social welfare professionals. Overall, this framework suggests that the social inequalities experienced by people with disabilities arise from the physical condition of the body and remain primarily an individual problem (Priestley 2005).

In contrast, social models of disability were developed in part to address the historical oppression and segregation of disabled individuals (Barnes 2012). These models emerged from numerous intellectual and political initiatives by activists associated with social movements of the 1970s, including the Independent Living Movement in the US and the Union of Physically Impaired Against Segregation in the UK. The models redefine disability, highlighting the importance of language. They point to the need to distinguish *impairment*, considered a medically classifiable condition, from *disability*, which concerns the social disadvantages experienced as a result of impairment (Barnes et al. 1999). Within a social model, disability refers to all the factors that create restrictive circumstances for people living with impairments; these range from individual prejudice and institutional discrimination, to inaccessible transportation and housing, to exclusionary practices in educational and employment institutions. From this perspective, disability is understood to exist through transactions *between* individuals and their environments, rather than *within* the individual alone.

The social model comprises various explanations of the processes through which inequalities occur. For example, there is the cultural approach in anthropology, which emphasizes the social construction and devaluing of human differences. Dominant social groups are portrayed as "normal" in cultural representations found in the media, in the prevailing ideology, and in the values and actions of policy-makers and other powerful individuals. In contrast, disability is labelled abnormal and deviant (Abberley 1993; Ingstad and Reynolds-Whyte 1995; Young 1990). Because dominant social values vary across societies and over time, cultural studies suggest that disability lacks a universal character and cannot be understood as a universal concept.

A distinct but related variation of the social model emphasizes structural causes, linking the exclusionary practices of social institutions to the requirements of a capitalist system of production. Rooted in Marxism, this model suggests that excluding people with impairments from social institutions, including the labour market, stems from the needs of industrial capitalism. People with disabilities are marginalized as workers because they are seen as more expensive for the company and less capable of meeting organizational demands; in other words, their labour cannot be exploited for profit (Abberley 1987; Hahn 1988; McFarlin et al. 1991; Robert and Harlan 2006).

While these two examples of social models of disability differ in whether the mode of production influences cultural representations of disability, or vice versa, they share an emphasis on the social rather than the individual causes of disability (Priestley 2005). Such models have had major influences on our understanding of disability, underscoring how society itself can create and perpetuate the oppression of people with disabilities (Oliver 1996). Within these models, social inequality for people with disabilities is seen as "a collective experience of discrimination and injustice, rather than as a personal tragedy affecting only individuals" (Priestley 2005: 380). Disability is seen as a social category associated with minority status, and is central to activism and political action aimed at eliminating oppression based on this status. In contrast to individual models, which point to assistance, adaptation, and coping as responses to supposed individual deficits, social models emphasize discrimination, exclusion, and oppression, and the need to protect human rights, increase inclusion, and enable full participation for people with disabilities (Priestley 2005).

Prevalence of Disability in Canada

The most recent profile of people with disabilities in Canada comes from the 2012 Canadian Survey on Disability (CSD) conducted by Statistics Canada. Given the theoretical discussion above, it is important first to understand how disability is defined and measured in practice. The definition of disability employed by the CSD comes from the World Health Organization's (WHO) conceptualization of "disability." The WHO uses "disability" as an umbrella term that subsumes impairments, daily activities and social participation, and limitations to personal activities. Disability is recognized as a complex and dynamic phenomenon, embodying more than health problems, and reflecting the interaction between components of the body and the self, on the one hand,

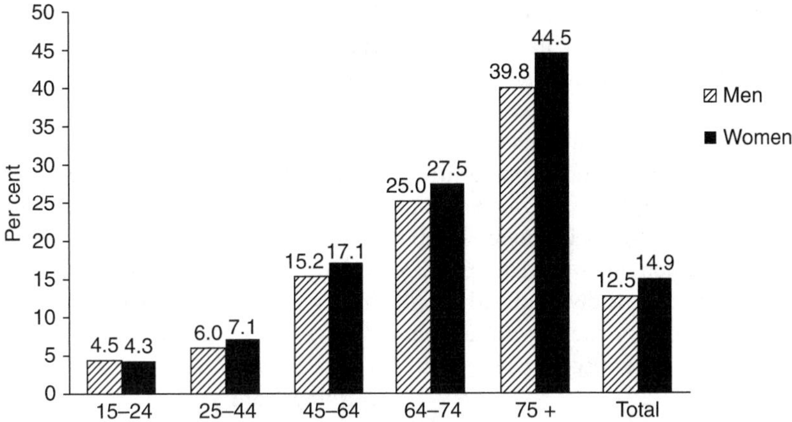

Figure 19.1 Prevalence of Disability in Canada by Age and Gender, 2012

Source: Arim (2015).

and social structures and environmental barriers, on the other hand (WHO 2015). Recognizing the importance of applying a social model of disability, Canadian scholars have revised the questions used in national disability surveys over time. The most recent 2012 CSD incorporates a more complete definition based on a social model (Arim 2015). Questions in the CSD assessed the presence of 10 types of impairment: seeing, hearing, mobility, flexibility, dexterity, pain-related, learning, developmental, mental health-related, and memory. However, the CSD did not consider someone to have a disability if, despite reporting some impairment, daily activities were not limited (Canadian Survey on Disability 2012).

Based on data from the 2012 CSD (Arim 2015), an estimated 3.8 million individuals, representing 14 per cent of Canadians aged 15 and over, have an impairment that limits their daily activities. As shown in Figure 19.1, the prevalence of disability varies by age and gender, from a low of 4 per cent among women aged 15–24 to a high of 45 per cent among women aged 75 and older. The average age of the onset of difficulty associated with a main impairment was 43. Thirteen per cent of Canadians with disabilities reported a disability that existed at birth. The vast majority of adult Canadians with disabilities reported more than one type of disability. Just over half were classified as having a mild or moderate disability, 23 per cent had a severe disability, and 26 per cent a very severe disability.

Disability across the Life Course

Numerous disciplines study the social aspects of disability, each taking a different approach and asking different questions. These include sociology, geography, health studies, gender studies, education, political science, and history. In addition, scholars in the growing field of disability studies employ interdisciplinary tools to understand the social determinants of the experience of disability. Another useful interdisciplinary approach comes from the work of life course scholars. Life course research emerged in the 1970s, partly in response to enormous social changes occurring at the time, including the growing diversity among North Americans and the greater variations in the ways people live their lives (Elder et al. 2003).

The life course perspective provides guiding paradigmatic principles that emphasize the intersection of individual lives with social structures and social change. Of particular relevance for disability are themes that highlight (1) the timing and duration of disability experiences for subsequent life chances and consequences; (2) the accumulation of risks and opportunities across the life course; and (3) the recognition that the life course is shaped by social policies and institutions that are unique to a particular time and place and that structure individual pathways and trajectories in domains such as education and employment. Below we discuss these three points in more detail.

First, the timing principle suggests that the same event can affect individuals differently and can change the meaning of the event, depending on when it occurs in history and in the individual life course (George 1993). The age and social conditions in which an individual experiences disability onset, as well as the length of time living with disability, are crucial considerations. There are many determinants of disability, including biological and genetic factors, along with social determinants such as employment and working conditions, socio-economic status, education, stress exposure, race and gender relations, access to health services, and health practices. As an example, advances in medicine, technology, and education in recent decades mean that persons acquiring impairments early in life now experience greater longevity. This has increased the proportion of people who are aging with impairments, relative to the proportion who first acquire impairments later in life (Putnam 2002). Consequently, researchers sometimes distinguish between aging with disability and aging into disability. Age of onset is important because it determines the set of social roles, institutions, and cultural norms that an individual needs to navigate. The life course of those who acquire impairments at birth or early in life is influenced by the intersection of their disabilities with educational institutions and youth culture and is therefore different from the life course of those who acquire impairments in middle age or later (Putnam 2002). The timing of impairment is important because it represents the point of entry into disabling social institutions and culture, and partly determines the form of the systematic barriers and oppression people encounter.

The timing of disability onset and the duration of disability relate to the second life course theme, which concerns the accumulation of risks and opportunities. A key explanation for the unfolding of inequality across the life course comes from theories of cumulative dis/advantage. These theories suggest that inequality is generated by a process in which initial relative advantages deriving from a more privileged social location lead to growing inequality among individuals or groups over time (Dannefer 2003; DiPrete and Eirich 2006; Merton 1968; O'Rand 1996). This accumulative process involves an unfolding series of opportunities for those in advantaged circumstances, along with an unfolding sequence of risk factors for those who exist in disadvantaged conditions. The latter group includes individuals whose future life chances are negatively influenced by exposure to disability. For example, a child growing up with an impairment acquired early in life may experience lower educational opportunity, which in turn creates disadvantages in employment and other life contexts, such as neighbourhood location; in addition, all of these disadvantages increase the chances of exposure to various stressors that can undermine future health and well-being (see, for example, Pearlin et al. 2005).

The third life course theme concerns social policies and institutions, and their roles in addressing the risks associated with an individual's progression through important life events, including disability. Disability policies are considered part of broader welfare state regimes, but these regimes differ across countries and time periods, especially in their level of generosity and support for various groups of citizens. Welfare state policies originally developed as a form of collective risk management to protect individuals from external risks and to help manage expected and unexpected circumstances associated with income loss, illness, and disability across the life course (Giddens 1999; O'Rand 2000, 2003). Over time, the generosity of these policies can be affected by many factors, including periodic economic crises or the election of conservative governments that perceive welfare state policies as the causes rather than the solutions to social problems. The 1980s, for example, saw rollbacks in government social support, as well as the shifting of responsibility for managing life course risks from the state to the individual (Barnes and Mercer 2010; O'Rand and Shuey 2007). State policies shape the broader context within which individuals live their lives, including individuals with disabilities. We turn now to a discussion of disability policy in Canada and other countries.

Policy Context, Policy Change

The social model of disability, as noted earlier, considers the ways that society can act as both a disabling force and a source of oppression. This model was developed most notably by Oliver in the 1980s, but its roots are traceable to Karl Marx's materialist approach, which connects social oppression to the mode of production. The history of the capitalist system of production is marked by fundamental changes in the organization of work, especially during the eighteenth and nineteenth centuries. These changes transformed the economic system from a "rural-based, co-operative system where individuals contributed what they could to the production process, to an urban, factory-based system, one organized around the individual waged labourer" (Oliver and Barnes 2012: 55). One consequence was that people with impairments were excluded from paid work, on the assumption that they were unable to keep up with the demands of the emerging factory-based system. People with impairments were once relatively easily incorporated into the economic and social life of rural communities, but were increasingly viewed as problems who, if they were not left to fend for themselves, were subjected to isolation and segregated within families or in residential institutions, including special schools, workhouses, and asylums (Morris 1969; Topliss 1979 in Oliver and Barnes 2012).

The social model of disability has important implications for social policy. Whereas the medical or individual model of disability stresses individual adaptation and coping strategies, and may entail exclusion and isolation within separate institutions, the social model requires change in the political, social, and physical environments in order to provide people with disabilities the opportunity to participate fully in society (Rioux and Samson 2006). Social inclusion thus becomes a public responsibility. Government policy and intervention should promote the removal of barriers and the adaptation of physical and social environments to assist individuals with physical or mental impairments. These initiatives include, for example, modifications in the workplace, accessibility and barrier-free designs incorporated into building codes, and adapted curricula within school systems. A second concern is advancing a human rights model of disability policy, which targets the systemic factors that prevent equal participation in society and generate economic and social disadvantages based on disability status (Rioux and Samson 2006).

Before the 1980s, policies at the national and international levels primarily reflected a medical model of disability that concentrated on prevention and rehabilitation. Rioux and Samson (2006) note that the shift to a social model of disability first appeared in 1982, with the United Nations (UN) establishment of international policy guidelines following the adoption of the World Programme of Action concerning Disabled Persons. These guidelines paved the way for recognition by the world's policy-makers that people with disabilities have the same rights as others to participate fully in society. In 1993, the UN adopted the Standard Rules on the Equalization of Opportunities for Persons with Disabilities, and the next decade and a half saw further strengthening of the UN's promotion of equal human rights for people with disabilities. In 2006, these efforts culminated in the Convention on the Rights of Persons with Disabilities, a human rights treaty that aimed to "promote, protect, and ensure the full and equal enjoyment of all human rights and fundamental freedoms by all persons with disabilities, and to promote respect for their inherent dignity" (United Nations 2006: 4). Governments participating in the Convention monitor programs, collect data, and report on efforts to create more inclusive and accessible societies. In Canada these requirements are satisfied in part by the Canadian Survey on Disability, the results of which are provided at different points in this chapter.

Canadian policies, for the most part, mirror the shifts in international policy guidelines established and developed by the UN as part of the international movement supporting disability rights (McColl et al. 2010). Canada does not currently have overarching national disability legislation, however, unlike such countries as the UK, Australia, and, most notably, the US. In 1990, the US established the Americans with Disabilities Act, which encourages the employment of individuals with disabilities and makes it illegal to discriminate in hiring, promotion, and employment. In contrast, the Canadian approach involves multiple human rights and anti-discrimination laws, regulations, and programs, which operate at both the federal and provincial levels. These combined initiatives promote greater accessibility for people with disabilities in education, employment, housing, and transportation, and also provide income support, health services, and tax relief (McColl et al. 2010). Fundamental rights and protections for persons with disabilities, in regard to such issues as employment equity and income support, are contained in three key pieces of legislation enacted in the 1980s: the Charter of Rights and Freedoms (1982), the Canadian Human Rights Act (1985), and the Employment Equity Act (1986). Despite the lack of overarching disability legislation in Canada (except in Ontario, which introduced the Accessibility for Ontarians with Disabilities Act in 2005), many observers feel that the current suite of federal and provincial statutes provides an adequate framework for promoting inclusion and integration and preventing discrimination against persons with disabilities (McColl et al. 2010).

Inequality in Education

> It is hard to overrate the importance of helping youngsters avoid being held back or placed in Special Education, because avoiding these placements makes a tremendous difference in their long term life chances. (Entwisle et al. 1997: 18)

Despite Canada's system of policy protections, the inequality experienced by persons with disabilities across many aspects of life remains a major issue for policy-makers and social activists. The education system offers an important illustration. The history of education for persons who have physical and mental impairments early in the life course is a story of devaluation and segregation. During the last half of the twentieth century, children with disabilities were socialized to have low expectations and aspirations regarding education and work, with their educational needs met by a segregated special education system (Barnes et al. 1999). In recent decades, disability activists, parents' groups, educators, and academics have increasingly challenged these notions, arguing that the segregated special education system should be abolished because of the lower expectations, social isolation, and inferior academic skills that it provides. Some policy-makers, parents, and professionals have countered that the existing system has advantages. These include the potential for specialized teacher training, flexible curricula, a more accessible environment, and regular contact with disabled peers, all of which could promote a more positive self-identity among children with disabilities (Barnes et al. 1999).

The debate over separate versus integrated schooling for students with disabilities has generated a large body of research on the mechanisms of educational stratification, including tracking or streaming, socialization practices, and stigmatization. Powell (2003) has discussed how sorting mechanisms within the education system constrain the achievement of students with disabilities. Early in life, gatekeeping educational policies apply bureaucratic rules, tracking systems, and sorting processes that create and sustain forms of social inequality across the life course (Powell 2003). These constraints begin with the "discovery" of children with impairments, or with difficulties in meeting normative learning and behavioural requirements of schools. These children are then selected for special education, removed from the regular classroom, and/or tracked into differentiated curricula. Those in lower tracks face restricted academic achievement, stigmatization, and dissimilar classroom cultures. These limiting factors, in turn, reduce the expectations of teachers, parents, and peers, and lower self-efficacy and feelings of competence among students (Ansalone 2001; Powell 2003).

Similar stigmatization and reduction of expectations occur for special education students, who have been identified as having educational needs that cannot be met through regular instructional practices. The needs of special education students are addressed through academic accommodations and/or modified educational programs. Their options range from full-day education placement in a regular class, with additional resources provided to support the student, to placement in a full-time special education class where the student remains segregated from the rest of the school. The proportion of students receiving special education assistance in Canada has increased in recent years. In Ontario, for example, the proportion increased from about 14 per cent of secondary students in 2001 to 23 per cent in 2013 (People for Education 2013). Research suggests that mobility out of special education is limited in part by lower expectations and a self-fulfilling prophecy (Eder 1981). The life course perspective highlights the negative implications of labelling and stigmatization on the future trajectories of work and identity for this increasing proportion of students. Research suggests that, compared to other Canadians, people with a disability took fewer courses at school, took longer to complete their schooling, and were more likely to discontinue their education (Arim 2015). In addition, nearly 40 per cent felt excluded at school, and almost one-third experienced bullying.

A snapshot of the overall picture of educational attainment in Canada shows significant differences between persons with and without disabilities. Based on data from the 2012 CSD, Arim (2015) finds that about 16 per cent of persons with disabilities are university-educated, compared to 31 per cent of persons without disabilities. Conversely, persons with disabilities are more likely to have obtained a high school degree (or less than a high school degree) as their highest level of educational attainment. As shown in Figure 19.2, these patterns hold even when we control for age. This control takes into account the overlap between age and disability and the existence of cohort differences in educational attainment; in other words, persons with disabilities are concurrently more likely to be older and to be members of birth cohorts with lower rates of university completion. Cohort differences in educational attainment are evident at the upper and lower levels. That is, persons with disabilities aged 45–65 have the lowest university completion rate (14 per cent versus 31 per cent for those without disabilities) but the highest rate of having ended their formal education with less than a high school diploma (22 per cent versus only 9 per cent for those without disabilities). CSD data also show that educational attainment varies by disability severity: persons with mild disabilities are more likely to be university graduates (21 per cent) than those with severe disabilities (12 per cent).

Inequality in Employment

Despite legislation aimed at ensuring equality in the workplace, people who enter the labour

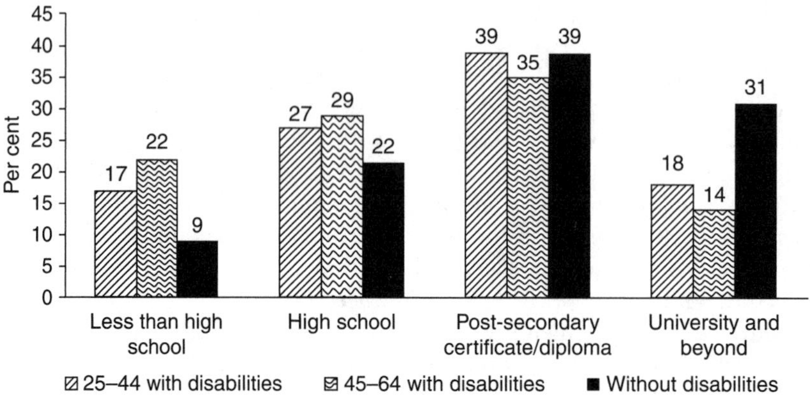

Figure 19.2 Highest Degree by Disability Status and Age

Source: Arim (2015).

force with a disability, or who develop a disability during their working lives, often face unique challenges and disadvantaged outcomes. Many factors explain employment inequalities for persons with disabilities. Employment-related challenges include discrimination in hiring, a lack of disability accommodation that makes it more difficult to continue to work, and negative assumptions from employers and co-workers about the capability of workers with disabilities, which present barriers to career advancement and job retention (Schur 2003; Schur et al. 2009). Based on estimates from the 2012 CSD (Arim 2015; Turcotte 2014), only 49 per cent of Canadians aged 25–64 with disabilities were employed, compared to 79 per cent of Canadians without disabilities. Figure 19.3 shows that people with disabilities were more likely than persons without disabilities to be out of the labour force (40 per cent versus 15 per cent) or unemployed (11 per cent versus 6 per cent). Labour force participation does vary greatly by disability severity,

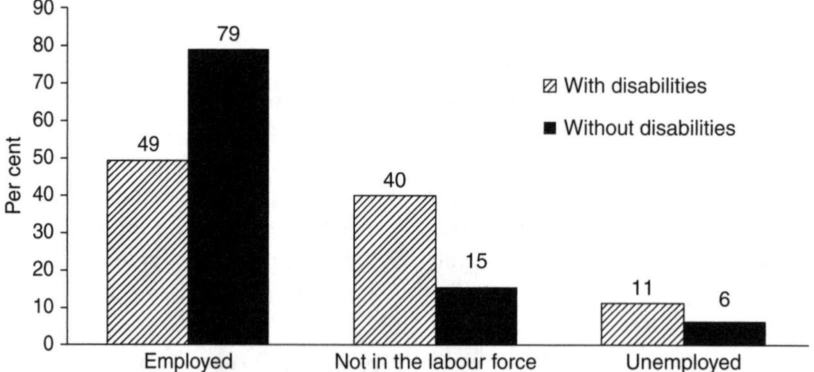

Figure 19.3 Employment Status by Disability Status, Canadians Aged 25–64

Source: Turcotte (2014).

however. For example, 68 per cent of Canadians aged 25–64 with mild disabilities are employed, which is only about 10 per cent less than the employment rate for Canadians without a disability (Turcotte 2014). The proportion declines to 54 per cent for those with a moderate disability, 42 per cent for severe disability, and 26 per cent for very severe disability.

Employment-related inequalities also vary with the timing of impairment in an accumulative fashion consistent with theories of cumulative dis/advantage. Employment outcomes across the life course are affected by educational attainment and skill acquisition early in life. Acquired human and social capital affects entry into and location within the labour market, which in turn affects career and income trajectories across the life course. For example, recent research (Lindsay et al. 2014) suggests that youth with disabilities may experience disadvantage and discrimination at labour market entry because employers believe that young workers with disabilities possess fewer "soft skills." Lack of such skills, which pertain to "personality, attitude, and behavior rather than to formal and technical knowledge," could affect communication abilities and overall job-readiness (Moss and Tilly 1996: 253). Institutional barriers also make it more difficult for youth with disabilities to participate in extracurricular sports and volunteer activities, which can enhance employment readiness skills and are often considered important for a well-rounded resumé (Lindsay et al. 2014). These employment barriers early in life can produce disadvantaged employment trajectories, with lower wages, precarious employment, fewer benefits, less opportunity for advancement, and a greater risk of poverty throughout the life course.

The nature of employment has important implications for job security, worker protections offered by unions and labour laws, wages, access to training, pensions, and other benefits. Workers with disabilities are over-represented in less secure, non-standard (e.g., part-time or temporary) employment (Baldwin and Schumacher 2002; Yelin and Trupin 2003). They are more likely to be in service jobs and less likely to be in managerial or professional jobs (Hale et al. 1998; Schur 2002). American research also shows lower levels of pay and benefit access (including health insurance and pension plans) among workers with disabilities (Schur 2002).

In 2012, 43 per cent of employed Canadians with disabilities thought they were disadvantaged in the workplace because of their condition; the same proportion reported needing a workplace accommodation to be able to work (Arim 2015). For workers with disabilities, formal definitions of "disability," established by various governmental and non-governmental organizations, affect employers' treatment of workers and their policies regarding disability in the workplace. In Canada, the 1985 Canadian Human Rights Act, in conjunction with the 1986 Employment Equity Act, prohibits workplace discrimination on the basis of disability, and makes employment opportunities and benefits accessible to designated disadvantaged groups, including persons with disabilities. Canadian legislation requires employers to alter workplace conditions to allow people with disabilities equal opportunities. The principle of *reasonable accommodation* applies, obliging employers to provide accommodations such as the removal of physical barriers, the use of assistive devices, and changes to the norms of productivity (such as modified duties and work schedules), provided these do not impose undue hardship on the employer. The existing laws are broad, however, and protections and accommodations are not universally offered to workers. Employers' decisions to accommodate are affected by perceptions of disability, including the belief that people with disabilities are less capable of meeting organizational demands, unable to work at a normal pace, capable of only limited tasks, and more expensive for the company (Abberley 1987; Hahn 1988; McFarlin et al. 1991; Robert and Harlan 2006). These perceptions affect employers' willingness to comply with worker accommodation requests (Florey and Harrison 2000). Recent research suggests that workers in precarious employment, such as temporary, part-time, and non-union jobs (where workers with disabilities are disproportionately concentrated), are more likely to have unmet accommodation needs (Shuey and Jovic 2013). In addition, workers in precarious jobs are less likely to disclose a disability or express their need for accommodation to their employer, and are more likely to have their job modification requests denied (Dyck and Jongbloed 2000; Harlan and Robert 1998).

Particularly vulnerable are older workers with a disability. They have lower labour force participation rates and higher unemployment rates than either younger adults with a disability or older adults without a disability (Statistics Canada 2001). Societal perceptions of aging overlap with perceptions about disability, so that ageism and age discrimination can compound the negative effect of disability for older workers. Research suggests that employees with less visible disabilities, many of which are associated with aging, are encouraged or coerced to stop working rather than ask for or receive accommodations that might allow their continued employment. Negative perceptions of aging, combined with stigmatization and perceptions about ability, are illustrated by statements from co-workers and employers, such as "if you can't do the job, then get out," and "if you're that sick, why don't you take an early retirement?" (Harlan and Robert 1998: 28). Individuals who acquire a disability later in life may view it as part of the normal aging process and not describe their health impairment as a disability or request accommodation. Research suggests that workers who attribute their limitations to aging are more likely to have unmet needs that, if accommodated, might help them to work longer (McMullin and Shuey 2006).

Economic Inequality

Disability theorists have argued that people with disabilities are an oppressed group. Oppression stems from the material disadvantages of poverty that can accompany impairment (Abberley 1987) and the marginalization that occurs because of exclusion or segregation in the education and employment spheres (Young 1990). The timing of disability onset is particularly important because it provides a crude marker for the life stage at which individuals are exposed to the structural barriers raised by disabling social institutions. Persons experiencing disability from birth or childhood begin to accumulate disadvantages early in life. These disadvantages carry across the life course into employment and beyond, and are visible in outcomes such as income and wealth. For others, disability onset occurs in early adulthood, which is typically the time at which educational attainment is completed and first jobs are sought. Others experience disability onset in mid-life, after employment is well underway. At this stage in the life course, the experience of disability can hamper workers' capacities to stay in their current jobs, reducing their wages and chances of promotion. As noted previously, disability onset in mid- to later life also makes it difficult to disentangle discrimination based on age from discrimination based on disability (McMullin and Shuey 2006). Without appropriate data tracing individuals over time, it is hard to establish whether disability affects economic security or whether economic security affects the chances of experiencing a disability. Hence, an important and heavily debated topic among health scholars is the extent to which health affects, or is affected by, socio-economic status. Because lower-class individuals are more likely to experience early health decline and disability, cross-sectional data comparing economic outcomes for persons with and without disabilities cannot easily determine the extent to which lower income levels among persons with disabilities are the result of disability or reflect the broader relationship between low socio-economic status and early health decline. Longitudinal data are required to answer this crucial question.

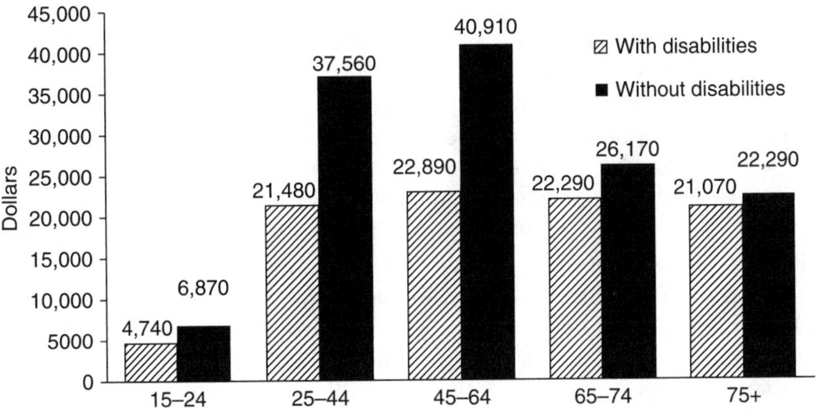

Figure 19.4 Median Total Income by Age and Disability Status

Source: Arim (2015).

That said, cross-sectional national survey data, including the CSD and the National Household Survey (NHS), can provide estimates of the economic inequality experienced by persons with disability in Canada. We know, for example, that persons of working age with disabilities are more likely than other Canadians to live in low-income households (Crawford 2013). As shown in Figure 19.4, recent evidence (Arim 2015) also reveals substantial differences in median income between people with disabilities and those without disabilities. The largest gap (about $18,000) occurs for those aged 45–64, which are the prime earnings years for most Canadians. The gap is smaller (less than $4,000) among adults aged 65–74, and even smaller (about $1,200) for those aged 75+. There are many possible explanations for why the gap narrows among older Canadians. Arim suggests that this pattern is partly due to government policies that provide income support to retirees, and also relates to the age of disability onset. Because the likelihood of disability onset increases with age, those aged 65 and older may be more recently affected by disability and therefore may not have been as adversely affected by loss of wages and pension contributions earlier in life, especially during their prime earning years. Another possible explanation is selective mortality; that is, people with a disability are less likely to live to older ages, and this reduces the appearance of inequality later in life (Willson and Shuey 2007). The narrower income gap among older Canadians could also occur because of differences in severity levels. The median income for persons with mild disabilities was $29,950, which is comparable to the $31,160 median income for persons without disabilities. However, the income gap grows as severity increases: among those with severe disabilities, median income is only $16,810, and for those with very severe disabilities only $14,390 (Arim 2015).

Conclusions

Many sources of oppression faced by Canadians with disabilities remain systematically embedded in our social institutions and culture. Nevertheless, since the 1970s we have seen major revisions to definitions and policies regarding disability in Canada. Academics, activists, and people with disabilities themselves have all worked towards greater inclusion and full participation of people with disabilities in our society. A major shift occurred in the 1980s, when traditional views of disability as an individual problem were gradually replaced by a social model that emphasized how society has disabled and excluded people with impairments. This shift was reflected in changing disability policies, which increasingly viewed social inclusion as a public responsibility and took a human rights approach to protecting, promoting, and improving the opportunities for full societal participation by people with disabilities.

Even so, despite the gains and policy protections currently in place, substantial inequities persist across many aspects of social life, and continue to be major issues for those who seek complete equality for people with disabilities. Structural inequalities in the educational and employment systems still result in greater risk exposure and lesser opportunity for people with disabilities across the life course. Canadians who experience disabilities early in life face educational and other institutional barriers that place them at risk of additional disadvantages that accumulate over time, affecting their employment chances, incomes, and wealth in mid-life and beyond. Those experiencing disability onset in mid-life are confronted with structural barriers in the workplace, which affect their wages, access to training, chances of promotion, and even their ability to work at all.

A final important point is that society's treatment of impairment and disability is not only a *source* of inequality in Canada, but also a *result* of broader systems of social stratification and inequality. There are many determinants of disability, including biological and genetic factors, social determinants such as employment and working conditions, socio-economic status, education, exposure to stress, access to health services, prenatal factors, and health practices. These determinants intersect with other social statuses, especially gender, race, and class of origin, all of which assign greater power, privilege, and resources to certain groups compared to others (McMullin 2010; Tilly 1998).

Life course scholars view disability as a process that intersects with both age and historical period. Hence, there are a multitude of pathways and trajectories of disability, and no universal experience of disability applies to everyone. Consequently, enacting real change for all of us who experience disability is a massive task. In advocating and promoting new policy initiatives, we should also recognize that disability is intertwined with the other major sources of inequality in our society. This means that reducing social inequality in all its forms is essential if we are to improve the well-being of all Canadians, including Canadians with disabilities.

Questions for Critical Thought

1. Why does income inequality persist despite Canadian legislation that protects against discrimination and advances the inclusion of people with disabilities?
2. In what ways does disability interact and overlap with other systems of inequality such as race, class, gender, and age?
3. What does a life course perspective contribute to our understanding of disability?
4. How might the life course of an individual differ depending on the age at which a disability is first experienced?

Recommended Readings

Barnes, Colin, and Geof Mercer. 2010. *Exploring Disability: A Sociological Introduction*, 2nd edn. Cambridge: Polity Press.

Oliver, Michael, and Colin Barnes. 2012. *The New Politics of Disablement*. New York: Palgrave Macmillan.

Stienstra, Deborah. 2012. *About Canada: Disability Rights*. Black Point, NS: Fernwood.

Thomas, Carol. 2007. *Sociologies of Disability and Illness: Contested Ideas in Disability Studies and Medical Sociology*. New York: Palgrave MacMillan.

Recommended Websites

Canadian Disability Policy Alliance:
http://www.disabilitypolicyalliance.ca/

Canadian Survey on Disability (CSD):
http://www.statcan.gc.ca/csd/

Council of Canadians with Disabilities:
http://www.ccdonline.ca/en/

Disability-related Policy in Canada Research Alliance:
http://www.disabilitypolicy.ca/

References

Abberley, P. 1987. "The concept of oppression and the development of a social theory of disability." *Disability, Handicap, and Society* 2, 1: 5–19.

———. 1993. "Disabled people and normality." In J. Swain, V. Finkelstein, S. French, and M. Oliver, eds, *Disabling Barriers—Enabling Environments*, pp. 107–15. London: Sage.

Ansalone, George. 2001. "Schooling, tracking, and inequality." *Journal of Children and Poverty* 7, 1: 33–47.

Arim, Rubab. 2015. "A profile of persons with disabilities among Canadians aged 15 years or older, 2012." Statistics Canada Publication 89-654-X. http://www.statcan.gc.ca/pub/89-654-x/89-654-x2015001-eng.htm. Accessed 28 May 2015.

Baldwin, M.L., and E.J. Schumacher. 2002. "A note on job mobility among workers with disabilities." *Industrial Relations* 41: 430–41.

Barnes, Colin. 2012. "The social model of disability: Valuable or irrelevant?" In N. Watson, A. Roulstone, and C. Thomas, eds, *The Routledge Handbook of Disability* Studies, pp. 12–29. London: Routledge.

——— and Geof Mercer. 2010. *Exploring Disability*, 2nd edn. Cambridge: Polity Press.

———, ———, and Tom Shakespeare. 1999. *Exploring Disability: A Sociological Introduction*. Cambridge: Polity Press.

Canadian Survey on Disability. 2012. Statistics Canada. www.statcan.gc.ca/csd/.

Crawford, C. 2013. "Disabling poverty and enabling citizenship: Understanding the poverty and exclusion of Canadians with disabilities." Winnipeg: Council of Canadians with Disabilities. http://www.ccdonline.ca/en/socialpolicy/poverty-citizenship/demographic-profile/understanding-poverty-exclusion/.

Dannefer, Dale. 2003. "Cumulative advantage/disadvantage and the life course: Cross-fertilizing age and social science theory." *Journal of Gerontology58B*, 6: S327–37.

DiPrete, T.A., and G.M. Eirich. 2006. "Cumulative advantage as a mechanism for inequality: A review of theoretical and empirical developments." *Annual Review of Sociology* 32: 271–97.

Dyck, I., and L. Jongbloed. 2000. "Women with multiple sclerosis and employment issues: A focus on social and institutional environments." *Canadian Journal of Occupational Therapy* 67: 337–46.

Eder, Donna. 1981. "Ability grouping as a self-fulfilling prophecy: A micro analysis of teacher–student interaction." *Sociology of Education* 54, 3: 151–62.

Elder, Glen H., Jr, Monica Kirkpatrick Johnson, and Robert Crosnoe. 2003. "The emergence and development of life course theory." In J. Mortimer and M. Shanahan eds, *Handbook of the Life Course*, pp. 3–19. New York: Kluwer Academic/Plenum.

Entwisle, Doris R., Karl L. Alexander, and Lisa S. Olson. 1997. *Children, Schools, and Inequality.* Boulder, Colo.: Westview Press.

Florey, A.T., and D.A. Harrison. 2000. "Responses to informal accommodation requests from employees with disabilities: Multistudy evidence of willingness to comply." *Academy of Management Journal* 43: 224–33.

George, Linda K. 1993. "Sociological perspective on life transitions." *Annual Review of Sociology* 19: 353–73.

Giddens, A. 1999. "Risk and responsibility." *Modern Law Review* 62: 1–10.

Goffman, Erving. 1963. *Stigma: Notes on the Management of Spoiled Identity.* London: Penguin.

Hahn, H. 1988. "The politics of physical differences: Disability and discrimination." *Journal of Social Issues* 44: 39–47.

Hale, T., H. Hayghe, and J. McNeil. 1998. "Persons with disabilities: Labor market activity." *Monthly Labor Review* 12: 1–12.

Harlan, S.L., and P.M. Robert. 1998. "The social construction of disability in organizations: Why employers resist reasonable accommodations." *Work and Occupations* 25: 397–435.

Ingstad, B., and S. Reynolds-Whyte. 1995. "Disability and culture: An overview." In B. Ingstad and S. Reynolds-Whyte, eds, *Disability and Culture*, pp. 3–31. Berkeley: University of California Press.

Lindsay, Sally, Tracey Adams, Robyn Sanford, Carolyn McDougall, Shauna Kingsnorth, and Dolly Menna-Dack. 2014. "Employers' and employment counselors' perceptions of desirable skills for entry-level positions for adolescents: How does it differ for youth with disabilities?" *Disability & Society* 29, 6: 1–15.

McColl, Mary Ann, Mike Schaub, Lauren Sampson, and Kevin Hong. 2010. "A Canadians with Disabilities Act?" *Report for the Canadian Disability Policy Alliance.* http://69.89.31.83/~disabio5/wp-content/uploads/2011/07/CDA-reformat.pdf. Accessed 28 May 2015.

McFarlin, D.B., J. Song, and M. Sonntag. 1991. "Integrating the disabled into the workforce: A survey of Fortune-500 company attitudes and practices." *Employee Responsibility and Rights Journal* 4: 107–23.

McMullin, Julie A. 2010. *Understanding Social Inequality: Intersections of Class, Age, Gender, Ethnicity, and Race in Canada*, 2nd edn. Toronto: Oxford University Press.

——— and Kim M. Shuey. 2006. "Ageing, disability and workplace accommodations." *Ageing & Society* 26: 831–47.

Merton, R.K. 1968. "The Matthew Effect in science." *Science* 159, 3810: 56–63.

Morris, P. 1969. *Put Away.* London: Routledge.

Moss, P., and C. Tilly. 1996. "Soft skills and race: An investigation of black men's employment problems." *Work and Occupations* 23: 252–76.

Oliver, Michael. 1983. *Social Work and Disabled People.* Basingstoke: Macmillan.

———. 1996. *Understanding Disability: From Theory to Practice.* Basingstoke: Macmillan.

——— and Colin Barnes. 2012. *The New Politics of Disablement.* New York: Palgrave Macmillan.

O'Rand, Angela M. 1996. "The precious and the precocious: Understanding cumulative disadvantage and cumulative advantage over the life course." *The Gerontologist* 36, 2: 230–8.

———. 2000. "Risk, rationality and modernity: Social policy and the aging self." In K.W. Schaie and J. Hendricks, eds, *The Evolution of the Aging Self: The Societal Impact on the Aging Process*, pp. 225–49. New York: Springer.

———. 2003. "The future of the life course: Late modernity and life course risks." In J.T. Mortimer and M. J. Shanahan, eds, *Handbook of the Life Course*, pp. 693–701. New York: Plenum.

——— and Kim Shuey. 2007. "Gender and the devolution of pension risks in the U.S." *Current Sociology* 55: 287–304.

Pearlin, L.I., S. Schieman, E.M. Fazio, and S.C. Meersman. 2005. "Stress, health and the life course: Some conceptual perspectives." *Journal of Health and Social Behavior* 46, 2: 205–19.

People for Education. 2013. *Mind the Gap: Inequality in Ontario's Schools*. People for Education Annual Report on Ontario's Publicly Funded Schools. http://www.peopleforeducation.ca/wp-content/uploads/2013/05/annual-report-2013-WEB.pdf/.

Powell, Justin. 2003. "Constructing disability and social inequality early in the life course: The case of special education in Germany and the United States." *Disability Studies Quarterly* 23, 2: 57–75.

Priestley, Mark. 2005. "Disability and social inequalities." In M. Romero and E. Margolis, eds, *The Blackwell Companion to Social Inequalities*, pp. 372–95. Oxford: Blackwell.

Putnam, Michelle. 2002. "Linking aging theory and disability models: Increasing the potential to explore aging with physical impairment." *The Gerontologist* 42, 6: 799–806.

Quinn, Peggy. 1995. "Social work education and disability: Benefiting from the impact of the ADA." *Journal of Teaching in Social Work* 12, 1, 55–71.

Robert, P.M., and S.L. Harlan. 2006. "Mechanisms of disability discrimination in large bureaucratic organizations: Ascriptive inequalities in the workplace." *Sociological Quarterly* 47: 599–630.

Rioux, Marcia H., and Rita M. Samson. 2006. "Trends impacting disability: National and international perspectives." In M.A. McColl and L. Jongbloed, eds, *Disability and Social Policy in Canada*, 2nd edn, pp. 112–42. Concord, Ont.: Captus Press.

Schur, L. 2002. "Dead-end jobs or a path to economic well-being? The consequences of non-standard work among people with disabilities." *Behavioral Sciences and the Law* 20: 601–20.

———. 2003. "Barriers or opportunities? The causes of contingent and part-time work among people with disabilities." *Industrial Relations* 42: 589–622.

———, D. Kruse, J. Blasi, and P. Blanck. 2009. "Is disability disabling in all workplaces? Workplace disparities and corporate culture." *Industrial Relations* 48: 381–410.

Shuey, Kim M. and Emily Jovic. 2013. "Disability Accommodation in Nonstandard and Precarious Employment Arrangements." *Work and Occupations* 40, 2: 174–205.

Statistics Canada. 2001. Education, Employment and Income of Adults with and without Disabilities—Tables, Table 5.1, "Total income of adults with disabilities, by sex and age groups, Canada, 2001." Catalogue no. 89-587-XIE. http://publications.gc.ca/Collection/Statcan/89-587-X/89-587-XIE2003001.pdf. Accessed 28 May 2015.

Thomas, Carol. 2007. *Sociologies of Disability and Illness: Contested Ideas in Disability Studies and Medical Sociology*. New York: Palgrave Macmillan.

Tilly, C. 1998. *Durable Inequality*. Berkeley: University of California Press.

Topliss, E. 1979. *Provision for the Disabled*, 2nd edn. Oxford: Blackwell.

Turcotte, Martin. 2014. "Persons with disabilities and employment." Statistics Canada Publication 75-006-X. http://www.statcan.gc.ca/pub/75-006-x/2014001/article/14115-eng.htm. Accessed 28 May 2015.

United Nations. 2006. *Convention on the Rights of Persons with Disabilities and Optional Protocol*. http://www.un.org/disabilities/default.asp?id=261. Accessed 26 May 2015.

Willson, Andrea E., Kim Shuey, and Glen H. Elder, Jr. 2007. "Cumulative advantage processes as mechanisms of inequality in life course health." *American Journal of Sociology* 112, 6: 1886–1924.

World Health Organization (WHO). 2015. "Disabilities." http://www.who.int/topics/disabilities/en/. Accessed 21 Feb. 2015.

Yelin, E., and L. Trupin. 2003. "Disability and the characteristics of employment." *Monthly Labor Review* 126: 20–31.

Young, L.M. 1990. *Justice and the Politics of Difference*. Princeton, NJ: Princeton University Press.

20 Regional Inequality in Canada: An Enduring Issue?

Mabel Ho and Catherine Corrigall-Brown

Introduction

Regions matter. The Organisation for Economic Co-operation and Development (OECD) *Regional Outlook* report found that, in 2010, Canada was home to the third-largest regional disparities among OECD nations (OECD 2014). Canada is a vast country with imposing natural and social barriers that separate regions from each other. There are also important regional differences in population composition, natural resources, and industrial structure. While these differences contribute to the unique and dynamic nature of our country, they also pose significant challenges and can lead to serious inequalities. These regional disparities are evident in differences in the economic and social well-being of Canadians living in the various provinces. In addition to these objective inequalities, there are regional disparities in the subjective feelings of frustration among citizens regarding their region's place in the Canadian federation. The people of Quebec have concerns about their language and cultural protection; Atlantic Canadians face continued economic uncertainty; northern Canadians face serious challenges in the delivery of social services; and some western Canadians feel politically alienated from the core of the country. In fact, it is hard to find a region of Canada that does not face its own unique and challenging issues.

While regional inequality is important, it does not always occupy a central place among Canada's political concerns. In times of expansion, when all regions are experiencing economic growth and when important national or international issues dominate the political agenda, there tends to be less discussion of regional inequality. Since the 1960s, governments have sought to deal with social problems and create conditions for socio-economic development on a regionally equitable basis. Optimists hoped that long-standing inequalities between regions could be resolved by government intervention. However, after extensive efforts to reduce regional disparities in Canada, inequalities still exist. Much has been learned, especially about what not to do and the ineffectiveness of certain policy options. At the same time, new issues have arisen, including globalization, the rise of the knowledge economy, the rapid movement to a technology-based post-industrial society, and the changing patterns in the ownership and investment of capital in the world. These issues pose new challenges, with implications for regional inequalities that are not yet clear.

In this chapter, we review the debate on regional inequality in Canada. In particular, we examine the following questions. What is the extent of regional inequality in Canada? How do social scientists explain this inequality? What have governments, especially at the federal level, done to address this inequality? How successful have these measures been in reducing regional disparities in Canada?

The Dimensions of Regional Inequality

The concept of regionalism entails the recognition of politically relevant divisions and territorial cleavages, which are often accompanied by a consciousness among residents that they have unique, regionally based interests (Schwartz 1974). While there is general agreement on the importance of regionalism and regional inequality in Canada (e.g., Brodie 1997; Skogstad 2000), the definition of region remains an important problem for assessing trends in inequality and for implementing policy. Successive governments have applied quite different interpretations of what constitutes a disadvantaged region. These definitional decisions are based as much on political grounds as on rational analyses of pertinent social and economic characteristics.

The larger the area encompassed by the term "region," the more likely it is to include significant internal variations or disparities. For example, the provinces within western Canada (British Columbia, Alberta, Saskatchewan, and Manitoba) have some characteristics in common, but also enormous differences. Similarly, the Atlantic provinces are often grouped together, but have notable differences, e.g., in their potential for the development of agriculture, forestry, manufacturing, or energy. In addition, vast differences exist in social and economic well-being within provinces. It is not uncommon, even in a small province, to have significant disparities, for example, in unemployment rates. Such is the case in Nova Scotia where Halifax, as of January 2015, had lower levels of unemployment (6.2 per cent) than the province as a whole (8.4 per cent) (Statistics Canada 2015).

At the other extreme, if a small, localized area is targeted (for example, a census district), policy solutions may be hindered because the underlying conditions contributing to the problem may require consideration of a broader geographic area. Can the problems of Cape Breton be resolved in isolation from the mainland of Nova Scotia? Can stagnation in eastern or northern Ontario be considered outside the context of developments in Toronto or Ottawa?

In practice, the province is most often used as the unit defining a region, because data are most readily available at the provincial level and less so for municipalities and other units. This approach is also occasioned by Canada's federal nature, and by the political and constitutional significance of provincial governments.

What are some indicators of regional inequality in Canada, using provincial-level data? Typically, economic measures are used and, among these, income and unemployment rates are most prevalent. Other economic measures often cited include rates of poverty and the productive capacity of each province; an example is provincial gross domestic product per capita, which measures the value of goods and services produced per person. Additional social indicators describe the educational level of the population, the health of the population (e.g., infant mortality rates), or living standards (e.g., a crowding index with respect to housing). Some contemporary evidence of regional inequality is shown in Tables 20.1–20.6.

Tables 20.1 and 20.2 provide data on income and unemployment rates by region, and show substantial inequalities on these measures. We see in Table 20.1 that the difference between the highest and lowest median income is $41,180 annually. This largest gap is the income difference between two northern regions, i.e., between Nunavut, which had a median total annual family income of $65,530 in 2012, compared to $106,710 in Northwest Territories. Table 20.2 reveals that

Table 20.1 Median Total Family Income, Canada, Provinces, and Territories (All Census Families) ($)

	2008	2009	2010	2011	2012
Canada	68,860	68,410	69,860	72,240	74,540
Newfoundland and Labrador	59,320	60,290	62,580	67,200	70,900
Prince Edward Island	61,010	62,110	63,610	66,500	69,010
Nova Scotia	61,980	62,550	64,100	66,030	67,910
New Brunswick	59,791	60,670	62,150	63,930	65,910
Quebec	63,830	64,420	65,900	68,170	70,480
Ontario	70,910	69,790	71,540	73,290	74,890
Manitoba	64,530	65,550	66,530	68,710	70,750
Saskatchewan	69,800	70,790	72,650	77,300	80,010
Alberta	86,080	83,560	85,380	89,830	94,460
British Columbia	67,890	66,700	66,970	69,150	71,660
Yukon	85,070	84,640	86,930	91,090	94,460
Northwest Territories	98,530	98,300	101,010	105,560	106,710
Nunavut	58,590	60,160	62,680	65,280	65,530

Note: Census families include couple families, with or without children, and lone-parent families.
Source: Statistics Canada, CANSIM Table 111-0009, http://www.statcan.gc.ca/tables-tableaux/sum-som/l01/cst01/famil108a-eng.htm.

Table 20.2 Unemployment Rates by Province, January 2015

Province	% Unemployed
Newfoundland and Labrador	11.4
Prince Edward Island	10.2
Nova Scotia	8.4
New Brunswick	10.0
Quebec	7.4
Ontario	6.9
Manitoba	6.0
Saskatchewan	4.5
Alberta	4.5
British Columbia	5.6

Source: Statistics Canada, CANSIM Table 282-0087, http://www.statcan.gc.ca/daily-quotidien/150206/t150206a003-eng.htm.

unemployment rates also vary considerably by province. Unemployment in January 2015 was highest in the Atlantic provinces (ranging from 8.4 to 11.4 per cent) and lowest in the West (ranging from 4.5 to 5.6 per cent). In fact, unemployment rates in Newfoundland and Labrador are two and a half times the rates in Alberta and Saskatchewan (4.5 versus 11.4 per cent). These patterns are consistent with statistics going back to the 1960s (Corrigall-Brown and Wien 2009: 337). It is obvious that economic outcomes for both individuals and families differ significantly by region. Just as it matters into which family we are born, so too does it matter where that family resides.

Explanations of Regional Inequality

There are a number of competing theoretical explanations of regional inequality. Below we examine three major perspectives: (1) the staples approach; (2) the modernization model; and (3) dependency theory. Each of these perspectives seeks to explain why inequalities exist and suggests what policies might remedy the situation. However, because these explanations are based on different theoretical interpretations, they point to different strategies for dealing with inequalities, some of which are not compatible with one another. Many analysts feel that no single explanation accounts fully for the patterns of regional inequality in Canada, and so these writers pragmatically suggest that some wisdom resides in most, if not all, the alternatives. Analysts also argue that some theories are better at explaining the origin of disparities in previous decades, while other approaches are more useful for contemporary conditions.

The Staples Approach

The staples approach argues that regional inequality develops largely because of differences in the endowments of natural resources across areas, and in the economies and policies created to support the development of these resources. Staples are "raw or semi-processed materials extracted or grown primarily for export markets" (Marchak 1985: 674). In view of Canada's historic reliance on staple production and export, it is not surprising that Canadian social scientists emphasize the role of staples in both regional development and regional inequality. The roots of the staples approach are found in the work of Mackintosh (1923) and Innis (1930, 1940, 1956), who examined successive staples, such as furs, cod, timber, and wheat, in order to understand their social, political, and economic impacts in the development of Canada's economy.

A given staple can become an engine of economic growth under various conditions. Simply discovering a valued resource may be the key. A change in technology or transportation may also make it economical to produce a staple that has been discovered but not yet exploited. As well, the demand (and price) for a resource may increase, depending on such factors as the level of need in importing countries or the availability from other suppliers. In any case, if the conditions are favourable, capital and labour will flow into the region to develop and export the staple.

Some work has attempted to elaborate on staples theory and delimit the conditions under which staples lead to economic development. Watkins (1977), in particular, has suggested that staples theory only has explanatory value if applied to "new" countries like Australia, New Zealand, or Canada. These countries historically have small populations in relation to their land mass and resources, and few inhibiting traditions. In this context, a region's prosperity depends not only on the availability and marketability of its natural resources, but also on the region's success in using the production or extraction of the staple in developing the rest of its economy. In other words, a region will prosper if it has a valued resource that can be profitably marketed abroad, and if it can extend appropriate linkages to other economic sectors, such as manufacturing and services, which in turn receive a stimulus from the export sector.

For example, if a lot of equipment is required to extract or produce the staple, and if that equipment can be locally manufactured, then the manufacturing sector will be stimulated. Also, if the natural resource can be processed locally rather than being exported in a raw state, then the regional economy will gain jobs and income. As well, if labour is attracted to the export sector and receives high wages, then a local demand for consumer goods will be created. The region's long-term economic development, therefore, depends on the extent to which the stimulus provided by the exploitation of the staple can be used to diversify the economy of the area. Provincial governments can actively encourage this by investing surpluses created from the exploitation of natural resources into other areas of the economy.

Unfortunately, it is in the nature of staple production that the demand for a given staple, and therefore its price, fluctuates over time and may eventually decline. Consumer preferences may change, new synthetic alternatives may be found, resources may be exhausted, production costs may increase, or other regions or countries may take over an established market. If the region has diversified its economy, the decline in the staple exporting sector is a less serious problem. Labour and capital freed up in the declining sector can be redeployed to other productive uses. Some migration away from the region can also be expected, depending on other factors, including government policies and opportunities elsewhere. It is more likely, however, that dependence on the staple production will continue, along with a reluctance to adjust to the situation. Attempts may be made to subsidize and protect the declining industry, rather than encouraging a search for alternative sources of economic growth. For example, the coal and steel industries in Cape Breton were the recipients of substantial subsidies over several decades, which sustained them long after they were economically viable. Governments may also seek to retain their population base, rather than encouraging migration from the region. Unless a new staple can be found and developed, the region may stagnate and decline.

There are two additional features of staple theory as it has been developed by Canadian political economists. First, the importance of staple production for a region or country is not restricted to its narrowly economic implications. Each staple, including the way its production is organized, leaves its imprint politically, socially, and culturally on the region. For example, the transition in Alberta from an economy dominated by farming to one dominated by energy production and export sped up urbanization in the province and encouraged the development of a large managerial/entrepreneurial class; ultimately, a populist-agrarian political regime was replaced with one more responsive to the new urban elite (Mansell 1986). Second, writers such as Innis (1956), Drache (1976), and Watkins (1977) have emphasized the negative implications of a staple economy. They note, in particular, the dependence on a foreign industrial centre through market and trade relations that are exploitative and constraining; the periodic crises and boom/bust periods; and the economic distortions induced in an area that lacks a diversified, self-reliant, and self-regulated economic base. We reconsider these themes when we discuss dependency theory in a later section.

Critics of the staples approach often suggest that this perspective provided important insights historically, when regional economies were centred on the fur trade, the cod fishery, or wheat farming. The critics suggest, however, that staple production has receded in importance over time, although energy production continues to be important in provinces like Alberta and Newfoundland and Labrador. Buckley (1958) dated the decline of the utility of the approach to as early as 1820. The Economic Council of Canada (1977: 8) concluded that "the maturing Canadian economy has reached the point where resources and transportation are no longer, as in the past, the only important determinants of regional variations in the well-being of Canadians, and we now have productive processes that are more complex and utilize natural resources somewhat differently."

Canadian sociologist Ralph Matthews (2014) has recently revisited the staples model, demonstrating that it continues to be important for our understanding of Canada's development. According to Matthews, four dimensions should be considered when applying staples theory: (1) the rise of neo-liberal government; (2) globalization and its consequences; (3) Aboriginal rights, titles, and entitlement; and (4) environmentalism. He argues that we can use staples theory in this more nuanced way to understand how "the social processes are influencing the economic ones" in contemporary times (Matthews 2014: 125).

The Modernization Model

Examination of the underdevelopment of Third World countries in the 1950s and 1960s led to the creation of the modernization or development model. This model suggests that certain traditional values and cultural practices in a country can restrict its development. From this perspective, development can only occur through the growth of the urban, industrial sector of the economy. The modernization approach suggests that the social relationships, culture, political institutions, and social structures appropriate to modern industrial society would spread from the (modern) centre to the (traditional) periphery. Increased mobility of individuals between country and city, mass communications and transportation, formal education, and the development of a modern state would all serve to disseminate rational, income-maximizing behaviour that would eventually help countries develop.

The modernization perspective was also applied to explain regional underdevelopment in advanced industrial societies, but with some modifications. While it is difficult to speak of development in Latin American countries without dealing with the overwhelming significance of the agriculture sector and the need for land reform, such is not the case in Canada. The debate in Canada also does not dwell as much on differences in progressive or traditional attitudes, values, and social structures between different parts of the country.

According to modernization theory, some regions of Canada are underdeveloped because their deficiencies stand in the way of improving their relative levels of employment and income in relation to other regions. Several causes have been identified for this underdevelopment: location in relation to markets and the resulting burden of transportation costs; lower rates of capital investment; shortcomings in infrastructure, such as roads, harbours, and hospitals; lower levels of investment in education and training of the workforce (human capital); inferior managerial quality; and lower levels of investment in new productive technology. Most of these factors contribute to the productivity of industry and thus to income and employment levels in the region.

The modernization model assumes that, under free market conditions, workers would move from areas with low incomes and few educational opportunities to areas with higher incomes and more educational opportunities. However, artificial impediments prevent this "natural" equalization from occurring. For example, if the minimum wage in poorer regions is higher than in other areas, or if employment insurance payments are more generous in amount and duration and more lenient in the terms for accessing them, then the incentives to leave the region are reduced. The same result occurs if the actions of unions, governments, or corporations keep wages unnaturally high in the region.

As these examples illustrate, the deficiency identified by modernization theorists is not limited to the disadvantaged area, but is also built into the policies and practices of national governments, unions, or corporations in interaction with the poorer region. Courchene (1994) concludes that, because the natural adjustment mechanisms of the market are not free to work as they should, provincial governments increasingly depend on federal transfers to sustain themselves, which worsens the problem. He suggests that the various problems interact. If wages are prevented from moving downward in a poor province, then unemployment remains high. This triggers an increasing influx of federal funds (e.g., employment insurance). However, the more money that flows in, the less incentive there is for the province or region to worry about the adequacy of wage adjustment, as well as labour and capital mobility. The result is a "vicious cycle" of inequality (Courchene 1986: 35; Courchene 1994).

Dependency Theory

Dependency theory first appeared in the late 1960s, and generated considerable intellectual excitement because it directly challenged the main tenets of modernization theory (Frank 1967; Wallerstein 1982). Articulated primarily by Latin American intellectuals, the approach contains two main arguments.

First, dependency theory suggests that underdevelopment is the result of exploitation by capitalist metropolitan centres. Far from being models of modernity to be emulated, the "developed" areas prosper at the expense of the "traditional" regions. Further, the exploitative relationship, e.g., between the US and Latin America, is reproduced within both developed and underdeveloped countries, thus accounting for regional inequality. One early application of the dependency perspective to Canada, by Davis (1971), divided the country into metropolitan areas (e.g., the urban industrial core) and satellite or hinterland areas (e.g., the North, the West, and Atlantic Canada). Davis argued that the metropolis continuously dominates and exploits the hinterland, but some groups in the hinterland tend to fight back against their metropolitan exploiters.

The second argument is that underdevelopment occurs when resources are drained from peripheral areas to a centre that controls the terms of trade. Thus, raw materials are exported from satellite regions at prices below their true value, and manufactured goods from the central area are sold back to the periphery at exorbitant prices. Richer areas concentrate on exporting industrial goods to the rest of the world, while poorer areas focus on trading primary commodities. However, the price of primary products tends to decline over time relative to the higher value-added industrial products (Greig et al. 2007). Hence, poorer countries and regions must export more primary products in order to purchase the same amount of industrial goods (Keily 1998: 8; Preston 1996); this process means that the poorer regions remain unable to catch up to the richer regions.

Financial institutions and multinational corporations play an important role in this process. Banks headquartered in core areas drain the peripheral regions of their savings and invest them elsewhere, while labour is attracted to the core when needed, but sent back to the periphery when not required. Often, the multinational corporation is regarded as the chief agent of exploitation, and the relationship between core and periphery is seen as uniformly negative. In more nuanced versions of this theory, multinationals that locate in a peripheral area and produce goods for local markets are acknowledged sources of growth and dynamism, since the multinationals must create some internal prosperity in order to sell their consumer goods. However, while some local wealth is generated, the area suffers substantial losses of capital resources through profit remittances, interest payments, and royalties. If the result is not uniform underdevelopment in the peripheral region, it is at best uneven or dependent development (Cardoso 1972).

Numerous Canadian studies in the dependency tradition emphasize these themes. Gidengil (1990) finds that, while central regions often show autonomous growth, peripheral regions only show growth in response to expansion at the centre. Other studies of particular regions in Canada support these findings, including examinations of the deindustrialization of the Atlantic provinces from 1890 to 1920 and their continuing underdevelopment (Acheson 1977; Forbes 1977; House 1981); agriculture and oil development on the prairies (Fowke 1968; Knuttila and McCrorie 1980); and First Nations–White interactions in the context of resource development in the Canadian North (Elias 1975; Kellough 1980).

In social terms, dependency theory focuses on the class structure of the metropolitan and satellite areas. While different analysts of particular regions or countries identify various kinds of social class constellations, all analyses identify dominant elites and subordinate labourers in both centre and periphery. Parts of the periphery elite are linked to the centre elite and serve as agents of the centre elite in satellite areas (Matthews 1980;

Table 20.3 Median Total Income (All Census Families), by Family Type, Canada, Provinces, and Territories (Relative to the Canadian Average, Canada = 100)

	2008	2009	2010	2011	2012
Canada	100	100	100	100	100
Newfoundland and Labrador	86	88	90	93	95
Prince Edward Island	89	91	91	92	93
Nova Scotia	90	91	92	91	91
New Brunswick	87	89	89	88	88
Quebec	93	94	94	94	95
Ontario	103	102	102	101	100
Manitoba	94	96	95	95	95
Saskatchewan	101	103	104	107	107
Alberta	125	122	122	124	127
British Columbia	99	98	96	96	96
Yukon	124	124	124	126	127
Northwest Territories	143	144	145	146	143
Nunavut	85	88	90	90	88

Note: Census families include couple families, with or without children, and lone-parent families.
Source: Calculated from Statistics Canada, CANSIM Table 111-0009, http://www.statcan.gc.ca/tables-tableaux/sum-som/l01/cst01/famil108a-eng.htm.

Stavenhagen 1974). In the Canadian context, Clement (1983) argues that a portion of the economic elite in our peripheral regions works for, and serves the interests of, central Canadian and American business interests in the region.

Dependency theory as an explanation for regional inequality in Canada has numerous critics. Some question the applicability to the Canadian context of a model articulated initially to explain underdevelopment in the Third World. In contrast to Third World countries, Canada is not generally characterized by low returns for labour (i.e., low wages) or low returns for exported resource products (Marchak 1985). Others have questioned whether the theory adds much to what has already been articulated, perhaps more appropriately for Canada, by staples theorists like Innis and Watkins. In many ways, the debate has moved to larger questions and broader perspectives, due to dissatisfaction with the rather simplistic dyadic relationships of dependency theory (Friedman and Wayne 1977).

Regional Disparities over Time

To enhance our understanding of regional inequality in Canada, we can compare income levels across the provinces and territories and consider trends over time. To do so, it is helpful to convert the median incomes in Table 20.1 to proportions relative to the overall Canadian median income for each year in the table (as shown in Table 20.3). We see in Table 20.3 that primarily the Atlantic region, and to a lesser degree Quebec and Nunavut, exhibit incomes below the Canadian median income during the recent period 2008–12; the highest median incomes are in the West, especially Alberta and Saskatchewan, and in parts of the North, specifically Yukon and the Northwest Territories. The relatively higher incomes in the West and North are partly traceable to well-paying jobs in the resource industries, which had been booming in those regions in recent years; for the North, these higher incomes are counterbalanced by the higher cost of living in that region (e.g., CBC News 2015a).

The current pattern of lower incomes in the Atlantic region and Quebec, and higher incomes in the West and North, has actually held true for a long time. The biggest change over time is that many regional gaps decreased substantially, especially compared to several decades ago. In 1961, for example, median incomes in the four Atlantic provinces were only about 60 to 70 per cent of the Canadian median (Corrigall-Brown and Wien 2009: 326); however, Table 20.3 shows that, by 2012, median incomes in the Atlantic region had risen to about 90 per cent of the Canadian median. Another big change is the relative income decline in Ontario, which in 1961 had the highest median income in Canada (Corrigall-Brown and Wien 2009), but stood right at the Canadian median in 2012.

Incomes in some provinces are boosted by federal government transfers. Table 20.4 shows federal support to the provinces and territories. Clearly, federal transfers have reduced some of the regional inequality. However, there is a substantial difference in the amount of federal support for each province. The three northern territories received relatively high levels in 2015–16 ($24,711 per person in Yukon to $40,352 per person in Nunavut). Federal support is much lower in the West and Ontario (ranging from $1,310 to $2,461). It is somewhat higher in the Atlantic provinces (from $3,221 to $3,758), the notable exception being Newfoundland and Labrador, which received only $1,312 per capita for 2015–16. Without these federal transfers, income inequality among the provinces would be much higher.

Although economic indicators of regional inequality are important, so, too, are social indicators. Inequality can manifest itself in ways that are external to the economy itself. A key social indicator is education level. Figure 20.1 shows rates of post-secondary certification across provinces. It is notable that some provinces have much higher levels of university degree attainment, while others have higher levels of college or other types of

Table 20.4 Federal Support to Provinces and Territories, Per Capita Allocation, Selected Years ($)

Province	2005–6	2010–11	2015–16
Newfoundland and Labrador	2,992	2,404	1,312
Prince Edward Island	2,954	3,459	3,758
Nova Scotia	2,415	2,778	3,221
New Brunswick	2,752	3,308	3,517
Quebec	1,583	2,180	2,461
Ontario	870	1,178	1,482
Manitoba	2,308	2,746	2,651
Saskatchewan	1,090	1,118	1,310
Alberta	674	905	1,310
British Columbia	1,091	1,128	1,310
Yukon	16,701	20,005	24,711
Northwest Territories	17,639	22,244	29,412
Nunavut	28,231	33,942	40,352

Source: Department of Finance Canada, http://www.fin.gc.ca/fedprov/mtp-eng.asp.

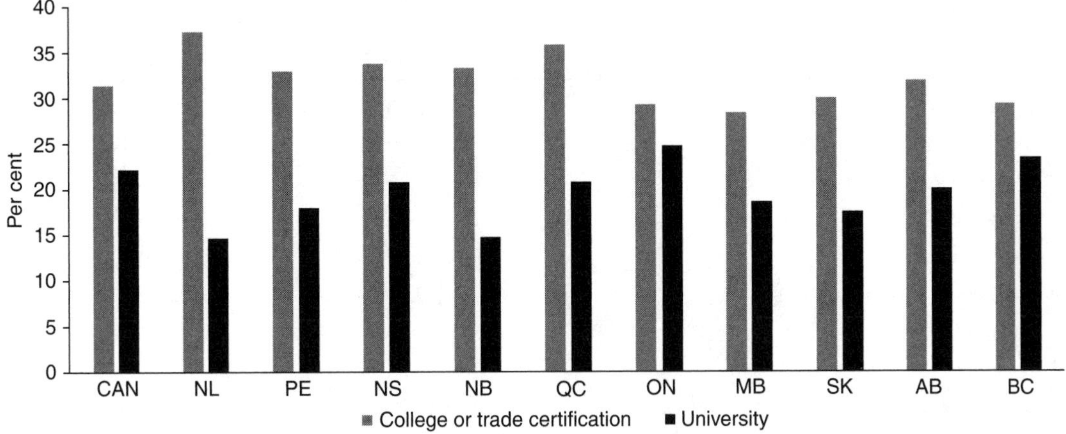

Figure 20.1 Percentages with Post-secondary Education, Canada and the Provinces, 2012

Source: HRSDC calculations based on Statistics Canada, Table 282-0004, "Labour force survey estimates (LFS), by educational attainment, sex and age group, annual (persons unless otherwise noted)," CANSIM (database).

non-university certifications. University certification is highest in Ontario and British Columbia, and lowest in Newfoundland and Labrador and New Brunswick. College certification is highest in Newfoundland and Labrador and Quebec, and lowest in Manitoba, Ontario, and British Columbia. While both types of certifications are evidence of continuing education, the earning outcomes of these different degrees can, in part, account for provincial differences in income.

Health inequalities can be measured in numerous ways. Three useful indicators are life expectancy, infant mortality, and food insecurity. First, even though health care is theoretically universal in Canada, some evidence, as shown in Table 20.5, suggests that people residing in economically disadvantaged regions tend to have shorter life expectancies, although the pattern is not strong. The lowest life expectancies clearly occur in Nunavut, which is the poorest of the three northern territories (recall Table 20.1); however, life expectancy is also somewhat below average in Yukon and the Northwest Territories, where incomes are relatively high, and also in Manitoba and Saskatchewan. A key factor is probably the lower life expectancies for some Aboriginal peoples, who represent a larger proportion of the population in these provinces and territories, especially Nunavut (Statistics Canada 2010; see Chapter 10 in this volume). Remoteness, and the resulting limited access to comprehensive health services, may also play a part in these regional patterns.

A somewhat similar outcome occurs for infant mortality (Table 20.6). The highest infant mortality clearly occurs in Nunavut, while relatively high rates also are evident in Yukon, Manitoba, and Saskatchewan for most years shown in the table. Patterns are mixed, however. One interesting finding is that, despite having incomes below the Canadian median, parts of the Atlantic region, particularly Prince Edward Island (4.2) and New Brunswick (3.5), are marked by some of the lowest infant mortality rates in the country.

A third health measure to consider is food insecurity, which refers to situations in which one or more household members have an insufficient quantity, quality, and variety of food in their diets. Statistics Canada's 2015 report on food insecurity found that 8.3 per cent of

Table 20.5 Life Expectancy in Years, Canada, Provinces, and Territories, 2009–11

	Males	Females
Canada	79.33	83.60
Newfoundland and Labrador	77.09	82.00
Prince Edward Island	78.15	82.90
Nova Scotia	78.05	82.64
New Brunswick	78.36	83.14
Quebec	79.43	83.55
Ontario	79.77	83.92
Manitoba	77.72	82.19
Saskatchewan	77.20	82.20
Alberta	79.06	83.45
British Columbia	80.25	84.40
Yukon	75.19	79.61
Northwest Territories	76.26	80.07
Nunavut	68.75	73.91

Source: Statistics Canada, Demography Division, http://www.statcan.gc.ca/pub/84-537-x/84-537-x2013005-eng.htm.

Table 20.6 Infant Mortality Rates (Both Sexes), Provinces and Territories, 2007–11

	2007	2008	2009	2010	2011
Canada	5.1	5.1	4.9	5.0	4.8
Newfoundland and Labrador	7.5	5.1	6.3	5.3	6.3
Prince Edward Island	5.0	2.0	3.4	3.6	4.2
Nova Scotia	3.3	3.5	3.4	4.6	4.9
New Brunswick	4.3	3.2	5.8	3.4	3.5
Quebec	4.5	4.3	4.4	5.0	4.3
Ontario	5.2	5.3	5.0	5.0	4.6
Manitoba	7.3	6.5	6.3	6.7	7.7
Saskatchewan	5.8	6.2	6.7	5.9	6.7
Alberta	6.0	6.2	5.5	5.9	5.3
British Columbia	4.0	3.7	3.6	3.8	3.8
Yukon	8.5	5.4	7.8	5.2	0.0
Northwest Territories	4.1	9.7	15.5	1.4	7.2
Nunavut	15.1	16.1	14.8	14.5	26.3

Note: The infant mortality rate is calculated as the number of deaths of children less than one year of age per 1,000 live births in the same year.
Source: Statistics Canada, CANSIM Table 102-0504, http://www.statcan.gc.ca/tables-tableaux/sum-som/l01/cst01/health21a-eng.htm.

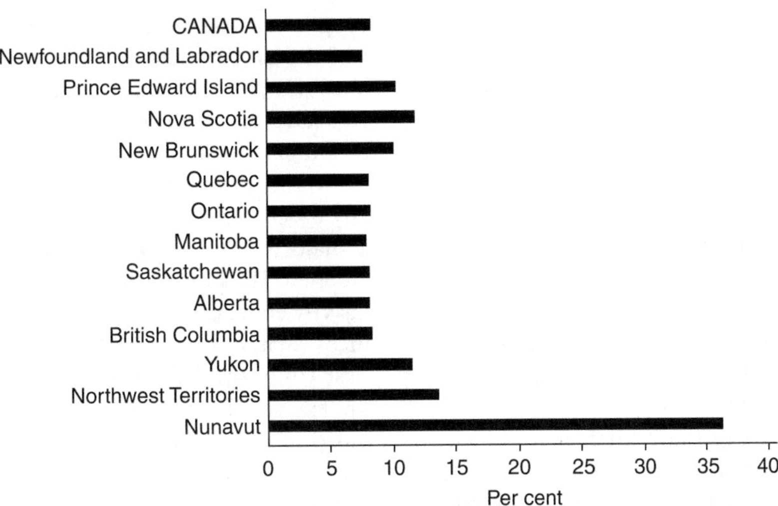

Figure 20.2 Percentage with Food Insecurity, Canada, Provinces, and Territories

Source: Statistics Canada, Canadian Community Health Survey, 2011–12, http://www.statcan.gc.ca/pub/82-625-x/2013001/article/11889/c-g/desc/desc04-eng.htm.

Canadian households (or 1.1 million in total) experienced food insecurity. Figure 20.2 reveals major differences in food insecurity across regions. Nunavut had the highest rate of food insecurity at 36.7 per cent, while the other northern territories were also high (13.7 per cent in the Northwest Territories and 12.4 per cent in the Yukon). In general, then, it appears that health inequality is higher in the North, especially Nunavut, than in most other regions of the country.

Political Outcomes of Regional Inequality

Inequality across the regions of Canada is important for a variety of reasons. Beyond our concerns about regional inequality for its own sake, it has many political consequences. Inequality, or the perception of inequality, affects how Canadians identify politically, and also the political party structure and electoral outcomes of the nation as a whole.

Canadians can identify themselves according to many criteria, including their nationality, their province, or their community of residence, and these subjective attachments can have real political implications. Canadians generally express a positive identification with both their nation and their province (Simeon 2004). Recent evidence suggests that Canadians outside Quebec primarily identify with the country as a whole (52 per cent) instead of their province (19 per cent). This is the reverse of what we find in Quebec, where 48 per cent of people identify more strongly with their province, compared to only 20 per cent with Canada as a whole (Valpy 2014). Other opinion poll evidence collected by Forum Research also indicates a relatively high regional identity in the Atlantic provinces (Carlson 2012).

Although westerners today tend to put their Canadian identity ahead of their provincial identifications (Carlson 2012), they sometimes believe that they are excluded from power at the centre. This is referred to as "western alienation." Between 1979 and 1997, at least 80 per cent of western Canadians agreed (either somewhat or strongly) that "the West usually gets ignored in national politics because the political parties depend mostly upon the voters in Quebec and Ontario" (Henry 2002). However, western Canadians' regional discontent declined between 2004 and 2008. For example, in 2008, British Columbians and Albertans were less likely to feel that their provinces were treated worse than other provinces. While regional discontent declined in western Canada, it increased in Ontario and Atlantic Canada in this period (Berdahl 2010).

The effects of these differences in identities and attitudes are evident in Canada's political party system and electoral outcomes. Canada's party system lost its pan-Canadian veneer in the 1990s. In particular, the elections of 1993, 1997, and 2000 produced a distribution of seats in the House of Commons with stronger regional parties than Canadians had seen for generations, and this meant more distinctive regional blocks of MPs from hitherto national parties. On the surface, at least, Canadian politics has seldom been so regionalized. Two regional parties formed in the 1990s and each held the position of official opposition in the federal Parliament: the sovereigntist Bloc Québécois after the 1993 election and the western-based Reform Party/Canadian Alliance after the 1997 and 2000 elections.

The federal-level Bloc Québécois manifested the most extreme version of regionalism: the desire for Quebec to secede from the country. This initiative has been closely linked to the separatist provincial party, the Parti Québécois, which was elected to govern Quebec for the first time in 1976. The level of nationalist sentiment has varied over time. For example, in the first referendum on Quebec sovereignty or separation, in 1980, only 40 per cent of Quebecers voted in favour. In the second referendum, in 1995, that figure rose to 49 per cent (Young and Archer 2002). By 2014, the proportion had declined to a still substantial 44 per cent (Perrella 2014). On the other hand, both the Bloc Québécois and the Parti Québécois have seen their political power reduced in recent elections.

Canadian politics continues to be regionally based. The 2011 federal election produced a majority Conservative government led by Stephen Harper, with Conservative support heavily concentrated in the three Prairie provinces, British Columbia, and Ontario. For the first time, the New Democratic Party (NDP), under Jack Layton, became the official opposition in Parliament, primarily because of the NDP's large and unprecedented majority in just one region: Quebec. For the first time, as well, the Liberal Party ran a distant third, ultimately leading the Liberals to choose a new leader: Justin Trudeau. In the 2015 federal election, regional divisions persisted, but there were also notable shifts, which led to the election of a majority Liberal government under Trudeau. The Conservatives held on to a majority of seats in the prairies, especially Alberta, where they have long dominated politically. The victorious Liberals did well in all the other regions, but especially in the Atlantic region, where they won every seat, in Ontario, where they won a strong majority, and in Quebec, where they replaced the NDP as the majority party (see the electoral map at http://www.elections.ca/content.aspx?section=res&dir=cir/maps2&document=index&lang=e). The regional concentration of party support, while it can vary over time, has been a persistent reality in Canadian politics.

Regions Today and in the Future

Canada's regions have undergone changes in development policies, which have occurred in three major phases since the 1960s (Bradford and Wolfe 2012). In the first wave, from the early 1960s to 1970s, regional inequality was addressed by paying more attention to remote areas and rural communities than to urban centres and inner-city neighbourhoods. The Canadian government dealt with regional disparities using centralized decision-making and a top-down approach. This was followed by the second wave, in the 1980s and 1990s, when the federal government decentralized, focusing its attention on developing assets and building capacities in different regions. More recently, the Harper government was part of a third wave, which Bradford and Wolfe have labelled the "new regionalism." This new regionalism is said to be concerned with innovation and evaluation. There is a need for "place-based" policies, whereby priorities are aligned and measurable with the involvement of multiple stakeholders, including community-based networks (Bradford and Wolfe 2012: 77). This approach was consistent with the regional policy changes currently happening in other OECD countries, and was intended to incorporate both local knowledge and accountability as key elements of policy implementation.

More specifically, the Harper government launched two new regional development agencies (RDAs) in 2009, one for northern Ontario (the Federal Economic Development Initiative for Northern Ontario, or FedNor), and one for southern Ontario (the Federal Economic Development Agency for Southern Ontario, or FedDev Ontario). The RDAs seek to apply development policies that build on regional economic assets and support business productivity (FedDev Ontario 2015). There also are other RDAs: the Atlantic Canada Opportunities Agency (ACOA); Canada Economic Development for Quebec Regions (CED); the Canadian Northern Economic Development Agency (CanNor); and the Western Economic Diversification Canada (WD). The future of the RDAs is uncertain, as funding has dwindled due to general budgetary pressures (Bradford and Wolfe 2012). In addition, the newly elected Trudeau Liberals have raised questions about whether the RDAs may ultimately be eliminated and replaced by a less centralized system for deciding on regional development policies (CBC News 2015b).

The future of Canada's disadvantaged regions will be shaped in large part by events and trends that impinge on regions from outside, as well as by internal dynamics. The relative success of regions increasingly depends, first, on how they integrate into continental and global markets, rather than the national market. As regional economies become inserted differently into the global economy, their links with the outside world will be crucial. In this sense, Canada will become less able to act as a giant "mutual insurance company" for different regions. Global pressures, the argument goes, will increasingly constrain federal policy instruments, including monetary, fiscal, trade, and redistributive policies. In this globalized political economy, it may well be harder to sustain the political commitment of wealthier provinces to assist poorer provinces through inter-regional redistribution (Savoie 2003).

In addition, global trade agreements further constrain the capacity of the federal government to deal with issues of regional inequality, because the federal government must conform to international trade rules before it can address the concerns of Canada's regions. Such considerations indicate that the study of regional inequality in Canada may be at a turning point. Perspectives and policies that have been prevalent for many years are increasingly being questioned, especially with respect to their results and usefulness in dealing with present and future issues arising from these global pressures.

Acknowledgement

We wish to thank Fred Wien for his important contributions to previous versions of this chapter.

Questions for Critical Thought

1. How is regional inequality related to other important forms of inequality in Canada, including class inequality, inequality in political power, racial and ethnic inequality, and other dimensions of inequality?
2. Regional inequality has important political implications, as discussed in this chapter. Go to http://www.elections.ca/content.aspx?section=res&dir=cir/maps2&document=index&lang=e. Using this map, consider the extent to which political parties in Canada are geographically concentrated. Why do you think this happens and how is this related to regional inequality?
3. One major issue in the North of Canada is food insecurity. A CBC News (2015a) story presents graphic and tabulated figures on the cost of basic food staples in Nunavut. How much do these same items cost in your local grocery store? What are the social implications of high food costs for individuals, families, and communities?
4. The following website lists regional development policies for each of Canada's major regions. Look up the policy for your region. What programs are instituted in your region to deal with inequality? How are these programs different from those in other parts of Canada? http://www.feddevontario.gc.ca/eic/site/723.nsf/eng/01690.html.

Recommended Readings

Clement, Wallace. 1983. *Class, Power, and Poverty: Essays on Canadian Society*. Toronto: Methuen.

Davis, A.K. 1971. "Canadian society and history as hinterland versus metropolis." In R.J. Ossenberg, ed., *Canadian Society: Pluralism, Change, and Conflict*, pp. 6–32. Scarborough, Ont.: Prentice-Hall.

Innis, Harold. 1956. *Essays in Canadian Economic History*. Edited by Mary Q. Innis. Toronto: University of Toronto Press.

Matthews, Ralph. 2014. "Committing Canadian sociology: Developing a Canadian sociology and a sociology of Canada." *Canadian Review of Sociology* 51, 2: 107–27.

Recommended Websites

Aboriginal Food Security in Northern Canada (2014):
http://www.scienceadvice.ca/uploads/eng/assessments%20and%20publications%20and%20news%20releases/food%20security/foodsecurity_fullreporten.pdf

National Household Survey:
http://www12.statcan.gc.ca/nhs-enm/index-eng.cfm

Regional development agencies across Canada:
http://www.feddevontario.gc.ca/eic/site/723.nsf/eng/01690.html

References

Acheson, T.W. 1977. "The Maritimes and 'Empire Canada'." In D.J. Bercuson, ed., *Canada and the Burden of Unity*. Toronto: Macmillan.

Berdahl, Loleen. 2010. *Whither Western Alienation? Shifting Patterns of Western Canadian Discontent with the Federal Government*. Calgary: Canada West Foundation.

Bradford, Neil, and David A. Wolfe. 2012. "Playing against type? Regional economic development policy in the Harper era." In G. Bruce Doern and Christopher Stonet, eds, *How Ottawa Spends 2012–2013: The Harper Majority, Budget Cuts, and the New Opposition*, pp. 71–88. Montreal and Kingston: McGill-Queen's University Press.

Brodie, Janine. 1997. "The new political economy of regions." In Wallace Clement, ed., *Understanding Canada: Building on the New Canadian Political Economy*, pp. 240–61. Montreal and Kingston: McGill-Queen's University Press.

Buckley, Kenneth. 1958. "The role of staple industries in Canada's economic development." *Journal of Economic History* 18 (Dec.): 439–50.

Cardoso, Fernando. 1972. "Dependency and development in Latin America." *New Left Review* 74 (July–Aug.): 83–95.

Carlson, Kathryn Blaze. 2012. "Canada Day poll: 15 things you should know about Canadian identity." *National Post*, 30 June. http://news.nationalpost.com/news/canada/canada-day-poll-15-things-you-should-know-about-canadian-identity.

CBC News. 2015a. "Food in Nunavut costs twice as much as Canadian average." 15 July. http://www.cbc.ca/news/canada/north/food-in-nunavut-costs-twice-as-much-as-canadian-average-1.3152896.

———. 2015b. "Liberals must offer clear vision without regional development ministers." 6 Nov. http://www.cbc.ca/news/canada/new-brunswick/regional-economic-development-agencies-future-1.3306222.

Clement, Wallace. 1983. *Class, Power, and Poverty: Essays on Canadian Society.* Toronto: Methuen.

Corrigall-Brown, Catherine, and Fred Wien. 2009. "Regional inequality: Causes and consequences." In Edward Grabb and Neil Guppy, eds, *Social Inequality in Canada: Patterns, Problems, and Policies*, 5th edn, pp. 324–44. Toronto: Pearson Education Canada.

Courchene, Thomas. 1986. "Avenues of adjustment: The transfer system and regional disparities." In Donald J. Savoie, ed., *The Canadian Economy: A Regional Perspective*, pp. 25–62. Toronto: Methuen.

———. 1994. *Social Canada in the Millennium: Reform Imperatives and Restructuring Principles.* Ottawa: Renouf.

Davis, A.K. 1971. "Canadian society and history as hinterland versus metropolis." In R.J. Ossenberg, ed., *Canadian Society: Pluralism, Change, and Conflict*, pp. 6–32. Scarborough, Ont.: Prentice-Hall.

Drache, Daniel. 1976. "Rediscovering Canadian political economy." *Journal of Canadian Studies* 11, 3 (Aug.): 3–18.

Economic Council of Canada. 1977. *Living Together: A Study of Regional Disparities.* Ottawa: Supply and Services Canada.

Elias, Peter. 1975. *Metropolis and Hinterland in Northern Manitoba.* Winnipeg: Manitoba Museum of Man and Nature.

FedDev Ontario. 2015. "Regional development agencies across Canada." Ottawa: Government of Canada. http://www.feddevontario.gc.ca/eic/site/723.nsf/eng/01690.html. Accessed 15 Apr. 2015.

Forbes, Ernest. 1977. "Misguided symmetry: The destruction of regional transportation policy for the Maritimes." In D.J. Bercuson, ed., *Canada and the Burden of Unity*, pp. 60–86. Toronto: Macmillan.

Fowke, Vernon. 1968. "Political economy and the Canadian wheat grower." In Norman Ward and Duff Spafford, eds, *Politics in Saskatchewan*, pp. 207–20. Toronto: Longmans Canada.

Frank, Andre Gunder. 1967. "Sociology of development and underdevelopment of sociology." *Catalyst* 3: 20–73.

Friedman, Harriet, and Jack Wayne. 1977. "Dependency theory: A critique." *Canadian Journal of Sociology* 2, 4 (Winter): 399–416.

Greig, Alastair, David Hulme, and Mark Turner. 2007. *Challenging Global Inequality: Development Theory and Practice in the 21st Century.* New York: Palgrave Macmillan.

Gidengil, Elisabeth. 1990. "Centres and peripheries: The political culture of dependency." *Canadian Review of Sociology and Anthropology* 27, 1: 23–48.

Henry, Shawn. 2002. "Revisiting western alienation: Towards a better understanding of political alienation and political behaviour in western Canada." In Lisa Young and Keith Archer, eds, *Regionalism and Party Politics in Canada*, pp. 77–91. Toronto: Oxford University Press.

House, Douglas. 1981. "Big oil and small communities in coastal Labrador: The local dynamics of dependency." *Canadian Review of Sociology and Anthropology* 18, 4 (Nov.): 433–52.

Innis, Harold. 1930. *The Fur Trade in Canada*. Toronto: University of Toronto Press.

———. 1940. *The Cod Fisheries*. Toronto: University of Toronto Press.

———. 1956. *Essays in Canadian Economic History*. Edited by Mary Q. Innis. Toronto: University of Toronto Press.

Keily, Ray. 1998. *Industrialization and Development: A Comparative Analysis*. London: UCL Press.

Kellough, Gail. 1980. "From Colonialism to Economic Imperialism." In J. Harp and J. Hofley, eds, *Structured Inequality in Canada*, pp. 343–77. Scarborough, Ont.: Prentice-Hall.

Knuttila, K.M., and J.N. McCrorie. 1980. "National policy and prairie agrarian development: A reassessment." *Canadian Review of Sociology and Anthropology* 17, 3 (Aug.): 263–72.

Mackintosh, W.A. 1923. "Economic factors in Canadian history." *Canadian Historical Review* 4, 1 (Mar.): 12–25.

Mansell, Robert. 1986. "Energy policy, prices, and rents: Implications for regional growth and development." In W. Coffey and M. Polese, eds, *Still Living Together*. Montreal: Institute for Research on Public Policy.

Marchak, Patricia. 1985. "Canadian political economy." *Canadian Review of Sociology and Anthropology* 22, 5 (Dec.): 673–709.

Matthews, Ralph. 1980. "The significance and explanation of regional differences in Canada: Towards a Canadian sociology." *Journal of Canadian Studies* 15, 2: 43–61.

———. 2014. "Committing Canadian sociology: Developing a Canadian sociology and a sociology of Canada." *Canadian Review of Sociology* 51, 2: 107–27.

Organisation for Economic Co-operation and Development (OECD). 2014. OECD *Regional Outlook 2014: Regions and Cities: Where Policies and People Meet*. Paris: OECD.

Perrella, Andre. 2014. "Support for Quebec sovereignty . . . outside of Quebec." http://www.lispop.ca/blog/2014/02/21/support-for-quebec-sovereignty-outside-of-quebec/.

Preston, P.W. 1996. *Development Theory: An Introduction*. Oxford: Clarendon Press.

Savoie, Donald J. 2003. "Regional development: A policy for all seasons and all regions." In François Rocher and Miriam Smith, eds, *New Trends in Canadian Federalism*, pp. 353–74. Peterborough, Ont.: Broadview Press.

Schwartz, Mildred A. 1974. *Politics and Territory*. Montreal and Kingston: McGill-Queen's University Press.

Simeon, Richard. 2004. "Canada: Federalism, language, and regional conflict." In Ugo M. Amoretti and Nancy Bermeo, eds, *Federalism and Territorial Cleavages*, pp. 92–122. Baltimore: Johns Hopkins University Press.

Skogstad, Grace. 2000. "Regional development policy" In Dietmar Braun, ed., *Public Policy and Federalism*. Burlington, Vt: Ashgate.

Statistics Canada. 2010. *Aboriginal Statistics at a Glance: Provincial/Territorial Distribution of Aboriginal Peoples*. http://www.statcan.gc.ca/pub/89-645-x/2010001/territorial-territoire-eng.htm.

———. 2015. "Labour force characteristics, seasonally adjusted, by census metropolitan area (3 month moving average)." Catalogue no. 71-001-XIE.

Stavenhagen, Rodolfo. 1974. "The future of Latin America: Between underdevelopment and revolution." *Latin American Perspectives* 9, 1 (Spring): 124–48.

Valpy, Michael. 2014. "Stop cheering—Quebec's sovereignty movement is far from finished." *Globe and Mail*, 10 Apr. http://www.theglobeandmail.com/globe-debate/stop-cheering-quebecs-sovereignty-movement-is-far-from-finished/article17912742/.

Wallerstein, Immanuel. 1982. "The rise and future demise of the world capitalist system: Concepts for comparative analysis." In H. Alavi and T. Shamin, eds, *An Introduction to the Sociology of "Developing Societies,"* pp. 29–53. Basingstoke: Macmillan.

Watkins, Mel. 1977. "The staple theory revisited." *Journal of Canadian Studies*, 12 (Winter): 83–95.

Young, Lisa, and Keith Archer, eds. 2002. *Regionalism and Party Politics in Canada*. Toronto: Oxford University Press.

PART IV

Some Consequences of Social Inequality

The preceding three parts have addressed the structure of social inequality in Canada, with a particular focus on important dimensions of disadvantage. These dimensions include the problems of class, power, and socio-economic status, as well as a broad range of crucial social justice factors that comprise race, ethnicity, language, ancestry, gender, sexual orientation, age, disability, and region. Some of the chapters in these parts have considered the significant *effects* or *consequences* of social inequality. For example, the chapters in Part I showed how the economic and class structures have changed as a consequence of the interplay involving corporate capitalists, the state leadership, and the struggle among classes. Other illustrations include the chapters on the effects on people's incomes of their gender, race, ethnicity, and educational attainment.

In addition to these social structural consequences of inequality, however, other important consequences that arise were not featured in Parts I, II, or III. These include the *consequences for people's experiences, outlooks, and behaviours*, many of which are significantly influenced by the structural dimensions of inequality. Our purpose in Part IV is to portray this second type of consequence. There is a wide array of such consequences, because social inequality touches so many aspects of people's lives. Therefore, the five chapters here do not provide a complete picture of the many consequences of social inequality, but they do offer some enlightening, intriguing, and crucial illustrations of how social inequality can and does shape the everyday lives of all Canadians.

The chapters here are limited to three kinds of consequences: (1) differences in people's *life chances*; (2) differences in Canadians' *attitudes or ways of thinking* about inequality and disadvantaged groups; and (3) differences in discriminatory *behaviour* in Canada.

We first deal with the issue of differences in life chances, starting with an aspect that is probably the most fundamental: health and life expectancy. Good health and living a long life are prized possessions in Canadian society, and undoubtedly *the* most prized possessions for most of us. Hence, the criterion of good health and life expectancy provides us with a strong test of our society's system of inequality. Finding evidence that differences in economic circumstances create differences in this area of life would clearly cast doubt on the idea that ours is a truly equal society. In Chapter 21, Gerry Veenstra offers an extensive review of recent evidence on the relationship between different forms of inequality and the health of Canadians. He finds that social class, gender, and race are all significant predictors of a broad range of health outcomes, including life expectancy, the incidence of chronic diseases, and self-reported health. The chapter also considers the explanations for why social inequality has such a sustained impact on health in Canada.

Chapter 22 considers another life chance issue, the serious problem of homelessness. Tracy Peressini's analysis reminds us that most Canadians, even if they are poor, take for granted certain basic comforts, including a roof over their heads and enough food to eat. She reviews the attempts to determine the number of homeless people in Canada, as well as their social background, personal characteristics, and life circumstances. Also considered are the possible explanations for homelessness, which include both social structural reasons and individual-level factors. Peressini goes on to discuss public policy, emphasizing that the major problem of affordable housing is left largely in local municipal or provincial hands, and is not a federal government responsibility. This has meant insufficient country-wide initiatives to solve the problem.

As noted above, social inequality can also produce other important consequences, which have to do with differences in people's *attitudes* or *ways of thinking*. Do the class locations and social statuses of Canadians affect their attitudes and beliefs about such questions as the acceptability of social inequality, or their level of intolerance or inclusion regarding disadvantaged minority groups? Questions of this type, which are considered in Chapters 23 and 24, probe the degree to which class and other forms of inequality shape our consciousness or awareness of social injustice in our own society.

Monica Hwang and Edward Grabb, in Chapter 23, present recent evidence concerning Canadians' beliefs about individualism and inequality, and whether these beliefs are related to people's social statuses or social backgrounds. Their analysis shows that Canadians tend to see inequality as a consequence of individual rather than group characteristics. On average, people agree with such ideas as the value of individual competition and hard work, the need for people to take responsibility for themselves, and the fairness of income differences based on individual performance or effort. Some evidence indicates that more advantaged people, e.g., those with higher income and higher occupational status, are more likely to hold such beliefs than are disadvantaged groups. However, the effects of social status are not strong, suggesting that the social background of Canadians has limited impact on the general belief that inequality based on individual differences is acceptable in our society.

Chapter 24 also considers how attitudes can be influenced by people's ranking on the different dimensions of inequality. Here, Robert Andersen examines the relationship between inequality and the level of acceptance or intolerance that people express towards certain minority groups in Canada. He considers recent survey data to see if people who are in deprived or disadvantaged circumstances, as judged by such measures as income, occupation, education, race, gender, and region, are more or less willing to have as their neighbours individuals from three designated minority groups: people of a different race, people of a different religion, and immigrants or foreign workers. The findings are especially relevant for assessing some claims in the literature that people of lower or working-class background are less tolerant of so-called "outgroups" than are other people. Andersen's research also reveals interesting patterns over time, and shows how intolerance patterns in Canada compare with trends in 92 other countries.

Finally, in Chapter 25, Philip Oreopoulos also deals with the problem of intolerance, this time in regard to the *discriminatory behaviour* faced by immigrant minorities in situations where they apply for jobs. Oreopoulos conducted a large-scale field experiment involving thousands of fictional resumés in response to actual online job postings across multiple occupations in Toronto. He constructed the resumés to represent recent immigrants from the three largest countries of origin—China, India, and Pakistan—and from Britain, as well as non-immigrants with and without ethnic-sounding names. Among his key results was the finding that interview request rates for English-named applicants with Canadian education and experience were more than three times higher than for resumés with Chinese, Indian, or Pakistani names with foreign education and experience. Overall, his analysis suggests considerable employer discrimination against applicants with ethnic names or with work experience solely outside of Canada.

Taken together, the chapters in this final part of the book provide convincing evidence that social inequality in Canada continues to be an important issue and a sober reality for many of its citizens. Despite the acknowledged freedoms and chances for success that exist in our society today, we still have a long way to go before complete equality, of either opportunity or condition, can be achieved.

21 Social Inequality and Health

Gerry Veenstra

Introduction

Social inequality in its various forms can have a multitude of detrimental effects on people's lives. Such inequalities can potentially influence a host of important life chances, including the probability of obtaining a university degree, getting a good job, adopting a child, or being victimized by crime. The purpose of this chapter is to explore the degree to which social inequalities in Canada affect one of the most fundamental life chances of all: good health. The main focus of the analysis is on relationships between gender, race or ethnicity, social class, and sexual orientation, on the one hand, and a range of health indicators, on the other. The discussion deals with a variety of arguments and explanations that populate the social determinants of health literature, and offers an indication of the extent to which health researchers have provided sound empirical evidence to assess these arguments and explanations.

The first section of the chapter describes associations between gender and health in Canada, delineating historical gender differences in life expectancy and contemporary gender differences in mortality and in various dimensions of physical and mental health (morbidity). The next section describes associations between race/ethnicity and health. Experiences of interpersonal and institutionalized racism, as well as the potentially intervening effects of social class, are particularly relevant to these associations. A description of the strong association between social class and health comes next, accompanied by explanations for this association that address material, psychosocial, and behavioural factors. The final section describes some of the health effects of sexual orientation, effects that may be at least partly explained by the presence of homophobia and heterosexism in Canadian society.

Gender and Health

Before the advent of industrial capitalism, Canadian men and women had very similar life expectancies (Clarke 2000). As recently as 1921, life expectancy was 60.6 years for females and 58.4 years for males, a difference of only 2.2 years. By the 1950s, the gender gap had risen to about 4.5 years in favour of females. By 1996, life expectancy was 81.4 years for females and 75.7 years for males, representing a major improvement for all Canadians over the preceding 75-year period, but with a larger gender gap in life expectancy of

5.7 years. The gender gap subsequently narrowed to just 4.0 years in 2011, with life expectancies of 83.5 years for females and 79.5 years for males. Canadian women clearly hold the edge over Canadian men when it comes to length of life, although the advantage recently appears to be waning.

Among causes of death, the rank ordering for the top 17 causes, as reported in Canadian health statistics in 2011, was very similar for men and women. This pattern suggests that men and women are dying for largely the same reasons. However, for 16 of the 17 causes of death, the age-standardized mortality rate for men was higher than the corresponding rate for women. (The one exception was Alzheimer's disease.) In particular, the cancer and heart disease mortality rates were much higher for men than for women. Trovato and Nirannanilathu (2007) showed that death from heart disease was the major contributor to the gender gap in life expectancy in 2000, followed by other cancers, accidents/violence, and lung cancer. Other circulatory diseases, breast cancer, prostate cancer, cirrhosis of the liver, and suicide made substantially smaller contributions to gender differences in mortality. Among unintentional injuries, motor vehicle accidents were especially important in accounting for higher mortality for men—especially young men—compared to women (Segall and Chappell 2000). During the teenage and young adult years, young men are much more likely than young women to die as the result of an accident, and even elderly men are more likely than elderly women to die from accidents due to falls, poisoning, drowning, choking, guns, or electrocution (Clarke 2000). Throughout the past century, the majority of deaths in the workplace were male deaths. In short, men appear to be more likely than women to die from nearly all of the major causes of death.

Various explanations have been posed to account for these gendered health inequalities. The "social acceptability" hypothesis suggests that women are more willing to accept the sick role than are men, by admitting sickness to others and accepting help from friends, family, and the health-care system (Gee and Kimball 1987). Women may also be more attentive to bodily sensations, more willing to talk about them, and more likely to seek care for each episode of an illness. A greater attention to minor signs and symptoms, and a greater willingness to take preventive and healing actions, may mean that health problems for women are less severe than for men of the same age (Clarke 2004).

Alternatively, the "risk" hypothesis suggests that men are socialized to engage in risky behaviours like hang-gliding, drinking and driving, and so forth. One American government project concluded that the prevalence of risk behaviours among adults was more common among men than among women for all but three of the 14 risk behaviours they studied. Some of these behaviours included smoking, drinking and driving, failing to use seat belts, not getting health screenings, and not being aware of medical conditions (Powell-Griner et al. 1997). A related explanation, the "healthy behaviours" argument, asserts that women are more likely than men to engage in healthful behaviours and lifestyles (Courtenay 2000). For example, women may be more likely to exercise, to control their weight, and to consume vitamin and mineral supplements. All of the explanations noted above are implicitly embedded in theories of masculinity and femininity, and essentially argue that adherence to popular norms of hegemonic masculinity and femininity is lethal for men's health and beneficial for women's health.

Although the mortality storyline in Canada suggests that males are unhealthier than females, the morbidity storyline is quite different. For example, based on data from the National Population Health Survey (NPHS) of 1994–5, Denton et al. (2004) reported significantly poorer health scores for Canadian women with regard to distress, self-rated health, functional health, and the presence of a chronic condition. McDonough and Walters (2001), also using data from the 1994–5 NPHS, found more distress and chronic conditions among women. Similarly, Janzen and Muhajarine (2003) analyzed data from the 1994–5 and 1996–7 waves of the NPHS to demonstrate poorer self-rated health and chronic conditions scores for women; the second of these associations persisted after stratifying the sample by age. Veenstra's (2011) analysis of data from the 2003 Canadian Community Health Survey also showed a slightly higher rate of reporting fair or poor self-rated health for women than for men, after controlling for age.

Overall, then, the empirical evidence shows consistently that Canadian women are more likely than Canadian men to report psychological distress, poor self-rated health, and the presence of a chronic condition. Various theories from the sociological literature on health inequalities have been employed to explain such gender differences in health. For instance, the "multiple roles" hypothesis suggests that, among women, taking on numerous duties (e.g., as parent, employee, sibling, caretaker, secretary for the choir) can result in role overload, role conflict, and excessive demands on time and energy that can contribute to higher levels of psychological distress and poorer physical health (Waldron et al. 1998). Similarly, the "nurturant" hypothesis suggests that women may experience more ill health than men due to excessive primary caregiver responsibilities, which typically fall to women in a patriarchal society. Providing care for others can lead to role strain, along with stress and time constraints that can lead women to neglect their own health needs (Segall and Chappell 2000).

Proponents of another hypothesis, the socio-economic status argument, claim that men tend to rank higher than women on measures of socio-economic status, such as income and occupational prestige, with subsequent negative effects for women's health. The reasons for such socio-economic differences are structural in nature and pertain to the history of patriarchy in Canada and elsewhere. Evidence indicates, for example, that women are not always rewarded in the marketplace for doing the same work as men; women often confront a "glass ceiling" that limits the status they can attain in a given organization; traditional "male" occupations tend to be of higher status than traditional "female" occupations; and so on. Women are also more likely to work at part-time jobs without benefits and opportunities for advancement and in jobs with less control over their duties and hours of work. Given the strong evidence for associations between socio-economic status and health in Canada, described later in this chapter, it is reasonable to conclude that gender differences in socio-economic status may at least partly explain gender differences in health.

Another hypothesis focuses on the "biased nature of medical research" argument. It suggests that women's health may tend to be worse than men's because much medical research has stemmed from male researchers studying male subjects. In previous generations, women's bodies were assumed to be similar to men's bodies, but they were said to be harder to research because of the additional complications introduced by menstruation, menopause, and pregnancy. Consequently, women have been traditionally under-studied in medical research, with treatments being developed for men that may not always apply to women.

Finally, there is the "under-reporting" hypothesis, which asserts that in many household surveys women are more likely to speak for the household as a whole than are men, which means that the morbidity characteristics of men are often under-reported (Clarke 2000). Prevalent norms of masculinity may also make men less likely to record for themselves the presence of an illness and/or report an illness to a survey researcher. The under-reporting explanation essentially suggests that survey findings sometimes provide inaccurate portrayals of health among men, so that what may appear to be poorer health scores for women are not actually the case.

Not all of these explanations have been subject to rigorous empirical investigation based on nationally representative Canadian data. Veenstra (2011) showed a reduction in the weak association between gender and self-rated health upon controlling for educational attainment and household income, suggesting that socio-economic status may mediate this gender–health association.

Denton et al. (2004) explored the degree to which various influences mediate the association between gender and health. These influences included structural factors (e.g., living alone, being a single parent, being of low income, working double days, and working in lower-status occupations), behavioural factors (e.g., smoking, drinking, and obesity), and psychosocial factors (e.g., stressful life events, childhood trauma, chronic stress in life domains, low self-esteem, less mastery, and less coherence). While some of these factors did help to account for the association between gender and self-rated health, most gender differences in functional health, distress, or chronic conditions were not explained by them. In a similar investigation, McDonough and Walters (2001) concluded that differential exposure to stressors played a small role in explaining gender differences in psychological distress, but had no effect on gender differences in self-rated health or chronic conditions. Finally, using the NPHS dataset, Janzen and Muhajarine (2003) sought to determine whether "breadth" of social role occupancy differentially affected the health of men and women. That is, these authors considered if single, double, or triple roles (involving various combinations of being married, having children at home, and working in the labour market) accounted for gender differences in health. The researchers found, however, that men were more likely than women to hold *both* single *and* triple roles, so that the role overload hypothesis could not be substantiated.

In summary, Canadian research based on nationally representative data reveals a somewhat higher risk of some forms of mental and physical illness for women than for men. In contrast, studies pertaining to mortality indicate higher age-standardized death rates for men than for women for nearly every major cause of death. Many explanations for gender differences in the health determinants literature have not yet been conclusively validated in the Canadian context. Nevertheless, theoretical perspectives that focus on contemporary manifestations of norms of masculinity and femininity seem especially promising.

Race, Ethnicity, and Health

Race is a social and political construct that has been used to distinguish among people on the basis of phenotypical (visible) physical characteristics such as skin colour. The word "race" appeared in the English language in the early seventeenth century; however, it was not until the eighteenth century that the term was used in Europe and North America to name and explain differences across human populations. Early racial typologies include those of Carolus Linnaeus, who in 1758 distinguished between European, American, Asiatic, and African races, and Johan Blumenbach, who in 1795 distinguished between Caucasian, Mongolian, American, Ethiopian, and Malay races. It turns out that the physical features used to delineate these racial categories do not correlate well with differences in genotype (in genetic makeup), and there are no systematic differences among these categories in regard to personality, intelligence, and so forth. Consequently, the term "race" is often placed in quotes by sociologists, to draw explicit attention to this problematic and to make it clear that racial groupings are inherently social, rather than biological, constructions. Ethnicity in turn is "a principle by which people are defined, differentiated, and organized around a shared awareness of their common ancestry as expressed in culture, physical attributes, language, historical experiences, and birthright" (Fleras 2010: 371). To the degree that racial identities have cultural dimensions, and that ethnic identities are shaped by relations of power, the concepts of race and ethnicity cannot be readily disentangled from one another.

How might "race" or ethnicity influence the health of Canadians? Individuals who do not belong to a society's economically and politically ascendant group, which in Canada comprises Whites of Western European ancestry, often possess discernible characteristics, such as language and dress. These characteristics can clearly locate them within a minority group and ultimately lead to experiences of racism. Racist experiences can affect health directly via the negative physical and psychological consequences of the interpersonal racial discrimination incurred during the course of everyday life. Racial oppression can become internalized in the mind and self, damaging self-esteem and potentially compromising and reducing the amount of social support available. Health can also be affected indirectly through processes of institutional racism, whereby minority groups identified and defined as biologically or culturally different are systematically excluded from certain social, political, and economic worlds (Karlsen and Nazroo 2002). In short, racism can influence how people are treated in many aspects of their lives, limiting their job, educational, recreational, marital, and family choices and chances. All these experiences and restrictions have the potential to affect health. Unfortunately, explanations predicated upon the occurrence of either interpersonal or institutional racism are not easily verified empirically because of inherent difficulties in recording experiences of discrimination that are not always recognized as such by survey respondents.

Although the body of existing research on racism and health in Canada is not large (Clarke 2004), many researchers have examined the health circumstances of Indigenous people in particular, that is, First Nations, Métis, and Inuit (who are typically referred to collectively as "Aboriginals" in Statistics Canada's health surveys). Shah (2004) notes that life expectancy in 2000 was 68.9 years for Aboriginal males (versus 76.3 years for Canadian males) and 76.3 years for Aboriginal females (versus 81.5 years for Canadian females). These differences in length of life between Aboriginal and other Canadians were somewhat narrower than they had been in previous decades but were still substantial. As for specific causes of death, data for 1996 indicated that First Nations and Inuit were 6.5 times more likely than the total Canadian population to die from injuries or poison, while evidence from 1994 showed that the suicide rate for Indigenous people aged 15–24 was eight times higher than that of any other group of Canadian youth (Shah 2004). Deaths from diabetes among Aboriginals are also especially high in comparison with the Canadian population (Young et al. 2000). It is apparent that life expectancies for Indigenous people are among the very lowest of all racial and ethnic groups in Canada.

In other research, Veenstra (2009) used data from the Canadian Community Health Survey (CCHS) of 2003 to show that, compared to White Canadians, there are higher risks of diabetes among Aboriginal, Black, Filipino, and South Asian Canadians, higher risks of hypertension among Aboriginal, Black, and Filipino Canadians, and higher risks of fair/poor self-rated health among Aboriginal, Chinese, and South Asian Canadians. He found that socio-economic status, as measured by educational attainment and household income, partly explained the associations between Aboriginal identification and these health indicators. These findings suggest that social and economic inequities pertaining to education, employment, and poverty may explain a significant portion of the health differential faced by Indigenous people in Canada.

Veenstra and Patterson (2016) combined data from nine cycles of the CCHS to examine health differentials between Black and White Canadians. They found that, after controlling for age, marital status, urban/rural residence, and immigrant status, Black respondents were more likely than White respondents to report diabetes and hypertension, Black women were less likely than White women to report cancer and fair/poor mental health, and Black men were less likely than White men to report heart disease. These health disparities were not explained by differences in socio-economic status (education and household income), health-related practices (smoking and regular physical activity), and body-mass index. Veenstra and Patterson (2016) speculate that the high rates of diabetes and hypertension among Black Canadians reflect experiences of racism, and that the low rates of heart disease and cancer among Black Canadians reflect survival bias, i.e., Black Canadians are less likely to survive heart disease and cancer long enough to participate in surveys like the CCHS.

Wu et al. (2003) used data from the National Population Health Survey of 1996–7 to predict depression. They found that, compared with English Canadians, respondents in the Chinese, East Asian, and Southeast Asian groups showed lower levels of depression, while respondents in the Aboriginal, French Canadian, Jewish, and "other White" categories experienced higher levels. The researchers also found that socio-economic status and social resources (in the form of various types of social support) did *not* mediate the association between racial/ethnic affiliation and depression. Marital status did mediate the association, however, with non-English Canadians being more likely to be unmarried. The authors speculated that marital relationships are a rich source of emotional and instrumental support, and that these relationships tend to encourage good health-care practices and oblige individuals to refrain from engaging in health-damaging behaviours. Again using the 1996–7 NPHS, Wu and Schimmele (2005) compared the worse functional health scores of Aboriginals, Arabs, West Asians, and "mixed-race" Canadians, as well as the worse self-rated health scores of Aboriginals, to the national average. When health behavioural and socio-economic factors were controlled, only the functional health disadvantage experienced by Arabic and West Asian Canadians disappeared, suggesting that socio-economic status and health behaviours do not explain the majority of the racial/ethnic health associations they identified in their analyses.

In summary, data on mortality rates and life expectancy indicate that Indigenous people in Canada suffer higher mortality rates than virtually all other Canadians. Research on morbidity again demonstrates exceptionally poor health outcomes for Indigenous people, and shows that this result is at least partly explained by socio-economic factors. Black, Filipino, and South Asian Canadians also appear to suffer inordinately poor health of one kind or another. In general, explanations for associations between race or ethnicity and health that point to socio-economic differentials and experiences of racism or discrimination appear to be especially pertinent for Black and Indigenous people in Canada.

Social Class and Health

Health research that employs the idea of social class, especially as conceived within the classical Marxist tradition (Marx and Engels 1970, 1976), is well developed in European nations such as the United Kingdom. However, no nationally representative study in the United States or Canada has used a Marxist conception of social class when assessing health patterns. Instead, virtually all of the North American research on social class and health has relied on socio-economic status measures (especially income, education, and occupation) in place of social class, and has used the terms "social class" and "socio-economic status" interchangeably. Socio-economic status indicators like income, education, and occupation are typically treated as continuously graded scales that serve to stratify individuals rather than groups (see, e.g., Grabb 2007). Education, as measured by highest educational level attained or number of years of education, is the most common indicator of socio-economic status in the health literature, in part because measures of education are easier to collect and because, beyond a certain age, formal educational credentials generally remain constant. Education also has a relatively low refusal rate on questionnaires (Liberatos et al. 1988), that is, more people are willing to disclose their level of education attainment. Annual income or wealth is also used frequently in health research, although these variables are far more difficult to measure. For example, questions about income have a high refusal rate on questionnaires (Liberatos et al. 1988) and income or wealth can be unstable over the life course (Benzeval and Judge 2001).

It is apparent that socio-economic status and social class should be clearly differentiated from one another, both conceptually and empirically, because they can manifest distinct, though often interrelated, associations with health. Since class relations privilege some groups in the labour market and then reward the members of these groups and their families with better incomes, greater opportunities for educational attainment, and/or jobs with higher prestige, socio-economic status likely intervenes between class position and health. However, to the extent that class relations influence the health of the members of some class groupings by pathways other than the accumulation of socio-economic resources, then class position and socio-economic status will be distinct determinants of health. Unfortunately, the degree to which social class and socio-economic status are distinct and complementary determinants of health in Canada is not known. The relationship between socio-economic status and health has been extensively researched in this country, however, and many explanations for it can be found in the health literature.

Possible explanations for the association between socio-economic status and health include the "spuriousness" argument, which suggests that some prior genetic cause such as physical size or intellectual capacity influences both socio-economic status and health. Adler et al. (1994) note, however, that some studies have controlled for height and find little evidence indicating that intelligence is related to health. Alternatively, the "drift" hypothesis suggests that illness starts a downward trajectory on the socio-economic status ladder, i.e., that causality goes from illness to lower socio-economic status rather than in the other direction. As Adler et al. (1994) show, two comprehensive reviews of the literature conclude that drift accounts for only a small proportion of the relationship between socio-economic status and health. A third hypothesis is the "level of analysis" argument, which proposes that wealthy people congregate spatially in neighbourhoods that tend to have *other* characteristics that can influence the heath of everyone who lives there, including lower crime rates, more green space, fewer bars, and more supermarkets. This explanation essentially argues that the association between socio-economic status and health reflects this higher-level contextual relationship, and so is not truly causal. Like the preceding explanations, this hypothesis has yet to receive much empirical support in the literature.

Most explanations, however, do accept the existence of some causal link between socio-economic status and health. Some researchers offer a "psychosocial" explanation that focuses on non-material factors associated with social status. According to this argument, because people are generally aware of where they stand relative to others in society, those who have low standing in everyday social interactions across multiple social contexts incur deleterious emotional and biological effects on their health. Researchers who adopt a materialist perspective argue that poor health reflects such material phenomena as adverse housing characteristics, bad environmental exposures, poor nutrition, and limited access to medical care, all of which stem from people's low economic standing (Lynch et al. 2004). There is also an "education" argument, which suggests that better-educated people tend to have more accurate information about what influences their health, and the related "health behaviours" argument, which claims that people of higher socio-economic status tend to engage in more healthful practices with regard to smoking, physical activity, dietary choices, substance abuse, and so on. However, Adler et al. (1994) note that the relationship between socio-economic status and health appears to persist, even after controlling for such health behaviours.

Whatever the explanation, an abundance of evidence demonstrates that socio-economic status is strongly related to health in Canada. This is true for a wide variety of health indicators pertaining to mortality, morbidity (including heart diseases, cancers, cardiovascular diseases, etc.), functional ability, and self-perceptions of health. Some research has shown that the socio-economic effect is particularly strong for young and middle-aged adults (Segall and Chappell 2000). Health researchers have also observed that individuals towards the top of the social "ladder" tend to have better health than those immediately below them at all stages of the ladder, but that this relationship weakens in strength as status increases (Wolfson et al. 1999).

Only a few of the many studies that investigate relationships between socio-economic status and health in Canada are touched upon here. Veenstra (2011, 2013) used the 2003 Canadian Community Health Survey to find strong effects of both educational attainment and household income on self-rated health and on the presence of hypertension. Indeed, of the multiple dimensions of inequality explored in these investigations, socio-economic status was by far the strongest predictor of health.

Studies focusing on psychosocial explanations for the effect of socio-economic status on health have recently captured the interest of many health researchers. Dunn et al. (2006) used a national survey sample collected by the Institute for Social Research at York University to assess the association between health and several socio-economic status measures. These measures included educational attainment, household income, personal income, perceived social standing relative to other Canadians and to Canadians of a previous generation, and actual social standing relative to others in the respondents' neighbourhoods of residence. As expected, results showed that socio-economic status was strongly associated with self-rated health. In support of the psychosocial argument, the researchers also found that perceived status relative to other Canadians was a strong predictor of self-rated health after controlling for age and gender, although perceived status relative to the previous generation was not related to health. Actual relative status was also strongly associated with self-rated health, particularly for comparisons with other neighbourhood residents located at the top of the income ladder. Dunn et al. could not control for socio-economic status when exploring the latter relationships, however, and so could not clearly distinguish between the relative strengths of the materialist and psychosocial explanations.

In summary, social class, at least as indicated by various socio-economic status measures, is among the strongest inequality-based determinants of health in Canada. The especially steep slope of the relationship between socio-economic status and health at the lower end of the status ladder provides support for a materialist perspective. On the other hand, the absence of a clearly identifiable status "cut-point," at which the relationship between socio-economic status and health disappears, supports the viability of the psychosocial perspective. It should also be noted that behavioural explanations are undoubtedly important when it comes to understanding the health effects of socio-economic status.

Sexual Orientation and Health

Negative attitudes towards people with non-heterosexual orientations range from homophobia to heterosexism. Homophobia refers to "any belief system that supports negative myths and stereotypes about homosexual people, or any of the varieties of negative attitudes that arise from fear or dislike of homosexuality" (Banks 2004: 6). Heterosexism refers to "a belief system that values heterosexuality as superior to and/or more natural than homosexuality; does not acknowledge the existence of non-heterosexuals; and assumes that all people are heterosexual" (Banks 2004: 6). Processes of homophobia and heterosexism can stratify people socially, economically, and politically by sexual orientation, and hence can affect the health of non-heterosexual Canadians.

Banks (2004) has identified several ways in which homophobia and heterosexism manifest themselves, all of which have the potential to explain health differences that separate lesbian, gay, bisexual, and transgender (LGBT) people from the heterosexual population. First, internalized homophobia refers to learned biases that people—including LGBT people themselves—incorporate into their own belief systems. External homophobia refers to observed and experienced expressions of internal biases, such as avoidance, verbal abuse, or violence directed towards non-heterosexual persons. Institutional homophobia refers to discriminatory actions on the part of societal institutions, including governments, educational institutions, and businesses, which adversely affect non-heterosexual people. Finally, cultural homophobia or heterosexism refers to social standards and norms that portray heterosexuality as "normal" or "moral" and that, as a result, can overtly depict non-heterosexual orientations as "deviant" or "abnormal." Such norms and negative depictions can be found almost everywhere in the media, in educational settings, and in religious systems, and can lead to the social exclusion of LGBT people.

Banks (2004) has delineated a series of ways in which experiences of homophobia and heterosexism might affect the health of non-heterosexuals. Many negative health effects arise from the chronic stress caused by repeatedly experiencing social stigmatization. For instance, LGBT people may be less likely than heterosexuals to possess strong familial social support or a strong sense of community, leaving them with fewer coping skills and resources for confronting and adapting to chronic stressors. They may suffer emotional distress from internalizing the negative attitudes towards homosexuality propagated in society, from the pressure to conceal their sexual identity, and from their fear of stigmatization. "Coming out" to their families, friends, and communities can be a stressful experience that leads to shame, anxiety, and social rejection.

Other explanations for the association between sexual orientation and health focus on health-relevant behaviours. For instance, certain self-destructive behaviours, such as risky sexual behaviours, violence-based behaviours, and suicide attempts, may be more prevalent among LGBT populations than among other Canadians. Substance abuse, which may be one means of coping with stress or painful emotional issues, also has negative health consequences. In addition, external homophobia can lead to verbal and physical attacks that have direct health effects. Finally, experiences of discrimination regarding employment, insurance, housing, and legal representation ultimately can have indirect health effects, especially since these experiences are connected to socio-economic disadvantage.

There are some studies of the health of gay, lesbian, and bisexual people in Canada, although these analyses have generally been limited by geographic area and sample selection. For instance, one study of young gay males in Vancouver has provided important insights into the possible health effects of sexual orientation (Botnick et al. 2002). Findings revealed that suicide attempts were high in this group, probably because of their relatively low levels of social support, socio-economic status, and self-esteem. Another study by Low-Beer et al. (2002) compared heterosexual, gay, and bisexual men living in the West End of Vancouver and found higher levels of HIV/AIDS in the non-heterosexual groups. Additional research by Myers et al. (1996), using a purposive sample of gay men from across Canada, revealed a relatively high incidence of sexual behaviours that placed the respondents at risk of poor health outcomes. However, given the somewhat selective nature of the samples involved, the results from these studies cannot be generalized to gay, lesbian, and bisexual people in Canada as a whole.

The first nationally representative Statistics Canada survey to ask a question about sexual orientation was the Canadian Community Health Survey. Pakula and Shoveller (2012) used CCHS data from 2007–8 to investigate associations between sexual orientation and mental health at the national level. They found that LGBT respondents were much more likely than heterosexual respondents to report a mood disorder, a relationship that was especially strong among men and among younger respondents. Veenstra (2011, 2013) used the 2003 version of the CCHS to find that gay, lesbian, and especially bisexual Canadians were more likely than heterosexual respondents to report fair or poor self-rated health, with bisexual respondents also more likely to report hypertension. However, problems encountered in the course of the latter investigations illustrate how difficult it can be to generate trustworthy empirical insights into this issue. For example, in the survey sample of respondents aged 25 and older, only 0.9 per cent of respondents selected the gay or lesbian option and only 0.5 per cent chose the bisexual option. These proportions are lower than those reported in similar studies from the United States (Cochran et al. 2003), Australia (Jorm et al. 2002), and the Netherlands (Bakker et al. 2006), where between 2 and 3 per cent of the general population report being gay, lesbian, or bisexual. In fact, all the survey research on this issue probably underestimates the proportion of people with non-heterosexual orientations, due to fear of stigmatization among survey respondents. Indeed, Banks (2004) has suggested that the actual proportion of non-heterosexuals in the population may be as high as 10 per cent. Veenstra (2011) compared the educational attainments and incomes of heterosexual, gay or lesbian, and bisexual respondents in his sample, and speculated that wealthy and well-educated gay or lesbian respondents may have been more willing than poor and less-educated gays or lesbians to report their actual sexual orientation in the CCHS. This outcome suggests that the sample of non-heterosexuals in the CCHS, which is supposed to be nationally representative, does not accurately represent the non-heterosexual population in Canada.

To summarize, the limited evidence available in Canada supports the contention that experiences of homophobia and encounters with heterosexism on the part of gay, lesbian, and bisexual Canadians are detrimental to various aspects of their mental and physical well-being. Further research along these lines is needed to understand more precisely how and for whom social inequality based on sexual orientation influences health in this country.

Conclusion

Health in Canada is an expensive business: in 2011, Canada spent fully 10.9 per cent of its gross domestic product (approximately $188 billion) on health care. Most Canadians associate the quality of the health-care system with the health of the population, implicitly assuming that the first strongly influences the second. However, when we consider that the biggest causes of death in Canada today are degenerative diseases such as cardiovascular disease and cancer, rather than the infectious diseases that were leading causes of mortality a century earlier, it becomes apparent that the nature and quality of Canada's health-care system may not play as large a role in promoting the health of Canadians as it once did. Preventive measures such as immunization and sanitation undoubtedly have had a tremendous effect in lowering mortality rates from infectious disease. Preventive measures for heart disease and cancer are not so easily enacted by a health-care system.

One of the major obstacles to any further increase in the life expectancy of Canadians is the continuing existence of social inequality. As shown in this chapter, inequalities based on gender, race or ethnicity, socio-economic status, and sexual orientation have important impacts on the health and well-being of many people in this country. Especially problematic are the negative health effects incurred by Indigenous Canadians, people with lower education, and those who have lower incomes. Forms of social inequality that translate into health inequalities are among the most egregious and inequitable of all. Many Canadians pay for these inequities with their health, and even with their lives.

The obstacles to ameliorating these problems may be difficult to overcome (Frankish et al. 1999). First, better theoretical models and better evidence are required for us to understand more fully the nature of the causal mechanisms that link social inequality to health in Canada. At the same time, though, causal models that are complex and multi-faceted could be more likely to deter changes in policy than to stimulate them. This could occur because the time frames necessary for addressing and ameliorating social inequality do not always fit nicely into the limited time windows that seem inherent to government electoral cycles and to changing political priorities. Another problem is identifying the appropriate government levels (municipal, provincial, federal) and divisions (social services, housing, taxation) that should take responsibility for initiating and sustaining real change. It could also be that too many Canadians see health care and health as the same thing. As a result, not enough of us may be ready to rally behind a movement towards reducing social inequality itself, which would in turn improve the aggregate health of Canadians in general. Recognizing the close links between social inequality and health should be one of the highest priorities for those policy-makers who seek a substantial improvement in the health of all Canadians.

Questions for Critical Thought

1. Social inequalities are inequalities between groups arising from relations of power. Which of the health inequalities and the explanations for them described in this chapter reflect unequal access to power and privilege and which reflect other kinds of factors?
2. In this chapter, health inequalities by gender, race or ethnicity, social class, and sexual orientation were presented separately. Looking through the chapter, what evidence is there that these factors are interconnected with one another as determinants of health? What other "intersections" involving gender, race or ethnicity, social class, and sexuality could also be investigated in future research on social inequalities in health?
3. Apart from health inequalities by gender, race or ethnicity, social class, and sexual orientation, what other forms of social inequality could also be considered? What would you expect to find regarding health inequalities for these other types of social inequality?
4. Does Canada spend too much on health care? If so, where and how could we spend the money better?

Recommended Readings

Bryant, Toba, Dennis Raphael, Ted Schrecker, and Ronald Labonte. 2011. "Canada: A land of missed opportunity for addressing the social determinants of health." *Health Policy* 101, 1: 44–58.

Davidson, Alan. 2014. *Social Determinants of Health: A Comparative Approach*. Toronto: Oxford University Press.

Frohlich, Katherine L., Nancy Ross, and Chantelle Richmond. 2006. "Health disparities in Canada today: Some evidence and a theoretical framework." *Health Policy* 79, 2–3: 132–43.

Segall, Alexander, and Christopher Fries. 2011. *Pursuing Health and Wellness: Healthy Societies, Healthy People*. Toronto: Oxford University Press.

Recommended Websites

California Newsreel, National Minority Consortia of Public Television, and Joint Center Health Policy Institute:
http://www.unnaturalcauses.org/

Centers for Disease Control and Prevention:
http://www.cdc.gov/socialdeterminants/FAQ.html

Public Health Agency of Canada:
http://www.phac-aspc.gc.ca/ph-sp/determinants/index-eng.php

World Health Organization:
http://www.who.int/social_determinants/en/

References

Adler, Nancy, Thomas Boyce, Margaret Chesney, Sheldon Cohen, Susan Folkman, Robert Kahn, and Leonard Syme. 1994. "Socio-economic status and health." *American Psychologist* 49, 1: 15–24.

Bakker, Floor, Theo Sandford, Ine Vanwesenbeeck, Hanneke Van Lindert, and Gert Westert. 2006. "Do homosexual persons use health care services more frequently than heterosexual persons? Findings from a Dutch population survey." *Social Science & Medicine* 63: 2022–30.

Banks, Christopher. 2004. *The C$st of Homophobia: Literature Review on the Economic Impact of Homophobia on Canada.* Saskatoon: Community–University Institute for Social Research.

Benzeval, M., and K. Judge. 2001. "Income and health: The time dimension." *Social Science & Medicine* 52: 1371–90.

Botnick, Michael, Katherine Heath, Peter Cornelisse, Steffanie Strathdee, Stephen Martindale, and Robert Hogg. 2002. "Correlates of suicide attempts in an open cohort of young men who have sex with men." *Canadian Journal of Public Health* 93, 1: 59–62.

Clarke, Juanne Nancarrow. 2000. *Health, Illness, and Medicine in Canada*, 3rd edn. Toronto: Oxford University Press.

———. 2004. *Health, Illness, and Medicine in Canada*, 4th edn. Toronto: Oxford University Press.

Cochran, Susan, J. Greer Sullivan, and Vickie Mays. 2003. "Prevalence of mental disorders, psychological distress, and mental health services use among lesbian, gay, and bisexual adults in the United States." *Journal of Consulting and Clinical Psychology* 71, 1: 53–61.

Courtenay, Will. 2000. "Constructions of masculinity and their influence on men's well-being: A Theory of gender and health." *Social Science & Medicine* 50: 1385–1401.

Denton, Margaret, Steven Prus, and Vivienne Walters. 2004. "Gender differences in health: A Canadian study of the psychosocial, structural, and behavioural determinants of health." *Social Science & Medicine* 58: 2585–600.

Dunn, James, Gerry Veenstra, and Nancy Ross. 2006. "Psychosocial and neo-material dimensions of SES and health revisited: Determinants of self-rated health in a Canadian national survey." *Social Science & Medicine* 62, 6: 1465–73.

Fleras, Augie. 2010. *Unequal Relations: An Introduction to Race, Ethnic, and Aboriginal Dynamics in Canada*, 6th edn. Toronto: Pearson Canada.

Frankish, C. James, Gerry Veenstra, and Glen Moulton. 1999. "Population health in Canada: Issues and challenges for policy, practice and research." *Canadian Journal of Public Health* 90, Supplement 1: S71–S75.

Gee, Ellen, and M. Kimball. 1987. *Women and Aging.* Toronto: Butterworths.

Grabb, Edward. 2007. *Theories of Social Inequality*, 5th edn. Toronto: Thomson Nelson.

Janzen, B., and Nazeem Muhajarine. 2003. "Social role occupancy, gender, income adequacy, life stage, and health: A longitudinal study of employed Canadian men and women." *Social Science & Medicine* 57: 1491–1503.

Jorm, Anthony, Ailsa Korten, Bryan Rodgers, Patricia Jacomb, and Helen Christensen. 2002. "Sexual orientation and mental health: Results from a community survey of young and middle-aged adults." *British Journal of Psychiatry* 180: 423–7.

Karlsen, Saffron, and James Nazroo. 2002. "Agency and structure: The impact of ethnic identity and racism on the health of ethnic minority people." *Sociology of Health and Illness* 24: 1–20.

Liberatos, P., B. Link, and J. Kelsey. 1988. "The measurement of social class in epidemiology." *Epidemiologic Reviews* 10: 87–121.

Low-Beer, S., K. Bartholomew, A. Weber, K. Chan, M. Landolt, D. Oram, A. Schilder, and R. Hogg. 2002. "A demographic and health profile of gay and bisexual men in a large Canadian urban setting." *AIDS Care* 14, 1: 111–15.

Lynch, J., G.D. Smith, S. Harper, M. Hillemeier, N. Ross, G.A. Kaplan, and M. Wolfson. 2004. "Is income inequality a determinant of population health? Part 1: A systematic review." *Milbank Quarterly* 82, 1: 5–99.

McDonough, Peggy, and Vivienne Walters. 2001. "Gender and health: Reassessing patterns and explanations." *Social Science & Medicine* 52, 4: 547–59.

Marx, Karl, and Friedrich Engels. 1970 [1846]. *The Communist Manifesto.* New York: Washington Square Press.

——and ——. 1976 [1846]. "The German ideology." In *Marx/Engels Collected Works*, vol. 5. New York: International Publishers.

Myers, T., G. Goden, J. Lambert, L. Calzavara, and D. Locker. 1996. "Sexual risk and HIV testing behaviour by gay and bisexual men in Canada." *AIDS Care* 8, 3: 297–310.

Pakula, Basia, and Jean A Shoveller. 2012. "Sexual orientation and self-reported mood disorder diagnosis among Canadian adults." *BMC Public Health* 13: 209: 1–7.

Powell-Griner, E., J. Anderson, and W. Murphy. 1997. "State- and sex-specific prevalence of selected characteristics—Behavioural risk factor surveillance system, 1994 and 1995." *Morbidity and Mortality Weekly Report* 46, 3: 1–31.

Segall, Alexander, and Neena Chappell. 2000. *Health and Health Care in Canada.* Toronto: Prentice-Hall.

Shah, Chandrakant P. 2004. "The health of Aboriginal peoples." In D. Raphael, ed., *Social Determinants of Health: Canadian Perspectives*, pp. 267–80. Toronto: Canadian Scholars' Press.

Trovato, Frank, and Lalu Nirannanilathu. 2007. "From divergence to convergence: The sex differential in life expectancy in Canada, 1971–2000." *Canadian Review of Sociology* 44, 1: 101–22.

Veenstra, Gerry. 2009. "Racialized identity and health in Canada: Results from a nationally representative survey." *Social Science & Medicine* 69, 4: 538–42.

——. 2011. "Race, gender, class, and sexual orientation: Intersecting axes of inequality and self-rated health in Canada." *International Journal for Equity in Health* 10: 3: 1–11.

——. 2013. "Race, gender, class, sexuality (RGCS), and hypertension." *Social Science & Medicine* 89: 16–24.

—— and Andrew C. Patterson. 2016. "Black–white health inequalities in Canada." *Journal of Immigrant and Minority Health* 18, 1: 51–7.

Waldron, I., C. Weiss, and M. Hughes. 1998. "Interacting effects of multiple roles on women's health." *Journal of Health and Social Behavior* 39: 216–36.

Wolfson, Michael, George Kaplan, John Lynch, Nancy Ross, and Eric Backlund. 1999. "The relationship between income inequality and mortality: An empirical demonstration." *British Medical Journal* 319: 953–7.

Wu, Zheng, Samuel Noh, Violet Kaspar, and Christoph Schimmele. 2003. "Race, ethnicity, and depression in Canadian Society." *Journal of Health and Social Behaviour* 44, 3: 426–41.

Wu, Zheng, and Christoph Schimmele. 2005. "Racial/ethnic variation in functional and self-reported health." *American Journal of Public Health* 95, 4: 710–16.

Young, T. Kue, Jeff Reading, Brenda Elias, and John O'Neil. 2000. "Type 2 diabetes mellitus in Canada's First Nations: Status of an epidemic in progress." *Canadian Medical Association Journal* 163, 5: 561–6.

22 The Homeless: Canada's Truly Disadvantaged

Tracy Peressini

Introduction

Homelessness is one of our most enduring and persistent problems. Like systems of stratification and inequality, homelessness exists in all societies in one form or another, and to some degree or another. The word "homeless" has been used to describe the poor and destitute in the developing world, as well as those who have been displaced by war, violence, environmental catastrophe, and economic depressions and recessions. According to a recent UN report (United Nations High Commissioner for Refugees 2014), almost 60 million people were considered to be homeless and/or refugees due to conflict and war. Some of these homeless have immigrated to Canada and other countries, only to find themselves homeless still. "Homelessness" is also a term that has been equally applied to describe those who have no home and/or who sleep rough—that is, those who live on the streets—due to personal troubles such as mental and physical health problems, addictions, family violence, child abuse and neglect, social dislocation and rejection, unemployment, and other social and economic hardships.

During the twentieth century the homeless were labelled with many names: hoboes, vagrants, knights of the road, the dispossessed, transient workers, skid row bums and alcoholics, and even "the houseless." Regardless of what we call them, they are among Canada's truly disadvantaged. They are present in every town, village, city, and urban centre across Canada, and recent reports indicate that their numbers are growing and their level of need is as pressing as ever.

Most people think homelessness is a simple, straightforward problem: if people don't have a home or a place to stay, then give them one and the problem is solved. In fact, though, it is a complex problem, because the homeless are often a hidden population whose composition varies over time, depending on an array of personal, social, and economic conditions.

It is important to understand, first of all, that the information and knowledge about homelessness are limited and, to a large degree, are based on anecdotal and experiential data. Researchers have spent a great deal of time focusing on the interesting stories and experiences of the homeless. However, these stories have limitations as a guide for creating programs and policies to address the problem. This has not stopped researchers from overgeneralizing their findings from small groups of homeless people to the larger population. In addition, much of this knowledge has not been replicated or validated, resulting in considerable variability in the numbers and rates reported. Therefore, there is a real and important need for better data and more complete information on Canada's homeless.

This chapter is organized around four basic questions. First, what is homelessness? Second, what is the composition of the homeless population; in other words, who are the homeless? Third, why are people homeless? Fourth, what is being done and what still needs to be done to address the problem? The chapter concludes by challenging the reader to think critically about the persistent problem of homelessness in Canada.

What Is Homelessness?

Surprisingly, this has not been the first question to be asked in public inquiries. Usually the default question in most investigations has been, *How many* homeless people are there? People are much more interested in using numbers as a means of estimating the severity of the problem. Most people are not interested in definitions as they tend to create boundaries for social inclusion and exclusion. However, we cannot determine the size of the population or the scope of the problem without first defining who is considered homeless and who is not. In this section we review the role that definitions play in estimating the extent of the problem in Canada. We also consider the new and uniquely Canadian definition of homelessness. Finally, we present an overview of the latest counts and estimates of the size and scope of Canadian homelessness.

The rising numbers of visibly homeless people on Canada's streets in the 1990s captured the nation's attention and concern. Researchers, policy analysts, social advocates, and service providers sought to determine how the problem should be addressed. It is unusual for so many stakeholders to be involved in a response to a social problem all at once. Typically, their involvement comes in stages, starting with people at the ground level, then service providers, and ending with government officials and policy analysts. Having all of the stakeholders participating at the same time resulted in what has been referred to as the "homelessness muddle" (Ellickson 1990: 45), which refers to a pool of differing definitions, methods for counting, agendas, and politics, all resulting in disagreement on what homelessness is, how many homeless people there are, and how to address the problem. On the one hand, social advocates and service providers prefer definitions that address the full spectrum of homelessness, including anyone from those who are at risk of homelessness (e.g., those who have some form of housing, but are at imminent risk of losing it) to those who are already without a permanent home. On the other hand, government officials and policy analysts prefer definitions that are restricted to those who currently lack a permanent place to live, typically those actually living on the street and/or living in shelters for the homeless. For example, using a broad definition of homelessness, American social advocates in the 1980s estimated that the homeless population was in excess of 1 million people (Hombs and Snyder 1982); at the same time, the US government, counting only street people and shelter users, estimated that between 250,000 and 350,000 people were homeless (US Department of Housing and Urban Development 1984). The debate over appropriate definitions has been one of the driving forces behind studies of homelessness since the early 1990s.

While opinions differ about numbers and rates, we are closer to a consensus over definitions. Most researchers and social advocates accept the United Nations definition of homelessness (see COH 2012), which indicates that people are homeless if they meet one of two criteria: (1) they have no home and live either outdoors or in emergency shelters or hostels; and (2) they live in homes that do not meet UN standards for a minimal home; (i.e., protection from the elements, access to safe water and sanitation, affordable price, secure tenure and personal safety, and accessibility to employment, education, and health care) (Springer 2000). In practice, however, many studies employ a variant of the narrower definition stipulated in the United States under the Stuart B. McKinney Homeless Assistance Act (COH 2012; US Congress, House of Representatives 1987). The Act defines homeless individuals as (1) persons who lack a fixed, regular, and adequate night-time residence; or (2) persons who have a primary night-time residence that is either a supervised or publicly operated shelter designed to provide temporary living accommodations (including welfare hotels, congregate shelters, and transitional housing for the mentally ill), an institution that provides temporary residence for individuals intended to be institutionalized, or a public or private place not designed for, or ordinarily used as, a regular sleeping accommodation for human beings (see Hirschl 1990: 444–5). The latter definition is used, in one form or another, in city censuses of the homeless across Canada.

Finally, after over 30 years of discussion and debate, working in conjunction with stakeholders at all levels, the Canadian Observatory on Homelessness (COH) developed what they say is a uniquely Canadian definition and typology of homelessness (COH 2012). The COH Working Group reviewed the gamut of conceptual definitions and argued for the use of a single definition of homelessness that: (1) gives us a common language to discuss, study, and respond to the problem; (2) is the foundation for consistent measurement of the size and scope of the problem; (3) creates a framework for evaluating progress and outcomes in terms of social research on homelessness and policy and program development to address the problem; (4) provides continuity and comparability across studies and jurisdictions so, for example, a program developed in one part of the country could be exported to and implemented in another part of the country; and (5) allows for stronger and more definitive policy responses to the problem (COH 2012).

The COH claims to have developed a "usable, understandable definition that is uniquely Canadian yet allows for national and international comparisons" (COH 2012: 1). As discussed below, this definition is not unique; moreover, it is highly politicized and subjective, subjective, and fails to provide guidelines that stakeholders can use to measure homelessness with any precision, accuracy, or consistency. The typology is a blend of the two definitions noted above. In this regard, it seems truly Canadian, because it is designed to be as inclusive as possible and to appease as many stakeholders and interested parties as possible. However, it does not provide instructions on how the typology can be used to measure the size and scope of the homeless population.

The COH Working Group (COH 2012: 1) defines homelessness as follows:

> Homelessness describes the situation of an individual or family without stable, permanent, appropriate housing, or the immediate prospect, means and ability of acquiring it. It is the result of systemic or societal barriers, a lack of affordable and appropriate housing, the individual/household's financial, mental, cognitive, behavioural or physical challenges, and/or racism and discrimination. That is, homelessness encompasses a range of physical living situations, organized here in a typology that includes 1) Unsheltered, or absolutely homeless and living on the streets or in places not intended for human habitation; 2) Emergency Sheltered, including those staying in overnight shelters for people who are homeless, as well as shelters for those impacted by family violence; 3) Provisionally Accommodated, referring to those whose accommodation is temporary or lacks security of tenure, and finally, 4) At Risk of Homelessness, referring to people who are not homeless, but whose current economic and/or housing situation is precarious or does not meet public health and safety standards. It should be noted that for many people homelessness is not a static state but rather a fluid experience, where one's shelter circumstances and options may shift and change quite dramatically and with frequency.

The core definition is summarized in the first sentence and basically describes what homelessness refers to: people who lack stable, permanent, appropriate housing, or who do not possess the ability to acquire it. This definition resembles the UN definition in that it is extremely broad; it ranges from those who are unhoused and unsheltered (e.g., street people), to those who are at risk of homelessness, the poor, the working poor, and those receiving government transfers (e.g., welfare, social security, disability support), with an emphasis on the at-risk population. This conceptualization does not easily yield guidelines for how to measure homelessness. It does not establish any boundaries or rules for deciding who will be counted as homeless and who will not. Therefore, the COH Working Group's argument that this definition is the foundation for consistent measurement across Canada is problematic, because it can be interpreted and used in numerous ways. The last part of the "definition" specifies a typology of housing arrangements, from those living on the streets, to those whose housing is precarious and unstable. While the typology of the Working Group is very detailed, its classification is not unique or new. It simply rehashes other previous efforts to define and measure homelessness (see Peressini et al. 2009; Taueber 1991).

Definitions are important because they directly affect how we count the homeless. If we choose to define homelessness from a broad perspective, then we produce an inflated estimate of the size of the population. If we choose to define homelessness from a narrower perspective, like that of the Stuart B. McKinney Act, which focuses purely on the street and sheltered homeless, then we obtain lower estimates, with no way to know the margin of error in the estimates. If we choose to parse the definition further by focusing purely on street dwellers (which local, regional, provincial, and federal governments prefer), then we end up with the smallest possible estimate of the homeless population. The choice of measure is crucial because it helps to determine the magnitude of the social response to addressing the problem (Fitzgerald et al. 2001: 121). The estimated size and composition of the homeless population guides government officials and policy analysts in determining the amount of funding that should be allotted for programs and services for the homeless (Springer 2000). Definitions, then, not only specify who will be counted, but also determine who "counts." The act of defining who is homeless results in a political and moral statement about who is worthy of public assistance and resources and who is not (Rossi 1989).

In 1995, Lynn McDonald, David Hulchanski, and I organized the first Canadian conference on methods for studying, counting, and understanding the homeless in Canada. The conference brought together community stakeholders, government officials, and university researchers, who agreed on similar definitions and typologies and operationalized them in terms of actual methods for estimating the homeless population. The primary recommendation from this conference was to develop a national database and tracking system of users of homeless services and programs, using a limited definition focusing on the recipients of shelters and food services (e.g., soup kitchens and drop-ins with meals). Over the next five years, the Canada Mortgage and Housing Corporation (CMHC) developed the tracking tool called The Homeless Individual and Family Information System, or HIFIS (see Peressini and Engeland 2004). In 2000, the responsibility for final development and implementation of the tool was transferred to the National Secretariat on Homelessness (Peressini and Engeland 2004), now called the Homelessness Partnering Strategy (HPS). HIFIS has been integrated into the National Homeless Information System (NHIS), which co-ordinates and amalgamates the collection of data using the HIFIS tool across communities and jurisdictions in Canada. Only recently have the data collected using this tool become available and been analyzed by the HPS.

In 2012, the HPS published the results of five years of data collected from participating shelters using HIFIS, combined with data collected from emergency homeless shelters by the city of Toronto (see also HPS 2015). Although HIFIS was designed for use in both services and shelters for the homeless, it has only been implemented in emergency shelters that chose to participate in the program. Some advocates and critics might argue that this provides only a very limited glimpse into the world of the homeless, but researchers have clearly demonstrated that those in shelters constitute the biggest component of the homeless population (Peressini et al. 2009; Dennis and Iachan 1993; Taueber 1991; Burnam and Koegel 1988). Furthermore, taking counts over an extended period of time, typically at least 30 days, means that those who are not captured on any single night may well be captured in the multiple counts that occur over this extended period (Peressini et al. 2009; Dennis and Iachan 1993; Taueber 1991; Burnam and Koegel 1988). Consequently, the longer that HIFIS runs in shelters, the more accurate its counts become. Unfortunately, HIFIS is not running in all of Canada's homeless shelters at present. Therefore, the results presented in the Homelessness Partnering Strategy (2012) National Shelter Study (NSS) are based on limited data.

There are 403 emergency homeless shelters in Canada, with a total of 15,400 beds (HPS 2012). The estimates from the NSS come from data collected in 96–123 shelters (about 25 to 30 per cent) between 2005 and 2009. Men, women, families, youth, and women with children are represented in this count; the NSS does not include shelters for battered women or transitional or so-called "second-stage" shelters that are available for six months to one year. The NSS estimates that 147,726 people used an emergency shelter in 2009. In addition, the NSS reports that 14,400 of the 15,400 beds were in use on any given night in 2009. While the absolute numbers did not change much over five years, the amount of time that people stayed in the shelter did, particularly in family shelters. The average length of stay doubled, from one to two months between 2008 and 2009. For people in the other types of shelter, the average stay was two to three days longer.

In summary, our best estimate of the homeless population is that about 147,000 people use an emergency shelter annually. Taking the annual figure and dividing by the number of nights in a year yields an average nightly count of 405 people staying in an emergency shelter. If we compare this to the bed count of 14,400, the problem of numbers and counting becomes apparent. The absolute number of people is relatively small, yet the level of demand and need, as reflected in bed nights, is significantly greater. It is also interesting that the only previous national count of the homeless produced similar estimates. In 1987, the Canadian Council on Social Development, in conjunction with the Canada Mortgage and Housing Corporation, conducted a national survey of temporary and emergency shelters, and reported that there were between 130,000 and 250,000 homeless Canadians (McLaughlin 1987). Gaetz et al. (2014: 5) speculate that there currently are 235,000 Canadians who experience homelessness annually, with over 35,000 homeless Canadians on any given night. Without specifying any source for their numbers, Gaetz et al. indicate that, of the 235,000 homeless Canadians, 5,000 are unsheltered, 180,000 were staying in shelters, and 50,000 were provisionally sheltered (e.g., in motels, transitional housing, or second-stage housing). Furthermore, of the 35,000 who are homeless on a nightly basis, 13,000–33,000 are chronically or episodically homeless. Clearly, the counts, numbers, rates, and percentages of homelessness vary considerably across sources, making it difficult to determine the extent of the problem and how to respond to it.

Who Is Homeless?

Most experts agree that the composition of today's homeless population differs significantly from that found in the first half of the twentieth century. Today's homeless are significantly more diverse and much more like other Canadians than we might expect. They come from all social classes and demographic groups: men and women, children and youth, families, students, seniors, immigrants and refugees, and Aboriginal peoples. They have experienced problems with poverty, unemployment, family violence, child abuse, divorce, mental illness, depression, physical disabilities, substance abuse, addictions, deviance, and criminalization. Nevertheless, most people still conjure up images of bag ladies, beggars, squeegee kids, and skid row alcoholics when thinking about the homeless. Street people are the most visible homeless people, but research suggests that they represent less than 10 per cent of the homeless population (Dennis and Iachan 1993). Most homeless persons actually do not live on the street; they live in temporary and emergency shelters, with friends and family, in their cars, indoors in public spaces, and in abandoned buildings. They also move into and out of public institutions, including group homes, psychiatric wards, shelters, and prisons. They are the invisible poor, and most never cross our paths in everyday life. As one homeless sole-support parent in Calgary once told a local reporter, "you can see me on the street and not know I'm homeless" (Slobodian 2002: B2).

For many, homelessness involves a complex process of exits from and returns to homelessness. It is partly the rapid turnover rate that prevents us from seeing the many different types of persons affected by homelessness. Researchers have found that most of the homeless experience multiple spells of homelessness, with initial periods of relatively short duration (usually 7–30 days), and subsequent periods of progressively longer duration (Piliavin et al. 1993). In most cases, homelessness is not a lasting condition but a short-term situation. No one chooses to be homeless, but extreme poverty and economic instability mean that it may take just one personal crisis—job loss, a missed child support payment, or illness—to deprive someone of housing. A key challenge is finding affordable housing, which is difficult because of wide-ranging changes and cuts in federal support for Canada's social safety net in recent decades, particularly for rent control and social housing (Gaetz 2012).

It is important to remember that the experience of homelessness is devastating and demoralizing. As Koegel, Burnam, and Farr (1990) have noted, homelessness involves a levelling process, in which personal and demographic characteristics have no observable impact on people's ability to adapt and survive on the streets. To be homeless is to be truly disadvantaged, regardless of age, sex, race, ethnic background, or any other demographic characteristic. That said, some demographic groups experience different durations of homelessness and different pathways into and out of homelessness.

Men are the most visible of Canada's homeless, and also constitute the largest demographic group. Almost all studies in Canada over the last several decades have found that men represent between 70 and 90 per cent of the homeless population (HPS 2012; Layton 2000). Researchers also report that mental illness, addictions, and disabilities are higher for men than for women (Gaetz 2012). Other studies have found a significant age effect, with younger men's addiction problems mainly involving drugs and older men reporting higher rates of drinking problems (Peressini 2007).

The NSS indicates significant gender and age differences in shelter users. The disparity in shelter use between men and women increases with age, with the proportion of older homeless men significantly higher than for older women and for younger men and women. Men make up progressively greater percentages of the homeless as age increases, with 63 per cent of youth, 76 per cent of adults, and almost 80 per cent of older adults being male. This study also found slight but significant changes in the shelter use population over the period of 2005–9, with the number of children and seniors increasing and adults aged 25–54 falling slightly.

Studies indicate that the age profile of Canada's homeless is in line with that of the general population, since most of the homeless are in the 25–54 age group (HPS 2012; Layton 2000). However, recent research suggests that the number of homeless children shelter users is also on the rise (HPS 2012). The NSS found that the number of children shelter users increased from 6,205 in 2005 to 9,459 in 2009. Youth and seniors are difficult populations to track because they are less likely to stay in or use shelter services. The NSS estimates that almost 30,000 youth and about 2,500 seniors used shelter services in 2009. Male youth and seniors are more likely to use emergency shelters than are their female counterparts (HPS 2012). Due to Old Age Security (OAS) and other programs for the elderly, seniors aged 65+ represent the smallest part of the homeless population; however, when they are homeless, they tend to require more intensive supports and services (Homeless Hub 2015).

Until recently, the research literature frequently discussed the preponderance of lesbian, gay, bisexual, transgender, queer, questioning, and two-spirited (LGBTQ2) youth among the homeless youth population, yet little data or evidence supported this observation. A recent street count in Toronto found that about 20 per cent of youth in the shelter system identified as LGBTQ2 (Homeless Hub 2015). It should be noted that only a fraction of youth, LGBTQ2 or otherwise, use the shelter system, so it is likely that 20 per cent is an underestimate.

Single women account for about one-fourth of Canada's shelter users (HPS 2012). Services and programs are generally developed to target women's homelessness, particularly women with children. Some speculate that the single female population is larger than estimates suggest, because they tend to be among the hidden homeless who share housing with families and friends, live in inadequate and unsafe housing, or, like youth, trade sex for a place to sleep (Homeless Hub 2015). Researchers often tie women's homelessness to poverty and men's homelessness to unemployment, mental problems, and addictions (Homeless Hub 2015).

Various reports claim that family homelessness is on the rise in Canada, but evidence supporting this claim appears sketchy and inconsistent. The supposed rise among homeless families and women could stem from changing definitions of homelessness and the inclusion of family shelters, welfare motels, second-stage shelters, and shelters for abused women in counts (Peressini 2009). Women's advocates have lobbied strongly for more programs, services, and safe, affordable housing for sole-support women and their families, presumably because they are more vulnerable than other marginalized groups.

Aboriginal people make up a disproportionate part of the urban homeless population. Like many of the other marginalized groups of homeless, the reported rates of homelessness for this group vary substantially across studies, from a low of 20 per cent of the homeless population to a high of 75 per cent, depending on the place or region studied. Although the evidence is largely anecdotal, a sizable proportion of the homeless population in some of Canada's cities consists of Aboriginal people (Begin et al. 1999; Beavis et al. 1997; Patrick 2014). The varying rates partly stem from the specific treaty rights of local bands and from provincial and federal policies regarding status and non-status eligibility for housing and support.

The number of immigrants and refugees who are homeless appears to be rising as well. Toronto (2001) reported a 6 per cent increase in the number of refugees and immigrants seeking admission to its shelter system over a two-year period, with most being families. Immigrants, refugees, and visible minorities are often among the hidden homeless, because they rarely seek help from mainstream services or programs. Consequently, the few studies that consider immigrants, refugees, and racialization are typically anecdotal, speculative, and sketchy. Therefore, we have little direct evidence documenting the homeless experiences of immigrants, refugees, visible minorities, and Aboriginal people.

Clearly, then, no single group of people characterizes Canada's homeless. While we know that the homeless come from all walks of life, more data collection and analysis are required before we can more fully understand who the homeless are, and how we can best proceed to eradicate the problem.

Why Are People Homeless?

One explanation for why people become homeless focuses on the individual's social, behavioural, emotional, and psychological deficits, emphasizing the role of personal pathology and disability. From this perspective, homelessness occurs because of *personal limitations*, or because there is something "wrong" with *the individual.* Mental or physical illness, physical disability, social alienation, social deviance, and disaffiliation (e.g., criminal behaviour, juvenile delinquency, and drug and alcohol abuse) are the causes, along with human capital deficits (e.g., little education, and low or inappropriate job skills and work experience). Researchers point to people's inability to care for themselves, because of incapacitation, choice, or a lack of social and personal resources (Bogard 2001; Hoch 2000). Studies carried out over the last decade and a half have supported these types of explanation. For example, US studies have shown that mental illness is correlated with homelessness, but only explains homelessness for 10 to 30 per cent of the population (Piliavin et al. 1993; Linhorst 1992). What, then, is the source of homelessness for the remaining 70 to 90 per cent of the population? Only some of those who have health problems, who have alcohol and drug abuse problems, or who have been released from prison become homeless.

To account for the many homeless who do not experience these types of personal problems, some researchers have argued that homelessness should be understood as a consequence of social, political, and economic structures that limit or restrict access to resources and opportunities. In this view, homelessness results from increased poverty and unemployment; declines in social and affordable housing; cuts to welfare and health-care programs; and the shift from a manufacturing economy to a service economy (Devine and Wright 1997). Hence, homelessness is said to arise when people cannot afford housing because they are unemployed, are on welfare, or work in minimum-wage jobs. Homelessness also occurs when housing costs increase due to market forces, e.g., when low vacancy rates are combined with insufficient building of new housing. Roth and Bean (1986) found that almost one-quarter of their sample listed unemployment as the major reason for their homelessness. However, another study of 60 major US metropolitan areas found inconsistent effects of housing availability and affordability on homelessness rates (Elliott and Krivo 1991). Research for another sample of American cities also showed no significant correlation between the rate of homelessness and the rates of poverty and unemployment (Tucker 1990).

Recent Canadian studies cite "systemic failure" as a major cause of homelessness. This is the "black hole" hypothesis, which states the homeless represent all those people who have fallen through the cracks in Canada's social safety net. Some homeless either don't qualify for, or have been disqualified from, various programs and supports. Other homeless may have no supports available to them, including recent immigrants and refugees, sex workers, and undocumented migrant workers. Systemic failures also stem from government cuts to anti-poverty programs, to welfare, and to other social services. In fact, some might argue that there is no such thing as homelessness. Instead, those who are labelled "homeless" are more properly seen as the poor, unemployed, uneducated, mentally ill, and disabled, or as people who have addiction problems, are racialized or criminalized, etc. Using the "homeless" label merely sidesteps the real issues creating the problems associated with homeless people. Perhaps, then, it might be useful to dispense with the term "homelessness" altogether and focus attention on the serious problems that vulnerable Canadians experience. These people occupy the bottom rung of our system of inequality, making them Canada's truly disadvantaged.

What Is to Be Done about the Homeless?

Currently, support for the homeless is generally provided in two ways. First, community and faith-based groups offer programs and services; these are almost always underfunded and the groups compete with each other for what little funding is available at the provincial and municipal levels. Second, charitable organizations, such as the United Way and the Salvation Army, also provide services and programs. The existing system is a skeletal structure of emergency and stop-gap measures that is rarely more than "three hots and a cot" (Feins and Fosburg 1999: 9-1). At present, funding for the federal Homelessness Partnering Strategy is largely spent on emergency and transitional housing for special needs groups, including women, children, families, and Aboriginal people, or on renovating the rundown buildings that traditionally have sheltered homeless men. Therefore, while funding provided through the HPS has a positive impact on the lives of homeless women, children, and families, it is doubtful that it will significantly reduce rates of homelessness for men, who constitute the majority of the homeless population.

One of the most controversial aspects of federal government initiatives is that neither poverty reduction nor the construction of new affordable housing is part of the HPS mandate. By focusing on the support of existing programs and services, the HPS reinforces the traditional stereotype that homelessness is a product of individual choice, incompetence, failure, or pathology, and not the result of inadequacies and inequalities in the welfare system and the availability of housing. This is a sore spot for many social advocates and service providers, who have consistently pointed to cuts and freezes in Canada's social programs—welfare, employment insurance, health care, social housing—as the prime reasons for rising rates of homelessness.

Currently, experts have focused their attention on affordable housing, arguing that the loss of funding for building affordable housing over the last 20 years—equivalent to 100,000 units—has put inordinate pressure on an already fragile social housing system. For example, in 1982 over 20,000 new social housing units were being built annually, but by 1995 the annual number had dropped to 1,000. After intense pressure from social activists, the number of new housing units had increased a decade later to only about 4,500 units annually. Critics argue that, at any time, there are close to three-quarters of a million households with extreme housing affordability problems that put them at imminent risk of homelessness (Gaetz 2012).

Given these considerations, local, regional, and federal governments have concentrated their time, energy, and money on the Housing First program, which is also referred to as "rapid rehousing." The idea is that the first step should be to get the homeless into housing, with the intention of providing supportive services once their housing is stabilized. By all accounts, this program has been a resounding success. The HPS carried out a demonstration project (see Mental Health Commission of Canada 2014) that showed that the Housing First approach effectively addresses homelessness, particularly chronic and episodic homelessness. Critics, however, argue that this amounts to a "warehousing" solution that is effective in reducing homeless visibility, but that, without support services in place, does little to address the core causes of people becoming and staying homeless.

The Homelessness Quandary

This chapter has sketched out our state of knowledge about homelessness, what has been done to address the problem, and what still needs to be done. Herein lies the homelessness quandary. After two decades of research, policy and program development, and social responses to the problem of homelessness, we are not much further ahead than we were when homelessness was declared a national disaster in 1998. We are certainly more aware, organized, and socially conscious. Nevertheless, for all the knowledge generated and tax dollars spent, the problem persists: many Canadians still find themselves unhoused, unsheltered, on the street, hungry, and in need. Even more compelling is the evidence that the current estimate of the size and scope of the problem is about the same as estimates from 1987. How can this be?

There are many possible answers to this question, but the most likely is that spending money on emergency and transitional services and programs is a band-aid, a temporary solution and a stop-gap measure. Such responses may be effective in reducing the visibility of homelessness, but do not address the underlying problem, which is insufficient affordable housing. In reality, there has been an affordable housing crisis in Canada since the mid-1980s, and it has worsened over the last three decades. We can apply whatever stop-gap measures we like, but without more affordable housing that puts people back into their communities, all we are doing is straining an overstressed emergency shelter and service system. Regardless of how effective Housing First has been, without significant federal support and funding to build new social housing, homelessness will continue to be a major social problem in Canada.

Questions for Critical Thought

1. How does not having a standardized definition or measure of homelessness affect our responses to the problem in Canada?
2. Who are the most vulnerable among the homeless? Why? How would you help them?
3. Thinking about solutions to the problem of homelessness, what would you focus on first (e.g., housing, programs and services, employment, education, prevention) and why?
4. What is the advantage of abandoning the label "homeless" and describing the real problems that are characteristic of Canada's truly disadvantaged?

Recommended Readings

Gaetz, Stephen, Tanya Gulliver, and Tim Richter. 2014. *The State of Homelessness in Canada 2014.* Toronto: Canadian Homelessness Research Network.

———, Bill O'Grady, Kristy Buccieri, Jeff Karabanow, and Allyson Marsolais, eds. 2013. *Youth Homelessness in Canada: Implications for Policy and Practice.* Toronto: Canadian Homelessness Research Network.

Hulchanski, J. David, Philippa Campsie, Shirley Chau, Stephen Hwang, and Emily Paradis, eds. 2009. *Finding Home: Policy Options for Addressing Homelessness in Canada.* Toronto: Canadian Homelessness Research Network.

Waegemakers-Schiff, Jeannette. 2015. *Working with Homeless and Vulnerable People: Basic Skills and Practice.* New York: Lyceum Press.

Recommended Websites

Canadian Alliance to End Homelessness:
http://www.caeh.ca/

Homeless Hub:
http://www.homelesshub.ca/

Homelessness Partnering Strategy:
http://www.esdc.gc.ca/eng/communities/homelessness/index.shtml

Mental Health Commission of Canada: National At Home Final Report:
http://www.mentalhealthcommission.ca/English/document/24376/national-homechez-soi-final-report?terminitial=38

Employment and Social Development Canada, "Feeling Home: Culturally-responsive approaches to Aboriginal homelessness":
http://www.esdc.gc.ca/eng/communities/homelessness/research/kdp/aboriginal/feeling_home.shtml

References

Beavis, M., N. Klos, T. Carter, and C. Douchant. 1997. *Literature Review: Aboriginal Peoples and Homelessness.* Ottawa: Canada Mortgage and Housing Corporation.

Begin, P., L. Casavant, and N.M. Chenier. 1999. *Homelessness.* Ottawa: Parliamentary Research Branch, Library of Parliament (PRB 99-1E).

Bogard, C. 2001. "Advocacy and enumeration." *American Behavioral Scientist* 45, 1: 105–20.

Burnam, M.A., and P. Koegel. 1988. "Methodology for obtaining a representative sample of homeless persons: The Los Angeles Skid Row Study." *Evaluation Review* 12, 2: 117–52.

Canadian Observatory on Homelessness (COH). 2012. *Canadian Definition of Homelessness.* Toronto: Canadian Homelessness Research Network. www.homelesshub.ca

Dennis, M.L., and R. Iachan. 1993. "A multiple frame approach to sampling the homeless and transient population." *Journal of Official Statistics* 14, 5: 1–18.

Devine, J.A., and J.D. Wright. 1997. "Losing the housing game: The levelling effects of substance abuse." *American Journal of Orthopsychiatry* 67, 4: 618–31.

Ellickson, R.C. 1990. "The homelessness muddle." *Public Interest* 99: 45–60.

Elliott, M., and L.J. Krivo. 1991. "Structural determinants of homelessness in the United States." *Social Problems* 38, 1: 113–31.

Feins, J.D., and L.B. Fosburg. 1999. "Emergency shelter and services: Opening a front door to the continuum of care." In *Practical Lessons: The 1998 National Symposium on Homelessness Research*, pp. 9-1–9-36. Washington: US Department of Housing and Urban Development.

Fitzgerald, S.T., M.C. Shelley, and P.W. Dail. 2001. "Research on homelessness." *American Behavioral Scientist* 45, 1: 121–48.

Gaetz, Stephen. 2012. *The Real Cost of Homelessness: Can We Save Money by Doing the Right Thing?* Toronto: Canadian Homelessness Research Network.

———, Tanya Gulliver, and Tim Richter. 2014. *The State of Homelessness in Canada 2014.* Toronto: Canadian Homelessness Research Network.

Hirschl, T. 1990. "Homelessness: A sociological research agenda." *Sociological Spectrum* 10: 443–67.

Hoch, C. 2000. "Sheltering the homeless in the US: Social improvement and the continuum of care." *Housing Studies* 15, 6: 865–76.

Hombs, M.E., and M. Snyder. 1982. *Homelessness in America: A Forced March to Nowhere.* Washington: Community for Creative Non-Violence.

Homeless Hub. 2015. http://www.homelesshub.ca/.

Homelessness Partnering Strategy (HPS). 2012. *The National Sheltering Survey.* Ottawa: Employment and Social Development Canada.

———. 2015. *Homelessness Strategy.* Ottawa: Employment and Social Development Canada. http://www.esdc.gc.ca/eng/communities/homelessness//index.shtml.

Koegel, P., A. Burnam, and R.K. Farr. 1990. "Subsistence adaptation among homeless adults in the inner city of Los Angeles." *Journal of Social Issues* 16, 4: 83–107.

Layton, J. 2000. *Homelessness: The Making and Unmaking of a Crisis.* Toronto: Penguin.

Linhorst, D.M. 1992. "A redefinition of the problem of homelessness among persons with a chronic mental illness." *Journal of Sociology and Social Work* 17, 4: 43–56.

McLaughlin, Mary Ann. 1987. *Homelessness in Canada: The Report of the National Inquiry.* Ottawa: Canadian Council on Social Development.

Mental Health Commission of Canada. 2014. *Annual Report 2013–14.* Oct. http://www.mentalhealthcommission.ca/English/document/61101/mhcc-annual-report-2013-14.

Patrick, C. 2014. *Aboriginal Homelessness in Canada: A Literature Review.* Toronto: Canadian Homelessness Research Network.

Peressini, T. 2007. "Perceived reasons for homelessness in Canada: Testing the heterogeneity hypothesis." *Canadian Journal of Urban Research* 16, 1: 112–26.

———. 2009. "Pathways into homelessness: Testing the heterogeneity hypothesis." In J. David Hulchanski et al., eds, *Finding Home: Policy Options for Addressing Homeless in Canada.* Toronto: Cities Centre, University of Toronto.

——— and J. Engeland. 2004. "The homelessness individuals and families information system: A case study in Canadian capacity building." *Canadian Journal of Urban Research* 13, 2: 347–61.

———, ———, and J. David Hulchanski. 2009. "Towards a strategy for counting the homeless." In J. David Hulchanski et al., eds, *Finding Home: Policy Options for Addressing Homeless in Canada.* Toronto: Cities Centre, University of Toronto.

Piliavin, I., M. Sosin, A.H. Westerfelt, and R.L. Matsueda. 1993. "The duration of homeless careers: An exploratory study." *Social Service Review* 67, 4: 576–98.

Rossi, P.H. 1989. *Down and Out in America: The Origins of Homelessness.* Chicago: University of Chicago Press.

Roth, D., and G. Bean. 1986. "New perspectives on homelessness: Findings from a statewide epidemiological study." *Hospital and Community Psychiatry* 37, 7: 712–19.

Slobodian, L. 2002. "A helter-shelter life: Hope, but no home." *Calgary Herald*, 8 June.

Springer, S. 2000. "Homelessness: A proposal for a global definition and classification." *Habitat International* 24: 475–84.

Taueber, C. 1991. "Enumerating homeless persons: Methods and data needs." In C. Tauber, ed., *Enumerating Homeless Persons: Methods and Data Needs.* Washington: US Department of Commerce, Bureau of the Census.

Toronto, City of. 2001. *The Toronto Report Card on Homelessness, 2001.* Toronto: City of Toronto.

Tucker, William. 1990. *The Excluded Americans: Homelessness and Housing Policies.* Washington: Regnery Gateway.

United Nations High Commissioner for Refugees. 2014. *World at War: Global Trends Forced Displacement in 2014.* http://unhcr.org/556725e69.pdf.

US Congress, House of Representatives. 1987. *Stewart B. McKinney Homeless Assistance Act, Conference Report to Accompany H.R. 558, 100th Congress, 1st Session.* Washington: US Government Printing Office.

US Department of Housing and Urban Development. 1984. *A Report to the Secretary on the Homeless and Emergency Shelters.* Washington: Office of Policy Development and Research.

23 What Do Canadians Think about Individualism and Inequality? The Effects of Social Status

Monica Hwang and Edward Grabb

Introduction

Canada is widely seen as one of the best societies in the world in which to live. Our country has consistently ranked near the top on the annual United Nations Human Development Index, which measures the overall quality of life in different nations, using measures like average life expectancy, educational attainment, and material standard of living. For many years Canada held the number-one ranking and, despite some recent declines, still ranked ninth among nations in the world as of 2015 (United Nations 2015). Nevertheless, regardless of this positive image, we know from the studies in this book that Canada has notable shortcomings when providing for the well-being of some citizens. Individuals often face significant problems of inequality due to their race, gender, class background, and other factors.

In this chapter, we consider how Canadians feel about social inequality and the role of the individual in their society. How does living in this prosperous but unequal society shape people's beliefs about such questions as whether inequality is acceptable or justifiable, and whether the government should intervene to assist individuals in need? Our main goal is to determine whether the social backgrounds or statuses of Canadians affect their attitudes about these important issues.

Individualism as a Dominant Value

Sociologists have long been interested in understanding the dominant system of values, or "dominant ideology," that prevails in different societies. Some writers follow Karl Marx's conception of dominant ideology, seeing it as the set of core beliefs held by the most powerful or dominant social class (Marx and Engels 1846, 1848; see Abercrombie et al. 1980). Other analysts use the term differently, to indicate the values that are embraced, not only by the most privileged or dominant groups, but by the population in general (Williams 1960: 409; Mann 1970; Grabb and Curtis 2010: 67, 261).

Regardless of which usage is preferred, most observers agree that, in democratic societies like Canada, no idea is more central to the dominant ideology than the belief in "individualism." Individualism has also been defined in different ways by social scientists. In the present analysis, it refers to the fundamental belief that all people have (or should have) the right, the freedom, and the responsibility to make their own way in society. There is debate about whether individualism in this sense is as strongly emphasized by Canadians as it is by other peoples, especially Americans; nevertheless, individualism is undoubtedly a core element in Canada's system of dominant values (Marchak 1988; Lipset 1990, 1996; Olsen 2002; Adams 2003; Grabb and Curtis 2010; Reutter et al. 2006).

The strong emphasis on individualism in contemporary democracies is evident in research on people's attitudes and beliefs. Some studies have considered beliefs about the individual's opportunity to succeed in life. For example, an analysis from the 1990s showed that 98 per cent of Americans believed everyone *should* have equal opportunity to get ahead (Inkeles 1997: 379). Early studies in the US found that about three-quarters of the population believed that equal, or at least considerable, opportunity actually *did* operate in their society (Mizruchi 1964; Huber and Form 1973; Kluegel and Smith 1986). While recent American evidence suggests some decline in this belief, as of 2007 about 70 per cent of respondents still agreed that all or most Americans have "an opportunity to succeed" (Stonecash 2007: 6).

Canadian research has also assessed people's views on why individuals succeed or get ahead in life. Analyses suggest that most Canadians also believe that individuals have considerable opportunity; one study showed that more than 80 per cent of Canadians emphasized individual qualities like ambition and hard work (along with getting a good education) as the main reasons for success, and saw background characteristics like class background, race, or gender as generally unimportant factors (Pammett 1996: 72–3; Curtis and Grabb 2004: 399). These findings parallel results in earlier Canadian studies (Johnstone 1969: 8–11; *Maclean's* 1998; Sniderman et al. 1996: 97–100) and in recent American research (Stonecash 2007: 8; Pew Research Center 2014: 10–11).

Other studies have looked at whether individual inequality is necessary or justifiable as an incentive for personal excellence and societal progress. Research in the US has generally found that most people see income inequality as an important motivation for individuals to work hard and achieve in life (e.g., Kluegel and Smith 1986: 106–7; Kelley and Evans 1993). Such attitudes are also evident in Canada, though to a lesser degree (Pammett 1996: 74–7; Osberg and Smeeding 2006).

Another body of research has considered people's attitudes about the relative merits of government assistance versus individual self-reliance when addressing problems of inequality. Several Canadian analyses indicate somewhat greater support for self-reliance than for government intervention. One study using 1990s national survey data found that only 43 per cent of Canadians thought the government should act to reduce income differences between high-income and low-income Canadians (Olsen 2002: 110). A subsequent analysis showed that, by 2002, this proportion had increased slightly, to 48 per cent (Centre for Research and Information on Canada 2002: 7). Although self-reliance is somewhat more highly valued by Americans than by Canadians (Olsen 2002: 110; Grabb and Curtis 2010: 180–2), most Canadians also take an individualistic perspective on this question.

The Effects of Social Status

Our key concern is whether social status or social background affects this Canadian tendency to have an individualistic view of inequality. Does being in a position of relative advantage or disadvantage, as judged by the different ranked social statuses that people occupy, influence people's beliefs about inequality and the value of individual responsibility?

Some might expect that privileged Canadians would be sympathetic about the plight of disadvantaged individuals, and would support policies to reduce inequality and increase government assistance to help the less fortunate. Others might expect that Canadians with higher social statuses will believe that individual differences in privilege are appropriate and should not be altered through government intervention or other initiatives. The latter hypothesis follows if we assume that advantaged people see their high positions as justifiable rewards for their own industry and achievement, believing that inequality is a natural consequence of individual differences in effort, ability, and acquired skills.

Previous studies indicate some support for the second hypothesis, although the patterns typically have not been strong. Early American research found that members of disadvantaged groups, such as racial minorities, women, and lower-income earners, were somewhat less likely than more privileged people to believe that inequality was based mainly on individual differences in effort or motivation (Huber and Form 1973: 97–104; Kluegel and Smith 1986: 100–2). US survey findings from 2007 also showed a modest effect of income level on individualist beliefs: 77 per cent of respondents earning $100,000 per year or more believed that most people have opportunity in American society, compared to just 66 per cent of those earning less than $50,000 annually (Stonecash 2007: 12). Another US survey conducted in 2012 by the Pew Research Center found a larger income effect, using a different measure of individualism. Results showed that Americans in the lowest quarter of household income were twice as likely as those in the highest quarter to believe that individual "hard work offers little guarantee of success" (46 per cent versus 23 per cent); the authors also noted, however, that this gap had not widened since an earlier survey in 1987, despite growing inequalities and increasing economic difficulties in the US since that time (Kohut and Dimock 2013: 9–10).

Research using 2002 Canadian survey data also found a modest income effect, this time regarding support for increasing government assistance to disadvantaged individuals; 50 per cent of people with household incomes below $40,000 per year favoured more government services, compared with 42 per cent of those with household incomes above $80,000 annually (Centre for Research and Information on Canada 2002: 6). The same study (pp. 6, 11) showed other social status effects: women were slightly more supportive than men of increased government services, and Quebecers were somewhat more supportive than other Canadians. Another analysis of Canadian survey data found only a weak relationship between a range of social statuses and commitment to individualist values; most Canadians, regardless of their income, employment status, education, gender, region, and other statuses, believed that individual factors like hard work and ambition were more important for getting ahead in Canada than were social background characteristics like race, gender, or having wealthy parents (Curtis and Grabb 2004: 401–3).

A more recent Canadian survey considered the related question of whether, because of growing economic inequality, Canada had become a "less fair society" in the last five years (Northrup and Jacobs 2014). Results (pp. 29–30) showed some moderate social status effects, with 39 per cent of respondents in the lowest income group strongly agreeing with this statement, compared to 28 per cent in the highest income group; also, 47 per cent of Quebecers strongly agreed, compared to less than 30 per cent in the rest of Canada. On the other hand, the effects of other social statuses, including education, gender, and employment status, were small or non-existent.

In this analysis, we reconsider the possible effects of social status on Canadian views about inequality and individualism, using a recent survey that includes numerous social statuses and more extensive measures of people's attitudes and beliefs.

Data and Methods

Sample

The data come from a 2006 sample of adult Canadians, collected as part of the World Values Surveys, a set of international surveys that, over the years, has involved more than 90 countries (World Values Survey Association 2012). The Canadian sample included 2,164 respondents and was weighted to make it representative of the national population.

Measuring Beliefs about Individualism and Inequality

Six questions from the survey were selected to assess beliefs about individualism and inequality. Five questions asked respondents to rate their views about two contrasting statements, using 10-point scales in which a score of 1 meant "you agree completely with the statement on the left" and a score of 10 meant "you agree completely with the statement on the right"; any number between 1 and 10 could be chosen if respondents' beliefs fell between the two extremes. These five items are:

1. "The government should take more responsibility to ensure that everyone is provided for" versus "People should take more responsibility for themselves."
2. "Competition is harmful. It brings out the worst in people" versus "Competition is good. It stimulates people to work hard and develop new ideas."
3. "Hard work doesn't generally bring success—it's more a matter of luck and connections" versus "In the long run, hard work usually brings a better life."
4. "Government ownership of business and industry should be increased" versus "Private ownership of business and industry should be increased."
5. "Incomes should be made more equal" versus "We need larger income differences as incentives for individual effort."

The sixth question used a different format, with respondents asked to consider a hypothetical situation in which "two secretaries of the same age, doing practically the same job" are paid differently because one secretary "is quicker, more efficient, and more reliable at her job." Respondents indicated if they thought it was "fair or not fair that the one secretary is paid more than the other."

The respondents who supported personal responsibility, competition, hard work, private enterprise, and larger income differences were assumed to be stronger believers in individualism and individually based inequality, as were respondents who said that it is fair to pay the more efficient and reliable secretary more money.

Measures of Social Status

We consider nine different social status measures. The first five deal with economic or socioeconomic factors: (1) *education* is the respondent's highest level of educational attainment, with the following categories: grade school or less, some high school, high school graduate, some post-secondary, and post-secondary graduate; (2) *income* is total household income from all sources, grouped into five categories ranked from lowest to highest; (3) *occupational status* is an eight-category measure ranging from unskilled manual workers to employers/owners; (4) *employment status* includes the unemployed, part-time, full-time, and self-employed workers; and (5) *subjective class identification* asks respondents to indicate the social class to which they think they belong, using four categories: lower class, working class, lower middle class, and upper middle class or higher. The remaining four social status variables are: (6) *race*, dichotomized into non-White and White respondents; (7) *gender*, dichotomized into female and male; (8) *language of interview*, which included Francophones and Anglophones; and (9) *region*, grouped into five categories: the Atlantic provinces, Quebec, Ontario, the Prairie provinces, and British Columbia.

Results

Overall Patterns

In Table 23.1, the numbers in the top row show the average scores for all respondents on the six attitude questions. We see that Canadians, while not extremely high on individualism, express relatively individualistic beliefs on every question.

Table 23.1 Responses to the Six Inequality Items by the Nine Social Statuses of the Respondents

	People Be Responsible	Competition Good	Hard Work Good	Private Ownership Increase	Income Differences Good	Pay Better Secretary More
All Respondents:	6.0/10	7.2/10	7.0/10	6.6/10	5.8/10	81%
Social Statuses:						
1. Education						
Grade school or less	5.8	6.6	7.2	6.4	5.6	65%
Some high school	6.1	7.0	6.9	6.5	5.6	77
High school grad.	6.1	7.2	7.1	**6.8**	5.7	78
Some post-sec	5.7	**7.5**	6.8	**6.8**	6.0	89
Post-sec. grad. or more	5.8	7.4	7.1	6.4	**6.2**	**90**
R-square	0.1%	0.9%	0.0%	0.0%	0.7%	2.7%
F	1.9	5.9***	1.3	3.3**	4.1**	16.3***
2. Income						
Lowest 1/5	5.5	6.9	7.0	6.6	5.2	70%
Fourth	5.8	7.1	6.6	6.4	5.6	75
Third	**6.4**	7.2	6.8	6.4	5.5	79
Second	6.0	7.0	7.0	6.5	5.9	81
Highest 1/5	6.1	**7.6**	**7.4**	**7.0**	**6.3**	**88**
R-square	0.5%	1.1%	0.6%	0.6%	2.2%	2.5%
F	5.9***	8.0***	5.7***	5.9***	11.0***	11.3***
3. Occupation						
Unskilled manual	4.9	6.8	6.7	5.3	5.5	72%
Semi-skilled manual	5.4	6.4	6.4	6.5	5.2	68
Skilled manual	6.0	7.2	6.7	6.7	5.9	77
Forepersons	6.4	7.7	**7.5**	6.2	6.2	84
Non-manual workers	5.9	7.0	6.9	6.5	5.6	87
Non-manual supervisors	**6.6**	7.2	7.2	6.5	**6.4**	89
Professional	6.1	7.4	7.2	6.7	6.0	86
Employer/owner	6.1	**8.2**	**7.5**	**7.5**	6.1	**90**
R-square	0.9%	2.8%	1.6%	1.9%	0.5%	2.5%
F	3.8***	8.6***	3.6***	7.7***	2.4*	5.3***
4. Employment						
Unemployed	5.5	6.8	6.7	6.4	5.4	71%
Part-time	5.4	6.9	6.9	6.3	5.4	78

Continued

Table 23.1 (Continued)

	People Be Responsible	Competition Good	Hard Work Good	Private Ownership Increase	Income Differences Good	Pay Better Secretary More
Full-time	6.1	7.2	7.0	6.6	5.9	82
Self-employed	**6.3**	**7.8**	6.9	**7.3**	**6.5**	**92**
R-square	0.7%	0.2%	0.1%	0.1%	0.2%	0.3%
F	6.8***	5.7***	0.9	4.5***	6.5***	6.3***
5. Subjective Class						
Lower class	5.1	6.6	6.6	6.7	5.4	62%
Working class	**6.1**	7.1	**7.1**	6.6	5.6	77
Lower middle	6.0	7.2	6.7	6.6	5.6	81
Upper middle+	**6.1**	**7.4**	**7.1**	6.6	**6.2**	**85**
R-square	0.1%	0.6%	0.0%	0.0%	1.1%	1.2%
F	3.8**	4.5**	4.3**	0.1	9.5***	10.1***
6. Race						
Non-White	5.4	7.0	6.8	6.2	**6.2**	80%
White	**6.1**	7.2	7.0	**6.7**	5.8	81
R-square	0.8%	0.1%	0.1%	0.5%	0.4%	0.0%
F	16.6***	2.2	2.3	10.7***	8.7**	0.4
7. Gender						
Female	6.0	7.0	6.8	6.5	5.8	79%
Male	6.0	**7.4**	**7.1**	6.7	5.9	82
R-square	0.0%	0.8%	0.3%	0.1%	0.1%	0.1%
F	0.3	17.3***	7.4**	2.0	1.2	3.0
8. Language						
Francophone	6.2	6.4	6.0	5.9	5.5	72%
Anglophone	6.0	**7.4**	**7.3**	**6.8**	**5.9**	**84**
R-square	0.1%	3.8%	5.6%	3.0%	0.7%	1.7%
F	2.5	81.8***	125.9***	63.0***	14.5***	35.3***
9. Region						
Quebec	6.1	6.4	6.0	5.9	5.6	72%
Atlantic	6.0	7.4	7.2	6.8	5.3	72
Ontario	6.0	7.3	7.3	6.8	6.0	**87**
Prairies	5.9	**7.5**	**7.5**	**7.0**	5.8	**87**
British Columbia	5.8	7.2	7.2	6.6	**6.2**	77
R-square	0.2%	4.5%	6.0%	3.6%	1.1%	3.0%
F	0.9	25.1***	34.3***	19.5***	5.8***	16.3***
Weighted N =	(2,123)	(2,123)	(2,132)	(2,062)	(2,112)	(2,097)

Notes: * indicates p <.05; ** indicates p <.01; *** indicates p <.001. For the first five items, scores are on a scale from 1 to 10. For the fifth item, the percentage is for respondents agreeing with the statement. In comparisons where the F value shows a statistically significant difference, the scores in bold type represent the most pro-individualist or pro-inequality responses.
Source: World Values Survey Association (2012).

For the five scales, the average responses are all above the mid-point (which is 5.5 on a scale from 1 to 10). This individualistic outlook is most evident in the questions about competition and hard work, with scores of 7.2 and 7.0. The scores on private enterprise and personal responsibility are lower, at 6.2 and 6.0, while the statement about larger income differences providing an incentive for individual effort produces a score of 5.8, which is only slightly above the mid-point. The lower score on this item could occur because this question is probably the most extreme, since respondents are not simply asked whether existing levels of income inequality are acceptable but whether income inequality should be increased even further.

The sixth and final question, concerning the secretaries' pay, suggests a very high level of support for the idea that inequality is acceptable to Canadians, provided it is based on individual performance. Fully 81 per cent say that the better-performing secretary should be paid more.

Overall, then, the findings are consistent with previous research showing that Canadians generally embrace an individualistic viewpoint about the problem of inequality and related issues like competition, hard work, personal responsibility, and government involvement.

Social Status and Beliefs about Individualism and Inequality

Table 23.1 also indicates whether the nine social statuses are related to the six beliefs about individualism and inequality. Throughout the table, bolded numbers are used to highlight the highest scores on all six beliefs for each of the nine social statuses. The results test the hypothesis that people with more advantaged backgrounds will be the most likely to take an individualistic perspective. If so, we should find the most individualistic attitudes among those who are more highly educated, earn higher incomes, have higher occupational status, are employed, have higher subjective class identification, are male, are White, speak English, and live in more prosperous regions (e.g., the Prairie provinces, Ontario, and British Columbia).

The findings show some support for this hypothesis, although the differences are typically not substantial, which is consistent with most of the previous studies reviewed earlier. Probably the clearest evidence that privileged Canadians hold more individualistic views occurs when we compare income groups. People with higher incomes tend to hold the most individualistic views on the six attitude questions, and all of these results are statistically significant (as shown by the F-tests). The biggest differences are for whether larger income differences are a good incentive—with a score of 6.3 for the highest income group and only 5.2 for the lowest income group—and for the secretary question, with 88 per cent of the highest income group supporting higher pay for the better secretary, compared to only 70 per cent of the lowest income group. A similar finding occurs for occupational status: for all six questions, people in more advantaged jobs, especially employers and owners, express significantly more individualistic responses than do people in unskilled jobs.

Somewhat weaker patterns occur for two other socio-economic status variables—subjective class identification and employment status. Still, on five of the six questions there is the same tendency for individualistic attitudes to be more common among the most advantaged group, i.e., those who identify as upper middle class or higher, and also among the full-time employed or self-employed. Education has the weakest effects of all the other socio-economic variables. Highly educated Canadians are more likely to support competition, higher pay for the better secretary, and using larger income differences as an incentive, but they are no more likely than the least educated to favour personal responsibility, private enterprise, or the value of hard work.

The results for the remaining four social statuses provide mixed support for the hypothesis that privileged groups hold a comparatively more individualistic attitude about inequality. There is a slight tendency for men to be more individualistic than women, but only for the two questions about competition and hard work. There is also a slight tendency for Whites to be more individualistic than non-Whites, but only for the two items about personal responsibility and private enterprise; moreover, on the value of larger income differences, the reverse pattern occurs, with non-Whites being slightly more supportive than Whites.

More consistent are the findings for the final two social status measures, i.e., language and region. For language, we see that Anglophone Canadians, while no different from Francophones on the personal responsibility item, have significantly more individualistic outlooks on the other five questions. A parallel pattern occurs for region, in that Quebec residents, most of whom are also Francophones, exhibit less individualistic beliefs than Anglophones on these same five questions. Taken together, the language and region results could reflect the more "statist" or "social democratic" nature of Quebec society, which for several decades has supported policies that increase government services for the poor and raise taxes for the wealthy (e.g., Grabb and Curtis 2010).

Another way to assess the effects of social status on the six attitude questions is to consider the R-square values reported in Table 23.1. These values indicate how much of the variability in each attitude can be accounted for, or explained, by the effects of each social status measure. The results show that *none* of the nine social statuses by itself has a very strong impact on any of the six attitudes. None of the R-square values is higher than 6 per cent, out of a possible 100 per cent, and all but a few values are below 2 per cent. These findings mean that the vast majority of the variability in Canadians' attitudes about individualism and inequality has nothing to do with their social statuses. Although it is not reported in the table, we also did multivariate analyses, in which we calculated the combined effects of all nine social status measures in accounting simultaneously for people's responses to each attitude question. The combined R-square values ranged from a low of 3 per cent for the personal responsibility item to a high of 8 per cent for the hard work item. These multivariate results underscore that, while social status differences play some role in explaining Canadian views about individualism and inequality, their impact is minor in comparison with other explanations.

Conclusion

Our results are generally consistent with earlier research on Canada's dominant belief system, especially on the value of individualism and the nature of inequality in our society. Like most previous studies, the findings show that most Canadians, while not extreme in their views, tend towards an individualistic perspective. The average person seems to believe in the virtues of individual competition, hard work, private enterprise, and personal responsibility, and also in the fairness of using income differences as incentives or rewards for individual effort and performance.

Our findings also parallel previous research in suggesting that people with more advantaged social backgrounds, in some cases, are more likely to embrace these beliefs about individualism and inequality than are people with less privileged status characteristics. This outcome is clearest when comparing Canadians with higher and lower socio-economic status, as judged by such measures as income, occupation, and, to some extent, subjective class identification and employment status. A similar pattern occurs for language and region, with more individualistic beliefs being expressed by Anglophones and residents of more prosperous regions, especially outside Quebec.

However, while the effects of social status are often significant, one of our most important findings is that these effects are generally not strong, and are especially weak for social statuses like gender, race, and education. The relatively weak or modest effects of social status are consistent with results from previous research showing that, even among relatively disadvantaged Canadians, people's beliefs lean towards the individualistic end of the continuum. Moreover, even when all the social status influences are considered in combination, they account for only a small proportion of the variability in attitudes that Canadians express about individualism and inequality.

The findings reported here suggest that people's beliefs about individual inequality are *dominant* in both senses of the term noted at the beginning of this chapter. That is, these beliefs tend to be held by more privileged Canadians, but also by the wider population. Most seem to agree that inequality in Canada is acceptable, justifiable, and perhaps even desirable, provided that it results from individual differences in hard work and involves a fair competition between people who have the opportunity to succeed, based on their own efforts and merits. In most people's minds, the system apparently works largely as it should, with little reason for wanting to change it. Such outlooks presumably lend ideological support to maintaining the status quo, which means that the dominant groups should continue to do well.

It may be that most Canadians tend to adopt the dominant ideology, with its emphasis on individualism and the acceptability of inequality, because most people are basically happy with their current situation, and because they do not see better alternatives in other societies. As noted at the beginning of this chapter, Canada has consistently been named by the United Nations as one of the best countries in the world, with a comparatively high level of material affluence and a generally good quality of life.

Nevertheless, given the clear evidence of structurally based inequalities and injustice in Canada, as illustrated in the chapters of this book, there is considerable room to speculate about why more Canadians, especially those facing poverty or discrimination, do not voice more discontent about the disadvantages and structural inequality in their society. Could it be, for example, that we see high-profile instances of poor people or minority group members who have achieved great success, leading us to conclude that Canada really is a land of opportunity? Some examples of these success stories include billionaire businessman Jimmy Pattison, former Governor General Michaëlle Jean, and entertainment figures like Céline Dion and Justin Bieber, all of whom started from humble beginnings. There is also evidence of broader opportunities for such upward social mobility, a term that refers to situations in which individuals achieve higher socio-economic statuses than their parents. Although this research shows that upward mobility mostly involves small gains and improvements (Wanner 2009), with few "rags-to-riches" stories like those of Pattison, Jean, and others, even this evidence of moderate opportunity in Canada could reinforce our individualistic beliefs about inequality.

We conclude with another crucial point to consider, however, which concerns the differences between perception and reality. Recent research shows that most Canadians do not have a true picture of inequality in their own country, and seriously underestimate how large the gap is between the rich and the poor, between the advantaged and the disadvantaged (Broadbent Institute 2014). A more accurate appreciation of how unequal we are, and a more complete awareness of the structural rather than the individual reasons behind this inequality, could reduce substantially the widespread acceptance of this central feature in our dominant belief system.

Questions for Critical Thought

1. The belief in individualism is a dominant value in Canada. Can you think of any others?
2. When people talk about equality and inequality, some make a distinction between equality of *opportunity* and equality of *condition*, which theoretically occurs in communist societies, for example. What pros and cons do you see in these two different conceptions of equality?

3. Many people believe that Canadians are less individualistic than Americans. What do you think of this supposed difference, and what examples can you think of to support your opinion?
4. We found that nine social characteristics had little impact in explaining why some Canadians have more individualistic beliefs than others do. Are there other social characteristics that might be more important explanations, and how might they be related to individualism?

Recommended Readings

Grabb, Edward, and James Curtis. 2010. *Regions Apart: The Four Societies of Canada and the United States*, 2nd edn. Toronto: Oxford University Press.

Kohut, Andrew, and Michael Dimock. 2013. *Resilient American Values: Optimism in an Era of Growing Inequality and Economic Difficulty.* Pew Research Center Working Paper, May. New York: Council on Foreign Relations.

Northrup, David, and Lesley Jacobs, assisted by Hugh McCague and Crystal Au. 2014. *The Growing Income Inequality Gap in Canada: A National Survey.* 31 Jan. Toronto: Institute for Social Research, York University, and Toronto Star.

United Nations. 2015. *Human Development Report 2015.* New York: United Nations Development Programme.

Recommended Websites

Broadbent Institute:
http://www.broadbentinstitute.ca/

Canadian Centre for Policy Alternatives:
https://www.policyalternatives.ca/

Pew Research Center, Global Attitudes and Trends:
http://www.pewglobal.org/

World Values Survey:
http://www.worldvaluessurvey.org/wvs.jsp

References

Abercrombie, Nicholas, Stephen Hill, and Bryan S. Turner. 1980. *The Dominant Ideology Thesis.* London: George Allen and Unwin.

Adams, Michael. 2003. *Fire and Ice: The Myth of Value Convergence in Canada and the United States.* Toronto: Penguin Canada.

Broadbent Institute. 2014. *The Wealth Gap: Perceptions and Misconceptions in Canada.* www.broadbentinstitute.ca/en/issue/wealth-gap-perceptions-and-misconceptions-canada.

Centre for Research and Information on Canada. 2002. *Portraits of Canada 2002.* Montreal: Canadian Unity Council.

Curtis, James, and Edward Grabb. 2004. "Social status and beliefs about what's important for getting ahead." In James Curtis, Edward Grabb, and Neil Guppy, eds, *Social Inequality in Canada: Patterns, Problems, Policies*, 4th edn, pp. 393–409. Toronto: Pearson Education Canada.

Grabb, Edward, and James Curtis. 2010. *Regions Apart: The Four Societies of Canada and the United States*, 2nd edn. Toronto: Oxford University Press.

Huber, Joan, and William Form. 1973. *Income and Ideology.* New York: Free Press.

Inkeles, Alex. 1997. *National Character. A Psycho-Social Perspective.* New Brunswick, NJ: Transaction.

Johnstone, John C. 1969. *Young People's Images of Canadian Society.* Studies of the Royal Commission on Bilingualism and Biculturalism, No. 2. Ottawa: Queen's Printer.

Kelley, Jonathan, and M.D.R. Evans. 1993. "The legitimation of inequality: Norms on occupational earnings in nine nations." *American Journal of Sociology* 99: 75–125.

Kluegel, James, and Eliot Smith. 1986. *Beliefs about Inequality.* New York: Aldine de Gruyter.

Kohut, Andrew, and Michael Dimock. 2013. *Resilient American Values. Optimism in an Era of Growing Inequality and Economic Difficulty.* Pew Research Center Working Paper, May. New York: Council on Foreign Relations

Lipset, S.M. 1990. *Continental Divide: The Values and Institutions of the United States and Canada.* New York: Routledge Press.

———. 1996. *American Exceptionalism.* New York: Norton.

Maclean's. 1998. "Taking the pulse of a nation." 110, 52 (5 Jan.).

Mann, Michael. 1970. "The social cohesion of liberal democracy." *American Sociological Review* 35:423–39.

Marchak, Patricia. 1988. *Ideological Perspectives on Canada*, 3rd edn. Toronto: McGraw-Hill Ryerson.

Marx, Karl, and Friedrich Engels. 1970 [1848]. *The Communist Manifesto.* New York: Washington Square Press.

——— and ———. 1976 [1846]. *The German Ideology.* In *Marx-Engels Collected Works*, vol. 5. New York: International Publishers.

Mizruchi, Ephraim. 1964. *Success and Opportunity.* New York: Free Press.

Northrup, David, and Lesley Jacobs, assisted by Hugh McCague and Crystal Au. 2014. *The Growing Income Inequality Gap in Canada: A National Survey.* 31 Jan. Toronto: Institute for Social Research, York University, and *Toronto Star.*

Olsen, Gregg M. 2002. *The Politics of the Welfare State: Canada, Sweden, and the United States.* Toronto: Oxford University Press.

Osberg, Lars, and Timothy Smeeding. 2006. "'Fair' inequality? Attitudes to pay differentials: The United States in comparative perspective." *American Sociological Review* 71: 450–73.

Pammett, Jon. 1996. "Getting ahead around the world." In Alan Frizzell and Jon Pammett, eds, *Social Inequality in Canada*, pp. 67–86. Ottawa: Carleton University Press.

Pew Research Center. 2014. *Emerging and Developing Economies Much More Optimistic Than Rich Countries about the Future.* http://www.pewglobal.org/files/2014/10/Pew-Research-Center-Inequality-Report-FINAL-October-9-2014.pdf.

Reutter, Linda, Gerry Veenstra, Miriam Stewart, Dennis Raphael, Rhonda Love, Edward Makwarimba, and Susan McMurray. 2006. "Public attributions for poverty in Canada." *Canadian Review of Sociology and Anthropology* 43: 1–22.

Sniderman, Paul, Joseph Fletcher, Peter Russell, and Philip Tetlock. 1996. *The Clash of Rights: Liberty, Equality, and Legitimacy in Pluralist Democracy.* New Haven: Yale University Press.

Stonecash, Jeffrey. 2007. *Inequality and the American Public: Results of the Fourth Annual Maxwell School Survey Conducted September, 2007.* Syracuse, NY: Campbell Public Affairs Institute, Maxwell School of Citizenship & Public Affairs, Syracuse University.

United Nations. 2015. *Human Development Report 2015.* New York: United Nations Development Programme.

Wanner, Richard. 2009. "Social mobility in Canada: Concepts, patterns, and trends." In Edward Grabb and Neil Guppy, eds, *Social Inequality in Canada: Pattern, Problems, and Policies*, 5th edn, pp. 116–32. Toronto: Pearson Education Canada.

Williams, Robin M., Jr. 1960. *American Society.* New York: Alfred Knopf.

World Values Survey Association. 2012. *Values Change the World—Survey Brochure.* http://www.iffs.se/wp-content/uploads/2012/12/WVS-brochure-web.pdf.

24 Economic Inequality and Acceptance of Minority Groups in Cross-National Perspective: Is Canada Uniquely Tolerant?

Robert Andersen

Introduction

Tolerance is widely considered a hallmark of Canadian society (Howard-Hassman 1999). But are Canadians really more tolerant than others? And is acceptance of minority groups equally distributed among the Canadian population, or are some groups less tolerant than others? Of particular concern is the role of economic inequality, which has a strong influence on a wide array of attitudes and behaviours, including tolerance (Andersen and Fetner 2008a). This concern has become even more relevant with the increase in inequality over the past few decades, which has characterized most modern societies (Nielsen and Alderson 1995; Firebaugh 2000; Goesling 2001), including Canada (Andersen and McIvor 2014; Banting and Myles 2013).

The present chapter assesses the relationship between economic inequality and ethno-religious tolerance in Canada and elsewhere. We address three general research questions related to this topic: (1) How is tolerance related to economic inequality, both within and across countries? (2) How does Canada compare to other countries in terms of average levels of tolerance? (3) Does inequality within Canada have implications for intolerance? These questions are answered using data from the World Values Survey (Inglehart et al. 2001) and contextual data from various sources. Before turning to the analysis, some theoretical perspectives need to be considered regarding the relationship between economic conditions and tolerance. Explored here are both the role of economic conditions at the individual level and how differences in national economies may also play a role.

The Role of Economic Conditions

Convincing evidence indicates that intolerance is largely related to perceptions that a minority "outgroup" poses a threat, whether real or imaginary, to the way of life of the majority (Sullivan, Piereson, and Marcus 1982). Economic inequality can play an important role in this regard. Specifically, those in lower economic positions have less economic security than those in higher economic positions, and hence may feel more vulnerable to people from groups other than their own (McClosky and Brill 1983). Many possible mechanisms could underlie this feeling of vulnerability, including (1) inter-group conflict, whether political or economic; (2) parochialism and ignorance; (3) working-class "authoritarianism" or conformism; and (4) relative deprivation.

Social Identity Theory and Inter-Group Conflict

According to social identity theory, these perceptions of threat are driven largely by inter-group conflict (Tajfel 1974). Although social identity theory is concerned specifically with the social-psychological mechanisms for how *perceived* threats shape attitudes—i.e., it does not assess whether these perceptions are actually justified—inter-group conflict can have real implications. For example, those in the working class might be intolerant of immigrants if they perceive—rightly or wrongly—that immigrants are more willing to work longer hours, in poorer conditions, and for less pay, all of which would give them a competitive advantage in the labour market. Intolerance among the working class, then, could stem from a fear that immigrants will take their jobs. At the same time, we might expect that those in professional occupations, most of which require significant formal education and skills, are more accepting of immigrants because they have less fear that they will compete with them for jobs.

Parochialism and Ignorance

Unjustified perceptions of threat can result from a lack of knowledge of the minority groups (Gibson 1986, 2006; Chong 1993; Weldon 2006). Research on social networks demonstrates that people with many social ties outside of their own group tend to have better knowledge of other groups (Granovetter 1973). Merton's (1957) distinction between "localite" and "cosmopolitan" individuals is also relevant in this regard. Localites are people who are largely in contact with others who are similar to themselves. In contrast, cosmopolitan individuals see themselves as belonging to a larger world. While Merton's work refers specifically to those living in larger urban centres, it is relatively straightforward to extend the idea to those with generally more diverse networks. We might expect localites to be more intolerant because they have less contact with people who have views different from their own, a pattern suggested in some studies (Andersen and Yaish 2003; Money 1999.)

People in lower socio-economic positions tend to have less diverse and less far-reaching social networks than those from higher socio-economic positions (Cote, Andersen, and Erickson 2015; Parkin 1967; Teather 1997; Eckstein 2001; Woldoff 2002; Entwisle et al. 2007). Although the gap has narrowed greatly over the past few decades, working-class people still tend to travel less, either for work or for leisure (Katz-Gerro 2002; Tomlinson 2003), participate less in voluntary associations (Curtis, Baer, and Grabb 2001; Andersen, Curtis, and Grabb 2006), and have fewer close contacts outside of work (Erickson 1996; Andersen and Heath 2002; Andersen, Yang, and Heath 2006). In short, individuals in lower socio-economic positions tend to have less exposure to, and probably less knowledge about, people who differ from themselves, compared with people in higher socio-economic positions.

Working-Class Authoritarianism

The most prominent theory predicting social class differences in tolerance is Lipset's working-class authoritarianism thesis (Lipset 1959, 1960; see also Grabb 1979, 1980; Billiet et al. 1996). Lipset suggested that social context can influence the development of particular predispositions that affect tolerance. He argued that the social and economic insecurity, and resulting family tension found disproportionately in the working class, can result in feelings of isolation from the dominant political and cultural values, which in turn inhibit the development of sophisticated views about social and political issues. This lack of sophistication can apparently lead to a preference for simple solutions to political and social problems and hence to traditionalism, moral conservatism, and hostility towards outgroups.

Some more recent applications of this theory suggest that working-class intolerance actually exists because the working class is more "conformist" rather than more "authoritarian" than other classes (Svallfors 2006). In this regard, Kohn (1977: 201) states that working-class individuals are less willing than other people to "allow others to step out of narrowly confined limits of what is proper and acceptable." Others argue that education, not social class, is largely responsible for differences in attitudes (Lipsitz 1965; Grabb 1979; Dekker and Ester 1987; Houtman 2003). Lipset himself acknowledged the theory's limitations in later work when he suggested that education, not class, plays the crucial role. More specifically, he stated: "a consistent and continuing research literature has documented relationships between low levels of education and racial and religious prejudice, opposition to equal rights for women, and with support of, and involvement in, fundamentalist religious groups" (Lipset 1981: 478).

Knowledge and Education

The rationale for a relationship between formal education and tolerance is compelling. Higher education is said to expose people to a more diverse range of cultures, ideas, and ways of life, with the result that highly educated individuals are presumed to be relatively more open-minded about social diversity (Stouffer 1955; Prothro and Grigg 1960; McClosky 1964; Davis 1975; McCutcheon 1985). Consistent with this idea, Jackman (1978) found that the more educated were more in favour of racial integration and ethnic equality than were the less educated (also Bobo and Zubrinsky 1996; Pedersen 1996; Gay 2006). Similarly, Quillian (1995) and Coenders and Scheepers (1998) demonstrated that highly educated individuals are much more likely than the less educated to express tolerance of immigrants (also Pedersen 1996; Semyonov et al. 2006; Haubert and Fussell 2006). A similar education effect has been found with respect to beliefs about gender equity (Ainsworth and Roscigno 2005; Cotter et al. 1999) and tolerance of homosexuality, both in Canada (Andersen and Fetner 2008b) and elsewhere (Overby and Barth 2002; Hicks and Lee 2006). Nevertheless, it is not completely clear whether education actually liberalizes people's beliefs or simply leads to better knowledge of social norms and values, resulting in "appropriate" liberal answers to survey questions (Jackman 1972).

Modernization, Economic Development, and Post-materialism

Much debate over the past few decades has focused on the declining importance of economic position—more specifically, of social class—as an explanation for social and political attitudes and behaviours in modern democracies (see Evans 1999). Some have argued that "class politics" is "dead" while others argue that class remains an important source of identity, though in different ways from the past. For example, postmodern explanations (e.g., Pakulski 1993; Pakulski and Waters 1996) argue that individualism has taken the place of class identities. Those who adhere to this thesis see several societal changes as being responsible for the declining significance of class. These include improved living standards for the working class, greater social and geographical mobility, increased opportunities for individual lifestyle choices, and the growth of mass communications, which have led to weaker and more diffuse patterns of personal interaction and a reduced reliance on locally based networks of support.

A variant of the individualization thesis, Inglehart's (1971, 1990, 1997) "post-materialist" thesis, argues that there has been considerable change in attitudes in modern democracies, with a shift away from material interests and towards so-called post-materialist values (Inglehart and Baker 2000). Post-materialist theorists hold that, as societies democratize, modernize, and obtain a high level of economic development, most people live economically secure lives and are thus freed from material concerns. As a result, individuals have moved away from collective material interests based on social class to more individualistic concerns related to lifestyle and freedom of expression, and thus have become more accepting of others. The theory implies that economic position has little impact on intolerance because even the less advantaged are comparatively free from material concerns.

The post-materialist thesis leads to two expectations: (1) given Canada's highly developed economy and degree of democratization, Canadians should exhibit relatively high levels of overall acceptance when compared to other national populations; and (2) because Canadians generally enjoy considerable wealth or affluence, post-materialism should be widespread, and so socio-economic status should have little impact on tolerance in Canada. Some existing research supports both of these ideas (Nevitte, Bakvis, and Gibbins 1989; Brym et al. 2004). Nevertheless, as we shall discuss below, there are also reasons to believe that post-materialism is less widespread than its proponents assume. At the very least, the theory's failure to consider explicitly how resources are distributed within societies prohibits it from explaining much of the story.

Contextual Inequality and Relative Deprivation

In contrast to the other theories discussed above, the theory of relative deprivation is concerned with relative, rather than absolute, economic conditions. From this view, those in lower economic positions can enjoy a relatively high standard of living and economic security and yet still be intolerant because of their relative position. In fact, some have argued that relative differences in economic conditions have more important consequences than absolute economic conditions (Runciman 1966; Griffin 1988). Originally coined by Stouffer (1949), relative deprivation refers to the discontent that individuals or groups feel if they think they are unfairly disadvantaged compared to other groups whom they view as enjoying unjust rewards. Merton (1957) expanded the concept, using it as the basis for his conception of anomie. He argued that the high rates of social mobility characteristic of developed societies raise people's expectations about their social and economic standing. Those who fail to reach their expectations are prone to feelings of dissatisfaction with society, leading them to protest against their situation. Relative deprivation has also been used to explain racial conflict (Vanneman and Pettigrew 1972), radical politics (Runciman 1966; Walker and Pettigrew 1984), and criminal activity (Lea and Young 1984; Box 1987; Young 1999).

In no country are economic resources distributed equally across the population. As other chapters in the present volume have shown, Canada is no exception. It is also very clear that not everyone experiences the freedom from material concerns that is so important to the post-materialist thesis discussed above. Moreover, economic inequality has risen dramatically in many countries (see Milanovic 2005), including Canada (Andersen and McIvor 2014), over the past few decades, so even if more people are free of material concerns, the relative distance between upper and lower economic classes has increased. Therefore, there is reason to suspect that the theory of relative deprivation may be even more relevant today than it was 30 years ago (see, e.g., Andersen 2012; Andersen and Curtis 2013). The mechanisms of the theory of relative deprivation suggest that differences in attitudes between those in high and low economic positions will be greatest when inequality is high. In short, this theory leads to the hypothesis that tolerance will be less well distributed throughout a society when inequality is high, and thus overall tolerance will be lower as a result.

New Evidence

We turn now to an analysis of the impact of economic inequality on tolerance in Canada and elsewhere. Specific attention is placed on overall levels of tolerance towards people of other races, people of other religions, and immigrants. We start by exploring the impact of economic inequality on tolerance within and across countries. Specifically, we assess the effects of individual-level and national-level economic indicators on tolerance across 92 countries. We also pay close attention to Canada's relative position in this regard. The chapter ends with an assessment of the relationship between economic position and tolerance within Canada.

Data Sources

To measure attitudes towards outgroups, we employ World Values Survey (WVS) data (Inglehart et al. 2001) collected from 238 surveys administered in 92 countries during the period from 1981 to 2005. The 92 countries included in the analysis represent a broad range of societies from all major geographic regions of the world and that vary widely in terms of economic development, level of inequality, and culture. All of the national samples were designed to be representative of the adult populations of the countries from which they were sampled. Data from two Canadian surveys—measured in 2000 and 2005—are included in the cross-national analysis. For the analysis of tolerance within Canada, we employ data from the 2005 WVS.

The WVS survey data were merged with information on the countries' levels of economic development and income inequality at the time of the survey. Economic development is tapped by GDP per capita, standardized to 2005 US dollars for each survey year. These data were taken from the World Bank (http://www.worldbank.org). Income inequality was measured using the Gini coefficient for household incomes. This measure has a theoretical range between 0 (where all households have equal income) and 1 (indicating complete income inequality, where one household has all of the income). The Gini indicators used for this study were obtained from the Luxembourg Income Study (LIS 2005) and the Standardized World Income Inequality Database (Solt 2009).

Dependent Variables

The analysis explores the effect of economic conditions on three dependent variables that tap the acceptance of outgroups. All three variables stem from a single question in the WVS: "On this list are various groups of people. Could you please sort out any that you would not like to have as neighbours?" We focus on three specific groups presented to the respondents: (a) "people of a different race," (b) "people of a different religion," and (c) "immigrants/foreign workers." Respondents were given two possible response choices. They could either mention or not mention the group as one that they would not want to have as neighbours. Those who mentioned a group were coded as "intolerant"; those who did not mention a group were coded as "tolerant."

Measures of Social Inequality

The main individual-level predictors in the statistical models are occupational class (which is often considered the best single indicator of social class), household income, and education. *Occupational class* is grouped into six categories: unskilled manual labour, skilled manual labour, routine non-manual labour, professionals, employers/owners, and an "other" category that includes those who are not working, such as students and homemakers. *Household income* is divided into quintiles. *Education* is divided into four categories: no education, elementary school, a high school diploma, and post-secondary qualifications.[1]

Results

Canada in Cross-National Perspective

We start by comparing the overall level of tolerance exhibited by Canadians with the levels expressed by people in other countries. As noted earlier, the post-materialist thesis suggests that acceptance of other groups should be positively

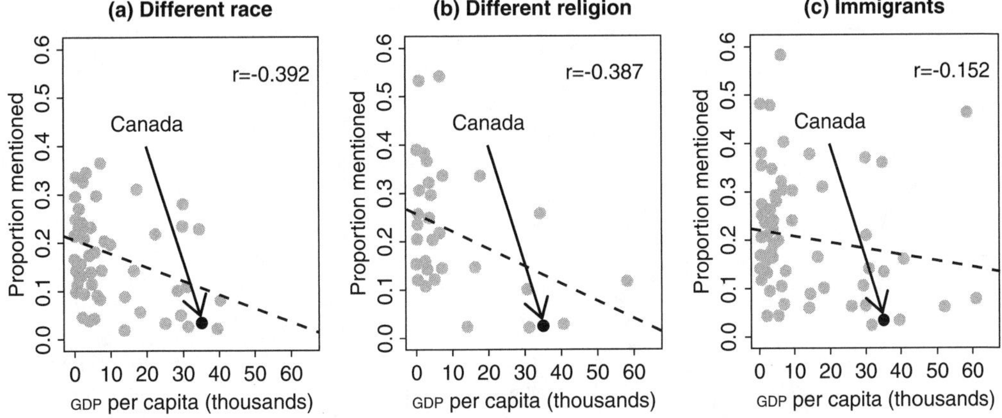

Figure 24.1 Cross-National Relationship between Ethno-Religious Intolerance and GDP per Capita (2007 US $)

Note: Shown are the proportions of the populations in each country responding that they would not want someone from the specified group as a neighbour.
Source: Author-generated through analysis of the World Values Surveys.

related to economic development. Given that Canada both is highly developed and has a long democratic tradition, we should expect levels of acceptance in Canada to be relatively high when compared to acceptance in other nations. To this end, Figure 24.1 plots the proportion of respondents in each country who would *not* want as neighbours someone from a different race, someone of a different religion, and immigrants, and relates these proportions to the country's GDP per capita (in US dollars). Also shown are the fitted lines from simple regressions of average intolerance on GDP per capita and their corresponding correlation coefficients.

There are two particularly noteworthy findings in Figure 24.1. First, for all three of the groups, the average level of intolerance is negatively related to the GDP per capita of the country. In other words, as the post-materialist thesis suggests, intolerance tends to decrease as economic development rises. The correlation coefficients indicate that the relationships with GDP per capita are particularly strong for intolerance of people from different races or religions. Second, compared with people from other countries, Canadians exhibit a very low level of intolerance of ethno-religious outgroups generally. Canada is rather unique not just in terms of its relative position to all other countries, but even among nations with similar levels of economic development.

We now turn to the relationship between national level-income inequality and intolerance. Figure 24.2 plots the proportion in each country that would not like to have people of a different race or religion, or immigrants, as neighbours, by the country's Gini coefficient for household incomes. Panels (a) and (b), which pertain to attitudes towards people of different races and religions, demonstrate a moderately strong positive relationship between inequality and intolerance. That is, people tend to be more tolerant if they live in more equal societies. On the other hand, no discernible relationship between national-level income inequality and tolerance of immigrants is apparent. Finally, as was the case with the effect of GDP per capita, we again see that Canadians tend to be much more tolerant on average than the country's level of inequality would suggest they would be.

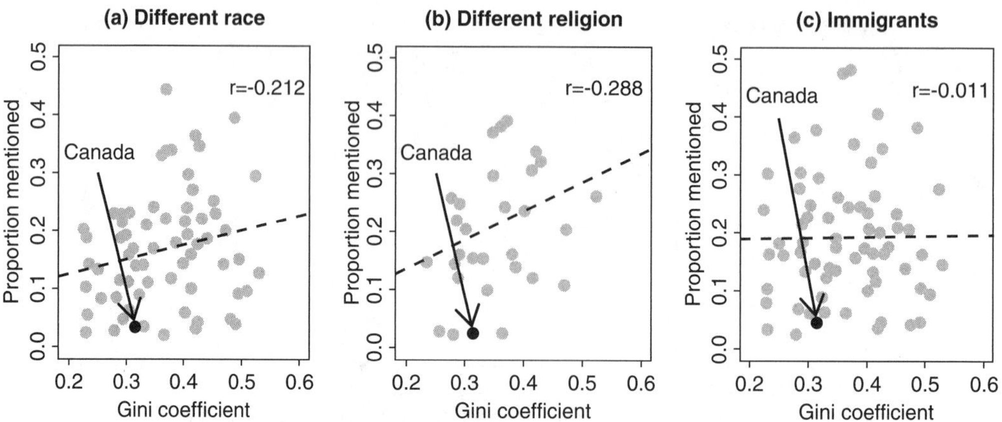

Figure 24.2 Cross-National Relationship between Ethno-Religious Intolerance and the Gini Coefficient for Household Incomes

Note: Shown are the proportions of the populations in each country responding that they would not want someone from the specified group as a neighbour.
Source: Author-generated through analysis of the World Values Surveys.

Figures 24.1 and 24.2 provide tentative evidence that national economic conditions influence attitudes towards ethno-religious outgroups. We find support for the post-materialist thesis in that acceptance of the three outgroups is highest in the richest countries. This is tentative evidence, then, that inequality across nations might account for at least some of the differences in intolerance. We also find support for the idea that intolerance is greatest when inequality is high. These findings should be interpreted cautiously, however, because they do not take into account the demographic composition of the countries being compared. It is possible that the relationships shown in Figures 24.1 and 24.2 reflect "compositional" effects rather than "contextual" effects. That is, without controlling for important individual-level predictors within countries, we cannot confidently claim that national economic conditions affect attitudes. It is possible that the patterns merely reflect country differences in the proportions of the types of people who are more likely to be tolerant. For this reason, we now turn to regression models that simultaneously predict intolerance from both important individual-level economic variables and national economic context.

Table 24.1 displays the results from fixed effect logistic regression models fitted to the WVS and national context data. By including "fixed effects" for countries (more simply put, country is controlled for in the models), we are able to control for any "leftover" influences related to unique country characteristics not included in the models. Several important conclusions can be based on these models. First, for all three dependent variables, individual-level economic conditions have the expected effect on attitudes. Those in less advantageous economic positions (e.g., low income, unskilled, and uneducated) tend to be more intolerant than their more educated and richer counterparts. Second, even after controlling for these individual-level predictors, the effects of economic conditions at the national level persist. Compared to more equal countries, less equal countries tend to be less tolerant; that is, people within less equal countries are more likely not to want immigrants and people of different

Table 24.1 Fixed Effects Logistic Regression Models Predicting Whether Respondents Would Not Like to Have a Neighbour of a Different Race or Religion, or Who Is an Immigrant

	Dependent Variable		
	Different Race	**Different Religion**	**Immigrants**
Income			
Lowest 1/5	0	0	0
Fourth	−0.14***	−0.13***	−0.13***
Third	−0.17***	−0.16***	−0.17***
Second	−0.19***	−0.17***	−0.17***
Highest 1/5	−0.14***	−0.003	−0.21***
Occupational class			
Unskilled manual	0	0	0
Skilled manual	−0.11***	−0.14***	−0.08***
Routine non-manual labour	−0.21***	−0.22***	−0.18***
Professionals	−0.21***	−0.18***	−0.10***
Employers/owners	−0.06***	−0.18***	−0.23***
Other	−0.02	−0.06**	0.04*
Educational qualifications			
None	0	0	0
Elementary school	−0.09***	−0.05***	−0.04***
High school graduate	−0.19***	−0.24***	−0.10***
Post-secondary	−0.21***	−0.42***	−0.24***
National economic context			
Gini coefficient	0.07***	0.18***	0.22***
GDP per capita	−0.19***	−0.16	0.44***
N (countries)	92	81	87
n (individuals)	295,522	184,267	288,851

*P-value<0.05; **P-value<.01; ***P-value<0.001.

Note: Although not shown here, models include fixed effects for country, survey year, and respondent's age and gender. The Gini coefficient and GDP per capita have been standardized so that the magnitude of their effects can be directly compared.

Source: Author-generated through analysis of the World Values Surveys.

races and religions to be their neighbours. On the other hand, having controlled for national-level income inequality and individual-level economic variables, GDP per capita now has variable influence on the three dependent variables. Although the expected negative relationship persists for attitudes towards people of different races and religions (the effect of the latter is not statistically significant), the effect is in the opposite direction for attitudes towards immigrants. Holding income inequality and individual-level economic conditions constant, intolerance towards

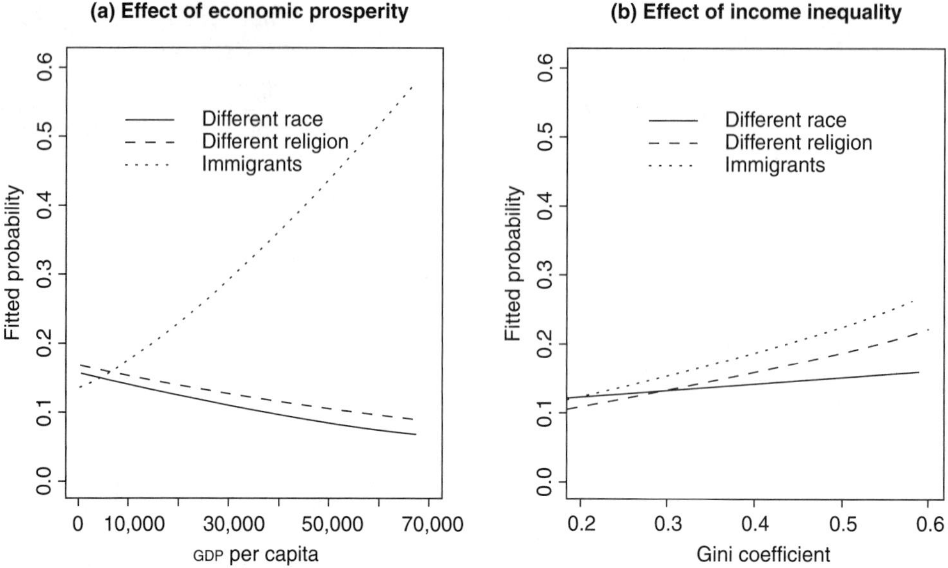

Figure 24.3 Effect Displays for the Relationship between National Economic Context and Probability of Accepting Minority Groups

Note: Fitted values derived from the fixed effects models reported in Table 24.1.
Source: Author-generated through analysis of the World Values Surveys.

immigrants is actually greater among rich countries than it is among poor ones.

The values shown in Table 24.1 represent logit coefficients, which are difficult to make complete sense of without some further calculations. To facilitate a better understanding of the effects of the two economic context variables, "fitted probabilities" calculated from these coefficients are presented in Figure 24.3. Panel (a) clearly displays the variable effects of GDP per capita on attitudes. As expected from the post-materialist thesis, the probability of intolerance of people of different races and religions decreases as economic prosperity rises. On the other hand, the probability of intolerance of immigrants dramatically *rises* as economic prosperity rises. Panel (b) of Figure 24.3 demonstrates the similar positive relationship that income inequality has with intolerance of all three of the groups under investigation. Still, as with the effect of economic prosperity, inequality has its strongest influence on attitudes towards immigrants. We will return to a discussion of these findings in the conclusion.

Inequality and Tolerance within Canada

We now turn to an assessment of the levels of intolerance within Canada. Table 24.2 assesses the bivariate relationships between intolerance and the individual-level economic variables. The p-value for the chi-square statistic in the last row for each variable indicates whether there is a statistically significant relationship with the dependent variable in question. The most remarkable finding in this table is the stark general differences between these results and the results shown in Table 24.1. The cross-national analysis clearly demonstrated that those in less advantaged economic conditions tend to be less tolerant. The tentative

Table 24.2 Percentage Indicating They Would Not Like to Have a Neighbour of a Different Race or Religion, or Who Is an Immigrant, by Socio-economic Characteristics, Canadian Respondents to the 2005 WVS

	% Reporting They Wouldn't Want Someone from the Following Groups as a Neighbour		
	Different Race	**Different Religion**	**Immigrants**
All respondents	2.6	2.1	3.9
Income			
Lowest 1/5	3.7	3.3	5.1
Fourth	4.0	3.1	4.4
Third	2.2	2.2	3.9
Second	1.7	1.1	4.6
Highest 1/5	1.5	1.5	2.5
p-value for chi-square test	0.37	0.53	0.71
Occupational class			
Unskilled manual	1.2	2.4	1.2
Skilled manual	1.8	3.6	5.4
Routine non-manual labour	2.1	1.4	2.1
Professionals	1.4	0.6	1.8
Employers/owners	1.2	0.0	1.4
Other	3.7	2.7	5.3
p-value for chi-square test	0.38	0.32	0.07
Educational qualifications			
None	9.4	9.4	21.0
Elementary school	2.7	2.7	4.6
High school graduate	2.1	1.5	2.7
Post-secondary	2.2	0.4	1.3
p-value for chi-square test	0.26	0.01	<0.001
N	1,171	1,171	1,171

Source: Author-generated through analysis of the World Values Surveys.

evidence in Table 24.2 suggests that this may not be the case in Canada, however. While the effects for occupational class and income are in the expected directions, they are not statistically significant. In other words, the differences are small enough that we cannot say that they are not due to chance alone. However, education does matter for tolerance, especially with respect to tolerance of immigrants. The proportion of respondents who do not want immigrants as neighbours decreases dramatically as the level of education increases. Especially intolerant are those with no formal educational qualifications: more than 20 per cent of this

Table 24.3 Type II Chi-Square Tests for Socio-economic Characteristics When All Are Included in Logistic Regression Models

Independent Variable (degrees of freedom)	Dependent Variable		
	Different Race	**Different Religion**	**Immigrants**
Educational qualifications (3)	0.75	3.59	13.45***
Occupational class (5)	2.16	4.43	4.21
Income (4)	0.47	0.53	2.82

*P-value<0.05; **P-value<.01; ***P-value<0.001.
Note: These are tests for the effect of each social status indicator controlling for all others. Models controlled for age, gender, marital status.
Source: Author-generated through analysis of the World Values Surveys.

group reported that they did not want to have immigrants as neighbours; none of the other education groups exceeded 5 per cent.

Thus far we have explored only the bivariate relationships between each of our predictors and the three dependent variables. It is possible that the failure to find strong effects of individual-level economic conditions is due to the lack of proper controls. To test more rigorously the impact of the individual-level economic variables, we turn to logit models, which allow us to assess the partial effects of each of the predictors on the dependent variables. In other words, these models enable us to control for the effects of all other variables when assessing the impact of any one predictor. *P*-values for chi-square tests for the effects of economic predictors are displayed in Table 24.3. The findings presented in this table are entirely consistent with the results shown in Table 24.2. Once again, the only statistically significant effect is that of education on attitudes towards immigrants. We can thus confidently conclude that the very high level of tolerance shown by Canadians generally is shared throughout its population.

Conclusions

Consistent with the post-materialist thesis, the analyses presented in this chapter demonstrate that intolerance towards people of different races and religions is related to the level of economic development in a country. On the other hand, in contrast to what the post-materialist thesis suggests, when we control for national-level income inequality, tolerance of immigrants tends to be lower in rich countries than in poor countries. The positive association between economic development and intolerance towards immigrants and foreign workers could be a reaction against the large increases in immigration across the rich nations of the world over the past few decades. Coincidentally, the rise in immigration has come at the same time as the rise in inequality within these countries. Although they are unrelated processes, the combination of increased immigration, especially of visual minorities, and the rise in inequality may have resulted in increased dissatisfaction with the perceived competition that immigrants might pose in the labour market. This dissatisfaction may have manifested itself as greater intolerance.

Consistent with the growing body of research on this issue, we also found strong evidence that national-level income inequality influences attitudes (Uslaner 2002; Uslaner and Brown 2002; Andersen and Fetner 2008a). Our findings suggest that, as income inequality rises, intolerance follows in tandem. The implications of this result are especially important given that inequality has risen drastically in most modern democracies, including Canada, over the past few decades. If governments wish to ensure the health of their democracies, they will need to think hard about formulating policies that limit inequality.

Our results also demonstrate that Canadians tend to be far more accepting of other races and religions than we would expect given Canada's levels of economic development and income inequality. Canadians also tend to be highly accepting of immigrants in comparison with people in most other nations, although Canadians are less tolerant towards immigrants than they are towards the other two groups. While we can only speculate, the generally high acceptance that Canadians express for immigrants and people of other races and religions may stem from the fact that, compared with people in most other nations, Canadians have a better knowledge of and more exposure to such groups in their daily lives. Given that Canada is among the most ethnically diverse nations in the world and has one of the largest foreign-born populations (e.g., Li 2003), we would expect Canadians to have greater than average knowledge and experience of ethno-religious groups different from themselves. It would be nearly impossible for Canadians to avoid contact with immigrants or people from racial groups that are different from their own, especially in large cities. This relatively high level of contact and interaction probably helps to enhance inter-group understanding and reduce perceptions of threat, which in turn promotes tolerance.

That Canadians are slightly less tolerant of immigrants and foreign workers than they are of people from other races or religions is almost surely related to economic considerations. Although the data employed in this study did not contain information on why respondents were intolerant, it seems likely that the higher level of intolerance for immigrants, and especially foreign workers, is related to the fact that they compete—or are believed to compete—with established Canadians for employment. While this competition may affect only a minority of Canadians, it is likely that some consider only whether immigrants, and especially foreign workers, are a possible threat or not, and not whether the probability of that threat is high. Moreover, immigrants and foreign workers often receive government assistance, which is something many Canadians disagree with generally (Andersen and Curtis 2013), and this could create ill feelings towards anyone perceived to be receiving it. On the other hand, it is difficult to construct a similar economic argument as to why Canadians would feel threatened by people of other races and religions. Still, it is important to remember that the level of tolerance of immigrants and foreign workers in Canada is extremely high—much higher than in almost every other nation we explored—and only slightly lower than levels of tolerance for people of other races and religions.

As with the cross-national findings, our findings within Canada are mixed regarding the impact of social inequality on intolerance. Variables most directly related to social class, i.e., occupational class and income, appear to have little or no effect on acceptance of immigrants and people of other races and religions in Canada. Given that most immigrants to Canada start with working-class jobs (Driedger 2003) and are increasingly non-White (Statistics Canada 2003), working-class Canadians are likely to have a much greater familiarity with immigrants and people of different races than are people in most other countries. In short, Canada's high level of tolerance is shared widely across the income distribution and social classes. Still, our findings also confirm previous research in showing that education has a consistent and positive relationship with acceptance of outgroups.

It is interesting to consider the possible implications of our findings and speculate about what might lie ahead. Social tolerance is widely considered to be crucial for the health of liberal democracy (Jones 2007). Given this, and considering that Canada is one of the most ethnically diverse countries in the world, it is not surprising that the Canadian state strongly promotes the acceptance of individual or group differences (White 2003; Merchant and Rich 2004; Mulder and Krahn 2005). It appears that the state's efforts have been quite successful. Other studies also have found that Canada is among the most tolerant nations in the world (Milligan, Andersen, and Brym 2014; Soroka and Roberton 2010). While these findings speak well for Canadian democracy, our level of tolerance could be threatened if inequality in Canadian incomes continues to rise. The mechanisms of the inequality effect are quite simple. When income inequality is high, people in lower economic positions must fight harder to get "their" share of resources. Differences among classes also become much more visible, increasing class identities and class polarization (Andersen and Curtis 2012). These conditions are ideal for the growth of intolerance. The implications are particularly strong for intolerance of immigrants, who may be perceived as taking away resources that native Canadians—especially the less educated—wish were theirs. Considering the results of this chapter, it is reasonable to suggest that the Canadian government would be wise to address the inequality issue if it wishes Canada to maintain its high level of tolerance.

Questions for Critical Thought

1. Canada has a reputation for being accepting of many different ethnic, racial, and religious groups. Do your own experiences, and those of your friends and family generally, fit this depiction of Canada? Discuss.
2. Studies generally show that higher education is a key factor that reduces intolerant or prejudiced attitudes towards ethnic, racial, and religious minorities. Some believe that this occurs because education increases people's awareness and appreciation of other cultures. Can you think of any other reasons why education has this apparent effect on attitudes?
3. Many Canadians believe that, in our multicultural society, we have far more progressive and tolerant attitudes than do Americans. Do you think this is true? Discuss.
4. This chapter raises doubts about the claim by some researchers that working-class people are more intolerant or prejudiced than other people. What do you think are the main origins of, or reasons behind, the existence of prejudice, discrimination, and intolerance in Canada?

Recommended Readings

Breton, Raymond. 2012. *Different Gods: Integrating Non-Christian Minorities into a Primarily Christian Society.* Montreal and Kingston: McGill-Queen's University Press.

Ekos Politics. 2013. "Attitudes to immigration and visible minorities: A historical perspective." 26 Feb. http://www.ekospolitics.com/wp-content/uploads/full_report_immigration_february_26_2013.pdf.

Reitz, Jeffrey G., Raymond Breton, Karen Kisiel Dion, and Kenneth L. Dion. 2009. *Multiculturalism and Social Cohesion: Potentials and Challenges of Diversity.* Amsterdam: Springer.

Satzewich, Vic. 2011. *Racism in Canada.* Toronto: Oxford University Press.

Soroka, Stuart, and Sarah Roberton. 2010. *A Literature Review of Public Opinion Research on Canadian Attitudes towards Multiculturalism and Immigration, 2006–2009.* Ottawa: Citizenship and Immigration Canada, Mar. http://www.cic.gc.ca/english/pdf/research-stats/2012-por-multi-imm-eng.pdf.

Recommended Websites

Canadian Centre for Diversity and Inclusion:
http://www.ccdi.ca/about/cidi-ccd-ccdi-merge/

Canadian Race Relations Foundation:
http://www.crr.ca/en/; http://www.crr.ca/fr/

Multicultural Canada:
http://www.multiculturalcanada.ca/

Tolerance.ca:
http://www.tolerance.ca/

Urban Alliance on Race Relations (Toronto):
http://urbanalliance.ca/

Note

1. Although not reported in the tables, the cross-national analysis also controls for age, gender, religiosity, and marital status.

References

Ainsworth, James, and Vincent Roscigno. 2005. "Stratification, school-work linkages, and vocational education." *Social Forces* 84, 1: 257–84.

Andersen, Robert. 2012. "Support for democracy in cross-national perspective: The detrimental effect of economic inequality." *Research in Social Stratification and Mobility* 30, 4: 389–402.

———, James Curtis, and Edward Grabb. 2006. "Trends in civic association activity in four democracies: The special case of women in the United States." *American Sociological Review* 71, 3: 376–400.

——— and Josh Curtis. 2012. "The polarizing effect of economic inequality on class identification: Evidence from 44 countries." *Research in Social Stratification and Mobility* 30: 129–41.

——— and ———. 2013. "Public opinion on redistribution in Canada, 1980–2005: The role of political and economic context." In Banting and Myles (2013: 141–64).

——— and Tina Fetner. 2008a. "Economic inequality and intolerance: Attitudes toward homosexuality in 35 democracies." *American Journal of Political Science* 52, 4: 942–58.

——— and ———. 2008b. "Cohort differences in tolerance of homosexuality: Attitudinal change in Canada and the United States, 1981–2000." *Public Opinion Quarterly* 72: 311–30.

——— and Anthony Heath. 2002. "Class matters: The persisting effects of contextual social class on individual voting behaviour in Britain, 1964–97." *European Sociological Review* 18, 2: 125–38.

——— and Mitch McIvor. 2014. "Rising inequality and its Impact in Canada: The role of national debt." In Brian Nolan et al., eds, *Changing Inequalities and Societal Impacts in Rich Countries: Thirty Countries' Experiences*, pp. 172–95. Oxford: Oxford University Press.

——— and Meir Yaish. 2003. "Social cleavages, electoral reform, and party choice: Israel's 'natural' experiment." *Electoral Studies* 22, 3: 399–423.

———, Min Yang, and Anthony Heath. 2006. "Class politics and political context in Britain, 1964–97: Have voters become more individualized?" *European Sociological Review* 22: 125–38.

Banting, Keith, and John Myles, eds. 2013. *Inequality and the Fading of Redistributive Politics*. Vancouver: University of British Columbia Press

Billiet, Jaak, Rob Eisinga, and Peer Scheepers. 1996. "Ethnocentrism in the Low Countries: A comparative perspective." *Journal of Ethnic and Migration Studies* 22, 3: 401–16.

Bobo, Lawrence, and Camille Zubrinsky. 1996. "Attitudes on residential integration: Perceived status differences, mere in-group preference, or racial prejudice?" *Social Forces* 74, 3: 883–909.

Box, Steven. 1987. *Recession, Crime and Punishment.* London: Macmillan.

Brym, Robert J., John W.P. Veugelers, Jonah Butovsky, and John Simpson. 2004. "Postmaterialism in unresponsive political systems: The Canadian case." *Canadian Review of Sociology and Anthropology* 41, 3: 291–318.

Chong, Dennis. 1993. "How people think, reason, and feel about rights and liberties." *American Journal of Political Science* 37, 3: 867–99.

Coenders, Marcel, and Peer Scheepers. 1998. "Support for ethnic discrimination in the Netherlands 1979–1993: Effects of period, cohort, and individual characteristics." *European Sociological Review* 14, 4: 405–22.

Cote, Rochelle, Robert Andersen, and Bonnie Erickson. 2015. "Social capital and ethnic tolerance: The opposing effects of diversity and competition." In Yaojun Li, ed., *The Handbook of Research Methods and Applications on Social Capital*, pp. 91–106. Cheltenham, UK: Edward Elgar.

Cotter, David, Joan Hermsen, and Reeve Vanneman. 1999. "Systems of gender, race, and class inequality: Multilevel analyses." *Social Forces* 78, 2: 433–60.

Curtis, James, Douglas Baer, and Edward Grabb. 2001. "Nations of joiners: Explaining voluntary association membership in democratic societies." *American Sociological Review* 66, 6: 783–805.

Davis, James A. 1975. "Communism, conformity, and categories: American tolerance in 1954 and 1972–73." *American Journal of Sociology* 81, 3: 491–514.

Dekker, Paul, and Peter Ester. 1987. "Working-class authoritarianism: A re-examination of the Lipset thesis." *European Journal of Political Research* 15, 4: 395–415.

Driedger, Leo. 2003. "Changing boundaries: Sorting space, class, ethnicity, and race in Ontario." *Canadian Review of Sociology and Anthropology* 40, 5: 593–621.

Eckstein, Susan. 2001. "Community as gift-giving: Collectivist roots of volunteerism." *American Sociological Review* 66, 6: 829–51.

Entwisle, Barbara, Katherine Faust, Ronald Rindfuss, and Toshiko Kaneda. 2007. "Networks and contexts: Variation in the structure of social ties." *American Journal of Sociology* 112, 5: 1495–1533.

Erickson, Bonnie. 1996. "Culture, class, and connections." *American Journal of Sociology* 102, 1: 217–51.

Evans, Geoffrey, ed. 1999. *The End of Class Politics? Class Voting in Comparative Context.* Oxford: Oxford University Press.

Firebaugh, Glenn. 2000. "The trend in between-nation income inequality." *Annual Review of Sociology* 26: 323–39.

Gay, Claudine. 2006. "Seeing difference: The effect of economic disparity on black attitudes toward Latinos." *American Journal of Political Science* 50, 4: 982–97.

Gibson, James. 1986. "Pluralistic intolerance in America: A reconsideration." *American Politics Quarterly* 14, 4: 267–93.

———. 2006. "Do strong group identities fuel intolerance? Evidence from the South African case." *Political Psychology* 27, 5: 665–705.

Goesling, Brian. 2001. "Changing income inequalities within and between nations: New evidence." *American Sociological Review* 66, 5: 745–61.

Grabb, Edward. 1979. "Working-class authoritarianism and tolerance of outgroups: A reassessment." *Public Opinion Quarterly* 43, 1: 36–47.

———. 1980. "Marxist categories and theories of class: The case of working-class authoritarianism." *Pacific Sociological Review* 23, 4: 359–76.

Granovetter, Mark. 1973. "The strength of weak ties." *American Journal of Sociology* 78, 6: 1360–80.

Griffin, David R. 1988. *Spirituality and Society: Postmodern Visions.* Albany: State University of New York Press.

Haubert, Jeannie, and Elizabeth Fussell. 2006. "Explaining pro-immigrant sentiment in the US: Social class, cosmopolitanism, and perceptions of immigrants." *International Migration Review* 40, 3: 489–507.

Hicks, Gary, and Tien-tsung Lee. 2006. "Public attitudes toward gays and lesbians: Trends and predictors." *Journal of Homosexuality* 51, 2: 57–77.

Houtman, Dick. 2003. "Lipset and 'working-class' authoritarianism." *American Sociologist* 34, 1–2: 85–103.

Howard-Hassman, Rhoda. 1999. "'Canadian' as an ethnic category: Implications for multiculturalism and national identity." *Canadian Public Policy* 25, 4: 523–37.

Inglehart, Ronald. 1971. "The silent revolution in Europe: Intergenerational change in postindustrial societies." *American Political Science Review* 65: 911–1017.

———. 1990. *Culture Shift in Advanced Industrial Society*. Princeton, NJ: Princeton University Press.

———. 1997. *Modernization and Postmodernization: Cultural, Economic, and Political Change in 43 Societies*. Princeton, NJ: Princeton University Press.

——— et al. 2001. "World Values Surveys and European Values Surveys, 1981–1984, 1990–1993, 1995–1997, and 1999–2000." Computer file, ICPSR version. Ann Arbor, Mich.: Institute for Social Research and Inter-university Consortium for Political and Social Research.

——— and Wayne Baker. 2000. "Modernization, cultural change, and the persistence of traditional values." *American Sociological Review* 65, 1: 19–51.

Jackman, Mary. 1978. "General and applied tolerance: Does education increase commitment to racial integration?" *American Journal of Political Science* 22, 2: 302–24.

Jackman, Robert. 1972. "Political elites, mass publics, and support for democratic principles." *Journal of Politics* 34, 3: 753–73.

Jones, Peter. 2007. "Making sense of political toleration." *British Journal of Political Science* 37, 3: 383–402.

Katz-Gerro, Tally. 2002. "Highbrow cultural consumption and class distinction in Italy, Israel, West Germany, Sweden, and the United States." *Social Forces* 81, 1: 207–29.

Kohn, Melvin L. 1977. *Class and Conformity. A Study in Values*. Chicago: University of Chicago Press.

Lea, John, and Jock Young. 1984. *What Is to Be Done about Law and Order?* Harmondsworth, UK: Penguin.

Li, Peter. 2003. *Destination Canada: Immigration Debates and Issues*. Toronto: Oxford University Press.

Lipset, Seymour Martin. 1959. "Democracy and working-class authoritarianism." *American Sociological Review* 24, 3: 482–502.

———. 1960. *Political Man: The Social Bases of Politics*. Garden City, NY: Doubleday.

———. 1981. *Political Man: The Social Bases of Politics*, expanded edition. Baltimore: Johns Hopkins University Press.

Lipsitz, Lewis. 1965. "Working-class authoritarianism: A re-evaluation." *American Sociological Review* 30, 1: 103–9.

Luxembourg Income Study (LIS). 2005. "Income inequality measures." http://www.lisproject.org/keyfigures/ineqtable.htm.

McClosky, Herbert. 1964. "Consensus and ideology in American politics." *American Political Science Review* 58, 2: 351–82.

——— and Alida Brill. 1983. *Dimensions of Tolerance: What Americans Believe about Civil Liberties*. New York: Basic Books.

McCutcheon, Allan L. 1985. "A latent class analysis of tolerance for nonconformity in the American public." *Public Opinion Quarterly* 49, 4: 474–88.

Merchant, David, and Paul Rich. 2004. "Canada and the Commonwealth: Does the Commonwealth have a future as well as a past?" *American Behavioural Scientist* 47, 10: 1319–28.

Merton, Robert. 1957. *Social Theory and Social Structure*. Glencoe, Ill.: Free Press.

Milanovic, Branko. 2005. *Worlds Apart: Measuring International and Global Inequality*. Princeton, NJ: Princeton University Press.

Milligan, Scott, Robert Andersen, and Robert Brym. 2014. "Assessing variation in tolerance in 23 Muslim-majority and Western countries." *Canadian Review of Sociology* 51, 3: 239–61.

Money, Jeannette. 1999. *Fences and Neighbors: The Political Geography of Immigration Control*. Ithaca, NY: Cornell University Press.

Mulder, Marlene, and Harvey Krahn. 2005. "Individual and community-level determinants of support for immigration and cultural diversity in Canada." *Canadian Review of Sociology and Anthropology* 42, 2: 421–44.

Nevitte, Neil, Herman Bakvis, and Roger Gibbins. 1989. "The ideological contours of 'new politics' in Canada: Policy, mobilization, and partisan support." *Canadian Journal of Political Science* 22, 3: 475–503.

Nielsen, François, and Arthur S. Alderson. 1995. "Income inequality, development, and dualism." *American Sociological Review* 60, 5: 674–701.

Overby, Marvin, and Jay Barth. 2002. "Contact, community context, and public attitudes toward gay men and lesbians." *Polity* 34, 4: 433–56.

Pakulski, J. 1993. "The dying of class or of Marxist class theory?" *International Sociology* 8, 3: 279–92.

——— and M. Waters. 1996. *The Death of Class*. London: Sage.

Parkin, Frank. 1967. "Working-class Conservatives: A theory of political deviance." *British Journal of Sociology* 18: 278–90.

Pedersen, Willy. 1996. "Working-class boys at the margins: Ethnic prejudice, cultural capital, and gender." *Acta Sociologica* 39, 3: 257–79.

Prothro, J.W., and C.W. Grigg. 1960. "Fundamental principles of democracy: Bases of agreement and disagreement." *Journal of Politics* 22, 2: 276–94.

Quillian, Lincoln. 1995. "Prejudice as a response to perceived group threat: Population composition and anti-immigrant and racial prejudice in Europe." *American Sociological Review* 60, 4: 586–611.

Runciman, W.G. 1966. *Relative Deprivation and Social Justice. A Study of Attitudes to Social Inequality in Twentieth Century England*. Berkeley: University of California Press.

Semyonov, Moshe, Rebeca Raijman, and Anastasia Gorodzeisky. 2006. "The rise of anti-foreigner sentiment in European societies, 1988–2000." *American Sociological Review* 71, 3: 426–49.

Solt, Frederich. 2009. "Standardizing the world income inequality database." *Social Science Quarterly* 90, 2: 231–42.

Soroka, Stuart, and Sarah Roberton. 2010. *A Literature Review of Public Opinion Research on Canadian Attitudes towards Multiculturalism and Immigration, 2006–2009*. Ottawa: Citizenship and Immigration Canada, Mar. http://www.cic.gc.ca/english/pdf/research-stats/2012-por-multi-imm-eng.pdf.

Statistics Canada. 2003. "Selected demographic and cultural characteristics." Topic based tabulation number 97F0010XCB2001044.

Stouffer, Samuel. 1949. *The American Soldier*. Princeton, NJ: Princeton University Press.

Stouffer, Stephen A. 1955. *Communism, Conformity, and Civil Liberties: A Cross-Section of the Nation Speaks Its Mind*. New York: Doubleday.

Sullivan, John, James Piereson, and George Marcus. 1982. *Political Tolerance and American Democracy*. Chicago: University of Chicago Press.

Svallfors, Stefan. 2006. *The Moral Economy of Class*. Stanford, Calif.: Stanford University Press.

Tajfel, Henri. 1974. "Social identity and intergroup behaviour." *Social Science Information* 13, 2: 65–93.

Teather, Elizabeth. 1997. "Voluntary organizations as agents in the becoming of place." *Canadian Geographer* 41, 3: 226–35.

Tomlinson, Mark. 2003. "Lifestyle and social class." *European Sociological Review* 19, 1: 97–111.

Uslaner, Eric. 2002. *The Moral Foundations of Trust*. Cambridge, UK: Cambridge University Press.

——— and Mitchell Brown. 2002. "Inequality, trust, and civic engagement." *American Politics Research* 33, 6: 868–94.

Vanneman, Reeve, and Thomas Pettigrew. 1972. "Race and relative deprivation in the urban United States." *Race* 13, 4: 461–86.

Walker, Iain, and Thomas Pettigrew. 1984. "Relative deprivation theory: An overview and conceptual critique." *British Journal of Social Psychology* 23 (Nov.): 301–10.

Weldon, Steven. 2006. "The institutional context of tolerance for ethnic minorities: A comparative multilevel analysis of Western Europe." *American Journal of Political Science* 50, 2: 331–49.

White, Linda. 2003. "Liberalism, group rights, and the boundaries of toleration: The case of minority religious schools in Ontario." *Canadian Journal of Political Science* 36, 5: 975–1003.

Woldoff, Rachel. 2002. "The effects of local stressors on neighborhood attachment." *Social Forces* 81, 1: 87–116.

Young, Jock. 1999. *The Exclusive Society: Social Exclusion, Crime and Difference in Late Modernity*. Thousand Oaks, Calif.: Sage.

25 Why Do Skilled Immigrants Struggle in the Labour Market? A Field Experiment with Thirteen Thousand Resumés*

Philip Oreopoulos

Recent immigrants struggle in Canada's labour market, with unemployment rates almost twice those of similarly aged non-immigrants. Table 25.1, using the 2006 Canadian census, shows this for immigrants arriving between 2001 and 2005. Median wages of recent immigrant workers are also 36 per cent lower compared to Canadian-born workers. Previous research finds little evidence for expecting that this wage gap will significantly narrow with host-country experience. While the immigrant–non-immigrant wage gap used to disappear (and sometimes even be reversed) after 10 to 15 years for immigrants arriving prior to the 1970s, wages of immigrants arriving in the 1990s were still about 25 per cent lower than wages of non-immigrants as of 2000 (Frenette and Morissette 2005).

Recent immigrants to other countries such as the United States also experience similar labour market disadvantages (Lubotsky 2007), but it is particularly noteworthy in the Canadian case that immigration policy focuses on attracting immigrants with superior levels of education, experience, and industry demand to offset anticipated skilled labour force shortages and encourage economic growth. More than half of today's immigrants enter Canada under a point system, which rates applicants based on their highest degree, language ability, age, whether they have work experience at occupations deemed "in demand," whether they already have a job offer, have worked or studied in Canada previously, and have cash at hand.[1] Virtually every adult immigrant who enters Canada under the point system now has at least an undergraduate degree. The overall percentage of recent immigrants with an undergraduate degree is about 60 per cent, compared to 20 per cent for those born in Canada of similar age (Statistics Canada 2008). Conditioning on highest degree completed, therefore, causes the relative wage gap between recent immigrants and non-immigrants to *increase*, from 36 per cent lower wages for immigrants to 48 per cent (Table 25.1).

The usual suspects for explaining the gap include the possibility that employers do not value foreign education as much as Canadian education. The point system treats any degree from any institution the same. Foreign experience may also be treated as inferior to Canadian experience, since less is known about the foreign

* Abridged from "Why Do Skilled Immigrants Struggle in the Labor Market? A Field Experiment with Thirteen Thousand Resumes." *American Economic Journal: Economic Policy* 3 (4): 148–171, 2011. Reprinted with permission.

Table 25.1 Unemployment and Earning Differences between Recent Immigrants and Non-Immigrants, Ages 25–39, from the 2006 Census

	(1) Unemployment Rate	(2) Mean Earnings for Positive Earners in Labour Force ($)	(3) Mean Earnings for Positive Earners in Labour Force ($)
Non-immigrants	0.059	39,841	33,000
Recent immigrants (0–4 years)	0.104	27,462	21,000
Ratio (non-immig./immig.)	0.57	1.45	1.57
Estimated ratio, conditional on age, schooling, and city	0.54	2.20	1.94
Sample size	127,149	119,275	119,275

Notes: The sample in Column 1 includes all individuals from the 2006 Public-Use Canadian Census, aged 25 to 39, in the labor force, and recorded either as a non-immigrant, or a recent immigrant (arrived within the last five years). The sample in Columns 2 and 3 is restricted further to individuals with positive earnings. All amounts are in 2005 Canadian dollars. The estimated ratio is computed by first regressing unemployment status or log earnings on immigrant status, plus fixed effects for age, highest degree, and city of residence. The unemployment rate and mean earnings are imputed using the immigrant coefficient from the regression, relative to the actual value for non-immigrants, and the ratio of this is reported in the table. For Column 3, quantile regression around the median is used instead of ordinary least squares.

employer and tasks involved. Other possibilities are that cultural and language differences have grown as the proportion of applications from Europe has decreased and the proportion from Asia and the Pacific has increased. Concerns about language proficiency may remain.

This paper presents results from an audit study of why Canadian immigrants arriving under the point system struggle in the labour market.[2] Thousands of resumés were sent online in response to job postings across multiple occupations in the Greater Toronto Area, after randomly varying characteristics on the resumés to uncover what affects employers' decisions on whether to contact an applicant. The resumés were constructed to represent plausibly recent immigrants under the point system from the three largest countries of origin (i.e., China, India, and Pakistan) and Britain, as well as non-immigrants with and without ethnic-sounding names (including Greek names). In addition to names, I randomized where applicants received their undergraduate degree, whether their job experience was gained in Toronto or Mumbai (or another foreign city), whether their job experience was from well-recognized multinational firms or large firms, whether they listed fluency in multiple languages (including French), whether they had additional education credentials, whether the credentials were accredited by a Canadian agency, whether resumés with foreign education or experience listed Canadian references or indicated permanent residency status, and whether they listed active extracurricular activities.

A related study by Bertrand and Mullainathan (2004) found that resumés sent to blue-collar jobs in Boston and Chicago with White-sounding first names (e.g., Emily and Greg) generated callbacks about 50 per cent more often than the same resumés sent with Black-sounding names (e.g., Lakisha and Jamal).[3] Whereas that study focused on callback differences between White and Black names, this one examines differences generated by manipulating a wider set of resumé characteristics to disentangle the many possible factors explaining why the non-immigrants are more successful in the labour market, even among those with bachelor degrees. I also explore more closely what mechanisms might underlie applicant discrimination, using predictions generated by alternative models of discrimination, and complement the audit study methodology with a qualitative approach that involves discussing results directly with recruiters and human resource managers.

Theories of Job-Applicant Discrimination

As a descriptive exercise, audit studies help quantify the magnitude to which characteristics such as work experience, schooling, and extracurricular activities influence reactions of prospective employers. An advantage of using resumés instead of actors seeking employment is that the investigator knows exactly what information employers have when deciding to contact an applicant back. Audit studies can also help reveal or rule out statistical discrimination, which arises when employers use observable characteristics as signals for inferring unknown information (Phelps 1972). For example, with limited time and budget, employers may make marginal decisions on whom to interview or telephone by using resumé name or country of education/experience to predict an applicant's language skills.

Since productivity expectations under this model are determined conditional on other information, listing additional resumé characteristics that correlate with unlisted skills reduces uncertainty and the need to infer. Applicants with ethnic-sounding names who have only Canadian experience and education, for example, are most likely Canadian-born, and should generate fewer language skill concerns than applicants with foreign experience or education. If employers are statistically discriminating, the callback gap between foreign-educated or foreign-named resumés and apparently Euro-Canadian resumés should fall by adding information related to unobservable skill. I also explore how the callback rate changes when changing a Canadian-experienced and Canadian-educated resumé with an English name to a Greek name, to increase the likelihood that the applicant is Canadian-born and to minimize language and communication concerns. Another prediction of the statistical discrimination model is that the callback rate gap between foreign-named or foreign-educated resumés and "Canadian" resumés should be larger in cases where jobs applied to require more of the skills being inferred from the name or immigrant status. For example, the callback rate gap for computer programmer jobs, which require less English/French language skills to perform well, should be smaller than for sales jobs.

Applications matched across a wide set of characteristics and sent to jobs that mostly require skills easily noted on a resumé should generate similar callback responses under the models of statistical discrimination mentioned above. If racial or ethnic differences remain, "taste"-based theories of employer discrimination may be at play. Employers may prefer hiring individuals from particular groups, independent of productivity. Another explanation for remaining callback differences may be through unconscious mistakes generated by unconditional biases or stereotypes. Some researchers suggest that, when employers sort through resumés, name discrimination can be unintentional (Stanley, Phelps, and Banaji 2008; Chugh 2004). Social psychologists differentiate between explicit attitudes, which describe one's expressed views, and implicit attitudes, which are unconscious mental associations between a target (such as immigrants) and a given attribute (such as poor communication skills). Implicit discrimination may operate subconsciously and cause people to make decisions in ways contrary to their own conscious and deliberative views (Ranganath, Smith, and Nosek 2008).

Several modern theories of prejudice align with this model. Crandall and Eshleman (2003), for example, describe how employers may believe that they are rejecting an applicant because of language skill concerns, when actually their implicit biases are driving the decision. An applicant's name or country of origin may trigger particular stereotypes that cause employers to overweight these concerns and underweight the offsetting factors on the resumé. While recruiters may consciously attempt to avoid discrimination and missing out on the best hire, subconscious beliefs and attitudes may influence assessments and decisions nonetheless. Pressure to avoid bad hires exacerbates these effects, as does the need to review resumés quickly. Employers may erroneously use unconditional productivity expectations to determine whether to call back an applicant rather than conditioning on other characteristics on the resumé.

Implicit discrimination can also arise from thinking in categories. Fryer and Jackson (2008) and Mullainathan (2002) note that types of experiences less frequent in the population are more coarsely categorized and more often lumped together. This can result in discrimination against minority groups even when there is no malevolent intent to discriminate. Employers less accustomed to seeing foreign-named or foreign-educated applicants with adequate language skills are more likely to lump all foreign-named and foreign-educated applicants into one category, even if other listed characteristics offset the concerns about language skills. This leads to a more general pattern of rejection for these applicants regardless of other listed skills.

Research Design

Thousands of randomly created resumés were sent by e-mail in response to job postings across multiple occupations in the Greater Toronto Area between April and November 2008. An additional set of resumés was sent across Toronto and Montreal between February and September 2009, in order to improve precision and consider effects from adding other attributes. The resumés were designed to represent typical immigrants who arrived recently under the Canadian point system from China, India, and Pakistan (the current top-three source countries) and from Britain, as well as non-immigrants with and without ethnic-sounding names (including Greek names).[4] They were constructed after consulting actual resumés of recent immigrants and online submissions.[5] The sample represents all jobs posted during these periods that accepted applications via direct e-mail and generally required three to seven years of experience and an undergraduate degree. Positions that specifically required at least a graduate degree, North American experience, or other further education were ignored.

With few exceptions, four resumés were sent to each employer over a two- to three-day period in random order. The first represented an applicant with an English-sounding name, Canadian undergraduate education, and Canadian experience (Type 0). The second resumé had instead a foreign-sounding name (Chinese, Indian, Pakistani, or Greek), but still listed Canadian undergraduate education and Canadian experience (Type 1). The third resumé included a foreign-sounding name (Chinese, Indian, or Pakistani), corresponding foreign undergraduate degree, and Canadian experience (Type 2). The fourth included a foreign-sounding name, foreign education, and some foreign experience (Type 3) or all foreign experience (Type 4). I also randomized applicants' alma maters, whether the applicants listed fluency in multiple languages (including French), whether they had additional Canadian education credentials, and whether or not their job experience was from well-recognized multinational firms or large firms. To address concerns regarding employers shying away from resumés with foreign credentials because of additional costs in contacting references or concerns about legal working status, I also randomized a subset of resumés with foreign experience that listed Canadian references (with local telephone numbers) and explicitly noted permanent residency status.

The English-sounding names on Type 0 resumés were picked randomly from a list of the most popular Anglophone surnames in Canada (Smith, Martin, Brown, Wilson, or Johnson), and matched randomly with one of four possible male names (Greg, John, Matthew, or Michael) or four possible female names (Alison, Carrie, Emily, or Jill) used previously by Bertrand and Mullainathan (2004).[6] Resumés with foreign education or experience from Britain had the same names. Greek names were either Lukas or Nicole Minsopoulos. The other resumés of Types 1 to 4 had names picked randomly among a list of 24 popular male and female names from China, India, and Pakistan.[7] In some cases, I used names with Chinese last names and English first names picked from these same lists. Tables 25.2a and 25.2b show the number of resumes sent and the number of callbacks received, by name and type. E-mail addresses were set up for all 44 names using both gmail.com and yahoo.ca accounts. The total sample size is 12,910 resumés, sent in response to 3,225 job postings.

Work experiences were constructed from actual resumés accessible online. The descriptions were sufficiently altered to create distinct sets that would not be associated with actual people, but I also tried to maintain original overall content and form. Each resumé listed the job title, job description, company name, and city location for an applicant's three most recent jobs covering four to six years, with the first job beginning in the same year as the applicant's undergraduate degree completion. The city listed was always the same (except for Type 3 resumés).[8] Experience sets were constructed for 20 different occupation categories, almost all the same as those used by the online job site workopolis.com.[9] Within each category, I created four different experience sets, whose job titles and corresponding job descriptions were randomly assigned to one of the four resumés sent to a single employer.[10] It is notable that this randomization not only made years of experience the same across immigrant and non-immigrant resumés (on average), but also made the description of this experience the same. In addition, company names were also independent of resumé type for about half the sample. International companies were chosen wherever possible to keep the experience sets identical across immigrant and non-immigrant resumés except for location (e.g., ABC Inc., Toronto versus ABC Inc., Mumbai). Where no obvious international company was available, I picked closely related companies in size and industry.

Since virtually all immigrants who arrived recently under the point system had at least a bachelor's degree, all resumés generated in this study did so as well. A job posting's occupation category determined the set of degrees to randomly pick. For example, resumés generated for a position as a financial analyst had a bachelor of arts either in economics or in commerce, while those for a software developer position had a bachelor's degree in computer science or in computer engineering. Alma mater was picked randomly from a list of about four universities in the same country as the applicant's corresponding name and in the same proximity to the applicant's location of experience. About half of the universities were listed in the 2008 QS World University Rankings' Top 200.[11] The other universities were less prestigious.

To assess whether additional Canadian educational credentials may offset lower callback rates from having foreign experience or foreign schooling, 20 per cent of resumés, except those of Type 4, were randomly assigned Canadian master's degrees. Master's degrees were occupation-specific and completed during the same three-year period as the applicant's most recent (Canadian) experience, so that it looked like the applicant was enrolled part-time while working full-time.

I also explored the role of accreditation by assigning some resumés with foreign education certificates by the fictitious "Canada International Skills Certification Board." Dietz et al. (2009) find that such certification reduces discrimination found by undergraduate students in judging whether to follow up with applicants from South Africa with White or African names. One concern with this earlier work is that students were specifically asked to focus on the quality of the resumé, potentially priming subjects to focus on productivity stereotypes. Our field setting considers a more real-world environment.

Language skills and extracurricular activities were also manipulated to help explore whether language or cultural concerns underlie callback differences. I randomly selected 20

Table 25.2a Number of Resumés Sent, by Resumé Type and Ethnicity

	Resume Type				
	0	1	2	3	4
Name, Ethnicity, and Sex	**English Name Cdn Educ. Cdn Exp.**	**Foreign Name Cdn Educ. Cdn Exp.**	**Foreign Name Foreign Educ. Cdn Exp.**	**Foreign Name Foreign Educ. Mixed Exp.**	**Foreign Name Foreign Educ. Foreign Exp**
English males					
Greg Johnson	394		37	36	33
John Martin	423		47	34	35
Matthew Wilson	404		38	37	36
Michael Smith	261		56	33	30
English females					
Alison Johnson	422		40	29	37
Carrie Martin	441		38	35	28
Emily Brown	254		48	41	58
Jill Wilson	427		42	24	42
Indian males					
Arjun Kumar		136	108	102	89
Panav Singh		150	107	79	76
Rahul Kaur		164	108	94	76
Samir Sharma		143	90	82	81
Indian females					
Maya Kumar		142	99	88	75
Priyanka Kaur		166	92	109	80
Shreya Sharma		135	93	83	98
Tara Singh		131	114	80	83
Pakistani males					
Ali Saeed		55	23	13	29
Asif Sheikh		63	19	23	25
Chaudhry Mohammad		43	19	20	16
Hassan Khan		63	18	23	23
Pakistani females					
Fatima Sheikh		54	17	15	25
Hina Chaudhry		73	17	30	21
Rabab Saeed		51	21	8	14
Sana Khan		64	22	16	34
Chinese males					
Dong Liu		154	99	74	79
Lei Li		128	86	96	87
Tao Wang		58	36	45	34
Yong Zhang		142	90	100	75

Chinese females					
Fang Wang		58	43	48	34
Min Liu		150	92	108	82
Na Li		132	101	90	69
Xiuying Zhang		176	104	75	103
Chinese/English males					
Allen Wang		59	25	20	20
Bill Zhang		58	18	21	37
Eric Wang		93	59	45	37
Jack Li		38	17	15	19
James Liu		49	25	22	21
Chinese/English females					
Amy Wang		44	26	16	18
Jennifer Li		49	27	22	17
Michelle Wang		96	59	46	56
Monica Liu		63	26	23	22
Vivian Zhang		69	20	21	28
Greek male					
Lukas Minsopoulos	168				
Greek female					
Nicole Minsopoulos	198				
Total	3,026	3,615	2,266	2,021	1,982

Notes: Cdn = Canadian, Educ = Country where bachelor's degree obtained, and Exp = country where job experience obtained. Mixed experience corresponds to first two jobs listed on resume as being from a foreign country, and most recent (third) job listed from Canada.

per cent of resumés in Toronto to list fluency in multiple languages and 60 per cent of resumés in Montreal. Resumés with English- or Greek-sounding names listed fluency in English and French. The other resumés listed fluency in English, French, and the applicant's mother tongue (Mandarin, Cantonese, Hindi, or Punjabi), depending on the applicant's ethnic origin name. In addition, 60 per cent of resumés listed active extracurricular activities. One of three possible sets was chosen listing characteristics such as volunteer initiative (e.g., Big Brother/Sister, Habitat for Humanity), social interests (e.g., competitive squash player, classical pianist), and proactive work skills (e.g., excellent common sense, judgment, and decision-making abilities). Table 25.3 shows average frequencies of these and other characteristics on the resumés sent for each type.

Clearly, resumés had to look different when sending to the same employer, so I also randomized each applicant's cover letter (i.e., a short, general message sent as a part of the e-mail text), and the e-mail subject line and the resumé file name; resumés were saved as pdf files unless Word documents were specifically requested. I randomized each resumé's layout, residential address, and telephone number; all possibilities were within Toronto or Montreal. Each applicant listed three previous jobs, with earlier years of experience being over two, three, or four years for each particular job, and with the most recent job always being listed as starting from the year the bachelor's degree was obtained.

Table 25.2b Number of Callbacks Received, by Resumé Type and Ethnicity

	Resume Type				
	0	1	2	3	4
Name, Ethnicity, and Sex	English Name Cdn Educ. Cdn Exp.	Foreign Name Cdn Educ. Cdn Exp.	Foreign Name Foreign Educ. Cdn Exp.	Foreign Name Foreign Educ. Mixed Exp.	Foreign Name Foreign Educ. Foreign Exp.
English males					
Greg Johnson	47		3	2	4
John Martin	48		5	3	4
Matthew Wilson	50		2	5	3
Michael Smith	29		3	4	1
English females					
Alison Johnson	66		5	5	5
Carrie Martin	82		6	6	3
Emily Brown	38		8	6	6
Jill Wilson	69		2	3	7
Indian males					
Arjun Kumar		13	13	3	5
Panav Singh		10	15	7	2
Rahul Kaur		15	10	6	5
Samir Sharma		14	7	9	4
Indian females					
Maya Kumar		19	8	6	2
Priyanka Kaur		13	11	6	4
Shreya Sharma		16	12	5	6
Tara Singh		20	12	4	6
Pakistani males					
Ali Saeed		3	6	0	1
Asif Sheikh		5	0	0	0
Chaudhry Mohammad		3	1	2	0
Hassan Khan		7	1	0	0
Pakistani females					
Fatima Sheikh		4	1	2	2
Hina Chaudhry		6	3	1	1
Rabab Saeed		3	1	0	0
Sana Khan		6	4	2	0
Chinese males					
Dong Liu		16	3	11	2
Lei Li		15	7	7	8
Tao Wang		7	5	4	3
Yong Zhang		15	9	6	5

Chinese females					
Fang Wang		11	5	5	2
Min Liu		19	9	11	10
Na Li		9	11	8	2
Xiuying Zhang		16	6	7	5
Chinese/English males					
Allen Wang		7	0	3	1
Bill Zhang		4	1	2	4
Eric Wang		9	2	4	0
Jack Li		0	1	1	1
James Liu		4	1	2	1
Chinese/English females					
Amy Wang		8	1	1	0
Jennifer Li		3	3	1	0
Michelle Wang		12	4	2	2
Monica Liu		9	2	1	0
Vivian Zhang		5	2	1	2
Greek male					
Lukas Minsopoulos		18			
Greek female					
Nicole Minsopoulos		19			
Total	429	363	211	164	119

Notes: Cdn = Canadian, Educ = Country where bachelor's degree obtained, and Exp = country where job experience obtained. Mixed experience corresponds to first two jobs listed on resume as being from a foreign country, and most recent (third) job listed from Canada.

A program by Lahey and Beasley (2009) was used to select randomly the characteristic codes of each resumé. Microsoft Office was used to transform these choices into text and mail-merge them onto actual resumé templates. Some resumé sets were dropped to avoid repeating names sent to the same employer. Research assistants developed a program to make the data-collection process more menu-driven. When a job posting was identified for the study (from an Internet site), a research assistant would open a dialog window prompting for the job's corresponding occupation. Phone numbers or e-mail addresses on the post were used to check that someone had not applied to this employer previously. A second window allowed the user to enter the job title, the job posting's source, the company name, contact information, and whether additional certificates needed to be added to the resume. The program then updated the data collection spreadsheet and created four resumés that could be edited for cosmetic quality (to ensure they fit cleanly on one or two pages). The output also included instructions for what cover letter, subject line, and file name to use. The resumés were saved as pdf files and e-mailed from the addresses of the corresponding names to the employer over a two- to three-day period in random order. Any application whose corresponding e-mail bounced, indicating it was never received, was dropped from the sample.

Multiple telephone numbers and two e-mail accounts for each name were set up to collect employer responses. Responses were classified as callbacks if the employer requested an applicant to contact them (not just for clarification). Responses were classified as requests for interviews if one was

Table 25.3 Proportion of Resumés Sent with Particular Characteristics, by Resumé Type

	(1)	(2)	(3)	(4)	(5)	(6)
		Resumé Type Sent				
		0	1	2	3	4
Characteristics of Resumé	Full Sample	English Name Cdn Educ. Cdn Exp.	Foreign Name Cdn Educ. Cdn Exp.	Foreign Name Foreign Educ. Cdn Exp.	Foreign Name Foreign Educ. Mixed Exp.	Foreign Name Foreign Educ. Foreign Exp.
Female	0.51	0.51	0.51	0.50	0.50	0.52
Top-200 world university	0.54	0.59	0.64	0.46	0.45	0.45
Extracurricular activities listed	0.60	0.60	0.61	0.60	0.59	0.61
Fluent in French and other languages	0.25	0.25	0.26	0.24	0.24	0.23
Canadian master's degree	0.17	0.20	0.20	0.21	0.20	0.00
Multinational firm work experience	0.25	0.28	0.23	0.24	0.26	0.26
High-quality work experience	0.31	0.33	0.31	0.30	0.30	0.31
Canadian references listed	0.03	0.00	0.00	0.00	0.09	0.08
Accreditation of foreign education	0.04	0.00	0.00	0.08	0.07	0.07
Permanent resident indicated	0.04	0.00	0.00	0.10	0.07	0.06
Name, ethnicity						
English-Canadian	0.23	1.00	0.00	0.00	0.00	0.00
English-British	0.07	0.00	0.00	0.15	0.13	0.15
Indian	0.26	0.00	0.32	0.36	0.35	0.33
Pakistani	0.07	0.00	0.13	0.07	0.07	0.09
Chinese	0.22	0.00	0.28	0.29	0.31	0.28
Chinese with English first name	0.11	0.00	0.17	0.13	0.12	0.14
Greek	0.03	0.00	0.10	0.00	0.00	0.00

Notes: Cdn = Canadian, Educ = country where bachelor's degree obtained, and Exp = country where job experience obtained. Mixed experience corresponds to first two jobs listed on resume as being from foreign country, and most recent (third) job listed from Canada. Top 200 World Ranking University according to the 2008 QS World Rankings (http://www.topuniversities.com/).

specifically mentioned. Employers that contacted an applicant twice were contacted themselves during off-hours by e-mail or phone message and told that the applicant had accepted another position and was no longer looking for employment.

I also recorded measures of language and social skills associated with each job using the Occupational Information Network (O*NET). The purpose was to examine whether callback differences across resumé types varied by the extent to which jobs require language or social skills. For each job title, I recorded the O*NET's corresponding skill measure for speaking, writing, and social perceptiveness.[12] Each variable ranges from possible values of 0 to 100. I created a summary variable by adding the three values for each job and using this measure to sort occupations into deciles.

With random assignment, simple comparisons of callback rates can identify relative effects of the different resumé characteristics. One exception is that small changes were made to the probability distribution of resumé characteristics over the two-year period of data collection. Applicants with Chinese last names but English first names, for example, were added in September 2008. Pakistani names were removed in February 2009, after finding similar results compared to applicants with Chinese or Indian names. Greek names were also randomly added in February 2009, as were permanent residency status, Canadian references, accreditation signals, and refined sets of experience to better distinguish by firm size and prestige. To account for these changes, I include in the regression an indicator variable for whether the resumé was sent between April and August 2008, September and November 2008, or February and September 2009. The findings are similar when allowing for separate period trends by resumé type, ethnicity, and city, but are somewhat less precise.

More specifically, I estimate regression equations in which the likelihood of callback from an employer is predicted based on resumé type and a variety of other resumé characteristics. The regression equations are designed to include the possibility of interactions between resumé types and other characteristics, to estimate, for example, whether callback differences between resumés with English and Chinese-sounding names become smaller when additional language skills or educational credentials are listed.[13]

Results

Table 25.4 shows the main results. The sample excludes foreign resumés with listed accreditation, local references, or permanent resident status for comparability with Canadian-experienced and Canadian-educated resumés. (The next table considers the impact of adding these characteristics.) Row 1 shows the estimated baseline callback rate of about 16.0 per cent for Type 0 resumés with English-sounding names, Canadian experience, and Canadian education in period 1 (April–August 2008).[14] Changing only the name to one with Indian origin lowers the callback rate by 4.5 per cent, to 11.5 per cent (s.e. = 1.2 per cent), and changing it to one with Pakistani or Chinese origin lowers it slightly more, to 11.0 per cent and 11.3 per cent, respectively. Overall, resumés with English-sounding names are 39 per cent more likely to receive callbacks than resumés with Indian, Pakistani, or Chinese names (Column 7). Switching applicants' names from English to Greek origins lowers callback rates by 4.0 per cent. The callback rate gap between English and Greek names is about the same as it is between English and other ethnic names and is significant at the 0.05 level.

The callback rate among Type 1 resumés with English first names and Chinese last names in Column 4 (e.g., Allen or Michelle Wang) is 12.5 per cent, which is significantly different from the callback rate among those with first and last English names (e.g., John or Carrie Martin), but also not significantly different from the callback rate among those with first and last Chinese names (e.g., Lei or Na Li). Many second-generation Chinese adopt and use an English-sounding name to make pronunciation easier for non-Chinese and to signal North American assimilation. Interestingly, this adoption does not significantly improve one's chances for a callback.

There appears to be no large difference in callback rates between Type 1 and Type 2 resumés,

Table 25.4 Estimated Callback Rates by Resumé Type and Ethnic Origin

	(1)	(2)	(3)	(4)	(5)	(6)	(7)
	Callback Rate for Type 0 Resumés with English Name, Canadian Experience, and Canadian Education						
Type 0 English name Cdn educ. Cdn exp.	**0.160**	**0.158**	**0.154**	**0.158**	**0.158**	**0.158**	**0.157**
	Callback Rates and Relative Differences by Ethnic Origin and Experience/ Education Location (Difference Compared to Type 0) [Standard Error of Difference] {Callback Ratio: Type 0/Type}						
	Indian	**Pakistani**	**Chinese**	**Chinese with English First Name**	**English-British**	**Greek**	**Indian/ Pakistani/ Chinese**
Type 1	**0.115**	**0.110**	**0.113**	**0.125**	**NA**	**0.118**	**0.113**
Foreign name	(−0.045)	(−0.050)	(−0.041)	(−0.033)		(−0.040)	(−0.044)
Cdn educ.	[0.012]***	[0.016]***	[0.013]***	[0.014]**		[0.019]**	[0.009]***
Cdn exp.	{1.39}	{1.44}	{1.40}	{1.26}		{1.34}	{1.39}
Type 2	**0.115**	**0.140**	**0.097**	**0.129**	**0.129**	**NA**	**0.110**
Foreign name	(−0.045)	(−0.018)	(−0.057)	(−0.029)	(−0.029)		(−0.047)
Foreign educ.	[0.015]***	[0.027]	[0.015]***	[0.019]	[0.019]		[0.011]***
Cdn exp.	{1.39}	{1.13}	{1.59}	{1.22}	{1.22}		{1.43}
Type 3	**0.075**	**0.078**	**0.101**	**0.098**	**0.157**	**NA**	**0.085**
Foreign name	(−0.085)	(−0.080)	(−0.053)	(−0.060)	(−0.001)		(−0.072)
Foreign educ.	[0.013]***	[0.020]***	[0.016]***	[0.020]***	[0.023]		[0.010]***
Mixed exp.	{2.13}	{2.05}	{1.58}	{1.61}	{1.01}		{1.85}
Type 4	**0.062**	**0.052**	**0.059**	**0.141**	**0.141**	**NA**	**0.059**
Foreign name	(−0.098)	(−0.106)	(−0.095)	(−0.017)	(−0.017)		(−0.098)
Foreign educ.	[0.013]***	[0.015]***	[0.014]***	[0.021]	[0.021]		[0.009]***
Foreign exp.	{2.58}	{3.04}	{2.61}	{1.12}	{1.12}		{2.71}

Notes: Cdn = Canadian, Educ = Country where bachelor's degree obtained, and Exp = country where job experience obtained. Mixed experience corresponds to first two jobs listed on resume as being from a foreign country, and most recent (third) job listed is from Canada. The table shows coefficient estimates from regressing callback status on resume type and two time indicators for when the sampling distribution of resumes changed (i.e., adding Pakistani and Greek names) with robust standard errors. Each column shows separate regression results after selecting on the sample of Type 0 resumes and Types 1–4 resumes with the indicated ethnic backgrounds. The first row indicates the callback rate estimate for Type 0 resumes during the first period of data collection. ***, **, and * indicate callback rate differences compared to Type 0 are statistically significant at the 1%, 5%, and 10% levels respectively.

which systematically differ only by whether they list a bachelor's degree from a Canadian university (Type 1) or a foreign university (Type 2). Both sets of resumés do not include Canadian names and foreign experience. Thus, conditional on listing four to six years of Canadian experience, employers do not seem to care if an applicant's education is from a foreign institution when deciding whether to contact the applicant for an interview.

In contrast, switching from job experience acquired in Canada to job experience acquired from a foreign country matters a lot. Types 2, 3, and 4 resumés all list foreign names and foreign degrees. The experience descriptions are also identical, but Type 4 resumés list previous job experience with companies located in foreign cities (e.g., ABC Inc., Mumbai instead of ABC Inc., Toronto) and Type 3 resumés list foreign cities for two of the three previous jobs (the most recent job is listed as being in Toronto). The callback rate for resumés that list almost all job experience from India, China, or Pakistan drops 2.5 per cent compared to resumés with all Canadian experience (from 11.0 per cent to 8.5 per cent), as shown in Column 7. Callback rates drop 5.1 per cent for resumés listing only foreign job experience. Interestingly, the resumés listing only British experience do not generate any significant fall in callback rates compared to Type 0 Canadian resumés (14.1 per cent compared to 15.8 per cent, as reported in Column 5).

For the remaining results, Types 2, 3, and 4 resumés exclude applicants with British experience and education, in order to focus on comparisons with the three largest immigrant groups from China, India, and Pakistan, and all resumés exclude applicants with Greek or English-Chinese names.

If concerns about language or other traits not directly observed explain the callback rate

Table 25.5 Estimated Effects on the Probability of Callback from the Inclusion of Resumé Characteristics

	(1) Type 0 English Name Cdn Educ. Cdn Exp.	(2) Type 1 Foreign Name Cdn Educ. Cdn Exp.	(3) Type 2 Foreign Name Foreign Educ. Cdn Exp.	(4) Type 3 Foreign Name Foreign Educ. Mixed Exp.	(5) Type 4 Foreign Name Foreign Educ. Foreign Exp.
Callback rate (for Type 0) and unconditional callback difference between other resumé types	0.157	−0.044 [0.009]***	−0.048 [0.010]***	−0.073 [0.009]***	−0.094 [0.009]***
Callback difference after conditioning on all resumé characteristics		−0.044 [0.009]***	−0.049 [0.010]***	−0.074 [0.010]***	−0.096 [0.009]***
Sample size	3,026	2,631	1,618	1,501	1,408

Notes: Panel A reports callback rate differences by resume type, relative to Type 0, with and without including control variables for applicant gender, an indicator that the applicant obtained her bachelor's degree from a university ranked in the Top 200 according to the QS University World Rankings, and whether the resume listed extracurricular activities, fluency in multiple languages (including French), a Canadian master's degree, Canadian references, Canadian government accreditation of an applicant's foreign degree, and permanent resident status. Panel 8 reports coefficient results from regressing callback status on these characteristics. Robust standard errors are reported. Cdn = Canadian, Educ = Country where bachelors degree obtained, and Exp = country where job experience obtained. Mixed experience corresponds to first two jobs listed on resume as being from a foreign country, and most recent (third) job listed from Canada. ***, **, and * indicate callback rate differences compared to Type 0 are statistically significant at the 1%, 5%, and 10% levels respectively.

gaps discussed above, adding information related to these concerns should help reduce the gap. Table 25.5 shows if this reduction occurs when conditioning on whether the applicant is female; graduated from a top-200 world ranked university (according to the 2008 QS University World Rankings); listed active social extracurricular activities (e.g., volunteer work, competitive sports, travel); has fluency in French, English, and a mother tongue (applicable for Indian- and Chinese-named resumés); graduated with an occupation-related Canadian master's degree; had job experience with large, prestigious, national firms or with multinational firms with establishments in all three countries; listed a reference with a Canadian

Table 25.6 Callback Rate Differences for Resumés Sent to Jobs with Different Language and Social Skill Requirements

(1) Language and Social Skill Requirement Decile	(2) Sample Occupations	(3) Callback Rate for English Name Cdn Educ. Cdn Exp.	(4) Callback Diff. for Foreign Name Cdn Educ. Cdn Exp.	(5) Ratio
1	Computer programmer	0.127	−0.034	1.4
	Maintenance technician		[0.020]*	
2	Accountant	0.148	−0.050	1.5
	Web developer		[0.026]*	
3	Bookkeeper	0.128	−0.050	1.6
	Systems administrator		[0.018]***	
4	Administrative assistant	0.128	−0.059	1.9
	Office administrator		[0.017]***	
5	Electrical engineer	0.122	−0.059	1.9
	Design assistant		[0.022]***	
6	Sales representative	0.157	−0.053	1.5
	Quality analyst		[0.018]***	
7	Financial analyst	0.254	−0.056	1.3
	Project manager		[0.028]**	
8	Account manager	0.183	−0.041	1.3
	Receptionist		[0.024]*	
9	Human resources manager	0.133	−0.029	1.3
	Collection officer		[0.025]	
10	Executive recruiter	0.162	−0.067	1.7
	Community counsellor		[0.028]**	

Notes: Job postings applied to were matched to Speaking, Writing, and Social O*NET defined occupation skill requirements (each with a 1-7 point continuous scale). All three measures were added to create an aggregate score, and used to separate the sample into deciles. Callback differences are estimated as in Table 4 Column 7. Cdn = Canadian, Educ = Country where bachelor's degree obtained, and Exp = country where job experience obtained. ***, **, and * indicate callback rate differences compared to Type 0 are statistically significant at the 1%, 5%, and 10% levels respectively.

phone number; listed education accredited by the (fictitious) Canada International Skill Certification Board (resumé Types 2, 3, and 4 only); or listed legal permanent residency status (resumé Types 2, 3, and 4 only). The table shows the callback rate between Type 0 resumés and other types with and without these dummy variable controls. The results clearly indicate that conditioning on these factors overall has virtually no impact on the callback rate by name, source country of education, or experience. Therefore, whether resumés include or exclude this information has no role regarding the impact that name, country of education, or experience has on reducing the likelihood of an employer's response.

Table 25.6 shows how callback rates differ, depending on whether the jobs applied for require above or below median language and social skills. Here I explore whether employers trying to hire in jobs requiring more intensive language or social skills are even less likely to interview immigrants, out of concerns that they have fewer of these skills than non-immigrants. I match each posting's job description with measures of speaking, writing, and social O*NET-defined occupational skill requirements and add these values together. I then run separate regressions for each decile to test for name differences between Type 0 resumés with English names and Type 1 resumés with Chinese, Indian, or Pakistani names. The table shows general consistency across language and social skill deciles. Across a wide range of occupations ranging from computer programmer and web developer, in the lower decile categories of O*NET language and social skills to receptionist and project manager in higher decile categories, the ratio in callback rates between resumés with English names and ethnic-sounding names remains about the same and statistically significant. Overall, however, the finding of significantly lower callback rates for resumés with foreign names occurs for occupations requiring higher language and social skill requirements.

Discussing Results with Recruiters

After finding significant levels of name discrimination, even for Greek names and across a wide range of jobs, I e-mailed a random sample of 300 employers from the sample of resumés to gain perspective from the recruiters themselves about what they think drives the results. I offered $25 amazon.ca gift certificates for responses to be used anonymously (and under guidance from University of Toronto's Ethics Review Board). I focused on the Chinese, Indian, and Pakistani name discrimination results for resumés with Canadian experience and education, and asked whether recruiters thought that the observed behaviour resulted from remaining productivity concerns or something else. I also noted that listing active extracurricular activities, volunteer work, and fluency in multiple languages (including French) did not significantly affect the findings, and these differences were found for many different job types.

Only 29 responded. Virtually all respondents said that employers often treat name, country of education, or experience as a signal that an applicant may lack critical language skills for the job. When asked specifically about why otherwise identical resumés except for name would generate a different response, typical responses were:

> The problem is the ability to communicate in English. Foreign-sounding names may be overlooked due to a perception that their English language skills may be insufficient on the job site.
>
> One reason for this to occur would be people's fear of strong accents not being understood by customers and/or co-workers.
>
> Name suggests candidate is not fluent in English, is the candidate eligible to work in Canada, will the candidate need extensive time off to return home to visit family/friends, will the employer be required to provide additional time off in recognition of cultural holidays.

Some recruiters also pointed out that they often face more pressure to avoid bad hires than they are awarded for exceptional ones. Negative hiring experiences with workers of a specific ethnicity also created less openness to people from that ethnicity in the future:

> The lesson and outcome of hiring someone who left the company angrily is to not hire anyone of the same ethnicity. The same politics work against all of us.

Some respondents also expressed difficulties evaluating the qualifications of someone with a non-English name:

> A good recruiter will call everyone because there may be times that people aren't represented as you'd picture them from their resumé. . . . When you're calling someone with an English-sounding name, you know what you're getting into. You know that you can call Bob Smith, and you can talk to him as quickly as you want to. It's less work because you know that his English will be fine. It also indicates that he's White-looking. The brown guy who was born here is not less desirable in the workplace, but it takes something more to know for sure that he speaks English without an accent. We'd have to make a phone call and test the water.

Conclusion

Three main descriptive findings emerge. First, Canadian-born individuals with English-sounding names are much more likely to receive a callback for an interview after sending their resumés compared to foreign-born individuals, even among those with foreign degrees from highly selective schools, or among those with the same listed job experience but acquired outside of Canada. The results show that 15.7 per cent of resumés sent with English-sounding names and Canadian education and experience received a callback from an employer, compared to only 6.0 per cent of resumés with foreign-sounding names from China, India, or Pakistan, and foreign experience and education. The callback gap lines up with overall unemployment differences. In 2006, the national unemployment rate for immigrants was 11.5 per cent, more than double the rate of 4.9 per cent for the Canadian-born population (Statistics Canada 2007). Much of the unemployment difference, therefore, may be due to immigrants not even making it to the interview stage in the job application process.

Second, employers value Canadian experience far more than Canadian education when deciding to interview applicants with foreign backgrounds. Among resumés with foreign names and foreign education, the callback rate climbs from 6.0 per cent to 8.5 per cent by listing just one previous job with a company located *inside* Canada rather than outside. Listing all job experience with companies located inside Canada leads to the callback rate increasing further, to 11.0 per cent. These substantial increases are especially noteworthy because they also occur when only job location differs, while keeping constant job descriptions and company names (e.g., ABC Inc., Toronto versus ABC Inc., Mumbai). Employers are much more interested in foreign-born applicants with more Canadian experience.

While Canadian experience is crucial in determining the likelihood of a callback, having a degree from a more prestigious foreign institution or acquiring additional schooling in Canada apparently does not significantly affect the chances of a callback. Conditional on listing four to six years of Canadian experience on a resumé, callback rates do not differ significantly by whether a resumé lists a bachelor's degree from a nearby Canadian university versus one from a foreign university. I also find little effect from indicating that an applicant graduated from a top-ranking school compared to a low-ranking one, even among resumés with degrees from Canadian institutions. This surprises me, since admission criteria vary widely by school. Perhaps employers do not pay close attention to education qualifications for resumés with several years of experience. I also find no effect from listing an additional Canadian master's degree. The recruiters with whom

I discussed these results were not surprised. All said that education plays only a minor role in deciding whether to call back for an interview, once an applicant has accumulated four to six years of experience.

Third, employers discriminate substantially by name. Employer contact falls by 4.4 per cent when switching from a Canadian resumé with a common English name to one with a common Chinese, Indian, Pakistani, or even Greek name (15.7 per cent to 11.3 per cent, respectively). This difference is substantial, and almost as large as that found by Bertrand and Mullainathan (2004) using resumés in the United States with Black- or White-sounding given names.

When asked what explains these findings, recruiters who responded said overwhelmingly that employers often treat names as a signal that an applicant lacks critical language skills for the job. Some recruiters, as noted above, also pointed out that they often face more pressure to avoid bad hires than they are awarded for exceptional ones. This leads to risk aversion and exacerbates the impact from even small signals of lower expected productivity.

The empirical evidence, however, does not easily corroborate the view that all the observed discrimination is statistically driven by concerns about language skills. The resumés sent were, on average, the same regarding description of job experience, years of schooling, style of resumé, and cover e-mail. The statistical discrimination model predicts that adding information related to important characteristics not listed on the resumé should reduce the degree of discrimination, yet I find little evidence of this. Listing of fluency in French, English, and mother tongue marginally increases callback rates for foreign-educated and foreign-experienced applicants, but has no impact for foreign-named applicants. Prominently recognized firms or large firms also do not reduce the gap in callback rates.

An interesting (and unexpected) finding is that switching applicants' names from English to Greek origins generates lower callback rates. The callback rate gap between English and Greek names is about the same as it is between English and Chinese names and significant at the 0.10 level. I believe employers probably view Greek-named applicants as Canadian-born, with little difference in English proficiency compared to the English applicant. A reinterpretation of the gap between English-named applicants and those with Indian, Pakistani, or Chinese names therefore is that recruiters place a premium on wanting to interview applicants with English names rather than a discount on those who are Indian, Pakistani, or Chinese.

Surprisingly, no recruiters who responded explicitly acknowledged the possibility that information on the resumé could offset or address their stated language concerns, despite efforts to point out this possibility. Most respondents seemed to assume an applicant with an Indian, Pakistani, or Chinese name was an immigrant, and justified the results based on language concerns. Those who expressed these concerns also failed to acknowledge that the cost to acquire more information about language skills is small. If employers are interested in a candidate but concerned about the applicant's language skills, they could contact the applicant by telephone to determine whether an interview would be worthwhile.

One direct policy recommendation is that employers should consider masking names on applications before making initial interview decisions. Masking names is easily implemented for employers that collect applications online. Recruiters can also request that applicants list name and contact information on a separate page at the end of a resumé, which can then be ignored or removed during the initial interview selection process. It would not be difficult to explore this practice on a trial basis to determine whether it leads to better hiring or turns out to be onerous with little perceived benefit. As a related example, Goldin and Rouse (2000) document how blind audition procedures (e.g., auditioning behind a screen) fostered impartiality in hiring and increased the proportion of women in symphony orchestras. Another implication is to develop hiring policies that involve contacting marginal applicants and initially assessing their language abilities, when in doubt.

It should not be overlooked, however, that many recruiters are clearly concerned that immigrants may lack critical language skills for performing well on the job. These concerns appear to be based on real productivity worries. We cannot rule out that the stated reasons for discrimination belie underlying prejudice. Nevertheless, employers state that they place high value on workers with strong communication skills, and it is worth considering additional ways to rank immigrant applicants who came to Canada under the point system higher, if they have these skills.

Acknowledgements

The author thanks Metropolis British Columbia for financial support, and is grateful for research assistance from Amit Dhand, Wei Gong, Adam Kowalczewski, Chris-Ann Monteiro, Monica Pu, and Ayaz Warraich. He also thanks Joanna Lahey, who provided her program to randomize resumé characteristics; Rishi Aurora, for computing service support; Diane Dechief, who helped with the qualitative analysis; and Marianne Bertrand Tarek Hussain, Dan-olof Rooth, Katherine Laird, and Joanna Lahey, who provided detailed suggestions.

Questions for Critical Thought

1. Describe the employers who engage in discrimination according to Oreopoulos's study.
2. What types of discrimination are measured in Oreopoulos's audit study? What types of discrimination are not measured?
3. According to Oreopoulos's study, if a job applicant has an Asian surname, what characteristics on the resumé will likely increase the chances of receiving a callback from an employer?
4. What types of policies might reduce the chances of discrimination such as measured in Oreopoulos's study?

Recommended Readings

Agocs, Carol, and Harish Jain. 2001. *Systemic Racism in Employment in Canada: Diagnosing Systemic Racism in Organizational Culture*. Toronto: Canadian Race Relations Foundation.

Block, Sheila, and Grace-Edward Galabuzi. 2011. *Canada's Colour Coded Labour Market: The Gap for Racialized Workers*. Ottawa and Toronto: Canadian Centre for Policy Alternatives and Wellesley Institute.

de Beijl, Roger Zegers, ed. 2002. *Documenting Discrimination against Migrant Workers*. Geneva: International Labour Office.

Esses, V.M., J. Dietz, and A. Bhardwaj. 2006. "The role of prejudice in the discounting of immigrant skills." In R. Mahalingam, ed., *Cultural Psychology of Immigrants*, pp. 113–30. Mahwah, NJ: Lawrence Erlbaum.

Recommended Websites

Canadian Human Rights Reporter:
http://www.cdn-hr-reporter.ca/hr_topics/race-discrimination

International Labour Organization:
http://www.ilo.org/

Toronto Region Immigrant Employment Council:
http://triec.ca

Notes

1. See Beach, Green, and Worswick (2007), Antecol, Kuhn, and Trejo (2006), or Borjas (1993) for more details about the Canadian point system (more formally called Federal Skilled Status Category). Language ability is evaluated based on an applicant's International English Language Test System (IELTS) score, or by submitting a written explanation detailing training in and usage of the English language. If an immigration officer believes that the written explanation is inadequate, he or she may require that the applicant take the IELTS instead.
2. Previous studies have attempted to explain the immigrant–native Canadian wage gap using a Blinder-Oaxaca-type decomposition methodology (e.g., Aydemir and Skuterud, 2005; Frenette and Morissette, 2005; Green and Worswick, 2010; Schaafsma and Sweetman, 2001). The general consensus view from this work appears to be that this wage gap in Canada exists mostly because of lower returns to foreign experience, especially among immigrants from Asia and the Pacific. This approach, however, does not offer details about what underlies these relationships, and whether indicating more specific skills or listing different kinds of job experience would alter the relationship.
3. See Riach and Rich (2002) for a review of the audit-study literature. Resumé audits have advantages over those with actors because they provide more control over the information employers use to make a decision. Although these types of studies only measure the interview-selection stage of the hiring process, they allow larger samples to be collected, and have more degrees of freedom to examine interactions and subgroups. Additional discrimination may arise after the interview selection stage.
4. According to the 2006 census, Chinese and South Asians made up more than 50 per cent of all immigrants with a bachelor's degree in Toronto, and 45 per cent of all individuals in the Greater Toronto Area were immigrants (Statistics Canada 2010).
5. A human resource director at a job placement organization in Bangladesh provided very helpful advice and a comprehensive set of anonymized resumés of individuals who qualified under the point system to immigrate to Canada. I also consulted resumés posted on www.workopolis.com and www.jobbank.ca.
6. The common Canadian surname list comes from a CBC article dated 26 July 2007, accessed on 12 March 2008: www.cbc.ca/news/background/namechange/common-surnames.html. The list comes from infoUSA, "which claims to have put together a directory of every telephone listing in Canada."
7. Chinese names were picked from a most common names list on the website http://zhidao.baidu.com/question/41504421.html. The web page cited the National Citizen Identity Information Center of China as the source. Indian names were gathered from the web page http://hinduism.about.com/library/babynames/bl-babynames-index.htm, and with consultation with one of my research assistants with Indian heritage. I saved these web pages, which are available on request.
8. The locations were Mississauga, Toronto, Beijing, Shanghai, Guangzhu, New Delhi, Mumbai, the province of Punjab, or London.
9. The categories were administrative, insurance, arts and media, biotech-pharmaceutical, marketing, e-commerce, production, education, retail, maintenance, programmer, civil engineering, electrical engineering, executive, finance, technology, human resources, computer, health care, and hospitality.
10. The main sites I used for this were workopolis.com and jobbank.ca.
11. See www.topuniversities.com.
12. Occupations were matched to these skill measures using O*NET's website, http://online.onetcenter.org/.
13. Specifically, I use versions of the following linear probability model:

$$y_{ijt} = \delta_0 + \delta_1 Resume\_Type_{ijt} + \delta_2 X_{ijt} + \delta_3 [Resume\_Type_{ijt} * X_{ijt}] + v_t + e_{ijt}$$

where y_{ijt} is an indicator variable for whether resumé *i* sent to job *j* posing in period *t* generated a callback, $Resume\_Type_{ijt}$ is an indicator variable for resumé type, with the indicator for Type 0 being omitted, X_{ijt} represents other resumé characteristics, and $Resume\_Type_{ijt} * X_{ijt}$ is the interaction term. Standard errors are corrected for possible heteroskedasticity and clustering by job.

14. Reflecting deteriorating economic conditions, callback rates fell, on average, 1.4 to 1.5 per cent for the two subsequent periods September–November 2008 and February–September 2009, respectively. As mentioned earlier, findings are similar when allowing for separate time trends by resumé and ethnic type, but are slightly less precise.

References

Antecol, Heather, Peter Kuhn, and Stephen J. Trejo. 2006. "Assimilation via prices or quantities? Sources of immigrant earnings growth in Australia, Canada, and the United States." *Journal of Human Resources* 41, 4: 821–40.

Aydemir, Abdurrahman, and Mikal Skuterud. 2005. "Explaining the deteriorating entry earnings of Canada's immigrant cohorts, 1966–2000." *Canadian Journal of Economics* 38, 2: 641–81.

Beach, Charles M., Alan G. Green, and Christopher Worswick. 2007. "Impacts of the point system and immigration policy levers on skill characteristics of Canadian immigrants." *Research in Labor Economics* 27: 349–401.

Bertrand, Marianne, and Sendhil Mullainathan. 2004. "Are Emily and Greg more employable than Lakisha and Jamal? A field experiment on labor market discrimination." *American Economic Review* 94, 4: 991–1013.

Borjas, George J. 1993. "Immigration policy, national origin and immigrant skills: A comparison of Canada and the United States." In David Card and Richard Freeman, eds, *Small Differences That Matter: Labor Markets and Income Maintenance in Canada and the United States*, pp. 21–44. Chicago: University of Chicago Press.

Chugh, Dolly. 2004. "Societal and managerial implications of implicit social cognition: Why milliseconds matter." *Social Justice Research* 17, 2: 203–22.

Crandall, Christian S., and Amy Eshleman. 2003. "A justification-suppression model of the expression and experience of prejudice." *Psychological Bulletin* 129: 414–46.

Dietz, Jorge, Victoria M. Esses, Chetan Joshi, and Caroline Bennett-AbuAyyash. 2009. *The Evaluation of Immigrants' Credentials: The Roles of Accreditation, Immigrant Race, and Evaluator Biases.* CLSRN Working Paper Number 18. Vancouver: Canadian Labour Market and Skills Researcher Network.

Frenette, Marc, and René Morissette. 2005. "Will they ever converge? Earnings of immigrant and Canadian-born workers over the last two decades." *International Migration Review* 39, 1: 228–57.

Fryer, Roland, and Matthew O. Jackson. 2008. "A categorical model of cognition and biased decision making." *B.E. Journal of Theoretical Economics* 8, 1: Article 6.

Goldin, Claudia, and Cecilia Rouse. 2000. "Orchestrating impartiality: The impact of blind auditions on female musicians." *American Economic Review* 90, 4: 715–41.

Green, David A., and Christopher Worswick. 2010. "Earnings of immigrant men in Canada: The roles of labour market entry effects and returns to foreign experience." In Ted McDonald, Elizabeth Ruddick, Arthur Sweetman, and Christopher Worswick, eds, *Canadian Immigration: Economic Evidence for a Dynamic Policy Environment*, pp. 77–110. Montreal and Kingston: McGill-Queen's University Press.

Lahey, Joanna H., and Ryan A. Beasley. 2009. "Computerizing audit studies." *Journal of Economic Behavior and Organization* 70, 3: 508–14.

Lubotsky, Darren. 2007. "Chutes or ladders? A longitudinal analysis of immigrant earnings." *Journal of Political Economy* 115, 5: 820–67.

Mullainathan, Sendhil. 2002. "A memory-based model of bounded rationality." *Quarterly Journal of Economics* 117, 3: 735–44.

Phelps, Edmund S. 1972. "The statistical theory of racism and sexism." *American Economic Review* 62, 4: 659–61.

Ranganath, Kate, Colin Smith, and Brian Nosek. 2008. "Distinguishing automatic and controlled components of attitudes from direct and indirect measurement methods." *Journal of Experimental and Social Psychology* 44: 386–96.

Riach, Peter A., and Judith Rich. 2002. "Field experiments of discrimination in the market place." *Economic Journal* 112: F480–F518.

Schaafsma, Joseph, and Arthur Sweetman. 2001. "Immigrant earnings: Age at immigration matters." *Canadian Journal of Economics* 34, 4: 1066–99.

Stanley, Damian, Elizabeth Phelps, and Mahzarin Banaji. 2008. "The neural basis of implicit attitudes." *Current Directions in Psychological Science* 17, 2: 164–70.

Statistics Canada. 2007. *The Canadian Immigrant Labour Market in 2006: First Results from Canada's Labour Force Survey*. Catalogue no. 71-606-XIE. Ottawa: Minister of Industry.

———. 2008. *Earnings and Incomes of Canadians over the Past Quarter Century*. Catalogue no. 97-563-X. Ottawa: Minister of Industry.

———. 2010. *Census of Canada, 2006: Public Use Microdata File of Ind*ividuals [computer file]. Catalogue no. 95M0028XVB. Ottawa: Statistics Canada.

Selected Glossary

Below is a list of selected key terms and concepts that are frequently used by theorists and researchers who study the topic of social inequality. It should be noted that complete agreement does not exist on precise definitions for many of these terms and concepts. However, the definitions provided below give the reader an indication of what most scholars in the field of social inequality typically mean when they use these terms and concepts.

Aboriginal Peoples All descendants of the original inhabitants of Canada, comprising subgroups that include registered Indians, non-status Indians, Métis, and Inuit. *See also* First Nations Peoples and Indigenous Peoples.

achieved status A position in a social organization, group, or structure that is mainly or partly acquired through personal effort, e.g., educational attainment, occupational status.

ascribed status A position in a social organization, group, or structure that is mainly or exclusively acquired at birth, and is largely beyond the person's ability to change or control, e.g., class of origin, ethnic background.

bourgeoisie The Marxian term for the large-scale capitalist class.

class A category of people, or the locations that the people occupy, within the economic structure, e.g., the capitalist class, the working class. In cases where people in a class take on the same subjective awareness of their common location, as well as other characteristics of a genuine social group, some scholars refer to such a group as a social class.

domination A power relation that is socially structured, i.e., is generally stable across time and place. *See also* power.

equality of condition A situation in which individuals or groups exist in the same general material circumstances as other individuals or groups.

equality of opportunity A situation in which individuals or groups all have the same chance to succeed (or fail) in a social system, especially in material terms. Equality of opportunity differs from equality of condition in that it does not require that all people have an equal degree of material or other success, and it ignores the fact that some people are advantaged and others disadvantaged from birth.

ethnicity A socially constructed attribute that derives from distinctive cultural characteristics, including national origin, language, and religion. *See also* race.

First Nations Peoples Descendants of the original inhabitants of Canada who used to be called "Indians." The latter word, however, is now considered inappropriate by those who see it as a mistaken attribution from Canada's colonial past; nonetheless, as a consequence of this past, "Indian" is still used in legislation (the Indian Act, the Constitution Act, 1982) and for federal classification purposes (e.g., status Indians).

gender A socially constructed attribute related to biological or physiological sex, but distinct from sex, in that gender refers to cultural and psychological traits arising from socially defined contexts. Whereas sex refers to males and females, for example, gender refers to masculine and feminine, and also to transgender identities that are distinguishable from the simple masculine–feminine dichotomy.

Indigenous Peoples An alternative term for Aboriginal Peoples. The word "Indigenous" is preferred to "Aboriginal" by some observers, who associate the latter term with the government's labelling and subjugation of Canada's original inhabitants.

intergenerational mobility Change in an individual's social status, usually occupational status, in comparison to the social status of the individual's parents. *See also* social mobility.

intragenerational mobility Change in an individual's social status, usually occupational status, during the individual's life course. *See also* social mobility.

petty bourgeoisie Marx's term for the small-scale capitalist class.

power The differential capacity to command resources and thereby to control social situations. These resources include, in particular, access to economic control (control over material resources), political control (control over human resources, people), and ideological control (control over ideas, knowledge, beliefs, information). Although it is often considered to be synonymous with power, some scholars use the term "domination" to denote socially structured power, i.e., stable power relations that endure across time and place.

prestige The degree of honour or deference attached to a particular social status, e.g., occupational prestige.

proletariat The Marxian term for the working class in the capitalist system.

race A socially constructed attribute that derives primarily from distinctive physical characteristics, such as skin colour. *See also* ethnicity.

racism A belief system or set of practices that encourages hatred, intolerance, prejudice, and discrimination toward groups or individuals deemed to be racially distinct and inferior, and typically held by members of dominant racial categories.

sex A biological distinction, conventionally between males and females, which is now understood to involve more differences than the simple male–female dichotomy conveys. *See also* gender.

social class An economic class that acquires a subjective awareness of their common location and other characteristics of a genuine social group; position in an economic hierarchy defined by occupation, education, or income that affects people's life chances. *See also* class.

social closure A situation in which a subordinate social group is denied or excluded from the same rights, opportunities, rewards, and privileges as a more dominant social group.

social inequality The existence of human or socially defined differences that are consequential for the rights, opportunities, rewards, and privileges experienced by individuals and groups in society.

social mobility Movement within a system of social inequality or social stratification, especially as gauged by changes in a person's occupational status. This movement can be up, down, or lateral. Researchers often distinguish between "intragenerational mobility," in which an individual changes jobs over time in her/his own career, and "intergenerational mobility," in which an individual attains a different job than that held by either or both of her/his parents.

social status A position in a social organization, social group, or social structure.

social stratification The depiction of social inequality as a ranked set of categories, or social strata. The ranking criterion can vary, but usually involves income level, educational attainment, occupational prestige, or some combination of these characteristics.

socio-economic status An individual's position in the overall socio-economic hierarchy, which is typically gauged by occupational status. It usually reflects a combination of the education and income level of the person's occupation, or of the household head's occupation. Socio-economic status is empirically related to class position, but many theorists see the concepts of class and socio-economic status as conceptually distinct.

visible minority As defined by Canada's Employment Equity Act, any "persons, other than Aboriginal peoples, who are non-Caucasian in race or non-white in colour."

Index